THE
DRAMATIC WORKS
OF
Richard Brinsley
Sheridan

The Screen Scene in *The School for Scandal*, painted by James Roberts, 1777

By courtesy of the Committee of the Garrick Club

THE
DRAMATIC WORKS
OF
Richard Brinsley Sheridan

EDITED BY

CECIL PRICE

VOLUME II

OXFORD
AT THE CLARENDON PRESS
1973

Oxford University Press, Ely House, London W. 1

GLASGOW NEW YORK TORONTO MELBOURNE WELLINGTON
CAPE TOWN IBADAN NAIROBI DAR ES SALAAM LUSAKA ADDIS ABABA
DELHI BOMBAY CALCUTTA MADRAS KARACHI LAHORE DACCA
KUALA LUMPUR SINGAPORE HONG KONG TOKYO

© *Oxford University Press 1973*

*Printed in Great Britain
at the University Press, Oxford
by Vivian Ridler
Printer to the University*

CONTENTS

NOTE

WHILE the present work was in the press, the Sheridan papers of the late Clare Sheridan came up for auction. A brief summary of their attractions, as far as they bear on Sheridan's plays, is to be found on pages 831, 834, 837, and 841.

LIST OF ILLUSTRATIONS

ABBREVIATIONS USED IN THE NOTES

Here and thronghout, place of publication is London unless otherwise noted

Add. MS.	Additional MS., British Museum.
Anderson Cat.	Sale catalogue of John J. Anderson, Jr., the Anderson Auction Co., and the Anderson Galleries, New York City.
Black	Clementina Black, *The Linleys of Bath* (rev. edn., 1926).
Boaden, *Kemble*	James Boaden, *Memoirs of the Life of John Philip Kemble, Esq.* (1825, 2 vols.).
Chatsworth MS.	Manuscript owned by the Duke of Devonshire, Chatsworth, Derbyshire.
Dowden	*The Letters of Thomas Moore* (ed. Wilfred S. Dowden, Oxford, 1964, 2 vols.).
Dufferin MS.	Manuscript owned by the Marchioness of Dufferin and Ava.
Egerton MS.	Egerton MS., British Museum.
Folger MS.	Manuscript in the Folger Shakespeare Library, Washington, D.C.
Frampton Cat.	*Catalogue of A Collection of Books Relating to English and Foreign Literature Forming The Library of Richard Brinsley Sheridan at Frampton Court* (Privately printed, 1884). Owned by Dr. R. Alston.
Garrick Corr.	*The Private Correspondence of David Garrick* (ed. J. Boaden, 1831–2, 2 vols.).
Garrick, *Letters*	*The Letters of David Garrick* (ed. D. M. Little and G. M. Kahrl, Cambridge, Mass., 1963, 3 vols.).
Harvard MS.	Manuscript in the Theatre collection of Harvard College Library.
Hodgson Cat.	Sale catalogue of Messrs. Hodgson, Chancery Lane, W.C.2.
Huntington MS.	Manuscript in the Henry E. Huntington Library, San Marino, California.
Kelly	*Reminiscences of Michael Kelly* (2nd edn., 1826, 2 vols.).
LeFanu MS.	Manuscripts owned by Mr. W. R. LeFanu.
Letters	*The Letters of Richard Brinsley Sheridan* (ed. C. Price, Oxford, 1966, 3 vols.).
The London Stage	*The London Stage, 1660–1800: Part 4, 1747–1776* (ed. G. W. Stone, Jr., Carbondale, Ill., 1962, 3 vols.).
MacMillan	*Catalogue of the Larpent Plays in the Huntington Library* (comp. D. MacMillan, San Marino, California, 1939).

M.L.N.	*Modern Language Notes* (Baltimore, Md., 1886–1969, 84 vols.).
Moore	Thomas Moore, *Memoirs of the Life of the Right Honourable Richard Brinsley Sheridan* (2nd edn., 1825, 2 vols.).
Moore, *Journal*	*Memoirs, Journal, and Correspondence of Thomas Moore* (ed. Lord John Russell, 1853–6, 8 vols.).
Nettleton and Case	*British Dramatists from Dryden to Sheridan* (ed. G. H. Nettleton and A. E. Case, 1939).
P.B.S.A.	*Papers of the Bibliographical Society of America* (New York, 1906–69, 63 vols.).
P.M.L.A.	*Publications of the Modern Language Society of America* (Baltimore, Md.,—Menasha, Wis., 1884–1968, 83 vols.).
Purdy	*The Rivals, A Comedy. As it was first Acted at the Theatre-Royal in Covent-Garden. Written by Richard Brinsley Sheridan Esq. Edited from the Larpent MS. by Richard Little Purdy* (Oxford, 1935).
Rae	*Sheridan's Plays now printed as he wrote them and his Mother's unpublished Comedy A Journey to Bath* (ed. W. Fraser Rae, 1902).
Rae, *Sheridan*	W. Fraser Rae, *Sheridan, A Biography* (1896, 2 vols.).
R.E.S.	*The Review of English Studies* (Oxford, 1925–69, 45 vols.).
Rhodes	*The Play and Poems of Richard Brinsley Sheridan* (ed. R. Crompton Rhodes, Oxford, 1928, 3 vols.).
Sichel	W. Sichel, *Sheridan* (1909, 2 vols.).
Sotheby	Sale catalogues of Messrs. Sotheby, London, and of the varying names of the firm from 1814 to 1969.
Speeches	*Speeches of the late Right Honourable Richard Brinsley Sheridan* (ed. 'A Constitutional Friend' [Sir John Philippart?], 1816, 5 vols.).
T.L.S.	*The Times Literary Supplement*, 1902–69.
Williams	Iolo A. Williams, *Seven XVIIIth Century Bibliographies* (1924).
Wm.	Dated watermark (or countermark) in the paper on which a manuscript is written.
W.T.	Typescript copies of letters and other MSS. of the Sheridan circle, formerly in the possession of Sophie, Lady Wavertree. These copies contain a number of obvious typing errors, and I have silently corrected them when quoting from the typescripts.
Yale MS.	Manuscript in the Yale University Library.

SOME DATES IN SHERIDAN'S LIFE

4 November 1751. Christened 'Thos. Brinsley Sheridan' at St. Mary's Church, Dublin.

1762–c. 1767–8. At Harrow School.

September 1770–August 1772. At Bath.

August 1772–March 1773. At Waltham Abbey.

13 April 1773. Married Elizabeth Linley at Marylebone Church.

17 and 28 January 1775. *The Rivals* acted at Covent Garden Theatre.

2 May 1775. *St. Patrick's Day* acted at Covent Garden Theatre.

21 November 1775. *The Duenna* acted at Covent Garden Theatre.

21 September 1776. Opened Drury Lane Theatre as principal manager.

24 February 1777. *A Trip to Scarborough* acted at Drury Lane Theatre.

March 1777. Elected a member of the Literary Club on the motion of Samuel Johnson.

8 May 1777. *The School for Scandal* acted at Drury Lane Theatre.

15 October 1778. *The Camp* acted at Drury Lane Theatre.

12 September 1780. Elected M.P. for Stafford.

27 March–1 July 1782. Under-Secretary of State for Foreign Affairs.

21 February–18 December 1783. Secretary to the Treasury.

7 February 1787. Made a celebrated speech on the Begums of Oude in the proceedings against Warren Hastings, and others (3–13 June 1788) on his impeachment.

November–December 1788. Confidential adviser to the Prince of Wales in the Regency crisis.

28 June 1792. Death of his first wife at Bristol Wells.

21 April 1794. Opened the rebuilt Drury Lane Theatre.

27 April 1795. Married Esther Ogle, daughter of the Dean of Winchester.

24 May 1799. *Pizarro* acted at Drury Lane Theatre.

November 1806. Succeeded Charles James Fox as M.P. for Westminster.

May 1807. Defeated in the Westminster election but became M.P. for Ilchester.

24 February 1809. Drury Lane Theatre destroyed by fire.

Autumn 1812. Defeated at the Stafford election, so losing a seat in Parliament.

7 July 1816. Died at Savile Row.

13 July 1816. Buried in Westminster Abbey.

VERSES TO
THE MEMORY OF GARRICK

VERSES TO THE MEMORY OF GARRICK

COMPOSITION

SHERIDAN probably took over some of his father's prejudices against Garrick, and as late as May 1775, he could say: 'To talk of Mr. G——['s] *selfishness—Cunning—Avarice*—and *Insincerity* is literally to advance a Position which no one that has ever had any Dealings with him will attempt to controvert.'[1] Within months, he was in active negotiation with Garrick for the purchase of his moiety of the Drury Lane Theatre, and initial dislike developed into warm friendship. In the summer of 1776, he succeeded Garrick as manager of the playhouse, and was very dependent on his goodwill for the next two and a half years. Sheridan consulted him on many occasions, and Garrick was able to help him with prologues as well as with financial backing. Besides, they enjoyed each other's company.

Consequently Sheridan was very moved by Garrick's death. He was chief mourner at the funeral, and is said to have spent the rest of the day in silence.[2] The *Monody* was a serious attempt to indicate the loss the British stage had suffered, and was greatly admired by Byron. Mrs. Siddons, too, said she was never able to read it without weeping.[3]

RECEPTION

The Monody recited on Thursday night at Drury-lane theatre by Mrs. Yates, in compliment to the memory of Mr. Garrick, is the production of Mr. R. B. Sheridan. As a friend to departed merit, a man of refined sentiment, and a powerful poet, the composition does him great credit. As the manager of the theatre in which Mr. Garrick trod the stage for so many years, to the delight of the age he lived in, the stile of its performance also reflects great honour upon the author of it. Both the form in which the Monody is given to the publick, and the Monody itself, may nevertheless be liable to some small share of critical objection. To begin with the latter, it is perhaps the first time that ever a Monody was written entirely in unvaried measure, we mean in heroic verse; in general we imagine Monodies partake of the nature of Odes, the number of feet being occasionally changed, and the verse shifting from short to long, and *vice versa*; we mention this, the rather because in the representation we conceive variety of metre would have had a pleasing effect, and both

---

[1] *Letters*, iii. 302.

[2] J. T. Smith, *Nollekens and his Times*, ed. Whitten (1920), i. 184.

[3] Mrs. Siddons to Sheridan, Oxford, 3 Mar. 1814 (Cutting in an extra-illustrated volume of Hawkins's *Life of Kean*, opp. p. 172, in the Folger Shakespeare Library).

relieved the ear of the audience, and the delivery of the speaker. The present Monody is otherwise ably constructed; the exordium is solemn and well adapted to the subject; the remarks on the perishable fame of an actor, and the comparative difference of the fate of the fame of the painter, sculptor, and poet, are solid, judicious, and elegantly expressed; the conclusion also is warm and noble. Throughout the composition, the soul and spirit of true poetry exist manifestly; all the thoughts are good; that of Shakespeare's monument, pointing out the grave of Garrick, is admirable, and that of architectural ruins giving the architect's fame additional grace from their decay, truly excellent. The introduction of several thoughts is happy, and most of the lines are beautifully turned. There is, however, discoverable, a laboriousness of metre, and an apparent artifice of composition throughout. With regard to the representation, pains have obviously been taken to render it great in effect. The Monody is divided into three parts, between each of which, and at the conclusion, solemn airs are sung by Mr. Webster, Mr. Gaudry, a Young Lady, and Mrs. Wrighten, supported by a band of choristers. The stage is formed in somewhat like the same shape that it assumed when Mr. Garrick was wont to speak his Ode to Shakespeare, excepting only, that now, instead of an air of hilarity and cheerfulness which then pervaded it, an air of solemnity and awful woe is cultivated. In the center of the perspective, amidst a thick grove of bays and cypress, stands a monumental pyramid representing the funeral pile of Mr. Garrick. The figures of tragedy and comedy appear as if in basso relievo, in positions expressive of their loss, while fame is mounting the skies with a medallion of Mr. Garrick, and the little Cupids are weeping over his urn beneath. The ground work of the basso relievo is decorated with the torch of Hymen, comic masks and symbols, tragic bowls, chains, etc. Before the pyramid Mrs. Yates with dishevelled hair and in a flowing robe of purple sattin, speaks the Monody. The singers are ranged on each side in compartments railed off with ballustrade. The *coup d'oeil* of the whole is good, but the monument, whether from its colouring, or from some other cause, does not produce the desired effect. The medallion also, which we understand to be an original picture of Mr. Garrick by Sir Joshua Reynolds, (the property of Sir Thomas Mills)[1] is scarcely distinguishable; we mean so distinguishable that the audience, did not the occasion tell them, could discover who it represented.

Mrs. Yates last night recited the Monody well in general, but we think she is capable of doing it more justice, as she is beyond compare the best declaimer on the English stage. We submit to her consideration the absolute necessity of her keeping up her voice to the end of the lines, and not dropping the last syllable; and also whether her speaking the whole

[1] Cf. *The Public Advertiser*, 4 May 1776; 'Verses from Sir Thomas Mills to Mr. Garrick, on receiving his Portrait, painted by Mr. Dance.'

would not have a better effect than her partially reading it. At any rate she should not quit the stage till the curtain drops. Her going off so *mal apropos*, destroyed the whole *deceptio visus*; and roused the minds of the audience from that enthusiasm of woe and reverence, into which the poet had wrought them, to the pitiful recollection that Mrs. Yates, the *Actress*, was hastening to her dressing-room to change her attire. The music is rather heavy, but not destitute of merit. The air sung by the Young Lady was most pleasing; as a new performer she acquitted herself very creditably. Her pipe is agreeable but not very powerful.

There is something so like Mr. Sheridan's thoughts respecting the perishing fame of an *actor*, in the poem of that name, written by the late Mr. Lloyd,[1] and something so noble in the sentiment, and bold in the expression, that we think it right to present the end of that poem to our readers. (*Morning Chronicle*, 12 Mar. 1779; reprinted *General Evening Post*, 11–13 Mar. 1779.)

A *Monody* to the memory of the late Mr. Garrick, written by Mr. Sheridan, junior, was spoken last night at this theatre;—The curtain rising to slow music, discovered in a cypress shade the mausoleum of our departed Roscius, on which were the figures of Melpomene and Thalia mourning his loss, over whom, appears Time supporting a Medallion with his portrait. Mrs. Yates, in the character of the Recording Muse, is seen in the center of a temporary orchestra, reclining on an urn, with her hair dishevelled. The introductory strain of music ceasing, she advanced and recited an invocation to the audience, to pay their tribute to his memory before any other offering was made to it; then the Chorus sang—

> His fame requires, we act a tenderer part;
> His *Memory* claims the tear you gave his *Art*!

The unequal effects of the different arts of *Poetry*, *Painting*, and *Sculpture*, are then beautifully described, in the course of which an elegant compliment is paid to Sir Joshua Reynolds, the *Raphael* of the present age: these arts however are represented as yielding objects; but not so the *Actor*'s art, for

> Feeble tradition is his memory's guard.

Here succeeds a forcible, and marking description of Mr. Garrick's acting powers, which the poet says were

> All perishable like the electric fire
> But strike the frame, and as they strike—expire!
> Incense, too choice, a bodied flame to bear,
> Its fragrance charms the sense, and blends in air!

---

[1] Robert Lloyd's closing lines in *The Actor* (1760), from 'Yet, hapless Artist! tho' thy skill can raise'.

Here a Trio by Mrs. Wrighten, Mr. Webster, and a young Lady, &c., succeeds; after which a second Poetic Exhortation is made to the audience, and the Monody concludes with a classical description of an intended Shrine, which the mournful Muse shall guard

> And with soft sighs disperse th' irreverend dust,
> That Time shall shake upon his sacred bust.

Such is the bare outline of one of the most elegant, and finished poems in the language, and which does equal honour to the living author, and the deceased worthy: It was admirable in recital—but we have no doubt the world will find fresh beauties in its perusal. . . . The musical parts were highly characteristic, and the chorusses full, and sublime. . . . The whole was received by a very crowded and brilliant audience, with very singular, and repeated bursts of applause. (*Morning Post*, 12 Mar. 1779.)

On drawing up the curtain a building is discovered on the stage, nearly in the form used at an oratorio, except that a vacant space, is left in the centre for the speaker (Mrs. Yates). Before the organ a mausoleum is erected, on which two fine figures of Tragedy and Comedy appear weeping over the urn of Mr. Garrick, and above is his portrait (a striking likeness) supported by a cherub.

. . . After hearing the beautifully pathetic lines in the Epilogue to the Rivals and to Semiramis, our expectations on this occasion were very high, but they are here far exceeded; and it is impossible not to express a wish (at which, however, the Comic Muse would exclaim in the most violent terms) that Mr. Sheridan would confine a greater part of his attention to poetical composition, as it seems reserved for him to give the last polish to harmony, force, and elegance of English verse. (*The Gazetteer*, 12 Mar. 1770.)

. . . The most singular Circumstance in Mr. Garrick's Life was, that he obtained a greater Share of Applause than any Man ever enjoyed, than any Man ever merited; and yet when his Name is associated with a Socrates, a Plato . . . even Poetry is ashamed of her Meannesses. . . .

The Monody by Mr. Sheridan, junior, is destitute of all poetical Merit except Versification. The Fable of it . . . is uninteresting; it is destitute of original Images; its Sentiments are trite, and its most plausible Passages are formed to catch Applause from the ignorant, not to obtain the Approbation of the Judicious.

If this Opinion should be important enough to be disputed, let the Monody be printed, and we pledge ourselves to prove *all* our Assertions to the Satisfaction of those Persons who are accustomed to read or attend to English poetry. Mr. Sheridan is a popular Writer; but in the Scales of Criticism, if Popularity were a Circumstance of Weight, Gay would rival Milton . . .

The Monody consisted of three Parts: An Exordium or Exhortation to praise Garrick; a most laboured and heavy Description of the Fates of Painters, Sculptors, Poets and Actors; and an Application or Inference (in the Pulpit style) that Garrick should have a better Fate than any of them.

In all our Lives, we never were more heartily tired by an Half Hour's Performance: though Mrs. Yates read, and Mr. Linley's Strains were sung. We do not mean to compare the Performances of the Reader and Musical Composer; but their different Pretensions helped to keep us awake; Mrs. Yates by her Art in giving Importance to an harmonious sentimental Trifle, and Mr. Linley by making us laugh at his Musick. For of all the drawling dismal Things we ever heard, this is the most destitute of musical Merit. But hush—it is *decreed* by the Powers of our *bleak* Parnassus, that no other Musick shall enter the Theatre. Melodious Jackson! . . . breathe thy heavenly Strains to the callous Ears of the stupid Devonians! Shade of the immortal Arne! . . . Dulness has *contracted* with Avarice; and no Music but—that is, *no Music* can even enter the Theatre. (*St. James's Chronicle*, 11–13 Mar. 1779.)

Verses occasioned by the MONODY *performed at Drury-Lane*

When Garrick's pageant pass'd along,
So star'd at by the gaping throng,
'Twas curious to observe each breast
With different sentiments imprest;
For nature like a looking-glass,
Reflects all objects as they pass,
By her own superficies.

The tradesman, in his haste delay'd,
Damns a nonsensical parade,
Of which he nothing had provided,
Nor e'en the smallest spoils divided,
   Not so the glover—

The distant peer in titles proud,
Expressed his discontent aloud;
Such pomp—procession—and such state,
Became the burials of the great;
He thought that due alone to birth,
Which memory dedicates to worth.
The wit found food enough for jokes,
He punn'd upon the scarfs and cloaks,

The hatband waving on the wind,
The streamers *starting* out behind;
Swearing to those who stood about him,
(Some had perhaps the sense to doubt him)
How well he the deceased had known,
'I us'd his house just as my own;
A month ago, he was in health, I
Din'd with him in the Adelphi.'
He nam'd the wits too as they pass'd,
In order on, from first to last;
With easy freedom through the whole ran,
From Sheridan, quite down to Colman.

The lawyer quits the empty court,
He to the shew too must resort,
Declaring he'd be bold to say,
'*Twas stopping up the King's Highway.*
As for the women they all said,
'Twas right to honour husbands—*dead,*
To give them, all they then could have,
A requiem in the *silent* grave.
The widow all applaud, whose woe,
Gratis, had given them the shew.
But chief of all, the undertaker
Wish'd that *Heaven would please to take her.*

Still in one point the croud agree,
The whole to be some mystery,
Which time perhaps might soon explain.
—*A Monody at Drury Lane*
Bespeaks the observation true,
'Twas Interest they had in view.—

So Garrick join'd in Shakespeare's praise
His drooping theatre to raise,
But every dunce could then foresee
The *reason* of the *Jubilee.*

R.F.[1]

Bedford Coffee-house, March 12.

(*Morning Chronicle,* 13 Mar. 1779.)

---

[1] 'R.F.' printed verses praising the Monody in the *Morning Post,* 13 March.

CHOICE OF TEXT

1. MANUSCRIPTS

There are several manuscript copies in existence. Commander and Mrs. Scarlett-Streatfeild possess a contemporary transcription, and the Folger Shakespeare Library has one in R. Butler's commonplace book (W. a. 166). The two most important, however, are in Lord Spencer's library at Althorp, and in the Henry E. Huntington Library (HM 17433).

(i) *The Spencer MS.*

This is one of several documents concerning the *Monody*. Sheridan's letter to Richard Rigby is there, apologizing for the fact that he was so irritated with the dedication he had prepared that he had thrown it in the fire, and written something much simpler in its place. Rigby enclosed it in a letter to Lady Spencer, commenting that he thought it 'but a lame excuse for idleness'.[1] There is a copy of the dedication to Lady Spencer present, but it bears William Linley's signature and the date '1812'. The music is to be found in nine pages, and there is also a printed text with music. One page contains the words, 'Mrs. Wrighten; Mr. Gaudry; Mr. Webster; Organ solo;' with the appropriate lines of music, and the signature, 'J. S. Gaudry Script. 1779'. The manuscript of the verses is in the hand of a copyist, but contains Sheridan's autograph corrections as well as his signature at the end.

(ii) *The Lord Chamberlain's MS.*

Under the title of *Monody*, it was submitted to the Lord Chamberlain's office on 10 March 1779, by Sheridan's father, Thomas Sheridan.

The last twenty lines of the printed text are not in this version, and the last four that were there have been deleted, see p. 461, n. 1, below.

2. PRINTED TEXTS

(i) 'Airs and Chorusses'

This consists of a four-page brochure of *The Airs and Chorusses, in the Monody, on the Death of Mr. Garrick. Set to Music by Mr. Linley.* 4to.[2]

(ii) *Of the text*

The title-page of the first edition reads:

VERSES | To the MEMORY of | GARRICK. | SPOKEN AS | A MONODY, | AT | The Theatre Royal in Drury-Lane. | [Short rule] | LONDON: | Published by T. EVANS, in the Strand; J. WILKIE, St. Paul's Church- | Yard; E. and C. DILLY, in the Poultry; A. PORTAL, opposite the New Church; and J. ALMON, Piccadilly. | M,DCC,LXXIX.

---

[1] *Letters*, i. 125-6.   [2] See pp. 846-7 below.

Collation: 4to. in half-sheets: [A]² [Frontispiece inserted between the leaves] [B]² C–D².

Contents: [1] Half-title: 'VERSES | To the MEMORY of | GARRICK. | (Price One Shilling.)'; [2] blank; [3] title; [4] blank; [5] Dedication; [6] blank; 7–15, text; [16] blank. The inserted frontispiece usually comes between p. [2] and p. [3]: it is by Loutherbourgh and is engraved by A. Albanesi. It is accompanied by the last six lines of the printed text.[1]

There are two issues of the first edition: 'Difference' appears in the dedication of the first, but it is corrected to 'Deference' in the second.

The second edition was published in the same year, but contains a few small differences mentioned in the textual footnotes of the present edition. A presentation copy, inscribed on the half-title 'From the Author' is listed in Bernard Quaritch's Catalogue 373 (1923), item 2226.

A copy of the third edition in the Folger Library (W. b. 479) prints the text found in the first edition.

Conclusion

I have accepted the first edition as copy-text and have admitted into it superior readings to be found in the Spencer MS. at Althorp.

The abbreviations employed are:

L   The Lord Chamberlain's MS. in the Huntington Library.
Sp.   Spencer MS.
79a   The first edition of 1779, first issue.
79b   The second edition of 1779.

The following appear in the printed editions of the monody, but are not given in the variants here: Suffe'rers (p. 459, l. 4); The'enduring (p. 460, l. 13); the'inspiring (p. 460, l. 17); the'according (p. 460, l. 26); the'Electric (p. 461, l. 13); the'irreverend (p. 462, l. 19).

---

[1] In the Morgan Library copy (call number W 25 B), this engraved page is an inch wider than the other pages, and has been folded back.

VERSES

To the MEMORY of

GARRICK.

[Price One Shilling.]

With thoughts that mourn, nor yet desire Releif,   With Looks that speak–He never shall return;
With meek Regret, and fond enduring Grief;   Chilling thy tender Bosom, clasp his Urn:
And with soft Sighs disperse the irreverend Dust,
Which Time may Strew upon his sacred Bust:

The frontispiece of *Verses to the Memory of Garrick*, engraved by Albanesi from
P. J. De Loutherbourg's design

VERSES

To the Memory of

GARRICK.

[Price One Shilling.]

With thoughts that mourn, nor yet desire Releif,   With Looks that speak—He never shall return,
With meek Regret, and fond enduring Grief;   Chilling thy tender Bosom, clasp his Urn:
And with soft Sighs disperse the irreverend Dust,
Which Time may Strew upon his sacred Bust:

The frontispiece of *Verses to the Memory of Garrick*, engraved by Albanesi from
P. J. De Loutherbourg's design

VERSES

To the MEMORY of

GARRICK.

SPOKEN AS

A MONODY,

AT

The Theatre Royal in Drury-Lane.

LONDON:

Published by T. EVANS, in the Strand; J. WILKIE, St. Paul's Church-
Yard; E. and C. DILLY, in the Poultry; A. PORTAL, opposite the
New Church; and J. ALMON, Piccadilly.

M, DCC, LXXIX.

TO THE RIGHT HONOURABLE

COUNTESS SPENCER,

Whose APPROBATION and ESTEEM were JUSTLY CONSIDERED by

Mr. GARRICK

AS THE HIGHEST PANEGYRICK
HIS TALENTS OR CONDUCT COULD ACQUIRE,
THIS IMPERFECT TRIBUTE TO HIS

MEMORY

IS, WITH GREAT DEFERENCE INSCRIBED
BY HER LADYSHIP's
MOST OBEDIENT
HUMBLE SERVANT,

RICHARD BRINSLEY SHERIDAN.

MARCH 25th, 1779.

If dying EXCELLENCE deserves a Tear,[1]
If fond Remembrance still is cherished here,
Can we persist to bid your Sorrows flow
For fabled Suff'rers and delusive Woe?
Or with quaint Smiles dismiss the plaintive Strain,   5
Point the quick Jest—indulge the Comic Vein—
Ere yet to buried ROSCIUS we assign—
One kind Regret—one tributary Line!

   His Fame requires we act a tenderer Part:—
His MEMORY claims the Tear you gave his ART!   10

   The general Voice, the Meed of mournful Verse,
The splendid Sorrows that adorned his Hearse,
The Throng that mourn'd as their dead Favourite pass'd,
The grac'd Respect that claim'd him to the last,
While SHAKESPEAR's Image from its hallow'd Base,   15
Seem'd to prescribe the Grave, and point the Place,—
Nor these,—nor all the sad Regrets that flow
From fond Fidelity's domestic Woe,—
So much are GARRICK's Praise—so much his DUE—
As on this Spot—One Tear bestow'd by YOU.   20

   Amid the Arts which seek ingenuous Fame,
OUR toil attempts the most precarious Claim!
To HIM, whose mimic Pencil wins the Prize,
Obedient Fame immortal Wreaths supplies:[2]
Whate'er of Wonder REYNOLDS now may raise,   25
RAPHAEL still boasts cotemporary Praise:[3]

21 Amid] *Sp.*, *79a*, *79b*; 'Mid all *L*

---

[1] Cf. N. Rowe, *The Ambitious Step-Mother* (1700), Prologue, l. 1:
       If Dying Lovers yet demand a tear.
[2] Brander Matthews drew attention (in *Sheridan's Comedies* (Boston, 1885), p. 36)
to Garrick's own use of this theme in the prologue to *The Clandestine Marriage*:
       The painter's dead, yet still he charms the eye,
       While England lives his fame can never die;
       But he who struts his hour upon the stage
       Can scarce protract his fame through half an age;
       Nor pen, nor pencil can the actor save;
       The art and artist have one common grave.
[3] Cf. p. 404, n. 1 above. See also the *Morning Chronicle*, 30 Dec. 1779.

Each dazling Light, and gaudier Bloom subdu'd,
With undiminish'd Awe HIS Works are view'd:
E'en Beauty's Portrait wears a softer Prime,
Touch'd by the tender Hand of mellowing Time.

The patient SCULPTOR owns an humbler Part,   5
A ruder Toil, and more mechanic Art;
Content with slow and timorous Stroke to trace
The lingering Line, and mould the tardy Grace:
But once atchieved—tho' barbarous Wreck o'erthrow
The sacred Fane, and lay its Glories low,   10
Yet shall the sculptur'd Ruin rise to Day,
Grac'd by Defect, and worship'd in Decay;
Th' enduring Record *bears* the Artist's Name,
Demands his Honors, and asserts his Fame.

Superior Hopes the POET's Bosom fire,—   15
O proud Distinction of the sacred Lyre!—
Wide as the inspiring PHOEBUS darts his Ray,
Diffusive Splendor gilds his VOTARY's Lay.
Whether the Song Heroic Woes rehearse,
With Epic Grandeur, and the Pomp of Verse;   20
Or, fondly gay, with unambitious Guile
Attempt no Prize but favouring Beauty's Smile;
Or bear dejected to the lonely Grove
The soft Despair of unprevailing Love,—
Whate'er the Theme—thro' every Age and Clime   25
Congenial Passions meet the according Rhyme;
The Pride of Glory—Pity's Sigh sincere—
Youth's earliest Blush—and Beauty's Virgin Tear.

Such is THEIR Meed—THEIR Honors thus secure,
Whose Arts yield Objects, and whose Works endure.   30
The ACTOR only, shrinks from Time's Award;
Feeble Tradition is HIS Memory's Guard;
By whose faint Breath his Merits must abide,
Unvouch'd by Proof—to Substance unallied!
Ev'n matchless GARRICK's Art to Heav'n resign'd,   35
No fix'd Effect, no Model leaves behind!

1 Light] *Sp.*, *79a*, *79b*; sight *L*   31 Time's] *Sp.*, *L*; Times *79a*, *79b*

   The GRACE of ACTION—the adapted MIEN
Faithful as Nature to the varied Scene;
Th' EXPRESSIVE GLANCE—whose subtle Comment draws
Entranc'd Attention, and a mute Applause;
GESTURE that marks, with Force and Feeling fraught,   5
A Sense in Silence, and a Will in Thought;
HARMONIOUS SPEECH, whose pure and liquid Tone
Gives Verse a Music, scarce confess'd its own;
As Light from Gems, assumes a brighter Ray
And cloathed with Orient Hues, transcends the Day!—   10
PASSION's wild Break—and FROWN that awes the Sense,
And every CHARM of gentler ELOQUENCE—
All perishable!—like the Electric Fire
But strike the Frame—and as they strike expire;
Incense too choice a bodied Flame to bear,   15
Its Fragrance charms the Sense, and blends with Air.
   WHERE then—while sunk in cold Decay he lies,
And pale Eclipse for ever close those Eyes!—
WHERE is the blest Memorial that ensures
Our GARRICK's Fame?—whose is the Trust?—'tis YOURS!   20

   And O! by every Charm his Art essay'd
To soothe your Cares!—by every Grief allay'd!
By the hush'd Wonder which his Accents drew!
By his last parting Tear repaid by you!
By all those Thoughts, which many a distant Night,   25
Shall mark his Memory with a sad Delight!—
Still in your Hearts' dear Record bear his Name;
Cherish the keen Regret that lifts his Fame;
To YOU it is bequeath'd, assert the Trust,
And to his WORTH—'tis all you can—be JUST.[1]   30

---

9 Gems] *Sp.*, *79a*, *79b*; Prisms *L*   15 choice] *Sp.*, *L*; pure *79a*, *79b*   16 with]
Sp., *79a*, *79b*; the *L*   18 And . . . close] *Sp.*; And . . . veils *79a*, *79b*; Death on
those Lips and Darkness in *L*   21 Charm] *Sp.*, *79a*, *79b*; Grace *L*   22 soothe]
Sp.; sooth *79a*, *79b*, *L*   24 his] *Sp.*, *79a*, *79b*; the *L*   27 Hearts'] *Sp.*;
heart's *79a*, *79b*; Hearts *L*   28 lifts] *Sp.*, *79a*, *79b*; stamps *L*

---

  [1] The Lord Chamberlain's MS. ends with 'JUST'. Sheridan added the following
lines, then cancelled them:

      Whether the Song heroic Woes rehearse,
      With Epic grandeur and the pomp of Verse,
      Or fondly gay, with unambitious guile,
      Attempt no Prize but fav'ring Beauty's smile.—

What more is due from sanctifying Time,
To chearful WIT, and many a favour'd RHYME,
O'er his grac'd Urn shall bloom, a deathless Wreath,
Whose blossom'd Sweets shall deck the Mask beneath.
For these,—when SCULPTURE's votive Toil shall rear   5
The due Memorial of a Loss so dear!—
O loveliest Mourner, Gentle MUSE! be thine
The pleasing Woe to guard the laurell'd Shrine.
As FANCY, oft by Superstition led
To roam the Mansions of the sainted Dead,   10
Has view'd, by shadowy Eve's unfaithful Gloom,
A weeping Cherub on a Martyr's Tomb—
Do thou, sweet MUSE, hang o'er HIS sculptur'd Bier,
With patient Woe, that loves the ling'ring Tear;
With Thoughts that mourn—nor yet desire Relief,   15
With meek Regret, and fond enduring Grief;
With Looks that speak—He never shall return!—
—Chilling thy tender Bosom clasp his Urn!
And with soft Sighs disperse the irreverend Dust,
Which TIME may strew upon his sacred Bust.   20

7 loveliest] *Sp.*; lovliest *79a, 79b*   13 Do] *Sp.*; So *79a, 79b*   14 ling'ring]
Sp.; lingering *79a, 79b*

THE CRITIC

THE CRITIC

The Critic was, above all, a topical satire. Some of its political jests had an edge that is now lost, and to appreciate them again we need to look at the state of the country just before the date of the first performance, 30 October 1779.

On 18 June the Spanish ambassador delivered to Lord Weymouth 'a paper in which it is declared that his Catholick Majesty intends to have recourse to arms under the groundless pretence of obtaining reparation for injuries supposed to have been received'.[1] The declaration of war did not arouse much local anxiety until 16 August, when news reached the Admiralty that the French and Spanish fleets had slipped past the British squadron and were in the Channel. There was alarm on the Exchange, and the *Public Advertiser* declared: 'a few days, in all human probability, must determine our very Existence as a free and independent People: Nay, perhaps, the Blow is already struck.'[2] Reports stated that the enemy fleet consisted of a hundred ships, 'including sixty of the line', and that they were within four leagues of Plymouth. Wagons of arms and ammunition started off from St. James's towards Devonshire, volunteer companies assembled, and invasion fever seized the country.[3] It did not die down until the middle of September, and even then there was much uneasiness about the future: 'Our fears of an invasion are dissipated for the present . . . The combined Fleet, it is true, has left the Channel, but it may still return; and while it continues to be so superior to ours, the Enemy may find an Opportunity of transporting Troops to our Coasts.'[4] People seriously doubted the country's ability to defend itself, and a number of letters on this theme appeared in the newspapers. In the *Public Advertiser*, 'Cato' spoke scathingly of Sandwich's inability 'to preserve a sufficient naval force for the security of the Kingdom'.[5] 'Brutus' satirized 'the rapid Progress of the inhabitants of Westminster and Middlesex in *military* discipline'.[6] 'Coriolanus' declared that it was evident that the plan for raising volunteer companies was quite inadequate to the country's needs.[7] 'Scipio' wrote gloomily on the infallible signs that England was a declining power; 'Historicus', on 'the critical situation in which the British Empire now stands'.[8] 'Capitilamis' denounced 'the plunderers and blunderers' in the government: 'Courage

---

[1] *Public Advertiser*, 21 June 1779.
[3] Ibid., 20, 24 Aug., 2 Sept. 1779.
[5] 3 Sept. [6] 6 Sept. [7] 11 Sept.

[2] Ibid., 18, 19 Aug. 1779.
[4] Ibid., 11 Sept. 1779.
[8] 23 and 28 Sept.

and true Valour abound in our Fleets and Armies, though a stigmatized Coward directs the War; and there are [those] who are wakeful and watchful for their Country's Good, though North sleeps in the Storm that his senseless misrule has raised. . . .'[1] Letters under Roman names were to be found in the newspapers almost as frequently as during Junius's attacks on an earlier administration.

The newspapers and one theatre also tried other methods of arousing patriotic feeling. The *Public Advertiser* and the *Lady's Magazine*,[2] for example, printed Queen Elizabeth's speech to her army encamped at Tilbury. Sadler's Wells drew 'immense audiences' with its performances of 'A New Musical Piece consisting of Airs, serious and comic, Recitatives, Choruses etc. called THE PROPHECY; or, QUEEN ELIZA-BETH AT TILBURY. In the course of which will be displayed a Transparency, representing the destruction of the Spanish Armada, and a Moving Perspective View representing the present GRAND FLEET'.[3] The nature of the entertainment may also be judged from one song that survives. It was given by Miss Dowson to 'great applause', and the last of its stanzas reads:

> To herself then let England be true,
> In spite of each threat and bravado,
> Protected by Heaven and you,
> I laugh at the Spanish Armada.[4]

Other poets, too, were busy. One of them wrote 'The Spanish Invasion', and an extract from it was printed in the *London Review*,[5] as a 'harangue by good queen Bess . . . when she appeared on horseback at the camp at Tilbury':

> Chiefs, heroes, nobles, subjects, warriors, friends,
> On whom our fate, next Providence depends,
> Think on your glorious and immortal sires!
> Think on their manly feats and martial fires!
> Like them, by dangers be not overaw'd,
> But learn to emulate what all applaud.
> When storms arise to stop your ready course,
> Stem the wild tempest; yield not to its force
> Great is the honour when you overthrow,
> By dint of courage, a superior foe!
> When magnanimity o'er fear prevails,
> And fate lends fortitude propitious gales!

---

[1] *Public Advertiser*, 5 Oct.

[2] 17 Sept.; and Sept. 1779, p. 453.

[3] *Morning Chronicle*, 29 Sept. 1779. Rhodes, ii. 182, was the first to note this entertainment, drawing his reference from *The Gazetteer*, 16 Aug. 1779.

[4] From a single sheet folio giving words and music, owned by the editor.

[5] x (1779), 403-4.

From weakness strength hath often met disgrace;
Nor is the swiftest sure to gain the race.
Valour may win what numbers seem to claim;
And skill through difficulties rise to fame.
In war, if disadvantage was unknown,
No hero to the public could be shewn.
The odds of pow'r, a disproportion'd fight,
Give greatest proofs of true intrinsic might.
I, though my sex might in my favour plead,
I, though a woman, will my army lead!
Brave ev'ry horror of a bloody field,
And boldly scorn, while life remains, to yield!
Perish before I see my people slaves,
To haughty tyrants, and to bigot braves!
To serve you, this is my intended plan:
My sex is woman, but my soul is man:
To you I both my purse and person bring:
A queen's my title; but my heart is king.

Its pomposity is equalled by its absurdity, but the speech does convey something of the feeling that England must stir herself to meet 'the haughty Don', as she had done in 1588.

Early in August, a newspaper correspondent calling himself 'Scribble-much' had recommended managers of country theatres 'to adopt the Practice of Sadler's Wells in producing something to raise the Spirits of our Countrymen at this alarming Crisis and trusts it will not be thought beneath the Attention of the Partners[1] of our Theatres Royal to pursue a similar Plan'.[2] But when there were no further alarms, people began to recover their composure and even to wonder if what had been seen off Plymouth were a phantom fleet. Covent Garden Theatre did not accept the advice of 'Scribble-much', but chose to laugh at the whole affair in a musical farce by Charles Dibdin, given there on 20 October and called *Plymouth in an Uproar*.

Drury Lane had to provide something to satisfy public interest and, ten days later, put on *The Critic*. There is some reason to believe, however, that Sheridan had not begun this afterpiece with the invasion in mind. The first newspaper reference to the new composition goes back to 2 October, when the *Morning Chronicle* reported: 'Mr. Sheridan's new farce, which is said to be a piece of ridicule against news-paper puffing, in the very articles which serve as puffs for it, we now hear will not be ready this fortnight.' This seems to indicate that, at the beginning of the month, the play had not been completed, and that, in its earliest form, it continued the satire on newspapers that Sheridan had begun in *The School for Scandal*. Possibly it comprised the present first act, without allusion

---

[1] Harris, of Covent Garden, and Sheridan had joined forces.
[2] *Public Advertiser*, 11 Aug. 1779.

to (or preparation for) the rehearsal. He certainly worked hardest on this part, and told Michael Kelly 'that he valued the first act more than any thing he ever wrote'.[1]

This would also explain why Sheridan gave the farce its title, one later questioned by a reviewer.[2] The choice is better appreciated when we realize that some allusion may have been intended to an occasional prelude of the same name that was acted before Cumberland's *Calypso* at Covent Garden on 20 March 1779:[3]

Mr. Cumberland, the author, wages a kind of *Irish fighting* war against newspaper printers in general, in hopes of thus covertly wounding an individual in that profession, who, once, it seems, shared his confidence, and only lost his friendship because he would not *puff* him, as the first poet, in this, or any other age. The prelude itself, abstracted from the malevolent design of this choleric man, is a wretched compound of self evident plagiarisms. . . .[4]

The prelude concerns Eustace, a naïve young poet from Newcastle, who calls on Type, a newspaper printer, to ask him to correct a tragedy he has written. He meets Ratsbane, who is amused by his innocence: 'Type a Critic! he has malice enough, if that were all; but as for his Learning . . . a Grocer's boy carries out more with him in his parcels, than Type does in his Pericranium. . . . His Heart [is] as black as his Ink.' In another encounter, three 'ill drest men' bring their paragraphs to Type: 'Gor'd by an over-drove Ox.—Run over, by a Brewer's dray.—Brought to life by the Humane Society!—Pshaw! let me have no more People brought to life— I desire Mr. MacMurdo you will not do your business by halves, and let me have some Variety in your next Casualties.' Eustace has some conversation with Type about his tragedy:

TYPE. Have you never a mad Scene in your Play?
EUSTACE. None. Is that necessary?
TYPE. Indispensible.
EUSTACE. But the Story does not admit of it.
TYPE. So much the worse for the Story, and the Story teller. A Tragedy without a mad Scene, is no more than a Coat without Buckram. Your heroics

---

[1] Kelly, ii. 322.

[2] George Colman the elder reviewed it in the *Monthly Review*, lxv (1781), 287, and said, 'We do not quite comprehend why this drama is entitled *The Critic*.' He might have found an answer in *The Rehearsal*, Act I, where Bayes says to Johnson: 'There are, now-a-days, a sort of persons they call critics, that, egad, have no more wit in them than so many hobby-horses; but they'll laugh at you, sir, and find fault, and censure things that, egad, I'm sure they are not able to do themselves. A sort of envious persons that emulate the glories of persons of parts, and think to build their fame by calumniating of persons.'

[3] The prelude called *The Critic* was not printed, and the only available text is the one sent to the Lord Chamberlain, now Larpent 472 in the Henry E. Huntington Library.

[4] *London Evening Post*, 20–23 Mar. 1779.

should have at least five kneelings, two faintings, and a fall plump on the floor, to make up the Pathos, or your Piece is lost. I'll tell you now, in the first Act, let her be in Love, deeply in Love. In the Second, d'ye see, deeper and deeper still. In the third, disappointed, Crossed, Circumvented. . . . In the Fifth, and last, mad, downright mad, frantic, raving. This, with a proper sprinkling of Fits, fallings, Stampings, Starings, Cursings, Prayings, Stabbings, and Poisonings, make up a good round rattling modern Tragedy.—As for Language, Bysse's art of Poetry,[1] or your own Common place book, if you have one, will set you up with Dialogue for all Subjects.

The prelude ends with Type's giving the tragedy to the corrector of the press with the injunction, 'If it has merit, look you, it must be wrote down; if it has none, 'tis no matter, leave it to its own damnation.'

It is only a trifle, and its main interest lies in its mention of certain subjects that Sheridan was to develop with such droll gaiety in his own farce. There is no proof that he ever saw the prelude, though he refers to *Calypso* in his letters.[2] Whether or not it gave Sheridan a start in his own composition would not be worth discussing if the prelude itself were not ascribed to Richard Cumberland.

Everyone interested in eighteenth-century literature knows that Sir Fretful Plagiary is based on Cumberland, and Sheridan even disclosed his reasons for satirizing him so personally:

Talking of Cumberland, he said that he had drawn the character of Sir Fretful Plagiary partly from that writer, and he quoted several passages intended to apply to him, especially that about attacking a friend; this he wrote with reference to Cumberland's abuse of himself (Sheridan) in the *St. James's Chronicle*, at the time that he was making great efforts for Cumberland at Drury Lane. He did not, however, intend that Parsons should dress after Cumberland, which that actor did, and so enraged Cumberland's son, a youth in the Guards, that he applied to General O'Hara to call Sheridan out. The General dissuaded the young gentleman from it, and afterwards mentioned the fact to Sheridan himself.[3]

Sheridan made this statement in 1814, and by that time was rather vague about the date of his 'great efforts' for Cumberland and the abuse in the newspaper. It may be that over a year separated the two: Cumberland was closest to him in January 1778 when *The Battle of Hastings* was accepted by Sheridan for production at Drury Lane after it had been rejected at Covent Garden. The greatest abuse that Sheridan suffered in the *St. James's Chronicle* occurred in a long notice of the *Monody* indicating that it was 'destitute of all poetical Merit except Versification'; this appeared in the issue of 11–13 March 1779, but there is no proof that it

---

[1] Edward Bysshe, *The Art of English Poetry* (1702).
[2] *Letters*, i. 125. *Calypso* was an opera with music by Butler.
[3] J. C. Hobhouse, Lord Broughton, *Recollections of a Long Life* (1909), i. 138.

was written by Cumberland. In fact, he declared in his *Memoirs*,[1] 'I solemnly protest that I have never written, or caused to be written, a single line to puff and praise myself, or to decry a brother dramatist, since I had life.' But Cumberland's ingratitude for help in the theatre was known to Garrick,[2] and we may doubt, like Edmond Malone, if we can place 'much confidence in the account'.[3]

Sheridan and he were temperamentally opposed. Cumberland was precise, methodical, vain, and quarrelsome, proud of his descent from Richard Bentley and of his own classical taste. Garrick said he was 'the man without a skin',[4] and Kelly thought him 'one of the most sensitive of men, when his own writings were spoken of; and, moreover, reckoned envious in the highest degree. He had an inveterate dislike of Mr. Sheridan, and would not allow him the praise of a good dramatic writer. . . .'[5] His attempts to hide his irritation were not very successful, as on the occasion when he read *The Battle of Hastings* to the Drury Lane company and Sheridan 'came in yawning at the fifth act, with no other apology than having sate up late two nights running. It gave me not the least offence.'[6] His own self-satisfaction is evident in his comments on the corrections he had made to this tragedy; they read as if they were to be spoken, in turn, by Puff and Sir Fretful: 'Edwina's[7] simile of the Tower (act the first) is made very impassioned; the conclusion of the fourth act was before your criticism came to hand entirely reformed, and I owed the correction to Miss Younge's protest against the simile of the *lightning*.'[7] In any contest between them,[8] Sheridan's cool wit was bound to be victorious:

When the 'School for Scandal' came out, Cumberland's children prevailed upon their father to take them to see it;—they had the stage box—their father was seated behind them; and . . . every time the children laughed at what was going on on the stage, he pinched them, and said, 'What are you laughing at, my dear little folks? You should not laugh, my angels; there is nothing to laugh at.'—And then, in an under tone, 'Keep still, you little dunces.'

---

[1] (2nd edn., 1807), i. 270.

[2] *Garrick Letters*, p. 999. Burney says that he was Garrick's aversion, 'and he must have hated Garrick cordially—though for fear posterity sh[oul]d know that Men such as Garrick and Sheridan were his Enemies, he praises them highly' (R. Lonsdale, *Dr. Charles Burney* (Oxford, 1965), p. 435).

[3] *The Farington Diary*, ed. J. Greig (1922–8), iii. 200–1.

[4] R. Cumberland, *Memoirs* (2nd edn., 1807), i. 347. A contemporary was more severe: 'His whole conversation is sadly disgusting, from irony and detraction, conveyed in a cunning sort of way', quoted in James Ogden, *Isaac D'Israeli* (Oxford, 1969), p. 77.

[5] Kelly, ii. 120.

[6] *Garrick Corr.* ii. 285.

[7] A reference to Edwina is to be found in the Crewe version of *The Critic*. See p. 544 below.

[8] It ended with a nice irony: they lie next to each other in the Poet's Corner.

Sheridan having been told of this, said, 'It was very ungrateful in Cumberland to have been displeased with his poor children, for laughing at *my comedy*; for I went the other night to see *his tragedy* and laughed at it from beginning to end.'[1]

This well-known anecdote takes on a new interest if we believe that the tragedy he alluded to in it (and in the mock-tragedy of his *Critic*)[2] was *The Battle of Hastings*.

Sheridan claimed, however, that he had founded Sir Fretful 'only partly' on Cumberland,[3] and some critics were swift to point out that the other part was drawn from his own character:

Mr. Sheridan, too, gives us to understand, that there is a certain author who is uneasy, miserable, and even tortured, by the attacks of nameless writers in the newspapers. Where's the satire of this? . . . I say, Sir, when Mr. Sheridan reads these things, he feels angry and offended—d——ns the newspapers, curses their Editors, and has exactly the same sensations he gives Sir Fretful Plagiary on the stage,—whom indeed, if I could suspect Mr. S. capable of an intentional *felo de se*, I should have thought a character well copied from himself.[4]

The point is a reasonable one, though Sheridan is also satirizing the vanity of authors in all ages.

People recognized victims other than Cumberland. Dangle represented Thomas ('Dapper') Vaughan, author of *The Hotel*, friend of Henry Bate, and something of a green-room gossip or theatrical 'dangler'.[5] The ridicule of the language of auctioneers was pointed at Robert Langford, who had made an effort to gain some financial control at Drury Lane.[6] George Colman, too, came in for mention, and the *Morning Chronicle* thought 'the touches on the Haymarket author and manager feeble'.[7]

---

[1] Kelly, ii. 121. The anecdote itself only expands the theme of two lines in *The Critic* (p. 504, ll. 10–11) and two in the prologue to Buckingham's *The Rehearsal*:

> Our poets make us laugh at tragedy;
> And with their comedies they make us cry.

[2] As suggested by H. Barton Baker, 'Richard Brinsley Sheridan', *Gentleman's Magazine*, ccxliii (1878), 312.

[3] This has been forgotten because of the 'malevolence' of Parsons's performance: 'In pantomiming the character, and in the exercise of his features, he was admirable. His face expressed envy, malice, and arrogance, so powerfully, that we felt compassion . . . and could not help thinking Mr. Sheridan had mistaken cruelty for justice.' (*Morning Chronicle*, 1 Nov. 1779.)

[4] 'A Touch and Away' in the *Morning Chronicle*, 4 Nov. 1779. A similar point is made in the *Public Advertiser*, 8 Nov. 1779.

[5] See Henry Angelo, *Reminiscences* (1830), ii. 411; and *Garrick Corr.* ii. 198. *The Town and Country Magazine*, xi (1779), 574–5, says, 'Mr. Dangle is likewise a faithful portrait of another well-known character, who pretends to be the patron of dramatic writers, as well as performers of every class, and yet his spleen being at least equal to his patronage, he fails not to execrate those very pieces he had recommended.'

[6] See *Letters*, i. 104–7, and 'Bobby the Fair' in the *Morning Post*, 1 Nov. 1779.

[7] *Morning Chronicle*, 1 Nov. 1779.

There were probably a number of other personal allusions that were readily understood in 1779, but are now forgotten. Sheridan was said to have 'boldly ventured to irritate the swarm of literary insects',[1] and seems to have seen himself as another Pope, bringing dunces up for judgement:

Violent disputes have lately arisen between the Author and certain Play writers, some of whom are also Cricks on Theatrical Subjects in News-papers. On Mr. Sheridan's Elevation into the Condition of Manager, these Persons, for obvious Reasons, outstepped a little the Modesty of Truth in his Praises, hoping for a Recompense in his Partiality and Favour: But it seems he has forgotten all of them, and even given some Reasons of Complaint. This has changed the general Language of the Papers on the important Subject of the Manager; brought out Imputations on his Abilities and Integrity; and even induced some of them to ascribe his Popularity to Depredations on the Property of others, which had been entrusted to his Care. To defend himself, and to be revenged on his Enemies, he has brought forth the Critick; in which he has *peached* and caricatured his old Friends most outrageously.

At the same time, this writer admitted that every man of letters was an enemy to another, and no seraglio 'exhibited more artifice, more perfidy'.[2]

A much greater opportunity for personal allusion and topical jest presented itself once Sheridan widened the scope of the farce to include the mock-tragedy. He had an excellent model in the Duke of Buckingham's *The Rehearsal*, which had 'always been used as a Vehicle to convey witty remarks on the failings of the performers through the part of Mr. Bayes; frequently by mimicking their Defects either in Oratory or Action, and almost always by telling them of some of the Negligences and Misconceptions. It has likewise conveyed a Stroke of Satire occasionally on the Manager, as well as Mr. Bayes. . . .'[3] In nine years between 1767 and 1776 it was revived on twenty-two occasions: Bayes was taken by Foote for ten performances at the Haymarket; by Lee and Shuter for two each at Covent Garden; and by Garrick and King for four each at Drury Lane.[4] *The Rehearsal* was intimately known to playgoers, and Sheridan intended it to be in their minds when they saw *The Critic*.[5] He was so successful that *The Rehearsal* was seldom revived after 1779, and its place in the Drury Lane repertoire was taken by *The Critic*.

[1] *Morning Post*, 5 Nov. 1779.

[2] *St. James's Chronicle*, 30 Oct.–2 Nov. 1779.

[3] From an unidentified newspaper cutting of 26 Aug. 1777, in 'Covent Garden and Drury Lane Scrapbooks', vol. ix (1776–7), in the Folger Shakespeare Library.

[4] See *The London Stage*, Part 4, pp. 1274, 1276, 1351, 1538, 1619, 1621, 1649, 1650, 1665, 1677, 1733–5, 1792, 1799, 1822, 1839, 1902–3, 1977, 1990.

[5] As is shown in his parodying some of its lines, introducing topicalities, and giving Puff to King: cf. p. 468, n. 2 above. For critics, see *An Index to Mankind* (1751), p. 53: 'By a Critic was generally understood a good Judge, but now, with us, it signifies no more than an unmerciful Fault-finder, two steps above a Fool, and a great many below a wise Man.'

The newspapers of the day noted the resemblance and also compared the farce with Fielding's *Pasquin* (1736), Garrick's *A Peep behind the Curtain: or, The New Rehearsal* (1767), and the anonymous *The Tailors, a Tragedy for Warm Weather* (1767).[1] More recent writers have pointed out similarities to Garrick's *A Meeting of the Company* (1774),[2] and Colman's *New Brooms*.[3] They prove that Sheridan was familiar with popular burlesque, and that in his new offering he gave a witty turn to some long accepted themes and conventions. He himself had tried his hand earlier in this genre, when associated with Halhed in the composition of *Ixion*.[4] He had also written a 'fragment of a scene' that Moore described as concerning 'a puffing author . . . intended to be a Scotchman'.[5] It includes several ideas, and a couple of lines, that were to be transferred to *The Critic*.[6]

Sheridan's ridicule of stage conventions is highly amusing even if it is unfair, and it is always well to remember that he laughed at himself as well as at other authors and leading tragedians. He wrote puffs for Drury Lane,[7] so was best able to enjoy his own joke when he made Puff (King) recite some lines that were supposed to have appeared in the newspapers: 'It is not in the power of language to do justice to Mr. King!—Indeed he more than merited those repeated bursts of applause which he drew from a most brilliant and judicious audience!'[8] The very local and topical nature of the comic effect[9] is apparent too in the idea that Puff (and not Sir Fretful) was the author of the mock-tragedy because King was manager of Sadler's Wells and, therefore, probably compiler of *The Prophecy; or, Queen Elizabeth at Tilbury*.[10]

The players themselves, either with Sheridan's connivance or without it, added to the general hilarity by making fun of their fellows. The *Morning Post* noted: 'Miss Pope's imitation of a well-known tragedy heroine in one of her *mad movements*, and Mr. Bannister's representation of the *flounder-like* death of as celebrated a tragedy hero, were very striking traits, and universally applauded.'[11] Miss Pope, as Tilburina, took off Mrs. Crawford, and Bannister, as Whiskerandos, amused the audience at the expense of 'Gentleman' Smith's mannerisms as Richard III.[12]

---

[1] *Morning Chronicle*, 1 Nov. 1779.

[2] E. P. Stein, *Three Plays by David Garrick* (New York, 1926), p. 116.

[3] Dane F. Smith, *The Critics in the Audience of the London Theatres from Buckingham to Sheridan* (Albuquerque, N. Mexico, 1953), pp. 122–7.

[4] See below, p. 793.   [5] Moore, i. 24–5.   [6] See below, p. 804.

[7] See the one in his own handwriting transcribed in Rae, *Sheridan*, ii. 6 n.; and cf. the *Morning Chronicle*, 5 Nov. 1779.   [8] See below, p. 515.

[9] The traditional 'business' was carried to the United States. Cf. William Dunlap, *A History of the American Theatre* (New York, 1832), p. 165: 'Hodgkinson, on playing Puff in the Critic, mentioned himself as is usual, it being intended by the author that the actor shall do so.'

[10] See Rhodes, ii. 181–2.   [11] 1 Nov. 1779.

[12] See *General Evening Post*, 30 Oct.–2 Nov. 1779.

They also seem to have mimicked other 'modern heroes and heroines of tragedy'.[1]

The farce was written to appeal most strongly to those who knew intimately current histrionic styles and theatrical devices as well as the tragedies and sentimental comedies of the past fifty years. Its range of reference was of greatest interest to the playhouse coterie, since, as the *London Evening Post* stated, only 'those deep in the knowledge of Green room anecdote, and the private character of authors and theatrical danglers, may bring home the application to particular people'.[2] Horace Walpole criticized it on just those grounds: '*The Critic*, I own, was not so new as I expected; and then my being ill versed in modern dramas, most of the allusions must have escaped me. Does not half the merit of *The Rehearsal* depend on the notes?'[3] An enthusiastic supporter of the theatre would deny this, for immediate recognition brings delight that is never to be equalled by the reading of footnotes.[4] An audience will either enjoy the joke or become resentful at missing the point.

The coterie nature of the entertainment was also obvious in the way that some of the functionaries from behind the curtain gratified the audience by making an appearance on the stage. At the same time, Sheridan laughed at the extravagant demands made on the playhouse by inexperienced dramatists: he even brought on the under-prompter, head-carpenter, and master-lamplighter. This is evident in a piece of dialogue given on the first night[5] but deleted later:

PUFF. So, this is a pretty dilemma indeed—do call the head Carpenter to me.
UNDER PROMPTER. Mr. Butler. [*Enter* CARPENTER *Drest*] Here he is Sir.
PUFF. Hey—this the head Carpenter?
UNDER PROMPTER. Yes Sir. He was to have walk'd as one of the Generals at the review, for the truth is Sir your Tragedy employs every body in the Company.
PUFF. Then pray Mr. General, or Mr. Carpenter what is all this?
CARPENTER. Why Sir you only Consider what my Men have to do—they have got to remove Tilbury Fort with the Cannon, and to sink Gravesend and the River, and I only desire three minutes to do it in.
PUFF. Ah, and they have cut out the Scene.
CARPENTER. Besides, could I manage it in less, I question if the Lamplighters could clear away the Sun in time.
PUFF. Do, call one of them here.

---

[1] *Morning Chronicle*, 1 Nov. 1779. But Sichel, i. 605, is wrong in saying that 'the soliloquy always to the pit' was a hit at J. P. Kemble. It could not have been: Kemble was only a provincial actor at that date.

[2] 30 Oct.–2 Nov. 1779.   [3] *Walpole Corr.* xxxiii (1965), 159.

[4] Holcroft thought of preparing a key to *The Critic*: see *Dublin University Magazine*, xlvi (1855), 46.

[5] From the manuscript submitted to the Lord Chamberlain, Larpent 494, in the Henry E. Huntington Library.

UNDER PROMPTER. Master Lamplighter. (*From without*) Mr. Goodwin.

LAMPLIGHTER. Here (*Enter* LAMPLIGHTER *as a River God with a* PAGE *holding up his train.*)

PUFF. Sir, your most obedient Servant—who the Devil's this?

UNDER PROMPTER. The Master Lamplighter Sir—he does one of the River Gods in the Procession.

PUFF. O a River God is he—Well, Sir, you want time here I understand.

LAMPLIGHTER. Three Minutes at least Sir, unless you have a Mind to burn the Fort.

PUFF. Then they have cut out the Scene.

CARPENTER. Lord Sir there only wants a little Business to be put in here just as long as while we have been speaking will do it.

PUFF. What then are you all ready now?

PROMPTER BEHIND. Yes, all clear.

PUFF. O, then we'll easily manage it.

UNDER PROMPTER. Clear the Stage.

PUFF. And do, General, keep a Sharp look out, and beg the River God, not to spare his Oil in the last Scene, it must be brilliant—Gentlemen I beg a thousand Pardons but—

SNEER. O dear these little things will happen.[1]

The farce, as presented on its first night, was in every sense a piece of pure theatre. Even the dresses were so exaggerated as to be ludicrous, and at least one comment on them was sarcastic: 'There is a vast deal of wit in the length of Miss Pope's train; and . . . the enormous ruffs of Raleigh and his companions contain some excellent repartees and bon-mots.'[2] But the aim was laughter and was amply achieved.

The scenery and the finale were directed to a rather different end. Ridicule of the preparations for defence in the sleeping sentinels and other signs of confusion gave place to a scene in which the arts of painter and machinist were found at their highest: the sea-view representing an action 'between the British fleet and the Spanish Armada, wherein after a great part of the latter are destroyed by fireships, the former appear triumphantly pursuing them to martial music playing *Britannia rules the Waves*'.[3] De Loutherburg excelled himself on this occasion, and the *London Evening Post* remarked: 'The deception of the sea was very strong, and the perspective of the ships, together with the mode of their sailing, truly picturesque. This great painter, in all his scenic productions,[4] seems to bring nature to our view, instead of painting views after nature.'[5] They aroused wonder that led easily into patriotic sentiment; but the farce concluded with a piece of pastoral spectacle of the rivers 'with their

---

[1] See below, p. 537. The passage would have appeared between lines 26 and 28.

[2] *Morning Chronicle*, 4 Nov. 1779.   [3] *Morning Post*, 1 Nov. 1779.

[4] His three other sets for *The Critic* were warmly praised: 'A view of the Thames'; 'Gravesend from Tilbury Fort'; and 'The Governor's tent in a grove'.

[5] 30 Oct.–2 Nov. 1779.

various symbols in their hands' and 'old Father Time bringing up in the rear in his chrystal car'. Then came a fête to honour Britannia on her victory: 'a dance of river nymphs and godlings'.[1] With such a variety of entertainment, there was bound to be something to please everyone.

RECEPTION

Sir Fretful Plagiary is a character whose outline is so boldly drawn, and whose component parts are so strongly etched in *aqua fortis*, 'that he who runs may *read him*!' It is certainly a high finished copy of the kind, and cannot fail to correct, in a great measure, the contemptible habits it so happily exposes. Mr. *Dangle* is another well-known copy from the town; a character affecting the patronage of every thing that is *theatrical*, from the playwright down to the lowest of the performers; one who by this means obtains the perusal of all plays in manuscript, and, however high they may stand in his own opinion, has so much the virtue of compliance, as to join any one afterwards in execrating every part of each piece, '*though the author is his very good friend*'.

Mrs. *Dangle* is represented as a violent stickler for the chaste, sentimental drama of latter days. *Sneer* is drawn a shrewd fellow of the world, who dryly ridicules the various absurdities of all his theatrical friends. Mr. *Puff* (the modern *Bayes* of the piece) is introduced as having a new tragedy in rehearsal, to which he comes to invite his friends *Dangle* and *Sneer*; but previous to their going, he gives them a humorous account of his mode of living by various stratagems, which he practised in the diurnal prints; viz. sometimes by advertising 'that he was burnt out, and lost his all—another, that he had lost the use of all his limbs, going round the next morning to his friends to receive the several contributions:—at other times, that he was a widow with four helpless babes; or that he had eleven husbands cruelly pressed from him, and was left destitute each time, eight months gone with child, &c. &c.' After this he got into the service of the auctioneers; to whose advertisements[2] he gave a fancy, and polish before unknown. (*Here were introduced several curious quotations from the advertisements of a certain Auctioneer y'cleped*, Bobby the Fair, *which threw the whole house into convulsions of laughter*.) He next assumed the character of puffer-general; whose art, in imitation of Shakespeare's variations on *Lyeinge*, he divides into the *puff direct* the *puff collusive*, the *puff evasive*, &c. &c.—to each of which he subjoins a case in point, as true in fact, as it proved humorous in recital. After a few laughable truisms on the general mode of manufacturing the daily prints, the first act concludes with *Puff* and his two friends being summoned to attend the rehearsal of his tragedy, the burlesque representation of which employs the remainder of the piece.—

[1] *Morning Post*, 1 Nov. 1779.   [2] Cf. p. 516, n. 1.

The scene of this mock tragedy is laid at Tilbury Fort, at the time of the Spanish Armada; the hero and heroine of which are *Whiskerandos*, nephew of the Spanish Admiral, taken by the Captain of an English privateer, and confined a prisoner in the fort, and *Tilburina*, the Governor's daughter.

It would be in vain to attempt a description of this part of the piece, the principal excellence of which must naturally consist in dumb shew, extravagant gestures, or the dullest of all tragic rhapsodies.—Our readers must be content, therefore, with a general observation on the whole. The *Tragedy Rehearsed*, evidently on the plan of the Duke of Bucking-ham's *Rehearsal*, is, in our opinion, superior to all the other imitations of that celebrated production. It is conceived with great fancy, and repre-sents *modern tragedizing* throughout, in a point of view too ridiculous not to secure, in some degree, its intended effect. The manner of bringing *Burleigh* on, and *Puff* discovering so much anxiety for the performer being perfect in a character that had not a syllable to utter, is an excellent conceit; nor was *Puff's* interpretation of that Prime Minister's *thoughts* by any means an ill-timed stroke of political satire.

The only objection to this mock tragedy, is its extreme length; brevity being, in our opinion, as much the *life of burlesque*, as it is the *soul of wit*; and therefore, notwithstanding the remonstrances of Mr. Puff, if the actors were permitted to cut away half as much more, the piece would find its improvement therein. Even the first act, tho' abounding with temporary strokes of wit and humour, appears tedious; this however might soon be remedied, by curtailing the tea-table *tête-a-tête* between Mr. *Dangle* and his wife, which has neither novelty, nor incident, to plead for its future existence. (*Morning Post*, 1 Nov. 1779.)

After so long a Dearth of dramatic Novelty, the Expectation of the Public, which had presaged every Excellence from the Pen of their favourite Author, was at length fully gratified by the representation on Saturday of *The Critic*, a Dramatic After-piece, in Three Acts.

. . . The first act ridicules the several Species of petty Patronage and mock-Consequence of a self-elected Critic, in the character of *Dangle*; and of bitter Pleasantry and merry Malice in the cold sarcastic Severity of *Sneer*. These Characters are introduced at *Dangle*'s Theatrical Levee, and are succeeded by *Sir Fretful Plagiary* whose name is a Definition of him-self. Upon him the Author seems to have employed the whole Force and finest Powers of his wit. He is at once original and striking. With an affected Candour he importunes his friends for Comments which his Vanity has predetermined him to reject. His false humanity is at perpetual Variance with his real Arrogance; and while this would-be Stoic of Parnassus affects to be above all petty Censure, and even to be diverted by it, he becomes doubly ridiculous by betraying the meanest Subservience

to those very Passions which he most affects not to feel. Whether Sir
Fretful Plagiary is drawn from Nature, or is only the coinage of Fancy,
we will not determine; but if the former is the Case, the Original certainly
bids as fair for an enduring Ridicule as Dryden in *Bayes*.

After a scene of such Novelty and Wit, however judicious it might at
first appear to lighten the Dialogue by the Intervention of some Incident,
we cannot however think that the Introduction of the Operatical Candidates
was in the least Degree necessary; or that any Relief was wanting to the
bold Humour of the succeeding Character.—Mr. *Puff* is the finished Portrait of the Art he professes . . . This Character is undoubtedly taken from
Nature, and is peculiar to the present times. It is not however the Portrait
of any single *Individual* but the display of the whole *Species*, whose ridiculous Abuse of the Liberty of the Press, though too low an Offence for serious
Severity, was of all others the properest Theme for the Author of The
School for Scandal; the News-papers having of late superseded the more
contracted Practice of private Defamation, by giving a wider Circulation to
secret Malice, and becoming the open Registers of anonymous Detraction.
With the liveliest display of this Science, the first Act of *The Critic* closes.

The second and third contain *The Rehearsal of the Tragedy*—and in
these, considering how much of the *general* Subject had originally been
pre-occupied by the Duke of Buckingham, and how frequently also
several Authors of a later Date have ridiculed the *particular* Affectations
of Tragic Writers, it is astonishing with what Novelty and Ingenuity the
striking Faults of our present Compositions in this Line are here satirized:
The tedious and unartificial Commencements of modern Tragedies, the
inflated Diction, the figurative Tautology, the *Feu de théâtre* of Embraces
and Groans, Vows and Prayers, florid Pathos, whining Heroism, and
above all, the Trick of Stage Situation, are ridiculed with a Burlesque
which perhaps may be thought rather too refined for the Multitude. . . .
(*The Public Advertiser*, 1 Nov. 1779.)

The Critic is avowedly the production of the author of *The School for
Scandal*; like that comedy it has a great deal of merit, but is nevertheless
liable to more objection than any one piece of Mr. Sheridan's writing. The
first act, though uncommonly long, teems with poignant satire, keen
wit, and sterling humour. The second and third are by no means as
pleasant as the first, but are not without their share of seasoning; their
extreme length, however, rendered them heavy and tiresome. Their
want of effect also is ascribable in some measure to the satire being too
much concealed—in a mock tragedy the bathos should float upon the
surface . . . and above all things, every burlesque exhibition should be
short, because when the humour is violently extravagant, it soon satiates.
With regard to play, conduct and characters, Mr. Sheridan has not
attempted the least originality, excepting only in the character of Sir

Fretful Plagiary which is directly and grossly personal. The *Rehearsal*, *Tragedy à la mode*, Garrick's *Peep behind the Curtain*, and various other pieces, are examples, after which the *Critic* has been formed; some of these pieces are very closely parodied, and even Shakespeare is struck at by this dramatic drawcansir, in the last words uttered by his Spanish enamorato. The character of Puff is a mixture of Spatter in the *English Merchant*, and Bayes in the *Rehearsal*, with some additional colouring. The ridicule upon newspapers is in many cases very just, but in the warmth of resentment, (for the whole piece is obviously rather an act of angry retaliation than a dramatic satire, founded on general principles) Mr. Sheridan has been carried too far. Possibly the satire on advertisements addressed to the affluent and humane, may deprive some worthy objects of that relief which their distresses might otherwise receive from the benevolent. . . .

The *Morning Chronicle* being particularly *advertized* in the *Critic*, it was our earnest wish to have been warranted to give the piece the *puff direct* . . . but 'truth to say', the *Critic* will not bear such an account, excepting only with regard to the performers, who deserved it richly. . . . (*Morning Chronicle*, 1 Nov. 1779.)

One who was present in the boxes at Drury-Lane Theatre on Saturday evening, has favoured us with the following remarks on the new entertainment of *The Critic*. The first is a most glaring impropriety of expression, in the two excellent performers of Puff and Sneer; the first mentioned the word God once, and the other spoke it twice in the same scene; however inadvertent the expressions, yet when spoke on the stage they should be by no means passed over without censure, let the abilities of the performer be ever so respectable. Another impropriety, was the very witty ridicule of certain dramatic plagiarists, who advertise that they have sold ten editions, before they have sold ten books, when in the very next and best painted scene in the whole piece, to the utter astonishment of the whole audience, we are presented with one of the most direct species of plagiarism that perhaps was ever exhibited on the English stage, viz. an exact, and to do the artist justice, a good representation of that very beautiful engraving of Queen Elizabeth at Tilbury, with the view of the Spanish Armada, which is annexed to Mr. Johnson's Ladies polite Lottery Pocket Book, for 1780, price 1s. 6d. and sold at No. 4 Ludgate-hill; now universally purchased, and in the highest estimation for its superior elegance, to any ladies pocket book ever published in these kingdoms; besides the beneficial chance delivered with it gratis, which entitles the purchasers to more certain advantages than many others sold for half a crown. Mr. King's description of his living comfortably by his misfortunes, and advertising sham distress in order to procure benefactions from the unwary, however wittily expressed, should most certainly be expunged, as it may prevent many humane hearts which do honour to our nature, from relieving the *really distressed objects* of Christian compassion: it is hoped the same maxim prevails on the stage; which does so much honour to our courts of justice; that it is better for ten villains to escape punishment, than that one innocent person should suffer. (*Morning Chronicle*, 1 Nov. 1779.)

The entertainment and effect of Mr. Sheridan's new dramatic piece, called *The Critic*, was last night considerably heightened and improved, in consequence of its having been judiciously altered and curtailed. The first act is now at least twenty minutes shorter in the time of representation, and Puff's character is, if anything, more lively and agreeable for his having been deprived of some of his long speeches, which without any addition to the force of the satire, served only to shew that Mr. Sheridan was determined not to let the merest trifle escape him, which he could convert into a severity against news-papers. The *Tragedy rehearsed* has also had the author's pruning knife applied to it, as well as that of the comedians, and being much compressed is more laughable, and pleasant than it was on Saturday evening.

. . . The ridicule of the Humane Society[1] has still a place in *The Critic*, which (as the piece promises to be exceedingly popular in the theatre) will be a lasting monument of one of the most laudable institutions of this century, and will at the same time, shew that Mr. Sheridan (the favourite comic writer of it) thought the successful efforts of a set of men to rescue their fellow creatures from premature death, merited only public scorn and derision. (*Morning Chronicle*, 2 Nov. 1779.)

The author of this piece is said to be the acting manager (Mr. Sheridan) the éclat of whose name, as a dramatic writer, drew one of the most crowded and brilliant audiences we ever remember to have sat at, at this time of the year; and, on the whole, we think they were not disappointed in their evening's entertainment. The first act, as Lord Dorset said of Mr. Congreve's comedy of Love for Love, 'has wit enough for seven comedies'. It abounded with true satire, and poignant observation; and, allowing for the character of Puff being heightened beyond the life, in order to produce stage effect, it is one of the most finished sketches we know of.

The tragedy parts rather failed in supporting that flow of laugh and humour occasioned by the first act, arising from the solemnity of *tragic burlesque* not being generally understood. To those, however, conversant in the bombast of most modern tragedies, it had its *point*, and (considering how difficult it was to keep clear of 'The Rehearsal' and 'The Peep

---

[1] Instituted in 1774 by Thomas Cogan (1736–1818) and William Hawes (1736–1808), 'for the recovery of persons apparently drowned'. It also attempted to resuscitate people struck by lightning and suffocated by charcoal and lime fumes. Cf. pp. 26–7 above.

behind the Curtain', two pieces evidently on this plan) we think [showed] its originality. If Mr. Sheridan had only given his first act by way of prelude (as we are told he originally intended) it would have been a *Chef d'Oeuvre*; at present, we think it would be much mended by leaving out the Concert scene, compressing the tragedy part, and *lending* some of the wit and humour of the first act, (which it can very well afford) to the last act. (*London Evening Post*, 30 Oct.–2 Nov. 1779.)

The Parodies on the Advertisements, theatrical Accounts, Letters etc. in the News-papers, are very good Imitations of *Anticipation*;[1] but they are too numerous, too long, and some of them very injudiciously levelled at the best Virtues of Humanity. The first Act is, however, on the Whole, well furnished with Wit and Humour, and extremely well calculated to keep the Audience in a Roar.

The second and third Acts consist of a Rehearsal, in which the Authour parodies such a Number of Passages, which most Men endeavour to forget, that the Entertainment becomes insufferably heavy and tiresome, and would effectually sink it, but for the Aid of De Loutherbourg, who has decorated it with the most charming Scenes. The famous *Rehearsal* of the Duke of Buckingham should have instructed the Authour to avoid this Fault.

The Piece seems to be an Object of great Attention and Expectation in the House; for almost all the best Performers are crowded into it, and they exert their utmost Abilities. The Dresses, Scenes, and Decorations are in the richest Style, and the Expense attending them must be very considerable.

If the Piece were much shortened, divested of personal Injuries, and Satyres on real Distress; it has traits of Character, flashes of Wit and Humour, and it is furnished with such Performers, Scenes, and other ornamental Circumstances, as could not fail of giving it great Success. (*St. James's Chronicle*, 30 Oct.–2 Nov. 1779.)

'Sir, That Part of your Satire, which (in The Critick) is levelled against *Stage-Trick*, *Situation* and *Pantomime*, is well directed; but how came you to omit that *great* Comedy Situation, in which a Screen is the principal *Person* on the Stage?...' ('Hah!' to Mr. Sheridan, in *St. James's Chronicle*, 11–13 Nov. 1779.)

Mr. Sheridan's last piece call'd the Critic, was perform'd here [the Theatre Royal, Bristol] on Monday for the first time, and receiv'd in a manner, that does equal credit to the discernment and judgment of our audience, and to the very uncommon abilities of its excellent author.[2]—

---

[1] By Richard Tickell (1751–93).
[2] The part of the first act dealing with the interpreter and the 'Italian Family' was included in the performance: see *Felix Farley's Bristol Journal*, 5 Feb. 1780.

It was generally consider'd that this entertainment was calculated only for the meridian of London, and that the wit and satire with which it abounds, were chiefly personal or local—but the great applause it has met with both here and at Bath, sufficiently proves, that tho' it be possible particular characters may have been intended to be ridiculed in it—yet that the satire is general and the characters and situations in themselves perfectly natural and highly entertaining. (*Felix Farley's Bristol Journal*, 12 Feb. 1780.)

This *Tragedy Rehearsed* proceeds too closely in the beaten track of the Duke of Buckingham's *Rehearsal*. The mode and objects of ridicule are generally the same; except that the Author of the *Critic* has too indiscriminately attacked Tragedy in general, and levelled some of his severest traits against the very best modern tragedy in our language, we mean the tragedy of *Douglas*! The theatrical rage, however, for *situation, attitude, discoveries, processions*, etc. is properly and humorously exposed.
Leaving, however, *the Tragedy Rehearsed . . .* we revert with pleasure to the first [act] of the three, which abounds with wit, humour, and a masterly display of character. *Mr.* and *Mrs. Dangle*, though not very original, are natural and spirited; *Sneer* is drawn with a finer pencil; the *Unintelligible Interpreter* is truly pleasant; and the treatise on panegyric, delivered by *Puff*, is lively, shrewd, and satirical, though rather narrative than dramatic. From his own delineation of his character in the first Act, we should not expect to see him dwindle into the Bayes of the two last. That part might perhaps have been more properly sustained by *Sir Fretful Plagiary*—for whose sake, we are inclined to believe that the whole piece was written. . . . (George Colman the Elder, reviewing the published version of *The Critic*, in the *Monthly Review*, lxv (1781), 287.)

We may almost say that he gave the Tragic Muse her death-wound in his entertainment of the Critic, which we have always considered as the offspring of a pen that had in vain attempted to write a tragedy, and therefore felt a malicious pleasure in decrying a species of composition which has been deemed superior to its own. (*The British Magazine*, iii (1783), 173.)

The Critic is surely nothing equal, as a satire, to *Tom Thumb*—and when we talk of *The Rehearsal*, it sinks to nothing. Fielding and Buckingham have taken in the whole round of tragedy, and properly conceived that Dryden, Lee, and the old standards, were fair game. What has Mr. Sheridan done? Why truly, except indeed where he chuses to ridicule Shakespeare—which, by the bye, I do not think an English audience would have suffered in any body else—he has exposed the puerile, modern stuff, which if it be deficient in merit, he—as a manager—must bear his share of reprehension for obtruding it on the public. The business of *Sir Plagiary* is severe enough; but, unfortunately, the very words he intends should give the deepest wound, recoils on himself—for they are a *plagiary. Puff*, is full of pointed observation, but that part of the piece is the first instance—as I before observed—where an audience have quietly sat down and consented to be laughed at by an author. As to the drift of the piece, it appears to be written with a view alone to discourage writers of tragedy; for there is no possible situation that can excite pity, terror, or any of those passions which it is the business of tragedy peculiarly to call forth, but this work, which 'professes to be critical,' attempts to laugh at— and really not always with success; for, if figure and imagery may at all be introduced in this species of writing, the criticism itself is more an object of ridicule than the thing it professes to criticise. In short, I defy Mr. Sheridan himself to write a tragedy so as to steer clear of his own lash; and how absurd must a man appear who provides a castigation for himself! The matter relative to the clock, at the beginning of *The Duenna*, shews evidently that he is vulnerable, as well as his neighbours; and as the circumstance goes to a reprobation of the unities, it were as modest to propose some better criterion before he invited us to explode the admitted standard: 'but one man may steal a horse better than another look over the hedge,' says the old proverb. Mr. Sheridan can write in any style, and to any degree of perfection he pleases, but his public writing, like his public speaking, is more *catching* than CAPTIVATING; it *dazzles*, but does not IMPRESS—it *charms*, but does not CONVINCE. In short, as that gentleman's aim is popularity, he does every thing for the moment, and it is a question, after he has sunk into ease and independence, from his natural indolence of mind, whether he will ever again be known but by a few eminent trifles written to grace the private cabinet, and make up the *delices* of the elegant and erudite.

Mr. Sheridan having most probably done with the stage, as an author, it is but fair to examine how far, in that capacity, he has been an acquisition to the public; and when we consider that he has deprived the world of the best singer, beyond all comparison, that we have ever heard, it is very doubtful whether what he has given be adequate to what he has taken away—and, admitting this, the public would rather have gained than lost had Mr. Sheridan originally kept to politics, and have had nothing to do with the theatre.

This gentleman, from his earliest youth, resolved to be at the top of his profession, be it what it might. May his integrity equal his abilities, and there is no situation but he will adorn! (*The Musical Tour of Mr. Dibdin* (Sheffield, 1788), pp. 262–3.)

[Regret is expressed that Sheridan did not make Sir Fretful Plagiary the author of the tragedy rehearsed] for although the character of Puff cannot be better supported than it is by Mr. King, the insensibility of the character will not admit of those striking displays of tortured vanity, which might have been exhibited by Sir Fretful Plagiary, had he been continued on the scene. (*The Theatrical Guardian*, 5 Mar. 1791.)

Oct. 30 1779: The Critic, though by some pronounced a *Snarler*, went off with great applause. ([W. C. Oulton], *The History of the Theatres of London . . . 1771 to 1795* (1796), i. 89.)

CHOICE OF TEXT

The textual interest of some of the versions of *The Critic* has already been mentioned.[1] Additional details concerning the more important manuscripts and printed copies are given below.

1. OF THE PROLOGUE

I have been unable to locate the original manuscript of the prologue, so I have taken the first edition of 1781 as copy-text, collating it with the versions in the Larpent and Crewe MSS.

2. OF THE SONGS

The *London Chronicle*, 30 October–2 November 1779, noted that in the second scene, 'we meet with an Italian musical family, who are introduced to Mr. Dangle by Monsieur le —— in order to procure them an engagement at the Opera house. They sing a couple of foreign airs and depart.' The *General Evening Post* of the same date recorded, 'They sing a trio and duet, which had a pleasing and *nouvelle* effect.'

The text of 1781 merely says that 'they sing trios, etc.' Whatever they did in that year, it is clear that in the early performances, Delpini, Miss Field, and Miss Abrams sang a trio in French. It reads:

Je suis sortis de mon paÿs
  pour jouer de ma Chitarre
	I left my Country and my Friends
	  to play on my Guitar

Qui fait tin tin tin	Which goes tang tang tang
Qui fait tintamarre.	Which goes tang tamarre.
Tout le monde icy m'appelle,	I here am known and call'd by all,

Toujours par le nom de ma joly
  Chitarre.
	By the name of my tinkling
	  Guittar.

Nanette un jour me dit mon coeur,	Little Nancy said to me one Day,
Jouer un peu de ta belle Chitarre.	Come and play on your Guittar.

The Italian duet sung by Miss Fields and Miss Abrams reads:

Lusinghiero m'ingannasti	Flat'rer why dost thou deceive me?
Mi tradisti O Dio per che	Why betray my constant love?

---

[1] See pp. 24–30 above.

Tu piangesti e sospirasti	Why with sighs and well feign'd Sorrow
Tu giurasti fede ame	Hast thou sworn thy faith to prove?
Traditore ingannatore	False betrayer, thou base deceiver,
Tutto il male vien da te.	Ev'ry grief I owe to thee.

Both are to be found in some sheets entitled:

> The | SONG and DUET | *Sung by* | *Sigr. Delpini, Miss Field, and Miss Abrams,* | in the Entertainment of the | *CRITIC* | As perform'd at the THEATRE-ROYAL in DRURY-LANE, | *Published by Permission of the Managers* | [with rules adjoining] Price 1s. 6d | LONDON | *Printed for S. A. and P. Thompson, No. 75, St. Paul's Church Yard.*

N.d. Folio. 7 pages. Yale University Library copy.

The text also includes another French trio sung in *The Critic*. Its English first line is 'A maiden blush of sweet fifteen.'

Rhodes, iii. 364–5, found the text of the Italian duet in *The Banquet of Thalia* (York, 1790), and was criticized by Alfred Loewenberg[1] for not realizing that the provincial text was neither original nor complete. Loewenberg himself drew attention to the music published by Longman and Broderip, presumably towards the end of 1779, with the title-page:

> The | Favorite Airs | in the | Critic | Sung with universal Applause | by Miss Field | Miss Abrahams and Sigr. Delpini | at the Theatre Royal Drury Lane | adapted for the | Voice, Harpsichord, Violin, | German Flute and Guittar. | By Sigr. Giordani | Price 1 : 6
>
> London Printed by Longman and Broderip No. 26 Cheapside | Music Sellers to the Royal Family.

N.d. Folio. 12 pages.

He thought the composer was probably Tommaso Giordani, rather than his brother, Giuseppe Giordani, called Giordanello.

Loewenberg expressed the view that 'the rather trifling nature of these lyrics makes it easy to see why Sheridan did not care to have them inserted in the printed edition of the play'. This seems true, but they certainly pleased the audience. In a letter concerning the first night of *The Critic*, Georgiana, Duchess of Devonshire, picked the songs out for mention:

> . . . the first act of the farce is quite charming, it occasion'd peals of laughter ev'ry minute. The other two, in which the tragedy is rehears'd (to ridicule the insipid tragedys *d'aujourd hui*) are very good, but not so entertaining and rather long, there is a very pretty french song and an Italian one introduced in the first act, in the second a view of Tilbury fort and the river which is vastly well done and in the last a sea fight which was too very pretty.[2]

It is not known who wrote the words of the songs.

---

[1] 'The Songs in "The Critic"', *T.L.S.*, 28 Mar. 1942, p. 168. Loewenberg also notes that 'Sheridan's name is not mentioned. The publisher's advertisements of new music at the end seem to confirm the date of publication (1779).'

[2] No. 256 in the Chatsworth MSS. The first three and a half lines are quoted in *Georgiana*, ed. the Earl of Bessborough (1955), p. 44.

3. OF THE ENTERTAINMENT

(i) '*A Rough Sketch*'

On 16 August 1818 William Linley wrote to Thomas Wilkie,[1] saying: 'I *had* in my possession two very curious Common Place books in Mr. Sheridan's own handwriting.—The one containing a rough sketch of some of the Scenes and Characters in the *Critic*. . . .' He appears to have given it to Charles Brinsley Sheridan, and it may possibly be (though the description is not really accurate) the next item.[2]

(ii) *The Frampton Court MS.*

This is listed in Sotheby's Catalogue of 2 July 1930, lot 634, as 'parts of Acts I and II, upwards of 70 pp. in the hand of R. B. Sheridan'. The description does not quite tally with the notes made by Rae, when he printed the manuscript.[3] He indicates that there were gaps in the first act, but that he copied the second and third in their entirety from the original. Since the manuscript is not now extant, we must assume that more of it was made available to Rae than was sent to the sale-room.

The collations reveal a surprising amount of agreement between its readings and those of the printed text of 1781. Some lines that Rae prints are crossed out in the Larpent MS. but reappear in the 1781 edition. This seems to be another case[4] of Sheridan's going back to his manuscript and preferring its readings to those admitted into the text for performance. At the same time it must be added that the instances which show this desire for literary finish are comparatively few.

(iii) *The Lord Chamberlain's Copy*

This was prepared by Drury Lane Theatre for examination by the Lord Chamberlain, and was accompanied by a letter signed by Sheridan and saying the 'Dramatic Piece of two Acts' would be performed if it met with approbation.[5] It is now Larpent MS. 494 in the Henry E. Huntington Library.[6] Apart from the prologue, it amounts to 128 pages of writing. Five copyists were employed in the task of transcription.

(iv) *Drury Lane Prompt-book for First Performance*

This has not been located. When the new Drury Lane Theatre was opened in 1812, the management borrowed a printed copy of *The Critic* from the Lyceum for its own use.[7] I think it likely that this was the Stokes copy, noted below.

---

[1] Add. MS. 29764, f. 26. See p. 9, above.
[2] Sichel, i. 506 n., describes an autograph manuscript of *The Duenna* at Frampton Court, which contained a 'rough sketch of a sea-battle' on the back of the copy-book.
[3] Rae, pp. 222–62. For his footnotes see pp. 231 and 236.
[4] As in *The Rivals*. See Purdy, pp. xlii–xliii.   [5] *Letters*, i. 128.
[6] See MacMillan, pp. 83–4.   [7] Noted in Folger MS. W. b. 381.

At the first performance, the scene between the Justice and his long-lost son does not appear to have been given, and it was not performed until 1 January 1780. This information is derived from the *London Packet*, 31 Dec. 1779–3 Jan. 1780: 'In the tragedy rehearsed, an underplot ridiculing the stage discoveries of parents and children at the end of many of our dramatic pieces, was introduced, which we understand was intended to be represented originally, but was omitted the first night on account of the extraordinary length of the whole—it was highly relished by the audience of Saturday evening, and is of a piece with the rest of the burlesque.'

(v) *The Crewe MS.*

This is a presentation copy with an inscription in Sheridan's own hand: 'To Mrs. Crewe | From the Author'. He has added the title: 'THE CRITIC | or | A Tragedy rehears'd | A Dramatic Peice in three Acts'. Only a few words of the text itself are in his handwriting.

Proof that this text is later than the Frampton Court and Larpent MSS. is to be found in II. i (p. 520, l. 28 below), and this correction in Sheridan's hand is incorporated in the printed edition of 1781.

The manuscript is in Yale University Library.

(vi) *The First Edition (1781)*

This presents a number of bibliographical problems,[1] but little textual difficulty. For the engraved title-page, see p. 491 below.

Collation: 8vo: π A⁴ B–G⁸ H².

A4, the half-title, is folded back to precede A¹ and is succeeded by an inserted leaf bearing the engraved title.

Contents: pp. [x]+98+[2].

[ ] half-title, '[swelled rule] THE | *CRITIC*; | OR, | *A Tragedy Rehearsed.* [swelled rule] | [PRICE ONE SHILLING AND SIX-PENCE.]'; [ ] blank; [ ] title; [ ] blank; [i] and ii, '*TO MRS. GREVILLE*' [dedicatory letter]; [iii and iv] Prologue; [v] Dramatis Personæ; [vi] blank; [1] and 2–98, text; [99] blank; [100] Publisher's advertisement of plays by Garrick.

(vii) *Presentation Copies*

The most interesting of these is owned by Mr. Robert H. Taylor and is on deposit in Princeton University Library.[2] On the blank opposite the title-page it bears the words in Sheridan's hand:

---

[1] For their discussion, see Williams, pp. 222–3; *The Rothschild Library* (Cambridge, 1954), ii. 502–3; Rhodes, ii. 241–63; Nettleton and Case, pp. 955–7; and William B. Todd, 'Sheridan's *The Critic*', *The Book Collector*, v (1956), 172–3.

[2] Sold at auction by Puttick and Simpson, London, 19 January 1916, lot 448.

To Stella
from the Author

Tale tuum Carmen Nobis, divino Poeta
Quale sopor fessis in Gramine quale per aestum
Dulcis aquae saliente restinguere rivo[1]

On the blank opposite the last page of the text Sheridan has written:

Te nostrae, Vare myricae
Te nemus omne canet—nec Phoebo gratior ulla est,—
Quam sibi quae Vari praescripsit pagina Nomen—[2]

The latter is clearly complimentary, and in no sense a comment on the text it faces. 'Stella' was Mary Isabella, wife of Charles Manners, Marquis of Granby and afterwards (1779) fourth Duke of Rutland. She is mentioned in 'A Portrait' (see p. 352, l. 17, above).

Mr. Robert H. Taylor also owns a copy of the first edition with the half-title and a presentation inscription, 'from the Author'. Inside the front cover is to be found a red morocco label reading 'From R. B. Sheridan to Geo. Steevens'. Steevens was dramatic critic for the *St. James's Chronicle* for some years,[3] and may have been responsible for the notice of *The Rivals* that appeared in its issue of 17–19 January 1775.[4] His library was sold in 1800, and lot 1398 (21 May) was a copy of *The Critic* (1781) with two other plays. It was purchased by Nicol, the booksellers. When C. F. Libbie auctioned James H. Brown's library on 12–14 April 1898, lot 1816 was described as a presentation copy of the first edition, bearing the words 'from the Author'. It may not be the same volume as Mr. Taylor's.

Another copy inscribed 'From the Author' in Sheridan's hand was in the possession of Earl Spencer.[5] It came up for sale as the property of George H. Holliday at Leavitt, Strebeigh and Co.'s auction in New York from 10 October 1870, as lot 2023, and was described as having the Wimbledon Park bookplate and being 'elegantly bound in crimson morocco, extra'. What appears to be the same volume was listed in one of the catalogues of the Anderson Auction Company's sales of Robert Hoe's library.[6] It was said to be a first edition (98 pp.) with the advertisement

---

[1] Correctly given, except in the last line:

dulcis aquae saliente sitim restinguere rivo.

(Virgil, *Eclogues*, v. 45–7.)

[2] Virgil, *Eclogues*, vi. 10–12.

[3] Charles Harold Gray, *Theatrical Criticism in London to 1795* (New York, 1931; repr. 1964), p. 207.   [4] See p. 42 above.

[5] It is probably the one described by G. G. Sigmond in *The Dramatic Works . . . of Sheridan* (1848), p. 87: 'In the library of Mr. Henry Bohn there exists a presentation copy to one of the Duke of Marlborough's family, with the undoubted autograph of the author.'

[6] New York, beginning 1 May 1911, lot 3009. Cf. the Hoe Library Catalogue (1905), iii. 70.

leaf, but without the half-title: 'straight grain morocco, sides richly tooled, centre inlay of green morocco, from the Spencer collection'.

One further item ought to be mentioned. It was described as an 'unbound, presentation copy from the author of *The Critic*', and was sold by the Anderson Auction Co., on 30 January 1908, lot 874.

(viii) *Prompt Copies*

Two of these are selected for description. One was the subject of part of an article by Mr. F. W. Bateson,[1] and is in Harvard College Library.[2] Both the half-title and advertisement leaf are missing. Sheet B includes the following readings: p. 4, l. 4: ends 'to get a', and p. 15, l. 17, is 'not always so'.

The other is an interleaved copy of the 1781 text of *The Critic*, with many deletions and corrections as well as full stage instructions. It was prepared by the Drury Lane copyist, Stokes, and is Folger Prompt C 53. It is of particular interest because it shows how bare the theatrical text could be: see pp. 26–7 above.[3]

Conclusion

I propose to use the first edition as copy-text, and to make few and minor corrections: Sheridan gave full authority to this version. I have printed collations with other texts, however, because they indicate the development of the work between 1779 and 1781, and have helped me to formulate texts of other plays where the documentation is more meagre.[4]

The following abbreviations are used in the textual notes on the play:

Rae   Rae's transcription of the Frampton Court MS.
L   The Lord Chamberlain's copy, Larpent MS. 494.
C   The Crewe MS. in Yale University Library.
1781 The first edition of 1781.[5]

---

[1] See p. 24, n. 2 above.   [2] *EC 75 Sh 534 C (1781/B).
[3] But gags continued to be introduced after Stokes's day. Bernard H. Dixon noted (in *The Theatre*, N.S. iv (1881), p. 210): 'Some of the old pieces, mostly farces, which keep possession of the stage, would seem to depend as much, if not more, on the introductions that have been made from time to time, as on the original dialogue; and as many of these refer to occurrences which have taken place since the date of the piece, they make what should be something like a picture of the past, a strange mass of absurd incongruity. The Rev. James Townley's "High Life below Stairs" and Sheridan's "Critic" are two instances of what I mean.'
[4] See pp. 28–30 above.
[5] The *Public Advertiser*, 4 Aug. 1781, advertised it as '*This Day is published*, Corrected and revised by the Author'; and reviewed it, three days later, as 'his so much admired, and so long looked for Dramatic Piece, the CRITIC.' The second edition was advertised in the same month in the *London Chronicle*, 25–28 Aug. 1781.

THE
C·R·I·T·I·C

OR

A Tragedy Rehearsed

A

Dramatic Piece

in three ACTS

as it is performed at the

THEATRE ROYAL in DRURY LANE

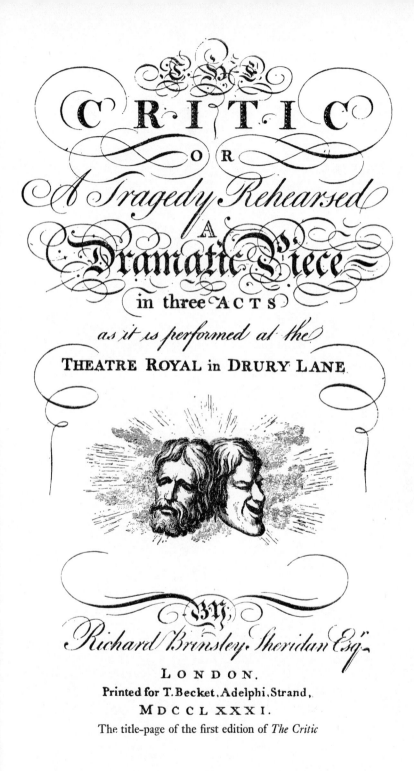

By

Richard Brinsley Sheridan Esq[r]

LONDON.

Printed for T. Becket, Adelphi, Strand,

MDCCLXXXI.

The title-page of the first edition of *The Critic*

TO Mrs. GREVILLE.[1]

MADAM,

In requesting your permission to address the following pages to you, which as they aim themselves to be critical, require every protection and allowance that approving taste or friendly prejudice can give them, I yet ventured to mention no other motive than the gratification of private friendship and esteem. Had I suggested a hope that your implied approbation would give a sanction to their defects, your particular reserve, and dislike to the reputation of critical taste, as well as of poetical talent, would have made you refuse the protection of your name to such a purpose. However, I am not so ungrateful as now to attempt to combat this disposition in you. I shall not here presume to argue that the present state of poetry claims and expects every assistance that taste and example can afford it: nor endeavour to prove that a fastidious conceal-ment of the most elegant productions of judgment and fancy is an ill return for the possession of those endowments.—Continue to deceive yourself in the idea that you are known only to be eminently admired and regarded for the valuable qualities that attach private friendships, and the graceful talents that adorn conversation. Enough of what you have written, has stolen into full public notice to answer my purpose; and you will, perhaps, be the only person, conversant in elegant literature, who shall read this address and not perceive that by publishing your particular approbation of the following drama, I have a more interested object than to boast the true respect and regard with which

I have the honour to be,

MADAM,

Your very sincere,

And obedient humble servant,

R. B. SHERIDAN.

---

[1] Frances Greville (born Macartney) was the wife of Richard Fulke Greville of Wilbury House, and mother of Sheridan's friend, Frances Crewe. Mrs. Greville was well known in literary circles for her 'Ode to Indifference'.

PROLOGUE.

By the Honorable RICHARD FITZPATRICK[1]

THE Sister Muses, whom these realms obey,
Who o'er the Drama hold divided sway,
Sometimes, by evil counsellors, 'tis said   5
Like earth-born potentates have been misled:
In those gay days of wickedness and wit,
When Villiers criticiz'd what Dryden writ,
The Tragick Queen, to please a tasteless crowd,
Had learn'd to bellow, rant, and roar so loud,   · 10
That frighten'd Nature, her best friend before,
The blust'ring beldam's company forswore.
Her comic Sister, who had wit 'tis true,
With all her merits, had her failings too;
And would sometimes in mirthful moments use   15
A style too flippant for a well-bred Muse.
Then female modesty abash'd began
To seek the friendly refuge of the fan,
Awhile behind that slight entrenchment stood,
'Till driv'n from thence, she left the stage for good.   20
In our more pious, and far chaster times!
These sure no longer are the Muse's crimes!
But some complain that, former faults to shun,
The reformation to extremes has run.
The frantick hero's wild delirium past,   25
Now insipidity succeeds bombast;
So slow Melpomene's cold numbers creep,
Here dullness seems her drowsy court to keep,
And we, are scarce awake, whilst you are fast asleep.

---

1 PROLOGUE] *1781*; Prologue to the Critic *L, C*   2 By ... FITZPATRICK]
1781; *om. L*; by a Friend *C* [S.]   3–6 THE Sister ... misled] *1781*; *om. L, C*
9 Queen] *1781*; Muse *L, C*   12 beldam's] *1781*; Beldame's *L*; Beldames *C*
19 that] *1781*; her *L, C*   23 faults] *1781*; Sins *L, C*   25 frantick] *1781*;
tragick *L, C*   28 Here ... court] *1781*; Her drowsy Court here Dulness seems
L, C   29 whilst] *1781*; while *L, C*

---

[1] 1748–1813. He was the second son of John, 1st Earl of Upper Ossory, and was
well known as soldier, wit, and friend of Fox. For Sheridan's invitation to him to see
and abuse *The Critic*, see *Letters*, i. 128–9.

Thalia, once so ill behav'd and rude,
Reform'd; is now become an arrant prude,
Retailing nightly to the yawning pit,
The purest morals, undefil'd by wit!
Our Author offers in these motley scenes,   5
A slight remonstrance to the Drama's queens,
Nor let the goddesses be over nice;
Free spoken subjects give the best advice.
Although not quite a novice in his trade,
His cause to night requires no common aid.   10
To this, a friendly, just, and pow'rful court,
I come Ambassador to beg support.
Can he undaunted, brave the critick's rage?
In civil broils, with brother bards engage?
Hold forth their errors to the publick eye,   15
Nay more, e'en News-papers themselves defy?
Say, must his single arm encounter all?
By numbers vanquish'd, e'en the brave may fall;
And though no leader should success distrust,
Whose troops are willing, and whose cause is just;   20
To bid such hosts of angry foes defiance,
His chief dependance must be, YOUR ALLIANCE.

1 behav'd] *1781*; bred *L, C*   and rude] *1781*; and so rude *L, C*   4 undefil'd]
1781, C; undefin'd *L*   5 motley scenes] *1781*; humble scenes *L, C*   6 A slight]
1781; A short *L, C*   7 Nor let the] *1781*; Nor let our *L, C*   8 give
the best] *1781*; may give good *L, C*   9 Although] *1781*; Yet though *L, C*
11–12 To this . . . support] *1781*; *transferred in L, C to follow line 18*   15 their
errors] *1781*; their foibles *L, C*   19 should] *1781*; need *L, C*

DRAMATIS PERSONÆ

DANGLE	Mr. Dodd.	
SNEER	Mr. Palmer.	
SIR FRETFUL PLAGIARY	Mr. Parsons.	
SIGNOR PASTICCIO RITORNELLO	Mr. Delpini.	5
INTERPRETER	Mr. Baddeley.	
UNDER PROMPTER	Mr. Phillimore.	

AND

PUFF	Mr. King.	
MRS. DANGLE	Mrs. Hopkins.	10
ITALIAN GIRLS	{ Miss Field, and the { Miss Abrams.	

Characters of the TRAGEDY

LORD BURLEIGH	Mr. Moody.	
GOVERNOR OF TILBURY FORT	Mr. Wrighten.	15
EARL OF LEICESTER	Mr. Farren.	
SIR WALTER RALEIGH	Mr. Burton.	
SIR CHRISTOPHER HATTON	Mr. Waldron.	
MASTER OF THE HORSE	Mr. Kenny.	
BEEFEATER	Mr. Wright.	20
JUSTICE	Mr. Packer.	
SON	Mr. Lamash.	
CONSTABLE	Mr. Fawcett.	
THAMES	Mr. Gawdry.	

AND   25

DON FEROLO WHISKERANDOS	Mr. Bannister, jun.	
1ST NIECE	Miss Collet.	
2D NIECE	Miss Kirby.	
JUSTICE'S LADY	Mrs. Johnston.	
CONFIDANT	Mrs. Bradshaw.	30

AND

TILBURINA	Miss Pope.

Guards, Constables, Servants, Chorus, Rivers,
Attendants, &c. &c.

1–34 DRAMATIS . . . &c. &c.] *1781*; *om. L, C*

THE CRITIC

ACT I

SCENE I

MR. *and* MRS. DANGLE *at Breakfast, and reading Newspapers.*[1]

DANGLE. [*reading*] 'BRUTUS to LORD NORTH.'[2]—'Letter the second on   5
the STATE OF THE ARMY'—Pshaw! 'To the first L— dash D of the
A— dash Y.'[3]—'Genuine Extract of a Letter from ST. KITT'S.'—
'COXHEATH INTELLIGENCE.'[4]—'It is now confidently asserted that
SIR CHARLES HARDY.'[5]—Pshaw!—Nothing but about the fleet, and
the nation!—and I hate all politics but theatrical politics.—Where's   10
the MORNING CHRONICLE?

MRS. DANGLE. Yes, that's your gazette.[6]

DANGLE. So, here we have it.——'*Theatrical intelligence extraordinary,*'
——'We hear there is a new tragedy in rehearsal at Drury-Lane Theatre,
call'd the SPANISH ARMADA, said to be written by Mr. PUFF, a   15
gentleman well known in the theatrical world; if we may allow ourselves to give credit to the report of the performers, who, truth to say,
are in general but indifferent judges, this piece abounds with the most
striking and received beauties of modern composition'—So! I am very
glad my friend PUFF's tragedy is in such forwardness.—Mrs. Dangle,   20
my dear, you will be very glad to hear that PUFF's tragedy——

---

8 INTELLIGENCE] *1781*; *Intelligence*—Pshaw! Politics!—*L, C*   12 Yes]*1781*; Aye *L, C*
13 So]*1781*; Yes *L, C*   17 report of the]*1781*, *L*; *om. C*   19 composition]*1781*,
C; composition, tho' truth to say we had rather see Tragedy on principles diametrically
opposite *L*   20 Mrs. Dangle]*1781*; O *C, L*   21 PUFF's]*1781*; Mr. Puff's *C, L*

[1] Cf. 'The Quidnuncs; a moral Interlude', in the *London Review*, ix (1779), 59. It
begins:
    MR. *and* Mrs. Quidnunc *are discovered sitting at a table*; *on which are scattered heaps
of newspapers. After taking up and throwing down one after another,* Quidnunc *speaks.*
    MR. Q. Confound these barren *chronicles*, I say. Why, there's no scandal in 'em, wife,
    to-day.

[2] 'Brutus' was one of the pseudonyms of 'Junius' in the political controversy of
1769–72. On 6 Sept. 1779, however, 'Brutus' wrote to the editor of the *Public Advertiser*,
satirizing the military discipline of the Westminster and Middlesex volunteers.

[3] John Montagu, 4th Earl of Sandwich (1718–92), first Lord of the Admiralty, and
a favourite target for abuse.   [4] See p. 707.

[5] 1716?–1780. Commander of the Channel Fleet.

[6] William Woodfall (1746–1803) was its dramatic critic and subjected the plays that
he saw to careful and dispassionate examination. The newspaper was said, in its issue of
5 Nov. 1777, to have 'the honour of taking the lead as a theatrical reviewer'.

MRS. DANGLE. Lord, Mr. Dangle, why will you plague me about such nonsense?—Now the plays are begun I shall have no peace.—Isn't it sufficient to make yourself ridiculous by your passion for the theatre, without continually teazing me to join you? Why can't you ride your hobby-horse without desiring to place me on a pillion behind you, Mr.   5
Dangle?

DANGLE. Nay, my dear, I was only going to read——

MRS. DANGLE. No, no; you will never read any thing that's worth listening to:—you hate to hear about your country; there are letters every day with Roman signatures, demonstrating the certainty of an   10
invasion, and proving that the nation is utterly undone.[1]—But you never will read any thing to entertain one.

DANGLE. What has a woman to do with politics, Mrs. Dangle?

MRS. DANGLE. And what have you to do with the theatre, Mr. Dangle? Why should you affect the character of a Critic? I have no patience with   15
you!—haven't you made yourself the jest of all your acquaintance by your interference in matters where you have no business? Are not you call'd a theatrical Quidnunc,[2] and a mock Mæcenas to second-hand authors?

DANGLE. True; my power with the Managers is pretty notorious; but is   20
it no credit to have applications from all quarters for my interest?—From lords to recommend fidlers, from ladies to get boxes, from authors to get answers, and from actors to get engagements.

MRS. DANGLE. Yes, truly; you have contrived to get a share in all the plague and trouble of theatrical property, without the profit, or even   25
the credit of the abuse that attends it.

DANGLE. I am sure, Mrs. Dangle, you are no loser by it, however; YOU have all the advantages of it:—mightn't you, last winter, have had the reading of the new Pantomime a fortnight previous to its performance? And doesn't Mr. Fosbrook[3] let you take places for a play before it is   30
advertis'd, and set you down for a Box for every new piece through the season? And didn't my friend, Mr. Smatter, dedicate his last Farce to you at my particular request, Mrs. Dangle?

MRS. DANGLE. Yes; but wasn't the Farce damn'd, Mr. Dangle? And to be sure it is extremely pleasant to have one's house made the motley   35
rendezvous of all the lackeys of literature!—The very high change of trading authors and jobbing critics!—Yes, my drawing-room is an absolute register-office for candidate actors, and poets without charac-

[1] See the letters of 'Coriolanus alter', 'Scipio', 'Honestus', 'Historicus', and 'Capitilamis' in the *Public Advertiser*, 18, 23, 27, 28, 30 Sept. and 5 Oct. 1779.

[2] Gossip. See also p. 497, n. 1, above.

[3] Thomas Fosbrook was still, officially, a numberer at Drury Lane Theatre, but must already have been acting in the position he held for many years there—that of 'Box, Book, and Housekeeper'.

ter; then to be continually alarmed with Misses and Ma'ams piping
histeric changes on JULIETS and DORINDAS, POLLYS[1] and OPHE-
LIAS; and the very furniture trembling at the probationary starts and
unprovok'd rants of would-be RICHARDS and HAMLETS!—And what
is worse than all, now that the Manager has monopoliz'd the Opera-   5
House,[2] haven't we the Signors and Signoras calling here, sliding their
smooth semibreves, and gargling glib divisions in their outlandish
throats—with foreign emissaries and French spies, for ought I know,
disguised like fidlers and figure dancers!

DANGLE. Mercy! Mrs. Dangle!   10

MRS. DANGLE. And to employ yourself so idly at such an alarming
crisis as this too—when, if you had the least spirit, you would have
been at the head of one of the Westminster associations[3]—or trailing a
volunteer pike in the Artillery Ground?[4]—But you—o'my conscience,
I believe if the French were landed to-morrow your first enquiry   15
would be, whether they had brought a theatrical troop with them.

DANGLE. Mrs. Dangle, it does not signify—I say the stage is 'the Mirror
of Nature,'[5] and the actors are 'the Abstract, and brief Chronicles of the
Time:'[6]—and pray what can a man of sense study better?—Besides, you
will not easily persuade me that there is no credit or importance in   20
being at the head of a band of critics, who take upon them to decide for
the whole town,[7] whose opinion and patronage all writers solicit, and
whose recommendation no manager dares refuse!

MRS. DANGLE. Ridiculous!—Both managers and authors of the least
merit, laugh at your pretensions.—The PUBLIC is their CRITIC—   25
without whose fair approbation they know no play can rest on the

3 probationary] *1781*; probation *L, C*   5 Manager has] *1781*; Managers have *L,
C*   10 Mercy!] *1781, C*; Marry *L*   17-19 I say . . . Besides] *1781*; *om. L, C*
20 not easily] *1781*; never *L, C*   22 and] *1781, C*; *om. L*   23 dares] *1781*;
dare *L, C*

----

[1] Dorinda was a character in Farquhar's *The Beaux Stratagem*, and Polly Peachum
appeared in Gay's *The Beggar's Opera*.
[2] Sheridan and Thomas Harris of Covent Garden Theatre had purchased the King's
Theatre, but Harris had withdrawn after one season. See *Letters*, i. 116 n. 3.
[3] The volunteer militia. The Duke of Northumberland reported to the King on
1 Sept., on the recruiting, and the subscriptions raised at the Guildhall. See *Public
Advertiser*, 2 Sept. 1779.
[4] Just north of Moorfields, and off Finsbury Square and Chiswell Street.
[5] Cf. Hamlet's 'mirror up to nature' (III. ii).
[6] *Hamlet*, II. ii.
[7] 'The pit is the grand court of criticism; and in the centre of it is collected that
awful body, distinguished by the title of The Town. Hence are issued the irrevocable
decrees; and here final sentence is pronounced on plays and players' (quoted from *The
Connoisseur*, ed. Colman the Elder and Bonnell Thornton, no. 43, 20 Nov. 1754, in
D. F. Smith, *The Critics in the Audience of the London Theatres from Buckingham to
Sheridan* (Albuquerque, N. Mexico, 1953), p. 95).

stage, and with whose applause they welcome such attacks as yours,
and laugh at the malice of them, where they can't at the wit.

DANGLE. Very well, Madam—very well.

Enter SERVANT.

SERVANT. Mr. Sneer, Sir, to wait on you.   5

DANGLE. O, shew Mr. Sneer up.   [*Exit* SERVANT.
Plague on't, now we must appear loving and affectionate, or Sneer will
hitch us into a story.

MRS. DANGLE. With all my heart; you can't be more ridiculous than you
are.   10

DANGLE. You are enough to provoke——

Enter MR. SNEER.

—Hah! my dear Sneer, I am vastly glad to see you. My dear, here's
Mr. Sneer.

MRS. DANGLE. Good morning to you, Sir.   15

DANGLE. Mrs. Dangle and I have been diverting ourselves with the
papers.—Pray, Sneer, won't you go to Drury-lane theatre the first night
of Puff's tragedy?

SNEER. Yes; but I suppose one shan't be able to get in, for on the first
night of a new piece they always fill the house with orders to support it.[1] 20
But here, Dangle, I have brought you two pieces, one of which you must
exert yourself to make the managers accept, I can tell you that, for 'tis
written by a person of consequence.

DANGLE. So! Now my plagues are beginning!

SNEER. Aye, I am glad of it, for now you'll be happy. Why, my dear   25
Dangle, it is a pleasure to see how you enjoy your volunteer fatigue,
and your solicited solicitations.

DANGLE. It's a great trouble—yet, egad, it's pleasant too.—Why,
sometimes of a morning, I have a dozen people call on me at breakfast
time, whose faces I never saw before, nor ever desire to see again.   30

SNEER. That must be very pleasant indeed!

DANGLE. And not a week but I receive fifty letters, and not a line in them
about any business of my own.

SNEER. An amusing correspondence!

4 SERVANT] *1781*, *C*; *om. L*   6 O] *1781*, *L*; *om. C*   11 You . . . provoke]
1781, *L*; *om. C*   20 fill] *1781*; cram *L*, *C*   25 Aye] *1781*; Aye, and *C*, *L*
27 solicitations] *1781*, *C*; solicitation *L*   34 An] *1781*; O, an *L*, *C*

---

[1] The privilege of free admission was greatly abused while Sheridan was manager
of Drury Lane Theatre. At the end of Oct. 1785, Sheridan's sister-in-law, Mary Tickell,
wrote that her mother 'raves about Orders that come in in Mr. Sheridan's Name every
Night—She threatens to write herself about it' (Folger MS. Y. d. 35, f. 177). Cf. *Letters*,
i. 140 n. 8; iii. 29–31.

DANGLE. [*reading*] 'Bursts into tears, and exit.' What, is this a tragedy!

SNEER. No, that's a genteel comedy, not a translation—only *taken from the French*; it is written in a stile which they have lately tried to run down; the true sentimental,[1] and nothing ridiculous in it from the beginning to the end.   5

MRS. DANGLE. Well, if they had kept to that, I should not have been such an enemy to the stage, there was some edification to be got from those pieces, Mr. Sneer!

SNEER. I am quite of your opinion, Mrs. Dangle; the theatre in proper hands, might certainly be made the school of morality; but now, I am 10 sorry to say it, people seem to go there principally for their entertainment![2]

MRS. DANGLE. It would have been more to the credit of the Managers to have kept it in the other line.

SNEER. Undoubtedly, Madam, and hereafter perhaps to have had it 15 recorded, that in the midst of a luxurious and dissipated age, they preserv'd *two* houses in the capital, where the conversation was always moral at least, if not entertaining!

DANGLE. Now, egad, I think the worst alteration is in the nicety of the audience.—No double entendre, no smart innuendo admitted; even 20 Vanburgh[3] and Congreve obliged to undergo a bungling reformation!

SNEER. Yes, and our prudery in this respect is just on a par with the artificial bashfulness of a courtezan, who encreases the blush upon her cheek in an exact proportion to the diminution of her modesty.

DANGLE. Sneer can't even give the Public a good word!—But what have 25 we here?—This seems a very odd——

---

1 'Bursts . . . exit.'] *1781*, *C*; *om. L*   tragedy!] *1781*, *C*; tragedies *L*   6 Well] *1781*; Aye *L*, *C*   11 people] *1781*; the people *L*, *C*   14 it] *1781*; *om. L*, *C*

---

[1] Cf. Richard Tickell's *The Wreath of Fashion, or, The Art of Sentimental Poetry* (1777), pp. 2–3:

> First, for true grounds of Sentimental lore,
> The scenes of modern Comedy explore;
> Dramatic Homilies! devout and sage,
> Stor'd with wise maxims, 'both for youth and age'. . . .
> But chief, let *Cumberland* thy Muse direct;
> High Priest of all the Tragic-comic sect!
> Mid darts and flames his Lover *cool*[*l*]*y* waits;
> Calm as a Hero, cas'd in *Hartley's plates*;
> 'Till damp'd, and chill'd, by sentimental sighs,
> Each stifled passion in a vapour dies.

[2] In an early fragment by Sheridan, quoted by Moore, i. 24–5, one of the characters says, 'it ever was my opinion that the stage should be a place of rational entertainment; instead of which, I am very sorry to say, most people go there for their diversion'. Cf. p. 804 below.

[3] See p. 556.

SNEER. O, that's a comedy, on a very new plan; replete with wit and
mirth, yet of a most serious moral! You see it is call'd 'THE RE-
FORMED HOUSEBREAKER;' where, by the mere force of humour,
HOUSEBREAKING is put into so ridiculous a light, that if the piece has
its proper run, I have no doubt but that bolts and bars will be entirely   5
useless by the end of the season.

DANGLE. Egad, this is new indeed!

SNEER. Yes; it is written by a particular friend of mine, who has discovered that the follies and foibles of society, are subjects unworthy
the notice of the Comic Muse, who should be taught to stoop only at   10
the greater vices and blacker crimes of humanity—gibbeting capital
offences in five acts, and pillorying petty larcenies in two.—In short,
his idea is to dramatize the penal laws, and make the Stage a court of
ease to the Old Bailey.

DANGLE. It is truly moral.   15

Enter SERVANT.

Sir Fretful Plagiary, Sir.

DANGLE. Beg him to walk up.—[*Exit* SERVANT.] Now, Mrs. Dangle,
Sir Fretful Plagiary is an author to your own taste.

MRS. DANGLE. I confess he is a favourite of mine, because every body   20
else abuses him.

SNEER. —Very much to the credit of your charity, Madam, if not of your
judgment.

DANGLE. But, egad, he allows no merit to any author but himself, that's
the truth on't—tho' he's my friend.   25

SNEER. Never.—He is as envious as an old maid verging on the desperation of six-and-thirty: and then the insiduous humility with which he
seduces you to give a free opinion on any of his works, can be exceeded
only by the petulant arrogance with which he is sure to reject your
observations.   30

DANGLE. Very true, egad—tho' he's my friend.

SNEER. Then his affected contempt of all newspaper strictures; tho', at
the same time, he is the sorest man alive, and shrinks like scorch'd
parchment from the fiery ordeal of true criticism: yet is he so covetous of
popularity, that he had rather be abused than not mentioned at all.   35

DANGLE. There's no denying it—tho' he is my friend.

SNEER. You have read the tragedy he has just finished, haven't you?

DANGLE. O yes; he sent it to me yesterday.

SNEER. Well, and you think it execrable, don't you?

1–2 and mirth] *1781*, C; *om.* L   11 and] *1781*, C; *om.* L   12 offences] *1781*,
C; Offendors L   larcenies] *1781*, C; larcenaries L   15 It . . . moral] *1781*;
That is to unite Poetry and Justice indeed L, C   19 own] *1781*; *om.* L, C
32 newspaper] *1781*, L; Newspapers C   34–5 yet . . . all] *1781*; *om.* L, C
38 to] *1781*; *om.* L, C

DANGLE. Why between ourselves, egad I must own—tho' he's my
friend—that it is one of the most——He's here [*Aside*]—finished and
most admirable perform——

[SIR FRETFUL *without*.] Mr. Sneer with him, did you say?

Enter SIR FRETFUL.   5

Ah, my dear friend!—Egad, we were just speaking of your Tragedy.—
Admirable, Sir Fretful, admirable!

SNEER. You never did any thing beyond it, Sir Fretful—never in your
life.

SIR FRETFUL. You make me extremely happy;—for without a compli-   10
ment, my dear Sneer, there isn't a man in the world whose judgment I
value as I do yours.—And Mr. Dangle's.

MRS. DANGLE. They are only laughing at you, Sir Fretful; for it was but
just now that—

DANGLE. Mrs. Dangle!—Ah, Sir Fretful, you know Mrs. Dangle.—My   15
friend Sneer was rallying just now—He knows how she admires you,
and—

SIR FRETFUL. O Lord—I am sure Mr. Sneer has more taste and
sincerity than to——A damn'd double-faced fellow!   [*Aside.*

DANGLE. Yes, yes,—Sneer will jest—but a better humour'd——   20

SIR FRETFUL. O, I know——

DANGLE. He has a ready turn for ridicule—his wit costs him nothing.—

SIR FRETFUL. No, egad,—or I should wonder how he came by it. [*Aside.*

MRS. DANGLE. Because his jest is always at the expence of his friend.

DANGLE. But, Sir Fretful, have you sent your play to the managers yet? 25
—or can I be of any service to you?

SIR FRETFUL. No, no, I thank you; I believe the piece had sufficient
recommendation with it.—I thank you tho'.—I sent it to the manager
of COVENT-GARDEN THEATRE this morning.

SNEER. I should have thought now, that it might have been cast (as the 30
actors call it) better at DRURY-LANE.

SIR FRETFUL. O lud! no—never send a play there while I live—harkee!
[*Whispers* SNEER.]

SNEER. *Writes himself!*—I know he does—

SIR FRETFUL. I say nothing—I take away from no man's merit—am   35
hurt at no man's good fortune—I say nothing—But this I will say—
through all my knowledge of life, I have observed—that there is not a
passion so strongly rooted in the human heart as envy!

2–3 He's . . . perform—] *1781*; transferred in L, C to precede '*Enter* SIR FRETFUL.' (line 5).
4 did you say?] *1781*; is he L, C   17 and] *1781*, C; *om*. L   19 *Aside*] *1781*;
om. L, C   23 *Aside*] *1781*; *om*. L, C   24 Because . . . is] *1781*; Aye, the
reason is because his Jests are L. *Transcribed in* C, *but then deleted with* always at the
expence of his friend.   27–8 sufficient recommendation] *1781*; recommendation
sufficient L, C   33 *Whispers* SNEER] *1781*; whispers L, C

SNEER. I believe you have reason for what you say, indeed.

SIR FRETFUL. Besides—I can tell you it is not always so safe to leave a play in the hands of those who write themselves.[1]

SNEER. What, they may steal from them, hey, my dear Plagiary?

SIR FRETFUL. Steal!—to be sure they may; and, egad, serve your best thoughts as gypsies do stolen children, disfigure them to make 'em pass for their own.[2]

SNEER. But your present work is a sacrifice to Melpomene, and HE, you know, never——

SIR FRETFUL. That's no security.—A dext'rous plagiarist may do any thing.—Why, Sir, for ought I know, he might take out some of the best things in my tragedy, and put them into his own comedy.

SNEER. That might be done, I dare be sworn.

SIR FRETFUL. And then, if such a person gives you the least hint or assistance, he is devilish apt to take the merit of the whole.—

DANGLE. If it succeeds.

SIR FRETFUL. Aye,—but with regard to this piece, I think I can hit that gentleman, for I can safely swear he never read it.

SNEER. I'll tell you how you may hurt him more—

SIR FRETFUL. How?—

SNEER. Swear he wrote it.

SIR FRETFUL. Plague on't now, Sneer, I shall take it ill.—I believe you want to take away my character as an author!

SNEER. Then I am sure you ought to be very much oblig'd to me.

SIR FRETFUL. Hey!—Sir!—

DANGLE. O you know, he never means what he says.

SIR FRETFUL. Sincerely then—you do like the piece?

SNEER. Wonderfully!

SIR FRETFUL. But come now, there must be something that you think might be mended, hey?—Mr. Dangle, has nothing struck you?

DANGLE. Why faith, it is but an ungracious thing for the most part to—

6 disfigure] *1781, C*; disguise *L*   8-9 and . . . never——] *1781*; and— *L, C*
17 I think] *1781; om. L, C*   25 SIR . . . Sir!—] *1781; om. L, C*   26 DANGLE
. . . says] *1781; om. L, C*   27 Sincerely then] *1781*; Pshaw now!—but sincerely *L, C*

[1] Cf. Thomas Holcroft's statement of 10 Dec. 1796: '. . . The reading of manuscripts I have found to be attended with danger. I once read two acts of a manuscript play, and was afterwards accused of having purloined one of the characters. The accusation had some semblance of truth: latent ideas floated in my mind, and there were two or three traits in the character drawn by me similar to the one I had read; though I was very unconscious of this when I wrote the character' (W. Dunlap, *A History of the American Theatre* (New York, 1832), p. 159).

[2] Moore, i. 276, sees a resemblance to Charles Churchill's lines in *The Apology* (1761), 234-5:

> Like gypsies, least the stolen brat be known,
> Defacing first, then claiming for his own.

SIR FRETFUL. —With most authors it is just so indeed; they are in general strangely tenacious!—But, for my part, I am never so well pleased as when a judicious critic[1] points out any defect to me; for what is the purpose of shewing a work to a friend, if you don't mean to profit by his opinion?					5

SNEER. Very true.—Why then, tho' I seriously admire the piece upon the whole, yet there is one small objection; which, if you'll give me leave, I'll mention.

SIR FRETFUL. SIR, you can't oblige me more.

SNEER. I think it wants incident.					10

SIR FRETFUL. Good God!—you surprize me!—wants incident!—

SNEER. Yes; I own I think the incidents are too few.

SIR FRETFUL. Good God!—Believe me, Mr. Sneer, there is no person for whose judgment I have a more implicit deference.—But I protest to you, Mr. Sneer, I am only apprehensive that the incidents are too 15 crowded.—My dear Dangle, how does it strike you?

DANGLE. Really I can't agree with my friend Sneer.—I think the plot quite sufficient; and the four first acts by many degrees the best I ever read or saw in my life. If I might venture to suggest any thing, it is that the interest rather falls off in the fifth.—					20

SIR FRETFUL. —Rises; I believe you mean, Sir.

DANGLE. No; I don't upon my word.

SIR FRETFUL. Yes, yes, you do upon my soul—it certainly don't fall off, I assure you—No, no, it don't fall off.

DANGLE. Now, Mrs. Dangle, didn't you say it struck you in the same 25 light?

MRS. DANGLE. No, indeed, I did not—I did not see a fault in any part of the play from the beginning to the end.

SIR FRETFUL. Upon my soul the women are the best judges after all!

MRS. DANGLE. Or if I made any objection, I am sure it was to nothing in 30 the piece; but that I was afraid it was, on the whole, a little too long.

SIR FRETFUL. Pray, Madam, do you speak as to duration of time; or do you mean that the story is tediously spun out?

MRS. DANGLE. O Lud! no.—I speak only with reference to the usual length of acting plays.					35

SIR FRETFUL. Then I am very happy—very happy indeed,—because the play is a short play, a remarkably short play:—I should not venture to

9 SIR] *1781*; *om. L, Rae, C*   13 Good God] *1781*; *om. L, C, Rae*   13 & 15 Mr. Sneer] *1781*; *om. L, C, Rae*   16 My dear] *1781*; Mr. *L, C, Rae*   17 my friend] *1781*; Mr. *L, C, Rae*   20 fifth] *1781*; fifth act *L, C, Rae*   23 upon my soul] *1781, C*; *om. L, Rae*   24 you] *1781, C, Rae*; *om. L*   25 didn't] *1781, C, L*; did *Rae*   37 remarkably] *1781, L*; remarkable *C*

[1] Sheridan quotes this phrase as 'Nothing is so pleasant as a judicious Critic who—', when inviting Fitzpatrick to see the play. Cf. *Letters*, i. 129.

differ with a lady on a point of taste; but, on these occasions, the watch, you know, is the critic.

MRS. DANGLE. Then, I suppose, it must have been Mr. Dangle's drawling manner of reading it to me.

SIR FRETFUL. O, if Mr. Dangle read it! that's quite another affair!— 5
But I assure you, Mrs. Dangle, the first evening you can spare me three hours and an half, I'll undertake to read you the whole from beginning to end, with the Prologue and Epilogue, and allow time for the music between the acts.

MRS. DANGLE. I hope to see it on the stage next.   10

DANGLE. Well, Sir Fretful, I wish you may be able to get rid as easily of the news-paper criticisms as you do of ours.—

SIR FRETFUL. The NEWS-PAPERS!—Sir, they are the most villainous— licentious—abominable—infernal—Not that I ever read them—No—I make it a rule never to look into a news-paper.   15

DANGLE. You are quite right—for it certainly must hurt an author of delicate feelings to see the liberties they take.

SIR FRETFUL. No!—quite the contrary;—their abuse is, in fact, the best panegyric—I like it of all things.—An author's reputation is only in danger from their support.   20

SNEER. Why that's true—and that attack now on you the other day——

SIR FRETFUL. ——What? where?

DANGLE. Aye, you mean in a paper of Thursday; it was compleatly ill-natur'd to be sure.

SIR FRETFUL. O, so much the better.—Ha! ha! ha!—I wou'dn't have it 25 otherwise.

DANGLE. Certainly it is only to be laugh'd at; for—

SIR FRETFUL. —You don't happen to recollect what the fellow said, do you?

SNEER. Pray, Dangle—Sir Fretful seems a little anxious—

SIR FRETFUL. —O lud, no!—anxious,—not I,—not the least.—I—But 30 one may as well hear you know.

DANGLE. Sneer, do *you* recollect?—Make out something.   [*Aside.*

SNEER. I will, [*to* DANGLE.]—Yes, yes, I remember perfectly.

7 and an half] *1781*; *om.* L, C   14 infernal] *1781*; *om.* L, C   15 news-paper]
1781; Paper L, C   18 No!] *1781*; O Lud! no L, C   23 compleatly] *1781*;
Damn'd L, C   27 Certainly it is] *1781*; O it's L, C   for—] *1781*, C; for—certainly
what Sir Fretful observes is Extreemly true, an Author of Eminence who is a Candidate
for fame ought to distrust— | *Sir Fret.* It wasn't in the Morning Post, I do sometimes see
that. | *Dangle.* No, I think not—I say he ought to distrust his own Merit, if it doesn't
create Envy sufficient— | *Sir Fret.* Nor the Morning Chronicle—I happen'd to have met
with that lately— | *Dangle.* No I'm sure not—Envy Sufficient I say to procure him the
Sanction of abuse from bad writers. | *Sir Fret.* The Gazetteer— | *Dangle.* I really didn't
take notice, as I knew you only laugh'd at these things,—therefore Mr. Sneer, a Man of
Sense—L   30 no] *1781*; *om.* L, C   32 *Aside*] *1781*, C; *om.* L   33 *to* DANGLE]
1781; *om.* L, C

SIR FRETFUL. Well, and pray now—Not that it signifies—what might the gentleman say?

SNEER. Why, he roundly asserts that you have not the slightest invention, or original genius whatever; tho' you are the greatest traducer of all other authors living. 5

SIR FRETFUL. Ha! ha! ha!—very good!

SNEER. That as to COMEDY, you have not one idea of your own, he believes, even in your common place-book[1]—where stray jokes, and pilfered witticisms are kept with as much method as the ledger of the LOST-and-STOLEN-OFFICE. 10

SIR FRETFUL. —Ha! ha! ha!—very pleasant!

SNEER. Nay, that you are so unlucky as not to have the skill even to *steal* with taste.—But that you gleen from the refuse of obscure volumes, where more judicious plagiarists have been before you; so that the body of your work is a composition of dregs and sediments— 15 like a bad tavern's worst wine.

SIR FRETFUL. Ha! ha!

SNEER. In your more serious efforts, he says, your bombast would be less intolerable, if the thoughts were ever suited to the expression; but the homeliness of the sentiment stares thro' the fantastic encumbrance of its 20 fine language, like a clown in one of the new uniforms!

SIR FRETFUL. Ha! ha!

SNEER. That your occasional tropes and flowers suit the general coarseness of your stile, as tambour sprigs would a ground of linsey-wolsey;[2] while your imitations of Shakespeare resemble the mimicry of Falstaff's 25 Page,[3] and are about as near the standard of the original.

SIR FRETFUL. Ha!—

SNEER. —In short, that even the finest passages you steal are of no service to you; for the poverty of your own language prevents their assimilating; so that they lie on the surface like lumps of marl[4] on a 30 barren moor, encumbering what it is not in their power to fertilize!—

SIR FRETFUL. [*after great agitation.*]——Now another person would be vex'd at this.

SNEER. Oh! but I wou'dn't have told you, only to divert you.

SIR FRETFUL. I know it—I *am* diverted,—Ha! ha! ha!—not the least 35 invention!—Ha! ha! ha! very good!—very good!

11 very pleasant] *1781*; *om. L, C*   20 stares] *1781*; stare *L, C*   22 Ha! ha!] *1781, C*; Ha! *L*   23 the general] *1781, C*; general *L*   27 Ha!] *1781, C*; Ha! ha! ha! *L*   36 very good] *1781*; *om. L, C*

[1] Cf. Buckingham's *The Rehearsal*, I. i: 'This is my book of *Drama Commonplaces*, the mother of many other plays.'

[2] Elaborate embroidery on a very ordinary fabric of wool and linen.

[3] *2 Henry IV*, II. ii. 75-7: 'Look, if the fat villain have not transformed him ape.'

[4] 'A kind of dry, soft, fossile earth, harsh to the touch; used to be cast on land, to make it more fruitful' (E. Chambers, *Cyclopædia* (5th edn., 1743), *under* 'marle').

SNEER. Yes—no genius! Ha! ha! ha!

DANGLE. A severe rogue! Ha! ha! ha! But you are quite right, Sir Fretful, never to read such nonsense.

SIR FRETFUL. To be sure—for if there is any thing to one's praise, it is a foolish vanity to be gratified at it, and if it is abuse,—why one is always 5 sure to hear of it from one damn'd good natur'd friend or another!

Enter SERVANT.

Sir, there is an Italian gentleman, with a French Interpreter, and three young ladies, and a dozen musicians, who say they are sent by LADY RONDEAU and MRS. FUGE. 10

DANGLE. Gadso! they come by appointment. Dear Mrs. Dangle do let them know I'll see them directly.

MRS. DANGLE. You know, Mr. Dangle, I shan't understand a word they say.

DANGLE. But you hear there's an interpreter. 15

MRS. DANGLE. Well, I'll try to endure their complaisance till you come.
[*Exit.*

SERVANT. And Mr. PUFF, Sir, has sent word that the last rehearsal is to be this morning, and that he'll call on you presently.

DANGLE. That's true—I shall certainly be at home. [*Exit* SERVANT.] 20 Now, Sir Fretful, if you have a mind to have justice done you in the way of answer—Egad, Mr. PUFF's your man.

SIR FRETFUL. Pshaw! Sir, why should I wish to have it answered, when I tell you I am pleased at it?

DANGLE. True, I had forgot that.—But I hope you are not fretted at 25 what Mr. Sneer——

SIR FRETFUL. —Zounds! no, Mr. Dangle, don't I tell you these things never fret me in the least.

DANGLE. Nay, I only thought——

SIR FRETFUL. —And let me tell you, Mr. Dangle, 'tis damn'd affronting 30 in you to suppose that I am hurt, when I tell you I am not.

SNEER. But why so warm, Sir Fretful?

SIR FRETFUL. Gadslife! Mr. Sneer, you are as absurd as Dangle; how often must I repeat it to you, that nothing can vex me but your supposing it possible for me to mind the damn'd nonsense you have been 35 repeating to me!—and let me tell you, if you continue to believe this, you must mean to insult me, gentlemen—and then your disrespect will affect me no more than the news-paper criticisms—and I shall treat it— with exactly the same calm indifference and philosophic contempt— and so your servant. [*Exit.* 40

SNEER. Ha! ha! ha! Poor Sir Fretful! Now will he go and vent his
philosophy in anonymous abuse of all modern critics and authors—
But, Dangle, you must get your friend PUFF to take me to the rehearsal
of his tragedy.

DANGLE. I'll answer for't, he'll thank you for desiring it. But come and 5
help me to judge of this musical family; they are recommended by
people of consequence, I assure you.

SNEER. I am at your disposal the whole morning—but I thought you had
been a decided critic in musick, as well as in literature?

DANGLE. So I am—but I have a bad ear.—Efaith, Sneer, tho', I am 10
afraid we were a little too severe on Sir Fretful—tho' he is my friend.

SNEER. Why, 'tis certain, that unnecessarily to mortify the vanity of any
writer, is a cruelty which mere dulness never can deserve; but where a
base and personal malignity usurps the place of literary emulation, the
aggressor deserves neither quarter nor pity.   15

DANGLE. That's true egad!—tho' he's my friend!

SCENE II

A Drawing Room, Harpsichord, &c. Italian Family, French Interpreter,
MRS. DANGLE *and* SERVANTS *discovered.*

INTERPRETER. Je dis madame, ja'i l'honneur to *introduce* & de vous 20
demander votre protection pour le Signor PASTICCIO RETORNELLO
& pour sa charmante famille.

SIGNOR PASTICCIO. Ah! Vosignoria noi vi preghiamo di favoritevi
colla vostra protezione.

1ST DAUGHTER. Vosignoria fatevi questi grazzie.   25

2D DAUGHTER. Si Signora.

INTERPRETER. Madame—*me interpret.*—C'est à dire—in English—
qu'ils vous prient de leur faire l'honneur—

MRS. DANGLE. —I say again, gentlemen, I don't understand a word you
say.   30

SIGNOR PASTICCIO. Questo Signore spiegheró.

8–9 but . . . well] *1781*, C; *om. L*   9 as in literature] *1781*; as literature C; *om. L*
10 So . . . ear] *1781*, C; *om. L*   13 where] *1781*; when L, C   16 egad]
1781; *om. L*, C   friend] *1781*, L; friend (*exe.*) C   18 *A . . . &c.*] *1781*, C;
om. L   18–19 *Italian . . . discovered*] *1781*; French Gent., Italian Family, & Mrs.
Dangle with Ritornello and Daughters C; Discover Mrs. Dangle, Monsieur, Signor
Pasticchio Ritornello and Daughters L   20 INTERPRETER] *1781*; *Monsieur* L, C
to] *1781*, L; *om.* C   21 votre] *1781*, C; vostra L   21–2 PASTICCIO . . . sa]
1781, C; Pasticchio Ritornello & pour La L   23 preghiamo] *1781*, L; pregtiambo
C   favoritevi] *1781*; favoriteri L; favorite C   25 1ST DAUGHTER] *1781*; 1st G
C; 1st L   grazzie] *1781*, C; Grazzy L   26 2D DAUGHTER] *1781*; 2nd G C;
2nd L   31 Questo . . . spiegheró] *1781*, C; Signore spia L

INTERPRETER. Oui—*me interpret.*—nous avons les lettres de recommendation pour Monsieur Dangle de——

MRS. DANGLE. —Upon my word, Sir, I don't understand you.

SIGNOR PASTICCIO. La CONTESSA RONDEAU e nostra padrona.

3D DAUGHTER. Si, padre, & mi LADI FUGE.   5

INTERPRETER. O!—*me interpret.*—Madame, ils disent—*in* English—
Qu'ils ont l'honneur d'etre protegés de ces Dames.—*You understand?*

MRS. DANGLE. No, Sir,——no understand!

Enter DANGLE *and* SNEER.

INTERPRETER. Ah voici Monsieur Dangle!   10

ALL ITALIANS. A! Signor Dangle!

MRS. DANGLE. Mr. Dangle, here are two very civil gentlemen trying to
make themselves understood, and I don't know which is the interpreter.

DANGLE. Ebien!

INTERPRETER. Monsieur Dangle—le grand bruit de vos talents pour⎫   15
la critique & de votre interest avec Messieurs les Directeurs a tous ⎬
les Theatres.   ⎪

SIGNOR PASTICCIO. Vosignoria siete si famoso par la vostra conos-   ⎭
censa e vostra interessa colla le Direttore da—

Speaking together.

DANGLE. Egad I think the Interpreter is the hardest to be understood of 20
the two!

SNEER. Why I thought, Dangle, you had been an admirable linguist!

DANGLE. So I am, if they would not talk so damn'd fast.

SNEER. Well I'll explain that—the less time we lose in hearing them the
better,—for that I suppose is what they are brought here for.   25

> [SNEER *speaks to* SIG. PAST.—*They sing*
> *trios,*[1] *&c.* DANGLE *beating out of time.*
> SERVANT *enters and whispers* DANGLE.

DANGLE. Shew him up.   [*Exit* SERVANT.

Bravo! admirable! bravissimo! admirablissimo!—Ah! Sneer! where will 30
you find such as these voices in England?

1 les] *1781*; des *L, C*   5 padre] *1781*; patri *L, C*   6 disent] *1781, C*;
diseus *L*   12 Mr. Dangle] *1781, C*; my dear *L*   16 Directeurs] *1781, C*;
directieurs *L*   19 colla le] *1781*; colle *L*; coll'le *C*   da] *1781, C*; ti both
Theatre *L*   22 linguist] *1781*; linguist, I am sure you write the Account of foreign
Literature in one of the Reviews. *L, C*   23–5 So . . . for] *1781*; Yes, but it is
not necessary to understand the Languages for that. Why reading the Books [Book—*C*]
is mere Journeymans Work, I get that done by the Sheet, and so Skim over a Translation
in Abstract *L, C*   26–8 SNEER . . . DANGLE] *1781, C*; *om. L*   29–30 Shew . . .
admirablissimo] *1781*; Bravo! admirable! bravissimo! *C*; *om. L*   30–1 Ah! . . .
such] *1781, C*; *om. L*   31 as these voices] *1781*; *om. L*; voices as these *C*
31–line 2, p. 511 in England . . . coming] *1781, C*; *om. L*

¹ See p. 484 above.

SNEER. Not easily.

DANGLE. But PUFF is coming.—Signor and little Signora's—obliga-
tissimo!—Sposa Signora Danglena—Mrs. Dangle, shall I beg you to
offer them some refreshments, and take their address in the next room.

[*Exit* MRS. DANGLE *with the* ITALIANS   5
and INTERPRETER *ceremoniously.*

Re-enter SERVANT.

Mr. PUFF, Sir.

DANGLE. My dear PUFF!

Enter PUFF.   10

My dear Dangle, how is it with you?

DANGLE. Mr. Sneer, give me leave to introduce Mr. PUFF to you.

PUFF. Mr. Sneer is this? Sir, he is a gentleman whom I have long panted
for the honour of knowing—a gentleman whose critical talents and
transcendant judgment——   15

SNEER. —Dear Sir——

DANGLE. Nay, don't be modest, Sneer, my friend PUFF only talks to you
in the stile of his profession.

SNEER. His profession!

PUFF. Yes, Sir; I make no secret of the trade I follow—among friends   20
and brother authors, Dangle knows I love to be frank on the subject,
and to advertise myself *vivâ voce.*—I am, Sir, a Practitioner in Panegyric,
or to speak more plainly—a Professor of the Art of Puffing,[1] at your
service—or any body else's.

SNEER. Sir, you are very obliging!—I believe, Mr. Puff, I have often   25
admired your talents in the daily prints.

PUFF. Yes, Sir, I flatter myself I do as much business in that way as any
six of the fraternity in town—Devilish hard work all the summer—
Friend Dangle? never work'd harder!—But harkee,—the Winter
Managers were a little sore I believe.   30

DANGLE. No—I believe they took it all in good part.

PUFF. Aye!—Then that must have been affectation in them, for egad,
there were some of the attacks which there was no laughing at!

SNEER. Aye, the humourous ones.—But I should think Mr. Puff, that
Authors would in general be able to do this sort of work for themselves.   35

2–3 Signor . . . Danglena] *1781*; *om. L, C*   3–4 Mrs. Dangle . . . them] *1781*,
C; *om. L*   4 some refreshments] *1781*; chocolate *C*; *om. L*   and take . . .
room] *1781, C*; *om. L*   5–6 *Exit . . . ceremoniously*] *1781*; *Exeunt Frenchman,*
and Italians Dangle complimenting in bad French and Italian C; *om. L*   7 *Re-*
enter] *1781, C*; *Enter L*   13 is this] *1781*; *om. L, Rae, C*   19 His] *1781*,
L, C; Of his *Rae*   31 No] *1781, L, C*; O no *Rae*   32 Aye] *1781, L, C*;
Ah *Rae*

---

[1] Sheridan was competent in this line himself. See Rae, *Sheridan*, ii. 6 n.

PUFF. Why yes—but in a clumsy way.—Besides, we look on that as an encroachment, and so take the opposite side.—I dare say now you conceive half the very civil paragraphs and advertisements you see, to be written by the parties concerned, or their friends?—No such thing—Nine out of ten, manufactured by me in the way of business.   5

SNEER. Indeed!—

PUFF. Even the Auctioneers now,—the Auctioneers I say, tho' the rogues have lately got some credit for their language—not an article of the merit their's![1]—take them out of their Pulpits, and they are as dull as Catalogues.——No, Sir;—'twas I first enrich'd their style—'twas I 10 first taught them to crowd their advertisements with panegyrical superlatives, each epithet rising above the other—like the Bidders in their own Auction-rooms! From ME they learn'd to enlay their phraseology with variegated chips of exotic metaphor: by ME too their inventive faculties were called forth.—Yes Sir, by ME they were instructed 15 to clothe ideal walls with gratuitous fruits—to insinuate obsequious rivulets into visionary groves—to teach courteous shrubs to nod their approbation of the grateful soil! or on emergencies to raise upstart oaks, where there never had been an acorn; to create a delightful vicinage without the assistance of a neighbour; or fix the temple of Hygeia[2] in 20 the fens of Lincolnshire!

DANGLE. I am sure, you have done them infinite service; for now, when a gentleman is ruined, he parts with his house with some credit.

SNEER. Service! if they had any gratitude, they would erect a statue to him, they would figure him as a presiding Mercury, the god of traffic 25 and fiction, with a hammer in his hand instead of a caduceus.—But pray, Mr. Puff, what first put you on exercising your talents in this way?

PUFF. Egad sir,—sheer necessity—the proper parent of an art so nearly allied to invention: you must know Mr. Sneer, that from the first time I tried my hand at an advertisement, my success was such, that for 30 sometime after, I led a most extraordinary life indeed!

SNEER. How, pray?

PUFF. Sir, I supported myself two years entirely by my misfortunes.

SNEER. By your misfortunes!

PUFF. Yes Sir, assisted by long sickness, and other occasional disorders; 35 and a very comfortable living I had of it.

1 Why yes] *1781, L, C*; Aye *Rae*   3 conceive] *1781, Rae*; think *L, C*   3–4 to be] *1781, C*; are *L, Rae*   20 neighbour; or] *1781, L, C*; Neighbour—waft salubrious Gales or *Rae*   24 if] *1781*; Egad if *L, C, Rae*   25 him as] *1781, L, C*; you as *Rae*

---

[1] See p. 471 above, and p. 516 n. below.

[2] This is possibly a glancing allusion to James Graham's, the quack doctor's, establishments in the Adelphi, the 'Temple of Health and Hymen', and later, in Pall Mall, 'the Electrical Temple of Health'. Graham's pretensions are ridiculed in Colman the elder's *The Genius of Nonsense* (1780).

SNEER. From sickness and misfortunes!—You practised as a Doctor, and an Attorney at once?

PUFF. No egad, both maladies and miseries were my own.

SNEER. Hey!—what the plague!

DANGLE. 'Tis true, efaith. 5

PUFF. Harkee!—By advertisements—'To the charitable and humane!'[1] and 'to those whom Providence hath blessed with affluence!'

SNEER. Oh,—I understand you.

PUFF. And in truth, I deserved what I got, for I suppose never man went thro' such a series of calamities in the same space of time!—Sir, I was 10 five times made a bankrupt, and reduced from a state of affluence, by a train of unavoidable misfortunes! then Sir, tho' a very industrious tradesman, I was twice burnt out, and lost my little all, both times!—I lived upon those fires a month.—I soon after was confined by a most excruciating disorder, and lost the use of my limbs!—That told very 15 well, for I had the case strongly attested, and went about to collect the subscriptions myself.

DANGLE. Egad, I believe that was when you first called on me.—

PUFF. —In November last?—O no!—I was at that time, a close prisoner in the Marshalsea,[2] for a debt benevolently contracted to serve a 20 friend!—I was afterwards, twice tapped for a dropsy, which declined into a very profitable consumption!—I was then reduced to—O no— then, I became a widow with six helpless children,—after having had eleven husbands pressed, and being left every time eight months gone with child, and without money to get me into an hospital! 25

SNEER. And you bore all with patience, I make no doubt?

PUFF. Why, yes,—tho' I made some occasional attempts at felo de se; but as I did not find those *rash actions* answer, I left off killing myself very soon.—Well, Sir,—at last, what with bankruptcies, fires, gouts,

---

9 in truth] *1781, C, Rae*; egad *L*   17 subscriptions] *1781, Rae*; subscription *L, C*
Between lines 25 and 26, Rae adds a speech: Dangle. Mercy on me—   27 occasional]
1781, C, L; judicious *Rae*   28 I did] *1781, C, L*; did *Rae*   those *rash actions*]
1781, L, C; them *Rae*

---

[1] Cf. 'To the Affluent and Humane' in the *Public Advertiser*, 18 Aug. 1779 'A Man of unblemished Character, having been a Housekeeper many Years, and carried on his Business with a Prospect of not knowing his present unhappy Situation; but through the Vicissitudes of Life, and unavoidable Misfortunes, together with the Decay of his Business, is reduced to the very lowest State of Adversity. He has a very large Family of small Children, all dependent on him for Support, and is unable to provide them with the common Necessaries of Life; it having pleased the Almighty frequently to afflict some of them with Sickness, which renders their Case extremely deplorable; they have been obliged to part with almost every Necessary for Bread . . . .' See p. 480 above.

[2] The debtors' prison on the south bank of the Thames and abutting Borough High Street, that ran to London Bridge.

dropsies, imprisonments, and other valuable calamities, having got together a pretty handsome sum, I determined to quit a business which had always gone rather against my conscience, and in a more liberal way still to indulge my talents for fiction and embellishment, thro' my favourite channels of diurnal communication—and so, Sir, you have   5 my history.

SNEER. Most obligingly communicative indeed; and your confession if published, might certainly serve the cause of true charity, by rescuing the most useful channels of appeal to benevolence from the cant of imposition.—But surely, Mr. PUFF, there is no great *mystery* in your   10 present profession?

PUFF. Mystery! Sir, I will take upon me to say the matter was never scientifically treated, nor reduced to rule before.

SNEER. Reduced to rule?

PUFF. O lud, Sir! you are very ignorant, I am afraid.—Yes Sir,—   15 PUFFING is of various sorts—the principal are, The PUFF DIRECT— the PUFF PRELIMINARY—the PUFF COLLATERAL—the PUFF COLLUSIVE, and the PUFF OBLIQUE, or PUFF by IMPLICATION.— These all assume, as circumstances require, the various forms of LETTER TO THE EDITOR—OCCASIONAL ANECDOTE—IMPARTIAL   20 CRITIQUE—OBSERVATION from CORRESPONDENT,—or ADVER-TISEMENT FROM THE PARTY.[1]

SNEER. The puff direct, I can conceive—

PUFF. O yes, that's simple enough,—for instance—A new Comedy or Farce is to be produced at one of the Theatres (though by the bye they   25 don't bring out half what they ought to do). The author, suppose Mr. Smatter,[2] or Mr. Dapper—or any particular friend of mine—very well; the day before it is to be performed, I write an account of the manner in which it was received—I have the plot from the author,—and only add—Characters strongly drawn—highly coloured—hand of a master—   30 fund of genuine humour—mine of invention—neat dialogue—attic salt! Then for the performance—Mr. DODD was astonishingly great

7–10 and your . . . imposition] *1781*, *C*; *om. L, Rae*   17–18 PUFF PRELIMINARY . . . IMPLICATION] *1781*, *C*, *L*; *the Puff direct—the Puff oblique—the Puff collateral, the Puff Preliminary, and the Puff Collusive Rae*   19 These . . . assume] *1781*, *L*, *C*; These all as circumstances require assume *Rae*   as . . . require] *1781*, *Rae*; *om. L*, *C*   various] *1781*; varied *L*, *C*, *Rae*   27 Dapper] *1781*, *C*; Flimsey *L*, *Rae* 28 to be] *1781*; *om. L*, *C*, *Rae*

---

[1] 'A kind of parody of Touchstone's dissertation on the lye in quarrelling. . . . The only proper object which appears to have been omitted, is what are called the house paragraphs for the theatres' (*General Evening Post*, 30 Oct.–2 Nov. 1779).

[2] 'Jack Smatter' was a character (played by the youthful Garrick) in James Dance's *Pamela* (1740), an adaptation of Richardson's novel.

in the character of SIR HARRY![1] That universal and judicious actor
Mr. PALMER, perhaps never appeared to more advantage than in the
COLONEL;[2]—but it is not in the power of language to do justice to
Mr. KING![3]—Indeed he more than merited those repeated bursts of
applause which he drew from a most brilliant and judicious audience!   5
As to the scenery—The miraculous power of Mr. DE LOUTHER-
BOURG's pencil[4] are universally acknowledged!—In short, we are at a
loss which to admire most,—the unrivalled genius of the author, the
great attention and liberality of the managers—the wonderful abilities
of the painter, or the incredible exertions of all the performers!—   10
SNEER. That's pretty well indeed, Sir.
PUFF. O cool—quite cool—to what I sometimes do.
SNEER. And do you think there are any who are influenced by this.
PUFF. O, lud! yes, Sir;—the number of those who go thro' the fatigue of
judging for themselves is very small indeed!   15
SNEER. Well, Sir,—the PUFF PRELIMINARY?
PUFF. O that, Sir, does well in the form of a *Caution.*—In a matter of
gallantry now—Sir FLIMSY GOSSIMER, wishes to be well with LADY
FANNY FETE—He applies to me——I open trenches for him with a
paragraph in the Morning Post.——It is recommended to the beautiful 20
and accomplished Lady F four stars F dash E to be on her guard
against that dangerous character, Sir F dash G; who, however pleasing
and insinuating his manners may be, is certainly not remarkable for the
constancy of his attachments!—in Italics.—Here you see, Sir FLIMSY
GOSSIMER is introduced to the particular notice of Lady FANNY— 25
who, perhaps never thought of him before—she finds herself publickly
cautioned to avoid him, which naturally makes her desirous of seeing
him;—the observation of their acquaintance causes a pretty kind of
mutual embarrassment, this produces a sort of sympathy of interest—
which, if Sir Flimsy is unable to improve effectually, he at least gains 30
the credit of having their names mentioned together, by a particular

1 SIR HARRY] *1781*, L, C; young Mr. Something *Rae*   2–3 than in the COLONEL]
1781, L, C; *om. Rae*   3 not in the power of] *1781*; impossible for L, C, *Rae*
6 DE] *1781*; *om.* L, C, *Rae*   10 exertions] *1781*, *Rae*, L; exertion C   12 O
cool] *1781*, *Rae*; O L, C   13 do] *1781*, L, C; *om. Rae*   who are] *1781*, C,
Rae; *om.* L   27 desirous of seeing] *1781*; desire to see L, C; desirous to see *Rae*

1 The best-known 'Sir Harry' was Sir Harry Wildair in Farquhar's *The Constant
Couple*, but the reference may be to Dodd as Sir Harry Bouquet in *The Camp*. He
created the part of Dangle.
2 The best-known 'Colonel' is Colonel Standard in *The Constant Couple* (taken by
Palmer from 8 May 1776). A 'Colonel Promise' and a 'Sir Harry Foxchase' are to be
found in Fielding's *Pasquin* (1736), but this satire had not been acted for many years.
3 See pp. 303–4, 473 above.
4 See p. 475 above.

set, and in a particular way,—which nine times out of ten is the full
accomplishment of modern gallantry!

DANGLE. Egad, Sneer, you will be quite an adept in the business.

PUFF. Now, Sir, the PUFF COLLATERAL is much used as an appendage
to advertisements, and may take the form of anecdote.—Yesterday as   5
the celebrated GEORGE BON-MOT was sauntering down St. James's-
street, he met the lively Lady MARY MYRTLE, coming out of the
Park,—'Good God, LADY MARY, I'm surprised to meet you in a white
jacket,—for I expected never to have seen you, but in a full-trimmed
uniform, and a light-horseman's cap!'—'Heavens, GEORGE, where   10
could you have learned that?'—'Why, replied the wit, I just saw a
print of you, in a new publication called The CAMP MAGAZINE,
which, by the bye, is a devilish clever thing,—and is sold at No. 3, on
the right hand of the way, two doors from the printing-office, the
corner of Ivy-lane, Paternoster-row, price only one shilling!'[1]   15

SNEER. Very ingenious indeed!

PUFF. But the PUFF COLLUSIVE is the newest of any; for it acts in the
disguise of determined hostility.—It is much used by bold booksellers
and enterprising poets.—An indignant correspondent observes—that
the new poem called BEELZEBUB'S COTILLION, or PROSER-   20
PINE'S FETE CHAMPETRE, is one of the most unjustifiable performances he ever read! The severity with which certain characters are
handled is quite shocking! And as there are many descriptions in it too
warmly coloured for female delicacy, the shameful avidity with which
this piece is bought by all people of fashion, is a reproach on the taste 25
of the times, and a disgrace to the delicacy of the age!—Here you see
the two strongest inducements are held forth;—First, that nobody
ought to read it;—and secondly, that every body buys it; on the strength
of which, the publisher boldly prints the tenth edition, before he had
sold ten of the first; and then establishes it by threatening himself with 30
the pillory, or absolutely indicting himself for SCAN. MAG.![2]

DANGLE. Ha! ha! ha!—'gad I know it is so.

PUFF. As to the PUFF OBLIQUE, or PUFF BY IMPLICATION, it is too
various and extensive to be illustrated by an instance;—it attracts in
titles, and presumes in patents; it lurks in the *limitation* of a subscrip- 35
tion, and invites in the assurance of croud and incommodation at public

---

1 set, and in a particular] *1781, C, Rae; om. L*   8 MARY, I'm] *1781, L, C;* 'Mary',
said George, 'I'm' *Rae*   11 the wit] *1781, C, Rae;* he *L*   15 price . . . shilling]
1781, L, C; om. Rae   16 Very] *1781;* Ah! that's very *L, C, Rae*   29 had] *1781,
Rae;* has *C, L*

---

[1] '*The Morning Post* . . . is memorable for teaching advertisers how to write; and what
Puff says in the *Critic*, has certainly its origin from the superior style in which auctions
were advertised in *The Morning Post*, which set every body mad for high-flown,
paragraphical descriptions of trifles' (*The Musical Tour of Mr. Dibdin* (Sheffield, 1788),
pp. 428–9).   [2] Scandalum magnatum: defaming the highest in the realm.

places; it delights to draw forth concealed merit, with a most disinterested assiduity; and sometimes wears a countenance of smiling censure
and tender reproach.—It has a wonderful memory for Parliamentary
Debates, and will often give the whole speech of a favoured member,
with the most flattering accuracy.[1] But, above all, it is a great dealer in   5
reports and suppositions.—It has the earliest intelligence of intended
preferments that will reflect *honor* on the *patrons*; and embryo promo-
tions of modest gentlemen—who know nothing of the matter themselves.
It can hint a ribband for implied services, in the air of a common report;
and with the carelessness of a casual paragraph, suggest officers into   10
commands—to which they have no pretension but their wishes. This,
Sir, is the last principal class in the ART of PUFFING——An art which
I hope you will now agree with me, is of the highest dignity—yielding
a tablature of benevolence and public spirit; befriending equally trade,
gallantry, criticism, and politics: the applause of genius! the register of   15
charity! the triumph of heroism! the self defence of contractors! the
fame of orators!—and the gazette of ministers![2]
SNEER. Sir, I am compleatly a convert both to the importance and
ingenuity of your profession; and now, Sir, there is but one thing which
can possibly encrease my respect for you, and that is, your permitting   20
me to be present this morning at the rehearsal of your new trage——
PUFF. —Hush, for heaven's sake.—*My* tragedy!—Egad, Dangle, I take
this very ill—you know how apprehensive I am of being known to be
the author.
DANGLE. 'Efaith I would not have told—but it's in the papers, and your   25
name at length—in the Morning Chronicle.
PUFF. Ah! those damn'd editors never can keep a secret!—Well, Mr.
Sneer—no doubt you will do me great honour—I shall be infinitely
happy—highly flattered——
DANGLE. I believe it must be near the time—shall we go together.   30
PUFF. No; It will not be yet this hour, for they are always late at that
theatre: besides, I must meet you there, for I have some little matters

---

1–3 delights . . . reproach] *1781, C, Rae; om. L*   4 often] *1781, C, Rae;* some-
times *L*   5 great] *1781, L, Rae;* good *C*   9 implied] *1781, Rae;* implicit *L,
C*   11 pretension] *1781, Rae;* pretensions *L, C*   12 in] *1781, L, C;* of *Rae*
An art] *1781;* and Practise *L;* a practice *C, Rae*   17 orators] *1781, C;* Patriots
L, Rae   18 Sir] *1781, Rae; om. L, C*   23 this] *1781, L, Rae;* it *C*   31 No]
1781, Rae; O no *L, C*

---

[1] 'Looking at Messrs. Dilly's splendid edition of Lord Chesterfield's miscellaneous
works, he [Johnson] laughed, and said, 'Here now are two speeches ascribed to him, both
of which were written by me' (J. Boswell, *Life of Johnson*, ed. G. B. Hill; revd., L. F.
Powell (Oxford, 1934), iii. 351). W. Woodfall was famous for his accurate reports.
[2] Boaden, *Kemble*, i. 67–8, sees a resemblance in manner of putting the points and in
cadence of language, to Isaac Barrow's *Second Sermon on Evil Speaking* (1678), p. 44.

here to send to the papers, and a few paragraphs to scribble before I go.
                                    [*Looking at memorandums.*
—Here is 'a CONSCIENTIOUS BAKER, on the Subject of the Army
Bread;' and 'a DETESTER OF VISIBLE BRICK-WORK, in favor of the
new invented Stucco;' both in the style of JUNIUS,[1] and promised for   5
to-morrow.—The Thames navigation too is at a stand.[2]—MISOMUD
or ANTI-SHOAL must go to work again directly.—Here too are some
political memorandums I see; aye—To take PAUL JONES,[3] and get the
INDIAMEN out of the SHANNON—reinforce BYRON[4]—compel the
DUTCH to—so!—I must do that in the evening papers, or reserve it for   10
the Morning Herald, for I know that I have undertaken to-morrow,
besides, to establish the unanimity of the fleet in the Public Advertiser,
and to shoot CHARLES FOX[5] in the Morning Post.—So, egad, I
ha'n't a moment to lose!
DANGLE. Well!—we'll meet in the Green Room.   [*Exeunt severally.*   15

END OF ACT I

2 *Looking at memorandums*] *1781*, *Rae*; *om. L, C*   7 Here] *1781, Rae*; oh here
L, C   8 aye] *1781, Rae*; are *L*; are *transcribed, then deleted, in C*   10 so]
1781, Rae; oh *L, C*   10–11 or ... Herald] *1781, Rae*; *om. L, C*   13 shoot
CHARLES FOX] *1781, Rae*; recover three Men for the Humane Society *L, C*   14 to
lose] *1781, Rae*; to lose—meet me at the theatre *C*; *om. L*   15 Well! ... Room]
1781, Rae; We will *C*; I won't indeed *L*   *L gives two further speeches:*
    Sneer. I shall be all impatience.
    Puff. Egad I think we shall surprise him hey?
Exeunt severally] *1781, C, Rae*; *om. L*

___

    [1] 'Junius' is believed to have been Sir Philip Francis (1740–1818), and his letters,
published in the *Public Advertiser* between 1769 and 1772, fiercely attacked George III
and his ministers. Coleridge thought the letter to the King 'almost faultless in composition': see *The Letters of Junius*, ed. C. W. Everard (1927), pp. lvi, 135–48. For
Sheridan's interest in 'Junius', see *Letters*, i. 3–4, 6, 8; iii. 159.
    [2] Trinity House was attacked in the newspapers for not dredging the Thames
adequately: see the *Public Advertiser*, 26 Oct. 1779.
    [3] John Paul Jones (1747–92), privateer, effectively menaced the shipping of Britain
on behalf of the American revolutionaries.
    [4] John Byron (1723–86), circumnavigator. He commanded the West Indies fleet,
1778–9.
    [5] Charles James Fox (1749–1806), a leader of the opposition to the King, particularly
attacking naval policy.

ACT II

SCENE I

The THEATRE

Enter DANGLE, PUFF, *and* SNEER, *as before the Curtain.*

PUFF. No, no, Sir; what Shakespeare says of ACTORS may be better 5
applied to the purpose of PLAYS; *they* ought to be 'the abstract and
brief Chronicles of the times.' Therefore when history, and particularly the history of our own country, furnishes any thing like a case in
point, to the time in which an author writes, if he knows his own
interest, he will take advantage of it; so, Sir, I call my tragedy The 10
SPANISH ARMADA; and have laid the scene before TILBURY FORT.

SNEER. A most happy thought certainly!

DANGLE. Egad it was—I told you so.—But pray now I dont understand
how you have contrived to introduce any love into it.

PUFF. Love!—Oh nothing so easy; for it is a received point among poets, 15
that where history gives you a good heroic out-line for a play, you may
fill up with a little love at your own discretion; in doing which, nine
times out of ten, you only make up a deficiency in the private history
of the times.—Now I rather think I have done this with some success.

SNEER. No scandal about Queen ELIZABETH, I hope? 20

PUFF. O Lud! no, no.—I only suppose the Governor of Tilbury Fort's[1]
daughter to be in love with the son of the Spanish Admiral.

SNEER. Oh, is that all?

DANGLE. Excellent, Efaith!—I see it at once.—But won't this appear
rather improbable? 25

PUFF. To be sure it will—but what the plague! a play is not to shew
occurrences that happen every day, but things just so strange, that tho'
they never *did*, they *might* happen.

---

2 SCENE I] *1781*, *Rae*, *C*; *om. L*   3 The THEATRE] *1781*; *om. L, C, Rae*
4 *Enter . . . Curtain*] *1781*; Dangle Puff and Sneer *L, Rae*; *for the version in C, see
p. 29*   5 No . . . Sir] *1781*; Sir, I say that *L, C*; I say that *Rae*   ACTORS]
1781; the actors *L, C, Rae*   7 Chronicles] *1781*; chronicle *L, C, Rae*   10 my]
1781, *Rae*; this *L, C*   14 it] *1781*, *C*; it, and that you know is as necessary
to a modern Tragedy as— | *Sneer.* Novelty to a Simile, and therefore you had better not
try to make Love on the Subject. *L*; *Rae prints 'it . . . subject', omitting 'Sneer', and
'Novelty' and reading 'one' for 'love'*   19 success] *1781*, *L, C*; Address *Rae*
26 what the] *1781*, *Rae*; what a *L, C*

---

[1] Built in the reign of Henry VIII to defend the mouth of the Thames. R. Brookes,
The General Gazetteer (8th edn., 1797), describes it as 'a regular fortification, which may
be termed the key to London'. He adds that it has 'a platform . . . on which are planted
106 guns'.

SNEER. Certainly nothing is unnatural, that is not physically impossible.

PUFF. Very true—and for that matter DON FEROLO WHISKERANDOS
—for that's the lover's name, might have been over here in the train of
the Spanish Ambassador; or TILBURINA, for that is the lady's name,
might have been in love with him, from having heard his character, or   5
seen his picture; or from knowing that he was the last man in the world
she ought to be in love with—or for any other good female reason.—
However, Sir, the fact is, that tho' she is but a Knight's daughter, egad!
she is in love like any Princess!

DANGLE. Poor young lady! I feel for her already! for I can conceive how   10
great the conflict must be between her passion and her duty; her love
for her country, and her love for DON FEROLO WHISKERANDOS!

PUFF. O amazing!—her poor susceptible heart is swayed to and fro, by
contending passions like—

Enter UNDER PROMPTER.   15

UNDER PROMPTER. Sir, the scene is set, and every thing is ready to
begin if you please.—¹

PUFF. 'Egad; then we'll lose no time.

UNDER PROMPTER. Tho' I believe, Sir, you will find it very short, for
all the performers have profited by the kind permission you granted   20
them.

PUFF. Hey! what!

UNDER PROMPTER. You know, Sir, you gave them leave to cut out or
omit whatever they found heavy or unnecessary to the plot, and I must
own they have taken very liberal advantage of your indulgence.   25

PUFF. Well, well.—They are in general very good judges; and I know I
am luxuriant.—Now, Mr. HOPKINS,² as soon as you please.

UNDER PROMPTER *to the Musick.* Gentlemen, will you play a few bars
of something, just to—

2 DON FEROLO WHISKERANDOS] *1781*; Don Whiskerondos *L*; Don *Rae*; Don Ferola
Whiskerandos *C*   4 the Spanish Ambassador] *1781*, *C*, *Rae*; *om. L*   TILBURINA]
1781, *C*, *L*; Tilburnia *Rae*   7 with] *1781*, *C*, *L*; *om. Rae*   12 DON FEROLO
WHISKERANDOS] *1781*; Don *C*, *Rae*; Don Whiskerondos *L*   13 O amazing] *1781*,
Rae; Amazing *L*; Oh *C*   28 to . . . Musick] *1781*, *C*; *To the Orchestra Rae*;
om. L   29 just to] *1781*; to *L*, *Rae*, *C*

¹ 'The purpose aimed at is effected by a kind of burlesque parody, of which there
are some thousand lines extended through the greater part of two acts. These must
have been a very tedious, laborious, and disgusting task; and the effect of this kind of
ridicule is so very strong, that it soon grows tiresome and disagreeable. The public
opinion of modern tragedy is already so very low, as appears by their general desertion,
that the game is hardly worth the pursuit' (*General Evening Post*, 30 Oct.–2 Nov. 1799).

² William Hopkins, prompter and copyist at Drury Lane Theatre, 1760–80.

PUFF. Aye, that's right,—for as we have the scenes, and dresses, egad,
we'll go to't, as if it was the first night's performance;—but you need
not mind stopping between the acts.   [*Exit* UNDER PROMPTER.

[*Orchestra play. Then the Bell rings.*]

Soh! stand clear gentlemen.—Now you know there will be a cry of   5
down!—down!—hats off! silence!—Then up curtain,—and let us see
what our painters have done for us.

SCENE II

The Curtain rises and discovers TILBURY FORT

Two Centinels asleep.   10

DANGLE. Tilbury Fort!—very fine indeed!
PUFF. Now, what do you think I open with?
SNEER. Faith, I can't guess—
PUFF. A clock.—Hark!—[*clock strikes.*] I open with a clock striking, to
beget an aweful attention in the audience—it also marks the time, which 15
is four o'clock in the morning, and saves a description of the rising sun,¹
and a great deal about gilding the eastern hemisphere.
DANGLE. But pray, are the centinels to be asleep?
PUFF. Fast as watchmen.
SNEER. Isn't that odd tho' at such an alarming crisis?   20
PUFF. To be sure it is,—but smaller things must give way to a striking
scene at the opening; that's a rule.—And the case is, that two great men
are coming to this very spot to begin the piece; now, it is not to be
supposed they would open their lips, if these fellows were watching
them, so, egad, I must either have sent them off their posts, or set them 25
asleep.
SNEER. O that accounts for it!—But tell us, who are these coming?—

2–3 but . . . acts] *1781, C, Rae; om. L*   3 *Exit . . .* PROMPTER] *1781, C; om.*
Rae, L   4 *Orchestra . . . rings*] *1781*; *Orchestre play L, C*; Orchestra *play Rae*
5 will be] *1781, C, Rae;* is *L*   7 us] *1781, L;* us. (*Curtain rises*) *Rae, C*
9 *The Curtain . . .* FORT] *1781;* TILBURY FORT *C, L;* Before Tilbury Fort *Rae*
10 *Two*] *1781; om. L, C, Rae*   14 *strikes*] *1781, Rae;* STRIKES FOUR *L, C*
16 o'clock] *1781, C, Rae; om. L*   21 To . . . but] *1781;* Aye, but *L, C, Rae*
22 that's a rule] *1781; om. L, C, Rae*   23 now] *1781, L, C; om. Rae*

¹ Cf. R. Cumberland, *The Battle of Hastings* (1778), III. i:
                    Invention never yok'd
            A fairer courser to Apollo's car,
            When with the zephyrs and the rosy hours
            Through heav'n's bright portal he ascends the east,
            And on his beamy forehead brings the morn.

PUFF. These are they—SIR WALTER RALEIGH, and SIR CHRISTO-
PHER HATTON.—You'll know Sir CHRISTOPHER, by his turning out
his toes—famous you know for his dancing. I like to preserve all the
little traits of character.—Now attend.

Enter SIR WALTER RALEIGH *and* SIR   5
CHRISTOPHER HATTON.

'SIR CHRISTOPHER.

'True, gallant Raleigh!—

DANGLE. What, they had been talking before?[1]
PUFF. O, yes; all the way as they came along.—I beg pardon gentlemen   10
[*to the Actors*] but these are particular friends of mine, whose remarks
may be of great service to us.—Don't mind interrupting them whenever
any thing strikes you. [*To* SNEER *and* DANGLE.]

'SIR CHRISTOPHER.

'True, gallant Raleigh!   15
But O, thou champion of thy country's fame,
There *is* a question which I yet must ask;
A question, which I never ask'd before—
What mean these mighty armaments?
This general muster? and this throng of chiefs?   20

SNEER. Pray, Mr. Puff, how came Sir Christopher Hatton never to ask
that question before?
PUFF. What, before the Play began? how the plague could he?
DANGLE. That's true efaith!
PUFF. But you will hear what he thinks of the matter.   25

'SIR CHRISTOPHER.

'Alas, my noble friend, when I behold
Yon tented plains in martial symmetry
Array'd.——When I count o'er yon glittering lines
Of crested warriors, where the proud steeds neigh,   30
And valor-breathing trumpet's shrill appeal,
Responsive vibrate on my listning ear;
When virgin majesty herself I view,[2]

4 attend] *1781*; observe *L, C, Rae*   11 *to the Actors*] *1781, C*; om. *L, Rae*
12 whenever] *1781, Rae*; when *L, C*   13 To . . . DANGLE] *1781, C*; om. *L, Rae*
23 he] *1781, Rae*; they *L, C*

---

[1] Cf. Buckingham's *The Rehearsal*, II. i:
Physician. Sir, to conclude.
Smith. What, before he begins?
Bayes. No, Sir; you must know, they had been talking of this a pretty while without.
[2] Queen Elizabeth reviewed her soldiers at Tilbury Fort in Aug. 1588. The speech
she made then was reprinted in the *Public Advertiser*, 17 Sept. 1779.

Like her protecting Pallas veil'd in steel,
With graceful confidence exhort to arms!
When briefly all I hear or see bears stamp
Of martial vigilance, and stern defence,
I cannot but surmise.—Forgive, my friend,   5
If the conjecture's rash——I cannot but
Surmise.——The state some danger apprehends!

SNEER. A very cautious conjecture that.

PUFF. Yes, that's his character; not to give an opinion, but on secure
grounds—now then.   10

'SIR WALTER.

'O, most accomplished Christopher.'——

PUFF. He calls him by his christian name, to shew that they are on the
most familiar terms.

'SIR WALTER.   15

'O most accomplish'd Christopher, I find
Thy staunch sagacity still tracks the future,
In the fresh print of the o'ertaken past.

PUFF. Figurative!

'SIR WALTER.   20

'Thy fears are just.

'SIR CHRISTOPHER.

'But where? whence? when? and what
The danger is——Methinks I fain would learn.

'SIR WALTER.   25

'You know, my friend, scarce two revolving suns,
And three revolving moons, have closed their course,
Since haughty PHILIP,[1] in despight of peace,
With hostile hand hath struck at ENGLAND's trade.

'SIR CHRISTOPHER.   30
'I know it well.

'SIR WALTER.

'PHILIP you know is proud, IBERIA's king!

4 vigilance] *1781*; *C*; preparation *L, Rae. In C* 'preparation' *is corrected to* 'vigilance'
in Sheridan's hand.   9 secure] *1781, C*; good *L, Rae*   10 now then] *1781,*
C, Rae; now and then *L*   18 past] *1781, Rae, C*; Post *L*   23 But . . .
what] *1781, L, Rae*; But whence? where? when? which? whose? *C, a correction in*
Sheridan's hand.   33 proud, IBERIA'S] *1781*; proud Iberia's, *L, C, Rae*

---

[1] Philip II, King of Spain (1527-98).

'SIR CHRISTOPHER.

'He is.

'SIR WALTER.

'——His subjects in base bigotry
And Catholic oppression held,——while we   5
You know, the protestant persuasion hold.

'SIR CHRISTOPHER.

'We do.

'SIR WALTER.

'You know beside,——his boasted armament,   10
The fam'd Armada,——by the Pope baptized,
With purpose to invade these realms——

'SIR CHRISTOPER.

                    '——Is sailed,
Our last advices so report.   15

'SIR WALTER.

'While the Iberian Admiral's chief hope,
His darling son——

'SIR CHRISTOPHER.

          '——Ferolo Wiskerandos hight——   20

'SIR WALTER.

'The same—by chance a pris'ner hath been ta'en,
And in this fort of Tilbury——

'SIR CHRISTOPHER.

                    '——Is now   25
Confin'd,—'tis true, and oft from yon tall turrets top
I've mark'd the youthful Spaniard's haughty mien
Unconquer'd, tho' in chains!

'SIR WALTER.

          'You also know——   30

DANGLE. —Mr. Puff, as he *knows* all this, why does Sir Walter go on telling him?

PUFF. But the audience are not supposed to know any thing of the matter, are they?

SNEER. True, but I think you manage ill: for there certainly appears no 35 reason why Sir Walter should be so communicative.

15 report] *1781*, L, C; advise *Rae*   17 Iberian] *1781*; Spanish L, C, *Rae*
20 Ferolo . . . hight] *1781*; Don Whiskerondos! L; Don Ferolo Whiskerandos C; Don—
Rae   26 from . . . top] *1781*, *Rae*; om. L, C   27 youthful] *1781*, *Rae*; om.
L, C   33 But] *1781*, *Rae*; Ay, but L, C   35 ill] *1781*; *Rae*; very ill L, C

PUFF. Fore Gad now, that is one of the most ungrateful observations I
ever heard—for the less inducement he has to tell all this, the more I
think, you ought to be oblig'd to him; for I am sure you'd know nothing
of the matter without it.

DANGLE. That's very true, upon my word.   5

PUFF. But you will find he was *not* going on.

'SIR CHRISTOPHER.

'Enough, enough,—'tis plain—and I no more
Am in amazement lost!——

PUFF. Here, now you see, Sir Christopher did not in fact ask any one   10
question for his own information.

SNEER. No indeed:—his has been a most disinterested curiosity!

DANGLE. Really, I find, we are very much oblig'd to them both.

PUFF. To be sure you are. Now then for the Commander in Chief, the
EARL OF LEICESTER! who, you know, was no favourite but of the   15
Queen's.—We left off—'in amazement lost!'—

'SIR CHRISTOPHER.

'Am in amazement lost.——
But, see where noble Leicester comes! supreme
In honours and command.   20

'SIR WALTER.

'And yet methinks,
At such a time, so perilous, so fear'd,
That staff might well become an abler grasp.

'SIR CHRISTOPHER.   25

'And so by heav'n! think I; but soft, he's here!

PUFF. Aye, they envy him.

SNEER. But who are these with him?

PUFF. O! very valiant knights; one is the Governor of the fort, the other
the master of the horse.—And now, I think you shall hear some better 30
language: I was obliged to be plain and intelligible in the first scene,
because there was so much matter of fact in it; but now, efaith, you have
trope, figure, and metaphor, as plenty as noun-substantives.

Enter EARL OF LEICESTER, THE GOVERNOR, *and others.*

'LEICESTER.   35

'How's this my friends! is't thus your new fledg'd zeal
And plumed valor moults in roosted sloth?

1 Fore Gad] *C, Rae, L*; for, egad *1781*   4 matter] *1781, L*; plot *C, Rae*
14 Commander in Chief] *1781, C, Rae*; Generalissimo *L*   29–30 the other . . .
horse] *1781, Rae*; *om. L, C*   34 *Enter . . . others*] *1781*; Ent Earl of Leicester &c.
L, C; Enter EARL OF LEICESTER, GOVERNOR, MASTER OF THE HORSE, KNIGHTS, &C. *Rae*
37 moults] *L, C*; moulds *1781, Rae*

Why dimly glimmers that heroic flame,
Whose red'ning blaze by patriot spirit fed,
Should be the beacon of a kindling realm?
Can the quick current of a patriot heart,   5
Thus stagnate in a cold and weedy converse,
Or freeze in tideless inactivity?
No! rather let the fountain of your valor
Spring thro' each stream of enterprize,
Each petty channel of conducive daring,
Till the full torrent of your foaming wrath   10
O'erwhelm the flats of sunk hostility!

PUFF. There it is,—follow'd up!

'SIR WALTER.

'No more! the fresh'ning breath of thy rebuke
Hath fill'd the swelling canvass of our souls!   15
And thus, tho' fate should cut the cable of   [*All take hands.*
Our topmost hopes, in friendship's closing line
We'll grapple with despair, and if we fall,
We'll fall in Glory's wake!

'EARL OF LEICESTER.   20

'There spoke Old England's genius!
Then, are we all resolv'd?

'ALL.

'We are——all resolv'd.

'EARL OF LEICESTER.   25

'To conquer——or be free?

'ALL.

'To conquer, or be free.

'EARL OF LEICESTER.

'All?   30

'ALL.

'All.

DANGLE. *Nem. con.* egad!
PUFF. O yes, where they *do* agree on the stage, their unanimity is
wonderful!   35

'EARL OF LEICESTER.

'Then, let's embrace——and now——

5 weedy] *1781, C*; pond-like *L, Rae*   12 PUFF . . . up!] *1781, Rae; om. L*
16 *All take hands*] *1781, Rae; om. L, C*   17 topmost] *1781, C; om. L, Rae*

SNEER. What the plague, is he going to pray?
PUFF. Yes, hush!—in great emergencies, there is nothing like a prayer!

'EARL OF LEICESTER.
   'O mighty Mars!

DANGLE. But why should he pray to *Mars*?   5
PUFF. Hush!

'EARL OF LEICESTER.
            'If in thy homage bred,
Each point of discipline I've still observ'd;
Nor but by due promotion, and the right   10
Of service, to the rank of Major-General
Have ris'n; assist thy votary now!

'GOVERNOR.
'Yet do not rise,——hear me!

'MASTER OF HORSE.   15
'And me!

'KNIGHT.
'And me!

'SIR WALTER.
'And me!   20

'SIR CHRISTOPHER.
'And me!

PUFF. Now, pray all together.

'ALL.
'Behold thy votaries submissive beg,   25
That thou will deign to grant them all they ask;
Assist them to accomplish all their ends,
And sanctify whatever means they use
To gain them!

SNEER. A very orthodox quintetto!   30
PUFF. Vastly well, gentlemen.—Is that well managed or not? Have you
   such a prayer as that on the stage?
SNEER. Not exactly.

[EARL OF LEICESTER *to* PUFF.]
But, Sir, you hav'nt settled how we are to get off here.   35

15–16 MASTER ... And me!] *1781*; *om. L, C, Rae*   23 PUFF ... together] *1781*;
om. L, C, Rae   26 will] *1781, L, C*; wilt *Rae*   34 *to* PUFF] *1781, Rae*;
om. L, C

PUFF. You could not go off kneeling, could you?[1]

[SIR WALTER *to* PUFF.]

O no, Sir! impossible!

PUFF. It would have a good effect efaith, if you could! exeunt praying!—
Yes, and would vary the established mode of springing off with a   5
glance at the pit.[2]

SNEER. O never mind, so as you get them off, I'll answer for it the audience
wont care how.

PUFF. Well then, repeat the last line standing, and go off the old way.

'ALL.   10

'And sanctify whatever means we use to gain them.   [*Exeunt.*

DANGLE. Bravo! a fine exit.

SNEER. Well, really Mr. Puff.——

PUFF. Stay a moment.——

THE CENTINELS *get up.*   15

'1ST CENTINEL.

'All this shall to Lord Burleigh's ear.

'2D CENTINEL.

''Tis meet it should.   [*Exeunt* CENTINELS.

DANGLE. Hey!—why, I thought those fellows had been asleep?   20

PUFF. Only a pretence, there's the art of it; they were spies of Lord
Burleigh's.

SNEER. —But isn't it odd, they were never taken notice of, not even by
the commander in chief.

PUFF. O lud, Sir, if people who want to listen, or overhear, were not   25
always conniv'd at in a Tragedy, there would be no carrying on any
plot in the world.

DANGLE. That's certain!

PUFF. But take care, my dear Dangle, the morning gun is going to fire.
[*Cannon fires.*   30

2 *to* PUFF] *1781, Rae, C; om. L*   4 could! exeunt] *1781*; could exeunt *L, C, Rae*
17 ear] *1781, L, Rae*; ear. (*Exit*) *C*   19 should] *1781, C*; should. The General it
seems is disapprov'd *L, Rae*   *Exeunt* CENTINELS] *1781*; Exit Centinels *L*; Exeunt
Rae; Exit *C*   21–2 it; they . . . Burleigh's] *1781, C*; it, I mean it to mark Lord
Burleigh's Character, who, you know was famous for his Skill in procuring Intelligence,
and employ'd all sorts of people as Spies. *L, Rae*   26 in a Tragedy] *1781, Rae,
L*; in Tragedy *C*   30 *fires*] *1781, L, Rae*; fire *C*

---

[1] Cf. Henry Jones, *The Earl of Essex* (1753), II. 1: *Enter Southampton | Southampton.*
(*kneeling*). Permit me, madam, to approach you thus.

[2] Cf. Garrick's 'tripping off the stage with a bridled head and an affected alertness'
(Robert Baker, *Remarks on the English Language* (2nd edn., 1779), p. xviii, quoted in
K. A. Burnim, *David Garrick, Director* (Pittsburgh, Pa., 1961), p. 55).

DANGLE. Well, that will have a fine effect.

PUFF. I think so, and helps to realize the scene.—   [*Cannon twice.*
What the plague!—*three* morning guns!—there never is but one!—aye,
this is always the way at the Theatre—give these fellows a good thing,
and they never know when to have done with it. You have no more   5
cannon to fire?

PROMPTER *from within.* No Sir.

PUFF. Now then, for soft musick.

SNEER. Pray what's that for?

PUFF. It shews that TILBURINA is coming; nothing introduces you a   10
heroine like soft musick.—Here she comes.

DANGLE. And her confidant, I suppose?[1]

PUFF. To be sure: here they are—inconsolable to the minuet in Ariadne![2]
(*Soft musick.*)

Enter TILBURINA *and* CONFIDANT.   15

'TILBURINA.

'Now has the whispering breath of gentle morn,
Bad Nature's voice, and Nature's beauty rise;
While orient Phœbus with unborrow'd hues,
Cloaths the wak'd loveliness which all night slept   20
In heav'nly drapery! Darkness is fled.
Now flowers unfold their beauties to the sun,
And blushing, kiss the beam he sends to wake them,
The strip'd carnation, and the guarded rose,
The vulgar wall flow'r, and smart gillyflower,   25
The polyanthus mean—the dapper daizy,
Sweet William, and sweet marjorum,——and all
The tribe of single and of double pinks![3]

1 Well ... effect] *1781*; Hey—Well ... effect *L, Rae*; *om. C here, but transferred to
l. 5, following Puff's 'with it', but spoken by Dangle.*   2 I think ... scene] *1781,
L, Rae*; *om. C*   Cannon twice] *1781*; *om. L, C, Rae*   3 What] *1781*; *om. L,
Rae*; Hey! what   *three* morning guns] *1781, C*; *om. L, Rae*   there ... one] *1781*,
om. C, L, Rae   aye ... way] *1781, C*; *om. L, Rae*   4–5 give ... with it] *1781, C*;
om. L, Rae   5 you ... no] *1781, C*; There are *L, Rae*   7 *from within*] *1781*,
C; *om. L*; *within Rae*   8 musick] *1781, C*; music (*musick*) *Rae*; Music (*Soft
Music*) *L*   11 comes] *1781, L, C*; comes—all in tune to the minuet in Ariadne
Rae   13 here ... Ariadne] *1781*; *om. L, C, Rae*   15 *Soft musick*] *1781*,
C; *om. L, Rae*   17–21 Now ... fled] *1781, Rae*; *om. L, C*   27 & in l. 7,
p. 530 marjorum] *1781*; margery *L, C*; marjory *Rae*

<hr>

[1] Common in French tragedy. Cf. Ambrose Philips, *The Distressed Mother* (1719),
an adaptation of Racine's *Andromaque*), IV:
Cephisa. Madam, I have no will but yours. My life
       Is nothing, balanc'd with my love to you.
[2] Handel's *Ariadne in Crete* (1734).
[3] Cf. Milton, *Lycidas*, ll. 139–51.

Now too, the feather'd warblers tune their notes
Around, and charm the listning grove.—The lark!
The linnet! chafinch! bullfinch! goldfinch! greenfinch!
——But O to me, no joy can they afford!
Nor rose, nor wall flow'r, nor smart gillyflower,   5
Nor polyanthus mean, nor dapper daizy,
Nor William sweet, nor marjoram——nor lark,
Linnet, nor all the finches of the grove!

PUFF. Your white handkerchief madam——
TILBURINA. I thought, Sir, I wasn't to use that 'till, 'heart rending woe.' 10
PUFF. O yes madam—at 'the finches of the grove,' if you please.

'TILBURINA.
'Nor lark,
Linnet, nor all the finches of the grove!   [*Weeps.*

PUFF. Vastly well madam!   15
DANGLE. Vastly well indeed!

'TILBURINA.
'For, O too sure, heart rending woe is now
The lot of wretched Tilburina!

DANGLE. O!—'tis too much.   20
SNEER. Oh!——it is indeed

'CONFIDANT.
'Be comforted sweet lady——for who knows,
But Heav'n has yet some milk-white day in store.

'TILBURINA.   25
'Alas, my gentle Nora,
Thy tender youth, as yet hath never mourn'd
Love's fatal dart.—Else wouldst thou know, that when
The soul is sunk is comfortless despair,
It cannot taste of merryment!   30

DANGLE. That's certain.

'CONFIDANT.
'But see where your stern father comes;
It is not meet that he should find you thus.

PUFF. Hey, what the plague!—what a cut is here!—why, what is become 35

3 greenfinch] *1781*, *L*, *Rae*; greyfinch *C*   5 gillyflower] *1781*, *Rae*, *C*; Gillyflower's *L*   10 Sir] *1781*, *Rae*; *om. L, C*   13–14 Nor lark, Linnet] *1781*; Nor
lark not Linnet *C*; *om. L, Rae*   20 'tis . . . much] *1781*; *om. L, C, Rae*   21 it
is indeed] *1781*; *om. L, C, Rae*   23 for who knows] *1781*; who knows *L, Rae*;
nor distrust *C*   28–30 Else . . . merryment] *1781*, *L*, *Rae*; *om. C*

of the description of her first meeting with Don Whiskerandos? his
gallant behaviour in the sea fight, and the simile of the canary bird?[1]
TILBURINA. Indeed Sir, you'll find they will not be miss'd.
PUFF. Very well.—Very well!
TILBURINA. The cue ma'am if you please.   5

'CONFIDANT.

'It is not meet that he should find you thus.

'TILBURINA.

'Thou counsel'st right, but 'tis no easy task
For barefaced grief to wear a mask of joy.   10

Enter GOVERNOR.

'How's this—in tears?——O Tilburina, shame!
Is this a time for maudling tenderness,
And Cupid's baby woes?——hast thou not heard
That haughty Spain's Pope-consecrated fleet   15
Advances to our shores, while England's fate,
Like a clipp'd guinea, trembles in the scale!

'TILBURINA.

'Then, is the crisis of *my* fate at hand!
I see the fleets approach——I see——   20

PUFF. Now, pray gentlemen mind.—This is one of the most useful
figures we tragedy writers have,[2] by which a hero or heroine, in consideration of their being often obliged to overlook things that *are* on
the stage, is allow'd to hear and see a number of things that are not.
SNEER. Yes—a kind of poetical second-sight!   25
PUFF. Yes—now then madam.

'TILBURINA.

'I see their decks
Are clear'd!——I see the signal made!
The line is form'd!——a cable's length asunder!   30
I see the frigates station'd in the rear;
And now, I hear the thunder of the guns!
I hear the victor's shouts——I also hear
The vanquish'd groan!——and now 'tis smoke——and now
I see the loose sails shiver in the wind!   35
I see——I see——what soon you'll see——

1 Don Whiskerandos] *1781*, *L*, *C*; Don *Rae*   2 behaviour] *1781*, *Rae*; bravery
L, *C*   20 fleets] *1781*, *L*, *Rae*; fleet's *C*   23 their . . . overlook] *1781*, *C*, *Rae*;
overlooking their being often obliged to *L*   29 signal] *1781*, *Rae*; Signal's *C*; Signals *L*

<hr>

[1] For the current delight in similes, see 'Simon Simile' on p. 210 above.
[2] Cf. Henry Jones, *The Earl of Essex*, I. i:
Raleigh (*to Burleigh*).   My heart exults; I see,
          I see, my lord, our utmost wish accomplish'd!
          I see great Cecil shine without a rival,
          And England bless him as her guardian saint.

'GOVERNOR.

'Hold daughter! peace! this love hath turn'd thy brain:
The Spanish fleet thou *canst* not see—because
——It is not yet in sight!

DANGLE. Egad tho', the governor seems to make no allowance for this   5
poetical figure you talk of.

PUFF. No, a plain matter-of-fact man—that's his character.

'TILBURINA.

'But will you then refuse his offer?

'GOVERNOR.   10

'I must—I will —I can—I ought—I do.

'TILBURINA.

'Think what a noble price.

'GOVERNOR.

'No more——you urge in vain.   15

'TILBURINA.

'His liberty is all he asks.

SNEER. All *who* asks Mr. Puff? Who is—

PUFF. Egad Sir, I can't tell.—Here has been such cutting and slashing, I
don't know where they have got to myself.   20

TILBURINA. Indeed Sir, you will find it will connect very well.

'——And your reward secure.

PUFF. O,—if they had'nt been so devilish free with their cutting here,
you would have found that Don Whiskerandos has been tampering for
his liberty, and has persuaded Tilburina to make this proposal to her 25
father—and now pray observe the conciseness with which the argument
is conducted. Egad, the *pro & con* goes as smart as hits in a fencing
match.[1] It is indeed a sort of small-sword logic, which we have borrowed
from the French.

'TILBURINA.   30

'A retreat in Spain!

'GOVERNOR.

'Outlawry here!

7 man] *1781*, *C*, *Rae*; *om. L*   17 asks] *1781*, *L*, *Rae*; asks (*kneels*) *C*   18 Who
is—] *1781*; *om. L*, *C*, *Rae*   24 you would have found] *1781*, *L*; you'd found *Rae*,
L; you'd find *C*   Whiskerandos] *1781*; Whiskerondos *C*; *om. L*, *Rae*

---

[1] Cf. *The Rehearsal*, III. i: *Bayes*. This, Sirs, might properly enough be called a
prize of Wit; for you shall see 'em come in one upon another snip snap, hit for hit,
as fast as can be.

'TILBURINA.

'Your daughter's prayer!

'GOVERNOR.

'Your father's oath!

'TILBURINA.   5

'My lover!

'GOVERNOR.

'My country!

'TILBURINA.

'Tilburina!   10

'GOVERNOR.

'England!

'TILBURINA.

'A title!

'GOVERNOR.   15

'Honor!

'TILBURINA.

'A pension!

'GOVERNOR.

'Conscience!   20

'TILBURINA.

'A thousand pounds!

'GOVERNOR.

'Hah! thou hast touch'd me nearly!

PUFF. There you see——she threw in *Tilburina*, Quick, parry cart with 25
England!—Hah! thrust in teirce a title!—parried by honor.—Hah! a
pension over the arm!—put by by conscience.—Then flankonade[1] with
a thousand pounds—and a palpable hit egad!

'TILBURINA.

'Canst thou——   30
Reject the *suppliant*, and the *daughter* too?

'GOVERNOR.

'No more; I wou'd not hear thee plead in vain,
The *father* softens—but the *governor*
Is fix'd!   [*Exit.* 35

DANGLE. Aye, that antithesis of persons—is a most establish'd figure.

2 prayer] *1781*, *Rae*; Prayers *L*, *C*   26 Hah! thrust] *1781*, *C*; thrust *L*, *Rae*
27 put] *1781*, *C*, *Rae*; Snap *L*   Then] *1781*, *C*, *Rae*; The *L*   28 pounds] *1781*,
C, *Rae*; Crowns *L*   *After line 28, L and Rae give an additional speech to Sneer*: Well
Push'd Indeed.   35 fix'd] *1781*; resolv'd *L*, *C*, *Rae*   36 Aye . . . figure]
1781, *L*, *Rae*; om. *C*

---

[1] The 'parry carte' and 'thrust in tierce' were fencing terms, as was the 'flanconade',
a thrust in the flank.

‘TILBURINA.

'Tis well,——hence then fond hopes,—fond passion hence;
Duty, behold I am all over thine——

‘WHISKERANDOS *without*.

‘Where is my love——my——   5

‘TILBURINA.

‘Ha!

‘WHISKERANDOS *entering*.

‘My beauteous enemy——

PUFF. O dear ma'am, you must start a great deal more than that;   10
consider you had just determined in favour of duty—when in a moment
the sound of his voice revives your passion,—overthrows your resolution, destroys your obedience.—If you don't express all that in your
start—you do nothing at all.

TILBURINA. Well, we'll try again!   15

DANGLE. Speaking from within, has always a fine effect.

SNEER. Very.

‘WHISKERANDOS.

‘My conquering Tilburina! How! is't thus
We meet? why are thy looks averse! what means   20
That falling tear——that frown of boding woe?
Hah! now indeed I am a prisoner!
Yes, now I feel the galling weight of these
Disgraceful chains——which, cruel Tilburina!
Thy doating captive gloried in before.——   25
But thou art false, and Whiskerandos is undone!

‘TILBURINA.

‘O no; how little dost thou know thy Tilburina!

4 *Rae inserts two further lines*:
    Whisk. (*Without*) Where is my love—My Tilb. . . . Ha! | *Tilb.* Ha!
8 *entering*] *1781*; *without* L, C; *om. Rae*   10 deal] *1781*, C, *Rae*; *om.* L
10-11 that; consider] *1781*, L, *Rae*; that—We have better Tragedy Starts than that in
the School for Scandal, consider—C   16-17 Speaking . . . Very] *1781*, L, *Rae*;
om. C   *Rae* (*omitting stage directions*), L, C, *insert after line 15*:
    Tilb. Behold I am all-over thine
    Don. (*without*) Where is my Love? my—
    Tilb. Ha!
    Don. (*entering*) My beauteous, Enemy!
19 How!] *1781*, C; (*Enter Don*) Ha! L; (*enter*) ha! *Rae*   20 Rae omits all after
'means', *and before* 'Hey day' (l. 19, p. 535)   21-line 12, page 535 That falling
. . . father] *1781*, L, C

'WHISKERANDOS.

'Art thou then true? Begone cares, doubts and fears,
I make you all a present to the winds;[1]
And if the winds reject you——try the waves.

PUFF. The wind you know, is the established receiver of all stolen sighs, 5
and cast off griefs and apprehensions.

'TILBURINA.

'Yet must we part?——stern duty seals our doom:
Though here I call yon conscious clouds to witness,
Could I pursue the bias of my soul,   10
All friends, all right of parents I'd disclaim,
And thou, my Whiskerandos, should'st be father
And mother, brother, cousin, uncle, aunt,
And friend to me!

'WHISKERANDOS.   15

'O matchless excellence!——and must we part?
Well, if——we must——we must—and in that case,
The less is said the better.

PUFF. Hey day! here's a cut!—What, are all the mutual protestations out?
TILBURINA. Now, pray Sir, don't interrupt us just here, you ruin our 20
feelings.
PUFF. *Your* feelings!——but zounds, *my* feelings, ma'am!
SNEER. No; pray don't interrupt them.

'WHISKERANDOS.

'One last embrace.——   25

'TILBURINA.

'Now,——farewell, for ever.

'WHISKERANDOS.

'For ever!

'TILBURINA.   30

'Aye, for ever.   [*Going*

PUFF. S'death and fury!—Gadslife! Sir! Madam! if you go out without
the parting look, you might as well dance out—Here, here!

5–6 stolen sighs, and] *1781, C; om. L*   10 soul] *1781, C;* Love *L*   11 right
of] *1781, C;* rights, all *L*   I'd] *1781, C;* I *L*   20 just] *1781; om. C, L*
22 *Your* . . . ma'am!] *1781; om. L, C, Rae*   31 Aye] *1781, C, Rae; om. L*
32 S'death and fury!] *1781; om. L, C, Rae*   33 here!] *1781, Rae;* here! (*calling
out*) *L, C*

[1] Henry Jones, *The Earl of Essex*, II:
Essex. I scorn the blaze of courts, the pomp of kings;
    I give them to the winds.

CONFIDANT. But pray Sir, how am *I* to get off here?

PUFF. *You*, pshaw! what the devil signifies how *you* get off! edge away at the top, or where you will—[*Pushes the confidant off.*] Now ma'am you see—

TILBURINA. We understand you Sir.   5

'Aye for ever.

'BOTH.

'Ohh!——   [*Turning back and exeunt.*
                                   [*Scene closes.*

DANGLE. O charming!   10

PUFF. Hey!—'tis pretty well I believe—you see I don't attempt to strike out any thing new—but I take it I improve on the established modes.

SNEER. You do indeed.—But pray is not Queen Elizabeth to appear?

PUFF. No not once—but she is to be talked of for ever; so that egad you'll think a hundred times that she is on the point of coming in.   15

SNEER. Hang it, I think its a pity to keep *her* in the green room all the night.

PUFF. O no, that always has a fine effect—it keeps up expectation.

DANGLE. But are we not to have a battle?

PUFF. Yes, yes, you will have a battle at last, but, egad, it's not to be by land—but by sea—and that is the only quite new thing in the piece.   20

DANGLE. What, Drake at the Armada, hey?

PUFF. Yes, efaith—fire ships and all—then we shall end with the procession.—Hey! that will do I think.

SNEER. No doubt on't.

PUFF. Come, we must not lose time—so now for the UNDER PLOT.   25

SNEER. What the plague, have you another plot?

PUFF. O lord, yes—ever while you live, have two plots to your tragedy.— The grand point in managing them, is only to let your under plot have as little connexion with your main plot as possible.—I flatter myself nothing can be more distinct than mine, for as in my chief plot, the   30 characters are all great people—I have laid my under plot in low life— and as the former is to end in deep distress, I make the other end as happy as a farce.—Now Mr. Hopkins, as soon as you please.

Enter UNDER PROMPTER.

UNDER PROMPTER. Sir, the carpenter says it is impossible you can go to   35 the Park scene yet.

1 But] *1781, L, Rae*; And *C*   2 *You*] *1781*; om. *L, C, Rae*   3 *Pushes . . . off*] *1781, C*; om. *L, Rae*   6 Aye for ever] *1781, L, C*; om. *Rae*   8 *Turning . . . exeunt*] *1781, C*; *Rae*; *staring back L*   12 I . . . it] *1781, C, Rae*; you see *L* 15 in] *1781, L, Rae*; on *C*   17 up] *1781, C, Rae*; up the *L*   18 battle] *1781, L, C*; battle neither *Rae*   21 What] *1781*; O ho! what *L, C, Rae* 26 What] *1781*; Hey! what *L, Rae*; Why what *C*   29 main] *1781, L, C*; chief *Rae*   35 carpenter says] *1781*; carpenters say *L, Rae, C*   you] *1781, L, Rae*; that you *C*

PUFF. The Park scene! No—I mean the description scene here, in the wood.

UNDER PROMPTER. Sir, the performers have cut it out.

PUFF. Cut it out!

UNDER PROMPTER. Yes Sir.   5

PUFF. What! the whole account of Queen Elizabeth?

UNDER PROMPTER. Yes Sir.

PUFF. And the description of her horse and side-saddle?

UNDER PROMPTER. Yes Sir.

PUFF. So, so, this is very fine indeed! Mr. Hopkins, how the plague could   10
you suffer this?

HOPKINS, *from within.* Sir, indeed the pruning knife—

PUFF. The pruning knife—zounds the axe! why, here has been such lopping and topping, I shan't have the bare trunk of my play left presently.—Very well, Sir—the performers must do as they please, but   15
upon my soul, I'll print it every word.

SNEER. That I would indeed.

PUFF. Very well—Sir—then we must go on—zounds! I would not have parted with the description of the horse!—Well, Sir, go on—Sir, it was one of the finest and most laboured things—Very well, Sir, let them go   20
on—there you had him and his accoutrements from the bit to the crupper—very well, Sir, we must go to the Park scene.

UNDER PROMPTER. Sir, there is the point, the carpenters say, that unless there is some business put in here before the drop, they shan't have time to clear away the fort, or sink Gravesend and the river.   25

PUFF. So! this is a pretty dilemma truly!—Gentlemen—you must excuse me, these fellows will never be ready, unless I go and look after them myself.

SNEER. O dear Sir—these little things will happen—

PUFF. To cut out this scene!—but I'll print it—egad, I'll print it every   30
word!   [*Exeunt.*

END OF ACT II

10 plague] *1781*; devil *L, C, Rae*   21 accoutrements] *1781, Rae, C*; accoutrement
L   25 or] *1781*; and *C*; *om. L, Rae*   sink . . . river] *1781, C*; *om. L, Rae*
26 truly] *1781*; indeed *L, Rae*; indeed! I suppose I must end the act here whether I
will or no *C*   26–31 Gentlemen . . . word!] *1781, C*; *for the passage in L and Rae
it replaced, see pp. 474–5.*   31 Exeunt] *1781, C, Rae*; *om. L*

ACT III

SCENE I

Before the Curtain.

Enter PUFF, SNEER, *and* DANGLE.

PUFF. Well, we are ready—now then for the justices.   5
         [*Curtain rises; Justices, Constables, &c. discovered.*
SNEER. This, I suppose, is a sort of senate scene.
PUFF. To be sure—there has not been one yet.
DANGLE. It is the under plot, isn't it?
PUFF. Yes. What, gentlemen, do you mean to go at once to the discovery   10
    scene?
JUSTICE. If you please, Sir.
PUFF. O very well—harkee, I don't chuse to say any thing more, but
    efaith, they have mangled my play in a most shocking manner!
DANGLE. It's a great pity!   15
PUFF. Now then, Mr. Justice, if you please.

                    'JUSTICE.

    'Are all the volunteers without?

                    'CONSTABLE.

                              'They are.   20
    Some ten in fetters, and some twenty drunk.

                    'JUSTICE.

    'Attends the youth, whose most opprobrious fame
    And clear convicted crimes have stampt him soldier?

                    'CONSTABLE.   25

    'He waits your pleasure; eager to repay
    The blest reprieve that sends him to the fields
    Of glory, there to raise his branded hand
    In honor's cause.

                    'JUSTICE.   30

    ''Tis well——'tis Justice arms him!
    O! may he now defend his country's laws

1 ACT III] *1781, C, Rae; om. L*   2–3 SCENE ... *Curtain*] *1781;* SCENE I.—
The Theatre, before the Curtain Rae; *Scene L, C*   4 *Enter* ... DANGLE] *1781, C,
Rae; om. L*   5 Well, we are] *1781, Rae;* Well, all's *C; om. L*   5–6 ready ...
rises] *1781, Rae, C; om. L*   6 Justices ... discovered] *1781, L, Rae;* then discover Justice Constable &c *C*   7 scene] *1781, Rae, C;* House *L*   8 To ...
yet] *1781; om. C, Rae, L*   9 It is] *1781, Rae, C;* O it is *L*   10 Yes. What,]
1781, Rae, C; What *L*   14 my play] *1781, Rae;* it *L, C*   24 clear convicted]
1781, L, Rae; complicated *C*   have stampt him] *1781, C;* has stamp'd for *L;* have
stamp'd for *Rae*   28—line 1, page 539 there ... all] *1781, Rae, C; om. L*

With half the spirit he has broke them all!
If 'tis your worship's pleasure, bid him enter.

'CONSTABLE.

'I fly, the herald of your will.   [*Exit* CONSTABLE.

PUFF. Quick, Sir!—   5
SNEER. But, Mr. Puff, I think not only the Justice, but the clown seems
    to talk in as high a style as the first hero among them.
PUFF. Heaven forbid they should not in a free country!—Sir, I am not
    for making slavish distinctions, and giving all the fine language to the
    upper sort of people.   10
DANGLE. That's very noble in you indeed.

Enter JUSTICE'S LADY.

PUFF. Now pray mark this scene.

'LADY.

'Forgive this interruption, good my love;   15
But as I just now past, a pris'ner youth
Whom rude hands hither lead, strange bodings seiz'd
My fluttering heart, and to myself I said,
An if our TOM had liv'd, he'd surely been
This stripling's height!   20

'JUSTICE.

'Ha! sure some powerful sympathy directs
Us both——

Enter SON *and* CONSTABLE.

'JUSTICE.   25
'What is thy name?

'SON.

'My name's TOM JENKINS[1]—*alias*, have I none—
Tho' orphan'd, and without a friend!

'JUSTICE.   30
'Thy parents?

'SON.

'My father dwelt in Rochester——and was,
As I have heard——a fishmonger——no more.

9 slavish] *1781, C, Rae*; slovenish *L*   16 pris'ner] *1781, C, L*; handcuff'd *Rae*
19 TOM] *1781*; Jack *L, C, Rae*   23 both] *1781, L, C*; both—for this youth. *Rae*
24 SON] *1781, L, Rae*; Lad *C*   28 TOM JENKINS] *1781*; John Wilkins *L,
C, Rae*   have I] *1781, Rae, L*; I have *C*   33-4 and was . . . more] *1781,
C, Rae*; *om. L*

---

[1] Cf. J. Home, *Douglas*, II: 'My name is Norval'.

PUFF. What, Sir, do you leave out the account of your birth, parentage
and education?

SON. They have settled it so, Sir, here.

PUFF. Oh! oh!

'LADY.   5

'How loudly nature whispers to my heart!
Had he no other name?

                              'SON.

                                    'I've seen a bill

Of his, sign'd *Tomkins*, creditor.   10

                              'JUSTICE.

'This does indeed confirm each circumstance
The gypsey told!——Prepare!

                              'SON.

'I do.   15

                              'JUSTICE.

'No orphan, nor without a friend art thou——
I am thy father,[1] *here's* thy mother, *there*
Thy uncle——this thy first cousin, and those
Are all your near relations!   20

                              'MOTHER.

'O ecstasy of bliss!

                              'SON.

'O most unlook'd for happiness!

---

4 Oh! oh!] *1781*; Oh! *L, C, Rae*   5 LADY] *1781, C, Rae*; Mother *L*   6–7 How
... name] *1781, Rae*; *these lines appear in L before line 1, but have been struck out. Line 7
is then printed after line 4. In C, line 7 appears before line 1, and is repeated after line 4.*
10 creditor] *1781*; *Following this in L appear five lines of dialogue that are heavily struck
out. They appear to make up the passage in C and Rae that reads:*
     Justice. Ha! By Heavn our Boy is now before us.
     Mother. Had he his Ears?
     Son. Lady for three long winters have I mourned their loss.
     Mother. It is! it is!
13 told!——Prepare!] *1781*; told—Quick loose | Those ignominious bonds—prepare *C,
L, Rae*   18 *there*] *1781, Rae*; there's *L, C*   19 Thy uncle] *1781, L, C*; your
uncle *Rae*   20 your] *1781, C, Rae*; thy *L*   22 bliss] *1781, Rae*; Bliss
(*Faints*) *L, C*

---

[1] Cf. R. Cumberland, *The West Indian*, v. viii:
Stockwell. I am your father.
Belcour. My father! Do I live?
Stockwell. I am your father.
Belcour. It is too much. . . .

'JUSTICE.
'O wonderful event!

> [*They faint alternately in each others arms.*

PUFF. There, you see relationship, like murder, will out.

'JUSTICE.   5
'Now let's revive——else were this joy too much!
But come——and we'll unfold the rest within,
And thou my boy must needs want rest and food.
Hence may each orphan hope, as chance directs,
To find a father—where he least expects!   [*Exeunt.* 10

PUFF. What do you think of that?
DANGLE. One of the finest discovery-scenes I ever saw.—Why, this
under-plot would have made a tragedy itself.
SNEER. Aye, or a comedy either.
PUFF. And keeps quite clear you see of the other.   15

Enter SCENEMEN, *taking away the Seats.*

PUFF. The scene remains, does it?
SCENEMAN. Yes, Sir.
PUFF. You are to leave one chair you know—But it is always awkward in
a tragedy, to have you fellows coming in in your playhouse liveries to 20
remove things—I wish that could be managed better.—So now for my
mysterious yeoman.

Enter A BEEFEATER.

'BEEFEATER.
'Perdition catch my soul but *I* do love thee.[1]   25

SNEER. Haven't I heard that line before?
PUFF. No, I fancy not—Where pray?
DANGLE. Yes, I think there is something like it in Othello.
PUFF. Gad! now you put me in mind on't, I believe there is—but that's
of no consequence—all that can be said is, that two people happened to 30
hit on the same thought—And Shakespeare made use of it first, that's
all.
SNEER. Very true.

1 JUSTICE] *1781*, C; Lady *Rae*; *om. L*   2 O . . . event] *1781*, C, *Rae*; *om. L*
3 *They . . . arms*] *1781*, C; *Faints Rae*; *om. L*   6 Now . . . joy] *1781*; See she
revives—this joy's C, L, *Rae*   8 my boy] *1781*; *om. L, Rae, C*   13 itself]
1781, C; in itself *Rae*; of itself *L*   16–21 *Enter . . . better*] *1781*, L, *Rae*;
om. C   17 The scene] *Rae*, *1781*; O the scene *L*   20 to have] *1781*; *om.*
L, Rae   21–2 So . . . yeoman] *1781*; *om. L, C, Rae*   23 A] *1781*; *om. L,*
Rae, C   29 Gad!] *1781*, L, *Rae*; And C   31 on] *1781*, L, C; upon *Rae*

1 *Othello*, III. iii.

PUFF. Now, Sir, your soliloquy—but speak more to the pit, if you please
—the soliloquy always to the pit—that's a rule.[1]

'BEEFEATER.

'Tho' hopeless love finds comfort in despair,
It never can endure a rival's bliss!   5
But soft——I am observ'd.   [*Exit* BEEFEATER.

DANGLE. That's a very short soliloquy.
PUFF. Yes—but it would have been a great deal longer if he had not been
observed.
SNEER. A most sentimental[2] Beefeater that, Mr. Puff.   10
PUFF. Hark'ee—I would not have you be too sure that he *is* a Beefeater.
SNEER. What! a hero in disguise?
PUFF. No matter—I only give you a hint—But now for my principal
character—Here he comes—LORD BURLEIGH in person! Pray,
gentlemen, step this way—softly—I only hope the Lord High Treasurer 15
is perfect—if he is but perfect!

Enter BURLEIGH, *goes slowly to a chair and sits.*

SNEER. Mr. Puff!
PUFF. Hush!—vastly well, Sir! vastly well! a most interesting gravity!
DANGLE. What, isn't he to speak at all?   20
PUFF. Egad, I thought you'd ask me that—yes it is a very likely thing—
that a Minister in his situation, with the whole affairs of the nation on
his head, should have time to talk!—but hush! or you'll put him out.
SNEER. Put him out! how the plague can that be, if he's not going to say
any thing?[3]   25
PUFF. There's a reason!—why, his part is to *think*, and how the plague!
do you imagine he can *think* if you keep talking?

2 the soliloquy . . . rule] *1781*; *om. L, C, Rae*   6 *Exit* BEEFEATER] *1781*, *C*; *Exit
Rae*; *om. L*   11 Hark'ee] *C, Rae*; Hearke *1781*; Hearkee *L*   12 What!] *1781*;
O what *C, L, Rae*   15 the Lord High Treasurer] *1781*; the Treasurer *C*; he *L,
Rae*   17 goes . . . a] *1781*, *Rae*; *goes to a L*; *brings down C*   19 Sir . . .
gravity] *1781*; *om. L, C, Rae*   21 thing] *1781*, *C, Rae*; *om. L*   25 any thing]
1781, *C, Rae*; something *L*   26 the plague] *1781*, *Rae*; *om. L, C*

---

[1] 'Their ridiculous practice of approaching the pit with an arch leer of familiarity
and communicating to their good friends, the company, every sentiment they have
been intrusted with by their poor cully, the author' (Aaron Hill and William Popple,
The Prompter (1734–6; repr. New York, 1966), ed. W. W. Appleton and K. A. Burnim),
p. 116).   [2] Sententious.
[3] Cf. Buckingham, *The Rehearsal*, v. i: *Johnson.* . . . if I were in your place
I would make 'em go out again without ever speaking one word.

DANGLE. That's very true upon my word!

[BURLEIGH *comes forward, shakes his head and exit.*

SNEER. He is very perfect indeed—Now, pray what did he mean by that?

PUFF. You don't take it?

SNEER. No; I don't upon my soul.   5

PUFF. Why, by that shake of the head, he gave you to understand that
even tho' they had more justice in their cause and wisdom in their
measures—yet, if there was not a greater spirit shown on the part of the
people—the country would at last fall a sacrifice to the hostile ambition
of the Spanish monarchy.   10

SNEER. The devil!—did he mean all that by shaking his head?

PUFF. Every word of it—If he shook his head as I taught him.

DANGLE. Ah! there certainly is a vast deal to be done on the stage by
dumb shew, and expression of face, and a judicious author knows how
much he may trust to it.   15

SNEER. O, here are some of our old acquaintance.

Enter HATTON *and* RALEIGH

'SIR CHRISTOPHER.

'*My* niece, and *your* niece too!

By heav'n! there's witchcraft in't——He could not else   20

Have gain'd their hearts——But see where they approach;

Some horrid purpose low'ring on their brows!

'SIR WALTER.

'Let us withdraw and mark them.   [*They withdraw.*

SNEER. What is all this?   25

PUFF. Ah! here has been more pruning!—but the fact is, these two
young ladies are also in love with Don Whiskerandos.—Now, gentlemen, this scene goes entirely for what we call SITUATION and STAGE
EFFECT, by which the greatest applause may be obtained, without the
assistance of language, sentiment or character: pray mark!   30

Enter the TWO NIECES.

'1ST NIECE.

'Ellena here!

She is his scorn as much as I—that is

Some comfort still.   35

1 word] *1781*; word. Now—hush!—close! L, *Rae*; word—He's not asleep is he? |
Puff.No, thinking for the Good of the Nation. *C*   2 exit] *1781*, *C*, *Rae*; *Exits L*
3 by that] *1781*, *C*; that *Rae*; *om. L*   6 the head] *1781*, *C*, *L*; his Head *Rae*
6–7 that even . . . wisdom in] *1781*, *C*; that tho' every thing was to be hoped for from
the Justice of their cause, and the wisdom of *L*; that even tho' everything was to be
hoped from the Justice of their cause and wisdom of *Rae*   13 certainly is] *1781*,
L, *Rae*; is certainly *C*   vast] *1781*, *C*, *Rae*; great *L*   14–15 and . . . to it]
1781, *C*; *om. L*, *Rae*   17 HATTON *and* RALEIGH] *1781*, *C*; SIR CHRISTOPHER HATTON
and SIR WALTER RALEIGH *Rae*; Raleigh & Hatton *L*   24 Let . . . *withdraw*] *1781*,
C, *Rae*; *om. L*   26 Ah! . . . pruning] *1781*, *Rae*; Here has been more clipping
L, *C*   35 still] *1781*, *L*, *Rae*; still (*aside*) *C*

PUFF. O dear madam, you are not to say that to her face!—*aside*, ma'am, *aside*.—The whole scene is to be *aside*.

'1ST NIECE.

'She is his scorn as much as I—that is
Some comfort still!   [*Aside.*   5

'2D NIECE.

'I know he prizes not Pollina's love,
But Tilburina lords it o'er his heart.   [*Aside.*

'1ST NIECE.

'But see the proud destroyer of my peace.   10
Revenge is all the good I've left.   [*Aside.*

'2D NIECE.

'He comes, the false disturber of my quiet.
Now vengeance do thy worst——   [*Aside.*

Enter WHISKERANDOS   15

'O hateful liberty—if thus in vain
I seek my Tilburina!

'BOTH NIECES.

'And ever shalt!

'SIR CHRISTOPHER AND SIR WALTER *come forward.*   20

'Hold! we will avenge you.

'WHISKERANDOS.

'Hold *you*——or see your nieces bleed!

[*The two nieces draw their two daggers to strike* WHISKERANDOS, *the two Uncles at the instant with their two swords drawn, catch their two* 25 *nieces' arms, and turn the points of their swords to* WHISKERANDOS, *who immediately draws two daggers, and holds them to the two nieces' bosoms.*

PUFF. There's situation for you!—there's an heroic group!—You see the ladies can't stab Whiskerandos—he durst not strike them for fear of their uncles—the uncles durst not kill him, because of their nieces—I have 30 them all at a dead lock!—for every one of them is afraid to let go first.

1–2 O . . . be aside] *1781*, L, Rae; om. C. Following this L and Rae add a speech: 1st Niece. Very true, Sir.   3 1ST NIECE] *1781*, Rae; Puff L; om. C   4 She . . . is] *1781*; She is his scorn as much as I L, Rae; om. C   5 Some . . . still [*Aside*] *1781*; om. C; 1st Niece | That is some comfort still L, Rae   7 I . . . love] *1781*; He scorns he knows Pollena's Love L; He scorns, I know Edwina's Love C; He scorns I know Ellena's love Rae   8, 11, 14 Aside] *1781*, C, Rae; om. L   16 O . . . thus] *1781*, C, Rae; om. L   18 BOTH NIECES] *1781*, Rae, C; BOTH L   19 shalt] *1781*, Rae, C; shall L   20 SIR . . . forward] *1781*, Rae, C; Draws their Daggers, then Enter Sir Christopher & Sir Walter Raleigh & catch their Arms, & Don F draws Two Daggers & holds them to their Breasts L   24–7 The . . . bosoms] *1781*, C; om. L, Rae   28 group] *1781*; Rae, C; Grief—L   You see] *1781*; You see I have them all at a deadlock L, C, Rae   30–1 I . . . lock] *1781*; om. L, C, Rae   31 for] *1781*; and L, C, Rae

SNEER. Why, then they must stand there for ever.

PUFF. So they would, if I hadn't a very fine contrivance for't—Now
mind——

> *Enter* BEEFEATER *with his Halberd.*

'In the Queen's name I charge you[1] all to drop   5
Your swords and daggers!

> [*They drop their swords and daggers.*

SNEER. That is a contrivance indeed.

PUFF. Aye—in the Queen's name.

'SIR CHRISTOPHER.   10
'Come niece!

'SIR WALTER.
'Come niece!   [*Exeunt with the two nieces.*

'WHISKERANDOS.
'What's he, who bids us thus renounce our guard?   15

'BEEFEATER.
'Thou must do more, renounce thy love!

'WHISKERANDOS.
'Thou liest——base Beefeater!

'BEEFEATER.   20
'Ha! Hell! the lie!
By heav'n thou'st rous'd the lion in my heart!
Off yeoman's habit!—base disguise!—off! off!

> [*Discovers himself, by throwing off his upper dress,
> and appearing in a very fine waistcoat.* 25

Am I a Beefeater now?
Or beams my crest as terrible as when
In Biscay's Bay I took thy captive sloop.

PUFF. There, egad! he comes out to be the very Captain of the privateer
who had taken Whiskerandos prisoner—and was himself an old lover of 30
Tilburina's.[2]

2 very fine] *1781*; good *L, C, Rae*   4 his] *1781, C, Rae*; *om. L*   8–9 That
. . . name] *1781, Rae*; *om. L, C*   12 WALTER] *L*; RALEIGH *1781, C, Rae*
13 *Exeunt . . . nieces*] *1781, Rae*; *Exeunt C*; Exit all, but Don Ferolo *L*   15 guard]
1781, Rae, L; Guards *C*   21 Hell] *1781, Rae*; *om. L, C*   23 off! off!] *1781,
Rae*; *om. L, C*   24–5 by . . . waistcoat] *1781, Rae*; *om. L, C*   28 thy] *1781,
Rae*; the *L, C*   30 Whiskerandos] *1781, Rae*; Don Ferolo *L, C*

---

[1] Henry Jones, *The Earl of Essex*, I:
Queen. We charge you on your duty and allegiance,
  To stop this vile proceeding.
[2] Cf. John Home, *Douglas*, IV:
Norval. Returning homewards by Messina's port,
  Loaded with wealth and honours bravely won,
  A rude and boist'rous captain of the sea
  Fastened a quarrel on him. Fierce they fought:

DANGLE. Admirably manag'd indeed.

PUFF. Now, stand out of their way.

'WHISKERANDOS.

'I thank thee fortune! that hast thus bestow'd
A weapon to chastise this insolent.   [*Takes up one of the swords.* 5

'BEEFEATER.

'I take thy challenge, Spaniard, and I thank
Thee Fortune too!—   [*Takes up the other sword.*

DANGLE. That's excellently contrived!—it seems as if the two uncles had
left their swords on purpose for them.   10

PUFF. No, egad, they could not help leaving them.

'WHISKERANDOS.

'Vengeance and Tilburina!

'BEEFEATER.

'Exactly so——   15
[*They fight—and after the usual number
of wounds given,* WHISKERANDOS *falls.*

'WHISKERANDOS.

'O cursed parry!——that last thrust in tierce
Was fatal——Captain, thou hast fenced well!
And Whiskerandos quits this bustling scene   20
For all eter——

'BEEFEATER.

'—nity—He would have added, but stern death
Cut short his being, and the noun at once![1]   25

PUFF. O, my dear Sir, you are too slow, now mind me.—Sir, shall I
trouble you to die again?

7 Spaniard] *1781, Rae; om. L, C*   and I thank] *1781, C, Rae; om. L*   8 Thee]
1781, Rae; thy *C; om. L*   Fortune too] *1781, C, Rae; om. L*   Takes ... sword]
1781; om. L; takes up the other *C*; takes up one of the swords *Rae*   9–11 That's ...
them] *1781, Rae; om. L, C*   15 Exactly so] *1781, Rae; om. L, C*   16–17 *They
...falls*] *1781, C, Rae*; FIGHT | Don Whiskerandos falls *L*   21 quits] *1781, Rae,
L*; quit *C*   scene] *1781, C, Rae*; Globe *L*   24 He would] *1781, C, Rae*; twould
L   stern] *1781, Rae; om. L, C*   25 noun] *1781, C, Rae*; Noise *L*   26 are]
1781, C, Rae; move *L*

The stranger fell, and with his dying breath
Declared his name and lineage. 'Mighty God!'
The soldier cried, 'My brother! Oh my brother!'

[1] Cf. Henry Brooke, *Gustavus Vasa, the Deliverer of his Country* (1739), III. ii:
Tell him—for once, that I have fought like him,
And wou'd like him have—
Conquer'd—he shou'd have said—but there, O there,
Death sto—pt him short.

'WHISKERANDOS.

'And Whiskerandos quits this bustling scene
For all eter——

'BEEFEATER.

'——nity—He would have added——   5

PUFF. No, Sir—that's not it—once more if you please—
WHISKERANDOS. I wish, Sir—you would practise this without me——
I can't stay dying here all night.
PUFF. Very well, we'll go over it by and bye——I must humour these
gentlemen!   [*Exit* WHISKERANDOS. 10

'BEEFEATER.

'Farewell——brave Spaniard! and when next——

PUFF. Dear Sir, you needn't speak that speech as the body has walked off.
BEEFEATER. That's true, Sir—then I'll join the fleet.
PUFF. If you please.   [*Exit* BEEFEATER. 15
Now, who comes on?

Enter GOVERNOR, *with his hair properly disordered.*

'GOVERNOR.

'A hemisphere of evil planets reign!
And every planet sheds contagious phrensy!   20
My Spanish prisoner is slain! my daughter,
Meeting the dead corse borne along——has gone
Distract!   [*A loud flourish of trumpets.*

But hark! I am summon'd to the fort,
Perhaps the fleets have met! amazing crisis!   25
O Tilburina! from thy aged father's beard
Thou'st pluck'd the few brown hairs which time had left!

[*Exit* GOVERNOR.

SNEER. Poor gentleman!
PUFF. Yes—and no one to blame but his daughter!   30
DANGLE. And the planets——

2 *Variants as p. 546, line 21.*   6 please] *1781*, C; Please, Don Whiskerandos
L, Rae   9 humour] *1781*, C, Rae; recover L   10 Exit WHISKERANDOS] *1781*,
Rae; *om.* L; Exit D. Ferola C   12 and when next] *1781*; *om.* L, C, Rae
13 Dear Sir] *1781*, Rae; *om.* L, C   speech] *1781*, L, Rae; Speech Sir C   15 Exit
BEEFEATER] *1781*, C, Rae; *om.* L   17 with . . . disordered] *1781*, C; *om.* L, Rae
19 reign] *1781*, C, Rae; sure L   20 And . . . phrensy] *1781*, C, Rae; are
reigning, Shedding their baneful influence round L   23 *A loud flourish of*]*1781*;
A Flourish of C; *om.* L, Rae   25 amazing crisis] *1781*, Rae; *om.* L, C   26 thy
aged father's] *1781*, Rae, C; thy father's L   27 Thou'st . . . left] *1781*, C; Thou'st
pluck'd the few black hairs which time had left Rae; which time had left | Thou'st
pluck'd the few black hairs L   29-31 Poor . . . planets] *1781*; *om.* L, C, Rae

PUFF. True.—Now enter Tilburina!—

SNEER. Egad, the business comes on quick here.

PUFF. Yes, Sir—now she comes in stark mad in white satin.

SNEER. Why in white satin?

PUFF. O Lord, Sir—when a heroine goes mad, she always goes into   5
white satin—don't she, Dangle?

DANGLE. Always—it's a rule.

PUFF. Yes—here it is—[*looking at the book.*] 'Enter Tilburina stark mad
in white satin, and her confidant stark mad in white linen.'

  Enter TILBURINA *and* CONFIDANT *mad, according to custom.*   10

SNEER. But what the deuce, is the confidant to be mad too?

PUFF. To be sure she is, the confidant is always to do whatever her
mistress does; weep when she weeps, smile when she smiles, go mad
when she goes mad.——Now madam confidant—but—keep your
madness in the back ground, if you please.   15

    'TILBURINA.

  'The wind whistles——the moon rises——see
  They have kill'd my squirrel in his cage![1]
  Is this a grasshopper!——Ha! no, it is my
  Whiskerandos——you shall not keep him——   20
  I know you have him in your pocket——
  An oyster may be cross'd in love!——Who says
  A whale's a bird?—Ha! did you call, my love?
  ——He's here! He's there!——He's every where!
  Ah me! He's no where!'   [*Exit* TILBURINA.   25

PUFF. There, do you ever desire to see any body madder than that?

SNEER. Never while I live!

PUFF. You observed how she mangled the metre?

DANGLE. Yes—egad, it was the first thing made me suspect she was out
of her senses.   30

---

1 True.] *1781, Rae*; *om. L, C* 7 it's a rule] *1781*; *om. L, C, Rae* 8–9 Yes
. . . linen] *1781*; *om. L, C, Rae* 10 Enter . . . custom] *1781, C*; Enter
Tilburina Mad & Confidant Mad *L*; *Enter* TILBURINA *and her* CONFIDANT *mad Rae*
14 madam confidant] *1781*; Ma'am *L, C, Rae* but] *1781, Rae, L*; but Confidante *C*
15 if you please] *1781*; *om. L, C, Rae* 20 Whiskerandos] *1781*; Ferolo *L*;
Friend *Rae*; Ferola *C* 25 *Exit* TILBURINA] *1781*; Exit Til *L*; *Exit Rae*; *Exit
Tilburina & Confidante C* 27 live] *1781, Rae, L*; live—and pray what becomes
of her? *C* 28–30 You . . . senses] *1781*; *om. L, Rae, C*

---

 1 Cf. R. Steele, *The Funeral*, v. iii: *Enter Widow in deep Mourning, with a dead
Squirrel on her Arm.* . . .
Widow. Poor Harmless Animal—Pretty ev'n in Death:

   . . . .

 But chearfully didst bear thy little Chain.

SNEER. And pray what becomes of her?

PUFF. She is gone to throw herself into the sea to be sure—and that brings us at once to the scene of action, and so to my catastrophe—my sea-fight, I mean.

SNEER. What, you bring that in at last?   5

PUFF. Yes—yes—you know my play is *called* the *Spanish Armada*, otherwise, egad, I have no occasion for the battle at all.—Now then for my magnificence![1]—my battle!—my noise!—and my procession!— You are all ready?

PROMPTER *within*. Yes, Sir.   10

PUFF. Is the Thames drest?

Enter THAMES *with two Attendants.*

THAMES. Here I am, Sir.

PUFF. Very well indeed—See, gentlemen, there's a river for you!—This is blending a little of the masque with my tragedy—a new fancy you 15 know—and very useful in my case; for as there *must be* a *procession*, I suppose Thames and all his tributary rivers to compliment Britannia with a fete in honor of the victory.

SNEER. But pray, who are these gentlemen in green with him.

PUFF. Those?—those are his banks.   20

SNEER. His banks?

PUFF. Yes, one crown'd with alders and the other with a villa!—you take the allusions?—but hey! what the plague! you have got both your banks on one side—Here Sir, come round—Ever while you live, Thames, go between your banks. (*Bell rings.*)[2]—There, soh! now for't! 25 —Stand aside my dear friends!—away Thames!

[*Exit* THAMES *between his banks.*

1 And . . . her] *1781*; *om. Rae, L, C*   2 She is gone] *1781*; O She goes *C*; *om. L, Rae*   to throw] *1781*; and throws *C*; *om. L, Rae*   2–3 herself . . . action] *1781, C*; *om. L, Rae*   3 and . . . catastrophe] *1781*; *om. C, L, Rae* 3–4 my . . . mean] *1781, C*; *om. L, Rae*   5 What, you] *1781*; What you do *C*; *om. L, Rae*   bring . . . last] *1781, C*; *om. L, Rae*   6–7 Yes . . . all] *1781, C*; *om. L, Rae*   8 my noise] *1781*; *om. L, C, Rae*   10 within] *1781, L, C*; *om. Rae* 12 Enter . . . Attendants] *1781*; Enter Thames *&* Men in Green *C*; *om. L, Rae* 14–15 This . . . tragedy] *1781, C*; *om. L, Rae*   15–16 a new . . . case] *1781*; *om. L, C, Rae*   16–18 for as . . . victory] *1781, C*; *om. L, Rae*   22–3 one . . . allusions] *1781, C*; *om. L, Rae*   24 Here . . . round] *1781*; Here here *Rae*; *om. L, C* 25 rings.)—There, soh!] *1781*; (*rings*) There *C*; (*rings*) Now but away *Rae*; *om. L* 26 Stand aside . . . Thames!] *1781*; *om. L, C, Rae*   27 Exit . . . banks] *1781*; *om. L, C*; Exit . . . banks. Curtain drops. Rae

---

1 Cf. Buckingham, *The Rehearsal*, v. i:
  Bayes. I'll shew you the greatest Scene that ever England saw: I mean not for words, for those I do not value; but for state, shew, and magnificence.
2 So that music would begin or a curtain fall.

[Flourish of drums——trumpets——cannon, &c. &c. Scene changes to the
sea——the fleets engage——the musick plays 'Britons strike home.'[1]—
Spanish fleet destroyed by fire-ships, &c.—English fleet advances—musick
plays 'Rule Britannia.'—The procession of all the English rivers and their
tributaries with their emblems, &c. begins with Handels water musick— 5
ends with a chorus, to the march in Judas Maccabæus.[2]—During this scene,
Puff directs and applauds every thing——then

PUFF. Well, pretty well—but not quite perfect—so ladies and gentlemen,
if you please, we'll rehearse this piece again to-morrow.

CURTAIN DROPS   10

FINIS

1–9 *Flourish . . .* to-morrow] *1781*, C; *om.* L, Rae   2 *the . . . engage] 1781*;
Engagement begins C   3 *advances] 1781*; appears C   4–5 *of . . . &c.]*
1781; *om.* C   6 *scene] 1781*; time C   7 *every thing] 1781*; &c. &c. C
10 CURTAIN DROPS] *1781*, C; Battle & Procession L

---

[1] Britons strike home, revenge your country's wrongs,
Fight and record yourselves in Druids' songs.

From *Bonduca* (1696), adapted by G. Powell[?] from Beaumont and Fletcher's play
of the same name, and set by Henry Purcell.

[2] Handel's oratorio *Judas Maccabeus* was first performed in London at Covent
Garden on 1 Apr. 1747.

A TRIP TO SCARBOROUGH

A TRIP TO SCARBOROUGH

COMPOSITION

SIR JOHN VANBRUGH's *The Relapse* was a favourite play on the English stage for seventy years after its first performance on 21 November 1696. Its country characters are mainly caricatures; they know nothing of conscience or reticence, and are as open in their deceit as in their desires. Even their parson, Bull, pays his devotions to money and influence. Morality does not interest them: they are earthy and brazen. The fine ladies and gentlemen of the town are represented by Lord Foppington and his younger brother, Tom Fashion, as well as by Amanda and Berinthia, Worthy and Loveless. Foppington is thoroughly self-satisfied, and foolish in that he is proud of being a fop and at the 'head of so prevailing a party'. Tom is determined to take advantage of his indolence to gain a fortune. Coupler, who assists Tom, also makes advances to him, and even in the Restoration theatre these would have been felt to be criminal, were it not that Tom was first played by a woman. The truest representative of the Restoration code is probably Berinthia, for when she is carried off by Loveless to be seduced, she cries out for help in the smallest of voices. Amanda, however, has scruples, and when Worthy tries to seduce her, cries, 'Then, save me, Vertue, and the Glory's thine.' She successfully rejects Worthy with the phrase, 'Repent, and never more offend', and leaves him to soliloquize: 'Sure, there's divinity about her; and she has dispens'd some portion on't to me. For what but now was the wild flame of Love . . . or the vile, the gross desires of Flesh and Blood, is in a moment turn'd to Adoration' (v. v). The turn is dramatic enough, but not quite plausible. In fact, we may detect in this scene some of the sentimentality that was to mar comedy in the eighteenth century.[1]

Jeremy Collier, however, bitterly attacked the play in 1698, in his *Short View of the Immorality and Profaneness of the English Stage*. He was disturbed that Berinthia had got off without censure[2] though she had almost corrupted Amanda and had been impudent and profane. In a more general complaint he deplored the frequent cursing and blasphemy,[3] as well as the abuse of religion and scripture that he thought evident in *The Relapse*. His main charge was that the moral was vicious, and that the play perverted 'the end of comedy, which as Monsieur Rapin observes ought to regard reformation, and publick improvement'.[4]

---

[1] But cf. P. Mueschke and J. Fleisher, 'A Re-evaluation of Vanbrugh', *P.M.L.A.* xlix (1934), 850–3.

[2] Collier, p. 220.   [3] Ibid., p. 231.   [4] Ibid., pp. 210–11.

In spite of Collier's attack, *The Relapse* went on being performed in the next seventy years, though following the custom of the times it was generally cut. It gradually lost favour once a greater delicacy in expression and subject matter was expected, and was acted in the London theatres only on one occasion in the ten years after 7 May 1766. To meet the common objections, John Lee abstracted the scenes concerning Foppington, Fashion, Coupler, Sir Tunbelly, and Miss Hoyden, and they were presented at Covent Garden Theatre on 27 April 1773 as a farce called *The Man of Quality*.[1] It was no great success, being given only eight times (and those, benefit nights) in the next three years. The *Biographia Dramatica* classed it as one of the 'three literary murders (which he is willing to call alterations)'.[2]

Sheridan's early interest in Vanbrugh's play is to be seen in a paraphrase of one of its lines in *The Rivals*,[3] but the first allusion to his revising *The Relapse* is probably a note in the *Morning Chronicle*, 8 February 1777, mentioning a comedy that was to come 'from the pen of the acting manager'. On 17 February he wrote to the Lord Chamberlain's office, seeking permission to perform the enclosed manuscript of *A Trip to Scarborough* '(alter'd from Sir John Vanbrugh)'.[4] A newspaper report amplified this by saying that the play was 'stripped of all exceptionable passages' and the performance would be 'considerably improved by new scenes and decorations'.[5] It was not well received at the first performance on 24 February but was again acted, and at its third representation was accepted by the town. Mrs. Robinson, who played Amanda, suggested many years later that the reason for its ill success was that the first-night audience had thought that it was going to see an entirely new piece,[6] but this is difficult to accept when we recall that the newspapers had made clear that it was an adaptation.[7] The weight of evidence indicates other reasons. The actors were, for the most part, incompetent and indifferent. The *Morning Chronicle* went so far as to say: 'It appears from a piece of Green-room secrecy, lately developed, that several of the worthy wights of a public Theatre, both male and female, who personated the characters of a certain comedy, had argued, among themselves, if possible, to insure the damnation of that comedy, from their negligence and uncorrectness in the representation.'[8] A letter-writer in the same newspaper noted that this

---

[1] The *Chester Chronicle*, 9 May 1777, advertised a performance of a new farce, *The Man of Quality*, 'taken from the new comedy called *The Trip to Scarborough*'. Clearly the company acted Lee's text, but hoped to attract attention by referring to Sheridan's work. Cf., also, W. S. Clark, *The Irish Stage in the County Towns, 1720 to 1800* (Oxford, 1965), p. 236.

[2] D. E. Baker, *Biographia Dramatica* (new edn., 1782), i. 280.

[3] See p. 124 above.

[4] *Letters*, i. 110.

[5] *General Evening Post*, 18–20 Feb. 1777.

[6] See p. 560 below.

[7] The *Morning Chronicle* and *Public Advertiser*, 24 Feb. 1777.

[8] 6 Mar. 1777.

referred to *A Trip to Scarborough*, but suggested that the play 'sank from its own weight'.[1]

When *A Trip to Scarborough* was first produced, Sheridan had been manager of Drury Lane for five months. At the beginning of this period the public had looked forward to new and brilliant entertainment to be provided by the author of *The Duenna*, and had grown increasingly dissatisfied at the mere revival of old plays. Sheridan had been plagued by a discontented company,[2] and had not yet written the new masterpiece expected of him. So *A Trip to Scarborough* was probably a hasty attempt to restore *The Relapse* to its old position by improving its structure and making its language and situations more acceptable to a late eighteenth-century audience.

Sheridan's immediate task was to make the Berinthia–Loveless and Coupler–Fashion scenes acceptable. The latter he dealt with expeditiously by creating, in Coupler's place, a professional match-maker named Mrs. Coupler. That removed offence as well as much unnecessary detail.

His handling of the Berinthia–Loveless relationship was less happy. The audience would not have liked her comic surrender: 'Help, help, I'm ravished, ruined, undone! O Lord, I shall never be able to bear it.' So Berinthia now trifles with Loveless to pique Townly:

BER. Come, come, let go my hand, or I shall hate you, I'll cry out as I live.
LOV. Impossible, you can't be so cruel.
BER. Ha! here's someone coming—begone instantly.

The edge is taken out of dialogue and situation; the lines are proper rather than *risqué*. Berinthia becomes an intriguer whose motives are above suspicion, and Sheridan entirely omits the pact she made with Worthy to help him seduce Amanda. Everything works out morally.

Sheridan was much more reluctant to cut the scenes concerning Lord Foppington, Sir Tunbelly, and Miss Hoyden. The reason is obvious: these three gave the play its stage life, and provided excellent parts for Dodd, Moody, and Mrs. Abington. Even so, he had to tidy up some of the speeches. He omits Foppington's remarks on Sunday as 'a vile day', and any note of his intention to bring in a bill to allow the players to act on the Sabbath as a relief from the entertainment provided by the churches. In the passage that follows this, Sheridan skilfully alters the effect of Foppington's lack of attention to the church service because of the fine women in front of him, by changing the reference from church-going to opera-going. Sir Tunbelly, too, is less objectionable. In his last speech in *The Relapse*, he declares, 'that noble peer, and thee, and thy wife, and the

---

[1] The *Morning Post*, 25 Feb. 1777, suggested that since *The Man of Quality* had been played as a farce for two or three years, that had 'naturally thrown a damp upon the old play'.

[2] Cf. *Letters*, i. 104–8.

nurse, and the priest—may all go and be damn'd together'; but at the end of *A Trip to Scarborough* he lapses into geniality and is glad that his daughter has luck on her side.

Sheridan undoubtedly improved the construction of the piece. Collier had complained that the plot was ill-contrived[1] and that the dramatic unities had been broken. Sheridan meets these criticisms by bringing in Townly, to take over the place of Worthy and some of the functions of Coupler. The result is that the Foppington–Fashion and Foppington–Tunbelly scenes are more closely linked. In addition, the empty verse of the first scene of the play and of Loveless's long soliloquy (III. ii) is eliminated. Unity of place is achieved by setting the action at Scarborough. All these changes, together with the skilful cutting of the Berinthia–Loveless–Amanda scenes, turn *A Trip to Scarborough* into a well-made play, very different from the awkward jauntiness of *The Relapse*.

Sheridan talked to Michael Kelly about Congreve's plays and remarked, 'they are like horses; when you deprive them of their vice, they lose their vigour'.[2] He knew, too, what *A Trip to Scarborough* had lost in the cutting, and confessed to Thomas Moore that the dialogue of Vanbrugh was quite inimitable.[3]

RECEPTION

The TRIP to SCARBOROUGH, presented last night at Drury-Lane Theatre, is an alteration of the comedy of the RELAPSE, which was not only replete with gross allusions, but exhibited so glaring a picture of vice and immorality, that it has long been deemed unfit for representation. Mr. Sheridan, impelled by a laudable desire to keep Sir John Vanbrugh among the authors, whose plays are in the stock list of the theatre, has given himself the trouble of altering the Relapse, and has, (considering the heap of indecency he had to remove), atchieved an Herculean task, but we fear to very little purpose. The comedy last night was exceedingly languid and dragging during the first three acts, and the humour of the two last was of a sort too low and gross to make amends for the dullness of those that preceded them. The chief alterations, (exclusive of verbal corrections and several additional speeches) consist of the removal of the first scene of the Relapse, the change of the sex of Coupler, the giving Worthy the name of Col. Townly, calling the Surgeon Mr. Probe, abridging the 4th act, introducing an entire new scene in the fifth, producing the *denouement* in a different and improved manner, and preserving the unity of place by laying the scene altogether in the country. A veneration for dead authors

---

[1] Collier, p. 231.

[2] Kelly, ii. 310.

[3] See the extra-illustrated copy in the Widener Library of Harvard University, of T. Moore, *Memoirs of . . . Sheridan*, vi. 33.

speaks great modesty and good sense; and the revival of their plays may be of essential service to the drama, as to living writers, they serve the double purpose of a model and a beacon; by the first they may be led to aim at producing beauties, and by the latter they may be warned from errors; Mr. Sheridan, therefore, merits the thanks of the town, let his effort to revive Vanbrugh, and preserve his play from oblivion, prove ever so unsuccessful. Indeed, it is but justice to say, that the audience were put out of temper by the want of importance in Mrs. Robinson, who though her beautiful face and form suited well for the poet's description of Amanda, spoke so low during the beginning of the play, that the company in the front boxes could hardly hear a syllable she uttered; add to this Mr. Moody, who would otherwise have played Sir Tunbelly well, was not quite perfect, and few of the performers seemed to feel themselves at ease during the representation. These are errors which will doubtless be amended in future; and with such amendment, the play will probably be found more palatable than it appeared to be yesterday evening. The *Trip to Scarborough* was preceded by a very long Prologue spoken by Mr. King; but whether the audience were less inclined to laugh than usual, or whether the Allegory, introduced in the Prologue, was not sufficiently intelligible, it was received with less glee than is generally shewn on such occasions. The play was well dressed, and the part of Hoyden remarkably well acted. (*Morning Chronicle*, 25 Feb. 1777.)

... Mr. Sheridan has evidently bestowed great labour on this play, and in our opinion more than it deserved; for it never struck us as a piece that merited half the attention. He has carefully expunged the gross indecencies with which the piece originally abounded, given a modern air to the whole dialogue, corrected the unities of time and place, and in short, taken as much pains as would have carried him, perhaps, thro' the composition of an entire new Comedy.—The moonlight scene is quite new, and, in our judgment, the best in the piece. (*Morning Post*, 25 Feb. 1777.)

When we consider that this very comedy received for many years the public sanction under another title, we cannot but wonder at the disapprobation shewn last night by some of the gods, who indiscriminately hissed the performers and the piece. Whatever may be the fate of The Trip to Scarborough, we are confident that the candor and generosity of an English audience, will never countenance the private malice of envious individuals. The characters were tolerably well supported. Mr. Dodd was not over brilliant in the part of Lord Foppington, yet deserved more praise than censure. Mr. Smith and Mr. Reddish did their parts all possible justice. Mrs. Robinson's acting had certainly a just claim to the encouragement of the audience. Her dress became her amazingly. We will venture to affirm that success cannot fail to attend her theatrical abilities, and to

baffle the wicked design of those who last night condemned her performance with the music of the tempter of Eve. Mrs. Yates was not dressed
according to her usual high taste. It is needless to add that Mrs. Abington
filled her part with her usual sprightliness and propriety. Her merit needs
no panegyric; every frequenter of the theatre knows that Mrs. Abington is
the life and soul of every comedy in which she performs. A new prologue
was delivered by Mr. King; it contained a fable, whereby the author
claimed the indulgence of the auditors. (*The Gazetteer*, 25 Feb. 1777.)

. . . The alterations, as far as we could distinguish, from the recollection
of the original, consist more of a judicious pruning of the *licentious* parts,
than any great additions, though there were some scenes that were much
mended for the better, particularly those of Loveless and Berinthia.

In respect to the performers, they generally exerted themselves to
please. Mr. Smith was as usual, easy and genteel in Loveless; Mrs. Yates
did everything that the part admitted of; Mrs. Robinson shewed at first
some diffidence in Amanda (and no wonder for so young a performer in a
new part) but towards the latter end, exerted herself with such spirit and
sensibility, as to obtain no inconsiderable share of applause. Reddish,
Dodd, and Moody acquitted themselves likewise very well in their
respective parts, particularly Dodd, who exhibited with true *sangfroid*, a
coxcomb of the first stile.

The character of Miss Hoyden, is so like Miss Prue [in Congreve's
Love for Love] that a less skilful actress than Mrs. Abington, would have
made no distinction in the playing of it; but this truly comic and judicious actress gave it every air of *novelty*, at the same time that she paid every
attention to the line of nature; in short, both characters are *country bumpkins*; yet from the circumstances of Miss Hoyden's birth, the strange
manner of her education, and her great remoteness from the capital, she
very properly gave this portrait a deeper shade of ignorance and rusticity.

The play, on the whole, was well received, by a very brilliant and
numerous audience, though on the giving it out for this night, there was
something like a hissing. Perhaps a few further alterations might insure it
more success, particularly in those scenes with Berinthia and Amanda,
which tho' sensible, wanted spirit and business. (*London Evening Post*,
22–25 Feb. 1777.)

The Trip to Scarborough was last night performed (for the second
time) and received throughout with most universal and uncommon
applause. (*The Gazetteer*, 26 Feb. 1777.)

[An anonymous letter-writer declares that at the third performance,
the players knew their parts better, and also praises the scenes between
Lord Foppington and Miss Hoyden.]

After all the stage has very few characters more humorous than the two we have mentioned. It is for this reason that the Relapse has always been considered as one of the most diverting comedies. Mr. Sheridan has heightened the value of this play by several additional beauties in the dialogue and in the plot. This play cannot fail to become a favourite of the town, in spite of all the opposition of the cabal, which endeavoured to nip it in the bud; and as Mrs. Abington says in the prologue to BON TON

'To bury the sweet baby in the pit.'
(*The Gazetteer*, 28 Feb. 1777.)

It was altogether an impossibility to make a good play of the Relapse, the dialogue being exceeding low, and unfit for the present age, and through the piece there is a very moderate share of the principal ingredients in comedy. To say the truth, the whole piece was so insufferably dull, as to provoke an hissing sentence from a too patient audience. . . . ('A new Correspondent' in the *Morning Chronicle*, 28 Feb. 1777.)

. . . it contains nothing of the humours of a modern watering place. . . . The best passages [of *The Relapse*] have [earlier] been selected and cut down into a farce, which was frequently acted during the last two seasons, under the title of the Man of Quality. This to be sure is an aukward circumstance, and ought to have been weighed before the revival was determined on,—but that it is not the principal reason is evident, for those passages were the only ones applauded on the revival, which, by the way, shews that there was more judgement in cutting the Relapse into a farce, than in reproducing it as a play. ('Probus' in the *Morning Chronicle*, 3 Mar. 1777.)

The Trip to Scarborough was on Saturday evening presented, for the fourth time, and was received by a numerous audience with that warmth of applause which Vanbrugh's wit and humour ought ever to command. The performers are not yet quite perfect in their parts, and we must necessarily confess, that scarcely any comedy has been so little indebted to the exertion and merit of the actors and actresses, as the *Trip to Scarborough*. Excepting the characters of Hoyden, Loveless, Lord Foppington, the Nurse, the Shoemaker, and Lory, there is not a well played part in the piece; and even Dodd, though he is, generally speaking, an excellent comedian, wants importance in Lord Foppington. . . . Mrs. Yates has new dressed Berinthia and, if possible, worse than before. She on Monday resembled a Bartholomew Fair Doll, price sixpence. (*Morning Chronicle*, 3 Mar. 1777.)

The alterations made by Mr. Sheridan were rather unfavourably received on the first and second representations; and we think very justly so, if the public disapprobation had been properly directed against those who served up the entertainment, instead of the person who provided it. (*London Magazine*, xlvi (1777), 126.)

For the sake of preserving, in some measure, the unity of place, the scene of this alteration from the *Relapse*, is laid at Scarborough; from which might have been expected some display of the manners and customs of an English Spaw; but no such delineation is attempted, nor is much more probability given to the incidents by shifting the scene of action; for though this expedient saves Vanbrugh's long journies to the country and back again, it throws an aukward air over some circumstances, particularly the levee of Lord Foppington, who would scarce appear surrounded with his tradesmen at Scarborough. Neither the adventure of Lord Foppington and his younger brother, nor the relapse of Loveless are much varied from the original: and perhaps even the amours of Worthy and Berinthia, the chief object of the alteration, might have been more materially improved. It is laudable however in those, who have the direction of our theatres, to keep the productions of our most eminent comic writers before the eye of the Public. (Notice of the printed text in the *Monthly Review*, lxv (1781), 373–4, by George Colman the elder.)[1]

An alteration of Vanbrugh's *Relapse*; but such a one as will add little to the reputation of the gentleman whose name it bears. Indeed, he has been heard in conversation to confess, that he had spoiled Vanbrugh's play. (D. E. Baker, *Biographia Dramatica, or, A Companion to the Playhouse* (new edn., 1782), ii. 379.)

Drury Lane this evening invites to the pleasant comedy, *The Trip to Scarborough*, retouched by the elegant pen of Sheridan, with the native ease and sensibility of the lovely Farren, and sprightly hoydening of that True Child of Nature, the spirited Jordan. (*The World*, 20 Apr. 1790.)

Respecting the getting up of this piece, the performers were extremely inattentive and factious; it is therefore no wonder that on the first and second representations the Comedy was unfavourably received. It was afterwards played to several crowded houses. ([W. C. Oulton], *The History of the Theatres of London . . . 1771 to 1795* (1796), i. 51.)

The second character which I played was Amanda, in 'A Trip to Scarbro'.' The play was altered from Vanbrugh's 'Relapse'; and the audience, supposing it was a new piece, on finding themselves deceived, expressed a considerable degree of disapprobation. I was terrified beyond imagination, when Mrs. Yates, no longer able to bear the hissing of the audience, quitted the scene, and left me alone to encounter the critic tempest. I stood for some moments as though I had been petrified: Mr.

---

[1] See B. C. Nangle, *The Monthly Review, First Series, 1749–1789, Indexes of Contributions and Articles* (Oxford, 1934), pp. 373–4.

Sheridan from the side wing, desired me not to quit the boards: the late Duke of Cumberland, from the stage-box, bade me take courage—'It is not you, but the play, they hiss', said his Royal Highness. I curtsied; and that curtsy seemed to electrify the whole house; for a thundering peal of encouraging applause followed,—the comedy was suffered to go on, and is to this hour a stock play at Drury-lane theatre. (*Memoirs of the late Mrs. Robinson, Written by Herself* (1801), ii. 3–5.)

Here and there through the dialogue, there are some touches from his pen—more, however, in the style of his farce than his comedy. (Moore, i. 199.)

CHOICE OF TEXT

I. OF THE PROLOGUE

A paragraph in a newspaper of 28 May 1777 reads:

As the second prologue to the Trip to Scarborough has been given to the papers,[1] the lovers of the *true poetical fancy* present their compliments to the author, and beg he will oblige them with the *first*. Lest he should not recollect it, it was that prologue, spoken on the first night of this revived comedy, by Mr. King, where that excellent comedian was under the necessity of making *many so strange faces*, to imitate the many strange animals, which were grouped in that performance.[2]

A draft of this first prologue by David Garrick is to be found (in another hand) in Folger MS. W. b. 464, ff. 132–4, and it serves to explain some of the newspaper's comments:

> Thus has our English Horace' writ,[3]
> Vanbrugh wants grace, who ne'er wants wit:
> And he your heart, will surely win
> Who leaves the wit and weeds out Sin:
> How this is done we soon shall know
> For well, or ill, or but So So
> You'll tell us Sirs before you go.
> His Right to please can have no flaw,
> Who makes you laugh without paw, paw.
> But some choice Spirits never fail,
> At ev'ry thing that's done to rail;
> And this chaste plan will roughly handle
> And curse it by bell, book and candle.
> Should the Muse come, without this fuss,

---

[1] See Mary E. Knapp, *A Checklist of Verse by David Garrick* (Charlottesville, Va., 1955), p. 52, for a list of printings in newspapers and magazines.

[2] 'Covent Garden Scrapbooks, 1740–1777' (Folger MS.), under '28 May 1777'.

[3] Pope, 'And Van wants Grace, who never wanted Wit' ('The First Epistle of the Second Book of Horace, Imitated', *Imitations of Horace* in *The Poems of Alexander Pope*, ed. J. Butt (repr. edn., 1961), iv. 219, l. 289).

In puris naturalibus,
With wanton Smiles and Tawdry Jokes,
They'd hang us up for pois'ning folks:
But such strange molds some Minds are cast in—
  No pleasing 'Em, or full, or fasting:
  For these a Fable now comes pat in—
I'll tell it—not in greek, or latin,
But in plain English—Once a *Steed*
  Thinking to give a good repast,
Resolv'd the Neighbourhood to feed
  With spirit and with Taste:
For ev'ry Beast that could be found
  He made fit preparation;
And sent his poney Servant round
  With Cards of Invitation.
The feast to dress and overlook
He hired a celebrated Cook,
  A fat experienc'd *Sow*
The best desert he wisely deems
Is Custard, Syllabub, and Creams,
  For those he hir'd a *Cow*
The guests arriv'd, soon fall to clawing;
So sharply set seem'd ev'ry Beast,
Such scrambling, tearing, licking, pawing,
You'd swear it was a City-feast.
Their bellies full, and turn'd their backs,
They then grow Critical and nice,
The *Monkey* first, the feast attacks
Thus Chattering,—not a single Slice
  Touch'd I of any meat,
  Then grinning self Conceit
  Damn it, I cannot Eat,
Where there is neither Taste nor meaning
  Right, purr'd the tabby *Cat*
(Who with her paw her face was cleaning)
  I dipp'd my whiskers in no dish,
  The meat was neither fresh nor fat,
  And not a bit of fish!
True reply'd Pug—beasts that love grass
  Never with us of Ton will pass;
I never knew a Horse, but was an Ass.
The *Buck*, the Parish *Bull*, and *Bear*,
With passions not quite pure and chaste,
The Dinner was not fit, they Swore
  For Beasts of tip-top taste:
The frisky *Goat*, among the rest
  Thus shook his Beard, said all was dress'd
  For puny Sickly Creatures;

Rich Sauces could do his Blood no harm,
He wish'd it to run brisk and warm,
   As suited Goatish Natures:
The *Bear* and *Hog*, with paunches full,
Said Cleanliness was their Aversion;
The *Ass* alone, though counted dull,
   Drew up his length of Ear,
And gravely bray'd without a Sneer,
That eating was a fine diversion;
The *Dog* o'er ev'ry Morsel growl'd;
And when his Skin was stuff'd he howl'd.
   A Fox who had their Tricks remark'd,
   In Anger rose, and thus he bark'd;
   A Halter for you Brutes—You cram,
   And then the Feast, and Feasters damn;
   Those sportive Kids, and pretty Lambs,
   Those modest Sheep, and worthy Rams,
   The Gentle Folks, who graze or browse,
   Deer, Oxen, Heifers, Calves, and Cows,
   Than you can boast much better blood
      Each reputable beast
      Enjoy'd and prais'd the Feast,
   And gratefully now chews the Cud.
   (*To the Audience*) Sweet Sirs, who smile with human features
Save this Night's Dish from brutal Creatures;
If here they come to roar, and royster
      And this poor Play
      Becomes their Prey
      They'll at one Sup
      Thus whip it up
As I would eat an Oyster.

An earlier version in Garrick's hand of much of the above, is Folger MS. W. b. 464, f. 122; and an even earlier one (in another hand) is Folger MS. W. a. 153 (3), ff. 3–7. A transition to the printed text (pp. 570–1 below), is to be seen in Folger MS. Y. d. 105 (2).[1]

2. OF THE PLAY

No copy bearing Sheridan's handwriting is available. The texts that appear to possess authority are:

(i) *The Lord Chamberlain's MS.*

This is now Larpent MS. 426 in the Henry E. Huntington Library, and comprises 141 pages plus the application to the Lord Chamberlain. William Hopkins wrote the letter on 17 February 1777, and it was signed by Sheridan.

---

[1] Probably the item described in Sotheby's Catalogue, 17–19 Feb. 1930, lot 200.

The text is in four hands: the first transcribes Acts I and II; the second, Acts III and IV; and the third and fourth divide the last act between them. The fourth hand is the one that wrote out a single page in the manuscript of *The School for Scandal* sent to the Lord Chamberlain.

Part of one of Berinthia's speeches in III. ii (p. 598), is marked for deletion by, and bears a comment in the hand of, Edward Capell, deputy examiner of plays in the Lord Chamberlain's office. The passage reads:

	. . . Look you Amanda, you may build Castles in the Air, and fume, and fret, and grow thin and lean, and pale, and ugly, if
This ought to be soften'd.	you please but I tell you, [no Man worth having is true to his Wife, or ever was or ever will be so.]

Sheridan probably accepted the suggestion as far as the acting version was concerned, but nevertheless included the offending passage in the printed text of 1781. It had been taken word for word from *The Relapse*.

In the same spirit of compromise, Vanbrugh's 'What the pox' became 'What the plague' in the copy sent to the Lord Chamberlain, though given back its Restoration flavour in the printed text of 1781.

Both the Larpent MS. and the 1781 edition contain (in II. i) Sheridan's justification for revising the play:

But, 'till that reformation can be wholly made, 'twould surely be a pity to exclude the productions of some of our best writers for want of a little wholesome pruning; which might be effected by any one who possessed modesty enough to believe that we should preserve all we can of our deceased authors, at least 'till they are outdone by the living ones.

The words are spoken by Loveless.

There are several slips in the Larpent MS. which suggest that part of it may have been copied by ear: 'a thorough procuring countenance' is given as 'a thorough procuring Countess', and 'venture yourself alone' becomes 'venture yourself along'.

(ii) *The printed edition of 1781*

It was advertised in the *London Chronicle*, 27–30 October 1781, under the heading '*This Day was Published*', and in phrasing that follows the title-page except where it reads 'As it is now performed'.

This text is close to that of the Larpent MS. and derives some authority from it, but also corrects some of its errors. The name of Wilkie on the title-page would appear to suggest that the publication was authorized by Sheridan, since John Wilkie had been responsible for bringing out Sheridan's earliest works. On this occasion, however, the publisher was George Wilkie, John's son. Apparently John Wilkie was in serious financial trouble in 1781, so much so that on 7 June, Strahan stopped printing for him and secured an agreement for the repayment of arrears of £1150. George Wilkie took over control and (with his brother Thomas) reduced the debt by some £670 before his father's death in July 1785.[1] So the edition looks genuine enough, and though it presents a number of bibliographical problems,[2] they hardly affect the text.

Some slips appear in the printed work that are not in the Larpent MS. For example, Lord Foppington refers early in the Larpent MS. to his 'bouquet' (I. i), and this is taken up later (III. i); but in the 1781 version he mentions 'my watches' (I. i), and later his 'bouquet' (III. i). Similarly, Lord Foppington's affected accent is not always rendered consistently: 'judge' and 'jedge', 'world' and 'waurld' appear very close to each other.[3] For the title-page, see p. 569.

Collation: 8vo. in half-sheets: [A]⁴ B–O⁴.

Contents: pp. [1–8] and 1–104.

[1] Half-title: see p. 567; [2] blank; [3] Title; [4] blank; [5] and 6, 'PROLOGUE | Written by DAVID GARRICK, Esq.'; [7] blank; [8] Dramatis Personæ; [1] and 2–104, text.

(iii) *The Inchbald Edition*

This differs only very occasionally from the text of the first edition of 1781, and the collations are included to indicate the minor variants and the fact that the first edition was very acceptable thirty years later. Mrs. Inchbald's version appeared in *The Modern Theatre; A Collection of Successful Modern Plays, As Acted at The Theatres Royal, London. Printed from the Prompt Books under the Authority of the Managers*, and published in the seventh volume (pp. 237–309) by Longman in 1811.

Conclusion

I accept the first edition of 1781 as copy-text, and admit into it variants provided by the Larpent MS. In the textual footnotes, I include readings from the Inchbald text and from the first quarto edition of *The Relapse* (1697), where relevant. The abbreviations used are:

L   The Lord Chamberlain's MS.
81   The first edition of 1781.
I   Mrs. Inchbald's edition.
Rel. The first quarto of *The Relapse* (1697).

The first edition of 1781 is also accepted as copy-text for the prologue. It is collated with the text in the *London Evening Post*, and with the draft in the Folger Shakespeare Library. Abbreviations employed in footnotes are:

81   The first edition of 1781.
Draft Folger MS. W. a. 154 (3), ff. 8–10, in Garrick's hand.
LEP   *The London Evening Post* text, 24–27 May 1777.

---

[1] Information from Professor Hernlund.   [2] Discussed by Williams, p. 221.
[3] Berinthia is wrongly named as the speaker of two lines, p. 610 below, ll. 29–30.

A

TRIP

TO

SCARBOROUGH

A

COMEDY.

[Price One Shilling and Sixpence.]

A

TRIP

TO

SCARBOROUGH.

A

COMEDY.

AS PERFORMED AT THE

THEATRE ROYAL

IN

DRURY LANE.

ALTERED FROM

Vanbrugh's Relapse; or, Virtue in Danger.

By RICHARD BRINSLEY SHERIDAN, Esq.

LONDON.

Printed for G. WILKIE, No. 71, St. Paul's Church-yard.

MDCCLXXXI.

PROLOGUE.

Written by DAVID GARRICK, Esq.
Spoken by Mr. KING.

WHAT various transformations we remark,
From East Whitechapel to the West Hyde-park!   5
Men, women, children, houses, signs, and fashions,
State, stage, trade, taste, the humours and the passions;
Th' Exchange, 'Change alley, wheresoe'er you're ranging,
Court, city, country, all are chang'd, or changing;
The streets sometime ago, were pav'd with stones,   10
Which, aided by a hackney coach, half broke your bones.
The purest lovers then indulg'd no bliss;
They run great hazard if they stole a kiss—
One chaste salute—the Damsel cry'd, *O fye!*
As they approach'd, slap went the coach awry,   15
—Poor Sylvia got a bump, and Damon a black eye.
But now weak nerves in hackney coaches roam,
And the cramm'd glutton snores unjolted home:
Of former times that polish'd thing a *Beau,*
Is metamorphos'd now, from top to toe;   20
Then the full flaxen wig, spread o'er the shoulders,
Conceal'd the shallow head from the beholders!
But now the whole's revers'd—each fop appears,
Cropp'd, and trimm'd up—exposing head and ears;
The buckle then its modest limits knew—   25
Now, like the ocean, dreadful to the view,
Hath broke its bounds, and swallows up the shoe;
The wearer's foot, like his once fine estate,
Is almost lost, th' *incumbrance* is so great.
Ladies may smile—are they not in the plot?   30
The bounds of nature have not they forgot?
Were they design'd to be, when put together,
Made up, like shuttlecocks, of cork and feather?
Their pale fac'd grand-mama's appear'd with grace,
When dawning blushes rose upon the face;   35

8 you're] *LEP, Draft*; your *81*   14–16 *One . . . eye*] *81, LEP*; *om. Draft*
18 unjolted] *81, LEP*; in Safety *Draft*   *Between lines 22 and 23, Draft prints*:
                  The Front so deck'd, with such important Grin
                  You'd swear there were some furniture within.
24 head and ears] *81, LEP*; both his head and ears *Draft*

No blushes now their once lov'd station seek,
The foe is in possession of the cheek!
No head of old, too high in feather'd state,
Hinder'd the fair to pass the lowest gate;
A church to enter now, they must be bent,   5
If ev'n they should try th' experiment.

   As change thus circulates throughout the nation,
Some plays may justly call for alteration;
At least to draw some slender cov'ring o'er
That graceless wit,[1] which was too bare before: 10
Those writers well and wisely use their pens,
Who turn our Wantons into Magdalens;
And howsoever wicked wits revile 'em,
We hope to find in you, their Stage Asylum.

3 head] *81*; heads *LEP, Draft*   6 If ev'n] *81*; If ever *LEP*; Provided *Draft*
7 As] *81, LEP*; If *Draft*   9 draw] *81, LEP*; cast *Draft*   14 their] *81,*
LEP; a *Draft*

---

[1] See p. 561, n. 3.

DRAMATIS PERSONÆ. [1]

Lord FOPPINGTON,	Mr. Dodd.
YOUNG FASHION,	Mr. Reddish.
LOVELESS,	Mr. Smith.
Colonel TOWNLY,	Mr. Brereton.
Sir TUNBELLY CLUMSEY,	Mr. Moody.
PROBE,	Mr. Parsons.
LORY,	Mr. Baddeley.
LA VAROLE,	Mr. Burton.
SHOEMAKER,	Mr. Carpenter.
TAYLOR,	Mr. Baker.
HOSIER,	Mr. Norris.
JEWELLER,	Mr. La Mash.
SERVANTS, etc.	Mr. Wrighten, Mr. Everard.
BERINTHIA,	Mrs. Yates.
AMANDA,	Mrs. Robinson.
MRS. COUPLER,	Mrs. Booth.
NURSE,	Mrs. Bradshaw.
MISS HOYDEN,	Mrs. Abington.
SERVANTS, etc.	Miss Platt, Mrs. Smith.

[1] The leading parts (Foppington, Fashion, Loveless, Clumsey, Probe, Lory, Berinthia, Amanda, and Hoyden) are noted in the *London Evening Post*, 22–25 Feb. 1777. The players who took the shoemaker, tailor, and nurse, are named in the Larpent MS. The remainder are taken from the general list printed in the playbill of the second performance, and are allocated by following the Dramatis Personæ printed with the text of 1781.

A TRIP TO SCARBOROUGH

A COMEDY

ACT I

SCENE I, *the Hall of an Inn*

Enter YOUNG FASHION *and* LORY—Postillion *following with*   5
a Portmanteau.

Y. FASHION. Lory, pay the post-boy, and take the portmanteau.

LORY. Faith, sir, we had better let the post-boy take the portmanteau and
pay himself.

Y. FASHION. Why sure there's something left in it.   10

LORY. Not a rag, upon my honour, sir—we eat the last of your wardrobe
at Newmalton[1]—and if we had had twenty miles farther to go, our next
meal must have been off the cloak-bag.

Y. FASHION. Why 'sdeath it appears full.

LORY. Yes, sir—I made bold to stuff it with hay, to save appearances, and   15
look like baggage.

Y. FASHION. What the devil shall I do!—harkee, boy, what's the chaise?

BOY. Thirteen shillings, please your honour.

Y. FASHION. Can you give me change for a guinea?

BOY. O yes, sir.   20

LORY. Soh, what will he do now?—Lord, sir, you had better let the boy
be paid below.

Y. FASHION. Why, as you say, Lory, I believe it will be as well.

LORY. Yes, yes; tell them to discharge you below, honest friend.

BOY. Please your honour, there are the turnpikes too.   25

Y. FASHION. Aye, aye; the turnpikes by all means.

BOY. And I hope your honour will order me something for myself.

Y. FASHION. To be sure, bid them give you a crown.

LORY. Yes, yes—my master doesn't care what you charge them—so get
along you——   30

BOY. Your honour promised to send the hostler——

LORY. P'shaw! damn the hostler—would you impose upon the gentleman's generosity?—[*Pushes him out*]—A rascal, to be so curst ready
with his change!

Y. FASHION. Why faith, Lory, he had near pos'd me.   35

6, 7, and 8 Portmanteau] *81, L, I*; portmantle *Rel.*

---

[1] Or Malton, a market town twenty-two miles from Scarborough.

LORY. Well, sir, we are arrived at Scarborough, not worth a guinea!—I hope you'll own yourself a happy man—You have outliv'd all your cares.

Y. FASHION. How so, sir?

LORY. Why you have nothing left to take care of.

Y. FASHION. Yes, sirrah, I have myself and you to take care of still. 5

LORY. Sir, if you could prevail with some-body else to do that for you, I fancy we might both fare the better for't—But now, sir, for my Lord Foppington, your elder brother.

Y. FASHION. Damn my elder brother!

LORY. With all my heart; but get him to redeem your annuity however.— 10 Look you, sir, you must wheedle him, or you must starve.

Y. FASHION. Look you, sir, I will neither wheedle him nor starve.

LORY. Why what will you do then?

Y. FASHION. Cut his throat, or get some one to do it for me.

LORY. Gad-so, sir, I'm glad to find I was not so well acquainted with the 15 strength of your conscience as with the weakness of your purse.

Y. FASHION. Why, art thou so impenetrable a blockhead as to believe he'll help me with a farthing?

LORY. Not if you treat him *de haut en bas* as you used to do.

Y. FASHION. Why how would'st have me treat him? 20

LORY. Like a trout—tickle him.

Y. FASHION. I can't flatter.

LORY. Can you starve?

Y. FASHION. Yes.

LORY. I can't—Good-bye t'ye, sir. 25

Y. FASHION. Stay—thou'lt distract me. But who comes here—my old friend, Colonel Townly?

Enter COLONEL TOWNLY.

My dear Colonel, I am rejoiced to meet you here.

TOWNLY. Dear Tom, this is an unexpected pleasure—what, are you 30 come to Scarbro' to be present at your brother's wedding?

LORY. Ah, sir, if it had been his funeral, we should have come with pleasure.

TOWNLY. What, honest Lory, are you with your master still?

LORY. Yes, sir, I have been starving with him ever since I saw your 35 honour last.

Y. FASHION. Why, Lory is an attach'd rogue; there's no getting rid of him.

LORY. True, sir, as my master says, there's no seducing me from his service, 'till he's able to pay me my wages. [*Aside.* 40

Y. FASHION. Go, go, sir—and take care of the baggage.

1 we] *81, I*; now we *L*   6 prevail] *81, I*; but prevail *L*   9 elder] *L, I, Rel.*; eldest *81*   20 have] *81, I, Rel.*; thou have *L*   29 meet] *81, I*; See *L*

LORY. Yes, sir—the baggage!—O Lord!—I suppose, sir, I must charge the landlord to be very particular where he stows this.

Y. FASHION. Get along, you rascal. [*Exit* LORY, *with the Portmanteau.* But, Colonel, are you acquainted with my proposed sister-in-law?

TOWNLY. Only by character—her father, Sir Tunbelly Clumsey, lives 5 within a quarter of a mile of this place, in a lonely old house, which nobody comes near. She never goes abroad, nor sees company at home; to prevent all misfortunes, she has her breeding within doors; the parson of the parish teaches her to play upon the dulcimer; the clerk to sing, her nurse to dress, and her father to dance:—in short, nobody has 10 free admission there but our old acquaintance, Mother Coupler, who has procured your brother this match, and is, I believe, a distant relation of Sir Tunbelly's.

Y. FASHION. But is her fortune so considerable?

TOWNLY. Three thousand a year, and a good sum of money independent 15 of her father beside.

Y. FASHION. 'Sdeath! that my old acquaintance, dame Coupler, could not have thought of me as well as my brother for such a prize.

TOWNLY. Egad I wouldn't swear that you are too late—his Lordship, I know, hasn't yet seen the lady, and, I believe, has quarrelled with his 20 patroness.

Y. FASHION. My dear Colonel, what an idea have you started?

TOWNLY. Pursue it if you can, and I promise you you shall have my assistance; for besides my natural contempt for his Lordship, I have at present the enmity of a rival towards him. 25

Y. FASHION. What, has he been addressing your old flame, the sprightly widow Berinthia?

TOWNLY. Faith, Tom, I am at present most whimsically circumstanced —I came here near a month ago to meet the lady you mention; but she failing in her promise, I, partly from pique, and partly from idleness, 30 have been diverting my chagrin by offering up chaste incense to the beauties of Amanda, our friend Loveless's wife.

Y. FASHION. I have never seen her, but have heard her spoken of as a youthful wonder of beauty and prudence.

TOWNLY. She is so indeed; and Loveless being too careless and insen- 35 sible of the treasure he possesses—my lodging in the same house has given me a thousand opportunities of making my assiduities acceptable; so that in less than a fortnight, I began to bear my disappointment from the widow, with the most Christian resignation.

3 *Exit . . . Portmanteau*] *81, I*; Exit Lory Laughing *L*   7–8 company . . .
prevent] *81, I, Rel.*; company—at home to prevent *L*   11 admission] *81, I*;
admittance *L, Rel.*   16 beside] *81, I*; besides *L*   19 late] *81, I*; late yet *L*
28 most] *81, I*; not *L*   29 here] *81, I*; hither *L*   36 possesses] *81, I*;
possess *L*   38 disappointment] *81, I*; disappointments *L*

Y. FASHION. And Berinthia has never appear'd?

TOWNLY. O there's the perplexity; for just as I began not to care whether I ever saw her again or not, last night she arrived.

Y. FASHION. And instantly reassumed her empire.

TOWNLY. No faith—we met—but the lady not condescending to give   5
me any serious reasons for having fool'd me for a month, I left her in a huff.

Y. FASHION. Well, well, I'll answer for't, she'll soon resume her power, especially as friendship will prevent your pursuing the other too far— but my coxcomb of a brother is an admirer of Amanda's too, is he?   10

TOWNLY. Yes; and I believe is most heartily despised by her—but come with me, and you shall see her and your old friend Loveless.

Y. FASHION. I must pay my respects to his Lordship—perhaps you can direct me to his lodgings.

TOWNLY. Come with me, I shall pass by it.   15

Y. FASHION. I wish you could pay the visit for me; or could tell me what I should say to him.

TOWNLY. Say nothing to him—apply yourself to his bag, his sword, his feather, his snuff-box; and when you are well with them, desire him to lend you a thousand pounds, and I'll engage you prosper.   20

Y. FASHION. 'Sdeath and furies! why was that coxcomb thrust into the world before me? O Fortune! Fortune! thou art a jilt, by Gad. [*Exit.*

SCENE II, *a Dressing Room*

LORD FOPPINGTON, *in his Night Gown, and* LA VAROLE.

LD. FOPPINGTON. Well, 'tis an unspeakable pleasure to be a man of   25
quality—strike me dumb!—even the boors of this Northern spa have learn'd the respect due to a title—La Varole!

LA VAROLE. Mi Lor——

LD. FOPPINGTON. You han't yet been at Muddy-Moat-Hall to announce my arrival, have you?   30

LA VAROLE. Not yet, mi Lor.

LD. FOPPINGTON. Then you need not go till Saturday.

[*Exit* LA VA.
as I am in no particular haste to view my intended Sposa—I shall sacrifice a day or two more to the pursuit of my friend Loveless's wife—   35
Amanda is a charming creature—strike me ugly; and if I have any discernment in the world, she thinks no less of my Lord Foppington.

---

5 give] *L, I*; giev *8I*　　　6 having fool'd] *8I, I*; fooling *L*　　　a] *8I, I*; *om. L*
9 pursuing] *8I, I*; perusing *L*　　　13 must] *8I, I*; must first, *L*　　　16 visit] *8I, I*;
Visist *L*　　　20 you prosper] *8I, I*; you'll prosper *L*　　　22 jilt] *8I, I*; Jade *L*

Enter LA VAROLE.

LA VAROLE. Mi Lor, de shoemaker, de taylor, de hosier, de sempstress, de peru, be all ready, if your lordship please to dress.

LD. FOPPINGTON. 'Tis well, admit them.

LA VAROLE. Hey, Messieurs, entrez.   5

Enter TAYLOR, *&c. &c.*

LD. FOPPINGTON. So, gentlemen, I hope you have all taken pains to shew yourselves masters in your professions.

TAYLOR. I think I may presume to say, Sir——

LA VAROLE. My Lor, you clown you!   10

TAYLOR. My Lord, I ask your Lordship's pardon, my Lord. I hope, my Lord, your Lordship will please to own, I have brought your Lordship as accomplished a suit of clothes as ever Peer of England wore, my Lord—will your Lordship please to try 'em now?

LD. FOPPINGTON. Ay; but let my people dispose the glasses so, that I   15
may see myself before and behind; for I love to see myself all round.

Whilst he puts on his clothes, enter YOUNG FASHION *and* LORY.

Y. FASHION. Hey-day! What the devil have we here?—Sure my gentle-man's grown a favourite at court, he has got so many people at his levee.

LORY. Sir, these people come in order to make him a favourite at court—   20
they are to establish him with the ladies.

Y. FASHION. Good Heav'n! to what an ebb of taste are women fallen, that it should be in the power of a laced coat to recommend a gallant to them!

LORY. Sir, Taylors and Hair-dressers are now become the bawds of the   25
nation—'tis they that debauch all the women.

Y. FASHION. Thou say'st true; for there's that fop now has not, by nature, wherewithal to move a cook maid: and by the time these fellows have done with him, egad he shall melt down a Countess—but now for my reception.   30

LD. FOPPINGTON. Death and eternal tartures! Sir—I say the coat is too wide here by a foot.

TAYLOR. My Lord, if it had been tighter, 'twould neither have hook'd nor button'd.

LD. FOPPINGTON. Rat the hooks and buttons, Sir, can any thing be   35
worse than this?—As Gad shall jedge me! it hangs on my shoulders like a chairman's surtout.

TAYLOR. 'Tis not for me to dispute your Lordship's fancy.

5 entrez] *81, Rel., I*; entrer *L*   13 accomplished] *81, Rel., I*; compleat *L*
26 that] *81, I; om. L, Rel.*   27 by] *81, Rel., I*; my *L*   28 the time] *81, I*;
that time *Rel., L*   31 tartures] *Rel., L*; tortures *81, I*   34 nor] *81, I*; or *L*
36 jedge] *81*; judge *I, [altered from 'jedge'] L*

LORY. There, Sir, observe what respect does.

Y. FASHION. Respect!—D—m him for a coxcomb—but let's accost him. —Brother, I'm your humble servant.

LD. FOPPINGTON. O Lard, Tam, I did not expect you in England— Brother, I'm glad to see you—but what has brought you to Scarbro'   5 Tam?—Look you, Sir, [*to the Taylor*] I shall never be reconciled to this nauseous wrapping gown; therefore, pray get me another suit with all possible expedition; for this is my eternal aversion—Well, but Tam, you don't tell me what has driven you to Scarbro'?—Mrs. Callicoe, are not you of my mind?   10

SEMPSTRESS. Directly, my Lord.—I hope your Lordship is pleased with your ruffles?

LD. FOPPINGTON. In love with them, stap my vitals!—Bring my bill, you shall be paid to-morrow.

SEMPSTRESS. I humbly thank your Lordship.   [*Exit* SEMP.   15

LD. FOPPINGTON. Heark thee, shoemaker, these shoes a'nt ugly, but they don't fit me.

SHOEMAKER. My Lord, I think they fit you very well.

LD. FOPPINGTON. They hurt me just below the instep.

SHOEMAKER. [*feeling his foot*] No, my Lord, they don't hurt you there.   20

LD. FOPPINGTON. I tell thee they pinch me execrably.

SHOEMAKER. Why then, my Lord, if those shoes pinch you I'll be d—n'd.

LD. FOPPINGTON. Why wilt thou undertake to persuade me I cannot feel!

SHOEMAKER. Your Lordship may please to feel what you think fit, but that shoe does not hurt you—I think I understand my trade.   25

LD. FOPPINGTON. Now by all that's great and powerful, thou art an incomprehensible coxcomb—but thou makest good shoes, and so I'll bear with thee.

SHOEMAKER. My Lord, I have work'd for half the people of quality in this town these twenty years, and 'tis very hard I shoudn't know when   30 a shoe hurts, and when it don't.

LD. FOPPINGTON. Well, prithee be gone about thy business. [*Exit* SHOE. Mr. Mendlegs, a word with you. The calves of these stockings are thicken'd a little too much; they make my legs look like a porter's.

MENDLEGS. My Lord, methinks they look mighty well.   35

LD. FOPPINGTON. Aye, but you are not so good a judge of those things as I am—I have study'd them all my life—therefore pray let the next be the thickness of a crown piece less.

MENDLEGS. Indeed, my Lord, they are the same kind I had the honour to furnish your Lordship with in town.   40

8 possible] *81, I*; manner of *Rel.*, *L*   11 Directly] *81, I*; O Directly *L, Rel.*
13 stap] *Rel.*, *L, I*; stab *81*   my bill] *81, I*; your bill *L, Rel.*   24-5 you
think . . . trade] *81, Rel., I*; you think I understand my trade *L*   26 great] *L,
Rel.*; good *81, I*   30 this] *81, I*; om. *L, Rel.*   34 they] *L, Rel, I*; thy *81*

LD. FOPPINGTON. Very possibly, Mr. Mendlegs; but that was in the beginning of the winter; and you should always remember, Mr. Hosier, that if you make a Nobleman's spring legs as robust as his autumnal calves, you commit a manstrous impropriety, and make no allowance for the fatigues of the winter.   5

JEW. I hope, my Lord, those buckles have had the unspeakable satisfaction of being honoured with your Lordship's approbation?

LD. FOPPINGTON. Why they are of a pretty fancy; but don't you think them rather of the smallest?

JEW. My Lord, they could not well be larger to keep on your Lordship's   10 shoe.

LD. FOPPINGTON. My good Sir, you forget that these matters are not as they used to be: formerly, indeed, the buckle was a sort of machine, intended to keep on the shoe; but the case is now quite reversed, and the shoe is of no earthly use, but to keep on the buckle.—Now give me   15 my watches, and the business of the morning will be pretty well over.

Y. FASHION. Well, Lory, what dost think on't?—a very friendly reception from a brother after three years absence!

LORY. Why, Sir, 'tis your own fault—here you have stood ever since you came in, and have not commended any one thing that belongs to him.   20

Y. FASHION. Nor ever shall, while they belong to a coxcomb.—Now your people of business are gone, brother, I hope I may obtain a quarter of an hour's audience of you?

LD. FOPPINGTON. Faith, Tam, I must beg you'll excuse me at this time, for I have an engagement which I would not break for the salvation of   25 mankind. Hey!—there!—is my carriage at the door?—You'll excuse me, brother.   [*Going.*

Y. FASHION. Shall you be back to dinner?

LD. FOPPINGTON. As Gad shall jedge me, I can't tell, for it is passible I may dine with some friends at Donner's.[1]   30

Y. FASHION. Shall I meet you there? for I must needs talk with you.

LD. FOPPINGTON. That I'm afraid may'nt be quite so praper;—for those I commonly eat with are a people of nice conversation; and you know, Tam, your education has been a little at large—but there are other ordinaries in the town—very good beef ordinaries—I suppose, Tam,   35 you can eat beef?—However, dear Tam, I'm glad to see thee in England, stap my vitals!   [*Exit.*

Y. FASHION. Hell and furies! Is this to be borne?

1 possibly] *Rel.*, *L*, *81*; possible *I*   4 manstrous— *81*; *L*; monstrous *I*
16 watches] *81*, *I*; Bouquet *L*   30 Donner's] *81*, *I*; *om. L*; Lacket's *Rel.*
32 so] *81*, *I*, *Rel.*; as *L*   35 the] *L*; *om. 81*, *I*

---

1 The Assembly Rooms at Scarborough: see Rhodes, i. 284 n. 1.

LORY. Faith, Sir, I could almost have given him a knock o' the pate myself.

Y. FASHION. 'Tis enough; I will now shew you the excess of my passion, by being very calm.—Come, Lory, lay your loggerhead to mine, and, in cold blood, let us contrive his destruction. 5

LORY. Here comes a head, Sir, would contrive it better than us both, if she would but join in the confederacy.

Y. FASHION. By this light, Madam Coupler; she seems dissatisfied at something: let us observe her.

Enter COUPLER. 10

COUPLER. Soh! I am likely to be well rewarded for my services, truly; my suspicions, I find, were but too just—What! refuse to advance me a paltry sum, when I am upon the point of making him master of a Galloon![1] But let him look to the consequences, an ungrateful, narrow-minded coxcomb. 15

Y. FASHION. So he is, upon my soul, old lady: it must be my brother you speak of.

COUPLER. Hah!—stripling, how came you here? What, hast spent all, hey? And art thou come to dun his Lordship for assistance?

Y. FASHION. No;—I want somebody's assistance to cut his Lordship's 20 throat, without the risque of being hang'd for him.

COUPLER. Egad, sirrah, I could help thee to do him almost as good a turn without the danger of being burnt in the hand for't.

Y. FASHION. How—how, old Mischief?

COUPLER. Why you must know I have done you the kindness to make up 25 a match for your brother.

Y. FASHION. I'm very much beholden to you, truly.

COUPLER. You may be before the wedding-day yet: the lady is a great heiress, the match is concluded, the writings are drawn, and his lordship is come hither to put the finishing hand to the business. 30

Y. FASHION. I understand as much.

COUPLER. Now you must know, stripling, your brother's a knave.

Y. FASHION. Good.

COUPLER. He has given me a bond of a thousand pounds for helping him to this fortune, and has promised me as much more in ready money 35 upon the day of the marriage; which, I understand by a friend, he never designs to pay me; and his just now refusing to pay me a part, is a proof of it. If, therefore, you will be a generous young rogue and secure me five thousand pounds, I'll help you to the lady.

5 cold] *81, I*; cool *L, Rel.*   19 art thou come] *81, I*; art come *L*   22 to ... almost] *81, Rel., I*; almost to do him *L*   28 be] *L*; om. *81, I*   35 this] *L, I*; his *81*   of the] *81, I*; of *L*   37 pay] *81, I*; advance *L*   38 a] *81, I*; om. *L*

[1] 'A ribbon of gold, silver or silk thread' (*O.E.D.*). Or 'galleon': cf. p. 158, l. 18.

Y. FASHION. And how the devil wilt thou do that?

COUPLER. Without the devil's aid, I warrant thee. Thy brother's face not one of the family ever saw; the whole business has been managed by me, and all the letters go thro' my hands. Sir Tunbelly Clumsey, my relation, (for that's the old gentleman's name) is apprized of his lord- 5 ship's being down here, and expects him to morrow to receive his daughter's hand; but the Peer, I find, means to bait here a few days longer, to recover the fatigue of his journey, I suppose. Now you shall go to Muddymoat-hall in his place. I'll give you a letter of introduction; and if you don't marry the girl before sun-set, you deserve to be 10 hang'd before morning.

Y. FASHION. Agreed, agreed; and for thy reward——

COUPLER. Well, well;—tho' I warrant thou hast not a farthing of money in thy pocket now—no—one may see it in thy face.

Y. FASHION. Not a souse, by Jupiter. 15

COUPLER. Must I advance then?—well, be at my lodgings next door this evening, and I'll see what may be done—We'll sign and seal, and when I have given thee some farther instructions, thou shalt hoist sail and be gone. [*Exit* COUP.

Y. FASHION. So, Lory; Providence thou seest at last takes care of merit: 20 we are in a fair way to be great people.

LORY. Aye, sir, if the devil don't step between the cup and the lip, as he uses to do.

Y. FASHION. Why, faith, he has play'd me many a damn'd trick to spoil my fortune; and, egad, I'm almost afraid he's at work about it again 25 now; but if I should tell thee how, thou'dst wonder at me.

LORY. Indeed, sir, I should not.

Y. FASHION. How dost know?

LORY. Because, sir, I have wondered at you so often, I can wonder at you no more. 30

Y. FASHION. No! what wouldst thou say if a qualm of conscience should spoil my design?

LORY. I would eat my words, and wonder more than ever!

Y. FASHION. Why faith, Lory, tho' I am a young Rake-hell, and have play'd many a rogueish trick, this is so full-grown a cheat, I find I must 35 take pains to come up to't——I have scruples.

LORY. They are strong symptoms of death. If you find they encrease, sir, pray make your will.

Y. FASHION. No, my conscience shan't starve me neither, but thus far I'll listen to it. Before I execute this project, I'll try my brother to the 40

5 lordship's] *L, 8r*; lordship *I*   7 here] *8r, I*; her *L*   9 his] *L, I*; this *8r*
15 souse] *L, 8r*; sous *I*   16 lodgings] *8r, L*; lodging *I*   20 takes] *8r, I*;
take *L*   merit] *8r, I*; men of merit *L, Rel.*   37–8 sir, pray] *8r, I*; pray Sir *L,
Rel.*   39 far] *8r, I; om. L*   40 listen] *8r, I*; hearken *L, Rel.*

bottom. If he has yet so much humanity about him as to assist me (tho'
with a moderate aid) I'll drop my project at his feet, and shew him how
I can do for him much more than what I'd ask he'd do for me. This one
conclusive trial of him I resolve to make.—

Succeed or fail, still victory's my lot,   ⎫   5
If I subdue his heart, 'tis well—if not   ⎬
I will subdue my conscience to my plot.   ⎭   [*Exeunt.*

END OF THE FIRST ACT

ACT II

SCENE I   10

Enter LOVELESS *and* AMANDA.

LOVELESS. How do you like these lodgings, my dear? For my part, I am
so well pleas'd with them, I shall hardly remove whilst we stay here, if
you are satisfied.

AMANDA. I am satisfied with every thing that pleases you, else I had not 15
come to Scarbro' at all.

LOVELESS. O! a little of the noise and folly of this place will sweeten the
pleasures of our retreat; we shall find the charms of our retirement
doubled when we return to it.

AMANDA. That pleasing prospect will be my chiefest entertainment,   20
whilst, much against my will, I engage in those empty pleasures which
'tis so much the fashion to be fond of.

LOVELESS. I own most of them are, indeed, but empty; yet there are
delights, of which a private life is destitute, which may divert an
honest man, and be a harmless entertainment to a virtuous woman: 25
good musick is one; and truly, (with some small allowance) the plays,
I think, may be esteemed another.

AMANDA. Plays, I must confess, have some small charms, and would
have more, would they restrain that loose encouragement to vice,
which shocks, if not the virtue of some women, at least the modesty of 30
all.

LOVELESS. But, 'till that reformation can be wholly made, 'twould surely
be a pity to exclude the productions of some of our best writers for
want of a little wholesome pruning; which might be effected by any
one who possessed modesty enough to believe that we should preserve 35

1 as] *81*, *L*; *om. I*   3 I'd] *81*, *I*; I *L, Rel.*   5 fail] *81*, *L*, *I*; no *Rel.*

all we can of our deceased authors, at least 'till they are outdone by the living ones.

AMANDA. What do you think of that you saw last night?

LOVELESS. To say truth, I did not mind it much; my attention was for some time taken off to admire the workmanship of Nature, in the face 5 of a young lady who sat some distance from me, she was so exquisitely handsome!

AMANDA. So exquisitely handsome!

LOVELESS. Why do you repeat my words, my dear?

AMANDA. Because you seem'd to speak them with such pleasure, I 10 thought I might oblige you with their echo.

LOVELESS. Then you are alarm'd, Amanda?

AMANDA. It is my duty to be so when you are in danger.

LOVELESS. You are too quick in apprehending for me. I view'd her with a world of admiration, but not one glance of love. 15

AMANDA. Take heed of trusting to such nice distinctions. But were your eyes the only things that were inquisitive? Had I been in your place, my tongue, I fancy, had been curious too. I should have ask'd her, where she liv'd (yet still without design) who was she pray?

LOVELESS. Indeed, I cannot tell. 20

AMANDA. You will not tell.

LOVELESS. By all that's sacred then, I did not ask.

AMANDA. Nor do you know what company was with her?

LOVELESS. I do not; but why are you so earnest?

AMANDA. I thought I had cause. 25

LOVELESS. But you thought wrong, Amanda; for turn the case, and let it be your story; should you come home and tell me you had seen a handsome man, should I grow jealous because you had eyes?

AMANDA. But should I tell you he was *exquisitely* so, and that I had gazed on him with admiration, should you not think 'twere possible I might 30 go one step further, and enquire his name?

LOVELESS. [*Aside.*] She has reason on her side, I have talk'd too much; but I must turn off another way. [*To her.*] Will you then make no difference, Amanda, between the language of our sex and yours? There is a modesty restrains your tongues, which makes you speak by halves 35 when you commend, but roving flattery gives a loose to ours, which makes us still speak double what we think. You should not, therefore, in so strict a sense, take what I said to her advantage.

AMANDA. Those flights of flattery, sir, are to our faces only; when women are once out of hearing, you are as modest in your commendations as 40 we are; but I shan't put you to the trouble of farther excuses;——if you

---

10 such] *81, Rel., I*; so much *L*   18–19 her, where] *81, I*; her Name, and where
L, Rel.   30 'twere possible] *81, I, Rel.*; *om. L*   31 further] *81, I*; farther
L, Rel.   33 off] *81, I*; it off *L, Rel.*   40 are once] *81, I*; once are *L, Rel.*

please, this business shall rest here, only give me leave to wish, both for your peace and mine, that you may never meet this miracle of beauty more.

LOVELESS. I am content.

Enter SERVANT. 5

SERVANT. Madam, there is a lady at the door in a chair, desires to know whether your Ladyship sees company? her name is Berinthia.

AMANDA. O dear!—'tis a relation I have not seen these five years, pray her to walk in. [*Exit* SERV.] Here's another beauty for you; she was, when I saw her last, reckoned extremely handsome. 10

LOVELESS. Don't be jealous now, for I shall gaze upon her too.

Enter BERINTHIA.

LOVELESS. [*Aside.*] Ha!—by Heav'ns the very woman!

BERINTHIA. [*Saluting* AMANDA.] Dear Amanda, I did not expect to meet with you in Scarbro'. 15

AMANDA. Sweet cousin, I'm overjoy'd to see you. [*To* LOV.] Mr. Loveless, here's a relation and a friend of mine, I desire you'll be better acquainted with.

LOVELESS. [*Saluting* BERINTHIA.] If my wife never desires a harder thing, Madam, her request will be easily granted. 20

Enter SERVANT.

SERVANT. Sir, my Lord Foppington presents his humble service to you, and desires to know how you do. He's at the next door, and if it be not inconvenient to you, he'll come and wait upon you.

LOVELESS. Give my compliments to his Lordship, and I shall be glad 25 to see him. [*Exit* SERV.] If you are not acquainted with his Lordship, Madam, you will be entertained with his character.

AMANDA. Now it moves my pity more than my mirth, to see a man whom Nature has made no fool, be so very industrious to pass for an ass.

LOVELESS. No, there you are wrong, Amanda; you should never bestow 30 your pity upon those who take pains for your contempt; pity those whom Nature abuses, never those who abuse Nature.

Enter LORD FOPPINGTON.

LD. FOPPINGTON. Dear Loveless, I am your most humble servant.

LOVELESS. My Lord, I'm your's. 35

LD. FOPPINGTON. Madam, your Ladyship's very humble slave.

LOVELESS. My Lord, this lady is a relation of my wife's.

6 lady] *81, I*; young lady *L, Rel.*   7 her] *81, I*; I think her *L, Rel.*   10 extremely] *81, Rel. I*; *om. L*   20 request] *81, L*; requests *I*   be easily] *I, 81, Rel.*; easily be *L*   24 to you] *81, I*; *om. L, Rel.*   27 Madam] *81, I*; *om. L* 32 never] *81, I*; but never *L, Rel.*   37 wife's] *81, I*; Wives *L*

LD. FOPPINGTON. [*Saluting her.*] The beautifullest race of people upon
earth, rat me. Dear Loveless, I am overjoyed that you think of continu-
ing here. I am, stap my vitals. [*To* AMANDA.] For Gad's sake, Madam,
how has your ladyship been able to subsist thus long, under the fatigue
of a country life?   5

AMANDA. My life has been very far from that, my Lord, it has been a
very quiet one.

LD. FOPPINGTON. Why that's the fatigue I speak of, Madam; for 'tis
impossible to be quiet, without thinking; now thinking is to me the
greatest fatigue in the world.   10

AMANDA. Does not your lordship love reading then?

LD. FOPPINGTON. Oh, passionately, Madam, but I never think of what
I read.

BERINTHIA. Why, can your lordship read without thinking?

LD. FOPPINGTON. O Lard, can your ladyship pray without devotion, 15
Madam?

AMANDA. Well, I must own, I think books the best entertainment in the
world.

LD. FOPPINGTON. I am so much of your ladyship's mind, Madam, that
I have a private gallery in town, where I walk sometimes, which is 20
furnished with nothing but books and looking glasses. Madam, I have
gilded them, and ranged them so prettily, before Gad, it is the most
entertaining thing in the world, to walk and look at them.

AMANDA. Nay, I love a neat library too, but 'tis, I think, the inside of a
book should recommend it most to us.   25

LD. FOPPINGTON. That, I must confess, I am not altogether so fand of,
far to my mind, the inside of a book is to entertain one's self with the
forced product of another man's brain. Now I think a man of quality
and breeding may be much more diverted with the natural sprauts of
his own; but to say the truth, Madam, let a man love reading never so 30
well, when once he comes to know the tawn, he finds so many better
ways of passing away the four-and-twenty hours, that it were ten thousand pities he should consume his time in that. Far example, Madam,
now my life, my life, Madam, is a perpetual stream of pleasure, that
glides through with such a variety of entertainments, I believe the 35
wisest of our ancestors never had the least conception of any of 'em.
I rise, Madam, when in town, about twelve o'clock. I don't rise sooner,
because it is the worst thing in the world for the complexion; nat that I
pretend to be a beau, but a man must endeavour to look decent, lest he
makes so odious a figure in the side-bax, the ladies should be compelled 40
to turn their eyes upon the play; so, at twelve o'clock I say I rise. Naw,
if I find it a good day, I resalve to take the exercise of riding, so drink

my chocolate, and draw on my boots by two. On my return, I dress;
and after dinner, lounge, perhaps to the Opera.

BERINTHIA. Your lordship, I suppose, is fond of music?

LD. FOPPINGTON. O, passionately, on Tuesdays and Saturdays, provided there is good company, and one is not expected to undergo the   5
fatigue of listening.

AMANDA. Does your lordship think that the case at the Opera?

LD. FOPPINGTON. Most certainly, Madam; there is my Lady Tattle,
my Lady Prate, my Lady Titter, my Lady Sneer, my Lady Giggle, and
my Lady Grin,—these have boxes in the front, and while any favourite   10
air is singing, are the prettiest company in the waurld, stap my vitals!
May'nt we hope for the honour to see you added to our society, Madam?

AMANDA. Alas, my Lord, I am the worst company in the world at a
concert, I'm so apt to attend to the music.

LD. FOPPINGTON. Why, Madam, that is very pardonable in the country, 15
or at church; but a monstrous inattention in a polite assembly. But I am
afraid I tire the company?

LOVELESS. Not at all; pray go on.

LD. FOPPINGTON. Why then, ladies, there only remains to add, that I
generally conclude the evening at one or other of the Clubs, nat that I   20
ever play deep; indeed I have been for some time tied up from losing
above five thousand pawnds at a sitting.

LOVELESS. But is'nt your Lordship sometimes obliged to attend the
weighty affairs of the nation?

LD. FOPPINGTON. Sir, as to weighty affairs, I leave them to weighty   25
heads; I never intend mine shall be a burthen to my body.

BERINTHIA. Nay, my Lord, but you are a pillar of the state.

LD. FOPPINGTON. An ornamental pillar, Madam; for sooner than
undergo any part of the burthen, rat me, but the whole building should
fall to the ground.   30

AMANDA. But, my Lord, a fine gentleman spends a great deal of his time
in his intrigues; you have given us no account of them yet.

LD. FOPPINGTON. [Aside.] Soh! She would enquire into my amours,
that's jealousy; poor soul! I see she's in love with me. [To her.] Why,
Madam, I should have mentioned my intrigues, but I am really afraid   35
I begin to be troublesome with the length of my visit.

AMANDA. Your lordship is too entertaining to grow troublesome any
where.

LD. FOPPINGTON. [Aside.] That now was as much as if she had said pray
make love to me. I'll let her see I'm quick of apprehension. [To her.]   40
O Lard, Madam, I had like to have forgot a secret I must needs tell your
ladyship. [To LOV.] Ned, you must not be so jealous now as to listen.

11 waurld] 81, I; Wauld L; world Rel.   22 pawnds] 81; pounds L; paunds I
28 for] 81, I; far L   36 be] 81, I; grow L, Rel.   39 had] 81, Rel., I; om. L

LOVELESS. Not I, my Lord, I am too fashionable a husband to pry into the secrets of my wife.

LD. FOPPINGTON. [*To* AMAN. *squeezing her hand.*] I am in love with you to desperation, strike me speechless!

AMANDA. [*Giving him a box o' the ear.*] Then thus I return your passion,— 5 an impudent fool!

LD. FOPPINGTON. Gad's curse, Madam, I'm a Peer of the Realm.

LOVELESS. Hey, what the Devil do you affront my wife, Sir? Nay then—— [*Draws and fights.*

AMANDA. Ah! What has my folly done?—Help! murder! help! Part them, 10 for Heaven's sake.

LD. FOPPINGTON. [*Falling back, and leaning on his sword.*] Ah! quite through the body, stap my vitals!

Enter SERVANTS.

LOVELESS. [*Running to him.*] I hope I han't killed the fool, however— 15 bear him up—where's your wound?

LD. FOPPINGTON. Just thro' the guts.

LOVELESS. Call a surgeon, there—unbutton him quickly.

LD. FOPPINGTON. Ay, pray make haste.

LOVELESS. This mischief you may thank yourself for. 20

LD. FOPPINGTON. I may so, love's the Devil, indeed, Ned.

Enter PROBE *and* SERVANT.

SERVANT. Here's Mr. Probe, sir, was just going by the door.

LD. FOPPINGTON. He's the welcomest man alive.

PROBE. Stand by, stand by, stand by; pray, Gentlemen, stand by; Lord 25 have mercy upon us! did you never see a man run through the body before? Pray stand by.

LD. FOPPINGTON. Ah! Mr. Probe, I'm a dead man.

PROBE. A dead man, and I by! I should laugh to see that, egad.

LOVELESS. Prithee, don't stand prating, but look upon his wound. 30

PROBE. Why, what if I won't look upon his wound this hour, sir?

LOVELESS. Why then he'll bleed to death, sir.

PROBE. Why then I'll fetch him to life again, sir.

LOVELESS. 'Slife! he's run thro' the guts, I tell thee.

PROBE. I wish he was run thro' the heart, and I should get the more credit 35 by his cure.—Now I hope you are satisfied?—Come, now let me come at him—now let me come at him—[*viewing his wound*] Oons! what a gash is here!—Why, sir, a man may drive a coach and six horses into your body!

LD. FOPPINGTON. Oh!

PROBE. Why, what the devil have you run the gentleman thro' with a 40 scythe?—[*aside*] A little scratch between the skin and the ribs, that's all.

9 *fights*] L; *fight 81, I*   38 into] *81, Rel., I;* thro' L

LOVELESS. Let me see his wound.

PROBE. Then you shall dress it, Sir—for if any body looks upon it I won't.

LOVELESS. Why thou art the veriest coxcomb I ever saw.

PROBE. Sir, I am not master of my trade for nothing.

LD. FOPPINGTON. Surgeon!   5

PROBE. Sir?

LD. FOPPINGTON. Are there any hopes?

PROBE. Hopes! I can't tell—What are you willing to give for a cure?

LD. FOPPINGTON. Five hundred paunds with pleasure.

PROBE. Why then perhaps there may be hopes; but we must avoid a   10
further delay—here—help the gentleman into a chair, and carry him to
my house presently—that's the properest place—[*aside*] to bubble him
out of his money.——Come, a chair—a chair quickly—there, in with
him.—[*they put him into a chair*]

LD. FOPPINGTON. Dear Loveless, adieu: if I die, I forgive thee; and   15
if I live, I hope thou wilt do as much by me.—I am sorry you and I
should quarrel, but I hope here's an end on't; for if you are satisfied,
I am.

LOVELESS. I shall hardly think it worth my prosecuting any farther, so
you may be at rest, sir.   20

LD. FOPPINGTON. Thou art a generous fellow, strike me dumb!—
[*aside*] but thou hast an impertinent wife, stap my vitals!

PROBE. So—carry him off—carry him off—we shall have him prate
himself into a fever by and by—carry him off.

[*Exit with* LD. FOPPINGTON *and* PROBE.   25

AMANDA. Now on my knees, my dear, let me ask your pardon for my
indiscretion—my own I never shall obtain.

LOVELESS. Oh, there's no harm done—you serv'd him well.

AMANDA. He did indeed deserve it; but I tremble to think how dear my
indiscreet resentment might have cost you.   30

LOVELESS. O, no matter—never trouble yourself about that.

Enter COLONEL TOWNLY.

TOWNLY. So, so, I'm glad to find you all alive—I met a wounded Peer
carrying off—for Heav'ns sake what was the matter?

LOVELESS. O, a trifle—he would have made love to my wife before my   35
face, so she obliged him with a box o'the ear, and I run him through the
body, that was all.

TOWNLY. Bagatelle on all sides—but pray, Madam, how long has this
noble Lord been an humble servant of your's?

AMANDA. This is the first I have heard on't—so I suppose 'tis his quality   40
more than his love has brought him into this adventure. He thinks his

8 a] *81, I*; your *Rel.*; you L   10 a] *81, I*; om. L   16 sorry] *81, I*; very sorry
L, *Rel.*   17 here's] *81, L, Rel.*; there's *I*   24 into] *81, I, Rel.*; to L

title an authentic passport to every woman's heart, below the degree of
a Peeress.

TOWNLY. He's coxcomb enough to think any thing; but I would not have
you brought into trouble for him.—I hope there's no danger of his life?

LOVELESS. None at all—he's fallen into the hands of a roguish surgeon, 5
who, I perceive, designs to frighten a little money out of him—but I saw
his wound—'tis nothing—he may go to the ball tonight if he pleases.

TOWNLY. I am glad you have corrected him without farther mischief, or
you might have deprived me of the pleasure of executing a plot against
his Lordship, which I have been contriving with an old acquaintance of 10
yours.

LOVELESS. Explain——

TOWNLY. His brother, Tom Fashion, is come down here, and we have it
in contemplation to save him the trouble of his intended wedding; but
we want your assistance. Tom would have called, but he is preparing 15
for his enterprize, so I promised to bring you to him—so, sir, if these
ladies can spare you—

LOVELESS. I'll go with you with all my heart—[*aside*]—tho' I could wish,
methinks, to stay and gaze a little longer on that creature—Good Gods!
how engaging she is—but what have I to do with beauty?—I have 20
already had my portion, and must not covet more.—[*To* TOWNLY]
Come, sir, when you please.

TOWNLY. Ladies, your servant.

AMANDA. Mr. Loveless, pray one word with you before you go.

LOVELESS. [*to* TOWNLY.] I'll overtake you, Colonel. [*Exit* TOWNLY]. 25
What would my dear?

AMANDA. Only a woman's foolish question, how do you like my cousin
here?

LOVELESS. Jealous already, Amanda?

AMANDA. Not at all—I ask you for another reason. 30

LOVELESS. [*Aside.*] Whate'er her reason be, I must not tell her true.
[*to her*]. Why, I confess she's handsome—but you must not think I
slight your kinswoman, if I own to you, of all the women who may claim
that character, she is the last would triumph in my heart.

AMANDA. I'm satisfied. 35

LOVELESS. Now tell me why you ask'd?

AMANDA. At night I will—Adieu.—

LOVELESS. [*Kissing her.*] I'm yours——   [*Exit.*

AMANDA. [*Aside.*] I'm glad to find he does not like her, for I have a great
mind to persuade her to come and live with me. 40

BERINTHIA. [*Aside.*] Soh! I find my Colonel continues in his airs; there
must be something more at the bottom of this than the provocation he
pretends from me.

4 for] *81, Rel., I*; about *L*

AMANDA. For Heav'ns sake, Berinthia, tell me what way I shall take to persuade you to come and live with me?

BERINTHIA. Why one way in the world there is—and but one.

AMANDA. And pray what is that?

BERINTHIA. It is to assure me—I shall be very welcome.   5

AMANDA. If that be all, you shall e'en sleep here tonight.

BERINTHIA. To-night!

AMANDA. Yes, to-night.

BERINTHIA. Why the people where I lodge will think me mad.

AMANDA. Let 'em think what they please.   10

BERINTHIA. Say you so, Amanda?—Why then they shall think what they please—for I'm a young widow, and I care not what any body thinks.
——Ah, Amanda, it's a delicious thing to be a young widow.

AMANDA. You'll hardly make me think so.

BERINTHIA. Puh! because you are in love with your husband—but that is   15
not every woman's case.

AMANDA. I hope 'twas yours at least.

BERINTHIA. Mine, say you?—Now I have a great mind to tell you a lye, but I shall do it so aukwardly, you'd find me out.

AMANDA. Then e'en speak the truth.   20

BERINTHIA. Shall I?—then, after all, I did love him, Amanda, as a Nun does penance.

AMANDA. How did you live together?

BERINTHIA. Like man and wife—asunder—he lov'd the country—I the town.—He hawks and hounds—I coaches and equipage.—He eating   25
and drinking—I carding and playing.—He the sound of a horn—I the squeek of a fiddle.—We were dull company at table—worse a-bed: whenever we met we gave one another the spleen, and never agreed but once, which was about lying alone.

AMANDA. But tell me one thing truly and sincerely—notwithstanding all   30
these jars, did not his death at last extremely trouble you?

BERINTHIA. O yes.—I was forced to wear an odious Widow's band a twelve-month for't.

AMANDA. Women, I find, have different inclinations:—prithee, Berinthia, instruct me a little farther—for I'm so great a novice,   35
I'm almost asham'd on't.—Not Heav'n knows that what you call intrigues have any charms for me—the practical part of all unlawful love is——

BERINTHIA. O 'tis abominable—but for the speculative, that we must all confess is entertaining enough.   40

AMANDA. Pray, be so just then to me, to believe, 'tis with a world of innocence I would enquire whether you think those, we call Women of

4 what] *81, I*; which *L*   15 Puh] *81, I*; Pah! *L*; Phu *Rel.*   32 Widow's]
L, I; Widows' *81*   34 prithee] *81, I*; but prithee *L, Rel.*

Reputation, do really escape all other men, as they do those shadows of 'em the beaus?

BERINTHIA. O no, Amanda—there are a sort of men make dreadful work amongst 'em—men that may be called the beaus' Antipathy— for they agree in nothing but walking upon two legs. These have brains 5 —the beau has none.—These are in love with their mistress—the beau with himself.—They take care of her reputation—he's industrious to destroy it—They are decent—he's a fop. They are men—he's an ass.

AMANDA. If this be their character, I fancy we had here e'en now a pattern of 'em both.   10

BERINTHIA. His Lordship and Colonel Townly?

AMANDA. The same.

BERINTHIA. As for the Lord, he's eminently so; and for the other, I can assure you there's not a man in town who has a better interest with the women, that are worth having an interest with.   15

AMANDA. He answers then the opinion I had ever of him—Heav'ns! what a difference there is between a man like him, and that vain nauseous fop, Lord Foppington—[*taking her hand*] I must acquaint you with a secret, cousin—'tis not that fool alone has talked to me of love.— Townly has been tampering too.   20

BERINTHIA. [*Aside.*] So, so!—here the mystery comes out!—Colonel Townly!—impossible, my dear!

AMANDA. 'Tis true, indeed!—tho' he has done it in vain; nor do I think that all the merit of mankind combined, could shake the tender love I bear my husband; yet I will own to you, Berinthia, I did not start at his 25 addresses, as when they came from one whom I contemned.

BERINTHIA. [*Aside.*] O this is better and better—well said innocence!— and you really think, my dear, that nothing could abate your constancy and attachment to your husband?

AMANDA. Nothing, I am convinced.   30

BERINTHIA. What if you found he lov'd another woman better?

AMANDA. Well!

BERINTHIA. Well!—why were I that thing they call a slighted wife; somebody should run the risk of being that thing they call—a husband.

AMANDA. O fie, Berinthia, no revenge should ever be taken against a hus- 35 band—but to wrong his bed is a vengeance, which of all vengeance——

BERINTHIA. Is the sweetest!—ha! ha! ha!—don't I talk madly?

AMANDA. Madly indeed!

BERINTHIA. Yet I'm very innocent.

AMANDA. That I dare swear you are.—I know how to make allowances for 40 your humour—but you resolve then never to marry again?

2 'em the] *L*, *Rel.*; *om. 81, I*   beaus] *81, I*; Beauxs *L*; beaux *Rel.*   4 beaus']
I; Beauxs *L*; beaus *81*   7 her] *L*, *Rel.*; their *81, I*   8 decent] *81, I*; descent *L*
16 had ever] *81, L*; ever had *I*   19 a] *81, L*; the *I*

BERINTHIA. O no!—I resolve I will.

AMANDA. How so?

BERINTHIA. That I never may.

AMANDA. You banter me.

BERINTHIA. Indeed I don't—but I consider I'm a woman, and form my 5
resolutions accordingly.

AMANDA. Well, my opinion is, form what resolution you will, matrimony
will be the end on't.

BERINTHIA. I doubt it—but A Heav'ns!—I have business at home, and
am half an hour too late. 10

AMANDA. As you are to return with me, I'll just give some orders, and
walk with you.

BERINTHIA. Well, make haste, and we'll finish this subject as we go.
[*Exit* AMANDA.

Ah! poor Amanda, you have led a country life! Well, this discovery is 15
lucky!—base Townly!—at once false to me, and treacherous to his
friend! and my innocent, demure, cousin, too!—I have it in my power
to be revenged on her, however. Her husband, if I have any skill in
countenance, would be as happy in my smiles, as Townly can hope to
be in her's.—I'll make the experiment, come what will on't.—The 20
woman who can forgive the being robb'd of a favour'd lover, must be
either an ideot or a wanton.

END OF ACT THE SECOND

ACT III

SCENE I 25

Enter LORD FOPPINGTON *and* LA VAROLE.

LD. FOPPINGTON. Hey, fellow—let my vis-a-vis[1] come to the door.

LA VAROLE. Will your lordship venture so soon to expose yourself to
the weather?

LD. FOPPINGTON. Sir, I will venture as soon as I can to expose myself 30
to the ladies.

LA VAROLE. I wish your lordship would please to keep house a little
longer; I'm affraid your honour does not well consider your wound.

LD. FOPPINGTON. My wound!—I would not be in eclipse another day,

9 A] *81*; O *L*; ah *I*   22 ideot] *81*; idoet *L*; idiot *L*

---

[1] 'A light carriage for two persons sitting face to face' (*O.E.D.*). In *The Relapse*
Lord Foppington refers to 'the coach'.

tho' I had as many wounds in my body as I have had in my heart. So mind, Varole, let these cards be left as directed. For this evening I shall wait on my father-in-law, Sir Tunbelly, and I mean to commence my devoirs to the lady, by giving an entertainment at her father's expence; and heark thee, tell Mr. Loveless I request he and his company will   5 honour me with their presence, or I shall think we are not friends.

LA VAROLE. I will be sure.   [*Exit.*

Enter YOUNG FASHION.

Y. FASHION. Brother, your servant, how do you find yourself to day?

LD. FOPPINGTON. So well, that I have ardered my carriage to the door;   10 —so there's no great danger of death this baut, Tam.

Y. FASHION. I'm very glad of it.

LD. FOPPINGTON. [*Aside.*] That I believe's a lye.—Prithee, Tam, tell me one thing—did not your heart cut a caper up to your mauth, when you heard I was run thro' the bady?   15

Y. FASHION. Why do you think it should?

LD. FOPPINGTON. Because I remember mine did so when I heard my uncle was shot thro' the head.

Y. FASHION. It then did very ill.

LD. FOPPINGTON. Prithee, why so?   20

Y. FASHION. Because he used you very well.

LD. FOPPINGTON. Well!—Naw, strike me dumb, he starv'd me—he has let me want a thausand women, for want of a thausand pound.

Y. FASHION. Then he hinder'd you from making a great many ill bargains—for I think no woman worth money that will take money. 25

LD. FOPPINGTON. If I was a younger brother, I should think so too.

Y. FASHION. Then you are seldom much in love?

LD. FOPPINGTON. Never, stap my vitals.

Y. FASHION. Why then did you make all this bustle about Amanda?

LD. FOPPINGTON. Because she was a woman of an insolent virtue—and 30 I thought myself piqu'd in honour to debauch her.

Y. FASHION. [*Aside.*] Very well. Here's a rare fellow for you, to have the spending of five thousand pounds a year. But now for my business with him.—Brother, tho' I know to talk of business (especially of money) is a theme not quite so entertaining to you as that of the ladies, my neces- 35 sities are such, I hope you'll have patience to hear me.

LD. FOPPINGTON. The greatness of your necessities, Tam, is the worst argument in the warld for your being patiently heard. I do believe you

2 I] *81, I*; as I *L*   3 and] *81, I*; *om. L*   7 sure] *81, I*; sure your Honor *L*
10 ardered] *81, Rel.*; order'd *L, I*   carriage] *L*; coach *81, I*   11 great] *L*; *om. 81,*
I baut] *81, Rel., I*; bout *L*   14 not] *81, L*; *om. I*   15 run] *L, Rel.*; ran *81, I*
bady] *81, Rel., I*; Body *L*   22 Naw] *81, Rel., I*; now *L*   23 has let] *81, I*;
lett *L*   thausand] *81, Rel., I*; thousand *L*   28 stap] *81, Rel., I*; stop *L*

are going to make a very good speech, but strike me dumb, it has the worst beginning of any speech I have heard this twelvemonth.

Y. FASHION. I'm sorry you think so.

LD. FOPPINGTON. I do believe thou art—but come, let's know the affair quickly.　　　　5

Y. FASHION. Why then, my case in a word is this.—The necessary expences of my travels have so much exceeded the wretched income of my annuity, that I have been forced to mortgage it for five hundred pounds, which is spent. So unless you are so kind as to assist me in redeeming it, I know no remedy but to take a purse.　　　　10

LD. FOPPINGTON. Why, faith, Tam, to give you my sense of the thing, I do think taking a purse the best remedy in the warld—for if you succeed you are relieved that way, if you are taken—you are relieved t'other.

Y. FASHION. I'm glad to see you are in so pleasant a humour; I hope I　15
shall find the effects on't.

LD. FOPPINGTON. Why, do you then really think it a reasonable thing that I should give you five hundred pawnds?

Y. FASHION. I do not ask it as a due, brother, I am willing to receive it as a favour.　　　　20

LD. FOPPINGTON. Then thou art willing to receive it any how, strike me speechless.—But these are d——n'd times to give money in; taxes are so great, repairs so exorbitant, tenants such rogues, and bouquets[1] so dear, that the Devil take me, I am reduced to that extremity in my cash, I have been forced to retrench in that one article of sweet pawder,[2]　25
till I have brought it dawn to five guineas a maunth—now judge, Tam, whether I can spare you five hundred pawnds?

Y. FASHION. If you can't I must starve, that's all.　　　　[Aside.
Damn him.

LD. FOPPINGTON. All I can say is, you should have been a better husband.[3]　30

Y. FASHION. Ouns!—If you can't live upon ten thousand a-year, how do you think I should do't upon two hundred?

LD. FOPPINGTON. Don't be in a passion, Tam, for passion is the most unbecoming thing in the warld—to the face. Look you, I don't love to say any thing to you to make you melancholy, but upon this occasion I　35
must take leave to put you in mind, that a running-horse does require more attendance than a coach-horse.—Nature has made some difference 'twixt you and me.

3 sorry] *81, I*; very sorry *L, Rel.*　　　9 so] *81, I*; so that *L, Rel.*　　　18 pawnds] *81*; pounds *L*; paunds *Rel., I*　　　21 Then] *81, I*; om. *L*　　　25 pawder] *81, Rel., I*; powder *L*　　　26 dawn] *81, Rel., I*; down *L*　　　maunth] *81, I*; Month *L*; manth *Rel.*

[1] See p. 395 n.
[2] 'Perfumed powder used as a cosmetic' (*O.E.D.*).　　　　[3] Manager.

Y. FASHION. Yes.—She has made you older. [*Aside.*] Plague take her.

LD. FOPPINGTON. That is not all, Tam.

Y. FASHION. Why, what is there else?

LD. FOPPINGTON. [*Looking first upon himself and then upon his brother.*] Ask the ladies. 5

Y. FASHION. Why, thou Essence-bottle, thou Musk Cat,—dost thou then think thou hast any advantage over me but what fortune has given thee?

LD. FOPPINGTON. I do, stap my vitals.

Y. FASHION. Now, by all that's great and powerful thou art the Prince of 10 Coxcombs.

LD. FOPPINGTON. Sir, I am praud at being at the head of so prevailing a party.

Y. FASHION. Will nothing then provoke thee?—Draw, Coward.

LD. FOPPINGTON. Look you, Tam, you know I have always taken you 15 for a mighty dull fellow, and here is one of the foolishest plats broke out, that I have seen a lang time. Your poverty makes life so burthensome to you, you would provoke me to a quarrel, in hopes either to slip through my lungs into my estate, or to get yourself run thro' the guts, to put an end to your pain, but I will disappoint you in both your designs; far 20 with the temper of a Philasapher, and the discretion of a statesman—I shall leave the room with my sword in the scabbard. [*Exit.*

Y. FASHION. So! farewell brother; and now conscience I defy thee.—— Lory!

Enter LORY. 25

LORY. Sir?

Y. FASHION. Here's rare news, Lory, his Lordship has given me a pill has purged off all my scruples.

LORY. Then my heart's at ease again. For I have been in a lamentable fright, sir, ever since your conscience had the impudence to intrude into 30 your company.

Y. FASHION. Be at peace; it will come there no more, my brother has given it a wring by the nose, and I have kick'd it down stairs. So run away to the inn, get the chaise ready quickly, and bring it to dame Coupler's without a moment's delay. 35

LORY. Then, sir, you are going straight about the fortune?

Y. FASHION. I am.—Away—fly, Lory.

LORY. The happiest day I ever saw. I'm upon the wing already.

[*Exeunt severally.*

---

1 Yes] *81, L; om. I*   4 *upon*] *81, I;* on *L*   12 praud] *L, Rel.;* proud *81, I*
17 lang] *81, I;* long *L, Rel.*   20 far] *81, Rel., I;* for *L*   21 Philasapher] *81,*
Rel., I; Philos[o]pher *L*   22 my sword in the] *81, I;* the sword in my *L*

SCENE II, A GARDEN

Enter LOVELESS *and* SERVANT.

LOVELESS. Is my wife within?

SERVANT. No, sir, she has been gone out this half hour.

LOVELESS. Well, leave me. [*Exit* SERVANT.] How strangely does my 5
mind run on this widow—never was my heart so suddenly seiz'd on
before—that my wife should pick out her, of all woman-kind, to be her
playfellow.—But what fate does, let fate answer for—I sought it not—
soh!—by heav'ns!—here she comes.

Enter BERINTHIA. 10

BERINTHIA. What makes you look so thoughtful, Sir? I hope you are not
ill.

LOVELESS. I was debating, madam, whether I was so or not, and that was
it which made me look so thoughtful.

BERINTHIA. Is it then so hard a matter to decide?—I thought all 15
people were acquainted with their own bodies, tho' few people know
their own minds.

LOVELESS. What if the distemper I suspect be in the mind?

BERINTHIA. Why then I'll undertake to prescribe you a cure.

LOVELESS. Alas! you undertake you know not what. 20

BERINTHIA. So far at least then you allow me to be a Physician.

LOVELESS. Nay, I'll allow you to be so yet farther, for I have reason to
believe, should I put myself into your hands, you would increase my
distemper.

BERINTHIA. How? 25

LOVELESS. Oh, you might betray my complaints to my wife.

BERINTHIA. And so lose all my practice.

LOVELESS. Will you then keep my secret?

BERINTHIA. I will.

LOVELESS. I'm satisfied. Now hear my symptoms, and give me your 30
advice. The first were these when I saw you at the play; a random
glance you threw, at first alarm'd me. I could not turn my eyes from
whence the danger came—I gaz'd upon you till my heart began to pant
—nay, even now on your approaching me, my illness is so increas'd,
that if you do not help me I shall, whilst you look on, consume to Ashes. 35
[*Taking her hand.*

BERINTHIA. [*Breaking from him.*] O Lord let me go, 'tis the plague, and
we shall be infected.

LOVELESS. Then we'll die together, my charming angel.

5 leave me] *81, I*; give me leave *L*   22 farther] *81, I; Rel.*; further *L*   37 Lord]
81, I; Lard *L, Rel.*

BERINTHIA. O Gad! the devil's in you. Lord, let me go—here's some-body coming.

Enter SERVANT.

SERVANT. Sir, my lady's come home, and desires to speak with you.

LOVELESS. Tell her I'm coming. [*Exit* SERVANT.]——[*To* BERINTHIA]   5
But before I go, one glass of nectar to drink her health.

BERINTHIA. Stand off, or I shall hate you, by heavens.

LOVELESS. [*Kissing her.*] In matters of love, a woman's oath is no more to
be minded than a man's.   [*Exit* LOV.

BERINTHIA. Um!   10

Enter TOWNLY.

TOWNLY. Soh! what's here—Berinthia and Loveless—and in such *close*
conversation!—I cannot now wonder at her indifference in excusing
herself to me!—O rare woman,—well then, let Loveless look to his
wife, 'twill be but the retort courteous on both sides.—[*To* BERINTHIA.]   15
Your servant, Madam, I need not ask you how you do, you have got so
good a colour.

BERINTHIA. No better than I used to have, I suppose.

TOWNLY. A little more blood in your cheeks.

BERINTHIA. I have been walking!   20

TOWNLY. Is that all? Pray was it Mr. Loveless went from here just now?

BERINTHIA. O yes—he has been walking with me.

TOWNLY. He has!

BERINTHIA. Upon my word I think he is a very agreeable man!—and
there is certainly something particularly insinuating in his address!   25

TOWNLY. So! so! she hasn't even the modesty to dissemble! Pray,
madam, may I, without impertinence, trouble you with a few serious
questions?

BERINTHIA. As many as you please; but pray let them be as little serious
as possible.   30

TOWNLY. Is it not near two years since I have presumed to address you?

BERINTHIA. I don't know exactly—but it has been a tedious long time.

TOWNLY. Have I not, during that period, had every reason to believe
that my assiduities were far from being unacceptable?

BERINTHIA. Why, to do you justice, you have been extremely trouble-   35
some—and I confess I have been more civil to you than you deserved.

TOWNLY. Did I not come to this place at your express desire? and for no
purpose but the honour of meeting you?—and after waiting a month
in disappointment, have you condescended to explain, or in the
slightest way apologize, for your conduct?   40

BERINTHIA. O heav'ns! apologize for my conduct!—apologise to you!—
O you barbarian!—But pray now, my good serious Colonel, have you
any thing more to add?

TOWNLY. Nothing, madam, but that after such behaviour I am less
surpris'd at what I saw just now; it is not very wonderful that the woman ⁵
who can trifle with the delicate addresses of an honourable lover, should
be found coquetting with the husband of her friend.

BERINTHIA. Very true—no more wonderful than it was for this *honourable* lover to divert himself in the absence of this coquet, with endeavouring to seduce his friend's wife! O Colonel, Colonel, don't talk of honor ¹⁰
or your friend, for heav'ns sake.

TOWNLY. S'death! how came she to suspect this!—Really madam, I
don't understand you.

BERINTHIA. Nay—nay—you saw I did not pretend to misunderstand
you.—But here comes the Lady—perhaps you would be glad to be ¹⁵
left with her for an explanation.

TOWNLY. O madam, this recrimination is a poor resource, and to
convince you how much you are mistaken, I beg leave to decline the
happiness you propose me.—Madam, your servant.

Enter AMANDA. [TOWNLY *whispers* AMANDA, *and exit.*]   ²⁰

BERINTHIA. He carries it off well however—upon my word—very well!
—how tenderly they part!——So, cousin—I hope you have not been
chiding your admirer for being with me—I assure you we have been
talking of you.

AMANDA. Fie, Berinthia!—my admirer—will you never learn to talk in ²⁵
earnest of any thing?

BERINTHIA. Why this shall be in earnest, if you please; for my part I
only tell you matter of fact.

AMANDA. I'm sure there's so much jest and earnest in what you say to
me on this subject, I scarce know how to take it.—I have just parted ³⁰
with Mr. Loveless—perhaps it is my fancy, but I think there is an
alteration in his manner, which alarms me.

BERINTHIA. And so you are jealous? is that all?

AMANDA. That all!—is jealousy then nothing?

BERINTHIA. It should be nothing, if I were in your case.   ³⁵

AMANDA. Why what would you do?

BERINTHIA. I'd cure myself.

AMANDA. How?

BERINTHIA. Care as little for my husband as he did for me. Look you,
Amanda, you may build castles in the air, and fume, and fret, and grow ⁴⁰
thin, and lean, and pale, and ugly, if you please, but I tell you, no man
worth having is true to his wife, or ever was, or ever will be so.

19 you] *8r, I*; *om. L*   30 scarce] *8r, L*; scarcely *I*   34 then] *8r, I*; than *L*

AMANDA. Do you then really think he's false to me? for I did not suspect him.

BERINTHIA. Think so!—I am sure of it.

AMANDA. You are sure on't?

BERINTHIA. Positively—he fell in love at the play.   5

AMANDA. Right—the very same—but who could have told you this?

BERINTHIA. Um——O—Townly!——I suppose your husband has made him his confidant.

AMANDA. O base Loveless!—and what did Townly say on't?

BERINTHIA. So, so—why should she ask that?——[*aside*]——say!—   10
why he abused Loveless extremely, and said all the tender things of you in the world.

AMANDA. Did he?—Oh! my heart!—I'm very ill—I must go to my chamber—dear Berinthia, don't leave me a moment.   [*Exit.*

BERINTHIA. No—don't fear.——So—there is certainly some affection 15
on her side at least, towards Townly. If it prove so, and her agreeable husband perseveres—Heav'n send me resolution!—well—how this business will end I know not—but I seem to be in as fair a way to lose my gallant Colonel, as a boy is to be a rogue, when he's put clerk to an attorney.   [*Exit.* 20

SCENE III, *a Country House*

Enter YOUNG FASHION *and* LORY.

Y. FASHION. So—here's our inheritance, Lory, if we can but get into possession—but methinks the seat of our family looks like Noah's ark, as if the chief part on't were designed for the fowls of the air, and the 25
beasts of the field.

LORY. Pray, sir, don't let your head run upon the orders of building here—get but the heiress, let the devil take the house.

Y. FASHION. Get but the house! let the devil take the heiress, I say—but come, we have no time to squander, knock at the door—   30
                                    [LORY *knocks two or three times.*
What the devil have they got no ears in this house?—knock harder.

LORY. I'gad, sir, this will prove some inchanted castle—we shall have the giant come out by and by with his club, and beat our brains out.
                                                      [*knocks again.* 35

Y. FASHION. Hush—they come—[*from within*] who is there?

LORY. Open the door and see—is that your country breeding?—

SERVANT. [*within*] Ay, but two words to that bargain—Tummas, is the blunderbuss prim'd?

Y. FASHION. Ouns! give 'em good words Lory—or we shall be shot here 40
a fortune catching.

13 my] *L, Rel., I;* the *81*   25 on't] *I,81, Rel.;* of it *L*   40 or] *81, I; om. L, Rel.*

LORY. Egad sir, I think you're in the right on't—ho!—Mr. what d'ye callum—will you please to let us in? or are we to be left to grow like willows by your moat side?

> [SERVANT *appears at the window with a blunderbuss.*

SERVANT. Weel naw, what's ya're business?   5

Y. FASHION. Nothing, sir, but to wait upon Sir Tunbelly, with your leave.

SERVANT. To weat upon Sir Tunbelly?—why you'll find that's just as Sir Tunbelly pleases.

Y. FASHION. But will you do me the favour, sir, to know whether Sir Tunbelly pleases or not?   10

SERVANT. Why look you d'ye see, with good words much may be done.—Ralph, go thy waes, and ask Sir Tunbelly if he pleases to be waited upon —and dost hear? call to nurse that she may lock up Miss Hoyden before the geats open.

Y. FASHION. D'ye hear that Lory?   15

Enter SIR TUNBELLY, *with Servants, armed with guns, clubs, pitchforks, &c.*

LORY. O (*Running behind his master*) O Lord, O Lord, Lord, we are both dead men.

Y. FASHION. Take heed fool, thy fear will ruin us.

LORY. My fear, sir, 'sdeath, sir, I fear nothing—[*aside*] would I were well 20
up to the chin in a horse pond.

SIR TUNBELLY. Who is it here has any business with me?

Y. FASHION. Sir, 'tis I, if your name be Sir Tunbelly Clumsey?

SIR TUNBELLY. Sir, my name is Sir Tunbelly Clumsy, whether you have any business with me or not—so you see I am not asham'd of my 25
name, nor my face either.

Y. FASHION. Sir, you have no cause that I know of.

SIR TUNBELLY. Sir, if you have no cause either, I desire to know who you are; for 'till I know your name, I shan't ask you to come into my house: and when I do know your name, 'tis six to four I don't ask you then.   30

Y. FASHION. [*Giving him a Letter*] Sir, I hope you'll find this letter an authentic passport.

SIR TUNBELLY. Cod's my life, from Mrs. Coupler.—I ask your Lordship's pardon ten thousand times—[*to his Servant*]—Here, run in a doors quickly; get a Scotch coal fire in the great parlour—set all the Turkey 35
work chairs in their places; get the brass candlesticks out, and be sure stick the socket full of laurel, run—[*turning to* YOUNG FASHION] My Lord, I ask your Lordship's pardon—[*to* SERVANT] and do you hear, run away to nurse, bid her let Miss Hoyden loose again. [*Exit* SERVANT.

---

2 left] *81, L*; left here *I*   6 sir] *81, Rel., I; om. L*   17 O] *81; om. L, I,* O
Lord, Lord, we] *81*; O Lord, O Lord, we *L*; O, O Lord, Lord, we *I*   20 fear,
sir] *81, Rel., I*; fear *L*   23 I] *81, Rel., I*; me *L*   be] *81, Rel., I*; is *L*
34 *Servant*] *81, I; servants L, Rel.*   36 brass] *81, I*; great Brass *L*

[*To* YOUNG FASHION] I hope your honour will excuse the disorder of my family—we are not used to receive men of your Lordship's great quality every day—pray where are your coaches and servants, my Lord?

Y. FASHION. Sir, that I might give you and your fair daughter a proof how impatient I am to be nearer akin to you, I left my equipage to follow   5
me, and came away post with only one servant.

SIR TUNBELLY. Your Lordship does me too much honour—It was exposing your person to too much fatigue and danger, I protest it was—but my daughter shall endeavour to make you what amends she can—and tho' I say it, that should not say it, Hoyden has charms.   10

Y. FASHION. Sir, I am not a stranger to them, tho' I am to her: common fame has done her justice.

SIR TUNBELLY. My Lord, I am common Fame's very grateful humble servant.—My Lord, my girl's young—Hoyden is young, my Lord; but this I must say for her, what she wants in art, she has by nature—   15
what she wants in experience, she has in breeding—and what's wanting in her age, is made good in her constitution—so pray, my Lord, walk in; pray, my Lord, walk in.

Y. FASHION. Sir, I wait upon you.   [*Exeunt thro' the gate.*

MISS HOYDEN *sola.*   20

MISS. Sure, nobody was ever used as I am. I know well enough what other girls do, for all they think to make a fool of me. It's well I have a husband a-coming, or I'cod I'd marry the baker, I would so.—Nobody can knock at the gate, but presently I must be lock'd up—and here's the young greyhound can run loose about the house all the day long, so she   25
can.—'Tis very well——

[NURSE, *without opening the door.*]

NURSE. Miss Hoyden, Miss, Miss, Miss, Miss Hoyden!

Enter NURSE.

MISS. Well, what do you make such a noise for, ha?—what do you din a   30
body's ears for?—can't one be at quiet for you?

NURSE. What do I din your ears for?—here's one come will din your ears for you.

MISS. What care I who's come?—I care not a fig who comes, nor who goes, as long as I must be lock'd up like the ale cellar.   35

NURSE. That, Miss, is for fear you should be drank before you are ripe.

MISS. O don't you trouble your head about that, I'm as ripe as you, though not so mellow.

NURSE. Very well—now I have a good mind to lock you up again, and not let you see my Lord tonight.   40

4 fair] *L*; *om. 81, I*   10 it] *81, I*; *om. L*   18 pray . . . in] *81, I*; *om. L*
19 *thro' the gate*] *81, I*; *om. L*   21 nobody was ever] *81, I*; never nobody was *L*

MISS. My Lord! why is my husband come?

NURSE. Yes, marry is he, and a goodly person too.

MISS. [*Hugging* NURSE] O my dear nurse, forgive me this once, and I'll never misuse you again; no, if I do, you shall give me three thumps on the back, and a great pinch by the cheek.   5

NURSE. Ah! the poor thing, see how it melts, it's as full of good nature as an egg's full of meat.

MISS. But my dear Nurse, don't lie now, is he come by your troth?

NURSE. Yes, by my truly is he.

MISS. O Lord! I'll go and put on my laced tucker, tho' I'm lock'd up a   10
month for't.   [*Exit running.*

END OF THE THIRD ACT

ACT IV

SCENE I

Enter MISS HOYDEN *and* NURSE.   15

NURSE. Well, Miss, how do you like your husband that is to be?

MISS. O Lord, Nurse, I'm so overjoy'd, I can scarce contain myself.

NURSE. O but you must have a care of being too fond, for men now-a-days, hate a woman that loves 'em.

MISS. Love him! Why do you think I love him, Nurse? I'cod, I would   20
not care if he was hang'd, so I were but once married to him.—No, that which pleases me, is to think what work I'll make when I get to London; for when I am a wife and a Lady both, I'cod I'll flaunt it with the best of 'em. Aye, and I shall have money enough to do so too, Nurse.

NURSE. Ah! there's no knowing that Miss, for though these Lords have   25
a power of wealth, indeed, yet, as I have heard say, they give it all to their sluts and their trulls, who joggle it about in their coaches, with a murrain to 'em, whilst poor Madam sits sighing and wishing, and has not a spare half crown to buy her a Practice of Piety.

MISS. O, but for that, don't deceive yourself, Nurse, for this I must say   30
of my Lord, he's as free as an open house at Christmas. For this very morning he told me, I should have six hundred a year to buy pins. Now, Nurse, if he gives me six hundred a year to buy pins, what do you think he'll give me to buy fine petticoats?

NURSE. Ah, my dearest, he deceives thee foul[l]y, and he's no better than   35
a rogue for his pains. These Londoners have got a gibberage with 'em,

10 and] *81, I*; *om. L, Rel.*   21 if] *81, L*; *om. I*   36 got] *81, I*; got such *L*

would confound a gipsey. That which they call pin-money, is to buy their wives every thing in the versal world, down to their very shoe-knots.—Nay, I have heard folks say, that some ladies, if they will have gallants, as they call 'em, are forced to find them out of their pin-money too. But, look, look, if his Honor be not coming to you.—Now, if I 5
were sure you would behave yourself handsomely, and not disgrace me that have brought you up, I'd leave you alone together.

MISS. That's my best Nurse, do as you'd be done by—trust us together this once, and if I don't shew my breeding, may I never be married but die an old maid. 10

NURSE. Well, this once I'll venture you.—But if you disparage me——

MISS. Never fear. [*Exit* NURSE.

Enter Y. FASHION.

Y. FASHION. Your servant, Madam, I'm glad to find you alone, for I have something of importance to speak to you about. 15

MISS. Sir, (my Lord, I meant) you may speak to me about what you please, I shall give you a civil answer.

Y. FASHION. You give me so obliging a one, it encourages me to tell you in a few words, what I think both for your interest and mine. Your father, I suppose you know, has resolved to make me happy in being 20 your husband, and I hope I may depend on your consent to perform what he desires.

MISS. Sir, I never disobey my father in any thing but eating green gooseberries.

Y. FASHION. So good a daughter must needs be an admirable wife.—I 25 am therefore impatient till you are mine, and hope you will so far consider the violence of my love, that you won't have the cruelty to defer my happiness so long as your father designs it.

MISS. Pray, my Lord, how long is that?

Y. FASHION. Madam—a thousand years—a whole week. 30

MISS. A week!—Why I shall be an old woman by that time.

Y. FASHION. And I an old man.

MISS. Why I thought it was to be to-morrow morning, as soon as I was up. I'm sure nurse told me so.

Y. FASHION. And it shall be to-morrow morning, if you'll consent? 35

MISS. If I'll consent! Why I thought I was to obey you as my husband?

Y. FASHION. That's when we are married. Till then I'm to obey you

MISS. Why then if we are to take it by turns, it's the same thing. I'll obey you now, and when we are married you shall obey me.

2 versal] *81, I*; Varsal *L*   9–10 never . . . maid] *81, I*; never be married *L*; be twice Married and die a Maid *Rel.*   19 a] *81, I*; *om. L, Rel.*   23 eating] *81, I*; eating of *L, Rel.*   30 years] *81, I*; year *L, Rel.*   35 morning] *81, I*; morning still *L, Rel.*   38 if we are] *I, 81, Rel.*; are we *L*

Y. FASHION. With all my heart. But I doubt we must get Nurse on our side, or we shall hardly prevail with the Chaplain.

MISS. No more we shan't indeed, for he loves her better than he loves his pulpit, and would always be a-preaching to her by his good will.

Y. FASHION. Why then, my dear, if you'll call her hither, we'll try to 5 persuade her presently.

MISS. O Lord, I can tell you a way how to perswade her to any thing.

Y. FASHION. How's that?

MISS. Why tell her she's a handsome, comely woman, and give her half-a-crown. 10

Y. FASHION. Nay, if that will do, she shall have half a score of them.

MISS. O Gemini, for half that she'd marry you herself.—I'll run and call her. [*Exit.*

Y. FASHION. Soh, matters go swimmingly. This is a rare girl I'faith. I shall have a fine time on't with her at London. But no matter—she 15 brings me an estate will afford me a separate maintenance.

Enter LORY.

Y. FASHION. So, Lory, what's the matter?

LORY. Here, Sir; an intercepted packet from the enemy—your brother's postillion brought it—I knew the livery, pretended to be a servant of Sir 20 Tunbelly's, and so got possession of the letter.

Y. FASHION. [*Looking at it.*] Ouns!—He tells Sir Tunbelly here, that he will be with him this evening, with a large party to supper,—'egad! I must marry the girl directly.

LORY. O Zounds, Sir, directly to be sure! Here she comes. 25
[*Exit* LORY.

Y. FASHION. And the old Jesabel with her. She has a thorough procuring countenance, however.

Enter MISS HOYDEN *and* NURSE.

Y. FASHION. How do you do, Mrs. Nurse?—I desired your young lady 30 would give me leave to see you, that I might thank you for your extraordinary care and conduct in her education; pray accept of this small acknowledgement for it at present, and depend upon my farther kindness when I shall be that happy thing her husband.

NURSE. [*Aside.*] Gold by Maakins!—Your Honour's goodness is too 35 great. Alas! all I can boast of is, I gave her pure good milk, and so your Honour would have said, an you had seen how the poor thing thrived— and how it would look up in my face—and crow and laugh it would!

2 with] *81, Rel.*; on *L*   15 But] *81, I, Rel.*; *om. L*   23 to supper] *81, I*; *om. L*   27 old] *81, I*; young *L*   28 countenance] *81, I*; countess *L*   30 do] *81, I*; do, good *L*   35 Maakins!] *81, I*; makings *Rel.*; the Akins *L*

MISS. [*To* NURSE, *taking her angrily aside.*] Pray one word with you·
Prithee, Nurse, don't stand ripping up old stories, to make one ashamed
before one's love; do you think such a fine, proper gentleman as he is,
cares for a fiddle-come tale of a child? If you have a mind to make him
have a good opinion of a woman, don't tell him what one did then, tell 5
him what one can do now. [*To him*]. I hope your Honour will excuse my
miss-manners, to whisper before you, it was only to give some orders
about the family.

Y. FASHION. O every thing, Madam, is to give way to business; besides,
good housewifery is a very commendable quality in a young lady. 10

MISS. Pray, Sir, are young ladies good housewives at London town? Do
they darn their own linnen.

Y. FASHION. O no;—they study how to spend money, not to save it.

MISS. I'cod, I don't know but that may be better sport, ha, Nurse!

Y. FASHION. Well, you shall have your choice when you come there. 15

MISS. Shall I?—then by my troth I'll get there as fast as I can. [*To*
NURSE.] His Honour desires you'll be so kind, as to let us be married
to-morrow.

NURSE. To-morrow, my dear Madam?

Y. FASHION. Aye faith, Nurse, you may well be surprised at Miss's 20
wanting to put it off so long—to-morrow! no, no,—'tis now, this very
hour, I would have the ceremony perform'd.

MISS. I'cod with all my heart.

NURSE. O mercy, worse and worse.

Y. FASHION. Yes, sweet Nurse, now, and privately. For all things being 25
signed and sealed, why should Sir Tunbelly make us stay a week for a
wedding dinner?

NURSE. But if you should be married now, what will you do when Sir
Tunbelly calls for you to be wedded?

MISS. Why then we will be married again. 30

NURSE. What twice, my child!

MISS. I'cod, I don't care how often I'm married, not I.

NURSE. Well—I'm such a tender hearted fool, I find I can refuse you
nothing. So you shall e'en follow your own inventions.

MISS. Shall I?—[*Aside.*] O Lord I could leap over the Moon. 35

Y. FASHION. Dear Nurse, this goodness of yours shall be still more
rewarded. But now you must employ your power with the Chaplain,
that he may do his friendly office too, and then we shall be all happy.
Do you think you can prevail with him?

NURSE. Prevail with him!—Or he shall never prevail with me, I can tell 40
him that.

Y. FASHION. I'm glad to hear it; however, to strengthen your interest

13 it] *L*; *om. 81, I*   14 ha] *81, I*; than t'other *L*   22 would] *81, I*; could *L*
36–7 yours . . . rewarded] *L*; your's shan't go unrewarded *81, Rel., I*

with him, you may let him know, I have several fat livings in my gift, and that the first that falls shall be in your disposal.

NURSE. Nay then, I'll make him marry more folks than one, I'll promise him.

MISS. Faith do, Nurse, make him marry you too, I'm sure he'll do't for   5
a fat living.

Y. FASHION. Well, Nurse, while you go and settle matters with him, your lady and I will go and take a walk in the garden.   [*Exit* NURSE.

Y. FASHION. [*Giving her his hand.*] Come, Madam, dare you venture yourself alone with me?   10

MISS. O dear, yes, Sir, I don't think you'll do any thing to me I need be afraid on.   [*Exeunt.*

SCENE II

Enter AMANDA, *her* WOMAN *following.*

MAID. If you please, Madam, only to say whether you'll have me buy   15
them or not?

AMANDA. Yes—no—go—Teazer!—I care not what you do—prithee leave me.   [*Exit* MAID.

Enter BERINTHIA.

BERINTHIA. What, in the name of Jove's the matter with you?   20

AMANDA. The matter, Berinthia? I'm almost mad; I'm plagued to death.

BERINTHIA. Who is it that plagues you?

AMANDA. Who do you think should plague a wife, but her husband?

BERINTHIA. O ho! is it come to that?—we shall have you with yourself a widow, by and bye.   25

AMANDA. Would I were any thing but what I am!—a base, ungrateful man, to use me thus!

BERINTHIA. What, has he given you fresh reason to suspect his wandering?

AMANDA. Every hour gives me reason.   30

BERINTHIA. And yet, Amanda, you perhaps at this moment cause in another's breast the same tormenting doubts and jealousies which you feel so sensibly yourself.

AMANDA. Heaven knows I would not!

BERINTHIA. Why, you can't tell but there may be some one as tenderly   35
attached to Townly, whom you boast of as your conquest, as you can be to your husband.

3 one, I'll] *81, Rel., I*; one *I, L*   10 alone] *81, Rel., I*; along *L*   12 *Exeunt*]
81, Rel., I; *Exit L*   28 reason] *81, L*; reasons *I*   34 Heaven knows] *81,
I*; Heavens *L*

AMANDA. I'm sure I never encouraged his pretensions.

BERINTHIA. Pshaw! Pshaw!—No sensible man ever perseveres to love, without encouragement. Why have you not treated him as you have Lord Foppington?

AMANDA. Because he has not presum'd so far. But let us drop the subject. 5
Men, not women, are riddles. Mr. Loveless now follows some flirt for variety, whom I'm sure he does not like so well as he does me.

BERINTHIA. That's more than you know, Madam.

AMANDA. Why, do you know the ugly thing?

BERINTHIA. I think I can guess at the person—but she's no such ugly 10 thing neither.

AMANDA. Is she very handsome?

BERINTHIA. Truly I think so.

AMANDA. Whate'er she be, I'm sure he does not like her well enough to bestow any thing more than a little outward gallantry upon her. 15

BERINTHIA. [*Aside.*] Outward gallantry.—I can't bear this.—Come, come, don't you be too secure, Amanda; while you suffer Townly to imagine that you do not detest him for his designs on you, you have no right to complain that your husband is engaged elsewhere. But here comes the person we were speaking of. 20

Enter TOWNLY.

TOWNLY. Ladies, as I come uninvited, I beg, if I intrude you will use the same freedom in turning me out again.

AMANDA. I believe, sir, it is near the time Mr. Loveless said he would be at home. He talked of accepting Lord Foppington's invitation to sup at 25 Sir Tunbelly Clumsey's.

TOWNLY. His Lordship has done me the honor to invite me also. If you'll let me escort you, I'll let you into a mystery as we go, in which you must play a part when we arrive.

AMANDA. But we have two hours yet to spare—the carriages are not 30 ordered 'till eight—and it is not a five minutes drive. So, Cousin, let us keep the Colonel to play piquet with us, till Mr. Loveless comes home.

BERINTHIA. As you please, Madam, but you know I have letters to write.

TOWNLY. Madam, you know you may command me, tho' I'm a very 35 wretched gamester.

AMANDA. O, you play well enough to lose your money, and that's all the ladies require—and so without any more ceremony, let us go into the next room and call for cards and candles. [*Exeunt.*

25 accepting] *L*; accepting of *81, I*   26 Clumsey's] *81, I*; Clumsey *L*   28 we]
L, I; me *81*   30 are] *81, I*; were *L*   34 letters] *L*; a letter *81, I*   35 very]
81, I; om. *L*

SCENE III

Enter LOVELESS.

LOVELESS. So—thus far all's well—I have got into her dressing-room, and it being dusk, I think nobody has perceived me steal into the house. 5 I heard Berinthia tell my wife she had some particular letters to write this evening, before we went to Sir Tunbelly's, and here are the implements for correspondence—how shall I muster up assurance to shew myself when she comes?—I think she has given me encouragement— and to do my impudence justice, I have made the most of it.—I hear a 10 door open and some one coming; if it should be my wife, what the Devil should I say?—I believe she mistrusts me, and by my life I don't deserve her tenderness; however I am determined to reform, tho' not yet. Hah!—Berinthia—so I'll step in here till I see what sort of humour she is in.   [*Goes into the Closet.* 15

Enter BERINTHIA.

BERINTHIA. Was ever so provoking a situation!—To think I should sit and hear him compliment Amanda to my face!—I have lost all patience with them both. I would not for something have Loveless know what temper of mind they have piqued me into, yet I can't bear to leave them 20 together. No—I'll put my papers away, and return, to disappoint them. [*Goes to the closet.*] O Lord! a ghost! a ghost! a ghost!

Enter LOVELESS.

LOVELESS. Peace, my Angel—it's no ghost—but one worth a hundred spirits.   25
BERINTHIA. How, sir, have you had the insolence to presume to——run in again—here's somebody coming.

Enter MAID.

MAID. O Lord, Ma'am, what's the matter?
BERINTHIA. O Heav'ns I'm almost frightened out of my wits!—I 30 thought verily I had seen a ghost, and 'twas nothing but a black hood pin'd against the wall.—You may go again, I am the fearfullest fool! [*Exit* MAID.

Re-enter LOVELESS.

LOVELESS. Is the coast clear?   35

5 it] *81, I*; it's *L*   7 the] *81, I*; her *L*   14 of] *81, I*; of a *L*   22 a ghost! a ghost! a ghost!] *81, I*; a Ghost! a Ghost! a Ghost, a Ghost. *L*   27 coming] *81, I, Rel.*; a coming *L*

BERINTHIA. The coast clear!—Upon my word I wonder at your assurance!

LOVELESS. Why then you wonder before I have given you a proof of it. But where's my wife?

BERINTHIA. At cards. 5

LOVELESS. With whom?

BERINTHIA. With Townly.

LOVELESS. Then we are safe enough.

BERINTHIA. You are so!—Some husbands would be of another mind were he at cards with their wives. 10

LOVELESS. And they'd be in the right on't too—but I dare trust mine.

BERINTHIA. Indeed!—And she, I doubt not, has the same confidence in you. Yet do you think she'd be content to come and find you here?

LOVELESS. 'Egad, as you say, that's true—then for fear she should come, hadn't we better go into the next room out of her way? 15

BERINTHIA. What—in the dark?

LOVELESS. Aye—or with a light, which you please.

BERINTHIA. You are certainly very impudent.

LOVELESS. Nay then—let me conduct you, my Angel.

BERINTHIA. Hold, hold, you are mistaken in your Angel, I assure you. 20

LOVELESS. I hope not, for by this hand I swear.

BERINTHIA. Come, come, let go my hand, or I shall hate you, I'll cry out as I live.

LOVELESS. Impossible!—you cannot be so cruel.

BERINTHIA. Ha!—here's some one coming—be gone instantly. 25

LOVELESS. Will you promise to return if I remain here?

BERINTHIA. Never trust myself in a room with you again while I live.

LOVELESS. But I have something particular to communicate to you.

BERINTHIA. Well, well, before we go to Sir Tunbelly's I'll walk upon the lawn. If you are fond of a Moon-light evening, you will find me 30 there.

LOVELESS. E'faith, they're coming here now.—I take you at your word.

[*Exit* LOVELESS *into the Closet.*

BERINTHIA. 'Tis Amanda, as I live—I hope she has not heard his voice. Tho' I mean she should have her share of jealousy in turn. 35

Enter AMANDA.

AMANDA. Berinthia, why did you leave me?

BERINTHIA. I thought I only spoil'd your party.

AMANDA. Since you have been gone, Townly has attempted to renew his importunities.——I must break with him—for I cannot venture to 40 acquaint Mr. Loveless with his conduct.

24 cannot] *81, I*; could not *L*   34 'Tis] *81, I*; His *L*   heard his] *L, I*; hheard s
81   35 her] *L, I*; er *81*   38 spoil'd] *81, I*; spoilt *L*

BERINTHIA. O no—Mr. Loveless mustn't know of it by any means.

AMANDA. O not for the world.——I wish, Berinthia, you would undertake to speak to Townly on the subject.

BERINTHIA. Upon my word it would be a very pleasant subject for me to
talk to him on.—But come—let us go back,—and you may depend on't   5
I'll not leave you together again, if I can help it.   [*Exeunt.*

Enter LOVELESS.

LOVELESS. Soh—so!—a pretty piece of business I have over-heard—
Townly makes love to my wife—and I'm not to know it for the world—
I must enquire into this—and, by Heav'n, if I find that Amanda has in   10
the smallest degree——Yet what have I been at here?—O s'death!
that's no rule.

> That wife alone, unsullied credit wins,
> Whose virtues can atone her husband's sins;
> Thus while the man has other nymphs in view,   15
> It suits the woman to be doubly true.   [*Exit.*

END OF THE FOURTH ACT

ACT V

SCENE I

A Garden—Moon Light   20

Enter LOVELESS.

LOVELESS. Now, does she mean to make a fool of me, or not?—I shan't
wait much longer, for my wife will soon be enquiring for me to set out
on our supping party.—Suspence is at all times the devil—but of all
modes of suspence, the watching for a loitering mistress is the worst— 25
but let me accuse her no longer—she approaches with one smile to
o'erpay the anxiety of a year.

Enter BERINTHIA.

O Berinthia, what a world of kindness are you in my debt!—had you
staid five minutes longer—   30

BERINTHIA. You would have been gone, I suppose.

LOVELESS. [*Aside.*] Egad she's right enough.

BERINTHIA. And I assure you 'twas ten to one that I came at all. In
short, I begin to think you are too dangerous a Being to trifle with; and

as I shall probably only make a fool of you at last, I believe we had better let matters rest as they are.

LOVELESS. You cannot mean it sure?

BERINTHIA. No!—why do you think you are really so irresistable, and master of so much address, as to deprive a woman of her senses in a few days acquaintance? 5

LOVELESS. O, no, Madam; 'tis only by your preserving your senses that I can hope to be admitted into your favour—your taste, judgment, and discernment, are what I build my hopes on.

BERINTHIA. Very modest upon my word—and it certainly follows, that the greatest proof I can give of my possessing those qualities, would be my admiring Mr. Loveless! 10

LOVELESS. O that were so cold a proof—

BERINTHIA. What shall I do more?—esteem you?

LOVELESS. O, no—worse and worse.—Can you behold a man, whose every faculty your attractions have engrossed—whose whole soul, as by enchantment, you have seiz'd on—can you see him tremble at your feet, and talk of so poor a return as your esteem! 15

BERINTHIA. What more would you have me give to a married man?

LOVELESS. How doubly cruel to remind me of misfortunes! 20

BERINTHIA. A misfortune to be married to so charming a woman as Amanda!

LOVELESS. I grant all her merit, but—'sdeath, now see what you have done by talking of her—she's here by all that's unlucky.

BERINTHIA. O Ged, we had both better get out of the way, for I should feel as aukward to meet her as you. 25

LOVELESS. Aye—but if I mistake not, I see Townly coming this way also —I must see a little into this matter. [*Steps aside*]

BERINTHIA. O, if that's your intention—I am no woman if I suffer myself to be outdone in curiosity. [*goes on the other side.* 30

Enter AMANDA.

AMANDA. Mr. Loveless come home and walking on the lawn!—I will not suffer him to walk so late, tho' perhaps it is to shew his neglect of me ——Mr. Loveless—ha!—Townly again!—how I am persecuted!

Enter TOWNLY. 35

TOWNLY. Madam, you seem disturbed!

AMANDA. Sir, I have reason.

TOWNLY. Whatever be the cause, I would to Heaven it were in my power to bear the pain, or to remove the malady.

AMANDA. Your interference can only add to my distress. 40

13 O] *81, I; om. L* 20 misfortunes] *81, L*; a misfortune *I* 29 if I] *L, I*; if *81*

TOWNLY. Ah! Madam, if it be the sting of unrequited love you suffer
from, seek for your remedy in revenge—weigh well the strength and
beauty of your charms, and rouse up that spirit a woman ought to bear
—disdain the false embraces of a husband—see at your feet a real lover
—his zeal may give him title to your pity, altho' his merit cannot claim   5
your love!

LOVELESS. [Aside] So, so, very fine, e'faith!

AMANDA. Why do you presume to talk to me thus?—is this your friendship to Mr. Loveless?—I perceive you will compel me at last to
acquaint him with your treachery.   10

TOWNLY. He could not upbraid me if you were—he deserves it from me
—for he has not been more false to you, than faithless to me.

AMANDA. To you!

TOWNLY. Yes, Madam; the lady for whom he now deserts those charms
which he was never worthy of, was mine by right; and I imagined too,   15
by inclination—Yes, Madam, Berinthia, who now——

AMANDA. Berinthia!—impossible!—

TOWNLY. 'Tis true, or may I never merit your attention.—She is the
deceitful sorceress who now holds your husband's heart in bondage.

AMANDA. I will not believe it.   20

TOWNLY. By the faith of a true lover, I speak from conviction.—This
very day I saw them together, and overheard——

AMANDA. Peace, Sir, I will not even listen to such slander—this is a poor
device to work on my resentment, to listen to your insidious addresses.
No, Sir; though Mr. Loveless may be capable of error, I am convinced   25
I cannot be deceived so grossly in him, as to believe what you now
report; and for Berinthia, you should have fixed on some more probable
person for my rival, than she who is my relation, and my friend: for
while I am myself free from guilt, I will never believe that love can
beget injury, or confidence create ingratitude.   30

TOWNLY. If I do not prove this to you——

AMANDA. You never shall have an opportunity—from the artful manner
in which you first shew'd yourself attentive to me, I might have been
led, as far as virtue permitted, to have thought you less criminal than
unhappy—but this last unmanly artifice merits at once my resentment   35
and contempt.   [Exit.

TOWNLY. Sure there's divinity about her; and she has dispensed some
portion of honor's light to me: yet can I bear to lose Berinthia without
revenge or compensation?—Perhaps she is not so culpable as I thought
her. I was mistaken when I began to think lightly of Amanda's virtue,   40
and may be in my censure of my Berinthia.—Surely I love her still; for
I feel I should be happy to find myself in the wrong.   [Exit.

15 was never] 81, I ne'er was L   imagined] 81, I; imagine L   33 attentive] L;
om. 81, I   41 my Berinthia] 81, I; Berinthia L

Enter LOVELESS *and* BERINTHIA.

BERINTHIA. Your servant, Mr. Loveless.

LOVELESS. Your servant, Madam.

BERINTHIA. Pray, what do you think of this?

LOVELESS. Truly, I don't know what to say.   5

BERINTHIA. Don't you think we steal forth two very contemptible creatures?

LOVELESS. Why tolerably so I must confess.

BERINTHIA. And do you conceive it possible for you ever to give Amanda the least uneasiness again?   10

LOVELESS. No, I think we never should, indeed.

BERINTHIA. We!—why, monster, you don't pretend that I ever entertain'd a thought.

LOVELESS. Why then, sincerely, and honestly, Berinthia, there is something in my wife's conduct which strikes me so forcibly, that if it 15
were not for shame, and the fear of hurting you in her opinion, I swear I would follow her, confess my error, and trust to her generosity for forgiveness.

BERINTHIA. Nay, prithee don't let your respect for me prevent you; for as my object in trifling with you was nothing more than to pique 20
Townly; and as I perceive he has been actuated by a similar motive, you may depend on't I shall make no mystery of the matter to him.

LOVELESS. By no means inform him—for tho' I may chuse to pass by his conduct without resentment, how will he presume to look me in the face again!   25

BERINTHIA. How will you presume to look him in the face again?

LOVELESS. He—who has dared to attempt the honour of my wife!

BERINTHIA. You—who have dared to attempt the honour of his mistress!—Come, come, be ruled by me who affect more levity than I have, and don't think of anger in this cause. A Readiness to resent injuries, 30
is a virtue only in those who are slow to injure.

LOVELESS. Then I will be ruled by you—and when you shall think proper to undeceive Townly, may your good qualities make as sincere a convert of him, as Amanda's have of me. When truth's extorted from us, then we own the robe of virtue is a graceful habit.   35

> Could women but our secret counsels scan—
> Could they but read the deep reserve of man—
> To keep our love—they'd rate their virtue high—
> They'd live together, and together die!   [*Exit.*

6 very] *L*; *om. 81, I*   8 tolerably so] *L, I*; tolerable—so *81*   17 error] *81,*
I; folly *L*   30 and] *81, I*; *om. L*   32 I will] *81, L*; will I *I*   34 extorted]
L; extended *81, I*   35 graceful] *L*; secret *81*; sacred *I*   37 read] *L*; reach
81, I   38 their] *81, L*; our *I*   39 They'd] *L*; They *81, I*

SCENE II—Sir Tunbelly's House

Enter MISS HOYDEN, NURSE, *and* Y. FASHION.

Y. FASHION. This quick dispatch of the chaplain's I take so kindly, it shall give him claim to my favour as long as I live, I assure you.

MISS. And to mine too, I promise you. 5

NURSE. I most humbly thank your honors; and may your children swarm about you, like bees about a honey-comb.

MISS. I'cod with all my heart—the more the merrier, I say—ha Nurse?

Enter LORY, *taking* Y. FASHION *hastily aside.*

LORY. One word with you, for Heav'ns sake. 10

Y. FASHION. What the Devil's the matter?

LORY. Sir, your fortune's ruin'd, if you are not married—yonder's your brother, arrived with two coaches and six horses, twenty footmen, and a coat worth fourscore pounds—so judge what will become of your Lady's heart. 15

Y. FASHION. Is he in the house yet?

LORY. No—they are capitulating with him at the gate—Sir Tunbelly luckily takes him for an impostor, and I have told him that we had heard of this plot before.

Y. FASHION. That's right: [*to* MISS] my dear, here's a troublesome 20 business my man tells me of, but don't be frighten'd, we shall be too hard for the rogue.—Here's an impudent fellow at the gate (not knowing I was come hither incognito) has taken my name upon him, in hopes to run away with you.

MISS. O the brazen-faced varlet, it's well we are married, or may be we 25 might never have been so.

Y. FASHION. [*Aside.*] Egad like enough.—Prithee, Nurse, run to Sir Tunbelly, and stop him from going to the gate before I speak with him.

NURSE. An't please your honour, my Lady and I had best lock ourselves up till the danger be over. 30

Y. FASHION. Do so, if you please.

MISS. Not so fast—I won't be lock'd up any more, now I'm married.

Y. FASHION. Yes, pray, my dear do, till we have seiz'd this rascal.

MISS. Nay, if you'll pray me, I'll do any thing. [*Exit* MISS *and* NURSE.

Y. FASHION. [*To* LORY.] Hark you, sirrah, things are better than you 35 imagine. The wedding's over.

LORY. [*Aside.*] The Devil it is, Sir!

Y. FASHION. Not a word—all's safe—but Sir Tunbelly don't know it, nor must not, yet. So I am resolved to brazen the business out, and have

20 *to* MISS] *81, I; om. L*   34 you'll] *81, I; you L*

the pleasure of turning the imposture upon his Lordship, which I
believe may easily be done.

Enter SIR TUNBELLY, *and* SERVANTS, *armed with clubs, pitch-forks, &c.*

Y. FASHION. Did you ever hear, Sir, of so impudent an undertaking?

SIR TUNBELLY. Never, by the Mass—but we'll tickle him, I'll warrant 5
you.

Y. FASHION. They tell me, Sir, he has a great many people with him,
disguised like servants.

SIR TUNBELLY. Ay, ay, rogues enow—but we have master'd them.—
We only fired a few shot over their heads, and the regiment scower'd 10
in an instant.—Here, Tommas, bring in your prisoner.

Y. FASHION. If you please, Sir Tunbelly, it will be best for me not to
confront the fellow yet, till you have heard how far his impudence will
carry him.

SIR TUNBELLY. 'Egad, your Lordship is an ingenious person. Your 15
Lordship then will please to step aside.

LORY. [*Aside.*] 'Fore Heaven I applaud my master's modesty.

[*Exe.* YOUNG FASHION *and* LORY.

Enter SERVANTS, *with* LORD FOPPINGTON, *disarmed.*

SIR TUNBELLY. Come—bring him along, bring him along. 20

LD. FOPPINGTON. What the pax do you mean, gentlemen, is it fair time
that you are all drunk before supper?

SIR TUNBELLY. Drunk, sirrah!—here's an impudent rogue for you.
Drunk, or sober, bully, I'm a Justice of the Peace, and know how to
deal with strollers. 25

LD. FOPPINGTON. Strollers!

SIR TUNBELLY. Aye, strollers.—Come, give an account of yourself.—
What's your name? Where do you live? Do you pay scot and lot?
Come, are you a freeholder or a copyholder?

LD. FOPPINGTON. And why dost thou ask me so many impertinent 30
questions?

SIR TUNBELLY. Because I'll make you answer 'em before I have done
with you, you rascal, you.

LD. FOPPINGTON. Before Gad, all the answer I can make to 'em, is,
that thou art a very extraordinary old fellow, stap my vitals! 35

SIR TUNBELLY. Nay, if you are for joking with Deputy Lieutenants,
we know how to deal with you.—Here, draw a warrant for him
immediately.

LD. FOPPINGTON. A warrant!—What the Devil is't thou would'st be at,
old gentleman? 40

1imposture] *I*; impostor *81, L*   3 with ... &c.] *81, I*; *om. L*   21 pax] *81, Rel., I*;
plague *L*   34 answer] *L, Rel.*; answers *81, I*   make] *81, I*; make thee *L, Rel.*
1thou art] *L*; you are *81, I*   36 you are] *L*; thou are *81*; thou art *I*

SIR TUNBELLY. I would be at you, sirrah, (if my hands were not tied as a Magistrate) and with these two double fists beat your teeth down your throat you dog you.

LD. FOPPINGTON. And why would'st thou spoil my face at that rate?

SIR TUNBELLY. For your design to rob me of my daughter, villain.   5

LD. FOPPINGTON. Rab thee of thy daughter! Now do I begin to believe I am in bed and asleep, and that all this is but a dream. Prithee, old father, wilt thou give me leave to ask thee one question?

SIR TUNBELLY. I can't tell whether I will or not, till I know what it is.

LD. FOPPINGTON. Why then it is, whether thou didst not write to my   10
Lord Foppington to come down and marry thy daughter?

SIR TUNBELLY. Yes, marry did I, and my Lord Foppington is come down, and shall marry my daughter before she's a day older.

LD. FOPPINGTON. Now give me thy hand, old dad, I thought we should understand one another at last.   15

SIR TUNBELLY. This fellow's mad—here, bind him hand and foot.

               [They bind him.

LD. FOPPINGTON. Nay, prithee Knight, leave fooling, thy jest begins to grow dull.

SIR TUNBELLY. Bind him, I say—he's mad—bread and water, a dark   20
room, and a whip, may bring him to his senses again.

LD. FOPPINGTON. Prithee, Sir Tunbelly, why should you take such an aversion to the freedom of my address, as to suffer the rascals thus to skewer down my arms like a rabbit? 'Egad, if I don't waken quickly, by all that I can see, this is like to prove one of the most impertinent   25
dreams that ever I dreamt in my life.   *[Aside.*

      Enter MISS HOYDEN *and* NURSE.

MISS. [*Going up to him.*] Is this he that would have run away with me? Fough! how he stinks of sweets![1]—Pray, father, let him be dragged thro' the horse-pond.   30

LD. FOPPINGTON. [*Aside.*] This must be my wife, by her natural inclination to her husband.

MISS. Pray, father, what do you intend to do with him—hang him?

SIR TUNBELLY. That, at least, child.

NURSE. Aye, and it's e'en too good for him too.   35

LD. FOPPINGTON. [*Aside.*] Madame la Governante, I presume; hitherto this appears to me one of the most extraordinary families that ever man of quality match'd into.

SIR TUNBELLY. What's become of my Lord, daughter?

6 Rab] *81, Rel.*; Rob *L, I*   thy] *L, I*; your *81*   do I] *81, Rel., I*; I do *L*
29 Fough!] *81, I*; faugh *L*   36 *Aside*] *81, I*; *om. L*   37 to me] *L*; to me
to be *81, Rel., I*

  ―――――――――
  [1] Scent.

MISS. He's just coming, Sir.

LD. FOPPINGTON. [*Aside.*] My Lord!—What does he mean by that, now?

Enter YOUNG FASHION *and* LORY.

LD. FOPPINGTON. Stap my vitals, Tam, now the dream's out. 5

Y. FASHION. Is this the fellow, Sir, that design'd to trick me of your daughter?

SIR TUNBELLY. This is he, my Lord; how do you like him? is not he a pretty fellow to get a fortune?

Y. FASHION. I find by his dress, he thought your daughter might be 10 taken with a beau.

MISS. O gemini! Is this a beau? Let me see him again. Ha! I find a beau is no such ugly thing, neither.

Y. FASHION. 'Egad, she'll be in love with him presently.—I'll e'en have him sent away to gaol. [*To* LORD FOP.] Sir, tho' your undertaking shews 15 you a person of no extraordinary modesty, I suppose you ha'n't confidence enough to expect much favour from me.

LD. FOPPINGTON. Strike me dumb, Tam, thou art a very impudent fellow.

NURSE. Look; if the varlot has not the frontery to call his Lordship, 20 plain Thomas.

SIR TUNBELLY. Come, is the warrant writ?

CHAPLAIN. Yes, Sir.

LD. FOPPINGTON. Hold, one moment.—Pray gentlemen—my Lord Foppington, shall I beg one word with your Lordship? 25

NURSE. O, ho, it's my Lord, with him now; see how afflictions will humble folks.

MISS. Pray, my Lord, don't let him whisper too close, lest he bite your ear off.

LD. FOPPINGTON. I am not altogether so hungry as your Ladyship is 30 pleased to imagine. [*To* Y. FASHION.] Look you, Tam, I am sensible I have not been so kind to you as I ought, but I hope you'll forgive what's past, and accept of the five thousand pounds I offer. Thou may'st live in extreme splendor with it, stap my vitals!

Y. FASHION. It's a much easier matter to prevent a disease, than to cure 35 it. A quarter of that sum would have secured your mistress, twice as much won't redeem her. [*Leaving him.*

SIR TUNBELLY. Well, what says he?

Y. FASHION. Only the rascal offered me a bribe to let him go.

SIR TUNBELLY. Aye, he shall go, with a halter to him—lead on, Con- 40 stable.

2 *Aside*] *81, I; om. L*   15 undertaking] *81*; understanding *L, Rel.*   20 varlot]
81, I; varlet *L, Rel.*   26 afflictions] *81, Rel., I;* Affliction *L*   33 accept] *L,*
Rel., I; except *81*

Enter SERVANT.

SERVANT. Sir, here is Muster Loveless, and Muster Colonel Townly, and some ladies, to wait on you.

LORY. [*Aside.*] So, Sir, What will you do now?

Y. FASHION. Be quiet—they are in the plot. [*To* SIR TUNBELLY.] Only   5
a few friends, Sir Tunbelly, whom I wish'd to introduce to you.

LD. FOPPINGTON. Thou art the most impudent fellow, Tam, that ever Nature yet brought into the world. Sir Tunbelly, strike me speechless, but these are my friends and my guests, and they will soon inform thee, whether I am the true Lord Foppington or not.   10

Enter LOVELESS, TOWNLY, AMANDA, *and* BERINTHIA.

Y. FASHION. So, gentlemen, this is friendly; I rejoice to see you.

TOWNLY. My Lord, we are fortunate to be the witnesses of your Lordship's happiness.

LOVELESS. But your Lordship will do us the honour to introduce us to   15
Sir Tunbelly Clumsey?

AMANDA. And us to your Lady.

LD. FOPPINGTON. Ged take me, but they are all in a story.

SIR TUNBELLY. Gentlemen, you do me great honour; my Lord Foppington's friends will ever be welcome to me and mine.   20

Y. FASHION. My love, let me introduce you to these ladies.

MISS. By goles,[1] they look so fine and so stiff, I am almost asham'd to come nigh 'em.

AMANDA. A most engaging young lady, indeed!

MISS. Thank ye, Ma'am!   25

BERINTHIA. And I doubt not will soon distinguish herself in the Beau Monde.

MISS. Where is that?

Y. FASHION. You'll soon learn, my dear.

LOVELESS. But, Lord Foppington——   30

LD. FOPPINGTON. Sir!

LOVELESS. Sir! I was not addressing myself to you, Sir; pray who is this gentlemen? He seems rather in a singular predicament.

SIR TUNBELLY. Ha, ha, ha!—So, these are your friends and your guests, ha, my adventurer?   35

---

2 Muster] *81, 1*; Master *L*   6 wish'd] *81*; wish *L, 1*   *After line 10, L prints*:
      SIR TUNBELLY. Well, here they come I see, let who wou'd invite them.
18 Ged] *81, 1*; Gad *L*   24 young] *L*; *om. 81, 1*   32 this] *81, 1*; the *L*
After line 33, L prints:
      TOWNLY. For so well dress'd a person a little od[d]ly Circumstanc'd Indeed
34 So] *81, 1*; *om. L*   and your] *81, 1*; and *L*   35 ha] *81, 1*; hey *L*

---

[1] By God. Lucy, in a similar situation to Miss Hoyden's, says 'Then I'll have Mr. Thomas, by goles', in Fielding's *Old Man Taught Wisdom*.

LD. FOPPINGTON. I am struck dumb with their impudence, and cannot positively say whether I shall ever speak again or not.

SIR TUNBELLY. Why, Sir, this modest gentleman wanted to pass himself upon me for Lord Foppington, and carry off my daughter.

LOVELESS. A likely plot to succeed, truly, ha, ha!　　　5

LD. FOPPINGTON. As Gad shall judge me, Loveless, I did not expect this from thee; come, prithee confess the joke; tell Sir Tunbelly that I am the real Lord Foppington, who yesterday made love to thy wife; was honour'd by her with a slap on the face, and afterward pink'd thro' the bady by thee.　　　10

SIR TUNBELLY. A likely story, truly, that a Peer wou'd behave thus!

LOVELESS. A curious fellow indeed! that wou'd scandalize the character he wants to assume; but what will you do with him, Sir Tunbelly?

SIR TUNBELLY. Commit him certainly, unless the bride and bridegroom chuse to pardon him.　　　15

LD. FOPPINGTON. Bride and bridegroom! For Gad's sake, Sir Tunbelly, 'tis tarture to me to hear you call 'em so.

MISS. Why, you ugly thing, what would you have him call us? dog and cat!

LD. FOPPINGTON. By no means, Miss; for that sounds ten times more　20
like man and wife, than t'other.

SIR TUNBELLY. A precious rogue this, to come a wooing!

Enter SERVANT.

SERVANT. There are some more gentlefolks below, to wait upon Lord Foppington.　　　25

TOWNLY. S'death, Tom, what will you do now?

LD. FOPPINGTON. Now, Sir Tunbelly, here are witnesses, who I believe are not corrupted.

SIR TUNBELLY. Peace, fellow!—Wou'd your Lordship chuse to have your guests shewn here, or shall they wait till we come to 'em?　30

Y. FASHION. I believe, Sir Tunbelly, we had better not have these visitors here yet; 'egad, all must out!　　　[*Aside.*

LOVELESS. Confess, confess, we'll stand by you.

LD. FOPPINGTON. Nay, Sir Tunbelly, I insist on your calling evidence on both sides, and if I do not prove that fellow an impostor——　35

Y. FASHION. Brother, I will save you the trouble, by now confessing, that I am not what I have passed myself for;—Sir Tunbelly, I am a gentleman, and I flatter myself a man of character; but 'tis with great pride I assure you, I am not Lord Foppington.

SIR TUNBELLY. Oun's!—what's this!—an impostor!—a cheat!—fire　40

3 this] *81, L*; the *I*　　　4 upon] *81, I*; on *L*　　　5 A . . . ha!] *I, 81*; Ha! ha! ha!—
a likely Plot to succeed truly. *L*　　　9 on] *81, I*; in *L*　　　10 bady] *I*; body *L, 81*
24–5 *These lines are omitted in L, but space is left for them.*　　　30 wait] *81, I*; wait
below *L*　　　35 an] *81, I*; to be an *L*　　　39 assure you] *L, I*; assure *81*

and faggots, Sir!—if you are not Lord Foppington, who the Devil are
you?

Y. FASHION. Sir, the best of my condition is, I am your son-in-law, and
the worst of it is, I am brother to that noble Peer.

LD. FOPPINGTON. Impudent to the last!   5

SIR TUNBELLY. My son-in-law! Not yet, I hope?

Y. FASHION. Pardon me, Sir, I am, thanks to the goodness of your
Chaplain, and the kind offices of this old gentlewoman.

LORY. 'Tis true, indeed, Sir; I gave your daughter away, and Mrs.
Nurse, here, was clerk.   10

SIR TUNBELLY. Knock that rascal down!—But speak, Jezabel, how's
this?

NURSE. Alas, your honour, forgive me!—I have been overreach'd in this
business as well as you; your Worship knows, if the wedding dinner
had been ready, you would have given her away with your own hands.   15

SIR TUNBELLY. But how durst you do this without acquainting me!

NURSE. Alas, if your Worship had seen how the poor thing begg'd and
pray'd, and clung and twin'd about me like ivy round an old wall, you
wou'd say I who had nurs'd it and rear'd it, must have had a heart of
stone to refuse it.   20

SIR TUNBELLY. Ouns! I shall go mad! Unloose my Lord there, you
scoundrels!

LD. FOPPINGTON. Why, when these gentlemen are at leisure, I shou'd
be glad to congratulate you on your son-in-law, with a little more
freedom of address.   25

MISS. 'Egad, tho'—I don't see which is to be my husband, after all.

LOVELESS. Come, come, Sir Tunbelly, a man of your understanding
must perceive, that an affair of this kind is not to be mended by anger
and reproaches.

TOWNLY. Take my word for it, Sir Tunbelly, you are only tricked into   30
a son-in-law you may be proud of; my friend, Tom Fashion, is as
honest a fellow as ever breath'd.

LOVELESS. That he is, depend on't, and will hunt or drink with you
most affectionately; be generous, old boy, and forgive them.

SIR TUNBELLY. Never—the hussey.—when I had set my heart on   35
getting her a title!

LD. FOPPINGTON. Now, Sir Tunbelly, that I am untruss'd, give me
leave to thank thee for the very extraordinary reception I have met with
in thy damn'd, execrable mansion, and at the same time to assure thee,
that of all the bumpkins and blockheads I have had the misfortune to   40
meet with, thou art the most obstinate and egregious, strike me ugly!

SIR TUNBELLY. What's this!—Ouns! I believe you are both rogues
alike!

7 I am] L; om. 81, I   39 thee] L; you 81, I   40 of] 81, I; if L

LD. FOPPINGTON. No, Sir Tunbelly, thou wilt find to thy unspeakable
mortification, that I am the real Lord Foppington, who was to have
disgraced myself by an alliance with a clod; and that thou hast match'd
thy girl to a beggarly younger brother of mine, whose title deeds might
be contain'd in thy tobacco-box.   5

SIR TUNBELLY. Puppy, puppy!—I might prevent their being beggars if
I chose it;—for I cou'd give 'em as good a rent-roll as your Lordship.

TOWNLY. Well said, Sir Tunbelly.

LD. FOPPINGTON. Aye, old fellow, but you will not do it; for that would be
acting like a Christian, and thou art a thorough barbarian, stap my vitals. 10

SIR TUNBELLY. Udzookers! Now six such words more, and I'll forgive
them directly.

LOVELESS. 'Slife, Sir Tunbelly, you shou'd do it, and bless yourself;
ladies what say you?

AMANDA. Good Sir Tunbelly, you must consent.   15

BERINTHIA. Come, you have been young yourself, Sir Tunbelly.

SIR TUNBELLY. Well, then, if I must, I must;—but turn that sneering
Lord out, however; and let me be revenged on somebody; but first,
look whether I am a barbarian, or not; there, children, I join your hands,
and when I'm in a better humour, I'll give you my blessing.   20

LOVELESS. Nobly done, Sir Tunbelly; and we shall see you dance at a
grandson's wedding, yet.

MISS. By goles tho', I don't understand this; what, an't I to be a lady
after all? only plain Mrs.— What's my husband's name, Nurse?

NURSE. 'Squire Fashion.   25

MISS. 'Squire, is he?—Well, that's better than nothing.

LD. FOPPINGTON. Now will I put on a Philosophic air, and shew these
people, that it is not possible to put a man of my quality out of countenance. Dear Tam, since things are thus fallen out, prythee give me
leave to wish thee joy; I do it *de bon coeur*, strike me dumb! You have 30
married into a family of great politeness and uncommon elegance of
manners; and your bride appears to be a lady beautiful in her person,
modest in her deportment, refined in her sentiments, and of a nice
morality, split my windpipe!

MISS. By goles, husband, break his bones, if he calls me names.   35

Y. FASHION. Your Lordship may keep up your spirits with your grimace,
if you please, I shall support mine by Sir Tunbelly's favour, with this
lady, and three thousand pounds a year.

LD. FOPPINGTON. Well, adieu, Tam; ladies, I kiss your hands; Sir
Tunbelly, I shall now quit thy den, but while I retain my arms, I shall 40
remember thou art a savage, stap my vitals!   [*Exit.*

5 thy] *81, I*; a *L*   7 chose] *81, I*; chuse *L*   9 you will] *81, I*; thou!—wilt *L*
10 stap] *81, I*; stop *L*   17 sneering] *81, I*; swearing *L*   32 her person] *L*;
person *81, I*   33 a nice] *L*; nice *81, I*   35 me] *81, I*; we *L*

SIR TUNBELLY. By the mass, 'tis well he's gone, for I shou'd ha' been provok'd by and by, to ha' dun'un a mischief;—Well, if this is a Lord, I think Hoyden has luck o' her side, in troth!

TOWNLY. She has, indeed, Sir Tunbelly, but I hear the fiddles; his Lordship, I know, had provided 'em.   5

LOVELESS. O, a dance, and a bottle, Sir Tunbelly, by all means.

SIR TUNBELLY. I had forgot the company below; well, what—we must be merry then, ha?—and dance and drink, ha?—Well, 'fore George, you shan't say I do things by halves; son-in-law there looks like a hearty rogue, so we'll have a night of it; and which of these gay ladies   10 will be the old man's partner, ha?—Ecod, I don't know how I came to be in so good a humour.

BERINTHIA. Well, Sir Tunbelly, my friend and I both will endeavour to keep you so; you have done a generous action, and are entitled to our attention; and if you shou'd be at a loss to divert your new guests, we   15 will assist you to relate to them the plot of your daughter's marriage, and his Lordship's deserved mortification, a subject which, perhaps, may afford no bad evening's entertainment.

SIR TUNBELLY. 'Ecod, with all my heart; tho' I am a main bungler at a long story.   20

BERINTHIA. Never fear, we will assist you, if the tale is judged worth being repeated; but of this you may be assured, that while the intention is evidently to please, British auditors will ever be indulgent to the errors of the performance.

FINIS.   25

4 I hear] *81, I*; then we have *L*   7 I] *81, I*; Lord I *L*   8, 11 ha?] *81, I*; hey? *L*
9 things] *81, I*; the thing *L*

PIZARRO

PIZARRO contemplating over the product of his new Peruvian Mine.
"Honor? Reputation? a mere Bubble! — will the praises of posterity charm my bones in the Grave? —pfha! my present
purpose is all! — O. Gold! Gold! for thee I would sell my native Spain, as freely as I would plunder Peru."

Gillray's caricature (1799) of Sheridan gloating over the takings from *Pizarro*

By courtesy of the Trustees of the British Museum

PIZARRO

COMPOSITION

Pizarro was adapted by Sheridan from a literal translation of Kotzebue's *Die Spanier in Peru*, itself a dramatic version of a theme from Marmontel's *Incas*.[1]

The earliest suggestion that he was engaged on some work of this kind is to be found in the *Chester Chronicle*, 21 December 1798, probably copied from a London newspaper: 'The friends of the Drama will hear with pleasure that Mr. Sheridan has been for some weeks employed on a play, which it is expected will shortly be performed at Drury Lane Theatre—The story is a German one.' This is amplified in a passage in the *Monthly Mirror*:[2]

> The rage for the works of Kotzebue in this country, induced Mr. Sheridan to procure a literal translation of the DEATH OF ROLLA, (which had been received with unbounded applause at the Theatre Royal, Vienna) with a view to alter and adapt it himself, to the English stage. After *tugging* at the dramatic *oar* for six weeks, he found a chasm in this play which even his genius could not supply, and, indeed had Mr. Sheridan been conversant with the history of Kotzebue's dramatic works, he would have known that the DEATH OF ROLLA is merely a sequel to CORA, or the VIRGIN of the SUN by the same author.[3]
>
> The INCAS of PERU, by MARMONTEL, is the story on which these plays are constructed, and it is so interesting and extensive, that the German author found it impossible to compress the matter within the compass of five acts; he, therefore first produced CORA, and afterwards the DEATH OF ROLLA, which even now continue to be played alternately, with unbounded applause, on the German stage.
>
> Mr. Sheridan, we understand, has not copied a single speech from Kotzebue; but after he had communicated the difficulty of the undertaking to a gentleman well informed in German literature, the mistake was pointed out; and the grandeur of the outline has induced Mr. Sheridan to attempt that which the vast mind of Kotzebue could not accomplish. . . . We heartily wish him success.

Much the same statement was made in *The Oracle*, 1 March 1799, but with a blunter conclusion: 'The two plays are alternately at the Imperial Theatre in Vienna; but Mr. Sheridan has formed the grand design of blending them into one.'

Some indication of the way in which he set about doing so appears in a letter[4] he wrote at this time, arranging to visit Staines: 'I will also bring Rolla which if we Stay sunday I will sample if Burgess[5] lets me

---

[1] Jean-François Marmontel (1723–99), *Les Incas, ou la destruction de l'empire du Pérou* (2 vols., 1777).   [2] 1st Ser. vii (1799), 38.

[3] *Die Spanier in Peru, oder Rolla's Tod* (1796), and *Die Sonnenjungfrau* (1788).

[4] *Letters*, ii. 109.   [5] Henry Burgess, his solicitor and boon companion.

dictate to him—for in this d——d Town there is not getting half an hour without interruption.' Sheridan had plenty to occupy his attention without the play: the finances of Drury Lane Theatre were in a precarious state, the actors and actresses pressed for payment,[1] and his agricultural improvements at his new estate at Polesden badly needed subsidies. A theatrical success—even though the end of the season was near—would ease life considerably for everyone connected with him, and give Sheridan himself new confidence in his own ability to meet and master every challenge.

In a letter[2] to his wife, of 24–27 March, he reported progress:

I have been going over Rolla with Kemble who is just returned from Scotland. All the Scenery Dresses and musick are going on.—Those are my motions. I go to my little Inn again with all-copying Burgess on Friday if the last Line of Rolla is compleat before I go to bed I will be with you on Saturday to Dinner.

Another two months passed before the play was acted, and there were constant grumbles by everyone connected with it at his dilatoriness in finishing off the text.

On 29 April, Mrs. Siddons's daughter, Sally, mentioned it in a letter to a friend:

We shall not leave London till late this Summer, if Mr. Sheridan's Play comes out, for it is to have all the attraction of splendid decoration, added to fine writing, and interesting incident: I long to see it. Mr. Sheridan told my Mother a fortnight ago that it would be ready in three weeks, but she has not yet seen her Part.[3]

On 10 May the theatre advertised that 'A New Play called Pizarro, which has been for some time in preparation, will be performed for the First Time on Wednesday the 22nd instant, with entirely new Scenes, Dresses, and Decorations.'[4]

Michael Kelly, who had been chosen by Sheridan to prepare the music, gave a heartfelt account of the tensions and frustrations suffered by those who were closest to Sheridan at this period:

Expectation was on tip-toe: and strange as it may appear, 'Pizarro' was advertised, and every box in the house taken, before the fourth act of the play was begun; nor had I one single word of the poetry for which I was to compose the music. Day after day was I attending on Mr. Sheridan, representing that time was flying, and that nothing was done for me. His answer uniformly was, 'Depend upon it, my dear Mic., you shall have plenty of matter to go on with to-morrow;' but day after day, that morrow came not, which, as my name was advertised as the composer of the music, drove me half crazy.'[5]

Then Sheridan came and took him from a dinner-party to see two scenes, Pizarro's tent and the Temple of the Sun. The stage was lit up as 'for

[1] Especially Moody and Mrs. Siddons.   [2] *Letters*, ii. 111.
[3] O. G. Knapp, *An Artist's Love Story* (1904), p. 191.
[4] *The Oracle*, 10 May 1799.   [5] Kelly, ii. 143.

a public performance', but the only people present, apart from themselves, were the painters and carpenters. Sheridan's explanation for dragging Kelly from his friends was, 'these bunglers of carpenters require looking after'.[1] But he also promised to meet Kelly next day and actually fulfilled the engagement:

My aim was, to discover the situations of the different choruses and the marches, and Mr. Sheridan's ideas on the subject; and he gave them in the following manner:—'In the Temple of the Sun,' said he, 'I want the virgins of the Sun, and their high priest, to chaunt a solemn invocation to their deity.'—I sang two or three bars of music to him, which I thought corresponded with what he wished, and marked them down. He then made a sort of rumbling noise with his voice (for he had not the slightest idea of turning a tune), resembling a deep gruff bow, wow wow; but though there was not the slightest resemblance of an air in the noise he made, yet so clear were his ideas of effect, that I perfectly understood his meaning, though conveyed through the medium of a bow, wow wow. Having done this, and pointed out their several situations, he promised me, faithfully, that I should have the poetry in a couple of days; and, marvellous to say, he actually did send me Cora's song, which Mrs. Jordan sang; and the trio, sung by Mrs. Crouch, Miss Decamp, and Miss Leak, 'Fly, away, time,'—which they made very effective. The poetry of the last, however, was written by my good friend, Mr. Richardson;[2] the song really by himself. Having extracted these, I saw that it was perfectly ridiculous to expect the poetry of the choruses from the author of the play; and as I knew a literary gentleman, whose poverty, if not his will, would consent to assist me, I gave him Mr. Sheridan's ideas, as I had caught them from his bow, wow, wows, and got him to write words to them, which he did very well. . . .[3]

The theatre's resources became even more strained, and Sheridan fobbed off its creditors with the excuse, 'there is not a shilling in the Treasury but what goes to bring out our famous Piece. This infallibly comes out next week.'[4] But the opening was postponed another two nights. Even Sheridan's greatest admirers grew exasperated with him. For example, Mrs. Bouverie wrote on 17 May to an acquaintance to say:

. . . The Sheridans are in Town; next week the long expected new Play called Pizarro . . . is to come out. It was originally ill translated by some one who sent it to Sheridan, and he has completely written it over again, and has altered it and added to it according to his fancy—they say it will be by much the best thing that has appeared for years, and the world are in high expectation—but like

[1] Ibid., ii. 144–5.
[2] Joseph Richardson (1755–1803), author of *The Fugitive* and friend of Sheridan.
[3] Kelly, ii. 145–6. Boaden, *Kemble*, ii. 238, says the lines 'were supplied by Grub, always happy to be employed'. John Grubb assisted in the direction of Drury Lane Theatre from 1795, and had been a member of the party at Staines in March, but he cannot really be said to be poor, except in the sense that Sheridan asked all his associates to 'invest' their money in Drury Lane Theatre.
[4] *Letters*, ii. 118.

Sheridan it comes out at the end of the Season, owing to his idleness. Poor Hester[1] has suffered agonies of mind about this Play, and continues as violently attached to him as ever. . . .[2]

At seven o'clock in the evening of 23 May,[3] just twenty-four hours before it was due to be performed, Sheridan submitted a copy of the play to John Larpent, the Lord Chamberlain's examiner, taking care to add 'the Form and Object of it is not only unexceptionable but such as [I] have no doubt may be honour'd with peculiar approbation'.[4] Larpent and his wife spent the next four hours reading it and 'were much interested and affected'.[5] Kelly, however, was more impressed by Sheridan's dilatoriness:

at the time the house was overflowing on the first night's performance, all that was written of the play was actually rehearsing, and that incredible as it may appear, until the end of the fourth act, neither Mrs. Siddons, nor Charles Kemble, nor Barrymore, had all their speeches for the fifth. Mr. Sheridan was up-stairs in the prompter's room, where he was writing the last part of the play, while the earlier parts were acting; and every ten minutes he brought down as much of the dialogue as he had done, piece-meal, into the green-room, abusing himself and his negligence, and making a thousand winning and soothing apologies, for having kept the performers so long in such painful suspense.

. . . No man was more careful in his carelessness; he was quite aware of his power over his performers, and of the veneration in which they held his great talents; had he not been so, he would not have ventured to keep them (Mrs. Siddons particularly) in the dreadful anxiety which they were suffering through the whole of the evening. Mrs. Siddons told me that she was in an agony of fright; but Sheridan perfectly knew, that Mrs. Siddons, C. Kemble, and Barrymore, were quicker in study than any other performers concerned; and that he could trust them to be perfect in what they had to say, even at half-an-hour's notice.[6]

The first part of this account seems very exaggerated until we remember that the doors of the playhouse were opened for the evening performance at three o'clock in the afternoon, and that Sheridan is known to have been busy revising the fifth act on 24 May. John Britton gives an interesting account of what happened:

. . . Further portions of the drama were afterwards produced, when Kemble, as manager, announced its first representation; fully expecting that the author would furnish the concluding scenes in time for study and rehearsal. Strange to say, on the morning of the promised performance, the termination of the piece was not decided on, and Mrs. Siddons had not been provided with the affecting speech, which, in the character of Elvira, she was to address Alonzo, on the death of her paramour, Pizarro. Even when the performance began, the author

[1] His second wife.
[2] National Library of Scotland MS. 3598, f. 93: Lynedoch collection.
[3] Mrs. Larpent's diary: Huntington MS. HM 31201.   [4] *Letters*, ii. 118.
[5] Huntington MS.   [6] Kelly, ii. 146–7.

was in his room at the theatre, meditating on, and writing the concluding
sentences, and it was not till the end of the first act that he placed them in the
hands of the famed actress, and Charles Kemble. . . .[1]

If the play had been sent to the Lord Chamberlain's examiner in as
unfinished a state as Kelly suggests, that fact would surely have been
mentioned in Mrs. Larpent's diary. Britton's account seems to me the
more credible because it contents itself with suggesting that Sheridan
was at work on revision even up to the beginning of the play.

It is hardly surprising that the first night was not a success, even though
it drew an immense crowd, attracted by 'the joint reputation of Sheridan
and Kotzebue, and the first dramatic attempt of the former, after an
interval of twenty years'.[2] The tragedy took almost five hours in the
representation, and the exhausted audience was irritated by lapses by
actors and stage hands that showed inadequate rehearsal. Suett gave a
wretched performance as Diego, and Mrs. Jordan appeared miscast as
Cora. Mrs. Siddons, so impressive in declamation, was uneasy as Elvira,
a part so different from her usual roles. Other players were uncertain of
their lines. John Kemble, however, was very moving, dignified in bearing
and noble in utterance, and Charles Kemble and Barrymore were also
warmly admired.[3]

The critics soon remarked that the play in general did not 'reflect
much credit on the dramatic judgment of Mr. Sheridan'.[4] He had once
again treated the first performance as a dress rehearsal, and might well
have repeated as excuse and justification his sentence in the preface to
The Rivals: 'Though I was not uninformed that the acts were still too
long, I flattered myself that, after the first trial, I might with safer judgment proceed to remove what should appear to have been most dissatis-
factory.' He was advised to cut the tragedy, and proceeded to do so.
At the second performance, it took an hour less in running time; at the
fourth, an hour and twenty minutes.[5] The alterations that he made in
four days were extensive, but meant that the tragedy now pleased audiences
so much that it was constantly acted until the beginning of July, and
went on to hold a place in the theatre's repertoire for the next sixty years.

At first, its success was partly topical. The invader might be viewed
by English audiences not as Spanish but French, and eager applause

[1] *The Auto-Biography of John Britton, F.S.A.* (1850), i. 130. Britton was keenly
interested in the subject, and wrote *Sheridan and Kotzebue. The Enterprising Adventures
of Pizarro. With criticisms on the Play* (1799).

[2] *The Times*, 25 May 1799.

[3] *The Times, The Oracle*, and the *Morning Herald*, of 25 May 1799.

[4] *The Times*, 29 May 1799.

[5] *Bell's Weekly Messenger*, 26 May 1799; *The Times*, 29 May 1799. The latter noted:
'*Pizarro* is nearly now what it ought to have been on the first night of performance,
had that mature attention been bestowed on it, for the want of which no talents, however great, can apologize.'

was given to every reference to King and Country. George III had not attended a performance at Drury Lane Theatre for four years but went there on 5 June, accompanied by the Queen, Princesses, and Duke and Duchess of York. Sheridan preceded them to their box with lighted tapers, and the wags remarked that he was now seen in a new light.[1] The highly moral and patriotic sentiments of *Pizarro* helped to qualify the impression he had made on the King by his early sympathy for the French Revolution and his work for reform.

The play's outlook was also humanitarian in its sympathies: 'It exposes to just indignation and abhorrence the savage cruelty of the Europeans, inflamed with the lust of gold and fury of conquest, and excites the pity and interest of humanity in favour of a peaceable and virtuous people.'[2] Sheridan drew on his long detestation of East India Company adventurers for his description of the Spaniards, and on his equally warm admiration for less sophisticated Englishmen for the part of virtuous Peruvians.

The appeal of situation and spectacle also ensured success.[3] The tragedy contained one of the most famous scenes of the century: 'the wooden bridge over the tremendous chasm of two mountains is one of the most picturesque and striking views that any stage has exhibited'.[4] It enabled Rolla to make an exciting escape from the Spaniards, crossing the bridge over the cataract with the child in his arms and the soldiers firing at him. 'Rolla tears from the rock the tree which supports the bridge, and retreats by the back ground, bearing the child.'[5]

This particular piece of stage business is not in Kotzebue's text, and seems to have called on the talents of Sheridan as inventor of situations, De Loutherbourg as painter of wild landscape, and Alexander Johnston as carpenter.[6] De Loutherbourgh was also credited with 'the principal scenery',[7] while other designs were executed by Marinari, Greenwood, Dematiar, Banks, and Blackmore. As early as 28 April *Bell's Weekly Messenger* had said of *Pizarro* 'the incidents and dialogue are his [Sheridan's] own, but the Machinist and Painter have done much'. They gave plenty of time to their work, and their most superb efforts, Pizarro's pavilion and the Temple of the Sun, were greatly admired.

---

[1] *The Oracle*, 25 May 1799.

[2] *Morning Herald*, 6 and 8 June 1799.

[3] *The Times*, 25 May 1799.

[4] *Morning Herald*, 27 May 1799. See also Sybil Rosenfeld and Edward Croft Murray, 'A Checklist of Scene Painters working in Great Britain and Ireland in the Eighteenth Century', *Theatre Notebook*, xix (1965), 110.   [5] *Pizarro*, v. ii.

[6] See K. Burnim and P. Highfill, Jr., 'Alexander Johnson, Machinist', *Theatre Notebook*, xxiii (1968-9), pp. 100-2.

[7] *Morning Herald*, 27 May 1799. Cf. J. Britton, *Sheridan and Kotzebue* (1799), p. 143, and A. Oliver and J. Saunders, 'De Loutherbourg and Pizarro, 1799', *Theatre Notebook*, xx (1965-6), 30-2. See also p. 160 of the same volume.

The operatic element in the play has been emphasized[1] because it is something that might easily be missed by anyone reading Ridgway's many editions of *Pizarro*, but what has not been adequately noted is that Sheridan drew on a long stage tradition for his musical and processional effects. As far back as Beaumont and Fletcher's *The Tragedy of Bonduca*, we can find preparations for sacrifice indicated in a significant stage direction: '*Musick. Enter in solemnity the Druids singing, the Second Daughter strewing flowers: then Bonduca, Caratach, Nennius and others*' (III. i). Ritual procession was used in even more elaborate form in Rowe's *The Ambitious Step-Mother* (1701), III. iii, in the hymn to the Sun God:

The Scene opening, shews the Altar of the Sun, Magas, and several other Priests attending. Solemn music is heard: then enter on one side, Memnon, Artaxerxes, Amnestris, and Attendants; on the other Side, the Queen, Mirza, Artaban, Cleone, Cleanthes, and Attendants: they all bow towards the Altar, and then arrange themselves on each side of the stage, while the following Hymn is performed in Parts, and Chorus by the Priests.

This seems to me to resemble Act II, Sc. ii of *Pizarro*, with its processional march of priests and virgins of the sun, taking their places on either side of the temple before the high priest approached the altar and invoked the 'Pow'r Supreme'. Kelly was no Mozart to give true sublimity to the voices of priests in the temple, nor Sacchini a Beethoven to render unforgettable a hymn to light; but the music of *Pizarro* served its purpose in helping to dignify the theme and involve the audience in an age-old ritual.

The text, then, gives but a bare notion of the attractiveness of *Pizarro* in the last years of the eighteenth century, hardly a tremor of the theatrical experience enjoyed by so many thousand spectators at Drury Lane Theatre. One of the most critical of them took care to record her impressions for posterity:

Pizarro with innumerable faults interests It is a Pastic[c]io—Opera, Tragedy,—very Showy A flash of Language which when examined is more Sound than Sense. forced violent Situations, and every thing brought forward to seize the Imagination—Judgment has Nothing to do in the business and reflection only brings forward Absurdity in every Scene. Kemble Acts Rolla in the most perfect manner. Mrs. Siddons acts Elvira well but rather too highly wrought. The whole is a magnificent Spectacle.[2]

RECEPTION

. . . The great expection excited by the name of the original Author, and above all by that of the English Editor was not disappointed. Never was there so much curiosity, so ardent a desire to see a play. The doors were

---

[1] Rhodes, iii. 8.   [2] Mrs. Larpent's diary, 14 Jan. 1800: Huntington MS.

besieged at three o'clock, and when they opened, the crowding and confusion were dreadful. Crowds at the pit and gallery doors are common,
but the crowd at the box door, last night, was equal to any that ever
happened even at them. The whole boxes were taken, yet thousands went
who had no places. The moment the doors were opened, it was announced
there was 'no room, and no money returned.' This made those who had
not places, turn back; and the conflict between those who wished to enter,
and those who wished to retire, was extremely distressing. Ladies of the
first fashion, in full dress, were fainting; some lost a shoe, others a hat;
the stair-case windows were broken; the door-keepers could not resist
the torrent, and many went in without paying; the outside of the doors
were surrounded by hundreds who dared not enter, and many went
away who had places rather than encounter the crowd.

It was nearly seven o'clock before the play began, and it was nearly
twelve before it concluded.

.   .   .

Such is the fable of this play, which, from the moment it was first
announced, excited the most lively expectation, and which has been
hailed as the pledge of returning taste and genius to the stage. Although
it be the original work of Kotzebue, it is Mr. Sheridan's by adoption,
and therefore he is responsible for its defects, though the world will not
allow him the exclusive merit of all its beauties. It is with diffidence we
come to judge of a work sanctioned by so great a name. . . .

.   .   .

The construction of the fable, and the combination of these characters,
some of which, particularly *Rolla* and *Elvira*, lay claim to novelty, are
distinguished by a general, not a universal, exercise of happy ingenuity.
It is satisfactory, however, to reflect, that wherever it falls short of excellence, there is no radical defect, and that our objections are only such as
require to be pointed out in order to be removed. The third act terminates
rather abruptly, Mrs. Jordan's song, however pretty in the elemental
strife that reigns around, loses all its charms; and in the last act particularly, the scenes are much too dilated. A judicious compressure is
therefore only wanting. We complain only of a luxuriance that may be
restrained, not of wants to be supplied.

The sentiment is derived from the very bosom of domestic and public
duties: the tender and pathetic scenes are finely wrought up from the
conjugal and parental virtues; those of sublimer cast from the energies
of a free, brave, and generous people, fighting for liberty against oppression. They are laid in nature, and as such, are as applicable to the present
day, as the age for which they are written. Here, however, the author
does not descend from his height to court applause, by adopting them
to existing circumstances; he draws from the pure fountain of nature,
without seeming to direct its course.—The justice, the truth and beauty

of the scene, where the Peruvian prisoner is interrogated by *Pizarro*, are
so conspicuous, and the whole so highly finished, that for the first three
acts we evidently perceive an author reserving his strength for some
great occasion. Accordingly in the fourth act the interest bursts upon the
audience, in the tender sorrows of *Kora*, followed up by a variety of
scenes, vying with each other in force and pathos. . . .

If any part can be particularly called Mr. Sheridan's, it is the language;
and here we trace no fault. There are no quaint conceits, no meretricious
glare, no parade of words, no specious phraseology. It is nature attired
by the Graces, in true expression with all the beauties of polished style
and classical purity.

The piece was listened to with the deepest interest, and received the
warmest applause throughout. In the fifth act, neither the scene shifters
nor some of the performers were very perfect; circumstances which gave
opportunity to rival carpenters and scene shifters to express disapprobation; but the piece concluded amidst thunders of *unanimous* applause. . . .
(*Morning Post*, 25 May 1799.)

A liberal mind will make much allowance for a first night; but, with all
the Stage deficiencies, there is a prolixity in the *Second* and *Third* Acts
which approximates to dullness and insipidity, and hence it is very evident
that the whole has, in the Play-house phrase, been hastily got up. This is
the only apology which can be admitted; for with Sheridan's extraordinary
powers in the Senate, and unrivalled genius on the Stage, what task is
then so arduous that he cannot accomplish—provided he turns his mind
and leisure to the attainment of his object. (*The Oracle*, 25 May 1799.)

PIZARRO, a new Tragedy in five acts, taken from Marmontel's History
of the *Incas*, was performed last night, for the first time. Kotzebue has
dramatized part of the same story; notwithstanding which we find in
PIZARRO a fund of literary novelty, though it boasts not much originality in
point of construction or plot.—Mr. Sheridan, from whose pen flows
spontaneously every thing that is the work of long study in others, is
said to be the author; and the writing, with a few exceptions, is certainly
worthy of his great talents. There are several admirable and impressive
speeches allotted to Mrs. SIDDONS, and Mr. KEMBLE, some of which produced an electrical effect upon the auditory: a patriotic address by the
latter, as Chief of the Peruvian Army is one of the most nervous pieces
of declamation, and most successful appeals to Patriotism, that has ever
distinguished the English Drama; the audience felt it as such, and the
applause bestowed upon it was tumultuously ecstatic. (*The Morning
Herald*, 25 May 1799.)

The Death of Rolla by Kotzebue, and the universal applause with which
it was received on the German Stage, induced our English Terence to
emulate his foreign contemporary in a similar exhibition. He has closely

adhered to the outlines, and has in most instances preserved the sentiments of the original piece, but the language is entirely re-written from
the translation with which he was furnished.

.   .   .

That *Pizarro* possesses genuine claims to public admiration, must
universally be admitted, but it must undergo very material alterations
and curtailments, before it can again be represented with the desired
effect. It is in its present state, a striking instance of neglect and precipita-
tion. The dialogue is too prolix, the business in a languishing state, and
the machinery was not perfectly conducted. It must appear extraordinary
that the author, perfectly versed as he is, in the minutiae of a theatre,
and who is the constant judge of the productions of others, should have
formed his own of materials so lengthened as to take up nearly five hours
in the representation.

.   .   .

Pizarro's pavillion, and the Temple of the Sun, are equal in point of
brilliant effect to the best scenes of any of our Theatres. (*Bell's Weekly
Messenger*, 26 May 1799.)

An anxious wish to gratify the curiosity excited in the public mind,
could alone have justified a critical analysis of Mr. Sheridan's *Pizarro*,
by adoption, on its first representation, accompanied by so many defects,
evidently the result of precipitancy. These, as might be expected from
the commanding taste and genius of the Editor, were, on Saturday night,
almost entirely removed. . . . The alterations alluded to principally consist
in the total exclusion of a light character given to Suett in the opening.
The prolixity of dialogue in the scenes that follow between *Pizarro* and
Elvira is also much compressed, and hence the bold and masculine
passions by which they are distinguished derive more vigour, and glow
with brighter ardor. It is in the last act, however, we find alteration most
busily and judiciously employed. Its two beautiful and leading incidents,
comprising the loss of little *Fernando*, and the death of *Rolla*, so much
injured, at first, by the abuse of machinery, in some instances, and its
want of facility in others, by a battle and mere ordinary scenes that
followed, of no very interesting nature; these blemishes being removed
by an almost entire new construction, the act now shines forth with all
its proper lustre, full of animation, dignity, and pathos. . . . While . . . the
scene between the captive Cacique and *Pizarro* boldly vies with those
in which *Rolla* pleads the cause of humanity with the centinel in the
dungeon, or nobly falls in its defence, his exhortation to the Peruvian
soldiers in the Temple of the Sun, bursts in, and justly claims superiority.

The awful pauses between each weighty sentence . . . the forceful
interest of every line, clothed with all the sacred dignity of truth . . .
penetrate . . . into the hearts of the audience. (*Morning Post*, 27 May 1799.)

The piece has been shortened since the second representation, but it still wants some curtailment. The performers were last night more mellow in their parts. (*Morning Post*, 28 May 1799.)

Mr. Wilberforce,[1] Mr. H. Thornton,[2] and a few of their acquaintances occupied a box to see *Pizarro* on Thursday night, for the benefit of Mrs. Siddons. Mr. Wilberforce has not been in a Theatre, except on the above night, for the last TWENTY YEARS; but, if we may judge by the marked applause which he bestowed on *Pizarro*, we shall expect to see him a constant visitor. (*Morning Post*, 31 May 1799.)

. . . Pizarro the 21st night has been as full nearly as the first. Pray send me any anecdotes you can pick up about Kotzebue. There is no other subject scarcely of conversation, by which you will understand that there are various opinions on the subject. The violent Ministerialists are angry that Sheridan should have such applause; the violent oppositionists are as angry at the loyalty of the Play; and the rigid and censorious are suspicious of such pure morality and mild religion from the pen of a person esteemed profligate. To bring up the rear, authors are jealous of his success, and cry out it is Kotzebue and not Sheridan's merit: so Sheridan says—I am but a translator; but then, such a translation! As soon as it comes out I will send it to you. William Lamb foolishly distrusts it—foolishly, because it is attributed to pique at the failure of the Epilogue; the poetry of this was pretty, but it wanted strength. (Lady Elizabeth Foster to Augustus Foster, 27 Dec. 1799, quoted in Vere Foster, *The Two Duchesses* (1898), p. 162.)

When a distemper extends its contagious influence, it is the business of the physician to investigate the cause, and prescribe a remedy. Mental diseases, however, are of so complicated a nature as to baffle human skill, and their baneful effects are particularly fatal when they overpower the sufferer under the semblance of amusement. Of this we have many proofs in gaming, dress, masquerades, etc. The most remarkable species of mental disease, which occasioned a temporary suspension of common sense in this capital, was imported in bundles of paper, inscribed with Teutonic characters, which, when translated into English, communicated the contagion to the higher ranks of society with the rapidity of the electric fluid. The first symptoms were a strange admiration of ghosts, mouldering castles, sulphurous flames, bloody daggers, and other terrific images of a distempered imagination. In this stage of the disease it may be denominated the *Spectromania*; but on the introduction of a larger quantity of the infectious matter, the dangerous symptoms increased, and it assumed a formidable appearance under the name of *Kotzebue-mania*.

[1] William Wilberforce (1759–1833), reformer and religious leader.
[2] Henry Thornton (1760–1815), reformer and friend of Wilberforce.

The unhappy wight who was destined to do this irreparable injury to the morals of his countrymen was one *Benjamin Thompson*. We are told that he concealed the papers impregnated with the infection for ten years, till, in a moment of enthusiasm, he sent them to the manager of one of the theatres, who administered the *virus* to the public.

This cruel disease, which has spared neither age nor sex in Germany, France, or England, takes its name from an empiric named *Kotzebue*. The patients were afflicted with a childish passion for noise, faintings, the startings and ravings of others deeply affected with the same disease, and a strong abhorrence of common sense. This species of madness induced the women of every rank to divest themselves of a great part of their clothes. They also cut off their hair, which would have contributed to the restoration of health had the disorder affected only the head; but unfortunately its principal malignancy operated on the heart, where it extinguished the light of morality which had been kindled by a virtuous education. While labouring under this delirium, what had formerly been considered crimes were metamorphosed into virtues, and religion and decency were thrown aside like old garments.

When the distemper became general, the people thronged to our places of public amusement, where the contagion was most powerful. Thither the old and the young, the grave and the gay, hastened, like insects, to flutter round the flame of licentiousness; to add to the absurdity, the very people who wasted their time and money in pursuit of a phantom were clamorous against the high price of provisions! The curious names given to different portions of the infectious matter induced the people to purchase it just as they do other quack medicines. They had not the most remote idea that what was introduced under the plausible name of theatric entertainments could have any pernicious influence, till fatal experience made them feel the imbecility produced by immoral dramas. On the introduction of the *Stranger*, our ladies thronged to behold the fair German who had made a fashionable slip. By a little conversation with her they not only caught the infection of the *Kotzebue-mania*, but they were convinced that adultery was merely an amiable weakness, though they had so often heard it mentioned by English moralists as the most execrable deviation from the path of honour, and totally subversive of social felicity. The next dose was administered by a very skilful female Quack, who gave it the name of *Lovers' Vows*, and by a happy termination demonstrated the beneficial consequences of seduction.

But this mental malady did not arrive at the greatest height till the introduction of *Pizarro*. The multitude thronged to see this monster. They held up their hands, opened their mouths, and gazed in stupid astonishment at the superb pageant that shone before their imagination. It was such a delightful enjoyment to sit at one's ease, and behold all the horrors, without encountering the dangers of a battle and a thunderstorm! There was so much enthusiastic loyalty in the speech of *Rolla*, that even the critic with difficulty traced the sentiments, and detected the plagiarism, in the more simple and dignified lines of Cowper.

Those physicians of taste known by the name of Reviewers had anxiously watched the progress of the *Kotzebue-mania* through every stage, till it arrived at a crisis, when they administered a variety of antidotes, some as correctives, and others as alteratives. When the feverish symptoms abated, the convalescents were gradually restored; and the public taste, thought yet *very poorly indeed*, will, it is to be hoped, recover from the imbecility brought on by this mental *apoplexy*.

It has been recommended, in order to prevent such fatal accidents in future, that all the productions of the Continent shall be examined by adequate judges previous to their being landed, and that the vessels shall perform quarantine.

Such was the progress of the *Kotzebue-mania*, which had a more pernicious effect on the health and morals of the community than gin, or even the nostrums of quackery. Indeed no disease has raged with such fatal malignancy in this capital since the plague in 1665. (*The Oracle*, quoted in *The Spirit of the Public Journals for 1802* (1803), pp. 93–6.)

It is one of the peculiar advantages of this character [Rolla], that a performer must be miserably deficient in his profession indeed, who does not represent it with a considerable degree of success.

The play of *Pizarro* is the production of a poet profoundly skilled in dramatic effect; and every line that is put into the mouth of the Peruvian hero, and every situation in which he is placed, is written and concerted to produce it. The part of Rolla, in the language of the profession, plays itself. Success in this part should be therefore considered as only an equivocal test of the merit of an actor. (*The Times*, 5 Oct. 1804.)

The great success which had attended The Stranger, and the still increasing taste for the German Drama, induced Mr. Sheridan, in the present year, to embark his fame even still more responsibly in a venture to the same romantic shores. The play of Pizarro was brought out on the 24th of May, 1799. The heroic interest of the plot, the splendour of the pageantry, and some skilful appeals to public feeling in the dialogue, obtained for it at once a popularity which has seldom been equalled. As far, indeed, as multiplied representations and editions are a proof of success, the legitimate issue of his Muse might well have been jealous of the fame and fortune of their spurious German relative. When the author of the Critic made Puff say, 'Now for my magnificence,—my noise and my procession!' he little anticipated the illustration which, in twenty years afterwards, his own example would afford to that ridicule. Not that in pageantry, when tastefully and subordinately introduced, there is anything to which criticism can fairly object:—it is the dialogue of this play that is unworthy of its author, and ought never, from either motives of profit or the vanity of success, to have been coupled with his name. The style in which it is written belongs neither to verse or prose, but is a sort of amphibious native of both,—neither gliding gracefully through the former element, nor walking steadily on the other. In order to give pomp to the language, inversion is substituted for metre; and one of the worst faults of poetry, a superfluity of epithet, is adopted, without that harmony which alone makes it venial or tolerable.

It is some relief, however, to discover, from the manuscripts in my possession, that Mr. Sheridan's responsibility for the defects of Pizarro is not very much greater than his claim to a share in its merits. In the plot, and the arrangement of the scenes, it is well known, there is but little alteration from the German original. The omission of the comic scene of Diego, which Kotzebue himself intended to omit,—the judicious suppression of Elvira's love for Alonzo,—the introduction, so striking in representation, of Rolla's passage across the bridge, and the re-appearance of Elvira, in the habit of a nun, form, I believe, the only important points in which the play of Mr. Sheridan deviates from the structure of the original drama. With respect to the dialogue, his share in its composition is reducible to a compass not much more considerable. A few speeches, and a few short scenes, re-written, constitute almost the whole of the contribution he has furnished to it. The manuscript translation, or rather imitation, of the 'Spaniards in Peru,' which he used as the ground-work of Pizarro, has been preserved among his papers;— and, so convenient was it to his indolence to take the style as he found it, that, except, as I have said, in a few speeches and scenes, which might be easily enumerated, he adopted, with scarcely any alteration, the exact words of the translator, whose taste, therefore, (whoever he may have been) is answerable for the spirit and style of three-fourths of the dialogue. Even that scene where Cora describes the 'white buds' and 'crimson blossoms' of her infant's teeth, which I have often heard cited as a specimen of Sheridan's false ornament, is indebted to this unknown paraphrase for the whole of its embroidery.

But though he is found to be innocent of much of the contraband matter, with which his co-partner in this work had already vitiated it, his own contributions to the dialogue are not of a much higher or purer order. He seems to have written down to the model before him, and to have been inspired by nothing but an emulation of its faults. His style, accordingly, is kept hovering in the same sort of limbo, between blank verse and prose;—while his thoughts and images, however shining and effective on the stage, are like the diamonds of theatrical royalty, and will not bear inspection off it. The scene between Alonzo and Pizarro, in the third act, is one of those almost entirely re-written by Sheridan;

and the following medley group of personification affords a specimen of the style to which his taste could descend:—'Then would I point out to him where now, in clustered villages, they live like brethren, social and confiding, while through the burning day Content sits basking on the cheek of Toil, till laughing Pastime leads them to the hour of rest.'

The celebrated harangue of Rolla to the Peruvians, into which Kemble used to infuse such heroic dignity, is an amplification of the following sentences of the original, as I find them given in Lewis's manuscript translation of the play:—

ROLLA. You Spaniards fight for gold; we for our country.
ALONZO. They follow an adventurer to the field; we a monarch whom we love.
ATALIB. And a god whom we adore!

This speech, to whose popular sentiments the play owed much of its success, was chiefly made up by Sheridan of loans from his own oratory. The image of the Vulture and the Lamb was taken, as I have already remarked, from a passage in his speech on the trial of Hastings:—and he had, on the subject of Invasion, in the preceding year (1798), delivered more than once the substance of those patriotic sentiments, which were now so spirit-stirring in the mouth of Rolla. For instance, on the King's Message relative to preparation for Invasion:—

The Directory may instruct their guards to make the fairest professions of how their army is to act; but of these professions surely not once can be believed. The victorious Buonaparte may say that he comes like a minister of grace, with no other purpose than to give peace to the cottager, to restore citizens to their rights, to establish real freedom, and a liberal and humane government. But can there be an Englishman so stupid, so besotted, so befooled, as to give a moment's credit to such ridiculous professions? . . .—What, then, is their object? They come for what they really want: they come for ships, for commerce, for credit, and for capital. Yes; they come for the sinews, the bones—for the marrow and the very heart's blood of Great Britain. But let us examine what we are to purchase at this price. Liberty, it appears, is now their staple commodity: but attend, I say, and examine how little of real liberty they themselves enjoy, who are so forward and prodigal in bestowing it on others.

The speech of Rolla in the prison scene is also an interpolation of his own,—Kotzebue having, far more judiciously, (considering the unfitness of the moment for a *tirade*,) condensed the reflections of Rolla into the short exclamation, 'Oh, sacred Nature! thou art still true to thyself,' and then made him hurry into the prison to his friend.

Of the translation of this play by Lewis, which has been found among the papers, Mr. Sheridan does not appear to have made any use;— except in so far as it may have suggested to him the idea of writing a song for Cora, of which that gentleman had set him an example in a ballad, beginning

Soft are thy slumbers, soft and sweet,
Hush thee, hush thee, hush thee, boy.

The song of Mr. Lewis, however, is introduced, with somewhat less
violence to probability, at the beginning of the Third Act, where the
women are waiting for the tidings of the battle, and when the intrusion
of a ballad from the heroine, though sufficiently unnatural, is not quite
so monstrous as in the situation which Sheridan has chosen for it. (Moore,
ii. 286–91.)

On the first night, notwithstanding, that it excited, in many scenes,
much just, and genuine applause, yet, in the last act, encountered so much
violent opposition, as then to give but little presage of its future triumphant career.
    Conversing with Sheridan's friend, Richardson, after the fall of the
curtain, he told me, that not only he himself was much vexed and disappointed by this unexpected reception, but that Sheridan, to whom every
species of dramatic opposition was then new, had retreated to the Piazza
Coffee House, greatly annoyed, and discomfited. . . .
    Mrs. Jordan, in *Cora*, was also a failure; and though Mrs. Siddons,
by her fine taste, and majestic manner, in a great degree elevated Kotzebue's *soldier's* trull, *Elvira* (that campaigning lady, with a lurking *penchant*
for Alonzo,) yet, that this *outré* character did not excite the slightest
interest, is rendered clearly evident by the fact, that a *loud laugh* saluted
the entrance of Mrs. Siddons, when, during the last scene, she presented
the overpowered, and disarmed *Alonzo*, with a sword. To this list of
failures among the *dramatis personae*, must be added R. Palmer, in
Valverde, who likewise excited his share of laughter on the occasion.
    However, on the second night, after certain alterations, and omissions,
(amongst which was the whole of the character of *Diego*, without whose
incumbrance, the play has ever since continued to be performed) the
beauties of Sheridan, and Kotzebue, heightened, and improved by the
splendid acting of John Kemble in *Rolla*, and Mrs. Siddons in *Elvira*,
burst on the audience with an unencumbered magnificence; and *Pizarro*
so decidedly succeeded, that I have heard, it produced to the treasury on
its first sixty nights, the enormous sum of thirty thousand pounds. (*The
Life and Times of Frederick Reynolds Written by Himself* (2nd edn., 1827),
ii. 262–3.)

CHOICE OF TEXT

The *Morning Herald*, 8 May 1799, noted: 'Mr. Sheridan has not, as
reported, furnished an entire new work, founded upon a play by Kotzebue,
but has, however, made such variations in the translation as will give it
quite a new cast. The work in reality, is suspected to come from the translator of *The Stranger*.' The first sentence seems to be founded on fact; the

accuracy of the second was vigorously denied in the same newspaper, three days later:

The Play of *Pizarro* we are now assured, is not taken from *Kora* and *Rolla*, as translated by Mr. Thompson, or any other translator; nor is there a single sentence or incident from the former in the forthcoming Drama; the entire is written by Mr. Sheridan, and has been in rehearsal for some time, but not in the Theatre, which has given rise to a number of rumours on the subject.

A report on the matter, printed just after Sheridan's death, is more illuminating:

This performance was sold to Mr. Sheridan by a German for £100, but the version was so unintelligible that little use could be made of it; but two other translations falling in his way he adopted them, and with a slight addition of his own, contrived to render the piece highly attractive. . . . It is said that not less than 29,000 copies of it were sold in a short space of time.[1]

Just how slight were his own additions will be discussed below in the section dealing with the text of the play itself. There, too, an attempt will be made to identify the three translations that Sheridan is said to have used.

The choice of texts may be made from the following:

1. OF THE PROLOGUE

In 1780 Sheridan had written a prologue for Lady Craven's *The Miniature Picture*,[2] and the eighty lines had been much admired. Georgiana, Duchess of Devonshire, said of the poem: 'Isn't it quite charming? Mr. Sheridan was diffident of its success in reading as he thought it only did for stage effect but tho it does wonderfully on the stage it surely reads vastly well too.'[3] Horace Walpole's praise was more qualified: 'There is a very good though endless prologue written by Sheridan.'[4]

Some criticism of this kind may have reached Sheridan's ears or he may have felt himself, in the intervening years, that the prologue was too extended. Whatever the reason, he was content to offer its first thirty lines as the prologue to *Pizarro* in 1799. He added two new lines to round it off.

I have not been able to locate Sheridan's manuscript of the 1799 version. The text, here, is taken from the first edition of *Pizarro*.

2. OF THE EPILOGUE

The epilogue was written by William Lamb, afterwards second Lord Melbourne, husband of Lady Caroline Lamb and prime minister to Queen Victoria.

---

[1] *New Monthly Magazine*, vi (1816), 358.
[2] Acted at Drury Lane Theatre on 24 May 1780.
[3] To her mother, 30 May 1780: Chatsworth MS. no. 296.
[4] *Walpole Corr.*, xxix. 44.

I have not located the original manuscript, and print the text from the first edition of the play.

3. OF CORA'S SONG

Moore, i. opp. 1, prints a lithograph by Netherclift of Sheridan's draft of these verses. The original is now Yale MS. Im Sh 53+W 825a, vol. 1, opp. p. viii. Three stanzas in Sheridan's hand, beginning 'But thou wilt wake again, my boy', appear in Sotheby's Catalogue, 3 July 1933, lot 222. The finished version of the song was published in the *Morning Herald*, 27 May, and *The Times*, 28 May 1799.

4. OF THE MUSIC

Since Sheridan omitted the musical directions and words of the chants from the first edition of the play, I propose to print them in the footnotes only.

The newspapers made clear that 'all the symphonies' were by Jan Ladislav Dussek,[2] meaning by the phrase that the music given before the play and during the intervals was his, and was 'admirably adapted for the occasion'.[3] The music of 'the German chorusses' and Cora's song were by Kelly. In his memoirs the latter claimed: 'I had the proud distinction of having my name joined with that of Mr. Sheridan, in its production, having been selected by him to compose the whole of the music.'[4] But Kelly's publication of *The Music of Pizarro* shows that work by Gluck, Cherubini, and Sacchini was also used.[5] The title-page reads:

The Music of | PIZARRO, | *A PLAY,* | *As now performing at the* | THEATRE ROYAL DRURY LANE, | [rule] with unbounded Applause, [rule] | *The Music Composed & Selected* | ᵇᵞ | MICHAEL KELLY. | Ent at Stationers' Hall. Pr. 6s. | *Published for Mr. Kelly, No. 9.* | *New Lisle Street, & to be held at* | *all the Music Shops.*
Folio
Contents: pp. [ii]+ 1–30.
[i] title-page; [ii] blank; 1–30, music and text.

1 For the 'alternative song', see Sichel, ii. 279, where it 'appears in a sort of blank verse intended to be transformed to rhyme':

> On a sad bed of leaves and moss my child is laid,
> Yet better bed than this chilled bosom, for
> Thou sleep'st, my babe, nor heed'st the tempest wild.
> This bosom is no couch for Peace or thee,
> Alas, alas! my babe, if thou wouldst rise,
> Seek any cradle but thy mother's breast.'

This appears to me to be the first draft of the last part of the song as printed in the first edition, and not in any sense an 'alternative song'. For another stanza, see Moore, ii. 292.

2 Bohemian pianist and composer (1760–1812). See the *Morning Herald*, 27 May 1799.
3 *The Times*, 25 May 1799. 4 Kelly, ii. 143.
5 pp. 3, 6–7: Christoph Gluck (1714–87), German composer, and Antonio Sacchini (1736–86), Italian composer. The chorus by Cherubini (1760–1842) is printed in *The Music of Pizarro*, pp. 21–4.

5. OF THE PLAY

Reports agree in suggesting that Sheridan began work on *Pizarro* after obtaining or being sent a literal translation of Kotzebue's *Die Spanier in Peru, oder Rolla's Tod*. The subsequent development of the play might be seen in the following texts:

(i) *Harvard MS. fms Thr 5 (* 46 M–261 F)*

The title reads:

> the Spaniards in Peru. | or. | the Death of Rolla. | a Tragic Play in five Acts | translated from the German | of. | Aug[ustu]s von Kotzebue

The title-page also contains the Dramatis Personæ but no cast list.

The manuscript was acquired by Harvard College Library on 15 April 1947, as a bequest from the New York bookdealer, Gabriel Wells. It was Phillipps MS. 10,857, and had also appeared in Sotheby's Catalogue, 18 June 1928, lot 856a.[1]

The manuscript is folio, and made up of 173 ff. (151 pages of writing). It is bound in half red morocco.

One hundred and twenty pages contain the anonymous translator's version of Kotzebue's tragedy. Sheridan has heavily corrected the first of them, and, on a further seventeen blank pages facing the translator's lines, has written out his own paraphase. Fourteen of these concern the first act; three, the second. Later pages of the translation contain a few phrases, carets, and corrections in Sheridan's hand.

So that we may see Sheridan at work on this version, I print below a passage from it that was entirely deleted from the text after the first performance, because it was badly received:[2]

Original translator	*Sheridan's adaptation (in his own hand)*
DIEGO. how can I forget the flower of the Spanish nation—	DI. Can I forget the Flower of the Spanish Nation.
PIZARRO. is thy master living?	PIZ. Thy Master lives and thrives I find
DIEGO. he is.	—what say you is his Force—
PIZARRO. how strong his forces?	D. 12,000 your mighty Excellence
DIEGO. twelve Thousand.	PIZ. And Alonzo leads them
PIZARRO. and Alonzo their leader?	D. Alonzo and Rolla—
DIEGO. Alonzo and Rolla.	PIZ. Who is this Rolla?
PIZARRO. who is this Rolla?	DI. O your Excellence—a most unheard
DIEGO. a Peruvian that can swing his club and Sword with much dexterity and swiftness.	of tremendous Devil of a Fellow—in War a mad Tiger and every Limb [?] a Whelp in Peace an unwean'd Lamb.
PIZARRO. I shall be glad to be acquainted with him, are they Friends?	He makes no more of his huge Battle-Axe than I should of a Tooth-pick—and

---

[1] Sotheby's Catalogues, 19 June 1893, lot 750, and 10 June 1896, lot 1079, list a manuscript that is not identical: 'R. B. Sheridan: *Pizarro, or The Spaniards in Peru*, translated into English with Sheridan's autograph corrections and rough draft of his own play. 120 leaves, Folio.'

[2] See pp. 629, 638 and 640, above.

DIEGO. Friends? O yes! an[d] also loves Donna Cora.

ELVIRA. who is Cora?

DIEGO. the wife of my Master.

PIZARRO. Alonzo Married?

VALVERDA. And with a Heathen? Abominable!

DIEGO. they nevertheless love one another—

VALVERDA. has she been Baptized?

DIEGO. No! but she is good and virtuous.

VALVERDA. what a rogue—

PIZARRO. is Cora in camp with him?

DIEGO. yes! and her infant boy, besides a number of other Women.

PIZARRO. I am glad to hear it, easier will be the Victory. Their whimpering damps courage and makes men cowards. (to Diego) are they prepared to fight?

DIEGO. tomorrow they make their offering—

PIZARRO. enough! be gone, the discovery saves thy life, (to the Guard) take him away—

DIEGO. (in going to Elvira) pray young Gentleman,* speak for me (Diego, with the Guard goes off)

PIZARRO. (thoughtful) yes! I am resolved!—first a council of war, then for Battle. Elvira, thou must retire

* Elvira 'in Man's clothes'.

He is as ready with his sword as your Ex[c]el[l]ency['s] Cook used to be with his Ladle—He is moreover the Idol of the Peruvians and Kinsman to the King.

PIZ. This Rolla and I must soon be known to each other his Prowess shall be tried—are Rolla and Alonzo Friends

DI. Friends! They are as Brothers and Rolla too loves Donna Cora.

PIZ. Who is Cora

DI. My Master Alonzo's Wife.

PIZ. Alonzo married and to a Heathen!

DI. And yet the[y] Love each other—yes Heathen she is or was—but 'twould Glad a Cherub's heart to see their Happiness!

PIZ. And Rolla loves her too—

DI. Loves her in Truth in Faith and innocence. His own Hopes Rolla resign'd in Friendship to Alonzo! and now his happiness is to witness theirs— 'tis thus I've heard my master speak it.

PIZ. Romantic Savage—

ELV. Is Cora in the Camp?

DI. Sweet Sir She is and with her her infant Boy and many wives and mothers more.

PIZ. That's well. Their whimpering Panics will abate the valour of their Warriors do they expect think you our assault?

DI. O not to Day—this Day the[y] offer up a solemn sacrifice—

PIZ. Enough—take him away—

DI. O sweet fair young Sir if you would but say a word in my favour—

PIZ. Were I to spare thy Life—thoudst desert again—

DI. O Lord! never Sir—I haven't made a meal since I have been with those Fellows. They kill no living thing— their only food is grain herbs fruit and milk and such like, and the varlets have allow'd me no other—

PIZ. well unbind the knave and let him feed

DI. There only mark his excellence unbind the knave and let him feed! Heaven bless your Excellence

PIZ. Take him away

GUARD. To the Gallows General—

DI. No to the Pantry you Rascal! mind his Excellence you Rogue—Heaven bless your Excellence—unbind the

> Knave and let him feed.   Exeunt.
> PIZ. Yes—I am resolved—a Council
> first for Form—sake—then the Attack
> —Elvira retire—

Had this been printed, it would have appeared, with some additional speeches, on p. 660 below, between lines 14 and 15.

It is clear from this extract that Sheridan followed the themes provided for him but tried to give them a histrionic liveliness.

Occasionally he added to the manuscript a word or phrase that was obviously intended to remind him to expand the version before him, and from this indication alone we may probably be justified in suggesting that the Harvard MS. is one of the earliest of the drafts he prepared.

By the side of the line, 'they fight for wretched Gold, we for our King and country', Sheridan has jotted down one word: 'Nelson'. He did not amplify it in any way in this manuscript but on a later occasion, inserted at this point the famous patriotic harangue of Rolla to the Peruvians that served, between 1799 and 1809, to rally public feeling in England against the French.

At the beginning of II. iv, where Alonzo says that if he should die in battle Rolla should take Cora as his wife, Sheridan has written, 'describe Rolla's love'. It is possible that he worked up a speech on this theme but that it was deleted after the first performance. A similar reminder is to be found in f. 5: 'early mark Pizarro's sarcastic character.'

The translation ends with what is v. iii, in the printed text, and the last two scenes of the latter are not to be found in the literal translation of Kotzebue. They were Sheridan's own invention.

There are various opinions as to who wrote the translation from which Sheridan worked. Sichel concluded[1] that it was the work of a Miss Phillips, but Rhodes thought it was by 'Maria Geisweiler—the married and single names (I believe) of the same writer'.[2] Rhodes based his opinion on Boaden, who really said, 'I am not quite sure, but I think he used a translation made for him by Mr. Geisweiler, a German possessing both languages, and who afterwards rendered Sheridan's alteration back into German.'[3] If the *New Monthly Magazine* report[4] that Sheridan had paid a German one hundred pounds for a translation is true, it would do much to support Boaden's opinion that Constantine Geisweiler was the original translator, though no note of such a payment can be found in Drury Lane records. He had opened a shop at 54 Pall Mall in 1799 'for the Sale of German, French, and Italian Books',[5] and brought out Maria Geisweiler's *The Noble Lie* and *Poverty and Nobleness of Mind*, both translations from Kotzebue. Clearly either Constantine or Maria might have been the

---

[1] Sichel, ii. 277, basing his opinion on Egerton MS. 1975, f. 130.
[2] Rhodes, iii. 9.
[3] Boaden, Kemble, ii. 237. See *Pizarro. Translated into German by Constantine Geisweiler. (With the English Text).* 1800.   [4] See p. 641 above.
[5] See *The Noble Lie* (1799), p. [44].

translator of *The Spaniards in Peru* (Harvard version), and the problem remains unsolved.

What the Drury Lane records reveal is the following:[1]

> May 6 Miss Plumtree for Span[iards] in Peru £25
> — 13 Miss Plum for Sp in Peru   £25

Anne Plumptre had sold her translation to the radical publisher, Richard Phillips, and Sheridan made an agreement with him by which Phillips should 'withhold the publication of the Spaniards in Peru for three weeks or till the day after the play called Pizarro shall have been performed at Drury Lane'.[2] *The Times*, 29 May, remarked that 'the translation of *The Spaniards in Peru* is now before the Public'; and a day earlier, the *Morning Herald* had declared, 'Miss Plumptre's Death of Rolla is the identical Pizarro of Drury Lane.'

The evidence appears sufficient for us to conclude that Sheridan made use of Anne Plumptre's translation. Her published version is not, however, the same as that in the Harvard MS.

Moore also found Matthew Gregory Lewis's translation among Sheridan's papers and declared that the only use Sheridan made of it was to pick up from it the idea of a song for Cora.[3] But Sheridan did not need to mark the manuscript to use it; he may well have consulted it for inspiration and different interpretations of Kotzebue's meaning.

(ii) *The translation examined by Moore*

Moore says that Sheridan was indebted to 'the unknown paraphrast'[4] (i.e. the original translator) for the whole of the embroidery, and much else in *Pizarro*. Rhodes pointed out, however, that Sheridan's behaviour on the first night suggested that many of the lines were his own, and that what Moore took to be 'the translator's original manuscript was nothing of the sort, but the transcript of an intermediate version by Sheridan before he had completed his plan of reconstruction'.[5] How many intermediate versions there were is not known, but one of them would have been that of 'all-copying Burgess'[6] and there may have been several others apart from those mentioned below. So it is impossible at present to decide exactly how much Sheridan contributed to the text.

---

[1] Add. MS. 29710, f. 139.

[2] Sotheby's Catalogue, 15 July 1891, lot 452.

[3] Moore, ii. 289–92. Cf. Byron on the subject: '*Pizarro* was a sore subject with him ['Monk' Lewis], and no wonder that he winced at the name. Sheridan, who was not very scrupulous about applying to himself *literary* property at least, manufactured his play without so much as an acknowledgment, pecuniary or otherwise, from Lewis's ideas' (*Medwin's Conversations of Lord Byron*, ed. E. J. Lovell, Jr., (Princeton, N.J., 1966), p. 191).

[4] Moore, ii. 288.   [5] Rhodes, iii. 11.   [6] See p. 626 above.

Moore mentioned in particular Cora's flowery speech describing the attractiveness of the child and 'the ecstasy of his birth'. The lines are not in the Harvard translation, and it seems much more likely that Sheridan himself wrote them. His letters contain many affectionate and whimsical references to his son, Charles, who was then three years old; and Cora's sentiments were clearly his. Nor was he averse to public attention being given to the boy. Charles was the child in the arms of Rolla in the well-advertised painting of John Kemble, commissioned by Sheridan and exhibited at the Royal Academy in April 1800.[1]

There is another passage described by Moore that deserves attention. In the same manuscript he found that the scene in the third act between Alonzo and Pizarro was 'one of those almost entirely rewritten by Sheridan'.[2] It is not to be found in Sheridan's hand in the Harvard MS., but Sichel mentions that one of its speeches was in the Frampton Court MS.

(iii) *The Frampton Court MS.*

Sichel says that the new motive given to Elvira in the second scene of the third act 'is Sheridan's own, so is Alonzo's declamation:—

No! Deserter I am none! I was not born among robbers, pirates, murderers! When those legions lured by the abhorred lust of gold, and by thy foul ambition urged, forgot the honour of Catalans and forsook the duties of humanity, they deserted me. I have not warred against my native land, but against those who have usurped its power. The banners of my country when first I followed arms beneath them, were Justice, Faith, and Mercy. If these are beaten down and trampled under foot—I have no country, nor exists the power entitled to reproach me with revolt.'[3]

Sichel adds, 'Here we catch Sheridan's voice against Napoleon', and goes on to make a more important statement: 'His manuscript is preserved among the papers at Frampton Court; part of it is in his wife's handwriting. It contains an alternative song. . . .'[4] The Frampton catalogue describes the manuscript as 'Pizarro, a Tragedy in Five Acts, a Manuscript copy of the Play, with corrections throughout, and some entire scenes in the handwriting of the author, 1 vol. folio, *yellow mor. Frampton* 1880.'[5] Much the same description appears in Sotheby's Catalogue, 2 July 1930, lot 635,[6] but with the addition of the words 'to which is added the text from the edition of his works edited by Tom Moore, 1821, the whole inlaid to folio size, morocco gilt, by Zaehnsdorf'. It now seems to be at the bottom of the Mediterranean.[7]

(iv) *The Lord Chamberlain's MS.*

We know from several sources[8] that this manuscript was brought to Larpent for licensing in the evening before the day of performance, and

---

[1] *Morning Herald*, 30 Apr. 1800, referring to item 193 in the exhibition.
[2] Moore, ii. 289.   [3] Sichel, ii. 278.   [4] Ibid., 279.
[5] Frampton catalogue, p. 137.   [6] Nominally sold to Kahn for seventy pounds.
[7] See p. 23 above.   [8] See p. 628 above.

must therefore have been in a fairly late state of development. If we may believe Britton, it differed from the text of the first performance in omitting the two scenes at the very end of the play. It may have included other changes, but they cannot be identified because the manuscript has not been available since it passed into Larpent's hands.

(v) *The text of the first performance*

This, too, has not been located, but some inkling of what it contained may be learned from a description of what was omitted from the first night's text, when the play was given its fourth performance on 28 May:

The most material alterations are those which have been made in the first and last acts. In the one, SUETT's ludicrous and trifling character is omitted, and the dialogue between *Pizarro* and *Elvira* deprived of an exuberance of sentiment, and an expansion of language, that impaired the vigour of the design, derives strength from compression, and conducts us with more spirit to the catastrophe. In the other, some episodes which did not possess even the merit of embellishment, are struck out, and the mind is led, with almost uninterrupted interest, to contemplate the heroic fate of *Rolla*. . . .[1]

(vi) *The first edition of 1799*

Sheridan had every incentive to get the text published quickly. The play was in every one's mouth, and people were so eager to read it that Sheridan's competitors were able to profit by his dilatoriness. As noted, Anne Plumptre's version was acclaimed 'the identical Pizarro of Drury Lane', and passed into a second edition on 1 June. Another translator, Thomas Dutton, advertised the superior merit of his work which was translated from an edition of Kotzebue's drama 'published not two months ago' and containing notes and alterations by Kotzebue himself as secured by Professor Boettiger of Weimar College.[2] Sheridan was moved, at last, to action, and on 17 June, William Powell, the Drury Lane prompter, inserted an advertisement in *The Oracle* that read:

Pizarro

Several Translations of the above Drama having been Published purporting, to be the Play of 'PIZARRO, OR THE DEATH OF ROLLA, as now performing at the Theatre-Royal, Drury Lane', the Public are informed, that the above Tragedy in actual representation at that Theatre, has not yet been printed, but that a correct Edition from the Prompter's Book will be Published in about ten days . . . —Theatre Royal, June 15.

Interest in the 'correct Edition' was increased by the reports that went about concerning the sum for which Sheridan had sold his copyright. On the same day, *The Oracle* said five hundred pounds and the *Morning Herald*, seven hundred guineas.[3] Whatever the sum, the 'correct Edition'

[1] *The Times*, 29 May 1799. [2] *The Oracle*, 3 June 1799.
[3] 15 June 1799.

was published by Ridgway of York Street at midday on 25 June,[1] and sold in enormous numbers. Twenty-one editions were issued in London in the remainder of that year.[2]

The manuscript from which it was drawn is not known to be extant, but the holograph dedication appeared in Sotheby's Catalogue, 16 August 1917, lot 322.

Sheridan was pleased with the edition, as is almost certain from the lines in the letter to his wife, quoted earlier: 'I never yet own'd or allow'd the printing of anything Play Poems or Speeches but two things to both which I put my name—viz. The Critic and a Political Pamphlet on the affairs of India—I put Pizzarro out of the Question. . . .'[3] For the title-page, see p. 651 below.

Collation: 8vo, in half-sheets: [A]⁴ B–L⁴.

Contents: pp. [viii]+76+[3].

> [i] title; [ii] blank; [iii] Advertisement; [iv] blank; [v] Dedication; [vi] blank; [vii] Prologue; [viii] Dramatis Personae; [1] and 2–76, text; [77–79] Epilogue; [80] blank.

Williams, p. 234, notes that the play 'was issued with Ridgway's four-page list of publications, dated 25 June 1799, bound up at the end'.

The normal collation given above is challenged by an entry in the American Art Association and Anderson Galleries' Catalogue, 4–5 December 1935. Lot 372 is described as a copy of *Pizarro* in contemporary wrappers, stitched, uncut, and possessing half-title, 'Advertisement' leaf, three pages containing the epilogue, and four pages of advertisements bound in at the front. It carried the inscription of Frank W. Coore, and was from the collection of Seth S. and Ward E. Terry. I have not seen this copy, nor have I found a half-title mentioned elsewhere.

(vii) *Folger MS. T. a. 41.*

A comparison of Rolla's lines in J. P. Kemble's very careful transcription of his part for performance, with the printed edition of 1799, shows a number of minor differences. The very first line provides an example:

Kemble	*1799*
And post those warriors	Then place them

---

[1] *The Oracle*, 25 June 1799.

[2] Carl J. Stratman, *Bibliography of English Printed Tragedy, 1565–1900* (Carbondale and London, 1966), p. 593.

[3] *Letters*, iii. 202. For his debt to Kotzebue, and the value of the other translations, see John Britton, *Sheridan and Kotzebue* (1799), pp. 69, 115, 124–31; Thomas Dutton, *Pizarro in Peru* (1799), pp. iii–v, 9–18, 34, 43, 53, 70–117; Myron Matlaw, 'English Versions of "Die Spanier in Peru",' *Modern Language Quarterly*, xvi (Seattle, 1955), 63–7; J. W. Donohue, Jr., *Dramatic Character in the English Romantic Age* (Princeton, 1970), Ch. VI.

Another reads:

And never was the Hour of Peril nigh . . . of my Toil and of my Fame . . . Energies which swell your Hearts? . . . these base Invaders would delude you;—your manly Spirit has compared, like mine, which in this War inspire their Souls and ours;—they fight for Power. . . .	Yet never was the hour of peril near . . . of my toil, my feelings and my fame! . . . energies which inspire your hearts? . . . these bold invaders would delude you—Your generous spirit has compared as mine has, the motives, which in a war like this, can animate *their* minds and OURS. THEY, by a strange frenzy driven, fight for power. . . .

Both come from Act II, but similar changes may be discovered in Act III, Sc. i:

Such as befits the Cause, the Monarch they obey;—their Shout is, Victory or Death;—their universal Cry, our King, our King, our Country, and our God!	Such as became the cause which they support; their cry is, Victory or death, our King! our country! and our God!

Sometimes, too, Kemble's 'You' becomes 'Thou' in the printed text. These frequent differences suggest, once again, that Sheridan intended the printed version to be more literary than the stage lines.

(viii) *A Covent Garden prompt book*

The Newberry Library possesses J. P. Kemble's prompt copy of *Pizarro* (Case Y 134, 188, vol. 17); and it is clear that Kemble wrote his notes on this 28th edition (1807) of Sheridan's text, at least eight years after the first performances at Drury Lane. The book contains a number of interesting cuts and emendations as well as some very full directions on positioning. These are in Kemble's hand; Sheridan's is not to be found anywhere.

Conclusion

Five manuscripts corrected by Sheridan, seem to have been available once: the Harvard text, the manuscript of 120 leaves, the translation examined by Moore that seems to have been in the Frampton Court collection, the Larpent copy, and the missing prompt-book for the first performance. Each one was probably thought to be an improvement on its predecessor, though not necessarily in the order I have named them. Sheridan's final rendering—for readers—was the first printed edition, and since it met with his approval, I have accepted it as copy-text.[1] I have also corrected one printer's error[2] and have changed 'Almagra' (p. 702, l. 15) to 'Almagro'. I have not been able to find a copy of the first edition 'on fine wove Paper, hot-pressed. Price 5s'; and have contented myself with the half-crown issue.

[1] For later Ridgway editions, see Stratman, op. cit., pp. 593–7. Their texts contain only minor changes. For example, p. 47 of the third edition prints 'arm, which unshaken' ('arm unshaken': 685, l. 5, below). The twenty-first edition (1799) contains seventeen changes, but there is no evidence to prove they are by Sheridan.

[2] p. 686, l. 34: 'all else his worthless'.

PIZARRO;

A

TRAGEDY,

IN FIVE ACTS;

AS PERFORMED AT THE THEATRE ROYAL IN

Drury-Lane:

TAKEN FROM THE GERMAN DRAMA OF

KOTZEBUE;

AND

ADAPTED TO THE ENGLISH STAGE

BY

RICHARD BRINSLEY SHERIDAN.

———————

London:

PRINTED FOR JAMES RIDGWAY, YORK STREET,
ST. JAMES'S SQUARE.

1799.

Price 2s. 6d.

A superior Edition, on fine wove Paper, hot-pressed, Price 5s.

ADVERTISEMENT

As the two translations[1] which have been published of Kotzebue's 'SPANIARDS IN PERU' have, I understand, been very generally read, the Public are in possession of all the materials necessary to form a judgment on the merits and defects of the Play performed at Drury Lane Theatre.

[1] See p. 648, above.

DEDICATION[1]

To Her, whose approbation of this Drama, and whose peculiar delight in the applause it has received from the Public, have been to *me* the highest gratification its success has produced—I dedicate this Play.

RICHARD BRINSLEY SHERIDAN.

[1] To his second wife, though *The Oracle*, 5 July 1799, reported that 'A good deal of wit is sported on Mr. Sheridan's Dedication of his Play; some say it is inscribed to the Queen, others to Mrs. Sheridan, others to Mrs. Siddons, and why not—Mrs. Jordan? Perhaps the fact is, that it is dedicated to no *earthly power*, but to *Melpomene*, who has rendered no small assistance on the occasion.'

PROLOGUE

WRITTEN BY RICHARD BRINSLEY SHERIDAN, ESQ.

SPOKEN BY MR. KING.

CHILL'D by rude gales, while yet reluctant May
Withholds the beauties of the vernal day;   5
As some fond maid, whom matron frowns reprove,
Suspends the smile her heart devotes to love;
The season's pleasures too delay their hour,
And winter revels with protracted power:
Then blame not, Critics, if, thus late, we bring   10
A Winter Drama—but reproach—the spring.
What prudent Cit dares yet the season trust,
Bask in his whisky, and enjoy the dust?
Hors'd in Cheapside, scarce yet the gayer spark
Achieves the Sunday triumph of the Park;   15
Scarce yet you see him, dreading to be late,
Scour the New Road, and dash thro' Grosvenor-gate:—
Anxious—yet timorous too!—his steed to show,
The hack Bucephalus of Rotten-row.
Careless he seems, yet, vigilantly sly,   20
Woos the stray glance of Ladies passing by,
While his off heel, insidiously aside,
Provokes the caper which he seems to chide.[1]
Scarce rural Kensington due honour gains;
The vulgar verdure of her walk remains!   25
Where white-rob'd misses amble two by two,
Nodding to booted beaux—'How'do, how'do?'
With gen'rous questions that no answer wait,
'How vastly full! A'n't you come vastly late?
'I'n't it quite charming? When do you leave town?   30
'A'n't you quite tir'd? Pray can we set you down?'
These suburb pleasures of a London May,
Imperfect yet, we hail the cold delay;
Should our Play please—and you're indulgent ever—
Be your decree—''Tis better late than never.'   35

---

[1] Samuel Rogers said, 'Sheridan was a great artist: what could be more happy in expression than the last of these lines? You may see it illustrated in the Park every Sunday' (*Recollections of the Table Talk of Samuel Rogers* (1856), p. 68).

DRAMATIS PERSONÆ

ATALIBA, *King of Quito*,	Mr. Powell.
ROLLA, ⎱ *Commanders of*	⎰ Mr. Kemble.
ALONZO, ⎰ *his Army*,	⎱ Mr. C. Kemble.
CORA, *Alonzo's Wife*,	Mrs. Jordan.
PIZARRO, *Leader of the Spaniards*,	Mr. Barrymore.
ELVIRA, *Pizarro's Mistress*,	Mrs. Siddons.
ALMAGRO,	Mr. Caulfield.
GONZALO, ⎱ *Pizarro's*	⎰ Mr. Wentworth.
DAVILLA, ⎰ *Associates*,	Mr. Trueman.
GOMEZ,	⎱ Mr. Surmont.
VALVERDE, *Pizarro's Secretary*,	Mr. R. Palmer.
LAS-CASAS, *a Spanish Ecclesiastic*,	Mr. Aickin.
An old blind Man,	Mr. Cory.
OROZEMBO, *an old Cacique*,	Mr. Dowton.
A BOY,	MASTER Chatterley.
A CENTINEL,	Mr. Holland.
ATTENDANT,	Mr. Maddocks.
PERUVIAN OFFICER,	Mr. Archer.

SOLDIERS, MESS. FISHER, EVANS, CHIPPENDALE, WEBB, &c.

The Vocal Parts by

MESSRS. KELLY, SEDGWICK, DIGNUM, DANBY, &c.—
MRS. CROUCH, MISS DE CAMP, MISS STEPHENS,
MISS LEAK, MISS DUFOUR, &c.

PIZARRO

ACT I

SCENE I

A magnificent Pavilion near PIZARRO's *Tent—a View of the Spanish Camp in the back Ground.*—[1] ELVIRA *is discovered sleeping under a canopy on one side of the Pavilion—*VALVERDE *enters, gazes on* ELVIRA, *kneels, and attempts to kiss her hand;* ELVIRA, *awakened, rises and looks at him with indignation.*

ELV. Audacious! Whence is thy privilege to interrupt the few moments of repose my harassed mind can snatch amid the tumults of this noisy camp? Shall I inform your master of this presumptuous treachery? shall I disclose thee to Pizarro? Hey!

VAL. I am his servant, it is true—trusted by him— and I know him well; and therefore 'tis I ask, by what magic could Pizarro gain your heart, by what fatality still holds he your affection?

ELV. Hold! thou trusty SECRETARY![2]

VAL. Ignobly born! in mind and manners rude, ferocious, and unpolished, though cool and crafty if occasion need—in youth audacious—ill his first manhood—a licensed pirate—treating men as brutes, the world as booty; yet now the Spanish hero is he styled—the first of Spanish conquerors! and for a warrior so accomplished, 'tis fit Elvira should leave her noble family, her fame, her home, to share the dangers, humours, and the crimes of such a lover as Pizarro!

ELV. What! Valverde moralizing! But grant I am in error, what is my incentive? Passion, infatuation, call it as you will; but what attaches *thee* to this despised, unworthy leader?—Base lucre is thy object,

---

[1] The Spanish conquest of Peru was not a new subject for the theatre. As far back as 1658, Davenant had published *The Cruelty of the Spaniards in Peru. Exprest by Instrumentall and Vocall Musick, and by Art of Perspective in Scenes.* In Sheridan's day, *The World*, 17 Apr. 1790, advertised a performance at Sadler's Wells of 'An entire new piece consisting of Song, Dance, and Recitative, aided by Picturesque Scenery, Machinery, etc., and called THE INCAS OF PERU; *or*, THE CHILDREN OF THE SUN'.

[2] 'As the Inca drew near the Spanish quarters, father Vincent Valverde, chaplain to the expedition, advanced with a crucifix in one hand, and a breviary in the other, and in a long discourse explained to him the doctrine of the creation . . .' (W. Robertson, *The History of America* (5th edn., 1788), iii. 34).

mean fraud thy means. Could you gain me, you only hope to win a higher interest in Pizarro—I know you.

VAL. On my soul, you wrong me; what else my faults, I have none to-wards you: but indulge the scorn and levity of your nature; do it while yet the time permits; the gloomy hour, I fear, too soon approaches.   5

ELV. Valverde, a prophet too!

VAL. Hear me, Elvira—Shame from his late defeat, and burning wishes for revenge, again have brought Pizarro to Peru; but trust me, he over-rates his strength, nor measures well the foe. Encamped in a strange country, where terror cannot force, nor corruption buy a single 10 friend, what have we to hope? The army murmuring at increasing hardships, while Pizarro decorates with gaudy spoil the gay pavilion of his luxury! each day diminishes our force.

ELV. But are you not the heirs of those that fall?

VAL. Are gain and plunder then our only purpose? Is this Elvira's 15 heroism?

ELV. No, so save me Heaven! I abhor the motive, means, and end of your pursuits; but I will trust none of you:—in your whole army there is not one of you that has a heart, or speaks ingenuously—aged Las-Casas, and he alone, excepted.   20

VAL. He! an enthusiast in the opposite and worse extreme!

ELV. Oh! had I earlier known that virtuous man, how different might my lot have been!

VAL. I will grant, Pizarro could not then so easily have duped you; forgive me, but at that event I still must wonder.   25

ELV. Hear me, Valverde.—When first my virgin fancy waked to love, Pizarro was my country's idol. Self-taught, self-raised, and self-supported, he became a hero; and I was formed to be won by glory and renown. 'Tis known that when he left Panama in a slight vessel, his force was not an hundred men. Arrived in the island of Gallo, 30 with his sword he drew a line upon the sands, and said, 'Pass those who fear to die or conquer with their leader.' Thirteen alone remained, and at the head of these the warrior stood his ground. Even at the moment when my ears first caught this tale, my heart exclaimed, 'Pizarro is its lord!' What since I have perceived, or thought, or felt! 35 you must have more worth to win the knowledge of.

VAL. I press no further; still assured that while Alonzo de Molina, our General's former friend and pupil, leads the enemy, Pizarro never more will be a conqueror. [*Trumpets without.*]

ELV. Silence! I hear him coming; look not perplexed.—How mystery 40 and fraud confound the countenance! Quick, put on an honest face, if thou canst.

PIZARRO. [*Speaking without*]. Chain and secure him; I will examine him myself.

PIZARRO *enters.*

(VALVERDE *bows*—ELVIRA *laughs.*)

PIZ. Why dost thou smile, Elvira?

ELV. To laugh or weep without a reason, is one of the few privileges
we women have.   5

PIZ. Elvira, I will know the cause, I am resolved!

ELV. I am glad of that, because I love resolution, and am resolved not
to tell you. Now my resolution, I take it, is the better of the two, because
it depends upon myself, and yours does not.

PIZ. Psha! trifler!   10

VAL. Elvira was laughing at my apprehensions that——

PIZ. Apprehensions!

VAL. Yes—that Alonzo's skill and genius should so have disciplined and
informed the enemy, as to——

PIZ. Alonzo! the traitor! How I once loved that man! His noble mother   15
entrusted him, a boy, to my protection. At my table did he feast—in
my tent did he repose. I had marked his early genius, and the valorous
spirit that grew with it. Often I had talked to him of our first adventures
—what storms we struggled with—what perils we surmounted. When
landed with a slender host upon an unknown land—then, when I told   20
how famine and fatigue, discord and toil, day by day, did thin our
ranks; amid close-pressing enemies, how still undaunted I endured
and dared—maintained my purpose and my power in despite of
growling mutiny or bold revolt, till with my faithful few remaining
I became at last victorious!—When, I say, of these things I spoke, the   25
youth, Alonzo, with tears of wonder and delight, would throw him on
my neck, and swear, his soul's ambition owned no other leader.

VAL. What could subdue attachment so begun?

PIZ. Las-Casas—he it was, with fascinating craft and canting precepts
of humanity, raised in Alonzo's mind a new enthusiasm, which forced   30
him, as the stripling termed it, to forego his country's claims for those
of human nature.

VAL. Yes, the traitor left you, joined the Peruvians, and became thy
enemy and Spain's.

PIZ. But first with weariless remonstrance he sued to win me from my   35
purpose, and untwine the sword from my determined grasp. Much
he spoke of right, of justice and humanity, calling the Peruvians our
innocent and unoffending brethren.

VAL. They!—Obdurate heathens!—They our brethren!

PIZ. But when he found that the soft folly of the pleading tears he dropt   40
upon my bosom fell on marble, he flew and joined the foe: then,
profiting by the lessons he had gain'd in wrong'd Pizarro's school, the
youth so disciplined and led his new allies, that soon he forc'd me—

Ha! I burn with shame and fury while I own it! in base retreat and foul discomfiture to quit the shore.

VAL. But the hour of revenge is come.

PIZ. It is; I am returned—my force is strengthened, and the audacious Boy shall soon know that Pizarro lives, and has—a grateful recollection 5 of the thanks he owes him.

VAL. 'Tis doubted whether still Alonzo lives.

PIZ. 'Tis certain that he does; one of his armour-bearers is just made prisoner: twelve thousand is their force, as he reports, led by Alonzo and Peruvian Rolla. This day they make a solemn sacrifice on their 10 ungodly altars. We must profit by their security, and attack them unprepared—the sacrificers shall become the victims.

ELV. [*Aside.*] Wretched innocents! And their own blood shall bedew their altars!

PIZ. Right! [*Trumpets without.*] Elvira, retire! 15

ELV. Why should I retire?

PIZ. Because men are to meet here, and on manly business.

ELV. O, men! men! ungrateful and perverse! O, woman! still affectionate though wrong'd! The Beings to whose eyes you turn for animation, hope, and rapture, through the days of mirth and revelry; and on whose 20 bosoms in the hour of sore calamity you seek for rest and consolation; THEM, when the pompous follies of your mean ambition are the question, you treat as playthings or as slaves!—I shall not retire.[1]

PIZ. Remain then—and, if thou canst, be silent.

ELV. They only babble who practise not reflection. I shall think—and 25 thought is silence.

PIZ. Ha!—there's somewhat in her manner lately—

[PIZARRO *looks sternly and suspiciously towards* ELVIRA, *who meets him with a commanding and unaltered eye.*]

Enter LAS-CASAS, ALMAGRO, GONZALO, DAVILLA, *Officers and Soldiers.* 30
—*Trumpets without.*

LAS-C. Pizarro, we attend your summons.

PIZ. Welcome, venerable father—my friends, most welcome. Friends and fellow-soldiers, at length the hour is arrived, which to Pizarro's hopes presents the full reward of our undaunted enterprise and long- 35 enduring toils. Confident in security, this day the foe devotes to solemn sacrifice: if with bold surprise we strike on their solemnity—trust to your leader's word—we shall not fail.

ALM. Too long inactive have we been mouldering on the coast—our stores exhausted, and our soldiers murmuring—Battle! Battle!—then 40 death to the arm'd, and chains for the defenceless.

[1] 'Elvira, who appeared a few minutes before, the enfeebled slave of her passion, assumes a dignity and resolution, which even shook the tyrant for a moment.' (*The Oracle*, 25 May 1799.)

DAV. Death to the whole Peruvian race!

LAS-C. Merciful Heaven!

ALM. Yes, General, the attack, and instantly! Then shall Alonzo, basking at his ease, soon cease to scoff our suffering and scorn our force.

LAS-C. Alonzo!—scorn and presumption are not in his nature.5

ALM. 'Tis fit Las-Casas should defend his pupil.

PIZ. Speak not of the traitor—or hear his name but as the bloody summons to assault and vengeance. It appears we are agreed?

ALM. *and* DAV. We are.

GON. All!—Battle! Battle!10

LAS-C. Is then the dreadful measure of your cruelty not yet compleat?—Battle!—gracious Heaven! Against whom?—Against a King, in whose mild bosom your atrocious injuries even yet have not excited hate! but who, insulted or victorious, still sues for peace. Against a People who never wronged the living Being their Creator formed: a People, who,15 children of innocence received you as cherish'd guests with eager hospitality and confiding kindness. Generously and freely did they share with you their comforts, their treasures, and their homes: you repaid them by fraud, oppression, and dishonour. These eyes have witnessed all I speak—as Gods you were received; as Fiends have you20 acted.¹

PIZ. Las-Casas!

LAS-C. Pizarro, hear me!—Hear me, chieftains!—And thou, All-powerful! whose thunders can shiver into sand the adamantine rock—whose lightnings can pierce to the core of the rived and quaking earth—25 Oh! let thy power give effect to thy servant's words, as thy spirit gives courage to his will! Do not, I implore you, Chieftains—Countrymen—Do not, I implore you, renew the foul barbarities which your insatiate avarice has inflicted on this wretched, unoffending race!—But hush, my sighs—fall not, drops of useless sorrow!—heart-breaking anguish,30 choke not my utterance—All I entreat is, send me once more to those you *call* your enemies—Oh! let me be the messenger of penitence from you, I shall return with blessings and with peace from them.—Elvira, you weep!—Alas! and does this dreadful crisis move no heart but thine?35

ALM. Because there are no women here but she and thou.

PIZ. Close this idle war of words: time flies, and our opportunity will be lost. Chieftains, are ye for instant battle?

ALL. We are.

---

¹ 'The speech of this good old Priest is one of the finest and most impressive in the whole Piece . . .' (*The Oracle*, 25 May 1799). The Harvard MS. reads: 'What a dreadful reflexion! a Battle—against whom? against a King, that a few days ago offered peace—against a nation, that in innocence, and with purity worship their Creator in their accustomed way and manner.'

LAS-C. Oh, men of blood!—[*Kneels*.] God! thou hast anointed me thy
servant—not to curse, but to bless my countrymen: yet now my blessing on their force were blasphemy against thy goodness.—[*Rises*]. No!
I curse your purpose, homicides! I curse the bond of blood by which
you are united. May fell division, infamy, and rout, defeat your pro-   5
jects and rebuke your hopes! On you, and on your children, be the
peril of the innocent blood which shall be shed this day! I leave you,
and for ever! No longer shall these aged eyes be feared by the horrors
they have witnessed. In caves, in forests, will I hide myself; with
Tigers and with savage beasts will I commune: and when at length   10
we meet again before the bless'd tribunal of that Deity, whose mild
doctrines and whose mercies ye have this day renounced, then shall
YOU feel the agony and grief of soul which tear the bosom of your
accuser now! [*Going*.]

ELV. Las-Casas! Oh! take me with thee, Las-Casas.   15

LAS-C. Stay! lost, abused lady! I alone am useless here. Perhaps thy
loveliness may persuade to pity, where reason and religion plead in
vain. Oh! save thy innocent fellow-creatures if thou canst: then shall
thy frailty be redeemed, and thou wilt share the mercy thou bestowest.
[*Exit*. 20

PIZ. How, Elvira! wouldst thou leave me?

ELV. I am bewildered, grown terrified!—Your inhumanity—and that
good Las-Casas—oh! he appeared to me just now something more
than heavenly: and you! ye all looked worse than earthly.

PIZ. Compassion sometimes becomes a beauty.   25

ELV. Humanity always becomes a conqueror.

ALM. Well! Heaven be praised, we are rid of the old moralist.

GON. I hope he'll join his preaching pupil, Alonzo.

PIZ. Now to prepare our muster and our march. At mid-day is the hour
of the sacrifice. Consulting with our guides, the route of your divisions   30
shall be given to each commander. If we surprise, we conquer; and if
we conquer, the gates of Quito will be open to us.

ALM. And Pizarro then be monarch of Peru.

PIZ. Not so fast—ambition for a time must take counsel from discretion.
Ataliba still must hold the shadow of a sceptre in his hand—Pizarro   35
still appear dependant upon Spain: while the pledge of future peace,
his daughter's hand, secures the proud succession to the crown I
seek.

ALM. This is best. In Pizarro's plans observe the statesman's wisdom
guides the warrior's valour.   40

VAL. [*Aside to* ELVIRA.] You mark, Elvira?

ELV. O, yes—this is best—this is excellent.

PIZ. You seem offended. Elvira still retains my heart. Think—a sceptre
waves me on.

ELV. Offended?—No!—Thou know'st thy glory is my idol; and this
will be most glorious, most just and honourable.

PIZ. What mean you?

ELV. Oh! nothing—mere woman's prattle—a jealous whim, perhaps:
but let it not impede the royal hero's course.—[*Trumpets without.*] 5
The call of arms invites you—Away! away! you, his brave, his worthy
fellow-warriors.

PIZ. And go you not with me?

ELV. Undoubtedly! I needs must be the first to hail the future monarch
of Peru. 10

Enter GOMEZ.

ALM. How, Gomez! what bring'st thou?

GOM. On yonder hill among the palm trees we have surprised an old
cacique; escape by flight he could not, and we seized him and his
attendant unresisting; yet his lips breathe nought but bitterness and 15
scorn.

PIZ. Drag him before us.

[GOMEZ *leaves the tent, and returns conducting* OROZEMBO *and* ATTEN-
DANT, *in chains, guarded.*
What art thou, stranger? 20

ORO. First tell me which among you is the captain of this band of robbers.

PIZ. Ha!

ALM. Madman!—Tear out his tongue, or else——

ORO. Thou'lt hear some truth.

DAV. [*Shewing his poniard.*] Shall I not plunge this into his heart? 25

ORO. [*To* PIZ.] Does your army boast many such heroes as this?

PIZ. Audacious!—This insolence has sealed thy doom. Die thou shalt,
grey-headed ruffian. But first confess what thou knowest.

ORO. I know that which thou hast just assured me of—that I shall die.

PIZ. Less audacity perhaps might have preserved thy life. 30

ORO. My life is as a withered tree—it is not worth preserving.

PIZ. Hear me, old man. Even now we march against the Peruvian army.
We know there is a secret path that leads to your strong-hold among
the rocks: guide us to that, and name thy reward. If wealth be thy
wish— 35

ORO. Ha! ha! ha! ha!

PIZ. Dost thou despise my offer?

ORO. Thee and thy offer!—Wealth!—I have the wealth of two dear
gallant sons—I have stored in heaven the riches which repay good
actions here—and still my chiefest treasure do I bear about me. 40

PIZ. What is that? Inform me.

ORO. I will; for it never can be thine—the treasure of a pure unsullied
conscience.

PIZ. I believe there is no other Peruvian who dares speak as thou dost.

ORO. Would I could believe there is no other Spaniard who dares act as thou dost!

GON. [*Aside.*] Obdurate Pagan!—How numerous is your army?

ORO. Count the leaves of yonder forest.   5

ALM. Which is the weakest part of your camp?

ORO. It has no weak part—on every side 'tis fortified by justice.

PIZ. Where have you concealed your wives and your children?

ORO. In the hearts of their husbands and their fathers.

PIZ. Know'st thou Alonzo?   10

ORO. Know him!—Alonzo!—Know him!—Our nation's benefactor!— The guardian angel of Peru!

PIZ. By what has he merited that title?

ORO. By not resembling thee.

ALM. Who is this Rolla, joined with Alonzo in command?   15

ORO. I will answer that; for I love to hear and to repeat the hero's name. Rolla, the kinsman of the King, is the idol of our army; in war a tiger, chased by the hunter's spear; in peace as gentle as the unweaned lamb. CORA was once betrothed to him; but finding she preferred Alonzo, he resigned his claim, and, I fear, his peace, to friendship and to CORA's   20 happiness: yet still he loves her with a pure and holy fire.

PIZ. Romantic savage!—I shall meet this Rolla soon.

ORO. Thou hadst better not! The terrors of his noble eye would strike thee dead.

DAV. Silence, or tremble!   25

ORO. Beardless robber! I never yet have trembled before God—why should I tremble before man?—Why before thee, thou less than man!

DAV. Another word, audacious heathen, and I strike!

ORO. Strike, Christian! Then boast among thy fellows—I too have murdered a Peruvian!   30

DAV. Hell and vengeance seize thee! [*Stabs him.*]

PIZ. Hold!

DAV. Couldst thou longer have endured his insults?

PIZ. And therefore should he die untortured?

ORO. True! Observe, young man—your unthinking rashness has saved   35 me from the rack; and you yourself have lost the opportunity of a useful lesson; you might have seen with what cruelty vengeance would have inflicted torments, and with what patience virtue would have borne them.

ELV. [*Supporting* OROZEMBO's *head upon her bosom.*] Oh! ye are monsters all. Look up, thou martyr'd innocent—look up once more, and bless   40 me ere thou diest. God! how I pity thee!

ORO. Pity me!—Me! so near my happiness! Bless thee, lady!—Spaniards— Heaven turn your hearts, and pardon you as I do. [OROZEMBO *is borne off dying.*]

PIZ. Away!—Davilla! If thus rash a second time—

DAV. Forgive the hasty indignation which—

PIZ. No more—unbind that trembling wretch—let him depart; 'tis well he should report the mercy which we show to insolent defiance.——Hark!—our troops are moving. 5

ATTENDANT. [*On passing* ELVIRA.] If through your gentle means my master's poor remains might be preserved from insult—

ELV. I understand you.

ATT. His sons may yet thank your charity, if not avenge their father's fate. [*Exit.* 10

PIZ. What says the slave?

ELV. A parting word to thank you for your mercy.

PIZ. Our guard and guides approach. [*Soldiers march through the tents.*] Follow me, friends—each shall have his post assigned, and ere Peruvia's God shall sink beneath the main, the Spanish banner, bathed in blood, 15 shall float above the walls of vanquish'd Quito. [*Exeunt.*

Manent ELVIRA *and* VALVERDE.

VAL. Is it now presumption that my hopes gain strength with the increasing horrors which I see appal Elvira's soul?

ELV. I am mad with terror and remorse! Would I could fly these dread- 20 ful scenes!

VAL. Might not Valverde's true attachment be thy refuge?

ELV. What wouldst thou do to save or to avenge me?

VAL. I dare do all thy injuries may demand—a word—and he lies bleeding at your feet. 25

ELV. Perhaps we will speak again of this. Now leave me.

[*Exit* VALVERDE.

ELV. [*Alone.*] No! not this revenge—no! not this instrument. Fie, Elvira! even for a moment to counsel with this unworthy traitor!—Can a wretch, false to a confiding master, be true to any pledge of love or 30 honour?—Pizarro will abandon me—yes; me—who, for his sake, have sacrificed—Oh, God!—What have I not sacrificed for him; yet, curbing the avenging pride that swells this bosom, I still will further try him. Oh, men! ye who, wearied by the fond fidelity of virtuous love, seek in the wanton's flattery a new delight, oh, ye may insult and leave 35 the hearts to which your faith was pledged, and, stifling self-reproach, may fear no other peril; because such hearts, howe'er you injure and desert them, have yet the proud retreat of an unspotted fame—of unreproaching conscience. But beware the desperate libertine who forsakes the creature whom his arts have first deprived of all natural 40 protection—of all self-consolation! What has he left her!—Despair and vengeance! [*Exit.*

END OF THE FIRST ACT

ACT II

SCENE I

A Bank surrounded by a wild Wood, and Rocks.—CORA, *sitting on the root of a tree, is playing with her Child.*—ALONZO *looks over them with delight and chearfulness.* 5

CORA. Now confess, does he resemble thee, or not?

AL. Indeed he is liker thee—thy rosy softness, thy smiling gentleness.

CORA. But his auburn hair, the colour of his eyes, Alonzo—O! my lord's image, and my heart's adored! [*Pressing the Child to her bosom.*]

AL. The little daring urchin robs me, I doubt, of some portion of thy 10 love, my Cora. At least he shares caresses, which till his birth were only mine.

CORA. Oh no, Alonzo! a mother's love for her dear babe is not a stealth, or taken from the father's store; it is a new delight that turns with quicken'd gratitude to HIM, the author of her augmented bliss. 15

AL. Could Cora think me serious?

CORA. I am sure he will speak soon: then will be the last of the three holydays allowed by Nature's sanction to the fond anxious mother's heart.

AL. What are those three? 20

CORA. The ecstacy of his birth I pass; that in part is selfish: but when first the white blossoms of his teeth appear, breaking the crimson buds that did incase them; that is a day of joy: next, when from his father's arms he runs without support, and clings, laughing and delighted, to his mother's knee; that is the mother's heart's next holyday: and sweeter 25 still the third, whene'er his little stammering tongue shall utter the grateful sound of, Father, Mother!—O! that is the dearest joy of all!

AL. Beloved Cora!

CORA. Oh! my Alonzo! daily, hourly, do I pour thanks to Heaven for the dear blessing I possess in him and thee. 30

AL. To Heaven and Rolla.

CORA. Yes, to Heaven and Rolla: and art thou not grateful to them too, Alonzo? art thou not happy?

AL. Can Cora ask that question?

CORA. Why then of late so restless on thy couch? Why to my waking 35 watching ear so often does the stillness of the night betray thy struggling sighs?

AL. Must not I fight against my country, against my brethren?

CORA. Do they not seek our destruction, and are not all men brethren?

AL. Should they prove victorious? 40

CORA. I will fly, and meet thee in the mountains.

AL. Fly, with thy infant, Cora?

CORA. What! think you a mother, when she runs from danger, can feel
the weight of her child?

AL. Cora, my beloved, do you wish to set my heart at rest?

CORA. Oh yes! yes! yes!   5

AL. Hasten then now to the concealment in the mountains; there dwells
your father, and there all our matrons and virgins, and our warriors'
offspring, are allotted to await the issue of the war. Cora will not alone
resist her husband's, her sisters', and her monarch's wish.

CORA. Alonzo, I cannot leave you: Oh! how in every moment's absence 10
would my fancy paint you, wounded, alone, abandon'd! No, no, I
cannot leave you.

AL. Rolla will be with me.

CORA. Yes, while the battle rages, and where it rages most, brave Rolla
will be found. He may revenge, but cannot save thee. To follow danger, 15
he will leave even thee. But I have sworn never to forsake thee but
with life. Dear, dear Alonzo! can you wish that I should break my vow?

AL. Then be it so. Oh! excellence in all that's great and lovely, in courage,
gentleness, and truth; my pride, my content, my all! Can there on
this earth be fools who seek for happiness, and pass by love in the   20
pursuit?

CORA. Alonzo, I cannot thank you: silence is the gratitude of true
affection: who seeks to follow it by sound will miss the track. [*Shout
without.*] Does the King approach?

AL. No, 'tis the General placing the guard that will surround the temple 25
during the sacrifice. 'Tis Rolla comes, the first and best of heroes.
[*Trumpets sound.*]

ROLLA.

ROL. [*as entering.*] Then place them on the hill fronting the Spanish
camp. [*Enters.*]   30

CORA. Rolla! my friend, my brother!

AL. Rolla! my friend, my benefactor! how can our lives repay the obligations which we owe you?

ROL. Pass them in peace and bliss.—Let Rolla witness it, he is overpaid.

CORA. Look on this child—He is the life-blood of my heart; but if ever 35
he loves or reveres thee less than his own father, his mother's hate fall
on him!

ROL. Oh, no more!—What sacrifice have I made to merit gratitude?
The object of my love was Cora's happiness.—I see her happy.—Is
not my object gain'd, and am I not rewarded? Now, Cora, listen to a 40
friend's advice. You must away; you must seek the sacred caverns, the
unprofan'd recess, whither, after this day's sacrifice, our matrons, and
e'en the Virgins of the Sun, retire.

CORA. Not secure with Alonzo and with thee, Rolla?

ROL. We have heard Pizarro's plan is to surprise us.—Thy presence, Cora, cannot aid, but may impede our efforts.

CORA. Impede!

ROL. Yes, yes. Thou know'st how tenderly we love thee; we, thy husband 5 and thy friend. Art thou near us? our thoughts, our valour—vengeance will not be our own.—No advantage will be pursued that leads us from the spot where thou art placed; no succour will be given but for thy protection. The faithful lover dares not be all himself amid the war, until he knows that the beloved of his soul is absent from the peril of 10 the fight.

AL. Thanks to my friend! 'tis this I would have urged.

CORA. This timid excess of love, producing fear instead of valour, flatters, but does not convince me: the wife is incredulous.

ROL. And is the mother unbelieving too?   15

CORA. No more—Do with me as you please. My friend, my husband! place me where you will.

AL. My adored! we thank you both. [*March without.*] Hark! the King approaches to the sacrifice. You, Rolla, spoke of rumours of surprise.— A servant of mine, I hear, is missing; whether surprised or treacherous, 20 I know not.

ROL. It matters not. We are every where prepared. Come, Cora, upon the altar 'mid the rocks thou'lt implore a blessing on our cause. The pious supplication of the trembling wife, and mother's heart, rises to the throne of mercy, the most resistless prayer of human homage. 25

[*Exeunt.*

SCENE II

The Temple of the Sun: it represents the magnificence of Peruvian idolatry: in the centre is the altar.—A solemn march.[1]*—The Warriors and King enter on one side of the Temple.—*ROLLA, ALONZO, *and* 30 CORA, *on the other.*

ATA. Welcome, Alonzo! [*To* ROLLA.] Kinsman, thy hand.—[*To* CORA.] Bless'd be the object of the happy mother's love.

CORA. May the sun bless the father of his people![2]

ATA. In the welfare of his children lives the happiness of their King. 35 Friends, what is the temper of our soldiers?

[1] 'Grand March in the Temple of the Sun [by] Kelly': see *The Music of Pizarro,* pp. 1–2.

[2] 'To those *Children of the Sun,* for that was the appellation bestowed upon all the offspring of the first Inca, the people looked up with the reverence due to beings of a superior order. They were deemed to be under the immediate protection of the deity from whom they issued' (W. Robertson, *The History of America* (5th edn., 1788), iii. 204).

ROL. Such as becomes the cause which they support; their cry is, Victory or death! our King! our Country! and our God!

ATA. Thou, Rolla, in the hour of peril, hast been wont to animate the spirit of their leaders, ere we proceed to consecrate the banners which thy valour knows so well to guard.   5

ROL. Yet never was the hour of peril near, when to inspire them words were so little needed. My brave associates—partners of my toil, my feelings and my fame!—can Rolla's words add vigour to the virtuous energies which inspire your hearts?——No—YOU have judged as I have, the foulness of the crafty plea by which these bold invaders   10 would delude you—Your generous spirit has compared as mine has, the motives, which, in a war like this, can animate *their* minds, and OURS.—THEY, by a strange frenzy driven, fight for power, for plunder, and extended rule—WE, for our country, our altars, and our homes.— THEY follow an Adventurer whom they fear—and obey a power which   15 they hate—WE serve a Monarch whom we love—a God whom we adore.—Whene'er they move in anger, desolation tracks their progress! —Where'er they pause in amity, affliction mourns their friendship!— They boast, they come but to improve our state, enlarge our thoughts, and free us from the yoke of error!—Yes—THEY will give enlightened   20 freedom to *our* minds, who are themselves the slaves of passion, avarice, and pride.—They offer us their protection—Yes, such protection as vultures give to lambs—covering and devouring them!—They call on us to barter all of good we have inherited and proved, for the desperate chance of something better which they promise.—Be our plain answer   25 this: The throne WE honour is the PEOPLE'S CHOICE—the laws we reverence are our brave Fathers' legacy—the faith we follow teaches us to live in bonds of charity with all mankind, and die with hope of bliss beyond the grave. Tell your invaders this, and tell them too, we seek no change; and, least of all, such change as they would bring us.   30
                                                      [*Trumpets sound.*

ATA. [*Embracing* ROLLA.] Now, holy friends, ever mindful of these sacred truths, begin the sacrifice. [*A solemn Procession commences from the recess of the Temple above the Altar—The Priests and Virgins of the Sun arrange themselves on either side—The High-Priest approaches the*   35 *Altar, and the solemnity begins—The Invocation of the High-Priest*[1] *is*

---

[1] The procession was accompanied by a march by Gluck. See Kelly, *The Music of Pizarro*, pp. 3–11, for this, and for the invocation, made up of 'Solo and Semi-Chorus':

[*High-Priest*: Mr. Sedgwick]

Oh pow'r Supreme! in mercy smile
With favor on thy Servants' toil!
Our hearts from guileful passions free
Which here we render unto thee!

Q

*followed by the Chorusses of the Priests and Virgins—Fire from above
lights upon the Altar.—The whole assembly rise, and join in the Thanksgiving.*] Our offering is accepted.—Now to arms, my friends, prepare
for battle.

Enter ORANO.　　　　5

ORA. The enemy!

ATA. How near?

ORA. From the hill's brow, e'en now as I o'er-looked their force, suddenly
I perceived the whole in motion: with eager haste they march towards
our deserted camp, as if apprised of this most solemn sacrifice.　　10

ROL. They must be met before they reach it.

ATA. And you, my daughters, with your dear children, away to the
appointed place of safety.

CORA. Oh, Alonzo! [*Embracing him.*]

AL. We shall meet again.　　　　15

CORA. Bless us once more, ere you leave us.

AL. Heaven protect and bless thee, my beloved; and thee, my innocent!

ATA. Haste, haste!—each moment is precious!

CORA. Farewell, Alonzo! Remember thy life is mine.

ROL. Not one farewell to Rolla?　　　　20

CORA. [*Giving him her hand.*] Farewell! The God of war be with you:
but, bring me back Alonzo.　　　　[*Exit with the Child.*

ATA. [*Draws his sword.*] Now, my brethren, my sons, my friends, I know
your valour.—Should ill success assail us, be despair the last feeling
of your hearts.—If successful, let mercy be the first.[1] Alonzo, to you　25

[*Priests and Virgins*]

[Kelly, Dignum, Mrs. Crouch, Miss Decamp, Stephens, Dufour, Leak]

> Oh pow'r supreme! in mercy smile
> With favor on thy Servants' toil!
> Our hearts from guileful passions free
> Which here we render unto thee.

[*Chorus of Priests and Virgins*: by Sacchini]

> Thou Parent Light but deign to hear
> 　The voices of our feeble choir;
> And this, our sacrifice of fear,
> 　Consume with thine own hallowed fire!

[*Thanksgiving*]

> Give praise, give praise, the God has heard,
> Our God most awfully rever'd!
> The altar his own flames enwreath'd!
> Then be the conquering sword unsheath'd,
> And victory sit on Rolla's brow,
> Our foes to crush—to overthrow!

[1] 'This patriotic address, which was greatly applauded, was concluded with a chorus;
at the end of which the Peruvians filed off the stage, led by Rolla, who told them, "that

I give to defend the narrow passage of the mountains. On the right of
the wood be Rolla's station. For me, strait forwards will I march to
meet them, and fight until I see my people saved, or they behold their
Monarch fall. Be the word of battle—God! and our native land.
[*A march.*][1]   [*Exeunt.* 5

SCENE III

The Wood between the Temple and the Camp.

Enter ROLLA *and* ALONZO.

ROL. Here, my friend, we separate—soon, I trust, to meet again in
     triumph.   10
AL. Or perhaps we part to meet no more. Rolla, a moment's pause;
     we are yet before our army's strength; one earnest word at parting.
ROL. There is in language now no word but battle.
AL. Yes, one word more—Cora!
ROL. Cora! Speak!   15
AL. The next hour brings us—
ROL. Death or victory!
AL. It may be victory to one—death to the other.
ROL. Or both may fall.
AL. If so, my wife and child I bequeath to the protection of Heaven and 20
     my King. But should I only fall, Rolla, be thou my heir.
ROL. How?
AL. Be Cora thy wife—be thou a father to my child.
ROL. Rouse thee, Alonzo! Banish these timid fancies.
AL. Rolla! I have tried in vain, and cannot fly from the foreboding which 25
     oppresses me: thou know'st it will not shake me in the fight: but give
     me your promise.
ROL. If it be Cora's will—Yes—I promise—[*Gives his hand.*]
AL. Tell her it was my last wish! and bear to her and to my son, my last
     blessing.   30
ROL. I will.—Now then to our posts, and let our swords speak for us.
     [*They draw their swords.*]
AL. For the King and Cora!
ROL. For Cora and the King!   [*Exeunt different ways. Alarms without.*

in case of a defeat, despair should be the last quality that should fill their bosoms; and
in case of victory, mercy should be the first!" A blind man next appeared' (*The Oracle*,
25 May 1799). If the report is correct, the text of the first night differed from the printed
version at this point, and immediately afterwards.

   1 Kelly, *The Music of Pizarro*, p. 12: by Thomas Shaw, conductor of the band.

SCENE IV

A View of the Peruvian Camp, with a distant View of a Peruvian Village. Trees growing from a rocky Eminence on one Side. Alarms continue.

Enter an OLD BLIND MAN *and a* BOY.　　　　　5

O. MAN. Have none returned to the camp?

BOY. One messenger alone. From the temple they all march'd to meet the foe.

O. MAN. Hark! I hear the din of battle. O! had I still retain'd my sight, I might now have grasp'd a sword, and died a soldier's death! Are we 10 quite alone?

BOY. Yes!—I hope my father will be safe!

O. MAN. He will do his duty. I am more anxious for thee, my child.

BOY. I can stay with you, dear grandfather.

O. MAN. But should the enemy come, they will drag thee from me, my 15 boy.

BOY. Impossible, grandfather! for they will see at once that you are old and blind, and cannot do without me.

O. MAN. Poor child! you little know the hearts of these inhuman men.— [*Discharge of cannon heard.*] Hark! the noise is near—I hear the dreadful 20 roaring of the fiery engines of these cruel strangers.—[*Shouts at a distance.*] At every shout, with involuntary haste I clench my hand, and fancy still it grasps a sword! Alas! I can only serve my country by my prayers. Heaven preserve the Inca and his gallant soldiers!

BOY. O father! there are soldiers running—　　　　　25

O. MAN. Spaniards, boy?

BOY. No, Peruvians!

O. MAN. How! and flying from the field!—It cannot be.

Enter two Peruvian SOLDIERS.

O speak to them, boy!—Whence come you? How goes the battle?　　30

SOL. We may not stop; we are sent for the reserve behind the hill. The day's against us.　　　　　[*Exeunt* SOLDIERS.

O. MAN. Quick, then, quick!

BOY. I see the points of lances glittering in the light.

O. MAN. Those are Peruvians. Do they bend this way?　　　　　35

Enter a Peruvian SOLDIER.

BOY. Soldier, speak to my blind father.

SOL. I'm sent to tell the helpless father to retreat among the rocks: all will be lost, I fear. The King is wounded.

O. MAN. Quick, boy! Lead me to the hill, where thou may'st view the plain. [*Alarms.*]

Enter ATALIBA, *wounded, with* ORANO, OFFICERS, *and* SOLDIERS.

ATA. My wound is bound; believe me, the hurt is nothing: I may return to the fight. 5

ORA. Pardon your servant; but the allotted priest who attends the sacred banner has pronounced that the Inca's blood once shed, no blessing can await the day until he leave the field.

ATA. Hard restraint! O! my poor brave soldiers!—Hard that I may no longer be a witness of their valour. But haste you; return to your com- 10 rades: I will not keep one soldier from his post. Go, and avenge your fallen brethren. [*Exeunt* ORANO, OFFICERS, *and* SOLDIERS.] I will not repine; my own fate is the last anxiety of my heart. It is for you, my people, that I feel and fear.

OLD MAN *and* BOY *advance.* 15

O. MAN. Did I not hear the voice of an unfortunate?—Who is it complains thus?

ATA. One almost by hope forsaken.

O. MAN. Is the King alive?

ATA. The King still lives. 20

O. MAN. Then thou art not forsaken! Ataliba protects the meanest of his subjects.

ATA. And who shall protect Ataliba?

O. MAN. The immortal Powers, that protect the just. The virtues of our Monarch alike secure to him the affection of his people and the benign 25 regard of Heaven.

ATA. How impious, had I murmured! How wondrous, thou supreme Disposer, are thy acts! Even in this moment, which I had thought the bitterest trial of mortal suffering, thou hast infused the sweetest sensation of my life—it is the assurance of my people's love. 30

BOY. [*Turning forward.*] O, father!—Stranger, see those hideous men that rush upon us yonder!

ATA. Ha! Spaniards!—And I—Ataliba—ill-fated fugitive, without a sword even to try the ransom of a monarch life.

Enter DAVILLA, ALMAGRO, *and Spanish* SOLDIERS. 35

DAV. 'Tis he—our hopes are answered—I know him well—it is the King!

ALM. Away! Follow with your royal prize. Avoid those Peruvians, though in flight. This way we may regain our line.

[*Exeunt* DAVILLA, ALMAGRO, *and* SOLDIERS, *with* ATALIBA *prisoner.* 40

O. MAN. The King! Wretched old man, that could not see his gracious form!—Boy, would thou hadst led me to the reach of those ruffians' swords!

BOY. Father! all our countrymen are flying here for refuge.

O. MAN. No—to the rescue of their King—they never will desert him.   5
[*Alarms without.*]

Enter Peruvian OFFICERS *and* SOLDIERS, *flying across the stage;* ORANO *following.*

ORA. Hold, I charge you! Rolla calls you.

OFFICER. We cannot combat with their dreadful engines.   10

Enter ROLLA.

ROL. Hold, recreants! cowards!—What, fear ye death, and fear not shame? By my soul's fury, I cleave to the earth the first of you that stirs, or plunge your dastard swords into your leader's heart, that he no more may witness your disgrace. Where is the King?   15

ORA. From this old man and boy I learn that the detachment of the enemy which you observed so suddenly to quit the field, have succeeded in surprising him; they are yet in sight.

ROL. And bear the Inca off a prisoner?—Hear this, ye base, disloyal rout! Look there! The dust you see hangs on the bloody Spaniards'   20 track, dragging with ruffian taunts your King, your father!—Ataliba in bondage. Now fly, and seek your own vile safety, if you can.

O. MAN. Bless the voice of Rolla—and bless the stroke I once lamented, but which now spares these extinguished eyes the shame of seeing the pale trembling wretches who dare not follow Rolla though to save their 25 King!

ROL. Shrink ye from the thunder of the foe—and fall ye not at this rebuke? Oh! had ye each but one drop of the loyal blood which gushes to waste through the brave heart of this sightless veteran! Eternal shame pursue you, if you desert me now!—But do—alone I go—alone—to 30 die with glory by my monarch's side!

SOLDIERS. Rolla! we'll follow thee. [*Trumpets sound;* ROLLA *rushes out, followed by* ORANO, OFFICERS, *and* SOLDIERS.]

O. MAN. O godlike Rolla!—And thou sun, send from thy clouds avenging lightning to his aid!—Haste, my boy; ascend some height, and 35 tell to my impatient terror what thou seest.

BOY. I can climb this rock, and the tree above. [*Ascends a rock, and from thence into the tree.*] O—now I see them—now—yes—and the Spaniards turning by the steep.

O. MAN. Rolla follows them?   40

BOY. He does—he does—he moves like an arrow!—now he waves his arm to our soldiers—[*Report of cannon heard.*] Now there is fire and smoke.

O. MAN. Yes, *fire* is the weapon of those fiends.
BOY. The wind blows off the smoke: they are all mixed together.
O. MAN. Seest thou the King?
BOY. Yes—Rolla is near him! His sword sheds fire as he strikes!
O. MAN. Bless thee, Rolla! Spare not the monsters.   5
BOY. Father! father! the Spaniards fly!—O—now I see the King
  embracing Rolla. [*Waving his cap for joy. Shouts of victory, flourish of
  trumpets, &c.*]
O. MAN. [*Falls on his knees.*] Fountain of life! how can my exhausted
  breath bear to thee thanks for this one moment of my life! My boy,   10
  come down, and let me kiss thee—My strength is gone! [*The* BOY
  having run to the OLD MAN.]
BOY. Let me help you, father—You tremble so——
O. MAN. 'Tis with transport, boy!   [BOY *leads the* OLD MAN *off.*

Shouts, Flourish, &c.   15

Enter ATALIBA, ROLLA, *and Peruvian* OFFICERS *and* SOLDIERS.

ATA. In the name of my people, the saviour of whose sovereign you have
  this day been, accept this emblem of his gratitude. [*Giving* ROLLA
  his sun of diamonds.] The tear that falls upon it may for a moment dim
  its lustre, yet does it not impair the value of the gift.   20
ROL. It was the hand of Heaven, not mine, that saved my King.

Enter ORANO, *and* SOLDIERS.

ROL. Now, soldier, from Alonzo?
ORA. Alonzo's genius soon repaired the panic which early broke our
  ranks; but I fear we have to mourn Alonzo's loss; his eager spirit   25
  urged him too far in the pursuit!
ATA. How! Alonzo slain?
IST SOL. I saw him fall.
2D SOL. Trust me I beheld him up again and fighting—he was then
  surrounded and disarmed.   30
ATA. O! victory, dearly purchased!
ROL. O Cora! Who shall tell thee this?
ATA. Rolla, our friend is lost—our native country saved! Our private
  sorrows must yield to the public claim for triumph. Now go we to
  fulfil the first, the most sacred duty which belongs to victory—to dry 35
  the widowed and the orphaned tear of those whose brave protectors
  have perished in their country's case.
                       [*Triumphant march, and exeunt.*

END OF THE SECOND ACT

ACT III

SCENE I

*A wild Retreat among stupendous Rocks.—*CORA *and her Child, with other Wives and Children of the Peruvian Warriors, are scattered about the scene in groups.—They sing alternately, Stanzas expressive* 5 *of their situation, with a* CHORUS, *in which all join.*[1]

1ST PERUVIAN WOMAN. Zuluga, seest thou nothing yet?

ZUL. Yes, two Peruvian soldiers, one on the hill; the other entering the thicket in the vale.

2D PER. WOMAN. One more has pass'd.—He comes—but pale and 10 terrified.

CORA. My heart will start from my bosom.

Enter a Peruvian SOLDIER, *panting for breath.*

WOM. Well! joy or death?

SOLD. The battle is against us. The King is wounded, and a prisoner. 15

WOM. Despair and misery!

CORA. [*In a faint voice.*] And Alonzo?

SOLD. I have not seen him.

1ST WOM. Oh! whither must we fly?

2D WOM. Deeper into the forest. 20

CORA. I shall not move.

ANOTHER PERUVIAN SOLDIER, [*without.*] Victory! victory!

He enters hastily.

Rejoice! Rejoice! We are victorious!

WOM. [*Springing up.*] Welcome! welcome! thou messenger of joy: but 25 the King!

SOLD. He leads the brave warriors, who approach.

[*The triumphant march of the army is heard at a distance.—The Women and Children join in a strain expressive of anxiety and exultation.—The Warriors enter singing the Song of Victory, in which all* 30

---

[1] Kelly, *The Music of Pizarro*, pp. 13-16, reads: 'Glee sung by Mrs. Crouch, Miss Decamp, Stephens, Dufour, and Leak [by Kelly].

> Fly away, fly away, fly away time,
> Nor be the Anxious hour delay'd.
> Fly away, fly away, fly away time,
> That soothes the heart by grief dismay'd.
> Should gastley Death Appear in view
> We can dare it.
> With friends we love So brave and true
> We will share it.
> Fly away, fly away, fly away time, etc.'

join.[1]—*The King and* ROLLA *follow, and are met with rapturous and affectionate respect.* CORA, *during this scene, with her Child in her arms, runs through the ranks searching and inquiring for* ALONZO.]

ATA. Thanks, thanks, my children! I am well: believe it; the blood once stopp'd, my wound was nothing. [CORA *at length approaches* ROLLA, 5 *who appears to have been mournfully avoiding her.*] Where is Alonzo?

[ROLLA *turns away in silence.*

CORA. [*Falling at the King's feet.*] Give me my husband, give this child his father.

ATA. I grieve that Alonzo is not here. 10

CORA. Hop'd you to find him?

ATA. Most anxiously.

CORA. Ataliba! is he not dead?

ATA. No! the Gods will have heard our prayers.

CORA. Is he not dead, Ataliba? 15

ATA. He lives—in my heart.

CORA. Oh King! torture me not thus! speak out, is this child fatherless?

ATA. Dearest Cora! do not thus dash aside the little hope that still remains.

CORA. The little hope! yet still there *is* hope! Speak to me, Rolla: *you* 20 are the *friend of truth.*

ROL. Alonzo has not been found.

CORA. Not found! What mean you? will not *you*, Rolla, tell me truth? Oh! let me not hear the thunder rolling at a distance; let the bolt fall and crush my brain at once.—Say not that he is not found: say at 25 once that he is dead.

ROL. Then should I say false.

CORA. *False!* Blessings on thee for that word! But snatch me from this terrible suspense. Lift up thy little hands, my child; perhaps thy ignorance may plead better than thy mother's agony. 30

ROL. Alonzo is taken prisoner.

CORA. Prisoner! and by the Spaniards? Pizarro's prisoner? Then is he dead.

ATA. Hope better—the richest ransom which our realm can yield, a herald shall this instant bear. 35

---

[1] Kelly, *The Music of Pizarro*, pp. 17–20, reads: 'Distant military march and chorus of Peruvians [by Kelly].

[*Warriors.*] Victory now has made us free;
    We haste, we haste, our friends to see!

[*Women.*] Hush! hush! don't you hear?
    Some footsteps near
    A distant march assails the Ear;—
    Hark! louder still from yonder Hill
    Encreasing sounds with terror fill—'

[Sung simultaneously.]

PER. WOM. Oh! for Alonzo's ransom—our gold, our gems!—all! all!—
Here, dear Cora,—here! here!

[*The Peruvian Women eagerly tear off all their ornaments, and run
and take them from their children, to offer them to* CORA.]

ATA. Yes, for Alonzo's ransom they would give all!—I thank thee, Father,   5
who hast given me such hearts to rule over!

CORA. Now one boon more, beloved monarch. Let me go with the
herald.

ATA. Remember, Cora, thou art not a wife only, but a mother too:
hazard not your own honour, and the safety of your infant. Among   10
these barbarians the sight of thy youth, thy loveliness, and innocence,
would but rivet faster your Alonzo's chains, and rack his heart with
added fears for thee.—Wait, Cora, the return of the herald.

CORA. Teach me how to live till then.

ATA. Now we go to offer to the Gods, thanks for our victory, and prayers   15
for our Alonzo's safety.   [*March and procession. Exeunt omnes.*

SCENE II

The Wood.

Enter CORA *and child.*

CORA. Mild innocence, what will become of thee?   20

Enter ROLLA.

ROL. Cora, I attend thy summons at th' appointed spot.

CORA. Oh my child, my boy!—hast thou still a father?

ROL. Cora, can thy child be fatherless, while Rolla lives?

CORA. Will he not soon want a mother too?—For canst thou think I   25
will survive Alonzo's loss?

ROL. Yes! for his child's sake.—Yes, as thou didst love Alonzo, Cora,
listen to Alonzo's friend.

CORA. You bid me listen to the world.—Who was not Alonzo's friend?

ROL. His parting words——   30

CORA. His parting words! [*Wildly.*] Oh, speak!

ROL. Consign'd to me two precious trusts—his blessing to his son, and
a last request to thee.

CORA. His *last* request! his *last*!—Oh, name it!

ROL. If I fall, said he—(and sad forebodings shook him while he spoke)—   35
promise to take my Cora for thy wife; be thou a father to my child.—
I pledged my word to him, and we parted.—Observe me, Cora, I
repeat this only, as my faith to do so was given to Alonzo—for myself,
I neither cherish claim [n]or hope.

CORA. Ha! does my reason fail me, or what is this horrid light that presses   40

on my brain? Oh, Alonzo! It may be thou hast fallen a victim to thy
own guileless heart—hadst thou been silent, hadst thou not made a
fatal legacy of these wretched charms——

ROL. Cora! what hateful suspicion has possessed thy mind?

CORA. Yes, yes, 'tis clear—his spirit was ensnar'd; he was led to the fatal 5
spot, where mortal valour could not front a host of murderers—He
fell—in vain did he exclaim for help to Rolla. At a distance you look'd
on and smil'd—You could have saved him—could—but did not.

ROL. Oh, glorious sun! can I have deserved this? Cora, rather bid me
strike this sword into my heart. 10

CORA. No! live! live for love! for that love thou seekest; whose blossoms
are to shoot from the bleeding grave of thy betray'd and slaughter'd
friend!—But thou hast borne to me the *last words* of my *Alonzo!* Now
hear *mine*—Sooner shall this boy draw poison from this tortured breast—
—sooner would I link me to the pallid corse of the meanest wretch 15
that perish'd with Alonzo, than he call Rolla father—than I call Rolla
husband!

ROL. Yet call me what I am—thy friend, thy protector!

CORA. [*Distractedly.*] Away! I have no protector but my God!—With
this child in my arms will I hasten to the field of slaughter—There 20
with these hands will I turn up to the light every mangled body—
seeking, howe'er by death disfigur'd, the sweet smile of my Alonzo:—
with fearful cries I will shriek out his name till my veins snap! If the
smallest spark of life remains, he will know the voice of his Cora, open
for a moment his unshrouded eyes, and bless me with a last look: But 25
if we find him not—Oh! then, my boy, we will to the Spanish camp—
that look of thine will win me passage through a thousand swords—
They too are men.—Is there a heart that could drive back the wife
that seeks her bleeding husband; or the innocent babe that cries for his
imprison'd father? No, no, my child, every where we shall be safe.— 30
A wretched mother bearing a poor orphan in her arms, has Nature's
passport through the world. Yes, yes, my son, we'll go and seek thy
father.   [*Exit with the Child.*

ROL. [*After a pause of agitation.*] Could I have merited one breath of thy
reproaches, Cora, I should be the wretch—I think I was not formed 35
to be.—HER safety must be my present purpose—then to convince
her she has wronged me!   [*Exit.*

SCENE III.

PIZARRO's *Tent.*

PIZARRO, *traversing the scene in gloomy and furious agitation.* 40

Well, capricious idol, Fortune, be my ruin thy work and boast. To myself I will still be true.—Yet ere I fall, grant me thy smile to prosper in one act of vengeance, and be that smile Alonzo's death.

Enter ELVIRA.

Who's there? who dares intrude? Why does my guard neglect their duty?   5

ELV. Your guard did what they could—but they knew their duty better than to enforce authority, when I refused obedience.

PIZ. And what is it you desire?

ELV. To see how a hero bears misfortune. Thou, Pizarro, art not now collected—not thyself.   10

PIZ. Wouldst thou I should rejoice that the spears of the enemy, led by accurs'd Alonzo, have pierced the bravest hearts of my followers?

ELV. No!—I would have thee cold and dark as the night that follows the departed storm; still and sullen as the awful pause that precedes Nature's convulsion: yet I would have thee feel assured that a new 15 morning shall arise, when the warrior's spirit shall stalk forth—nor fear the future, nor lament the past.

PIZ. Woman! Elvira!—Why had not all my men hearts like thine?

ELV. Then would thy brows have this day worn the crown of Quito.

PIZ. Oh! hope fails me while that scourge of my life and fame, Alonzo, 20 leads the enemy.

ELV. Pizarro, I am come to probe the hero farther: not now his courage, but his magnanimity—Alonzo is your prisoner.

PIZ. How!

ELV. 'Tis certain; Valverde saw him even now dragged in chains within 25 your camp. I chose to bring you the intelligence myself.

PIZ. Bless thee, Elvira, for the news!—Alonzo in my power!—then I am the conqueror—the victory is MINE!

ELV. Pizarro, this is savage and unmanly triumph. Believe me, you raise impatience in my mind to see the man whose valour, and whose genius, 30 awe Pizarro; whose misfortunes are Pizarro's triumph; whose bondage is Pizarro's safety.

PIZ. Guard!—[*Enter Guard.*]—Drag here the Spanish prisoner, Alonzo! —Quick bring the traitor here.   [*Exit Guard.*]

ELV. What shall be his fate?   35

PIZ. Death! death! in lingering torments! protracted to the last stretch that burning vengeance can devise, and fainting life sustain.

ELV. Shame on thee! Wilt thou have it said that the Peruvians found Pizarro could not conquer till Alonzo felt that he could murder?

PIZ. Be it said—I care not. His fate is sealed.   40

ELV. Follow then thy will: but mark me; if basely thou dost shed the blood of this brave youth, Elvira's lost to thee for ever.

PIZ. Why this interest for a stranger? What is Alonzo's fate to thee?

ELV. His fate!—nothing!—thy glory, every thing!—Think'st thou I could love thee stript of fame, of honour, and a just renown?—Know me better.

PIZ. Thou shouldst have known ME better. Thou shouldst have known, that, once provoked to hate, I am for ever fixed in vengeance.— 5 [ALONZO *is brought in, in chains, guarded.* ELVIRA *observes him with attention and admiration.*]—Welcome, welcome, Don Alonzo de Molina; 'tis long since we have met: thy mended looks should speak a life of rural indolence. How is it that amid the toils and cares of war thou dost preserve the healthful bloom of careless ease? Tell me thy secret. 10

AL. Thou wilt not profit by it. Whate'er the toils or cares of war, peace still is *here.* [*Putting his hand to his heart.*]

PIZ. Sarcastic boy!

ELV. Thou art answered rightly. Why sport with the unfortunate?

PIZ. And thou art wedded too, I hear; aye, and the father of a lovely 15 boy—the heir, no doubt, of all his father's loyalty; of all his mother's faith.

AL. The heir, I trust, of all his father's scorn of fraud, oppression, and hypocrisy—the heir, I hope, of all his mother's virtue, gentleness, and truth—the heir, I am sure, to all Pizarro's hate. 20

PIZ. Really! Now do I feel for this poor orphan; for fatherless to-morrow's sun shall see that child. Alonzo, thy hours are numbered.

ELV. Pizarro—no!

PIZ. Hence—or dread my anger.

ELV. I will not hence; nor do I dread thy anger. 25

AL. Generous loveliness! spare thy unavailing pity. Seek not to thwart the tiger with his prey beneath his fangs.

PIZ. Audacious rebel! Thou renegado from thy monarch and thy God!

AL. 'Tis false.

PIZ. Art thou not, tell me, a deserter from thy country's legions—and, 30 with vile heathens leagued, hast thou not warred against thy native land?

AL. No! Deserter I am none! I was not born among robbers! pirates! murderers!—When those legions, lured by the abhorred lust of gold, and by thy foul ambition urged, forgot the honour of Castilians, and 35 forsook the duties of humanity, THEY deserted ME. I have not warred against my native land, but against those who have usurped its power. The banners of my country, when first I followed arms beneath them, were Justice, Faith, and Mercy. If these are beaten down and trampled under foot—I have no country, nor exists the power entitled to reproach 40 me with revolt.

PIZ. The power to judge and punish thee at least exists.

AL. Where are my judges?

PIZ. Thou wouldst appeal to the war council?

AL. If the good Las-Casas have yet a seat there, yes; if not, I appeal to
Heaven!

PIZ. And to impose upon the folly of Las-Casas, what would be the
excuses of thy treason?

ELV. The folly of Las-Casas!—Such, doubtless, his mild precepts seem   5
to thy hard-hearted wisdom!—O! would I might have lived as I will
die, a sharer in the follies of Las-Casas!

AL. To him I should not need to urge the foul barbarities which drove
me from your side; but I would gently lead him by the hand through
all the lovely fields of Quito; there, in many a spot where late was   10
barrenness and waste, I would show him how now the opening blossom,
blade, or perfumed bud, sweet bashful pledges of delicious harvest,
wasting their incense to the ripening sun, give chearful promise to the
hope of industry. This, I would say, is my work! Next I should tell
how hurtful customs, and superstitions strange and sullen, would often 15
scatter and dismay the credulous minds of these deluded innocents;
and then would I point out to him where now, in clustered villages,
they live like brethren, social and confiding, while through the burning
day Content sits basking on the cheek of Toil, till laughing Pastime
leads them to the hour of rest—this too is mine!—And prouder yet—   20
at that still pause between exertion and repose, belonging not to
pastime, labour, or to rest, but unto Him who sanctions and ordains
them all, I would show him many an eye, and many a hand, by gentleness from error won, raised in pure devotion to the true and only God!—
this too I could tell him is Alonzo's work!—Then would Las-Casas clasp 25
me in his aged arms; from his uplifted eyes a tear of gracious thankful-
ness would fall upon my head, and that one blessed drop would be to
me at once *this* world's best proof, that I had acted rightly *here*, and
surest hope of my Creator's mercy and reward *hereafter*.

ELV. Happy, virtuous Alonzo! And thou, Pizarro, wouldst appal with   30
fear of death a man who thinks and acts as he does!

PIZ. Daring, obstinate enthusiast! But know the pious blessing of thy
preceptor's tears does not await thee here: he has fled like thee—like
thee, no doubt, to join the foes of Spain. The perilous trial of the next
reward you hope, is nearer than perhaps you've thought; for, by my   35
country's wrongs, and by mine own, tomorrow's sun shall see thy
death.

ELV. Hold!—Pizarro—hear me!—If not always *justly*, at least act always
greatly. Name not thy country's wrongs—'tis plain they have no share
in thy resentment. Thy fury 'gainst this youth is private hate, and   40
deadly personal revenge; if this be so—and even now thy detected
conscience in that look avows it—profane not the name of justice or
thy country's cause, but let him arm, and bid him to the field on equal
terms.

PIZ. Officious advocate for treason—peace!—Bear him hence—he knows his sentence.

AL. Thy revenge is eager, and I'm thankful for it—to me thy haste is mercy. For thee, sweet pleader in misfortune's cause, accept my part- ing thanks. This camp is not thy proper sphere. Wert thou among yon 5 *savages*, as they are called, thou'dst find companions more congenial to thy heart.

PIZ. Yes; she shall bear the tidings of thy death to Cora.

AL. Inhuman man! that pang at least might have been spared me; but thy malice shall not shake my constancy. I go to death—many shall 10 bless, and none will curse my memory. Thou still wilt live, and still wilt be—Pizarro. [*Exit, guarded.*

ELV. Now by the indignant scorn that burns upon my cheek, my soul is shamed and sickened at the meanness of thy vengeance.

PIZ. What has thy romantic folly aimed at? He is mine enemy, and in 15 my power.

ELV. He is in your power, and therefore is no more an enemy. Pizarro, I demand not of thee virtue—I ask not from thee nobleness of mind— I require only just dealing to the fame thou hast acquired; be not the assassin of thine own renown. How often have you sworn that the 20 sacrifice which thy wondrous valour's high report had won you from subdued Elvira, was the proudest triumph of your fame? Thou knowest I bear a mind not cast in the common mould—not formed for tame sequestered love—content 'mid household cares to prattle to an idle offspring, and wait the dull delight of an obscure lover's kind- 25 ness—no! my heart was framed to look up with awe and homage to the object it adored; my ears to own no music but the thrilling records of his praise; my lips to scorn all babbling but the tales of his achieve- ments; my brain to turn giddy with delight, reading the applauding tributes of his monarch's and his country's gratitude; my every faculty 30 to throb with transport, while I heard the shouts of acclamation which announced the coming of my hero; my whole soul to love him with devotion! with enthusiasm! to see no other object—to own no other tie—but to make HIM my WORLD! Thus to love is at least no common weakness.—Pizarro!—was not such my love for thee? 35

PIZ. It *was*, Elvira!

ELV. Then do not make me hateful to myself, by tearing off the mask at once—baring the hideous imposture that has undone me!—Do not an act which, howe'er thy present power may gloss it to the world, will make thee hateful to all future ages—accursed and scorned by 40 posterity.

PIZ. And should posterity applaud my deeds, think'st thou my mouldering bones would rattle then with transport in my tomb?—This is renown for visionary Boys to dream of—I understand it not. The fame I value shall uplift my living estimation—o'erbear with popular support the envy of my foes—advance my purposes, and aid my power.

ELV. Each word thou speakest—each moment that I hear thee—dispels the fatal mist through which I've judged thee. Thou man of mighty name, but little soul, I see thou wert not born to feel what genuine 5 fame and glory are—yes, prefer the flattery of thy own fleeting day to the bright circle of a deathless name—yes, prefer to stare upon the grain of sand on which you trample, to musing on the starred canopy above thee. Fame, the sovereign deity of proud ambition, is not to be worshipped so: who seeks alone for living homage, stands a mean 10 canvasser in her temple's porch, wooing promiscuously from the fickle breath of every wretch that passes, the brittle tribute of his praise. He dares not approach the sacred altar—no noble sacrifice of his is placed there, nor ever shall his worship'd image, fix'd above, claim for his memory a glorious immortality.   15

PIZ. Elvira, leave me.

ELV. Pizarro, you no longer love me.

PIZ. It is not so, Elvira. But what might I not suspect—this wondrous interest for a stranger!—Take back thy reproach.

ELV. No, Pizarro; as yet I am not lost to you—one string still remains, 20 and binds me to your fate. Do not, I conjure you—do not for thine own sake, tear it asunder—shed not Alonzo's blood!

PIZ. My resolution's fixed.

ELV. Even though that moment lost you Elvira for ever?

PIZ. Even so.   25

ELV. Pizarro, if not to honour, if not to humanity, yet listen to affection; bear some memory of the sacrifices I have made for thy sake. Have I not for thee quitted my parents, my friends, my fame, my native land? When escaping, did I not risk in rushing to thy arms to bury myself in the bosom of the deep? Have I not shared all thy perils, heavy 30 storms at sea, and frightful 'scapes on shore? Even on this dreadful day, amid the rout of battle, who remained firm and constant at Pizarro's side? Who presented her bosom as his shield to the assailing foe?

PIZ. 'Tis truly spoken all. In love thou art thy sex's miracle—in war 35 the soldier's pattern—and therefore my whole heart and half my acquisitions are thy right.

ELV. Convince me I possess the first—I exchange all title to the latter, for—mercy to Alonzo.

PIZ. No more!—Had I intended to prolong his doom, each word thou 40 utterest now would hasten on his fate.

ELV. Alonzo then at morn will die?

PIZ. Think'st thou yon sun will set?—As surely at his rising shall Alonzo die.

ELV. Then be it done—the string is crack'd—sundered for ever.—But mark me—thou hast heretofore had cause, 'tis true, to doubt my resolution, howe'er offended—but mark me now—the lips which, cold and jeering, barbing revenge with rancorous mockery, can insult a fallen enemy, shall never more receive the pledge of love: the arm unshaken 5 by its bloody purpose, shall assign to needless torture the victim who avows his heart, never more shall press the hand of faith!—Pizarro, scorn not my words—beware you slight them not!—I feel how noble are the motives which now animate my thoughts—who *could* not feel as I do, I condemn—who, feeling so, yet *would* not act as I SHALL, I 10 despise!

PIZ. [*After a pause, looking at her with an affected smile of contempt.*] I have heard thee, Elvira, and know well the *noble* motives which inspire thee—fit advocate in virtue's cause!—Believe me, I pity thy tender feelings for the youth Alonzo!—He dies at sun-rise!   [*Exit.* 15

ELV. 'Tis well! 'tis just I should be humbled—I had forgot myself, and in the cause of innocence assumed the tone of virtue. 'Twas fit I should be rebuked—and by Pizarro. Fall, fall, ye few reluctant drops of weakness—the last these eyes shall ever shed. How a woman can love Pizarro, thou hast known too well—how she can hate, thou hast yet 20 to learn. Yes, thou undaunted! Thou, whom yet no mortal hazard has appalled! Thou, who on Panama's brow didst make alliance with the raving elements, that tore the silence of that horrid night—when thou didst follow, as thy pioneer, the crashing thunder's drift, and stalking o'er the trembling earth, didst plant thy banner by the red volcano's 25 mouth! Thou, who when battling on the sea, and thy brave ship was blown to splinters, wast seen—as thou didst bestride a fragment of the smoking wreck—to wave thy glittering sword above thy head— as thou wouldst defy the world in that extremity!—Come, fearless man—now meet the last and fellest peril of thy life—meet! and survive 30 —an injured woman's fury, if thou canst.   [*Exit.*

END OF THE THIRD ACT[1]

[1] Kelly, *The Music of Pizarro*, pp. 21–4, adds words for a chorus by Cherubini, sung by the priests at sacrifice:

> To thee be praise
> O Glorious Sun,
> Beneath whose beams
> The field was won!
> Raise high the voice,
> With shouts rejoice.

Rhodes, iii. 59, prints this as Scene iv, and says that it appears in the editions (1823) of Dolby and of Hughes.

ACT IV

SCENE I

A Dungeon in the Rock, near the Spanish Camp.—ALONZO *in Chains.*—
A CENTINEL *walking near the Entrance.*

ALONZO. For the last time, I have beheld the shadow'd ocean close   5
upon the light.—For the last time, thro' my cleft dungeon's roof,
I now behold the quivering lustre of the stars.—For the last time, O
sun! (and soon the hour) I shall behold thy rising, and thy level beams
melting the pale mists of morn to glittering dewdrops.—Then comes
my death, and in the morning of my day, I fall, which—No, Alonzo,   10
date not the life which thou hast run, by the mean reck'ning of the hours
and days, which thou hast breath'd: A life spent worthily should be
measured by a nobler line—by deeds—not years—Then woud'st thou
murmur not—but bless the Providence, which in so short a span, made
THEE the instrument of wide and spreading blessings, to the helpless   15
and oppress'd!—Tho' sinking in decrepid age—HE prematurely falls,
whose memory records no benefit conferred by him on man: They
only have lived long, who have lived virtuously.

Enter a SOLDIER—*shews the* CENTINEL *a Passport, who withdraws.*

ALONZO. What bear you there?   20
SOL. These refreshments I was order'd to leave in your dungeon.
AL. By whom order'd?
SOL. By the lady Elvira; she will be here herself before the dawn.
AL. Bear back to her my humblest thanks; and take thou the refresh-
ments, friend—I need them not.   25
SOL. I have served under you, Don Alonzo.—Pardon my saying, that
my heart pities you.   [*Exit.*
AL. In Pizarro's camp, to pity the unfortunate, no doubt requires forgive-
ness.—[*Looking out*] Surely, even now, thin streaks of glimmering light
steal on the darkness of the East.—If so, my life is but one hour more.— 30
I will not watch the coming dawn; but in the darkness of my cell, my
last prayer to thee, Power Supreme! shall be for my wife and child!—
Grant them to dwell in innocence and peace; grant health and purity
of mind—all else is worthless. [*Enters the Cavern.*]
CEN. Who's there? answer quickly! who's there?   35
ROL. A Friar, come to visit your prisoner.

ROLLA *enters, disguised as a Monk.*

ROL. Inform me, friend—Is not Alonzo, the Spanish prisoner, confined
in this dungeon?

CEN. He is.

ROL. I must speak with him.

CEN. You must not.

ROL. He is my friend.

CEN. Not if he were your brother.   5

ROL. What is to be his fate?

CEN. He dies at sun-rise.

ROL. Ha!—then I am come in time.

CEN. Just—to witness his death.

ROL. Soldier—I must speak with him.   10

CEN. Back,—back.—It is impossible!—

ROL. I do entreat you, but for one moment!

CEN. You entreat in vain—my orders are most strict.

ROL. Even now, I saw a messenger go hence.

CEN. He brought a pass, which we are all accustomed to obey.   15

ROL. Look on this wedge of massive gold—look on these precious gems.
—In thy own land they will be wealth for thee and thine, beyond thy
hope or wish. Take them—they are thine.—Let me but pass one minute
with Alonzo.

CEN. Away!—woud'st thou corrupt me?—Me!—an old Castilian!—I   20
know my duty better.

ROL. Soldier!—hast thou a wife?

CEN. I have.

ROL. Hast thou children?

CEN. Four—honest, lively boys.   25

ROL. Where did'st thou leave them?

CEN. In my native village—even in the cot where myself was born.

ROL. Do'st thou love thy children and thy wife?

CEN. Do I love them! God knows my heart,—I do.

ROL. Soldier! imagine thou wer't doom'd to die a cruel death in this   30
strange land—What would be thy last request?

CEN. That some of my comrades should carry my dying blessing to my
wife and children.

ROL. Oh! but if that comrade was at thy prison gate—and should there
be told——thy fellow soldier dies at sun-rise,—yet thou shalt not for   35
a moment see him—nor shalt thou bear his dying blessing to his poor
children or his wretched wife,—what would'st thou think of him, who
thus cou'd drive thy comrade from the door?

CEN. How!

ROL. Alonzo has a wife and child—I am come but to receive for *her*, and   40
for her *babe*, the last blessing of my friend.

CEN. Go in.—[*Retires.*]

ROL. Oh! holy Nature! thou do'st never plead in vain—There is not, of
our earth, a creature bearing form, and life, human or savage—native

of the forest wild, or giddy air—around whose parent bosom, THOU hast not a cord entwined of power to tie them to their offspring's claims, and at thy will to draw them back to thee. On iron pennons borne—the blood-stain'd vulture, cleaves the storm—yet, is the plumage closest to her heart, soft as the Cygnet's down, and o'er her unshell'd brood, the 5 murmuring ring-dove sits not more gently!—Yes—now he is beyond the porch, barring the outer gate! Alonzo!—Alonzo!—my friend! Ha!—in gentle sleep!—Alonzo—rise!

AL. How!—Is my hour elaps'd?—Well, [*returning from the recess*,] I am ready.   10

ROL. Alonzo,—know me.

AL. What voice is that?

ROL. 'Tis Rolla's.

AL. Rolla!—my friend!—[*Embraces him.*] Heavens! how could'st thou pass the guard? Did this habit——   15

ROL. There is not a moment to be lost in words;—this disguise I tore from the dead body of a Friar, as I pass'd our field of battle—it has gain'd me entrance to thy dungeon—now take it thou, and fly.

AL. And Rolla——

ROL. Will remain here in thy place.   20

AL. And die for me!—No!—Rather eternal tortures rack me.

ROL. I shall not die, Alonzo.—It is *thy* life Pizarro seeks, not Rolla's— and from my prison soon will thy arm deliver me;—or, should it be otherwise—I am as a blighted Plantain standing alone amid the sandy desart—Nothing seeks or lives beneath my shelter—Thou art a husband, 25 and a father—The being of a lovely wife and helpless infant hang upon thy life—Go!—Go!—Alonzo!—Go—to save—not thyself—but Cora, and thy child!—

AL. Urge me not thus, my friend—I had prepar'd to die in peace.

ROL. To die in peace!—devoting her you've sworn to live for,—to mad- 30 ness, misery, and death!—For, be assured—the state I left her in forbids all hope, but from thy quick return.

AL. Oh! God!

ROL. If thou art yet irresolute, Alonzo—now heed me well.—I think thou hast not known that Rolla ever pledg'd his word, and shrunk from its 35 fulfilment.—And, by the heart of truth I swear, if thou art proudly obstinate to deny thy friend the transport of preserving Cora's life, in thee,—no power that sways the will of man shall stir me hence;— and thou'lt but have the desperate triumph, of seeing Rolla perish by thy side,—with the assur'd conviction, that Cora, and thy child, are 40 lost for ever.

AL. Oh! Rolla!—you distract me!

ROL. A moment's further pause, and all is lost—The dawn approaches —Fear not for me—I will treat with Pizarro as for surrender and

submission;—I shall gain time, doubt not—while thou, with a chosen
band, passing the secret way, may'st at night return—release thy
friend, and bear him back in triumph.—Yes—hasten—dear Alonzo!—
Even now I hear the frantic Cora call thee!—Haste!—Haste!—Haste!

AL. Rolla, I fear your friendship drives me from honour, and from right. 5

ROL. Did Rolla ever counsel dishonour to his friend?

AL. Oh! my preserver!—[*Embracing him.*]

ROL. I feel thy warm tears dropping on my cheek—Go!—I am rewarded
—[*Throws the Friar's garment over* ALONZO.]—There!—conceal thy
face; and that they may not clank, hold fast thy chains—Now—God 10
be with thee!

AL. At night we meet again.—Then,—so aid me Heaven! I return to
save—or—perish with thee!   [*Exit.*

ROL. [*alone.*] He has pass'd the outer porch—He is safe!—He will soon
embrace his wife and child!—Now, Cora, did'st thou not wrong me? 15
This is the first time throughout my life I ever deceived man—Forgive
me, God of truth! if I am wrong—Alonzo flatters himself that we shall
meet again—Yes—There! [*lifting his hands to heaven*] assuredly, we
shall meet again:—there possess in peace, the joys of everlasting love,
and friendship—on earth, imperfect, and embitter'd.—I will retire, 20
lest the guard return before Alonzo may have pass'd their lines.
                                        [*Retires into the Recess.*

Enter ELVIRA.

ELV. No—not Pizarro's brutal taunts—not the glowing admiration which
I feel for this noble youth, shall raise an interest in my harrass'd bosom 25
which honour would not sanction. If he reject the vengeance my heart
has sworn against the tyrant, whose death alone can save this land—
yet, shall the delight be mine to restore him to his Cora's arms, to his
dear child, and to the unoffending people, whom his virtues guide,
and valour guards.—Alonzo, come forth!   30

Enter ROLLA.

Ha!—who art thou?—Where is Alonzo?

ROL. Alonzo's fled.

ELV. Fled!

ROL. Yes—and he must not be pursued—Pardon this roughness, [*seizing* 35
her hand]—but a moment's precious to Alonzo's flight.

ELV. What if I call the guard?

ROL. Do so—Alonzo still gains time.

ELV. What if thus I free myself? [*Shews a dagger.*]

ROL. Strike it to my heart—Still, with the convulsive grasp of death, 40
I'll hold thee fast.

ELV. Release me—I give my faith, I neither will alarm the guard, nor cause pursuit.

ROL. At once, I trust thy word—A feeling boldness in those eyes assures me that thy soul is noble.

ELV. What is thy name? Speak freely—By my order the guard is remov'd 5 beyond the outer porch.

ROL. My name is Rolla.

ELV. The Peruvian Leader?

ROL. I was so yesterday—To-day, the Spaniard's captive.

ELV. And friendship for Alonzo, moved thee to this act? 10

ROL. Alonzo is my friend—I am prepared to die for him. Yet is the cause a motive stronger far than friendship.

ELV. One only passion else could urge such generous rashness.

ROL. And that is——

ELV. Love? 15

ROL. True!

ELV. Gallant!—ingenuous Rolla!—Know that my purpose here was thine; and were I to save thy friend——

ROL. How!—a woman bless'd with gentleness and courage, and yet not Cora! 20

ELV. Does Rolla think so meanly of all female hearts?

ROL. Not so—you are worse and better than we are!

ELV. Were I to save thee, Rolla, from the tyrant's vengeance—restore thee to thy native land—and thy native land to peace—would'st thou not rank Elvira with the good? 25

ROL. To judge the action, I must know the means.

ELV. Take this dagger.

ROL. How to be used!

ELV. I will conduct thee to the tent where fell Pizarro sleeps—The scourge of innocence—the terror of thy race—the fiend, that desolates 30 thy afflicted country.

ROL. Have you not been injur'd by Pizarro?

ELV. Deeply as scorn and insult can infuse their deadly venom.

ROL. And you ask that I shall murder him in his sleep!

ELV. Would he not have murder'd Alonzo in his chains? He that sleeps, 35 and he that's bound, are equally defenceless. Hear me, Rolla—so may I prosper in this perilous act as searching my full heart, I have put by all rancorous motive of private vengeance there, and feel that I advance to my dread purpose in the cause of human nature, and at the call of sacred justice. 40

ROL. The God of Justice sanctifies no evil as a step towards good. Great actions cannot be achieved by wicked means.

ELV. Then, Peruvian! since thou do'st feel so coldly for thy country's wrongs, this hand, tho' it revolt my soul, shall strike the blow.

ROL. Then is thy destruction certain, and for Peru thou perishest!—
Give me the dagger!

ELV. Now follow me;—but first—and dreadful is the hard necessity—
you must strike down the guard.

ROL. The soldier who was on duty here?   5

ELV. Yes, him—else, seeing thee, the alarm will be instant.

ROL. And I must stab that soldier as I pass?—Take back thy dagger.

ELV. Rolla!

ROL. That soldier, mark me, is a man.—All are not men that bear the
human form. He refus'd my prayers—refus'd my gold—denying to 10
admit me—till his own feelings brib'd him.—For my nations' safety,
I would not harm that man!

ELV. Then he must with us—I will answer for his safety.

ROL. Be that plainly understood between us:—for, whate'er betide our
enterprize, I will not risk a hair of that man's head, to save my heart- 15
strings from consuming fire.   [*Exeunt.*

SCENE III

The inside of PIZARRO's *Tent.*—PIZARRO *on a Couch, in disturbed sleep.*

PIZ. [*in his sleep.*] No mercy, traitor.—Now at his heart!—Stand off
there, you—Let me see him bleed!—Ha! ha! ha!—Let me hear that 20
groan again.

Enter ROLLA *and* ELVIRA.

ELV. There!—Now, lose not a moment.

ROL. You must leave me now.—This scene of blood fits not a woman's
presence.   25

ELV. But a moment's pause may—

ROL. Go!—Retire to your own tent—and return not here—I will come
to you—Be thou not known in this business, I implore you!

ELV. I will withdraw the guard that waits.   [*Exit* ELVIRA.

ROL. Now have I in my power the accurs'd destroyer of my country's 30
peace: yet tranquilly he rests.—God!—can this man sleep?

PIZ. [*in his sleep.*] Away! away!—Hideous fiends!—Tear not my bosom
thus!

ROL. No:—I was in error—the balm of sweet repose he never more can
know.—Look here, ambition's fools!—Ye, by whose inhuman pride, 35
the bleeding sacrifice of nations is held as nothing—behold the rest
of the guilty!—He is at my mercy—and one blow!—No!—my heart
and hand refuse the act: Rolla cannot be an assassin!—Yet Elvira must
be saved! [*Approaches the Couch.*] Pizarro! awake!—

PIZ. [*Starts up.*] Who?—Guard!—   40

ROL. Speak not—another word is thy death—Call not for aid!—this arm
will be swifter than thy guard.

PIZ. Who art thou? and what is thy will?

ROL. I am thine enemy! Peruvian Rolla!—Thy death is not my will, or
I could have slain thee sleeping.

PIZ. Speak, what else?

ROL. Now thou art at my mercy—answer me! Did a Peruvian ever yet   5
wrong or injure thee, or any of thy nation? Didst thou, or any of thy
nation, ever yet shew mercy to a Peruvian in your power? Now shalt
thou feel—and if thou hast a heart, thou'lt feel it keenly!—a Peruvian's
vengeance! [*Drops the dagger at his feet*] There!

PIZ. Is it possible! [*Walks aside confounded.*]   10

ROL. Can Pizarro be surprised at this? I thought Forgiveness of Injuries
had been the Christian's precept—Thou seest, at least, it is the Peruvian's practice.

PIZ. Rolla—thou hast indeed surpris'd—subdued me. [*Walks again aside
as in irresolute thought.*]   15

Re-enter ELVIRA, [*not seeing* PIZARRO].

ELV. Is it done? Is he dead? [*Sees* PIZARRO] How!—still living! Then
I am lost! And for you, wretched Peruvians! mercy is no more!—Oh!
Rolla! treacherous, or cowardly?—

PIZ. How can it be, that—   20

ROL. Away Elvira speaks she knows not what! Leave me [*to* ELVIRA] I
conjure you, with Pizarro.

ELV. How!—Rolla, do'st thou think I shall retract—or that I meanly will
deny, that in thy hand *I* plac'd a poignard to be plung'd into that
tyrant's heart? No:—my sole regret is, that I trusted to thy weakness, 25
and did not strike the blow myself.—Too soon thou'lt learn that mercy
to that man is direct cruelty to all thy race!

PIZ. Guard! quick! a guard, to seize this frantic woman.

ELV. Yes, a guard! I call them too! And soon I know they'll lead me to
my death. But think not, Pizarro, the fury of thy flashing eyes shall   30
awe me for a moment!—Nor think that woman's anger, or the feelings
of an injur'd heart, prompted me to this design—No! Had I been only
influenced so—this failing, shame and remorse would weigh me down.
But tho' defeated and destroyed, as now I am, such is the greatness of
the cause that urged me, I shall perish, glorying in the attempt, and   35
my last breath of life shall speak the proud avowal of my purpose—
to have rescued millions of innocents from the blood-thirsty tyranny of
ONE—by ridding the insulted world of THEE.

ROL. Had the act been noble as the motive—Rolla would not have shrunk
from its performance.   40

Enter GUARDS.

PIZ. Seize this discover'd fiend, who sought to kill your Leader.

ELV. Touch me not, at the peril of your souls;—I am your prisoner, and
will follow you.—But thou, their triumphant Leader, shalt hear me.
Yet, first—for thee, Rolla, accept my forgiveness: even had I been the
victim of thy nobleness of heart, I should have admir'd thee for it—
But 'twas myself provok'd my doom—Thou would'st have shielded   5
me.—Let not thy contempt follow me to the grave. Didst thou but know
the spell-like arts, by which this hypocrite first undermin'd the virtue
of a guileless heart! how, even in the pious sanctuary wherein I dwelt,
by corruption and by fraud, he practis'd upon those in whom I most
confided—'till my distemper'd fancy led me, step by step, into the   10
abyss of guilt——

PIZ. Why am I not obey'd?—Tear her hence!

ELV. 'Tis past—but didst thou know my story, Rolla, thou would'st
pity me.

ROL. From my soul I do pity thee!   15

PIZ. Villains! drag her to the dungeon!—prepare the torture instantly.

ELV. Soldiers—but a moment more—'Tis to applaud your General—
It is to tell the astonished world, that, for once, Pizarro's sentence is an
act of justice: Yes, rack me with the sharpest tortures that ever agoniz'd
the human frame; it will be justice. Yes—bid the minions of thy fury— 20
wrench forth the sinews of those arms that have caress'd, and——even
have defended thee! Bid them pour burning metal into the bleeding
cases of these eyes, that so oft—oh, God!—have hung with love and
homage on thy looks—then approach me bound on the abhorred
wheel—there glut thy savage eyes with the convulsive spasms of that 25
dishonour'd bosom, which was once thy pillow!—Yet, will I bear it all;
for it will be justice, all! And when thou shalt bid them tear me to my
death, hoping that thy unshrinking ears may at last be feasted with the
music of my cries, I will not utter one shriek or groan—but to the last
gasp, my body's patience shall deride thy vengeance, as my soul defies 30
thy power.

PIZ. [*Endeavouring to conceal his agitation.*] Hear'st thou the wretch whose
hands were even now prepared for murder?

ROL. Yes! And if her accusation's false, thou wilt not shrink from hearing
her: if true, thy barbarity cannot make *her* suffer the pangs thy con- 35
science will inflict on *thee*.

ELV. And now, farewell, world!—Rolla, farewell!—Farewell, thou condemn'd of Heaven! [*to* PIZARRO;]—for repentance and remorse, I
know, will never touch thy heart.—We shall meet again.—Ha! be it
thy horror here, to know that we shall meet hereafter! And when thy 40
parting hour approaches—hark to the knell, whose dreadful beat will
strike to thy despairing soul. Then, will vibrate on thy ear the curses of
the cloister'd saint from whom you stole me. Then, the last shrieks
which burst from my mother's breaking heart, as she died, appealing

to her God against the seducer of her child! Then the blood-stifled
groan of my murder'd brother—murdered by thee, fell monster!—
seeking atonement for his sister's ruin'd honour.—I hear them now!
To me, the recollection's madness!—At such an hour,—what will it
be to thee?   5

PIZ. A moment's more delay, and at the peril of your lives——

ELV. I have spoken—and the last mortal frailty of my heart is past.—
And now, with an undaunted spirit, and unshaken firmness, I go to
meet my destiny. That I could not *live* nobly, has been PIZARRO's
ACT. That I will *die* nobly, shall be my OWN.   [*Exit, guarded.* 10

PIZ. Rolla, I would not thou, a warrior, valiant and renown'd, should'st
credit the vile tales of this frantic woman. The cause of all this fury—
O! a wanton passion for the rebel youth Alonzo, now my prisoner.

ROL. Alonzo is not now thy prisoner.

PIZ. How!   15

ROL. I came to rescue him—to deceive his guard—I have succeeded;—
I remain thy prisoner.

PIZ. Alonzo fled!—Is then the vengeance dearest to my heart never to be
gratified?

ROL. Dismiss such passions from thy heart; then thou'lt consult it's   20
peace.

PIZ. I can face all enemies that dare confront me—I cannot war against
my nature.

ROL. Then, Pizarro, ask not to be deem'd a hero—To triumph o'er ourselves, is the only conquest, where fortune makes no claim. In battle,   25
chance may snatch the laurel from thee, or chance may place it on thy
brow—but in a contest with yourself, be resolute, and the virtuous
impulse must be the victor.

PIZ. Peruvian! thou shalt not find me to *thee* ungrateful, or ungenerous—
Return to your countrymen—You are at liberty.   30

ROL. Thou do'st act in this, as honour, and as duty, bid thee.

PIZ. I cannot but admire thee, Rolla; I wou'd we might be friends.

ROL. Farewell.—Pity Elvira!—Become the friend of virtue—and thou
wilt be mine.   [*Exit.*

PIZ. Ambition! tell me what is the phantom I have follow'd? where is   35
the one delight which it has made my own? My fame is the mark of
envy—my love the dupe of treachery—my glory eclips'd by the boy I
taught—my revenge defeated and rebuked by the rude honour of a
savage foe—before whose native dignity of soul I have sunk confounded
and subdued! I would I cou'd retrace my steps—I cannot—Would I   40
could evade my own reflections!—No!—thought and memory are my
Hell.   [*Exit.*

END OF THE FOURTH ACT

ACT V

SCENE I

*A thick Forest—In the background, a Hut almost covered by Boughs of Trees—A dreadful Storm, with Thunder and Lightning.—*CORA *has covered her Child on a Bed of Leaves and Moss—Her whole appearance* 5 *is wild and distracted.*

CORA. O nature! thou hast not the strength of love. My anxious spirit is untired in its march; my wearied, shivering frame, sinks under it. And, for thee, my boy—when faint beneath thy lovely burthen, could I refuse to give thy slumbers that poor bed of rest! O my child! were 10 I assured thy father breathes no more, how quickly would I lay me down by thy dear side—but down—down for ever. [*Thunder and lightning.*] I ask thee not, unpitying storm! to abate thy rage, in mercy to poor Cora's misery; nor while thy thunders spare his slumbers will I disturb my sleeping cherub. Though Heaven knows I wish to hear 15 the voice of life, and feel that life is near me. But I will endure all while what I have of reason holds.

SONG.[1]

Yes, yes, be merciless, thou Tempest dire;
　Unaw'd, unshelter'd, I thy fury brave: 20
I'll bare my bosom to thy forked fire,
　Let it but guide me to ALONZO's grave!

O'er his pale corse then while thy lightnings glare,
I'll press his clay-cold lips, and perish there.

But thou wilt wake again, my boy,   25
Again thou'lt rise to life and joy,
　Thy father never!——
Thy laughing eyes will meet the light,
Unconscious that eternal night
　Veils his for ever.   30

On yon green bed of moss there lies my child,
　Oh! safer lies from these chill'd arms apart;
He sleeps, sweet lamb! nor heeds the tempest wild,
　Oh! sweeter sleeps, than near this breaking heart.

Alas! my babe, if thou would'st peaceful rest,   35
Thy cradle must not be thy mother's breast.

---

[1] See Kelly, *The Music of Pizarro*, pp. 25–8. It was by Kelly himself to words by Sheridan. Kelly prints 'kiss' for 'press' (l. 24); 'But' for 'Yet' (p. 696, l. 1).

Yet, thou wilt wake again, my boy,
Again thou'lt rise to life and joy,
　Thy father never!——
Thy laughing eyes will meet the light,
Unconscious that eternal night   5
　Veils his for ever.   [*Thunder and lightning.*]

CORA. Still, still, implacable! unfeeling elements! yet still dost thou
sleep, my smiling innocent! O, death! when wilt thou grant to this
babe's mother such repose? Sure I may shield thee better from the
storm; my veil may——   10
　While she is wrapping her mantle and her veil over him, ALONZO's *voice*
　is heard at a great distance.
AL. Cora!
CORA. Hah!!! [*rises.*]
AL. [*again*] Cora!   15
CORA. O, my heart! Sweet Heaven deceive me not!—Is it not Alonzo's
voice?
AL. [*nearer*] Cora!
CORA. It is—it is Alonzo!
AL. [*nearer still*] Cora! my beloved!——   20
CORA. Alonzo!—Here!—here!—Alonzo!   [*Runs out.*

Enter two *Spanish* SOLDIERS.

1ST SOL. I tell you we are near our out-posts, and the word we heard
just now was the countersign.
2D SOL. Well, in our escape from the enemy, to have discover'd their   25
secret passage thro' the rocks, will prove a lucky chance to us—Pizarro
will reward us.
1ST SOL. This way—The sun, though clouded, is on our left. [*Perceives
the child.*] What have we here?—A child!—as I'm a soldier.
2D SOL. 'Tis a sweet little babe. Now would it be a great charity to take   30
this infant from its pagan mother's power.
1ST SOL. It would so—I have one at home shall play with it.—Come
along.   [*Takes the child.*
                                                    [*Exeunt.*

Re-enter CORA *with* ALONZO.   35

CORA. [*speaking without*] This way, dear Alonzo. Now am I right—there
—there—under that tree. Was it possible the instinct of mother's heart
could mistake the spot! Now will you look at him as he sleeps, or shall
I bring him waking with his full blue laughing eyes to welcome you at
once—Yes—yes.—Stand thou there—I'll snatch him from his rosy   40
slumber, blushing like the perfum'd morn.

She runs up to the spot, and, finding only the mantle and veil, which she tears from the ground, and the child gone, [shrieks] and stands in speechless agony.

AL. [*running to her*] Cora!—my heart's beloved!

CORA. He is gone!   5

AL. Eternal God!

CORA. He is gone!—my child! my child!

AL. Where did you leave him?

CORA. [*Dashing herself on the spot.*] Here!

AL. Be calm, beloved Cora—he has wak'd, and crept to a little distance—   10
we shall find him—Are you assured this was the spot you left him in?

CORA. Did not these hands make that bed, and shelter for him?—and is
not this the veil that covered him?

AL. Here is a hut yet unobserved.

CORA. Ha! yes, yes! there lives the savage that has rob'd me of my child—   15
[*Beats at the door, exclaiming*] Give me back my child—restore to me
my boy!

Enter LAS CASAS *from the Hut.*

LAS C. Who calls me from my wretched solitude?

CORA. Give me back my child! [*Goes into the hut, and calls*] Fernando!   20

AL. Almighty powers! do my eyes deceive me! Las Casas!!!

LAS C. Alonzo,—my belov'd young friend!

AL. My rever'd instructor. [*Embracing.*]

CORA. [*Return'd.*] Will you embrace this man before he restores my boy?

AL. Alas, my friend—in what a moment of misery do we meet!   25

CORA. Yet his look is goodness and humanity.—Good old man, have
compassion on a wretched mother—and I will be your servant while
I live.—But do not, for pity's sake—do not say, you have him not—
do not say, you have not seen him.   [*Runs into the Wood.*]

LAS C. What can this mean?   30

AL. She is my wife.—Just rescued from the Spaniards' prison, I learn'd
she had fled to this wild forest—Hearing my voice, she left the child,
and flew to meet me—he was left sleeping under yonder tree.

LAS C. How! did you leave him?—[CORA *returns.*]

CORA. O, you are right!—right!—unnatural mother, that I was—I left   35
my child—I forsook my innocent——but I will fly to the earth's brink,
but I will find him. [*Runs out.*]

AL. Forgive me, Las Casas, I must follow her: for at night, I attempt
brave Rolla's rescue.

LAS C. I will not leave thee, Alonzo—you must try to lead her to the   40
right—that way lies your camp—Wait not my infirm steps,—I follow
thee, my friend.   [*Exeunt.*

SCENE II

*The Out-Post of the Spanish Camp.—The back ground wild and rocky,
with a Torrent falling down the Precipice, over which a Bridge is
formed by a fell'd Tree.*   [*Trumpets sound without.*

ALMAGRO. [*Without.*] Bear him along—his story must be false. [*Entering.*]   5
ROLLA [*in Chains*] *brought in by* SOLDIERS.

ROL. False!—Rolla, utter falsehood!—I would I had thee in a desert
    with thy troop around thee;—and I, but with my sword in this un-
    shackled hand!—[*Trumpets without.*]
ALM. Is it to be credited that Rolla, the renown'd Peruvian hero—   10
    shou'd be detected like a spy, skulking thro' our camp?
ROL. Skulking!
ALM. But answer to the General—he is here.

Enter PIZARRO.

PIZ. What do I see! Rolla!   15
ROL. O! to thy surprise, no doubt.
PIZ. And bound too!
ROL. So fast, thou need'st not fear approaching me.
ALM. The guards surpris'd him, passing our out-post.
PIZ. Release him instantly.—Believe me, I regret this insult.   20
ROL. You feel then as you ought.
PIZ. Nor can I brook to see a warrior of Rolla's fame disarm'd—Accept
    this, tho' it has been thy enemy's. [*Gives a sword.*] The Spaniards know
    the courtesy that's due to valour.
ROL. And the Peruvian, how to forget offence.   25
PIZ. May not Rolla and Pizarro cease to be foes?
ROL. When the sea divides us; yes!—May I now depart?
PIZ. Freely.
ROL. And shall I not again be intercepted?
PIZ. No!—let the word be given that Rolla passes freely.   30

Enter DAVILLA *and* SOLDIERS, *with the* CHILD.

DAV. Here are two soldiers, captived yesterday, who have escap'd from
    the Peruvian hold,—and by the secret way we have so long endeavoured
    to discover.
PIZ. Silence,—imprudent!—Seest thou not—? [*pointing to* ROLLA.]   35
DAV. In their way, they found a Peruvian child, who seems——
PIZ. What is the imp to me?—Bid them toss it into the sea.
ROL. Gracious heaven! it is Alonzo's child!—give it to me.
PIZ. Ha! Alonzo's child!—Welcome, thou pretty hostage.—Now Alonzo
    is again my prisoner!   40
ROL. Thou wilt not keep the infant from its mother?

PIZ. Will I not!—What, when I shall meet Alonzo in the heat of the
victorious fight—think'st thou I shall not have a check upon the valour
of his heart, when he is reminded that a word of mine is this child's
death?

ROL. I do not understand you.   5

PIZ. My vengeance has a long arrear of hate to settle with Alonzo!—and
this pledge may help to settle the account.

ROL. Man! Man!—Art thou a man?—Could'st thou hurt that innocent?
—By Heaven! it's smiling in thy face.

PIZ. Tell me, does it resemble Cora?   10

ROL. Pizarro! thou hast set my heart on fire—If thou do'st harm that
child—think not his blood will sink into the barren sand—No!—faithful to the eager hope that now trembles in this indignant heart—'twill
rise to the common God of nature and humanity, and cry aloud for
vengeance on its accurs'd destroyer's head.   15

PIZ. Be that peril mine.

ROL. [*Throwing himself at his feet*] Behold me at thy feet—Me, Rolla!—
Me, the preserver of thy life!—Me, that have never yet bent or bow'd
before created man!—In humble agony I sue to you—prostrate I
implore you—but spare that child, and I will be your slave.   20

PIZ. Rolla! still art thou free to go—this boy remains with me.

ROL. Then was this sword Heaven's gift, not thine! [*Seizes the* CHILD]—
Who moves one step to follow me, dies upon the spot.
                                      [*Exit, with the* CHILD.

PIZ. Pursue him instantly—but spare his life. [*Exeunt* ALMAGRO *and*   25
SOLDIERS.] With what fury he defends himself!—Ha!—he fells them
to the ground—and now——

Enter ALMAGRO.

ALM. Three of your brave soldiers are already victims to your command
to spare this madman's life; and if he once gains the thicket——   30

PIZ. Spare him no longer. [*Exit* ALMAGRO.] Their guns must reach
him—he'll yet escape—holloa to those horse—the Peruvian sees them—
and now he turns among the rocks—then is his retreat cut off.
     [ROLLA *crosses the wooden bridge over the cataract, pursued by the* SOL-
     DIERS—*they fire at him—a shot strikes him*—PIZARRO *exclaims*——   35

PIZ. Now! quick! quick! seize the child!—
     [ROLLA *tears from the rock the tree which supports the bridge, and
     retreats by the back ground, bearing off the child.*]

Re-enter ALMAGRO.

ALM. By Hell! he has escaped!—and with the child unhurt.   40

DAV. No—he bears his death with him—Believe me, I saw him struck
upon the side.

PIZ. But the child is sav'd—Alonzo's child! Oh! the furies of disappointed vengeance!

ALM. Away with the revenge of words—let us to deeds—Forget not we have acquired the knowledge of the secret pass, which thro' the rocky cavern's gloom brings you at once to the strong hold, where are lodg'd 5 their women, and their treasures.

PIZ. Right, Almagro! Swift as thy thought draw forth a daring and a chosen band—I will not wait for numbers.—Stay, Almagro! Valverde is informed Elvira dies to-day?

VAL. He is—and one request alone she——   10

PIZ. I'll hear of none.

VAL. The boon is small—'tis but for the noviciate habit which you first beheld her in—she wishes not to suffer in the gaudy trappings, which remind her of her shame.

PIZ. Well, do as thou wilt—but tell Valverde, that at our return, as his 15 life shall answer it, to let me hear that she is dead.

[*Exeunt, severally.*]

SCENE III

ATALIBA's *Tent.*

Enter ATALIBA, *follow'd by* CORA *and* ALONZO.   20

CORA. Oh! Avoid me not, Ataliba! To whom, but to her King, is the wretched mother to address her griefs?—The Gods refuse to hear my prayers! Did not my Alonzo fight for *you?*—and will not my sweet boy, if thou'lt but restore him to me, one day fight thy battles too?

AL. Oh! my suffering love—my poor heart-broken Cora!—you but 25 wound our Sovereign's feeling soul, and not relieve thy own.

CORA. Is he our Sovereign, and has he not the power to give me back my child?

ATA. When I reward desert, or can relieve my people, I feel what is the real glory of a King—when I hear them suffer, and cannot aid them, 30 I mourn the impotence of all mortal power. [*Voices behind*] Rolla! Rolla! Rolla!

Enter ROLLA, *bleeding, with the* CHILD, *follow'd by Peruvian* SOLDIERS.

ROL. Thy child! [*Gives the* CHILD *into* CORA's *arms, and falls.*]

CORA. Oh God!—there's blood upon him!   35

ROL. 'Tis my blood, Cora!

AL. Rolla, thou diest!

ROL. For thee, and Cora—[*Dies.*]

Enter ORANO.

ORANO. Treachery has revealed our asylum in the rocks. Even now the
foe assails the peaceful band retired for protection there.

AL. Lose not a moment!—Swords be quick!—Your wives and children
cry to you—Bear our lov'd hero's body in the van—'Twill raise the   5
fury of our men to madness.—Now, fell Pizarro! the death of one of
us is near!—Away! Be the word of assault, Revenge and Rolla—[*Exeunt.*
[*Charge.*

SCENE IV

A romantic part of the Recess among the Rocks—[Alarms] *Women are* 10
seen flying, pursued by the Spanish Soldiers,—The Peruvian Soldiers
drive the Spaniards back from the Field.—The Fight is continued on
the Heights.

Enter PIZARRO, ALMAGRO, VALVERDE, *and Spanish* SOLDIERS.

PIZ. Well!—if surrounded, we must perish in the centre of them—Where 15
do Rolla and Alonzo hide their heads?

Enter ALONZO, ORANO, *and Peruvians.*

AL. Alonzo answers thee, and Alonzo's sword shall speak for Rolla.

PIZ. Thou know'st the advantage of thy numbers.—Thou dar'st not
singly face Pizarro.   20

AL. Peruvians, stir not a man!—Be this contest only our's.

PIZ. Spaniards!—observe ye the same.   [*Charge.*
They fight. ALONZO's *shield is broken, and he is beat down.*

PIZ. Now, traitor, to thy heart!
At this moment ELVIRA *enters, habited as when* PIZARRO *first beheld* 25
*her.—*PIZARRO, *appalled, staggers back.—*ALONZO *renews the Fight,*
and slays him.   [*Loud shouts from the Peruvians.*

ATALIBA *enters, and embraces* ALONZO.

ATA. My brave Alonzo!

ALM. Alonzo, we submit.—Spare us! we will embark, and leave the 30
coast.

VAL. Elvira will confess I sav'd her life; she has sav'd thine.

AL. Fear not. You are safe. [*Spaniards lay down their arms.*]

ELV. Valverde speaks the truth;—nor could he think to meet me here.—
An awful impulse which my soul could not resist, impell'd me hither. 35

AL. Noble Elvira! my preserver! How can I speak what I, Ataliba,
and his rescued country, owe to thee? If amid this grateful nation
thou would'st remain——

ELV. Alonzo, no!—the destination of my future life is fix'd. Humbled
in penitence, I will endeavour to atone the guilty errors, which, however mask'd by shallow cheerfulness, have long consum'd my secret
heart—When, by my sufferings purified, and penitence sincere, my
soul shall dare address the Throne of Mercy in behalf of others,—for   5
thee, Alonzo—for thy Cora, and thy child,—for thee, thou virtuous
Monarch, and the innocent race you reign over, shall Elvira's prayers
address the God of Nature.—Valverde, you have preserved my life.
Cherish humanity—avoid the foul examples thou hast view'd.—
Spaniards returning to your native home, assure your rulers, they   10
mistake the road to glory, or to power.—Tell them, that the pursuits
of avarice, conquest, and ambition, never yet made a people happy, or
a nation great.—[*Casts a look of agony on the dead body of* PIZARRO *as
she passes, and exit.*]   [*Flourish of Trumpets.*
VALVERDE, ALMAGRO, *and Spanish* SOLDIERS, *exeunt, bearing off*   15
PIZARRO's *Body.—On a signal from* ALONZO, *flourish of Music.*
AL. Ataliba! think not I wish to check the voice of triumph—when
I entreat we first may pay the tribute due to our lov'd Rolla's memory.

A solemn March[1]—Procession of Peruvian Soldiers, bearing ROLLA's
Body on a Bier, surrounded by Military Trophies. The Priests and   20
*Priestesses attending chaunt a Dirge[2] over the Bier.—*ALONZO *and*
CORA *kneel on either side of it, and kiss* ROLLA's *hands in silent agony—*
*In the looks of the King, and of all present, the Triumph of the Day is
lost, in mourning for the fallen Hero.*   [*The Curtain slowly descends.*

[1] See Kelly, *The Music of Pizarro*, p. 29, 'Dead March'. No composer is named.
[2] Kelly, *The Music of Pizarro*, p. 30, reads: 'Sung by Mrs. Crouch, Miss Decamp,
Miss Dufour, Miss Leak, Miss Menage:

> Let the tears of gratitude and woe
> For the brave Rolla ever flow!'

It was by Kelly himself.

EPILOGUE

WRITTEN BY THE HON. WILLIAM LAMB

SPOKEN BY MRS. JORDAN

ERE yet Suspense has still'd its throbbing fear,
Or Melancholy wip'd the grateful tear,   5
While e'en the miseries of a sinking State,
A Monarch's danger, and a Nation's fate,
Command not now your eyes with grief to flow,
Lost in a trembling Mother's nearer woe;
What moral lay shall Poetry rehearse,   10
Or how shall Elocution pour the verse
So sweetly, that its music shall repay
The lov'd illusion, which it drives away?
Mine is the task, to rigid custom due,
To me ungrateful, as 'tis harsh to you,   15
To mar the work the tragic scene has wrought,
To rouse the mind that broods in pensive thought,
To scare Reflection, which, in absent dreams,
Still lingers musing on the recent themes;
Attention, ere with contemplation tir'd,   20
To turn from all that pleas'd, from all that fir'd;
To weaken lessons strongly now imprest,
And chill the interest glowing in the breast—
Mine is the task; and be it mine to spare
The souls that pant, the griefs they see, to share;   25
Let me with no unhallow'd jest deride
The sigh, that sweet Compassion owns with pride—
The sigh of Comfort, to Affliction dear,
That Kindness heaves, and Virtue loves to hear.
E'en gay THALIA will not now refuse   30
This gentle homage to her Sister-Muse.
   O ye, who listen to the plaintive strain,
With strange enjoyment, and with rapturous pain,
Who erst have felt the *Stranger*'s[1] lone despair,
And *Haller*'s settled, sad, remorseful care,   35
Does *Rolla*'s pure affection less excite
The inexpressive anguish of delight?

[1] See p. 788 below.

Do *Cora*'s fears, which beat without control,
With less solicitude engross the soul?
Ah, no! your minds with kindred zeal approve
Maternal feeling, and heroic love.
You must approve; where Man exists below,   5
In temperate climes, or 'midst drear wastes of snow,
Or where the solar fires incessant flame,
Thy laws, all-powerful Nature, are the same:
Vainly the Sophist boasts, he can explain
The causes of thy universal reign—   10
More vainly would his cold presumptuous art
Disprove thy general empire o'er the heart:
A voice proclaims thee, that we must believe,
A voice, that surely speaks not to deceive;
That voice poor *Cora* heard, and closely prest   15
Her darling infant to her fearful breast;
Distracted dar'd the bloody field to tread,
And sought *Alonzo* through the heaps of dead,
Eager to catch the music of his breath,
Though faltering in the agonies of death,   20
To touch his lips, though pale and cold, once more,
And clasp his bosom, though it stream'd with gore;
That voice too *Rolla* heard, and, greatly brave,
His *Cora*'s dearest treasure died to save,
Gave to the hopeless Parent's arms her child,   25
Beheld her transports, and expiring smil'd.
That voice ye hear—Oh! be its will obey'd!
'Tis Valour's impulse and 'tis Virtue's aid—
It prompts to all Benevolence admires,
To all that heav'nly Piety inspires,   30
To all that Praise repeats through lengthen'd years,
That Honour sanctifies, and Time reveres.

THE END

THE CAMP

A Musical Entertainment

THE CAMP

COMPOSITION

THE first reference to *The Camp* is to be found in *The Gazetteer*, 9 October 1778: 'A new entertainment, in two acts, called The Camp, has been for some time preparing, and will be speedily performed.'

Readers could have guessed its nature without difficulty, if only because newspapers and magazines of the past six months had contained many allusions to the military camp at Coxheath, near Maidstone, Kent. Genuine concern in the public prints about national defence and the recruitment of volunteers was accompanied by amusement at the invasion of the camp itself by a coterie of fashionable ladies led by Georgiana, Duchess of Devonshire. They dressed in military style, took delight in watching the exercises, and had their own mess. They suffered little hardship for we know from Georgiana's letters[1] that the Duke had a warm fire in his tent, and that on at least one occasion the company dined on turtle. The festivities were ridiculed in the anonymous doggerel of *The Camp Guide*:[2]

> And we not less daunted, will hew and will hack,
> And to take surer aim, we lay on our back!
> We drop to soft music, 'tis true, I assure ye,
> Like the troop of fam'd Bays, you've seen at old Drury.
> At —— gay camp, we're in hopes to have plays,
> And Breslaw's[3] expected here, one of these days.

The eyes of the country were on Coxheath.

Some playhouses had already taken advantage of the patriotic spirit that ran through the land. York Theatre presented *The Volunteers* with a suitable song:[4]

> Young and old together pressing,
> Rich and poor, prepare for fight,
> And to have a common blessing,
> One and all in arms unite!

Sadler's Wells put on 'an entertainment of music and dancing (never yet performed) called *A Trip to Coxheath* to conclude with a distant view of the camp, and a roast beef chorus'.[5] The time had come for the patent houses to do their part in rousing the country.

---

[1] *Georgiana*, ed. the Earl of Bessborough (1955), pp. 35–40.
[2] *In a Series of Letters, from Ensign Tommy Toothpick to Lady Sarah Toothpick, and from Miss Nelly Brisk, to Miss Gadabout* (1778), p. 5.   [3] Conjuror.
[4] *Morning Chronicle*, 13 Oct. 1778.   [5] *Public Advertiser*, 6 Aug. 1778.

Sheridan's father had now joined the Drury Lane company as acting manager, and he had earlier[1] shown a keen interest in spectacle as a means of drawing an audience. Perhaps he was responsible for sending Philippe de Loutherbourg, one of the most inventive painters of the day, to Coxheath to inspect the camp there[2] and make designs so that it could be represented in the London playhouse. In 1767 Thomas Linley had written five songs for Thomas Hull's *The Royal Merchant*, that had a martial air about them, and could be easily adapted for use in the new entertainment.[3] What was also needed was 'a plan and dialogue'. Many writers have claimed that this was written by Sheridan; others have ascribed it to Richard Tickell, and some have suggested that Sheridan and Tickell or Sheridan and Burgoyne collaborated in manufacturing it.[4]

For seventeen years it was taken for granted that Sheridan was the author. In the month of the first performance, at least four reports attributed it to him, with varying degrees of certainty. The *Morning Post*, 16 October 1778, declared: 'This petit piece is said to be the production of Mr. Sheridan, who tacked the dialogue part of it together, in order to introduce Mr. *Loutherbourgh*'s scenic spectacle of Coxheath Camp, with a kind of dramatic propriety; and in which he has been very successful.' The *St. James's Chronicle*[5] was of the opinion that 'the Dialogue appears to be the Work of Mr. Sheridan'. The *Town and Country Magazine*[6] said that 'the dialogue, tho' written by Mr. Sheridan, can only be considered as a temporary *jeu d'esprit*'. The *London Magazine*[7] mentioned that 'the plan and dialogue of this excellent performance are attributed to Mr. Sheridan'.

The first suggestion that it was definitely not Sheridan's work was made in 1795, when the York Theatre manager and busybody, Tate Wilkinson, published some recollections:

As to that excellent piece, *The Camp*, I do aver, in opposition, it is not fit for the stage, nor has ever yet succeeded: Mr. Sheridan never wrote a line or espoused it; it was a catchpenny for the time. . . . Mr. Linley was under the necessity of purloining the old music from 'The Royal Merchant'. . . . Mr. Sheridan's name was foisted into the newspapers to give it sanction.[8]

It ought to be noted, at once, that Wilkinson's statements were published in the same year as the first edition—a pirated one—of *The Camp*, and that the text printed in it does Sheridan little credit. If Wilkinson meant to condemn this particular printing, he had some justice on his side. In other respects, his assertions can be proved to be inaccurate. Linley

[1] Esther K. Sheldon, *Thomas Sheridan of Smock-Alley* (Princeton, 1967), p. 223.
[2] Folger MS. W. b. 282 records a payment of £160 to De Loutherbourg on 15 Nov. 1779 'for Expences to Derbyshire and Coxheath'.
[3] See p. 716 below.   [4] See Rhodes, ii. 271-2, 302-5.
[5] 15-17 Oct. 1778.   [6] x (1778), 545.
[7] xlvii (1778), 438.   [8] *The Wandering Patentee* (York, 1795), iv. 195.

hardly purloined the music, since he had written it himself.[1] *The Camp* was so very successful at Drury Lane Theatre that in its first sixty-eight performances it took more money than *The Critic* did in a similar period.[2]

Wilkinson's claim that Sheridan 'never wrote a line or espoused it' must therefore be treated with reserve, but the views of Thomas Moore may be accorded greater respect. He put them in downright fashion: 'This unworthy trifle (as appears from a rough copy of it in my possession) was the production of Tickell.'[3] Sichel called the entertainment 'an operetta by Tickell', and added that it 'only owed revising touches to Sheridan, and a copy of the play in the author's handwriting, with Sheridan's corrections, is to be found among his papers'. The only correction mentioned by Sichel occurs when 'an eye like the King of Prussia' becomes apparently 'a blood-spill eye'.[4] This is not to be found in any of the versions I have seen and looks as if it were an afterthought. Perhaps we should also remember that a manuscript in Tickell's hand was not necessarily composed by him, and that Sheridan was not particular about who copied his drafts as long as he could comfort himself with the idea of correcting them later.

If we may believe W. T. Parke's *Musical Memoirs* (1830), Sheridan showed as much interest in the success of *The Camp* as in any play undoubtedly by him:

Mr. Sheridan, on the spur of the moment, wrote a musical piece in two acts, called 'The Camp', produced at Drury Lane on the 15th of October, 1778. This agreeable piece, which had an uncommon run, displayed a variety of military evolutions, very beautiful scenery designed by J. P. Loutherburg, and some pretty music composed by Mr. Linley. At one of the rehearsals Bannister as Serjeant Drill, sung a song to the rustics to induce them to list, beginning.

> Great Caesar once renown'd in Fame,
> For a mighty arm and a laurel'd brow,
> With his Veni, vidi, vici, came,
> And conquer'd the world with his row dow dow.

The song ended: Bannister, as a further inducement, had to go through the manual exercise, giving the word himself, which he did in plain, intelligible terms, thus: 'Shoulder your arms!—Present your arms!' and was proceeding, when Sheridan, running up to him, exclaimed, 'That won't do at all, Mr. Bannister; it is very unsoldierlike—you speak to be understood; they never do that on the parade.'[5]

[1] See F. W. Bateson, 'Notes on the Text of Two Sheridan Plays', *R.E.S.* xvi (1940), 312–14.
[2] G. W. Williams, 'A New Source of Evidence for Sheridan's Authorship of *The Camp* and *The Wonders of Derbyshire*', *Studies in Philology* (Chapel Hill), xlvii (1950), 620. It was performed fifty-four times in its first season.
[3] Moore, i. 264–5. [4] Sichel, i. 443, 610, but see p. 831 below.
[5] i. 12. Parke (1762–1847) was a soprano chorister at Drury Lane in 1775, and played viola and oboe at Vauxhall Gardens. The music of *The Camp* contains two marches by 'Mr. Parke', probably his brother, John Parke (1745–1829). The period is likely to have left a strong impression on the youth's memory.

Parke's suggestion that the entertainment was written 'on the spur of the moment' is borne out by the theatre's correspondence with the Lord Chamberlain's office. Two days before the first performance, Sheridan signed a letter written by William Hopkins and asking for the Lord Chamberlain's approval of 'the following New Entertainment in Two Acts'.[1] Just what was enclosed is not clear, but the manuscript bears the docketing: 'R[eceived] 7th Novr. 1778. but approved by the Lord Chamberlain in Octr.'[1] The manuscript itself was not complete, and it seems likely that only an outline was presented to the licenser on the first occasion. Speed appears to have been essential and it would not be surprising if Sheridan had called on Tickell for some help or had asked Burgoyne to write some lines for a reappearance by O'Daub, the Irish painter.[2]

The Drury Lane account books, however, do not contain references to specific payments for the dialogue, and this has been interpreted, from the conventions employed in the ledgers, to mean that the lines were written by Sheridan himself.[3] The theory is convincing enough to deserve serious consideration.

The Larpent text too bears out the attribution. Sheridan's particular tone can be heard in the satire on fraudulent contractors and on the impact of the camp on fashionable life. Rhodes found in the description of the military lady's toilet (II. iii), 'the germ' of the epilogue written afterwards by Sheridan for Hannah More's tragedy, *The Fatal Falsehood* (1779). He went on to assert that 'its presence is a great argument in favour of his authorship of *The Camp*'.[4] A better one is that the lines were probably part of a poem on women that Sheridan was busily composing in 1778,[5] but probably never completed. It would be quite characteristic of him to lift something from this for immediate use, and it is worth notice that he commonly drafted his thoughts in prose before converting them into verse.

What the entertainment might have become had he found time to develop and polish his work can only be guessed, but it was essentially a topical, co-operative venture, brought out with zest to meet the needs of the moment. I see no objection to the idea that other writers may have had some hand in it, even though I believe that Sheridan was responsible for many of the lines. There are certainly some that are commonplace enough to have been written by anybody. Yet the plan and dialogue were important only because they introduced situations, drilling, choruses,

---

[1] *Letters*, i. 122–3. [2] See Rhodes, ii. 272, 303–5.
[3] G. W. Williams, op. cit., pp. 622–8, suggests that the book-keeping system of the theatre was regular except in the case of Sheridan's own plays; that Tickell and Burgoyne were charged standard sums when their plays were given for their benefits in other years, but that no authors' benefits were recorded in the accounts for this season. This leads to an assumption that Sheridan was the author of *The Camp* because he received £200 (5 Nov.) and £300 (4 Feb.) to cover amounts due to him.
[4] Rhodes, iii. 277. [5] *Letters*, i. 121–2.

scenery. The most discussed part of the show was, in fact, one of the devices used by De Loutherbourgh: 'In the beautiful perspective view of the Coxheath camp exhibited last night . . ., by a kind of magic peculiar to himself, he makes the different battalions, composed of small figures, march out in excellent order, into the front of their lines to the astonishment of every spectator.'[1] How this was done is not made clear to the reader, but it may have taught Sheridan that scenic tricks and illusions would serve him well when literary invention was at a standstill, and wit and wisdom were busy elsewhere. The point was to be made a year later by Puff: 'Now, gentlemen, this scene goes entirely for what we call SITUATION or STAGE EFFECT, by which the greatest applause may be obtained, without the assistance of language, sentiment or character.'[2]

RECEPTION

In entertainments of this kind, contrary to those of a more perfect dramatic species, the eye is to take the lead of the mind; and provided the scenery is well produced, it is hypercritical to enter theatrical caveats against the fable, characters, etc., of the piece. This being permitted we look upon 'The Camp' to be a very agreeable entertainment, and bids fair to dispute a run of favour with 'The Jubilee,'[3] which was so long the idol of the public.

The main story, detached from the other incidents, is very thin, but at the same time simple and affecting; and as we have before observed, it not being so necessary that those incidents should lead to the dénouement of the piece, they afford enough of business to keep up the attention of the audience. The plot is this— . . . .

This little fable is supported by many laughable and humourous incidents and sketches of characters. Amongst the latter are a Macaroni Officer, a Camp Contractor, a good blundering Irishman, etc., all of which were well performed, and received by an overflowing audience with very great and singular applause.

The three first scenes, though overlooked from an eager expectation of the grand view of Coxheath, were pleasant, beautiful landscapes; but the grand view must be seen to be felt: It does every degree of credit to this very ingenious foreigner.

Miss Walpole had great merit in her disguised character of a recruit; she was one of the prettiest breeches figures that a painter could wish for, and she went through her exercise with an ease and exactness very

---

[1] *Morning Post*, 16 Oct. 1778. Cf. Sybil Rosenfeld, 'The *Eidophusikon* Illustrated', *Theatre Notebook*, xviii (1963–4), 54. It is also worth noting that De Loutherbourg's painting of 'The troops at Warley Common reviewed by his Majesty, 1778', was item 15 in the Royal Academy exhibition of 1780. See the *Town and Country Magazine*, xii (1780), 256. [2] *The Critic*, III. i.

[3] By David Garrick, and produced at Drury Lane on 14 October 1769.

extraordinary for a lady. Parsons, Moody, and Mrs. Wrighten, exerted themselves to please, and succeeded very happily.

Mr. Webster's songs were not in general fitted for his voice, which (though an excellent one) is too guttural for fine notes, or shakes in piano; his song, to the tune of 'Kate of Aberdeen,' suffered in these particulars; in other respects both he and Bannister made very soldier-like appearances.

In short, the Camp at Drury-lane is upon the whole very likely to rival the Camp at Coxheath, and the Managers (though they don't deal in brown bread) to exceed the profits of the Contractors. (*The London Evening Post*, 15–17 Oct. 1778.)

The Piece opens with a View of the Road to the Camp at Coxheath . . . where Nell, a kind of Billingsgate Moralist, lays about her and scolds, and moralises at a most uncommon Rate. This Scene is succeeded by the Introduction of O'Daub, an Irish Painter, who is accosted by Gauge, and who says he is come to *take* the Camp. A very tolerable Dialogue ensues principally in the Irish manner. . . .

[Gauge says he supplied lime instead of flour. This] must be allowed for Wit. But the Author is too much delighted with his Conceit to let it pass in proper Time; he compares them again to a smooth Half-Crown; and again to bald Veterans, until every Man of Taste is wearied out with what would otherwise have pleased him.

. . . The Piece concludes with a View of the Right Wing of The Camp, and the Regiments in Motion, which exceeds every Thing in Scenery we have ever seen. The Dialogue appears to be the Work of Mr. Sheridan, junior. It has the Excellencies and Blemishes of that Writer. It is sprightly, ornamental, and yet level to the tinselled or untinselled Vulgar; but the witty Passages are indiscriminately dispersed; and held out too ostentatiously for Persons of Judgment and Taste.

The Characters are drawn from Fancy more than Observation. The French Suttler is particularly exceptionable; as Mr. Sheridan might have been furnished with Models in that Kind at Coxheath, from which a very masterly Sketch might have been given. The Music was *prepared* by Mr. Linley, who has more Judgement in giving Effect to Compositions, than Genius in producing them.

But the Writer and the Composer are so totally eclipsed by the Painter that the Entertainment of the *Camp*, will always be attributed to the Talents of Mr. de Loutherbourgh. (*St. James's Chronicle*, 15–17 Oct. 1778.)

On a Subject that promised so little Theatrical Entertainment, as *The Camp*, we were most agreeably surprised, Yesterday Evening, with a Dramatic Exhibition of very great Merit in every Point of View. The Dialogue is throughout witty and humorous, without sinking into Vulgarity, which, from the Situations and Characters, might have been apprehended. The Music is extremely sprightly and pleasing; the Overture most happily expressive of the martial Jollity and Festivity of our domestic Military Preparations. The Trio at the End of the first Act is in the highest Stile of Musical Composition, and does the greatest Honour to Mr. Linley.

The concluding Scene was received with the greatest Acclamations we ever remember. It seemed scarcely possible to give an exact View of the Camp at Coxheath so beautiful an Effect . . . .

Gauge, a country exciseman, takes advantage of his Kentish connections, to unite to his Vocation the Cheats of Smuggling, and the petty Tricks of a *Subaltern Contractor*; which he describes to *O'Daub*, the Irish painter, so famous in the *Fete Champetre*, and who is sent down by the Managers of Drury Lane to *take the Camp*; an Expedition which terminates in the ludicrous Circumstance of his being taken for a Spy.

The Ground-work of the plot is very simple, yet interesting. A Farmer's Daughter escapes from her Suffolk Relations (who were persuading her to a Marriage of Interest) in Pursuit of her Lover at the Camp, with a view to gaining his Discharge; but becomes so charmed with the Military Life, and the Protection shown her by Ladies of Quality who are down there, that she determines to marry her Soldier, and share his Toils. A Macarony Connoisseur rallies the Ladies on their Military Appearance, and by several well timed Witticisms, enlivens this pleasing Entertainment. (*Public Advertiser* and *The Oracle*, 16 Oct. 1778; and *London Chronicle*, 17–20 Oct. 1778.)

. . . The dialogue is happily hit off; the humour of it, is of the standard of the *Jubilee*, but the incidents of the present piece are not quite so comic. . . .

It cannot but have cost the managers great pains, as well as a considerable deal of money; it does their judgment, their ability, and their assiduity abundant credit. . . .

Mr. Webster sung the air to the tune of *Kate of Aberdeen* well, but it would have a better effect if he sung it in a more simple stile. (*Morning Chronicle*, 16 Oct. 1778.)

Miss Walpole's ballad is a very beautiful one; and the trio that concludes the first act, a very spirited, and masterly composition.—The first movement of the overture is bold, and striking, and the last, in which the drum and fife are very happily introduced, has a very noble effect indeed, and was encored.

. . . Miss Walpole . . . went through a part of the manual exercise in a style that would have done credit to any corps of regulars.

... Miss Farren, Miss Cuyler, and Mrs. Robinson, appeared to much advantage in their *Amazonian* attire. (*Morning Post*, 16 Oct. 1778.)

... Indeed the whole of the second act is by no means equal to the first.

The concluding chorus is rather oddly formed, and had not an effect equal to what might have been expected from the real merit of the composer. (*The Gazetteer*, 16 Oct. 1778.)

... The military manœuvres now commence, and afford much entertainment, as well on account of their novelty as the dexterity with which they were performed. Most of the airs are very well adapted, though not many of them are new. A prologue was spoken by Mr. Palmer, and ascribed to Mr. Garrick. The overture was set by Mr. Linley; but the chief merit of this performance is due to M. de Loutherbourg, whose fine representation of Cox-heath Camp does great honour to him as an artist. Indeed, the whole performance seems chiefly designed to introduce the happy effects of that great master's pencil, as the dialogue, tho' written by Mr. Sheridan, can only be considered as a temporary *jeu d'esprit*. (*Town and Country Magazine*, x (1778), 544–5.)

... Palmer [the manager of the Bath Theatre] goes on bravely. I wish, however, Sheridan would write no more, for nothing now will go down but 'School for Scandal' and 'Duenna'. 'The Camp' too is just pitched, and as many go to see it as did to Coxheath. (J. Taylor to David Garrick, from Bath, 14 Jan. 1779: Boaden, *Garrick Corr.* ii. 331.)

The Theatres but barren of entertainment this winter, and C[ovent] G[arden] barren of profit as well as entertainment. The Camp, wretched Stuff as it is, has assisted D[rury] L[ane]. (George Colman the elder to Joseph Lefanu, 4 Dec. 1778: a letter in the collection of Mr. W. R. LeFanu.)

The Camp, a farce by Sheridan, [was] intended to create much merriment in the galleries, an object which it completely attained. (*The Cyclopaedian Magazine* (Dublin, 1808), ii. 67.)

It is not a little extraordinary, however, that no public disavowal of this contemptible production was ever made on the part of the person most affected by the imputation, and to whom this forcible remonstrance was addressed when the entertainment came out at Drury Lane. 'At this impending moment,' says an anonymous writer, 'is it wise, is it honourable, in a poet of such talents as Mr. Sheridan, to vilify and throw disgrace on the national character; to sink the virtue of courage in its own esteem, and hold it forth in colours that tend to make us shun and despise instead of admiring it? *Bombast* is much more pardonable than *burlesque*. The first may exalt a weak mind, but the second must depress a strong one: and as courage, if it is not to be acquired, is at least to be improved, I would rather see another Lee write one Alexander, than a thousand Sheridans write a thousand *Camps*.'

Next to the folly of writing such a piece was the indiscretion of suffering it to disgrace the stage at a period when the country was distracted by party, and menaced by a combination of foreign foes, who were bent upon its destruction, or at least upon the annihilation of its naval power and commercial interests. It is hard to account for the apathy of Mr. Sheridan, and the little concern which he had for his reputation, when he could permit a farce of this description to pass current in the world as the effusion of his genius. If the piece was really his composition, prudence would have hinted the propriety of concealing its origin; and if it was not his performance, he acted very unjustly to himself, as well as disrespect-fully to the public, in omitting to disavow what was universally ascribed to his pen by the daily papers, by the frequenters of the theatre, and even by his most intimate friends. (John Watkins, *Memoirs of the Public and Private Life of the Right Honourable R. B. Sheridan* (2nd edn., 1817), i. 226–7.)

CHOICE OF TEXT

1. OF THE PROLOGUE

Only the first seventeen lines are included in the Larpent MS., and the original in Tickell's hand has not been located. It was printed in a number of newspapers, and I have accepted the version in the *St. James's Chronicle*, 20–24 October 1778, as copy-text, collating it with the texts given in the *Public Advertiser*, 23 October 1778, and the *Town and Country Magazine*, x (1778), 550–1, as well as with the fragment in the Larpent MS.

2. OF THE SONGS

Under the title of 'New Music', the *Public Advertiser*, 17 November 1778, contained an advertisement of the following work as published that day. The engraved title-page of the book reads:

> The | CAMP | *An Entertainment as performed at the* | THEATRE ROYAL in DRURY LANE, | Composed by | *Thomas Linley* | [rule] Price 5s. [rule] | LONDON | *Printed for S & A Thompson No 75 St Paul's Church Yard* | N.B. The favorite Song in the School for Scandal is Printed at the end of this Book by permission of the Author.

Oblong 4to.

Contents: pp. [iv]+27 of engraved music: p. [28] is blank.
[i] title; [ii] Blank; [iii] 'Advertisement | $*_*^*$ The Words of the following Airs Trios etc. introduced in the Entertainment of the CAMP are many of them taken from the Comic Opera of the ROYAL MERCHANT Set by the

same Composer, some of the Musick of which was found particularly applicable to the Subject of this Piece. | T.L.'; [iv] blank; 1–27, text.

The words of five of the songs given here were based on and close to the texts given in *The Royal Merchant . . . Printed for William Griffin* (1768). They were: 'Now coaxing, caressing' (Thompson, p. 6); 'Great Caesar' (Thompson, p. 7); 'Yet ere you're permitted' (Thompson, p. 8); 'What can our wisest heads provide' (Thompson, p. 12); and 'When the loud voice of War' (Thompson, p. 19).

The other four had new words: 'When war's alarms' (Thompson, p. 11); 'O Joy when the trumpets sound' (Thompson, p. 13); 'My Nancy leaves the rural train' (Thompson, p. 17); and 'The fife and drum sound merrily' (Thompson, p. 18).[1]

By this publication, the songs and music became available to other theatres. *Harlequin Volunteer, Or, A Trip to Coxheath* was performed at the Theatre Royal, Richmond Green, on 24 July 1779, and it 'introduced the Songs, Trios, and Grand Chorusses, composed by Mr. Linley, and sung last season at the Theatre Royal in Drury Lane, in the entertainment of *The Camp*'.[2] A performance at Bristol Theatre on 20 December 1779 was advertised with the footnote, 'The SONGS of the CAMP may be had at the Printing-Office in Small street, and at the Theatre.'[3]

The earliest copies I can discover[4] for sale at Drury Lane Theatre probably belong to 1803. They seem to have been intended to cater for demand to be expected from the revival of *The Camp* on 28 November 1803 and on fifteen other nights in that season. They were put out by Mrs. Lowndes, the Drury Lane Theatre printer, and the title-page reads:

SONGS, | TRIOS, CHORUSES, &c. | IN THE | MUSICAL ENTERTAINMENT | OF | *THE CAMP*, | AS IT IS PER-FORMED AT | THE THEATRE ROYAL, DRURY-LANE. | [swelled rule] | LONDON. | Printed for C. LOWNDES, (No 66,) Drury-Lane. | And Sold in the Theatre. | [swelled rule] | PRICE SIXPENCE.

Five of the songs are the same; the others contain some variants.

3. OF THE ENTERTAINMENT

(i) *Moore's 'rough copy'*

Moore's description[5] suggests that the manuscript he saw was wholly in the hand of Richard Tickell. It is possible, however, that he really referred to the next item.

---

[1] Mrs. Vlasto kindly informs me that two of the songs, 'The fife and drum' and 'When war's alarms', are in Corri's *Select Collection of the most admired Songs* (*c.* 1779), ii. 19–20, in the Rowe Music Library, King's College, Cambridge.

[2] Cutting in a Folger Library scrap-book.

[3] *Felix Farley's Bristol Journal*, 18 Dec. 1779. The *Journal* printing-office was in Small Street.

[4] The Lilly Library copy bears a handwritten date 'Oct. 22—1803'.

[5] See p. 709 above.

(ii) *A copy revised by Sheridan*

I have already quoted part of Sichel's description.[1] In a footnote he added, 'The amendments are mostly excisions, and recasting of styles.'[2] Sheridan's revision of his own work is largely of this kind, and this might make us assume that *The Camp* is bound to be his own composition, were it not for the fact that he revises other people's plays (e.g. Fielding's *The Fathers*) in the same way.

Sichel mentioned that the manuscript was among Sheridan's papers, but it is not listed in the Frampton catalogue and its present whereabouts is unknown.[3]

(iii) *The Lord Chamberlain's MS.*

Although this manuscript was not deposited at the Lord Chamberlain's office until three weeks after the first performance of the entertainment, the text is incomplete. This is revealed when we compare its lines with the summary of the story printed in the *Morning Chronicle*, 16 October 1778. The prologue soon peters out; blanks are left for songs and sometimes they are written in attenuated form; the scene between William and Nell at the beginning of the second act and their piece of dialogue at the end of that act are entirely omitted. It hardly seems likely that the transcriber would have left out both by accident, and the only reasonable explanation I can think of is that they had not been written when the manuscript was sent off for first inspection on 13 October. Why they were not inserted when the copy was sent to the examiner a second time is difficult to understand.

The gaps make the sequence of songs odd in two places. The first song in the manuscript is 'What can their wisest heads provide', but it is clear from the newspapers as well as Thompson and the version of 1795, that some change of order took place before performance, and that 'Now coaxing, caressing' became the first number. The other peculiarity also concerns 'Now coaxing, caressing', for it appears in the manuscript as one stanza followed by a long flourish, suggesting it might be the end of the scene. Comparison with the newspapers and other texts shows that this position was reserved, at the first performance, for 'O the Joy'.

The transcriber made a number of errors of spelling and sense: it seems certain, for example, that when he wrote 'The camp for you', he should have written 'The camp jargon'.

In spite of the very defective nature of this manuscript, it is the best text in existence. It contains some witty and satirical lines that suggest that Sheridan might have made more of the theme.

---

[1] See p. 709 above.   [2] Sichel, i. 610 n. 1.   [3] But see p. 831 below.

It is Larpent MS. 457 in the Henry E. Huntington Library, is in one hand throughout, and consists of thirty folios of writing.

(iv) *The text of the first performance*

This has not been located. A copy was reported to have been made available to the Liverpool Theatre in June 1779:

The Scenery, which has been generally allowed to be a very exact picture of the Encampment, is designed by the celebrated Mons. Lout[h]erbourgh, from which Mr. Hodgings (by the permission of the Drury Lane managers) was at the request of Mr. Younger, permitted to take a copy; and those Gentlemen have to their other favours, added that of giving him the dialogue of the Piece, which is not yet published.[1]

(v) *The pirated (and first) edition of 1795*

This seems to represent a transcription of the text at performance and, as Mr. F. W. Bateson[2] has suggested, one taken 'surreptitiously and by ear'. He supports his case by showing that 'tasty' becomes 'testy' (I. i), and 'course', 'cause' (I. ii). I have found another example to strengthen the argument: 'soaping' (I. i) becomes 'soaking'. In general, the text correctly repeats some words, but also adds very many that have no obvious authority. As in the pirated versions of *The School for Scandal*, paraphrasing is very frequent, so little purpose is served if an editor prints variants. Where the text is most useful is in providing lines for William and Nell, but even there we may assume that they are an elaboration of the original. The compiler goes in for broader strokes of comedy or sentiment, blunting the subtler points of the original, and obviously appealing to a less sophisticated audience. He does not understand the allusion to 'Capability' Brown so he omits it and makes nonsense of the line. Sir Harry Bouquet affectedly draws attention to the 'Parade, pomp, and circumstance of glorious war', but the compiler humourlessly gives the line as it stands in *Othello*. He tries to increase the sentimental appeal by stressing the circumstances in which Nancy runs way, and is so anxious to give O'Daub an Irish bull that he makes him say (and there is no sign of this in the Larpent MS.), 'I'm going to take a side front view of it.'[3]

Possibly this text was written up soon after the first season, though many years passed before it was printed. *The Camp* was so successful that it must have been in great demand outside London. The performance at Liverpool was sanctioned because Younger was influential, but it is unlikely that permission of this sort was granted often. Even so, *The*

---

[1] *Williamson's Liverpool Advertiser*, 18 June 1779. See, also, J. L. Hodgkinson and Rex Pogson, *The Early Manchester Theatre* (1960), p. 96, for a Manchester performance by the same company.

[2] 'Notes on the text of Two Sheridan Plays', *R.E.S.* xvi (1940), 313.

[3] I. i.

Camp was acted at Belfast on 26 November 1779,[1] in Bristol on 20 December,[2] at Dublin on 27 March 1780,[3] at Colchester on 12 September 1780,[4] and, no doubt, elsewhere. An unauthorized text was probably handed on from manager to manager and grew more corrupt with each transcription.

The title-page reads:

THE | CAMP, | A | *MUSICAL ENTERTAINMENT,* | AS PERFORMED AT THE | THEATRE ROYAL, DRURY LANE. | [Ornamental rule] | BY R. B. SHERIDAN, ESQ. | [Ornamental rule] | 𝕷𝖔𝖓𝖉𝖔𝖓: | PRINTED IN THE YEAR | M,DCC,XCV.

Collation: 8vo. A⁶–B⁸.

Contents: pp. [1–3]+4–28.

[1] Title; [2] Dramatis Personæ;[5] [3]–28, text.

A number of texts are derived from this one. The nearest in date has previously been overlooked, but is interesting because it suggests a possible printer of the 1795 version. The title-page reads:

THE | CAMP, | A MUSICAL ENTERTAINMENT | AS PERFORMED AT | THE THEATRE ROYAL, DRURY-LANE. | [Ornament] | BY R. B. SHERIDAN, ESQ. | [Ornament] | LON-DON: | PRINTED—AND SOLD BY J. ROACH, | RUSSEL-COURT, DRURY LANE. | [Short rule] | 1803.

Collation: 8vo. A–B⁶ C².

It differs from the 1795 version in a few instances in spelling, punctuation, and typography, but they are of little significance.[6]

Other editions derived from the 1795 text were published by Murray in the *Works* (1821),[7] by the Columbian Press in the *Dramatic Works of . . . Sheridan* (Greenock, 1828), and in George Daniel's version of the entertainment in Cumberland's *British Theatre* (*c.* 1833).

Rhodes made much of the fact that his text was based on Cumberland, but that he inserted into it passages recovered from the Greenock edition.[8] All this was quite unnecessary since the resulting text was almost exactly the same as that to be found in the edition of 1795, mentioned, but

---

[1] W. S. Clark, *The Irish Stage in the County Towns, 1720–1800* (Oxford, 1965), p. 241.   [2] See p. 716, above.

[3] *Freeman's Journal* (Dublin), 21–23 Mar. 1780.

[4] G. O. Rickword, 'Sheridan's Plays: A Note on the Colchester Stage, 1775–1785', *The Essex Review*, lviii (1949), 137–40.

[5] It includes Suett as 'Boy', Miss Pope as Lady Sash, and Mrs. Ward as Lady Gorget. The leading characters are otherwise the same as those in the 1778 list, though Baddeley had died in 1794.

[6] 'Lanturnburg' (p. 8) becomes in 1803, 'Lanternberg'; 'by gar' (p. 9), 'be gar'; 'sorrow on me' (p. 15), 'sorrow me'. The cast list is of the 1803 performances at Drury Lane, and includes William and the Corporal as separate persons.

[7] This is touched up slightly in spelling. Among the improved forms are (p. 16) 'Lantenberg'; (p. 17) 'Bouillard'; (p. 18) 'begar'; (p. 23) 'flour'; (p. 25) 'réveille'; (p. 65) 'bouilli'.   [8] Rhodes, ii. 266, 306.

obviously not collated, by him. His deduction that Daniel's copy was taken from the prompt-book of Drury Lane Theatre now seems unlikely to be correct.

Conclusion

I have used the Larpent MS. as copy-text, but have admitted into it the scene concerning William and Nell (pp. 740–2 below) from the 1795 version, and ll. 9–34 on p. 748, as well as ll. 6–17 on p. 750. I have corrected spelling errors[1] when they appear to be those of the copyist rather than of Sheridan. I have also admitted readings from the Thompson's edition of the words of the songs, and have been guided by this work and by the newspaper accounts of the first performance in deciding on the order of the musical items and development of the plot.

The following abbreviations are used in the textual footnotes of the entertainment:

L   The Lord Chamberlain's MS.

Th.   Thompson's edition: see pp. 715–16 above.

R.M.   [Thomas Hull and Thomas Linley] *The Royal Merchant: An Opera founded on Beaumont and Fletcher. As it is performed at the Theatre Royal, in Covent Garden. London: Printed for William Griffin, in Catharine-Street, in the Strand.* MDCCLXVIII.

1795   The version of the entertainment described on p. 718 above.

The abbreviations used in the textual notes to the prologue are:

SJC   *St. James's Chronicle*, 22–24 October 1778.

PA   *Public Advertiser*, 23 October 1778.

TC   *Town and Country Magazine*, x (1778).

L   The Lord Chamberlain's MS.

---

[1] I have normalized the following: 'gett' (pp. 725, 727, 730); 'sais' (p. 726); 'Majesties' and 'Majestie's' (pp. 724, 732); 'gott' (pp. 728, 731); 'Jewell' (pp. 729, 732); 'Forgott' (p. 730); 'Forreign' (p. 732); 'Brittish' (p. 733); 'Prushia' (p. 734); 'forreigner' (p. 744); 'exagaration' (p. 745); 'Cressent' (p. 745); 'Connoiscenti' (p. 745); 'Decipline' (p. 746). I have also normalized 'O'Daub'.

DRAMATIS PERSONÆ[1]

SERJEANT	Mr. Bannister
CORPORAL [WILLIAM]	Mr. Webster
O'DAUB	Mr. Moody
GAUGE	Mr. Parsons
MONSIEUR BLUARD [BOUILLARD, BOUILLE, BOULARD]	Mr. Baddeley
COUNTRYMEN	Mr. Wrighten, Mr. Burton, and Mr. Waldron
RECRUITS	Mr. Carpenter, Mr. Fawcett, Mr. Holcroft, and Mr. Chaplin
COMMANDER IN CHIEF AT THE CAMP	Mr. Farren
OFFICERS OF REGIMENTS	Mr. R. Palmer,[2] Mr. Lamash, and Mr. Kenny
SIR HARRY BOUQUET [PLUME, CHARLES PLUME]	Mr. Dodd
NELLY	Mrs. Wrighten
LADY SASH	Miss Farren
LADY PLUME	Mrs. Robinson
MISS GORGET [LADY GORGET]	Mrs. Cuyler
NANCY	Miss Walpole
COUNTRYWOMEN [including 'SMART GIRL' and 'MARGERY']	Mrs. Love, Mrs. Booth, Miss Kirby, and Mrs. Bradshaw.

[1] The cast list is taken from the *Morning Chronicle*, 16 Oct. 1778, but has been adjusted to contain the names given in the Larpent MS. and other sources. 'Sir Harry Bouquet', for example, is called 'Sir Charles Plume' in the *Morning Chronicle*; 'Sir Harry Plume' in the *Public Advertiser*, 16 Oct. 1778; 'Sir Charles Bouquet' in the *St. James's Chronicle*, 15–17 Oct. 1778; and 'Sir Henry Bouquet' in the printed version of 1803. The newspapers may have jumped to the conclusion that his surname was Plume, because Lady Plume calls him 'Brother'. For the contemporary significance of 'Bouquet', see p. 395 above, n. 2.

[2] He was painted in character for the Royal Academy exhibition of 1779: see the *London Chronicle*, 24–27 Apr. 1779.

PROLOGUE

Written by Richard Tickell, Esq.

The Stage is still the Mirror of the Day,
Where Fashion's Forms in bright Succession play;
True to its End, what Image can it yield   5
In Times like these, but the embattled Field?
What juster Semblance than the glittering Plains
Of village Warriors, and heroic Swains?
Invasions, Battles, now fill Rumour's Breath,
From Camps to Fleets, from Plymouth to Coxheath.   10
Through every Rank some pannic Terrors spread,
And each in varied Phrase express their Dread.
   At 'Change, no vulgar Patriot Passions fright
The firm and philosophick—Israelite:
Ask him his Hopes—' 'Tis all de shame to me!   15
I fix my Wishes by my Policy.
I'll do you Keppel;[1] or increase de Barters,
You will, I'll underwrite de Duke de Chartres.'[2]
Miss Tittup,[3] gasping from her stiff French Stays,
'Why, if these French shou'd come, we'll have French Plays: 20
Upon my Word, I wish these Wars wou'd cease.'
—Settling her Tucker, while she sighs for Peace.—
   With wilder Throbs the Glutton's Bosom beats,
Anxious and trembling, for West India Fleets,
Sir *Gobble Greenfat*[4] felt, in Pangs of Death,   25

12 each in] *SJC*, *PA*, *TC*; in each *L*   15 shame] *SJC*; same *L*, *TC*, *PA*
20 Why] *SJC*, *PA*, *TC*; Well *L*

---

[1] Augustus Keppel (1725–86), afterwards 1st Viscount Keppel, was Commander-in-Chief of the Fleet.

[2] Louis-Philippe-Joseph, Duc d'Orléans (1747–93), is better known as 'Philippe Egalité'. He commanded the blue squadron in the Battle of Ouessant on 27 July 1778.

[3] An arrogant woman in Garrick's farce, *Bon Ton; or, High Life Above Stairs* (1775). A line from George Colman's prologue to *Bon Ton* may have prompted Tickell's phrasing:

> The club's *bon ton. Bon ton*'s a constant trade
> Of rout, festino, ball, and masquerade:
> 'Tis plays and puppet-shews; 'tis something new;
> 'Tis losing thousands ev'ry night at Loo:
> Nature it thwarts, and contradicts all reason;
> 'Tis stiff French stays, and fruit when out of season.

[4] The epicure's delight, greenfat of turtle.

The ruling Passion taint his parting Breath:
Such in the latest as in all the past;
'O save my Turtle, Keppel!'—was his last.—
No Pang like this the Macaroni racks;
Calmly he dates the Downfall of Almack's.[1]   5
'As Gad's my Judge, I shall be glad to see
Our Paris Friends here, for Variety.
The Clubs are poor; let them their Louis bring;
The Invasion wou'd be rather *a good Thing*.'
    Perish such Fears! What can our Arms oppose,   10
When Female Warriours join our martiall'd Beaus.
Fierce from the Toilet, the plum'd Bands appear;
Miss struts a Major, Ma'am a Brigadier;
A spruce *Bonduca*[2] simpers in the Rear.
Unusual Watch *her Femmes de Chambre* keep,   15
Militia Phantoms haunt her in her Sleep:
She starts, she wakes, she quivers, kneels, and prays,
'Side-saddle, my Horse! ah! lace up my Stays![3]
Soft, soft; 'twas but a Dream; my Fears are vain;
And Lady *Minikin*'s[4] herself again.'—   20
    Yet hold; nor let false Ridicule profane
These fair Associates of th'embattled Plain:
Victorious Wreaths their Efforts justly claim,
Whose Praise is Triumph, and whose Smiles are Fame.

---

2 Such] *SJC*, *TC*; Search *PA*

---

[1] The aristocratic gaming club in Pall Mall, afterwards Brooks's.

[2] *Bonduca*, a tragedy by Beaumont and Fletcher, was revised by George Colman for performance in the summer season of 1778 at the Haymarket. It dealt with the aggressive Queen of Britain, better known as Boadicea.

[3] A distant parody of
> Give me another horse,—bind up my wounds,—
> Have mercy, Jesu!—Soft! I did but dream.—(*Richard III*, v. iii.)

[4] The heroine of Garrick's *Bon Ton*. She detests her husband and flirts with Colonel Tivy because fashion dictates her behaviour.

THE CAMP

SCENE 1st. *A Lane near the Camp*

Country People crossing the Stage with Provisions.

1ST MAN. Come, Deame, come, we are full late for the Subtler's[1] Market. 5

2ND MAN. Make haste, they are all before us.

OLD MAN. Why Robin,—why do'sn't come on?—

ROBIN. Lord Feather, why it been't my fault; the blind Colt has come down again—and there they lie, the Colt, my Mother, and the Chickens all in the Slough.— 10

OLD MAN. Why don't you run and help 'em you Dog?

ROBIN. I ha' help'd up the Colt, and if you please, now I'll see after the Chickens and my Mother.—

OLD MAN. Out you rogue—here's neighbour Harrow has help'd her.

Enter MARGERY *and* COUNTRYMAN. 15

MARGERY. Ah! you unlucky Varlet! As sure as can be Jan, the Rogue put the Beast out of the road on purpose,—and down we came with such a Bang!

OLD MAN. Aye!—What a mercy the chickens escap'd! —but put on Margery,—put on—or the Subtlers will be all serv'd before we 20 get to Camp. Ah! you Dog! I shall have you press'd at last.

ROBIN. Lord Feather, it been't my fault,—you know the Colt hasn't had an Eye these Eight years.

Enter more country women and smart Girls.[2]

1ST WOMAN. Come Madge, let's see what luck your face will have—Ah! 25 neighbour, nothing gets a good price, like putting a good face on't, ha! ha!—

2ND WOMAN. Aye, Aye,—these soldier won't buy o' the ugly ones— There's Goody Grub sends a poor lean Wench; and her scare-crow face drives away all the Customers, tho' her Fowl are the fattest in the 30 Market.

---

[1] Victualler. The spelling is an old form which Sheridan may have used, though 'tt' in his handwriting is commonly mistaken for 'bt'.

[2] This phrase certainly seems to have been in the prompt-book of Drury Lane Theatre, for an advertisement of a performance there, on 15 Oct. 1803, includes in the cast, 'Smart Girl: Mrs. Scott' (Drury Lane Scrapbook, Beaufoy Collection, Folger Shakespeare Library). No such words are used in the 1795 text or its derivatives.

1ST WOMAN. So! Here I see your Kinsman's Wife, Nell coming, Ah
Deame! that Wench spoils the Market,—whenever she comes, with her
honesty and her Nonsense; why she says she loves the Soldiers so,
that she'd sell to them for Nothing.—

2ND WOMAN. Aye! A Churlish Jade! she'll neither cheat herself, nor   5
let us cheat with Credit.—

Enter NELL.

NELL. So! What are you plotting there? hey now! I warrant how to take
in the poor Soldiers, and get double price for your worst Bargains.—

1ST WOMAN. Mind your own Business Nell.—   10

NELL. Why now an't you asham'd to take in the honest Fellows so?—

GIRL. Lord Nell, what need you meddle?—

NELL. Indeed! Pert-face—what I suppose I don't know why you are
disguised so.—yes, yes, the Soldiers pay for this Ribbond and Beads.

MAN. The Wench is turn'd Fool I think.—   15

NELL. Indeed Master Grinder! come out here, you shrivell'd sneaking
Sot! I believe I know your Tricks too. Wer'n't you caught last week,
soaping Nest Eggs to sell 'em for new laid ones—hey!—and didn't
you sit in the Stocks last Saturday for Robbing the Squire's Rookery,
to make your Pidgeon Pyes—you Rogue—hey?—   20

1ST WOMAN. Faith, Nell, if you go on in this way we'll inform our
Exciseman of it, so we will.—

MAN. Aye, aye,—We'll tell Master Gauge, and I warrant he'll find some
way to make her repent it.—

NELL. Yes, he's a pretty Protector. I'm sure I wish our Village had never 25
seen him—why you know now, he was but a sort of a broken Attorney
at Rochester, and bought this place[1] with his Vote, where he is both an
Exciseman and a Smuggler at once—Just as they say Mr. Squire's
Gamekeeper is the greatest Poacher in the Parish.

2ND WOMAN. 'Ecod there he comes—and now I believe you'll alter your 30
Note Nell.

NELL. Shall I? You'll see that.

2ND WOMAN. Oh! Master Gauge!

Enter GAUGE.

Hey dey! what the Plague is there a civil war broke out among ye?   35

1ST WOMAN. Here, Master Gauge, Nell has been rating us for cheating
the Soldiers.—

2ND WOMAN. Aye, and she says you encourage us in it.—

GAUGE. Encourage you in it—to be sure I do—in the way of Trade.—

MAN. Yes, yes,—in the way of Trade.   40

[1] Position.

GIRL. Yes, Master Gauge, and she abuses me because I go to Market
like a Christian, and says I do it to make the better Bargain—

GAUGE. Aye, and you're in the right on't—your Mother's a sensible
Woman Child—yes, yes, Dame, take plenty in your Baskets, and sell
your Ware off at the sign of your Daughter's Face.—   5

1ST WOMAN. So I say.—

GAUGE. Aye, Aye! Soldiers are Tasty customers, and this is the Market
where the Fair Trader will always have the best share.—

1ST WOMAN. Very true.

GAUGE. To be sure—that is the way to thrive—I hate to see an awkward   10
Gawky come sneaking into the Market, with her half-price Countenance, and never able to get above twice the value of her Goods.—

NELL. I have no patience.—An't you asham'd, Master Gauge—you, who
have a Post under Government, and carry his Majesty's Ink-horn, to go
to teach the Country Folks all the Court Tricks of preying on your best 15
Friends—Odd I wish I was on a Court Marshall against such Fellows
as you, who stoop to plunder a Knap-sack, and thrive by defrauding
your Defenders—You should have your deserts from the Cat o'Nine
Tails, and run the Gauntlet from Cox-heath to Wharley Common.—

GAUGE. Oons! here's a Jade—No respect to Office—stand back Neigh-   20
bours—stand back—she's an arrant Scold, I'll threaten her with the
Ducking Stool.—Here you Nell, hold your Tongue you Baggage, and
here's a Pound of Smuggled Hyson in hand, and I'll owe you an India
Handkerchief.—

NELL. Here good People—here's a Bribe[1]—You Paltry petty Fool—   25
here's influence and Corruption.—

GAUGE. Come, Neighbours, she talks Libels, and it's illegal to listen to
her—quick, quick,—I'll prosecute the first man that hears another
word.—

NELL. There's a pretty Fellow to be in Office—But I suppose he thinks 30
it a part of his duty to imitate his betters.—

SONG[2]

Now coaxing, caressing,
Now vexing, distressing,
As fortune delights to exalt or confound.   35

---

34 vexing, distressing] *Th., R.M.*; wheedling, distressing *1795*; flatt'ring and pressing *L*
35 As] *Th., R.M., 1795*; Tis *L*   delights to] *1795, R.M.*; their Hopes can *L*

---

[1] The 1795 text reads:
Gauge. . . . and, throw you a silk handkerchief into the bargain.
Nell. Here's a rogue! Bear witness neighbours he has offered me a bribe;—a pound
of tea. . . .
[2] Thompson prints three stanzas. Only two are given in *The Royal Merchant*, and
in the 1795 and *c.* 1803 versions of *The Camp*. The third stanza in Thompson is the

Her smile or her frown
Sets them up, knocks them down
Turning, turning, turning, as the wheel goes round.

We see by this sample,
On those they would trample,
Whom Fortune, hard fortune, has thrown to the ground;   5
To those rais'd on high,
Fawn, flatter and lye
Turning, turning, etc.

O fye Master Ga[u]ge,   10
Quit the tricks of the age,
Scorn the slaves that to fortune, false fortune are bound,
Their cringes and bows,
Protestations and vows,
Turning, turning, etc.   15

GAUGE returns [peeping in]

GAUGE. Let me see—is the Coast Clear? what a Termagant it is? refuse
a Bribe too! where the Devil could she learn that? Hey dey! who have
we got here? Let me see—by his Dress he should be a Smuggler or
a Subtler. As I live O'Da[u]b the Irish Painter![1] Ha! my old friend 20
O'Da[u]b! what brings you to Cox-heath?

Enter O'DAUB.

O'DAUB. Ah! My little Gauge! to be sure I'm not in luck.—I will want
an Interpreter to shew me the Views about here, and by my Soul I'll
force you to accept the Office.   25
GAUGE. Why, what's your Errant O'Daub?—

---

2 Sets them] *Th.*, *L*, *1795*; sets you *R.M.*   knocks them] *Th.*, *L*, *1795*; knocks you
R.M.   3 the] *Th.*, *L*, *1795*; her *R.M.*   5 they] *Th.*; you *R.M.*   8 Fawn]
Th.; We fawn *R.M.*

---

same as the second in the 1795 version. The Larpent MS. includes only the first stanza.
The edition of *c.* 1803 adds a completely different second stanza, as follows:
But master Exciseman,
Tho' you're such a wise-man,
With smirk, and with frown, and ink-horn profound,
I defy your court tribes,
All your cant, all your bribes,
Turning, turning, turning, as the wheel goes round.

[1] 'The Irish Painter' was the name of a character (also called O'Daub), who appeared
in Burgoyne's *The Maid of the Oaks* (1774). Although he came on merely in Act I,
Sc. ii, he had forty lines to say and a song, 'Then away to Champetre', to sing. The
part was very effectively performed by Moody. The play itself celebrated the marriage
of Lord Stanley, and the 'fête champêtre' that he had given on 9 June 1774, to mark
the occasion, at The Oaks, Epsom.

O'DAUB. Upon my conscience a very dangerous one—John the Painter's Job[1] was a Joke to it—I'm come to take the Camp.—

GAUGE. The Devil you are.—

O'DAUB. Aye,—and to bring it away with me too.

GAUGE. Indeed!—   5

O'DAUB. Aye,—And here's my Military Chest—these are my Colours you know.

GAUGE. Oh! I guess your Errand then.—

O'DAUB. Faith it's a foolish one—you must know I got such Credit at the Fete Champetre there that little Roscius recommended me to the 10 Managers of Drury Lane Theatre,[2] and so I am now a kind of a Deputy Superintendent under Mr. Leatherbag[3] the great painter; that is, as soon as he executes any thing, I design it my Jewel.

GAUGE. And what—are they going to bring the Camp on the Stage?

O'DAUB. You have it—Cox-heath by Candle light[4] my Jewel!   15

GAUGE. And will that Answer?

O'DAUB. Oh to be sure it won't answer,—What! when a gentleman may have a warm seat and see the whole Tote[5] of it for Two Thirteens, and it has cost me above Three Guineas already, and I came the cheapest way too, by Three of us going halves in the Maidstone Diligon[6] 20 My Dear.

GAUGE. Well, and what do you think of the Sight?

O'DAUB. Upon my soul I don't know what to make on't,—so, I'm come here, to be a little farther off, that I may have a clearer view of it;—I think it only looks like my Cousin O'Doyley's great—Bleach-yard at 25 Antrim—Thunder and wounds! What outlandish looking Creature is this coming here?

GAUGE. O this is Monsieur Bluard the French Subtler, who has a very commodious Booth in the Front of the line—no bad Acquaintance let me tell you, if you love Camp Bouillie and Soup Maigre.[7]   30

[1] James Aitken (1752–77), was tried on 7 Mar. 1777 and convicted of setting fire to the Portsmouth dockyard. See the *Gentleman's Magazine*, xlvii (1777), 121–4.

[2] The *Morning Chronicle*, 16 Oct. 1778, paraphrases this as, O'Daub, 'having gained great applause as a painter in the *Fête Champêtre*', was recommended by David Garrick to his successors.   [3] De Loutherbourgh.

[4] Cf. the prologue to F. Pilon's *The Invasion*, given at Covent Garden Theatre on 4 Nov. 1778:

> The muse in change and fashions still delighting,
> Now raves of nothing but of camps and fighting,
> Of mines, of ambuscades, and heroes slain,
> Arm'd cap-a-pie on the embattled plain
> Of Covent-Garden, or of Drury Lane.
> One night a Camp by candle light she shews.
> Next an Invasion, without wounds or blows.

[5] Sum.   [6] Diligence, or public stage-coach.

[7] Gruel, but 'bouillon gras' (clear soup) and 'bouillon maigre' (vegetable soup) may be meant.

Enter BLUARD.

Ah! Monsieur Gauge, I am so very glad to find you, by Gar I was hunt
you all over the Camp—I have been thro' Berkshire;—Cross Suffolk,
and all over Yorkshire, and hear no word of you.

O'DAUB. Thro' Berkshire, and Suffolk, and Yorkshire!—What the Devil 5
does he mean?

GAUGE. Only thro' their Regiments.—

BLUARD. By Gar, I am all eat up—I have depend on you for a supply,
and there be one, two, three Brigade Dinner all order to day—besides
two great Alderman, with their Lady from London. 10

GAUGE. Oons! Monsieur Bluard, I can't help it, I have done the best
I could for you, and you must detach a Party of Waiters to forage at
Maidstone.

BLUARD. O Mon Dieu—and I have not one thing in the House.

O'DAUB. Oh then Master Gauge, I must look somewhere else for my 15
Dinner.

BLUARD. O no—Monsieur.—I have ev'ry Ting ready for you in one
Moment.

O'DAUB. Ha!—ha!—thank you.—But pray now if your Countrymen were to come, wouldn't you be puzzled a little which side to 20
wish for?

BLUARD. Par bleu—No puzzle at all—I always wish for the
strongest.

GAUGE. O! my friend Bluard is above prejudice I assure you.

BLUARD. Diable! prejudice! I love de English very well—I ver much 25
obliged to dem—I love my Countrymen very vel and ver much obligee
too—de English be beat I take a my heel and run with them—and if
I can't run fast enough—by Gar I stop make de bow to Monsieur
Broglio[1]—and ha my chers countrymen—I am charm to get away to you.

GAUGE. Well said Monsieur Bluard! 30

BLUARD. But I do assure you Monsieur Gauge, upon my word and
Credit—indeed—I never will Desert de English—while they win—de
Battle—no, no,—I have too much honour for do that—Monsieur—
shall I have the honour to get you de little repast. Monsieur Gauge
persuade your Friend—I must be gone—Bon jour Monsieur—no, no, 35
Monsieur Gauge, I never vil forsake your Camp if you vin the Battle—
never, never—   [*Exit.*

O'DAUB. Your servant Mr. Bluard—tho' faith to do him justice he seems
to have forgot the fashion of his Country—for when he determines to
be a Rogue, he has the honesty to own it my dear. 40

GAUGE. O he has too much Conscience by half.

---

[1] Victor-Francis, duc de Broglie (1715–1804), maréchal de France.

O'DAUB. But pray what connection have you with the Subtlers—you are no Victualler sure?

GAUGE. No,—but I deal with them in a variety of ways, and in a Subaltern capacity supply the Camp with Various Articles.

O'DAUB. Indeed!   5

GAUGE. Aye,—But harkee—I do nothing but by *Contract*.

O'DAUB. A Contractor! What the Devil! sure you are not risen to such preferment as that?

GAUGE. No, no—Not in your first rate way[1]—no, no, mine are only Rank and file Contracts as I may say, and egad tho' they are good things,   10 I have now and then got into a scrape with 'em too.

O'DAUB. As how?

GAUGE. Why you must know, sometime since, I Contracted with a certain Serjeant of Militia to furnish the Brigade with hair Powder.

O'DAUB. Hair Powder!—very well—and you sent him flour I suppose.   15

GAUGE. Flour! Oons! I should have got nothing by that.—no, no I went to the fountain head—I had recourse to the Chalk Pit instead of the Mill, and supply'd the Corps with a plentifull Stock of Lime.

O'DAUB. With Lime! what the plague! and wasn't the Cheat found out?[2]

GAUGE. Why, we did pretty well during the fine Weather, but unluckily 20 one day, the men being caught in a damn'd soaking Shower, our heads were *slack'd* in an instant, the Smoak ran along the line, and in less than a Week the whole Regiment were as bald as Coots.—

O'DAUB. A cross accident indeed!

GAUGE. O! a Cursed Scrape—narrowly escaped the Halbert for't—   25 however I told my friend the Serjeant, that I had done his Men service, for they look'd like young Recruits before, and now they might pass for Veterans, for their Pates are all as smooth as an old half Crown.—

O'DAUB. You lost the Contract tho'?   30

GAUGE. I did.—however I got another soon after which has made me amends.—*A Shaving Contract* with a company of Granadiers.

O'DAUB. Faith I never knew you practised that Business.

---

[1] 'The only vast contracts for ordinary supplies and necessaries of life were those connected with the arming, victualling, and clothing of the Army and Navy. Cloth factors and grain merchants, ironmasters and timber dealers, pulled every possible wire to obtain Government orders . . .' (L. B. Namier, *The Structure of Politics at the Accession of George III* (2nd edn., 1965), p. 46.) Cf. N. Baker, *Government and Contractors* (1971), ch. X.

[2] Some satirical lines referring to Admiral Keppel's acquittal were put in later:

'On Tuesday evening, at Drury Lane Theatre, in the entertainment of The Camp, when Mr. Gage the exciseman, was relating his having sent lime for the soldiers' hair instead of flour . . . he added "but as I knew I was in the wrong, I demanded a court martial on the serjeant". The stroke was felt, and the audience marked their approbation by three loud plaudits' (*London Evening Post*, 11-13 Feb. 1779).

GAUGE. O No! I never handled a Razor in my life, but Ignorance in the
Articles agreed on is nothing in a Contract.—I shave by Deputy—had
Sam Sickle down from London, a Dev'lish determined hand—has the
swing of a Scyth[e], and will mow you a Company in the beat of a
Reveillé.   5

O'DAUB. Upon my Conscience it's a very pretty way this of working at
second hand, I wish myself could paint by Proxy.—

GAUGE. Aye,—and the best of it is this Job may lead to greater advantages; for turning my thoughts to the Subject,—I have lately with the
assistance of a most ingenious Mechanick, invented an Engine, or sort   10
of Razor Mill, by which a whole Platoon may be shaved at a time.
It will save a World of Trouble—tho' I shan't make it publick, unless
I can get a Patent for my Pains:—But what say you? shall we go and
have a Bottle of this Frenchman's Wine, and drink his Majesty's
health.   15

O'DAUB. With all my heart My Dear—and another to the two Camps
if you will.

GAUGE. Which Two?—

O'DAUB. The one at Cox-heath—and the other at Drury lane to be sure
my Jewel.   [*Exeunt.* 20

Scene near the Camp

Enter COUNTRY LADS *and* RECRUITS *etc.*

1ST LAD. I tell you—I will certainly list,—I have made up my mind on't.

2ND LAD. Well, well,—I'll say no more.

1ST LAD. Besides the Camp lies so handy to me, that there mayn't be   25
such an opportunity again.

2ND LAD. Why it does look main Jolly to be sure! 'Tis all one as a Fair
I think. But if I were to List now, I think I should like hugely to belong
to a Regiment of Horse, and I believe there is one of the Grandest
Troops come lately; I seed two of the Officers Yesterday, mighty   30
delicate looking Gentlemen.

1ST LAD. Aye!

2ND LAD. Yes, they are dress'd quite different from the others—their
Jackets are pretty much the same—but they wear a sort of a Pettycoat
as it were, with a great Hat and Feathers, and a Mortal sight of hair—   35
I suppose they be some of your outlandish Troops, your Foreign
Hessians, or such like.—

1ST LAD. Like enough.—But here comes the Serjeant we're looking for;
a rare Jolly Dog, and sings he does, louder than his own Drum, See
how brave they March.—Oons! walking's a mighty dull way of going   40
after all.—

Enter SERJEANT *and* SOLDIERS *Marching etc.*[1]

SONG and CHORUS

I

Great Cæsar once renown'd in fame
For a mighty Arm and a Laurell'd Brow   5
With his Veni Vidi, Vici, came
And he conquer'd the World with his
    Row dow, dow[2]
Chorus. Row, dow, dow; row, dow, dow,
    And he conquer'd the world, *etc.*   10

2

Thus should our Vaunting Enemies come[3]
And Winds and Waves their Course allow
In Freedom's Cause we'll beat our drum
And they'll fly all at the Sound of our row dow dow   15
Chorus. Row, dow, dow, *etc.*

3

Then come my Lads our Glory share
Whose honest hearts British Valor avow
At Honor's call to Camp repair   20
And follow the Beat of my Row dow dow.
Chorus. Row, dow, dow, etc.

1ST LAD. There! well, can you resist now?
SERJEANT. Come my Lads, now is your time to shew your love for
    your Country—If you are Lads of Spirit, you will never stay to be   25
    scratch'd off a Church door for the Militia, or Smuggled aboard a

5 Laurell'd] *L, R.M., Th.*; laurel *1795*   7 he] *L, 1795; om. Th., R.M.*
12 Thus] *L, Th.*; Then *1795*   13 Course] *L, Th.*; cause *1795*   14 Cause]
L, Th.; Flag *1795*   we'll] *Th., 1795*; will *L*   15 all at] *L*; from the *1795*;
at the *Th.*   our] *Th., 1795*; my *L*   18 Glory] *L, Th.*; Bounty *1795*
20 At . . . call] *L, Th.*; In Freedom's cause *1795*

   [1] 'A serjeant, with his suite come on; the serjeant sings an air, and several rustics
enter at the drumhead' (*Morning Chronicle*, 16 Oct. 1778).
   [2] The choruses do not appear in the Larpent MS. and are printed from the 1795
text. The Thompson version prints 'Chorus with side drum'.
   [3] The second and third stanzas in *The Royal Merchant* (III. v) are different:

            So I a modern Caesar come,
               To make oppressive tyrants bow;
            In freedom's cause I beat my drum,
               And the wood resounds to my row-dow-dow.

            Usurping Wolfort strait I spy,
               Above the rose I speak it now;
            His coward troops I've forc'd to fly,
               And the tyrant yields to my row-dow-dow.

Man of War by a Press-Gang, when you may have the Credit of a
Volunteer, and the Bounty money too.

1ST LAD. Serjeant, I'm your man.

2ND LAD. Aye, and I too then.

SERJEANT. That's my Hero! Sir, you'll be an honour to Cox-heath— 5
Well my Lad, what say you?

3RD LAD. I can't leave the Farm.

SERJEANT. The Farm! what, can you set yourselves to sow and plough
only for the Monsieurs to come and reap. Let your Fields be fallow
this year, and I'll insure you double Crops all your life after—here 10
Corporal!—Expound.—Now here's a fellow made for a Soldier!
there's a leg for a Spatterdash—with an eye[1] like the King of Prussia.—

4TH LAD. Aye, Master Serjeant,—but I hant the air, and the—

SERJEANT. Air! Oons! come to the Drill, and in a month you'll have the
Crest of a War Horse; why lookee there at long Ralph—he han't 15
been with us a Fortnight and see what a presence, there's Dignity—O
there's Nothing like the Drill for Grace—[*hits him with the Ratan*][2]

4TH LAD. Give us your hand Serjeant.

SERJEANT. Well said Captain! Corporal here—and now for a few
Questions my Lads.— 20

SONG and CHORUS[3]

[SERJEANT]

Yet ere you're permitted to list with me
Answer me straight twice Questions three

---

[1] See p. 709 above.

[2] 'A stick carried in the hand and used for beating someone with' (*O.E.D.*).

[3] Parodying the lines in *The Royal Merchant* (II. iv):

Prig. Yet ere you're admitted to live as we,
    Answer us bold twice questions three.

Hub. Expound to me speedily what they are,
    Then hear me my answer with truth declare.

Prig. First, can you steal well?

Hub.   Featly, featly!

Hig. Ven'son, and dress it?

Hub.   Neatly, neatly!

Prig. Eat it when done so?

Hub.   Sweetly, sweetly!

Hig. ⎱ The answer is honest, bold and fair

Prig. ⎰ So bow to the King, for his subjects you are

Hig. Next, can you drink well?

Hub.   Guggly, guggly!

Prig. Treat a fair wench well?

Hub.   Smugly, smugly!

Hig. Kiss her on straw, too?

Hub.   Snugly, snugly!

1ST COUNTRYMAN[1]

No lies Master Serjeant we'll tell to you
For tho' we're poor Lads, we be honest and true.

SERJEANT

First can you drink well?   5

1ST COUNTRYMAN

Cheerly, cheerly.

SERJEANT

Each man his gallon?

1ST COUNTRYMAN   10

Nearly, Nearly.

SERJEANT

Love a sweet Wench too?

1ST COUNTRYMAN

Dearly, dearly.   15

SERJEANT

The Answer is honest, bold and fair
So drink to the King for his Soldiers you are.

SERJEANT *and* SOLDIERS (*chorus*)

The answer is honest *etc*   20

SERJEANT

When Bullets are whizzing around your head
You'll bravely march on wherever you're led?

2ND COUNTRYMAN[2]

To Death we'll rush forward without delay,   25
If good Master Serjeant you'll show us the way.

SERJEANT

Next can you swear well?

COUNTRYMAN

Bluffly—Bluffly.   30

SERJEANT

Handle a Frenchman?

COUNTRYMAN

Roughly, Roughly.

2 to] *L, Th.*; unto *1795*   3 we're] *L, Th.*; we be *1795*   we be] *L, Th.*; we're
1795   13 too] *Th., 1795; om. L*   19–20 SERJEANT . . . honest *etc.*]
Th., 1795; Recruits etc./—Soldiers we are.—*L*   25 we'll] *L, 1795; om. Th.*
26 Master] *Th., 1795;* Mr. *L*

---

[1] The Larpent MS. adds 'Mr. Fawcet'.

[2] Thompson prints '2nd Recruit'; the version of 1795, '2nd Countryman', and the
Larpent MS. 'Countyman'. Holcroft mentions in his *Life of Thomas Holcroft*, ed. E.
Colby (1925), i. 190, that he 'had no opportunity of exerting his talents till the Camp
came out . . . when he endeavoured, as he expresses himself, *to make a part* of a foolish
recruit, and succeeded; in consequence of which his salary was raised to thirty shillings
weekly'.

SERJEANT

Frown at a cannon?

COUNTRYMAN

Gruffly, gruffly.

SERJEANT   5

The Answer is honest, bold and fair,
So drink to the King whose Subjects you are.[1]

SERJEANT. Well answer'd my Lads, and you shall have your Accoutrements out of hand.

Enter NELL.   10

SERJEANT. Ha! honest Nell! how dos't my Girl?
NELL. As well as the Rogues of our Village will let me Mr. Serjeant.
—well but I'm glad to see you have had such success with your Recruiting Drum—Odds my life these honest Fellows are of the true Sort—
They're worth a Regiment of Press'd men.   15
SERJEANT. Aye, so they are, but I have pick'd up one Lad who has been
enquiring for you, and says he knew you formerly in Suffolk.—
NELL. Aye!—
SERJEANT. Yes.—Where's the Suffolk boy? the Rogue's always loitering
behind, tho' he said he was coming here to join his Regiment[2]—Oh 20
here he comes.

Enter NANCY.

NELL. Odd, it is a dainty looking youth for a Soldier.—
NANCY. Serjeant you didn't think I was lost—you know you may trust
me.   25
SERJEANT. No, no, my Boy, I don't think you'll desert.
NELL. 'Efaith I do think I recollect his face tho'—
SERJEANT. There's the Young Woman you were enquiring for—
NANCY. Do then, let me stay and speak to her, I'll follow immediately.—
NELL. As sure as can be I do believe it is—   30
SERJEANT. Come then my Boys and let me shew you the Camp.—I shall
have an eye to this Lad—Come my Lads.

A March[3] and Chorus   [*Exeunt.*

NANCY. Nelly, have you forgot me?
NELL. I don't know unless you tell me who you are—But I believe by 35
your Laughing you are not what you seem to be, for all your Musket
and Belt—

---

[1] The 1795 version adds 'Huzza! Huzza! Huzza!'
[2] The West Suffolk Regiment of Militia was in camp at Coxheath.
[3] Thompson, pp. 24–5, gives 'Marches perform'd by the Regimental Band in the
Entertainment of the CAMP. [One of them] Composed by Mr. Parke.'

NANCY. I am not indeed!

NELL. Then Mr. Recruit can you tell me any News of a little Suffolk Cousin of mine call'd Nancy Grainger?—

NANCY. The best News I can tell you of her is, that she's very happy to find you here, and kisses you with all her heart.— 5

NELL. My dear Nancy, I am so glad.—But hold—I must take care of my Character.—Well, you are a brave Girl—and this is the gallantest Freak—for I suppose you are here out of pure Love—for your King and Country.

NANCY. Why, you wouldn't believe me if I was to tell you a lie.—So the 10 deuce take the Camp for robbing me of my dear William, Just as I was to have gain'd a right, never to part with him again.

SONG

NANCY

When War's alarms entic'd my Willy from me 15
My poor Heart with grief did sigh,
Each fond remembrance brought fresh sorrow on me,
I woke ere yet the Morn was nigh,
    No other could delight him,
    Ah! why did I e'er slight him, 20
Coldly answering his fond tale,
    Which drove him far
    Amid the rage of war
And left silly me thus to bewail.
But I no longer tho' a maid forsaken, 25
    Thus will mourn like yonder Dove,
But ere the lark to-morrow shall awaken,
    I will seek my absent love.
    The Hostile Country over,
    I'll fly to seek my lover, 30
Scorning ev'ry threat'ning fear,
    Nor distant Shore
    Nor Cannons' roar
Shall longer keep me from my Dear.

NELL. Ha! ha!—and do you believe I don't know your Story? do you 35 think on *Suffolk's* coming so near Fareham, I didn't find out my old acquaintance Will?—

16 poor] L, Th.; fond 1795　　18 Morn] Th., 1795; Morning L　　20 e'er] L; e're Th.; ere 1795　　21 Coldly] L, Th.; Cool[l]y 1795　　23 Amid] Th., 1795; Amidst L　　25 tho'] Th.; like L; thus 1795　　26 Thus will] L, Th.; Nor will I 1795　　27 But] L; For 1795, Th.　　awaken] Th., 1795; awake him L　　28 I will] Th.; I'll L; I'll go 1795　　29 The hostile country] L, Th.; The distant hills all 1795　　30 seek] Th., 1795; meet L　　33 roar] L, Th.; loud roar 1795

NANCY. Is he well? and did he tell you how he lov'd me?

NELL. Yes, yes,—I have had the whole Story over, and he told me too,
how since his Absence your Father with a true Farmer's Conscience
wanted you to be false hearted and marry his Neighbour the rich Miller,
and I believe o' my Conscience it was my good advice that prevented   5
his Deserting to go to you.

NANCY. O then I needn't inform you why I gave them the Slip, or how
I got into this disguise—but Nell tell me, don't you think it possible
for him to procure his discharge?—¹

NELL. No,—but I think he would deserve to be shot if he try'd for't—   10

NANCY. Lord then, what shall I do?

NELL. Do!—marry him at the Drum head as soon as you can, and if he
behaves well to you, you'll not find the Camp life so hard as you
expect.—

SONG   15

[NELL]

What can our wisest heads provide,
For the child we doat on dearly,
But a merry soul and an honest heart,
In a lad who loves her dearly,   20
Who with kisses and chat
And all all that,
Will sooth her late and early?
If the truth she'll tell,
When she knows him well,   25
She'll swear she loves him dearly.
Let the prude at name or sight of man,
Pretend to rail severely;
But alack a day! unseen she'll play
With the lad who loves her dearly.   30
Say old men what they will,
'Tis a lover still

17 our] *Th.*, *R.M.*, *1795*; their *L*   18 we] *Th.*, *R.M.*, *1795*; they *L*   dearly]
Th., *1795*, *L*; nearly *R.M.*   23 her] *L*, *Th.*, *R.M.*; him *1795*   24 she'll] *L*,
R.M.; she *Th.*, *1795*   27 name] *Th.*, *L*; the name *1795*   28 Pretend to]
Th., *1795*; In Publick *L*   31 what] *L*, *Th.*; whate'r *1795*

---

¹ *The Public Advertiser*, 16 Oct. 1778, describes this part of the story as: 'A farmer's
daughter escapes from her Suffolk relatives (who were persuading her to a marriage of
interest) in pursuit of her lover at the camp, with a view to gaining his discharge.'
There is no mention of a 'marriage of interest' in the 1795 version.

Makes day and night roll cheerly
What makes our May
All holiday,
But the lad we doat on dearly?[1]

NELL. But come, as I know you have been brought up a little too tenderly   5
for a Corporal's Wife, and understand some of your fine Needlework,
and all that,—I'll tell you what I'll do for you,—There are three or Four
Great Ladies who are often so kind as to take notice of me,—tho' by
the bye they are so condescending and goodnatur'd, that you'd never
guess 'em for Folks of fashion, and I am sure if they knew your story,   10
and how you were brought up, they'd do something in your behalf,
so I'll try to bring you to 'em.

NANCY. Dear Nell, I will be guided by you, for tho' my heart hasn't
fail'd me yet, I shall be so afraid of being discover'd at the Camp.
Here comes the Serjeant whose Party I join'd on the way—[*Shouldering*   15
her Musket]

NELL. As I live, I can't help laughing to see how smart you handle
your Arms.

NANCY. O I am Mistress of all the Exercise I assure you.

Enter SERJEANT.   20

[SERJEANT]. Why Nell, I believe you are going to run away with my
little Soldier here.—

NELL. Never fear Serjeant, he's in no danger from me.

NANCY. She thinks I have learn'd nothing since I listed. But ask the
Serjeant if I mightn't pass muster in the Lines.   25

SERJEANT. As handy a Lad as ever was, come, come, look at him Nell.

The Exercise[2]

NELL. Well done Indeed! odds me at this rate his Majesty need never
want Soldiers.

1 day and night] *Th.*, *1795*; night and day *L*   4 But] *1795*; *om. L, Th.*

---

¹ The second stanza in *The Royal Merchant* (II. i) is entirely different:
With the wretch estrang'd to social joys
Old time may loiter queerly,
Unable woman's worth to prize,
He ne'er can love her dearly:
But, what is't makes the flight he takes
By us felt more severely,
And life too short for play and sport?—
The girl we doat on dearly.

² 'On the Serjeant's return, she goes through her exercise, to shew her friend Nelly
her expertness in her new profession' (*Morning Chronicle*, 16 Oct. 1778). 'Miss Walpole,
in performing the military exercise, met with great applause' (*Town and Country
Magazine*, x (1778), 544).

NANCY. O then I have learn'd Something—But Courage—for my part I shall be happy in actual Service. hey! Serjeant! in smoke and fire, storming and wounding hey!—

TRIO

O the Joy when the Trumpets sound,   5
And the March beat around,
When the Steed tears the ground,
And shouts to the skies resound.
On glittering Arms the Sun Beams playing,
     Heighten the Soldier's Charms,   10
The Fife, the Spirit stirring Fife,
And the roll and the Rub a Dub
     Of the distant Drum.[1]
Cry, hark: the Enemy come
To arms, to arms, the attack's begun.   15

Act 2d.

Scene 1st

A Grove near the Camp[2]

Enter NELL, *speaking without.*

William! come speak to him another time, sure nothing could be more 20 lucky; however, I must obey their ladyships' instructions, and keep him in ignorance, that they may be present at the discovery. Poor fellow, it's almost a pity too, when one has it in one's power to make him so happy.

Enter WILLIAM.   25

WILLIAM. I am sorry Nell to make you wait, but it was an old friend.

11 the Spirit . . . Fife] *L, Th.; om. 1795*   12 and the Rub a Dub] *L, Th.; om. 1795*   14 come] *Th., 1795*; comes *L*

---

[1] Cf. J. Dryden, *King Arthur: or, the British Worthy* (1691), I. iii:

> Come if you dare, our Trumpets sound;
> Come if you dare, the Foes rebound:
> We come, we come, we come, we come,
> Says the double, double, double Beat of the Thund'ring Drum.

[2] This scene is not in the Larpent MS., and is printed from the 1795 version, which may be not very close to the original. The setting was certainly different, for the *Morning Chronicle*, 16 Oct. 1778, reported: 'The second act opens with a view of the Star Inn, on the Heath. William comes on with Nelly, who gives him hopes of seeing his beloved Nancy.'

NELL. Aye, aye, some one from Suffolk, I suppose, who has brought
you news of your dear Nancy.

WILLIAM. I wish it had; it's unaccountable that I don't hear from her.

NELL. Unaccountable? not at all: I suppose she has changed her mind.

WILLIAM. No Nelly, that's impossible, and you would think so, had you 5
heard how she plighted her faith to me, and vowed, notwithstanding
her parents were my enemies, nothing but death should prevent our
union.

NELL. O, I beg your pardon; if her father and mother indeed are against
you, you need not doubt her constancy. But come, don't be melancholy, 10
I tell you I want to have you stay somewhere near the Inn,[1] and perhaps
I may bring you some intelligence of her.

WILLIAM. How! dear Nell?

NELL. Tho' Indeed I think you are very foolish to plague yourself so,
for even had Nancy loved you well enough to have carried your knap- 15
sack, you would have been very imprudent to have suffered her.

WILLIAM. Aye, but prudence, you know, is not a soldier's virtue. It's
our business to hold life itself cheap, much more the comforts of it.
Shew me a young fellow in our regiment who, if he gains the heart of
a worthy girl, and [is] afraid to marry her for want of a little wealth, 20
[and] I would have him drummed out of the regiment for discretion.

NELL. Very fine! but must not the poor girl share in all your fatigues and
mishaps.

WILL. There Nell I own is the objection, but tenderness and affection
may soften even these; yet if my Nancy ever makes the trial, though 25
I may not be able to prevent her from undergoing hardships, I am sure
my affection will make her wonder at their being called so; I wish
I could once boast that the experiment was made.

AIR[2]

My Nancy leaves the rural train 30
A camp's distress to prove,
All other ills she can sustain,
But living from her love.

Yet, dearest, tho' your Soldier's there,
Will not your spirits fail, 35
To mark the hardships you must share,
Dear Nancy of the dale.[3]

30 leaves] *Th.*; quits *1795*   35 Will] *Th.*; Would *1795*

---

[1] Presumably the Star Inn on Coxheath.
[2] Sung to the tune of 'Kate of Aberdeen': see p. 712 above.
[3] Cf. Thomas Arne's song, 'Sweet Nan of the vale' (1751).

Or should you, love, each danger scorn,
   Ah! how shall I secure,
Your health, 'mid toils which you were born
   To soothe, but not endure,

A thousand perils I must view,   5
   A thousand ills assail,
Nor must I tremble e'en for you,
   Dear Nancy of the dale.

Scene 2nd[1]

Enter O'DAUB   10

Well to be sure this Camp is a pretty Comical Place, with their Drums
and their Fifes, and their Jigs and their Marches, and the Ladies in
their Regimentals[2]—upon my Conscience I believe they'd Form a
Troop of Cavalry if there was any hope of an Invasion.—But now I am
alone by myself, it's high time I should begin to be after taking my   15
Place. Well—here's Some of the Directions for it.—Now I can't think
what make[s] my hand shake so unless it is Mr. Booliard's Wine that
has got into my head—So—so—let me Study my orders a little, for
I'm not used to this Stage Business. P.S. and O.P.—who the Devil
now is to understand that?—O but here's the Explanation here, P.S.   20
—the Prompter's Side and O.P.—opposite the Prompter—I'm to mark
down the Side as it's to be on one Side or t'other. Very well—P.S.
and O.P. Somewhere here about is certainly the best Point to take it
from.

Enter SERJEANT, SOLDIERS *and* TWO COUNTRY MEN   25

1ST COUNTRYMAN. There! your Ships!—that's he.
2D. COUNTRYMAN. Aye, that's he sure enough, I have seen him Skulking about these two days, and if he ben't a Spy, I'll suffer hanging.
SERJEANT. He certainly must be a Spy by his drawing figures.
2D. COUNTRYMAN. Do your honors seize him, or the whole Camp may   30
   be blown up before you're aware.
O'DAUB. Prompter's side.
SERJEANT. Hush! and we shall convict him out of his own mouth.
O'DAUB. P.S.—Yet the Star and Garter[3] must certainly be P.S.[4]

1 scorn] *Th.*; share *1795*   3 were] *Th.*; are *1795*

---

[1] The 1795 version adds, 'An open View near the Camp'.
[2] See p. 707 above.
[3] The inn at Coxheath, shown in the previous scene and probably in this one, too.
[4] *The Critick . . . A Literary Catchpenny by R. B. Sheridan, Esquire* (London,
1780), p. 2, says 'it was from him [Thomas Sheridan] that *Young Pretender* [R.B.S.] got
the joke of O.P. and P.S. that told so much in *The Camp*, last season. . . .'

SERJEANT. P.S.—What the Devil does he say?

1ST COUNTRYMAN. Treason you may Swear by our not understanding him.—

O'DAUB. Aye, and then O.P. will have the advantage.

SERJEANT. O.P.—That's the old Pretender—A Damn'd French Jacobite Spy—my Life on't!   5

2D. COUNTRYMAN. And P.S. Prince Steward I suppose.[1]

SERJEANT. Like enough.

O'DAUB. Memorandum—the Officers' Quarters are in the Rear of the Line.

2D. COUNTRYMAN. Mark that.   10

O'DAUB. Nota bene—The Generals' Tents are all Houses.

1ST COUNTRYMAN. Remember.

O'DAUB. Then the Park of Artillery—O Burn the Artillery—we shall make nothing of that.

SERJEANT. There! a Villain—He'll burn the Artillery will he?   15

O'DAUB. Well faith this Camp is easier taken than I thought.

SERJEANT. Is it so Rogue?—But you shall find the difference. What a Providential Discovery!

O'DAUB. To be sure the People must like it; and in the Course of the Season, I hope we shall Surprize his Majesty.   20

SERJEANT. O the Villain! Seize him directly. Fellow you're a dead man if you Stir.

CORPORAL. We seize you for a Spy.

O'DAUB. A Spy! pho, get about your Business.

SERJEANT. Bind him, and blindfold him if he resist.   [*They bind him.* 25

2D. COUNTRYMAN. Aye Bind him, Bind him for certain, and Search him. I warrant his Pockets are Cramm'd with Powder, Matches, and Tinder Boxes.

O'DAUB. Tunder and Nouns, what do you mean?

1ST COUNTRYMAN. Hold him fast.   30

O'DAUB. Why here now are Ladies Coming, who know me—here's Lady Sarah Sash, Lady Plume, who were at the Fetè Champetre and will give me a character.

SERJEANT. Why Villain! your papers have prov'd you to be a Spy, and sent by the Old Pretender.   35

O'DAUB. O Lord! O Lord!

SERJEANT. Why you Dog, why didn't you say that the Camp was easier taken than you thought?

2D. COUNTRYMAN. Aye—Deny that.

---

[1] 'While he [O'Daub] is making laughable observations on the necessary points of perspective laid down in his instructions, as to which views as are to stand upon the stage P.S. and O.P., the serjeant and his recruits steal behind him, and misinterpret what he says, supposing that he means the Old Pretender by O.P. and the Pretender's Son by P.S.' (*Morning Chronicle*, 16 Oct. 1778.)

SERJEANT. Aye, and that you would burn the Artillery and surprize his Majesty,—So come you had better Confess who Employ'd you, before you're hang'd.

O'DAUB. Hang'd for a Spy! To be sure my Self is got into a pretty Scrape here.—I tell you Mr. Soldier or Serjeant, or what the Devil you are—   5
that upon my Conscience and Soul I am Nothing but a poor Painter Employ'd by Monsieur de Lantherburgh.

SERJEANT. There's a Dog! Confesses himself a Foreign Emissary Employ'd by Marshal Leatherbag.

2D. COUNTRYMAN. O He'll be convicted on his Tongue; you may   10
swear 'un a Foreigner by his Lingo.

1ST COUNTRYMAN. Aye, bring 'un away, I long to see un hanging.

O'DAUB. O, If I will be shot—The Devil go with the Theatre and Managers.   [*Exeunt.*

Scene 3d[1]   15

Enter LADY PLUME, LADY SARAH SASH,
MISS GORGET *etc.*[2]

LA. PLUME. O my dear Lady Sarah indeed you were too Severe and I'm sure if Miss Gorget had been bye she'd be of my Opinion.

LA. SASH. Not in the least.   20

LA. PLUME. You must know She has been rallying my poor brother Sir Harry Bouquet for not being in the Militia, and so ill naturedly.

MISS GORGET. Upon my word, I think Sir Harry deserves it for he is himself perpetually ridiculing the Camp.

LA. SASH. So he is indeed, and all I said was that he look'd so French,   25
and so finical that I thought he ran a risk of being mistaken for another Female Chevalier.[3]

LA. PLUME. Yet we must confess our Situation is open to a little Raillery —a few Elegancies of accommodation are certainly wanting, tho' one's Toilet is not absolutely as Sir Harry affirms spread on a Drum head.   30

LA. SASH. He vows there is an Eternal Confusion between our Lords' Camp Equipage, and our dressing Apparatus—between Stores Military and Millinery—such a description he gives—on the same Shelf

---

[1] 'Scene 2d' in the Larpent MS.

[2] 'Lady Sash, Lady Plume and Lady Gorget, appear in the next scene *en militaire*, and after some laugh among themselves, Sir Charles Plume enters, who not relishing the humour of the camp, complains of the infectious manners of it having pervaded the whole county of Kent . . .' (*Morning Chronicle*, 16 Oct. 1778). The *Town and Country Magazine*, x (1778), p. 545, refers to 'Miss Gorget' and 'Sir William Plume', but *St. James's Chronicle*, 15–17 Oct. 1778, calls them 'Lady Gorget' and 'Sir Charles Bouquet'. The names given in the text above are from the Larpent MS. The version of 1795 prints 'Lady Gorget' and 'Sir Harry Bouquet'.

[3] Charles D'Éon de Beaumont (1728–1810), chevalier. He was a captain of dragoons, engaged in military and political intrigue, who afterwards adopted women's clothes.

Cartri[d]ges and Cosmetics, Pouches and Patches—here Stands of
Arms, and there a file of Black Pins.[1] In one Drawer Bullet mo[u]ds
and Essence Bottles,[2] Pistol and Tweezer Cases with Battle Powder
mix'd with Mareshal.[3]

MISS GORGET. O Malicious Exaggeration. 5

LA. PLUME. But pray Lady Sarah, don't renew it. See he's coming to
join us again.

Enter SIR HARRY BOUQUET

SIR H.B. Now Lady Sarah, I beg a Truce. Miss Gorget I am rejoyced to
meet you at this delectable Spot, where according to Lady Sarah Sash, 10
my sister, Lady Plume you may be amused with such eternal[4] Variety.

LA. SASH. You see Lady Plume he perseveres.[5]

MISS GORGET. I assure you Sir Harry, I should have been against you
in your Raillery.

SIR H.B. Nay as Gad's my judge I admire the place of all things—Here 15
is all the Parade, Pomp, and Circumstance of Glorious War[6]—Mars
in a Vis a Vis[7]—and Bellona giving a Fete Champetre.

LA. PLUME. Now but seriously Brother, what can make you Judge so
differently of the Camp from everybody else.

SIR H.B. Why then Seriously I do think it, the very worst plann'd thing 20
I ever beheld, for instance now the Tents are all ranged in a Strait
Line. Now Miss Gorget, can any thing be worse than a strait Line?
Isn't there a horrid uniformity in this infinite Vista of Canvas? No
Curve no break—and the Avenue of Marquees—abominable!

LA. SASH. O to be sure a Square—a Circus or a Crescent[8] would have 25
been a vastly better form.

MISS GORGET. What a pity Sir Harry wasn't Consulted!

SIR H.B. As Gad's my Judge I think so—or Brown[9]—for there is great
Capability in the Ground.

LA. SASH. A Camp Cognoscente! positively Sir Harry we will have you 30
publish a treatise on Military Virtu.

[1] Cf. Pope, *The Rape of the Lock* (1714), i. 137-9:

> Here Files of Pins extend their shining Rows,
> Puffs, Powders, Patches, Bibles, Billets-doux.
> Now awful Beauty puts on all its Arms.

[2] The Larpent MS. reads 'Essence Bullets', but this is probably a misreading of
Sheridan's hand. The 1795 version gives 'essence bottles'. Cf. *A Trip to Scarborough*,
III. i (p. 595, l. 6 above): 'Thou essence-bottle'.

[3] 'Marechal': scent or scented hair powder. [4] 'dismal', *1795*.

[5] 'A Macarony Connoisseur rallies the ladies on their Military Appearance and by
several well-turned witticisms enlivens this pleasing entertainment' (*Public Advertiser*,
16 Oct. 1778). [6] See p. 718 above. [7] See p. 592, n.1 above.

[8] As in the designs of John Wood (1705?-54), and his son, at Bath.

[9] Lancelot Brown (1715-83), landscape gardener known as 'Capability' Brown.

SIR H.B. Very well—But now how will you excuse this, the Officers' Tents all close to the Common Soldiers—what an Arrangement is that? Now if I might have advised, there certainly should have been one part for the Cannaille and a *West End* of the Camp for the Noblesse and persons of a Certain Rank.   5

MISS GORGET. Very right, I hope you would have thought of proper Members for Hazard and Quinze.

LA. PLUME. To be sure with Festive Tents and Opera Pavilion.

SIR H.B. Egad the only Plan that could make the place Sufferable for a Week—well certainly the Greatest possible Defect in a General is 10 *want of Taste.*

LA. SASH. Undoubtedly—and Conduct Discipline and humanity are no Attonement for it.

SIR H.B. None in nature.

LA. PLUME. But Sir Harry it is rather unlucky that the Military Spirit 15 is so universal for you will hardly find any one to Side with you.

SIR H.B. Universal indeed! and the Ridicule of it is to see how this Madness has infected the whole Road—from Travelling to Maidstone.[1] The Camp jargon[2] is as Current all the Way as bad Silver. The very Postil[l]ions that drove me, talk of their Cavalry [which] refuses to charge 20 on a Trot uphill,[3] the turnpikes seem'd converted into Redoubts, and the Dogs demand the Counter Sign from my Servants instead of their Tickets—then when I got to Maidstone I found the very Waiters had a Smattering of Tactics, for enquiring what I could have for Dinner, a most drill'd Drawer reviewing his Bill of fare with the Air of a Field 25 Marshall propos'd an advanced Party of Soup and Bouille to be follow'd by the main body of Ham and Chickens, flank'd by a Fricasee with Sallads in the intervals, and a Corps de reserve of Sweatmeats, and whipt Sillabubs to form a hollow Square in the Centre.

LA. PLUME. Ha! ha! ha! but Sir Harry I am sorry to find you have so 30 strong a dislike to every thing that's Military—for unless you would contribute to the fortune of our little Female Recruit—

SIR H.B. Madam most willingly.—and very apropos here comes your Ladyship's Rustic Protege and has brought I see the little Soldier with her, as you desired her.   35

Enter NELL *and* NANCY.

NELL. Here—here—Nancy—make your Court'sy or your Bow to these Ladies who have so kindly promised to protect you.

---

[1] This makes sense as it stands, but it is not impossible that Sheridan wrote 'Tunbridge to London'. The 1795 version prints 'Maidstone to London'.

[2] The Larpent MS. gives 'The Camp for you!' but this looks like a misreading of Sheridan's handwriting. Probably the 1795 version, 'the camp jargon', is correct.

[3] '. . . the very postboys declaring that "they won't *charge* their *cavalry* upon a *precipice*", when ordered to drive fast up hill' (*Morning Chronicle*, 16 Oct. 1785).

NANCY. Simple Gratitude is the only return I can make but I am sure
these Ladies who have hearts to do so good natur'd a Deed, will excuse
my not being able to acknowledge it as I ought.

NELL. She means and please your Ladyships that she will always
acknowledge your Ladyship's Goodness to the last hour of her Life,   5
and as in Duty bound we will pray for your Ladyship's happiness and
your Ladyship's prosperity—that's [what] she means.

LA. PLUME. Very well, but Nancy you are Satisfied that your Soldier
should continue in his Duty?

NELL. O Yes, your Ladyship, she's quite Satisfied.   10

NANCY. I have seen him Madam, and I wish for Nothing now but to be
enabled to continue with him in a proper Character.

NELL. Yes, your Ladyship, that's all She wishes.

SIR H.B. Upon my word a pretty little Rural Romance. I think your
Ladyship should appoint her your own Aid de Camp.   15

LA. PLUME. Well Child we are all your Friends, and you may assure
your William, you shall be no Sufferer by your Constancy.

NELL. There Nancy—Say Something.

LA. SASH. But are you Sure you will be able to bear the hardships of the
Situation.   20

NELL. O yes my Lady, She's quite Sure, and She can tell you So in a
Song too.

NANCY. My heart is now so chearful, that indeed I don't know how
otherwise to Comply.

SONG[1]   25

The Fife and Drum sound merrily,
   A Soldier, a Soldier's the Lad for me,
   With my true Love, I soon will be,
For who so kind, and true as he.

With him in every toil I'll share,   30
   To please him shall be all my Care.
      Each peril I'll dare,
      All hardships I'll bear
For a Soldier, a Soldier's the Lad for me.

Then if kind heaven preserve my love,   35
What rapturous joy shall his Nancy prove,
Swift thro' the Camp shall my footsteps bound,
To meet my William with conquest crown'd.

26 sound] *Th.*; sounds *L, 1795*   28 will] *L, Th.*; shall *1795*   33 hardships]
L, Th.; hardship *1795*   34 For] *Th.*; *1795*; *om. L*   36 joy] *Th.*; joys *1795*
his] *Th.*; *om. 1795*

1 The Larpent MS. adds 'By Miss Walpole'.

Close to my faithful bosom prest,
Soon shall he hush his cares to rest,
Clasp'd in these arms,
Forget war's alarms,
For a Soldier, a Soldier's the lad for me.[1]

5

SIR H.B. Very well, and very Spirited egad—you see Ladies how your Military example has diffused itself.

MISS GORGET. I hope we shall make a Convert of you yet Sir Harry.

LA. PLUME. Now Nancy, you must be ruled by us.

NANCY. As I live there's my dear William!   10

LA. PLUME. Turn from him—you must.

NANCY. O, I shall discover myself—I tremble so unlike a soldier.

Enter NELL *with* WILLIAM.

NELL. Why I tell you, William, the ladies want to ask you some questions.   15

SIR HARRY. Honest corporal, here's a little recruit, son to a tenant of mine, and, as I am told, you are an intelligent young fellow, I mean to put him under your care.

WILLIAM. What the boy, your honour? Lord bless you sir, I shall never be able to make any thing of him.   20

NANCY [*aside*]. I am sorry for that.

L. SASH. Nay corporal, he's very young.

WILLIAM. He is under-size, my lady, such a stripling is fitter for a drummer than a rank and file.

SIR HARRY. But he's straight and well made.   25

NANCY. I wish I was ordered to right about.

WILLIAM. Well I'll do all in my power to oblige your ladyship. Come youngster, turn about—ah, Nelly!—tell me, is't not she?

SIR HARRY. Why don't you march him off?

NELL. Is he undersize corporal? O, you blockhead!   30

NANCY. O ladies, pray excuse me!—My dear William! [*runs into his arms.*]

NELL. They'll never be able to come to an explanation before your ladyships—Go, go and talk by yourselves. [*they retire up the stage.*]

Enter SERJEANT DRUM[2] *etc.*   35

SERJEANT. Please your Ladyship—we have taken a Sort of a Spy this Morning—who has the assurance to deny it, tho' he Confesses he is an Irish Painter—I have undertaken however to present this for him to Lady Sarah Sash. [*gives a paper*]

---

[1] The last nine lines of the song are omitted in the Larpent MS. So, too, are lines 9–34 on this page.

[2] This is the Larpent reading, but it is probably a mistake for 'Serjeant Drill'.

SIR H.B. What appears against him.

SERJEANT. A great many Suspicious Circumstances please your honour, he has an O to his name and we took him with a Draught of the Camp in his hand.

LA. SASH. Ha! ha! ha! this is ridiculous enough—'tis O'Daub the Irish 5 painter, who diverted us some time ago, at the Fete Champetre[1]— honest Serjeant we will See your Prisoner and I fancy you may release him.

SERJEANT. He is this way, and please your Ladyship.

SIR H.B. What's to be done this way? 10

SERJEANT. The Line your Honour turns out and perhaps as there are Some pleasure Tents[2] pitch'd in the Front of the Line—these Ladies will condescend to hear a March and Chorus, which Some Recruits are practising against his Majesty comes to the Camp.

LA. SASH. Come Sir Harry you will grow in love with a Camp Life yet. 15

SIR H.B. Your Ladyship will be utterly tired of it first, I'll answer for't.

LA. SASH. No No.

SIR H.B. Yes on the first bad Weather you'll give orders to Strike your Toilets, and each secure a Retreat to Tunbridge.

THE MARCH[3] 20

Finale[4]

SERJEANT[5]

While the loud voice of War,
Resounds from afar,
Songs of Triumph and Duty[6] we'll pay; 25
When our Monarch appears,
We'll give him three Cheers,

[1] See p. 728, n. 1 above.

[2] 'At length they all adjourn (to a grand tent in front of the line) on the invitation of the Serjeant to see the various regiments exercised, and to hear a song intended to be sung when his Majesty reviews the camp' (*Morning Chronicle*, 16 Oct. 1778).

[3] The 1795 version prints: 'A march while the scene changes to a View of the Camp.' Cf. the *Morning Chronicle*, 16 Oct. 1778: 'the scene then draws and discovers a most striking and exact representation of the right wing with different regiments in motion, and after a variety of military manœuvres, the whole concludes with a grand song and chorus.'

[4] This appears to be based on Prig's air and chorus in *The Royal Merchant* (I. iii). The first stanza (of four) reads:

At the crowning our king,
We all revel and sing,
For with pleasure our duty we pay;
We give him three cheers,
Till we rattle his ears,
'Tis huzza! and huzza! and huzza!

[5] Omitted in the Larpent MS. [6] 'duty and triumph' *1795*.

Chorus[1]   With huzza, and huzza, and huzza;
               May true Glory still wave her bright
                   banners around,
               Still with Fame, Power and Freedom Old
                   England be crown'd.[1]—   5

WILLIAM[2]

Inspir'd by my Love all Dangers I'll prove
No Perils shall William dismay,
If Nancy but smile the reward of my Toil,

Chorus.   Huzza! *etc.*[3]   10

NANCY[3]

Brave Sons of the Field
Whose Valor's our shield
Love and Beauty your toils shall repay,
In War's fierce alarms,   15
Inspir'd by those Charms,

Chorus.   Huzza! *etc.*[3]

FINIS

1 With] *L, 1795; om. Th.*   and huzza, and] *L, Th.;* huzza! huzza! *1795*   9 If
. . . Toil] *Th.;* In war's fierce alarms, inspir'd by those charms *1795*   12 Brave]
Th.; Ye *1795*   13 Valor's] *Th.;* bright valour's *1795*   15 In . . . alarms]
Th.; Inspir'd by the charms *1795*   16 Inspir'd . . . Charms] *Th.;* of war's
fierce alarms *1795*

---

1 Only the first stanza is given in the Larpent MS.
2 In the 1795 version, Nancy's stanza precedes William's. 'William' is omitted in
the Larpent MS.
3 Omitted in the Larpent MS.

THE GLORIOUS FIRST OF JUNE

A Piece in One Act

THE GLORIOUS FIRST OF JUNE

COMPOSITION

In a letter of 28 June 1794 Sheridan congratulated his friend J. W. Payne[1] on his part in the naval battle of 1 June: 'I wish you joy of the Victory, and of your own Lawrels—we shall get the poor mens widows above a thousand Pounds[2] by the Theatrical Benefit which I am doing all I can for.' He was a member of the committee of fourteen influential people,[3] who organized the theatrical entertainment given on 2 July for the relief of the widows and children of the men killed in action, and called *The Glorious First of June*.

Moore puts Sheridan's activities in this connection in their proper context:

Together with the political contests of this stormy year, he had also on his mind the cares of his new Theatre, which opened on the 21st of April. . . . He found time, however, to assist in the rapid manufacture of a little piece called 'The Glorious First of June,' which was acted immediately after Lord Howe's victory, and of which I have found some sketches in his hand-writing,—though the dialogue was no doubt supplied . . . by Cobb, or some other such *pedissequus* of the Dramatic Muse. The piece was written, rehearsed, and acted within three days. The first operation of Mr. Sheridan towards it was to order the mechanist of the theatre to get ready two fleets. It was in vain that objections were started to the possibility of equipping these paste-board armaments in so short an interval—Lord Chatham's order to Lord Anson was not more peremptory. The two fleets were accordingly ready at the time, and the Duke of Clarence attended the rehearsal of their evolutions.[4]

One of the sketches—really an outline—is given by Moore:

Scene I.—Miss *Leake*—Miss *Decamp*—Welsh.[5]

Short dialogue—Nancy persuading Susan to go to the Fair, where there is an entertainment to be given by the Lord of the Manor—Susan melancholy because Henry, her lover, is at sea with the British Admiral—*Song*—Her old mother scolds from the cottage—her little brother (*Welsh*) comes from the house with a message—laughs at his sister's fears and sings—*Trio*.

Scene II.—*The Fair.*

Puppet-show—dancing bear—bells—hurdy-gurdy—recruiting party—song and chorus.

Ballet—D'Egville.

Susan says she has no pleasure, and will go and take a solitary walk.

---

[1] *Letters*, ii. 12.   [2] He paid £1,310 into Angerstein's bank, for the fund.
[3] Including the Duke of Leeds, the Duke of Bedford, and the Earl of Mulgrave.
[4] Moore, ii. 250–2.   [5] Moore calls him 'Walsh'.

Scene III.—*Dark wood.*

Susan—gipsy—tells her fortune—recitative and ditty.

Scene IV.

Sea-Fight—hell and the devil!

Henry and Susan meet—Chorus introducing burden, 'Rule Britannia.'[1]

The outline differs from the Larpent text in a number of ways and may have been meant to be a rough guide to James Cobb, who probably had his own ideas on the subject. At any rate, he brought in the favourite comedian, Dicky Suett, in one of his best-loved parts, by resurrecting Lawyer Endless from Prince Hoare's farce, *No Song, No Supper*. That Cobb was responsible for the development of the story is clear from some of his later correspondence with the Drury Lane managers,[2] but Sheridan does not seem to have been satisfied with the result, and 'gave the dialogue on scraps of paper out of the boxes during rehearsal'.[3] The only known copy of the text was made available to the Lord Chamberlain's examiner on the day before performance,[4] and next evening Mrs. Larpent recorded in her journal that her husband 'read loud a farce the 1st of June'.[5]

Michael Kelly refers to it in his *Reminiscences*:

It was well suited to the purpose, and was a sequel to 'No Song, No Supper'; it was all got up in three days. Mr. Joseph Richardson wrote an elegant prologue on the occasion, which was spoken, with great feeling, by John Kemble; the piece concluded with a grand sea-fight, and a sumptuous fête, in honour of our glorious victory. Storace and myself gave it some new songs; but the music was chiefly old. I had to represent the character of Frederick; and as I was so much employed in writing the music, I begged Mr. Sheridan (who wrote a good many speeches for it), to make as short a part for me, and with as little speaking in it as possible. He assured me he would.

In the scene in which I came on, to sing a song (written by Cobb), 'When in war on the ocean we meet the proud foe' there was a cottage in the distance, at which (the stage direction said) I was to look earnestly, for a moment or two; and the line which I then had to speak was this:

'There stands my Louisa's cottage, she must be either in it, or out of it.' The song began immediately, and not another word was there in the whole part. This sublime and solitary speech produced a loud laugh from the audience.

When the piece was over, Mr. Sheridan came into the green-room, and complimented me on my quickness, and being so perfect in the part which he had taken so much pains to write for me. . . .[6]

The song, given by Kelly in the part of Splicem, was printed in *Songs, Duetts, Choruses, in . . . The Glorious First of June*, p. 8:

[1] Moore, ii. 250–1.

[2] Add. MS. 25915, f. 6: 'For the afterpiece of "The First of June".'

[3] Moore, *Journal*, ii. 303.

[4] J. P. Kemble's letter of application is with the play in Larpent MS. 1032 in the Henry E. Huntington Library.

[5] Huntington Library MS. 31201, vol. 1: 2 July 1794.   [6] Kelly, ii. 62–3.

When in war on the ocean, we meet the proud foe,
With ardour for conquest our bosoms do glow,
Shou'd they see on our vessels Old England's flag wave,
'Tis worthy of Britons, who conquer to save.

Their tri-colour'd ensigns we view from afar,
With three cheers they're welcom'd by each British tar;
Whilst the Genius of Britain still bids us advance,
Our great guns like thunder bid defiance to France.

But mark our last broadside; she sinks, down she goes;
Quickly man all our boats, they no longer are foes,
To snatch a brave fellow from a wat'ry grave,
Is worthy a Briton, who conquers to save.

Happy land, thou hast now in defence of thy rights,
Brave HOWE, who the man and the hero unites;
The friend to the wretched, the boast of the brave,
He lives still to conquer, and conquer to save.

This cannot be fitted easily into the Larpent version, so we must accept
the idea that the text of the first performance was fuller than that submitted to the Lord Chamberlain. Further support is given to this notion
by the printed version (p. 9),[1] in the 'Quintetto', sung by 'Splicem,
Countrymen, Mary and Susan':

> Th'eventful hour is near at hand,
> That must my destiny command:
> Ah! could I purchase fortune's smile,
> Whole years of future pain and toil
> I'd yield to her capricious power,
> And bribe her for that single hour.

Cobb made no charge for his work on *The Glorious First of June*, though
he was certainly responsible for part of it. Sheridan's revision may have
been fairly thorough, but no manuscript or printed text is extant to show
the nature of the 'good many speeches' he wrote for this musical entertainment. What is now available may well be mostly Cobb's.

When Kelly refers to Frederick and Louisa, he is thinking of the parts
played by himself and Mrs. Crouch in *No Song, No Supper*. The characters do not reappear in *The Glorious First of June*, so we must assume that
Kelly made a jesting allusion to his earlier part and that it was quickly
taken up by the audience.

---

[1] And by the fact that the printed version apportions the songs between two acts,
whereas the Larpent title includes the description, 'A Piece in One Act'.

RECEPTION

The new Piece, which may be fairly exempted from passing the ordeal of criticism, as having been written so much on the spur of the occasion, that the copy, we understand, was not delivered to the Prompter till Monday morning, comes from the pen of Mr. Cobb, who has the merit at least of keeping pace with the original idea of Mr. Sheridan, by making it perfectly appropriate to the transaction it is to celebrate. . . .

The dialogue is extremely neat and pointed, and the story a sort of continuation of *No Song No Supper*, aided by some very charming selections and compositions of Storace is shortly this: *William* promises to take care of the family of the gallant but unfortunate *Henry*, who has fallen in an engagement at sea. The Robin of *No Song No Supper*, a shipmate of *William's*, upbraids him with sculking from his duty. Roused by these remonstrances, *William* resolves to go on board of a ship in Lord Howe's fleet—*Robin*, who is also going in the same expedition, leaves his purse with the unfortunate family, and commissions *Susan*, the Sweet-heart of *William*, to deliver a keep sake to his *Margaretta*; she, jealous of *Robin*, follows him to the cottage. From this incident arise some situations which tend to strengthen the interest of the plot. The pathetic scenes of the piece are relieved by the introduction of our old friend *Lawyer Endless* and a *Commodore Broadside*, who on the return of *Robin* and *William* from the glorious engagement of the 1st of June, gives a splendid *fete* in honour of the Victory, which concludes the Entertainment.

The scenery is extremely beautiful, the Sea fight may be deemed the most complicated, as well as striking spectacle ever exhibited. (*The Times*, 3 July 1794.)

This grand and interesting spectacle—*a national tribute to national heroism*—having received the full varnish of rehearsals, shone on Thursday night with a glow of lustre, as at once to dazzle and captivate. Kelly's 'Conquer to Save' was such animated harmony that it electrified the feelings. The shipping was managed with so much skill, that an honest tar in the gallery, fired at the deception, exclaimed, '*Dowse my lights, how I should like to be among them.*' The absence of Merlin's trumpery and the Opera dancers, were entirely forgotten in the fresh touches of sentiment which enlivened the piece, and the superior resplendency of the fire-works. (*The Times*, 5 July 1794.)

The principal scenes are a representation of the Action. The immense Stage of Drury is turned into a Sea, and the two Fleets are seen manoeuvring. Nothing can surpass the enchantment of this exhibition.—It is not the usual mockery of pasteboard Ships. The vessels are large, perfect models of the ships they represent, and made with such minute beauty, as to be worthy of a place in the most curious collection. All the manoeuvres of the day are executed with nautical skill,—the lines are formed;—they bear down on each other; the firing is well managed, and kept up warmly for some time on both sides; at length, the French line is broken, several of their ships dismasted—boarded—taken,—and two sunk, as on the real occasion; and the expanse of sea affords a variety, which it is not easy for the mind to conceive possible for mere scenic representation. With the scenery is connected a very interesting story, which concludes with a Fete, in honour of the glorious triumph of the British Flag. The rejoicings are rapturous; all kinds of frolic and mirth take place that are characteristic of true British humour. Here dances are introduced, in the first style of excellence ever witnessed on an English stage; the performers being the first Opera dancers in the kingdom.[1] A grand scene is now introduced at the back of the stage, which presents a beautiful transparency of Lord Howe, under which is the name of the noble Admiral, formed with brilliant lamps, and a painting of Britannia holding the Cap of Liberty; while Neptune in a splendid and elegant habiliment, surveys the stage, and the yards of the two men of war are manned by their hands. The conclusion was a brilliant display of Fire-Works, one of which exhibited the words RULE BRITANNIA in capital characters, a shower of fire descending from each letter, while the Song was given by the performers in full chorus.

Several eminent persons have thought it a worthy occasion to club their talents in aid of this national Fete. The Duke of Leeds[2] composes one song, the Earl of Mulgrave[3] another. The prologue comes from the chaste and classical pen of Mr. Richardson,[4] and Mr. Sheridan's eloquence may be easily traced in the dialogue. (*The Salopian Journal*, 9 July 1794.)

CHOICE OF TEXT

Very little choice is offered. Two of the songs ('O'er the vast surface' and 'Our line was form'd') were printed in *The Times*, 4 July 1794, and others appeared in *Songs, Duetts, Choruses, &c In a New and Appropriate Entertainment, called THE GLORIOUS FIRST OF JUNE*, published by the Drury Lane Theatre printer, Mrs. Lowndes, and sold in the playhouse.[5] It has been noted, however, that most of them are not in the Larpent MS.[6]

[1] Mademoiselle Hillisberg and Madam de Caro of the King's Theatre.
[2] Francis Osborne, 5th Duke of Leeds (1751–99).
[3] Henry Phipps, 1st Earl of Mulgrave (1755–1831).
[4] Joseph Richardson (1755–1803), an intimate friend of Sheridan.
[5] Rhodes, iii. 317. The Huntington Library has a copy (K-D 253).
[6] MacMillan, p. 171.

In fact the copy sent to the Lord Chamberlain is very defective, short of songs, and probably without the contributions that Sheridan scribbled out during rehearsals. Sixty years later, the piece was described as 'so hastily prepared, that a portion of it had been performed whilst another was not yet written'.[1] Nevertheless, it is the only text that survives.

It consists of thirty-two pages overall, of which one contains the dramatis personæ and another the application to the Lord Chamberlain. Of the remainder, twenty pages have writing on them, though they also reveal a number of blank spaces. Except for J. P. Kemble's letter to the Lord Chamberlain, the manuscript is written in one hand.

No copy of Richardson's prologue is included in it.

Conclusion

I have printed the Lord Chamberlain's text (LA MS. 1032) almost as it stands, but have admitted into it a few variants drawn from the songs as printed in *The Times*, 4 July 1794, and the *Town and Country Magazine*, xii (1780), 14, as well as material from *Songs, Duetts. . . .*

The prologue was written by Joseph Richardson, and is printed from the copy submitted to the Lord Chamberlain. Substantives from the version in *Literary Relics of the late Joseph Richardson, Esq. . . . The Whole Collected and Prepared for the Press by Mrs. Richardson, his Widow* (1807), pp. 167–9, are inserted. The following abbreviations are used in listing variants:

L   The copy of the prologue submitted to the Lord Chamberlain: LA MS. 2474 in the Huntington Library. It is entitled 'Occasional Prologue', and is separated from the Larpent copy of the play.

Relics   Richardson's, *Literary Relics* . . . . (1807).

[1] J. Adolphus, *Memoirs of John Bannister, Comedian* (1839), i. 343.

DRAMATIS PERSONÆ[1]

COMMODORE BROADSIDE [CHACE]	Mr. Palmer
TOM OAKUM	Mr. Bannister
ROBIN	Mr. Barrymore
WILLIAM	Mr. C. Kemble
BEN	Mr. Sedgwick
BOWLING	Mr. Kelly
OLD COTTAGER	Mr. Cook
LABOURER	Mr. Dignum
ENDLESS	Mr. Suett
DICK	Mr. Hollingsworth
COTTAGER'S SON	Master Welch
COTTAGER'S WIFE	Mrs. Booth
MARY	Miss De Camp
SUSAN	Miss Leak
MARGARETTA	Miss Storace
COTTAGER'S youngest daughter	Miss Menage

[1] From *The Times*, 3 July 1794. It differs from the cast list given in the Larpent MS.

PROLOGUE

Of all the Virtues which enamour'd Fame
Connects for ever with a Briton's Name
None sounds more sweetly from her trump than thee,
Thou first, best excellence, Humanity—   5
Say shall a light, which from its beaming Sphere
Dispels the mist of sad misfortune's Tear,
Pierces the worst abodes which Miseries haunt,
And chears the languid eye of drooping want;
Shall it, tonight with feebler lustre shine,   10
When Justice joins her rites at pity's shrine?
No, every eye with generous drops bedew'd,
Shall own that bounty here, is gratitude.

    Ye hapless Orphans, doom'd no more to share
The fond protection of a father's care;   15
Ye widow'd mourners, doom'd, no more to know
The shelt'ring kindness which the brave bestow;
To-night our tenderest Sympathy shall prove,
(Our Sympathy! a sad exchange for love)
That when those slaughter'd heroes you bemoan,   20
Your sacred griefs you do not bear alone,
For in each British heart, your sorrows are their own.

    Ye Gallant spirits who to Heaven are fled,
Now rank'd, now honour'd, with the glorious dead,
If of your former being aught survive,   25
And Memory hold her fond Prerogative,
How will your heighten'd Natures Joy to see
Old England safe—Old England safe and free!
Sav'd by that Valour which dismiss'd from earth,
Claims from above, the Meed of Patriot worth—   30
These the grac'd ornaments that deck your Bier,
The Brave man's Sigh, and gentle beauty's Tear;
Glory itself at such a shrine may bow,
And what is Glory, but a Name for Howe!
Pity's sweet records, still shall bear his Name,   35
Exalting Conquest into nobler Fame:

---

4 more . . . than] *Relics*; so sweetly on her Trump as *L*   8 which] *Relics*; where *L*
12 with] *Relics*; in *L*   14 hapless] *Relics*; helpless *L*   20 those . . . bemoan]
Relics; o'er Heroes lost, you sadly moan *L*   23 who . . . are] *Relics*; that to
heav'n have *L*   25 aught] *Relics*; ought *L*   26 hold] *Relics*; holds *L*
29 Valour] *Relics*; Spirit *L*   33 itself] *L*; herself *Relics*

Touch'd by her hand, the Victor's wreaths assume
A softer Verdure, and a richer Bloom.
As when the Sun impetuous, pours his ray,
And dazzles Nature with redundant day,
If on some lonely spot his Beams he throws,   5
Where, dress'd in Sweets retires the bashful Rose,
We feel his gentler virtue in the Flower,
And love his Mildness, while we own his Power.
Divided Eulogy this night imparts
To British Spirit, and to British Hearts: 10
Those who assert their injur'd Country's cause,
Those who crown Valour with its best Applause,
Alike in cherish'd memory shall live
They who have won the Laurel, *you* who give.

2 softer] *Relics*; fresher *L*   7 gentler virtue] *Relics*; soften'd Beauty *L*   14 won
the Laurel] *Relics*; gain'd the wreath, and *L*

THE GLORIOUS FIRST OF JUNE

Scene 1. An Orchard before a Cottage on the Coast of Devonshire

Enter an OLD COTTAGER, *his wife,*—MARY, SUSAN, *two little* GIRLS *and a* BOY.   5

OLD COTTAGER. Alas our poor Henry! we have lost him, the truest friend
—the best Son.—

SUSAN. The kindest brother.

MARY. The fondest father and the most affectionate husband—

COTTAGER'S WIFE. My boy—who was the support of us all—   10

OLD COTTAGER. But he died Gloriously—fighting for his King and
Country—that is my consolation.

COTTAGER'S WIFE. Consolation indeed!—and we might all have Starved
Gloriously had it not been for his friend and Messmate, William.

MARY. Generous William! to quit his Ship, the Service and Commander   15
he loved that he might perform his promise to my poor Henry—and
support his helpless Parents and destitute family.

SUSAN. And he has fulfill'd that promise nobly—for five months has
William's daily labour been our support.

GIRL. He is too good to us I think, he works too hard.   20

BOY. So he does, Sister—and I am sorry for it—for he is so kind to us
all—he loves me so well.

GIRL. Not better than me—William certainly loves me, and I am sure he
loves my sister,—you know he does Sister Susan—you know what I over-
heard him say when you received the Love letter from Lawyer Endless. 25

COTTAGER'S WIFE. Aye, and I hope he'll shew his love by staying at
home to take care of us all instead of going to Sea again after glory.

BOY. Indeed, Grandmother; I hope not—William has promised that
whenever he goes to Sea again he will take me with him—and I am
sure I was born for a Sailor—for I love fighting.   30

COTTAGER'S WIFE. Hold your Tongue, Sirrah.

GLEE

MARY, SUSAN, BOY, *and* COUNTRY MAN.

Adieu to the village delights
    Which lately my fancy employ'd,   35
No longer the country invites,
    To me all its pleasures are void.

Adieu to the health-breathing hill,
Thou canst not my comfort restore,
For ever adieu my dear Will,
My Henry alas! is no more.[1]

GIRL. What would you do in a Battle, brother?   5
BOY. Do! I could carry a cartridge as well as a bigger man.
GIRL. A French man would swallow you up at a mouthful.
BOY. Swallow me!—I'd fight three of them, damme if I wouldn't.

SONG[2]

When 'tis night and the mid watch is come   10
And chilling Mists hang o'er the darken'd main
And Sailors think of their far distant home
And of those friends they ne'er may meet again
　　　But when the fight's begun
　　　Each standing at his Gun   15
Should any thought of them come o'er your mind
Think only should the day be won
　　　How 'twould cheer
　　　Their hearts to hear
That their old companion he was one.   20

2

When the rising Sun the day proclaims
And golden rays adorn the bright'ning wave
And ev'ry noble Seaman's heart remains
Resolv'd to conquer and his country save   25
　　　And when the fight's begun, etc.[3]

3

Or my lads if you a mistress kind
Have left on shore, some pretty Girl and true,

12 And] L; Then T. and C. Mag.   13 meet] L; see T. and C. Mag.   15 stand-
ing] L; serving T. and C. Mag.   17 Think only] L; We think but T. and C. Mag.
18 'twould] L; 'twill T. and C. Mag.   22–6 When . . . etc.] L; om. T. and C.
Mag.

---

[1] From Songs, Duetts, Choruses, &c. In . . . The Glorious First of June, p. 5.
[2] Originally written by Sheridan for a revival of Henry Woodward's pantomime,
Fortunatus (1753), at Drury Lane Theatre on 3 Jan. 1780. New scenes were then added
concerning the recent siege of Fort Omoa in Honduras, and 'When 'tis night' was one
of the patriotic songs rendered by Bannister. Text is given in the Town and Country
Magazine, xii (1780), 14. See pp. 782–4 below.
[3] In the chorus to stanza 2, read ''twill cheer' in its fifth line.

Who many a night sits list'ning to the wind
And sighs to think how it may fare with you
But when the fight's begun, *etc.*[1]

During the Song the GIRL *goes out and, at the end, returns.*

GIRL. Here comes our dear William.   [*Enter* WILLIAM. 5
BOY. Then I'll run and get his supper ready.
GIRL. Indeed you won't the Old Sea Captain in the village gave me some
   Strawberries today—and I have sav'd them all for him—And Sister
   Susan finds the cream, as I know you'll like it William.   [*Exit.*
MARY. [*to* WILLIAM.] My best of friends you are fatigued—this excessive 10
   toil overcomes you.
BOY. I don't believe William has had any dinner.
WILLIAM. Indeed you are mistaken—Labour preserved my health—and
   I have been fortunate today—we are rich—my wages are encreased
   this week. Here my friends we can afford to sup handsomely tonight. 15
                                              [*Re-enter* GIRL.
GIRL. Oh, mother, I am so frightened—there are some sailors talking
   together at the corner of the Orchard—I am afraid they want to rob us.
WILLIAM. Sailors! my mind misgives me—
COTT. WIFE. My dear boy, they are after you—they certainly are—hide 20
   yourself directly.
WILLIAM. Conceal myself!—and when my country demands—
SUSAN. Will you then desert us?

SONG

SUSAN   25

Oh stay, my love—my William dear
Ah! whither art thou flying
Nor think'st thou of my parents here
Nor heed'st thy Susan Sighing
Thy country's cause and honour's call   30
Are words that but deceive thee
Thou see'st my Tears, how fast they fall
Thou must not William leave me.

2

Who'll o'er them watch, if thus we part   35
In sickness or in sorrow

1 sits list'ning] *L*; doth listen *T. and C. Mag.*   3 But] *L*; Oh! *T. and C. Mag.*

---

[1] In the chorus to this stanza, read (in the third line) 'Should any thought of her';
(in the fifth) 'How 'twill chear her heart'; (in the sixth) 'That her own sailor he was one'.

In some cold shed with breaking heart
Where will thy Comfort borrow
Neglected left, no William nigh
To cheer, protect, relieve them
I helpless thrown aside to die   5
Thou must not William leave them.

3

And me—ah think, a Summer flown
Perhaps we part for ever
The fondest hearts that e'er were known   10
Unpitying Death will sever
Then why or waste or throw away
('Twill pass too soon, believe me)
One day of love, one little day
Thou must not William leave me.   15

MARY. Oh William, do not let us lose you. Remember your promise to
poor Henry, you are our only friend our only support, I do not speak
for my own sake, but see my poor father—look at Henry's Orphan'd
little ones.

WILLIAM. Do with me what you will.   [*Exeunt into house.* 20

Enter MARGARETTA.

MARG. Oh, Robin, Robin—rover as you are, I cannot help loving you.—
how often have you sworn that I alone had the power of making you
happy! Did I ever cease to exert that power—but Man ever will be
ungrateful—and what is worse, all their ingratitude cannot cure our 25
folly in loving them.

SONG

What a silly fool is woman
    Who believes in faithless man
Yet by some strange fate alas   30
    We still are duped, do all we can.
To every female, vowing sighing
Coaxing, swearing, truth belying
Kneeling, dressing, dancing, singing
The varied peal of flattery ringing   35
When of their falsehood, proof is brought
They kneel and sigh, and all's forgot
What a silly fool etc.

Lovely maidens Ah! beware
E'en now they spread the artful Snare   40
What a silly fool etc.   [*Exit.*

Scene 2. The Park, belonging to Commodore Chace's house

Enter ENDLESS *and* DICK.

ENDLESS. I tell you Dick I am in love—furiously in love—Oh Susan, Susan, lovely! Dear—

DICK. Why I thought Master Endless you had enough of love in your 5
last adventure with Mrs. Crop.[1]

ENDLESS. When I was found in the Sack! Ha! ha! ha! that was a good Joke for me.

DICK. Aye, aye, master, how was that?

ENDLESS. I establish'd my reputation for Intrigue.—the woman Ogled 10
me—the men envied me—I was quizzed at the Country meetings affronted by all the Country Squires in the neighbourhood—and contrived to be threshed by half a dozen of 'em.

DICK. And was that a good Joke?

ENDLESS. Excellent—for I made my fortune by assault and battery.— 15
but here comes Old Commodore Chace, Now Dick bow very low to him—he loves subordination—A fine stupid honest Old fellow—I count his credulity a hundred a year in my pocket.

Enter COMMODORE CHACE *and* TOM OAKUM.

DICK *bows very low and Exit.*   20

Good morrow to my noble Commodore—my kind patron how does my good master?

COMMODORE. So—so—as well as an Old Hull can be that has been disabled these Twenty years.—I say Tom Oakum, is it not twenty years ago since that damn'd Splinter knockt me down when I was in the 25
Dreadnought?

TOM. Twenty years next Midsummer ant please your honour.

COMMODORE. The Mounseers boarded us twice and were driven back again.—Ah, we fought it stiffly, yard arm and yard arm!—whenever my spirits are at low water mark, I bring my remembrance to bear 30
upon that engagement.

TOM. And it does your honour more good than a bucket full of Doctor's stuff.

ENDLESS. I was just coming to wait on your honour, on a little private business.   35

COMMODORE. Tom Oakum where's your new Song?

TOM. I'll fetch it [*Exit* TOM].

ENDLESS. To tell your honour the truth, I fear I must distrain for farmer Russet's rent—I can't get the money by fair means.

[1] Dorothy Crop, wife of the honest farmer, George Crop, appears in Prince Hoare's comic opera, *No Song, No Supper*, acted at Drury Lane Theatre, 16 Apr. 1790. So does Endless.

COMMODORE. Give him time, give him time!—

ENDLESS. He is as poor as a Church mouse.

COMMODORE. And how should it me otherwise—the old man lost his
    sheet Anchor in his Son Henry—poor fellow he is gone to the bottom
    —and the family have ever since had wind and Tide against them.   5

ENDLESS. The farm is vilely managed—I had some thoughts of marrying
    the eldest daughter Susan—and taking the farm into my own hands—
    —merely to manage it for your honour.

COMMODORE. That's kind of you, Endless,—but the Girl—

ENDLESS. Is proud and lazy like all the rest of the family.   10

COMMODORE. Proud and lazy!—that's bad—that's bad.

ENDLESS. I think I must distrain.—and then they have got a great
    lubberly fellow in the house—they call him William, he deserted from
    a man of war.

COMMODORE. What! do they harbour a deserter?   15

ENDLESS. Yes they do.

COMMODORE. Encourage a lubber to Skulk from the service of his
    Country.—

ENDLESS. Aye, and swear he shan't go to sea.

COMMODORE. But I say he shall.   20

ENDLESS. I knew your honour would say so—and so I have sent after
    him—and to tell you the truth I have distrain'd for the Rent.—[*Aside*]
    He is in a rare humour for my purpose.

COMMODORE. Why as to the Rent—

ENDLESS. The deserter—a fine able Seaman, but they make him a   25
    skulker.

COMMODORE. Ah!—

ENDLESS. I'll take care of him your honour. [*Aside*] It will do, It will do.
                                                [*Exit.*

COMMODORE. To encourage idleness and desertion from his Majesty's   30
    Service! But Russet's poor—yet such an example—

Enter TOM *and* SAILORS.

TOM. Here's the Song your honour, and here's the Boat's crew of the
    Brunswick who have follow'd your honour's old Cockswain Tom
    Pipes[1] to give you a cheer before they sail—and they'll bear abob.   35

Enter Boat's crew.

SONG[2] *and CHORUS*

O'er the vast surface of the deep
Britain shall still her Empire keep

---

[1] He bears the name of the reticent bosun's mate who looks after Commodore
Trunnion in Smollett's *Peregrine Pickle* (1751).
[2] By the Duke of Leeds. Sung by Bannister as 'Tom Oakum'.

Her heav'n descended Charter long
The fav'rite theme of Glory's Song
Shall still proclaim the blest decree
That Britons Ever shall be free.

2   5

Tho' Hostile bands in fierce array
Dare to dispute her Sov'reign sway,
The Savage fury nurs'd in gore
Boasts to despoil her silver Shore
Heav'n still supports its blest decree   10
That Britons ever shall be free.

3[1]

Hail happy Britain favour'd Isle
Where freedom, Arts, and Commerce smile
Long may thy George in glory prove   15
The transports of a Nation's love
Long reign to guard the blest decree
That Britons ever shall be free.

Enter MARY *and* SUSAN.

COMMODORE. Hey day—Two strange sail hove in sight.—You Tom 20
Oakum what Ship a hoy?

TOM. Under old Russet's command your honour.

MARY. Oh Sir! you who have the Character of being the friend of the
unfortunate, be our protector.

SUSAN. That wicked Lawyer Endless—   25

COMMODORE. Avast—avast—what of Lawyer Endless—I know him
well.

MARY. Indeed, Sir, you do not know him.

SUSAN. We have lost our only friend in William.—

COMMODORE. Look ye, my Lasses—I am told that you are proud and 30
lazy—now d'ye mark me—I don't like idleness—I hate useless hands
abroad.—we are all Shipmates in this world, and as for those that won't
take a spell at the Pumps—heave 'em overboard to the sharks I say.

MARY. Believe me, we do not merit this reproach—Endless is our bitter
enemy. Here is the rent for which we are indebted.—[*Offers money*]

---

[1] *The Times*, 4 July 1794, prints four stanzas, and this is the last in its version. The
third reads:

> 'Twas thus with HOWE, illustrious name!
> Still adding to a life of fame,
> Thro' Gallia's proud Armada broke,
> And Albion's wrath in thunder spoke,
> While Vict'ry sanction'd the decree,
> That 'Britons ever shall be free.'

COMMODORE. You are got rich suddenly.

SUSAN. We owe it to the Generosity of an honest Seaman the friend of my William.

COMMODORE. William!—That is the Skulker—but the Press Gang will give an Account of him. 5

MARY. No Sir—he is going a Volunteer to serve under a brave Captain who honours him by his friendship.

COMMODORE. Eh! You Tom Oakum—make sail after Endless, tell him to haul his wind—I must see into this.

SUSAN. Oh, Sir. 10

COMMODORE. Say no more, my Lasses—keep your money till I ask for it.—Don't think I want to be bribed by a fine speech to do an Act of Justice.

DUETT

MARY *and* SUSAN 15

Our hearts with joy expanding
Your voice our fate commanding
Most grateful thanks demanding
Accept the tribute due

Whatever good befalling 20
We still shall think of you
Adieu

Whatever good befalling
Our gratitude recalling
We still shall think of you. 25

Scene 3. The Sea fight

Scene 4. The Orchard before the Cottage

Enter MARGARETTA *and* CICELY.

MARGARETTA

Never, never, when you've won us 30
Can we trust in faithless man?
From our constant love you shun us
And we're duped do all we can.

Soon the passion you pretended,
Like a magic charm is ended, 35
While we're grieving, sobbing, crying;

You're to others kneeling, sighing,
Wheedling, vowing, weeping, dying,
To betray where'er you can.
   Never, never, etc.

Silly maidens, here take warning,   5
Vows of love, with prudence scorning,
   Never, never, etc.[1]

CICELY. Indeed my dear Margaretta your Jealousy of Robin is very absurd.

MARG. Don't talk so sister.—did we not watch him? did we not see him 10 loiter about the house—Nay did he not talk to a pretty young Woman—give her money—

CICELY. Here comes the very girl we saw him converse with.

Enter SUSAN *and* OLD COTTAGER.[2]

MARG. Now then to discover—   15

CICELY. I fancy she'll soon discover you are no Gypsey.

MARG. My dear handsome young Lady—shall I tell your fortune?

SUSAN. Alas! I wish you could.

MARG. You are born to great luck—let me see your hand and I'll tell you more.   20

DIALOGUE DUETT

MARGARETTA *and* SUSAN

MARG. Of lovers you'll have plenty,
Be married ere you're twenty,
The youth whom most you favour   25
   Is gone hence afar;
An honest farmer wooes you,
A lawyer too pursues you,
But ah! your heart's enslaver   30
   Is a British Tar.
His country's cause espousing,
The trump of glory rousing
His valour's best emotion,
   He'll a conqu'ror prove.   35
But ah! the fatal story!
That heart which pants for glory,
Inconstant as the ocean.

SUSAN. And is he false in love?

---

[1] From *Songs, Duetts, Choruses, &c. In . . . The Glorious First of June*, p. 11.
[2] The Larpent MS. prints 'Cooke' in place of 'OLD COTTAGER'.

MARG. This morning I espied you,
   By magic art descried you
   The Sailor's gift receiving,
    He gave a purse of gold.
SUSAN. I'll pay it where 'tis owing   5
   A keepsake too bestowing,
   My kindred wants relieving.
MARG. Your gratitude thus raising
   His whole bounty praising
   Your heart so fond believing.   10
SUSAN. I to my William true.
MARG. The traitor's love disdaining
   That keepsake, why retaining,
BOTH. In trust this pledge receiving,
    Is Margaretta's due.[1]   15

     Enter BEN *and* OTHER SAILORS.

BEN. Huzza! Old England for ever, we have Conquer'd.
MARG. Is Robin safe?
BEN. You'll see him ashore presently.—Ah! my Girls such an Engage-
  ment.   20
MARY. Tell us all about it.

       SONG

       BEN[2]

  Our line was form'd, the French lay to,
  One Sigh I gave to Poll on Shore,
  Too cold I thought our last Adieu—   25
  Our parting Kisses seem'd too few,
   If we should meet no more.
  But love, avast! my heart is Oak
  Howe's daring Signal floats on high;
  I see through roaring cannon's smoke—   30
  Their Awful line subdued and broke
  They strike they sink they fly.[3]

24 Our] *Times*; The *L* to] *Times*; too *L*   25 One] *Times*; A *L*
30 daring] *Times*; om. *L* 31 I see] *Times*; om. *L* 32 Their] *Times*; The *L*

---

[1] From *Songs, Duetts, Choruses, &c. In . . . The Glorious First of June*, pp. 12–13.
[2] *The Times*, 4 July 1794, notes that it was by the Earl of Mulgrave, and was sung by Sedgwick.
[3] *The Times*, 4 July 1794, prints two other stanzas. One of them reads:
   My limb struck off, let soothing art
    The chance of war to Poll explain:
   Proud of the loss, I feel no smart,
   But as it wrings my Polly's heart
    With sympathetic pain.

Now (danger past) we'll drink and Joke,
Sing 'Rule Britannia'; 'Hearts of Oak!'
And Toast before each Martial tune—
Howe and the Glorious first of June.

BEN. But we must go and give a cheer to my old commander Commodore 5
Broadside.   [*Exeunt.*

Scene 5

(*Enter* ROBIN *with a crutch and his Arm in a sling and Patch on his face*).

ROBIN. O poor William! how sorry I am for him! I have had all the sport
—all the fun! He'll never forgive himself being absent, when he sees 10
the knocks I've got how the Rogue will envy me, what a damn'd lucky
fellow I was to be in the thick of it.

Enter WILLIAM.

WILLIAM. Robin how glad am I to see you, give me your hand.
ROBIN. There, and the best is I have but one to give you—O William 15
what a fight and what sport you have lost—Ah, my boy—we were
favourites of fortune, Four Ships of the Line upon us at once—Damme
the shot crossed us at every point of the Compass—fore and aft my lad
—There we lay—Old Tom Steady at the helm never mov'd a muscle
tho' his old friend Bob tumbled upon him from the round Tops as 20
dead as a herring—Tom never changed his quid till the Main top-
mast went by the board—Then a damn'd Shot from the Frenchman's
Stern Chaser killed Jack Mainstay and then, as we passed under the
Stern of the Queen Charlotte—I'm sure I was doing my best for an
honest fellow call'd out to me, well done, stick to them Robin.   25
WILLIAM. You heard this?—
ROBIN. As plainly as the Cannon's roar.
WILLIAM. Now Robin, pity me no more—I was that honest fellow.—In
one word I felt your reproaches—I was stung by your generosity,
I went to my post, and I have shared your danger and your glory.   30
ROBIN. May I never sail again, but now I'm a happy fellow I would
share everything with a messmate I love as I do you William. Damme,
but I'd give you half my Wounds if I could.—but avast who comes here.

Yet she will think (with love so tried)
Each scar a beauty in my face,
And as I strut with martial pride,
On timbertoe by Polly's side,
Will call my limp a grace.

Enter the COMMODORE, TOM OAKUM, *the* OLD COTTAGER
and his Family, and MARGARETTA, *who talks aside*
with ROBIN.

COMMODORE. Victory! Victory!—'Hearts of Oak are our Ships—Hearts
of Oak are our men'[1]—Let me see the brave fellows. 5

SAILORS. Heaven bless you, noble commodore.—Huzza! Huzza!
Huzza!—

Enter ENDLESS.

ENDLESS. Bless us! bless us!—what surprising news. I give you joy
most noble commodore, congratulations are your due. 10

COMMODORE. Yes, and you damn'd knavish lubber—you curs'd land
Shark, I'll give you your due.—Here my lads lay hold of this mis-
creant—I have detected him in the worst Act of Oppression—in
grinding a poor Sailor's family—seize him, and give him a good wholesome Ducking. 15

ENDLESS. Take care Commodore what you do—you are a Justice and
must know this is against law.

COMMODORE. I'll not wait to consider whether it is Law or not—I'm
sure it is Justice Tom.—and you shall see the Sentence carried into
execution. 20

TOM. Bless your honour once more for that I say.

ENDLESS. My Sentence!—I have had no Trial—I claim a trial by my
Peers.

COMMODORE. They are not to be found—at least I hope so.

ENDLESS. I demand a Copy of my Indictment. 25

TOM. He shall be ducked your honour.

ENDLESS. I move in arrest of Judgement.

SAILORS. Duck him—Duck him—

ENDLESS. I move for a new Trial.

COMMODORE. Execute the Sentence, 30

SAILORS. Huzza! etc.

FETE

[1] Chorus from the song 'Come, cheer up, my lads, 'tis to glory we steer', by William
Boyce (1710–79), and sung in Garrick's *Harlequin's Invasion* (1759). The original read
'Heart of oak'

REVISALS

WILLIAM JERDAN noted:[1] 'Sheridan once told me in conversation that, as manager of Drury Lane Theatre, he made it a rule to read (I presume glance over) all the manuscripts sent in, and he never yet found one drama so wretchedly bad that he could not pick something good out of it.'[2] Sheridan undoubtedly tried to improve many of the plays that were put before him, and with his acute stage sense sometimes saw possibilities that did not occur to the authors. More frequently his corrections were merely verbal. He had also learned one lesson himself that he applied thoroughly: brevity and appropriateness must be the aims. Consequently we find M. P. Andrews referring humorously and wryly in his preface to *Dissipation* (1781) to something that struck other potential dramatists: 'Mr. Sheridan, it must be confessed, has taken away several witty things from this comedy.'

All the unacted plays in the following list come from the collection placed in P. G. Patmore's hands by 'a valued friend'[3] and now in the British Museum.[4] Three (*Ixion*, *A Fairy Opera*, and *Renaud d'Ast*) are given separate consideration, but the rest are dealt with rather summarily.

Selima and Azor (first acted 5 December 1776)

In the 'Advertisement' to this 'dramatic romance' in three acts,[5] the author, Sir George Collier,[6] wrote:

. . . He was absent from England at the Time it was brought on the Stage, and he is very sensible that the uncommonly favourable Reception it met with from the Public, must be principally owing to the great Justice done the Piece by the Managers, and by the Performers; but most particularly to the Taste and Judgment of Mr. SHERIDAN, in several judicious Alterations; and to the excellent Music of Mr. LINLEY; to both of whom the Author has pleasure in making this public Acknowledgment. Jan. 18, 1784.

---

[1] *Men I Have Known* (1866), p. 402.

[2] The phrasing reminds one of a similar statement by another great comic writer: 'The mind should be accustomed to make wise reflections, and draw curious conclusions as it goes along; the habitude of which made Pliny the younger, affirm: "That he never read a book so bad, but that he drew some profit from it." ' (Sterne, *Tristram Shandy*, Ch. 20.)

[3] Possibly the actor Horatio Saker. See his collection of plays offered for sale at auction by Puttick and Simpson, 22 July 1861, lot 1535.

[4] Add. MSS. 25906–26036.   [5] *Selima and Azor, A Persian Tale* (1784).

[6] 1738–95. Naval commander. Senior officer at Halifax, Nova Scotia, 1776–9. Later Vice-Admiral.

The Lord Chamberlain's MS. of the play (now Larpent MS. 421 in the Huntington Library) contains many alterations, probably by Sheridan.

The Tempest (4 January 1777)

Shakespeare's *The Tempest* was revived at Drury Lane, early in Sheridan's management, and was very successful. It gave De Loutherbourgh further opportunities, as is indicated in a newspaper report:

. . . being in a great measure a play of spectacle, [*The Tempest*] was got up with great credit to the managers, who spared no expense in the decorations. The storm scene, which formerly began the play, is now very judiciously transferred to the second act, which introduced, in our opinion, the King of Naples and his companions to the audience more in the order of narration.[1]

This version was not printed and the prompt-book does not seem to be extant, but some of the other alterations introduced are known from further newspaper accounts of performances.[2] *The Morning Post*, 13 January 1777, suggested that Sheridan was responsible for the changes.

The whole question is discussed by Professor Carroll Camden in an article[3] on a publication of four leaves called *Songs and Chorusses in The Tempest . . .*,[4] which she thinks (with good reason) was sold in the theatre when this version was acted. She points out, too, that two of the songs were not otherwise printed until J. P. Kemble brought out a new edition in 1789. They are:

> Arise! ye Spirits of the storm,
>   Appal the guilty eye;
> Tear the wild waves, ye mighty winds,
>   Ye fated lightnings fly,
> Dart thro' the tempest of the deep,
>   And rocks and seas confound,
> Hark how the vengeful thunders roll,
>   Amazement flames around,
> Behold! the fate-devoted bark
>   Dash'd on the trembling shore;
> Mercy the sinking wretches cry!
> Mercy!—they're heard now more.[5]

---

[1] *General Evening Post*, 20–23 Sept. 1777.

[2] See C. B. Hogan, *Shakespeare in the Theatre, 1701–1800* (Oxford, 1952–7), ii. 637.

[3] 'Songs and Chorusses in The Tempest', *Philological Quarterly*, xli (1962), 114–22.

[4] The copy in the Fondren Library of Rice University is not, however, unique. There are copies at the Folger and Huntington Libraries.

[5] Professor Camden suggests that this may have been inspired by the Devil's song in II. iii of the Dryden–Davenant–Shadwell version.

The other song is by Ariel in Act 1:

> O bid your faithful Ariel fly
> To the farthest Indies sky,
> And then, at thy afresh command,
> I'll traverse o'er the silver sand.
>
> I'll climb the mountains, plunge the deep,
> I like mortals, never sleep:
> Whate'er it be, not with ill-will,
> But merrily, merrily, merrily.

To this information, I ought to add that 'the music of *The Tempest*', by Sheridan's brother-in-law, Tom Linley, is to be found in J. S. Gaudry's[1] transcription in Egerton MS. 2493.

Gay, *The Beggar's Opera* (8 November 1777)

The reason for the revision is explained by W. C. Oulton:

The *Beggar's Opera* was performed at each theatre in the form of a *moral* tale, although the *indecent* scenes remained. This alteration was suggested by Mr. GARRICK, who thereby imagined to do away all prejudices against the piece; accordingly the poet and the manager in their stage-closet conversation, agreed to do poetical justice (as they called it) and *Macheath* was sentenced to heave ballast upon the river for three years; but the absurdity of this conclusion struck every impartial person. . . . To complete the *moral* turn of this now-spoiled opera, a well painted scene representing Woolwich, and the Justitia hulk,[2] was introduced. The managers however perceiving the absurdity of their alterations, began to reduce them, so that by degrees, the opera was restored to its primitive state.[3]

As far as I can discover, Macheath was sentenced to heave ballast in the Covent Garden performances,[4] and not in those at Drury Lane. Sheridan, instead, wrote a revised version of Scene 16 that embodied some of the original lines as well as a number of new ones. The manuscript is extant[5] and reads:

PLAYER. But, honest friend, I hope you don't intend that Macheath shall be really executed.

---

[1] Gaudry was professional music-copyist at Drury Lane Theatre. See p. 311 above.

[2] 'Moored off Woolwich Warren, as one of the receptacles for the convicts sentenced to labour for limited periods on the Thames' (*Morning Chronicle*, 8 Nov. 1777).

[3] *The History of the Theatres of London . . . 1771 to 1795* (1796), i. 70–1.

[4] *Morning Post*, 27–28 Oct. 1777. See the 'View of Convicts at work on the Thames', *London Magazine*, lvi (1777), 228, and LA MS. 438 in the Huntington Library.

[5] In the Harvard College Theatre collection. It is in Sheridan's hand, and is unpublished. Where the manuscript is defective, the words are supplied from a copy made by William Hopkins, also in the Harvard collection. Both are in fMS. Thr 5. 8.

BEGGAR. [Most certainly, sir. To make the piece perfect, I was for doing strict poetical justice. Macheath is to be hanged.] And for the other personages of the drama, the audience must suppose they were all either hang'd or transported—and for the same reason.

PLAYER. Why then, my good friend this [is] a downright deep tragedy—the catastrophe [is manifestly wrong, for an opera must end happily.]

BEGGAR. I despise any [Laws for Dramatic Auth]ors be they laid down by Moderns or Ancients, which Counteract the Laws of the Country, Moral Justice, and the Peace and Welfare of Society.[1]

PLAYER. And yet, friend, how many greater men than your hero, who fall under your description, are seen smiling at all public places; and walk as safely and boldly in the face of day, as if the starving, murdering, and cheating thousands were look'd upon as so many virtues.

BEGGAR. Whenever I [lay my Scene in Asia among] Profligate Nabobs—[or in England you k]now among whom I mean?—I [will treat them with as] little ceremony as I do my Highwayman.—Whoever—be he what he may—will be misled by Criminal Passions, and abetted by false Friends as Criminal as those Passions they shall not escape *me* tho' they may the laws.

> Tho' Gold from Law may take out the Sting
> The High and the Low alike I will string
> Upon Tyburn Tree

PLAYER. This [is being a patriot] indeed.

BEGGAR. I think so[, Sir,—nor shall the want] of a better Coat weaken the feelings of my heart or the Conviction of my understanding.

PLAYER. Bravo, bravissimo!

BEGGAR. I'll sooner lose the whole Profits of my Opera as much as I want them. —The Managers at the request of the Public may do what they please—But my Macheath is dead in Law.—And tho' Taste, Custom and Fashion, all the arguments of Aristotle and [with all] the Examples of all the [Operas? that ever were wr]itten, should differ, with [me, yet *my* Macheath] shall suffer. By this Act of Justice, [and the] forfeit of One Life, some Thousands may be preserv'd.

> No Crimes are flatter'd in my honest page;
> And for the boast and honour of the Age
> At least let Justice triumph on the Stage.

End of the Opera

There is nothing in the report in the *Morning Chronicle*, 10 November 1777, to suggest that these lines were actually spoken at the first performance. The notice runs:

The Beggar's Opera of Drury-lane Theatre is an alteration of Gay—not a very violent one, but just enough to shew that the Managers of that house are also ready to pay attention to the voice of parliament and the complaints of the good

---

[1] 'The Legislature hath long complained of the pernicious Consequences arising to the low Public from the heroick Character of Macheath; and the *Cork Cutter's Son* and *Sixteen-String Jack*, confessed upon their Examinations, that they had resolved to take to the Road, from the Idea of a Highwayman's Life as drawn by Gay.' ('T.W.' in *St. James's Chronicle*, 23–25 Oct. 1777.)

and virtuous respecting the immoral tendency of the Opera in its original form. As it was performed on Saturday we found the scene of the thieves over their bottle and glass purged of the most pernicious of those left-handed maxims and plausible pleas urged by the company in defence of highway robbery.—The long speech of Mrs. Trapes is also curtailed of the looser parts,—and at the end of the Opera a new reason is assigned by the Beggar for reprieving Macheath, namely, in order to *reform* him. This last alteration, the Player asks the Beggar how the Town will approve;—to which the latter replies, 'an act of mercy will always be acceptable to an English audience.' There is something pleasing in this compliment, upon first hearing it, but on maturer consideration, we question whether it may not be deemed an appeal to the heart, to sacrifice the understanding. If Macheath be not punished, we do not find the desired end of altering the Opera at all effected. . . . Symphonies were on Saturday evening added to several of the airs, and the harmony made more full, by Mr. Linley, which had a very pleasing effect, particularly the accompanyment of the horns in several places. It may be right in point of stage effect.

The references to reforming Macheath and to mercy being acceptable to English audiences seem to me to indicate that Sheridan abandoned the lines calling for the hanging of Macheath, even though they had been copied out by William Hopkins and were ready for the performers. Fortunately the Harvard collection also contains another set of lines in Sheridan's hand that tallies with the description of the last scene printed by the *Morning Chronicle*. Once again some lines from the original are mingled with new ones:

BEGGAR. The Play as I at first intended it would have happily carried the most excellent moral 'twould have been that the lower sort of[1] people have their vices in a degree, as well as the rich, and that they are punished for them.

PLAYER. True—but then suppose in order to preserve poetical and moral justice at once you were to mediate between the impropriety of violating the Laws of Drama, and the injustice of suffering vice to triumph with impunity.

BEGGAR. What do you mean?

PLAYER. Why—instead of *hanging* your Hero, is it not possible to *reform* him?

BEGGAR. Why 'tis possible to be sure but wouldn't the reformation be rather sudden—?[2]

PLAYER. O not in the least for a theatrical one—and in this kind of Drama, 'tis no matter how absurdly things are brought about.[3]

BEGGAR. True, then do yon Rabble there run cry a reprieve.[4] But will not the reflecting Part of the Audience be apt to censure the Pardoning Macheath as an encouragement to Vice?

[1] Sheridan writes 'etc.' at this point, and the copyist goes back to an earlier version to complete the sentence.

[2] The other copyist (not William Hopkins) writes, possibly from Sheridan's second thoughts: 'It may be *possible*—but would not the reformation appear rather sudden?'

[3] 'about' is added from the second copyist's manuscript.

[4] The second copyist writes: 'Very true, Sir. So, yon rabble there [run?] and cry a reprieve. (*A Reprieve, etc. within.*)'

PLAYER. Not in the least—if you suppose your Hero possess'd of Feeling enough to be reclaimed by such unexpected lenity—an English Audience will never[1] find injustice in an act of mercy.

This may have been cut down even more before presentation, for the *London Chronicle*, 11 November 1777, noted:

The only alteration in the piece is judiciously introduced in about six lines between the Manager and the Poet; the former of whom, in reply to the latter's insisting on strict poetical justice being done, proposes restoring Macheath to society, under the idea of his repentance for his former vices and follies; observing, that abandoned must that character be indeed, on whom such mercy has not a proper influence! This modest deviation from the original, as it was due to morality, met with the universal approbation of the whole theatre.

I am inclined to accept the *Morning Chronicle* report as more reliable, but must admit that I have not been able to find a revised version in Sheridan's hand of 'the thieves over their bottle' or of Mrs. Trapes's long speech.

Fielding, *The Fathers* (30 November 1778)

The 'Advertisement', prefacing the printed version of *The Fathers, or, the Good-Natur'd Man* (1778), makes clear the circumstances in which this play was found and afterwards produced:

The Comedy now published, was written by the late Henry Fielding some years before his death. The author had shown it to his friend Mr. Garrick; and entertaining a high esteem for the taste and critical discernment of Sir Charles Williams,[2] he afterwards delivered the manuscript for his opinion. At that time appointed Envoy Extraordinary to the Court of Russia, Sir Charles had not leisure to examine the play before he left England. . . . Sir Charles died in Russia, and the manuscript was lost. . . .

About two years ago Thomas Johnes, Esq.;[3] member for Cardigan, received from a young friend, as a present, a *tatter'd manuscript play*, bearing, indeed, some tokens of *antiquity*, else the present had been of little worth, since the young gentleman assured Mr. Johnes, that it was 'a damn'd thing!'—Notwithstanding this unpromising character, Mr. Johnes took the dramatick foundling to his protection with much kindness; read it; determin'd to obtain Mr. Garrick's opinion of it; and for that purpose sent it to Mr. Wallis,[4] of Norfolk-Street, who waited upon Mr. Garrick with the manuscript, and asked him, if he knew whether the late Sir Charles Williams had ever written a play?—Mr. Garrick cast his eye upon it—'The lost sheep is found! This is Harry Fielding's Comedy!' cry'd Mr. Garrick, in a *manner* that evinced the most friendly regard for the memory of the author.

---

[1] 'never' is added from the second copyist's manuscript.
[2] Sir Charles Hanbury Williams (1708–59), diplomatist and satirical poet.
[3] 1748–1816; founder of the Hafod Press, and translator of Froissart.
[4] 1713–1800. He was Garrick's solicitor.

This recognition of the play was no sooner communicated to Mr. Johnes, than he, with the most amiable politeness, restored his foundling to the family of Mr. Fielding.

Two gentlemen, of the most distinguished dramatic talents of the age, have shewn the kindest attention to the fragment thus recovered. To the very liberal and friendly assistance of Mr. Sheridan, and to the Prologue and Epilogue, written by Mr. Garrick, is to be attributed much of that applause with which the public have received the Fathers; or, The Good-Natur'd Man.

The identification of the manuscript is mentioned by Garrick in a letter[1] written as far back as 3 January 1776, but production was delayed partly because of Garrick's quarrel with Sir John Fielding over permission given to William Addington to prepare the play for performance,[2] and partly by Garrick's retirement from the direction of Drury Lane Theatre.

It would be useful to know the extent of the changes made by William Addington in the 'tatter'd manuscript play', but this will be revealed only when its present location is discovered. The copy made for Albany Wallis[3] is also missing. The one manuscript in existence is the Lord Chamberlain's copy, submitted by Sheridan for his approval on 25 November 1778, not far short of three years after the retrieval of *The Fathers*. It is now Larpent MS. 461 in the Huntington Library, and John Payne Collier noted that in this text 'various corrections and improvements . . . are in the hand writing of Sheridan'.[4]

I do not think that all the corrections are in his hand. Some may have been made by a copyist, and others, by Sheridan's first wife. Sheridan himself contributed a minimum of seventy-five words scattered in eighteen different places in the text, and most of his changes try to give the phrasing a greater clarity. He alters 'beyond credit' to 'beyond credibility', and 'tho' he be scarce over shoes' to 'tho' he wan't over the instep'. He writes 'a measure seldom attended with success' in place of Fielding's 'a step I am not us'd enough to take'. Sheridan's phrases were normally, though not invariably, accepted by the printer of the first edition.

When *The Fathers* was produced, general opinion suggested that Sheridan had not been sufficiently attentive to its needs. The *Morning Chronicle* put the point of view clearly:

. . . If Fielding's plays, prepared for representation under his own eye, were deemed imperfect, it is no wonder that a comedy, found in manuscript by accident, and brought upon the stage many years after his death, should be liable to objection. *The Fathers, or The Good-Natured Man*, has already been declared to be an orphan, and, what is worse (notwithstanding the boasted assistance it is said to have received) it is evident it either has had no guardian, or one that has not done his duty by it. Were the case otherwise, it surely never would have been

---

[1] *Garrick Letters*, p. 1064.   [2] Ibid., pp. 1072–5.
[3] W. L. Cross, *History of Henry Fielding* (New Haven, 1918), iii. 100–3.
[4] MacMillan, p. 78.

suffered to have made its appearance in the rickety and deformed shape in which it was exhibited yesterday evening. The play is a motley mixture of beauties and defects, and resembles an old-fashioned aigrette made up of some brilliants and some false stones, originally very ill set, and which has been suffered to lie by till the form of it was totally out of fashion. The defects unfortunately are radical; the fable being exceedingly poor, and ill-managed; and the conduct of it not more absurd than unnatural. On the other hand, the characters are some of them boldly drawn, and highly finished; the dialogue witty, humourous and well-turned; the sentiments sterling, and the satire and ridicule pointed at their proper objects, dishonest cunning and egregious folly.[1]

The *Morning Post* was equally severe at Sheridan's expense: 'We were surprized to find that there was not a single new scene painted for the piece; but this we could have overlooked, if we thought the manager had paid a friendly attention to the drama itself, which we fear is not the case.'[2] In general, the reviewers blamed Sheridan for not presenting the play more effectively, so that Fielding's family would have drawn real financial benefit from good houses and many performances.

Obviously Sheridan went to some trouble over the text, but he did not give it the full professional attention that the public expected.

Woodward, *Fortunatus* (3 January 1780)

Henry Woodward's pantomime, *Fortunatus*, was given its first performance on 26 December 1753 at Drury Lane Theatre. It was revived, there, in 1780 'with alterations and three new scenes',[3] that concerned the recent siege of Fort Omoa in the Bay of Honduras:

This famous siege is thus represented:—A grand scene, so designed as to exhibit the inside of the fort, with the guns mounted, the exterior of one of the bastions, with the fosse and counterscarp, and the harbour and the British fleet, at one view, is first discovered. By the happy contrivance of this scene (which is a fresh proof of Mr. De Louterbourgh's great abilities as an artist), the audience see the mode of defence used by the besieged, and the British tars in the act of scaling the walls of the fort, at the same time. The assailants proving successful as to the outworks, which they carry, the scene changes to the interior of the fort, in which is represented the singular instance of an English seaman's bravery, recited in Capt. Dalrymple's dispatch[4] from Omoa, a Spaniard found without arms being furnished with a cutlass by a sailor, who afterwards conquers him and then spares his life. This over, the scene changes again, and the surrender of the fort in form by the Spanish Governor's delivery of the keys of it, is exhibited; after which the whole entertainment finishes with Mr. Vernon's singing 'Rule Britannia', assisted by Mr. Gaudry, and the chorus supported by most of the singing performers of the Theatre.

---

[1] *Morning Chronicle*, 1 Dec. 1778. [2] *Morning Post*, 1 Dec. 1778.
[3] The *London Chronicle*, 1–4 Jan. 1780.
[4] Dalrymple (of the Loyal Irish Volunteers) sent a dispatch on 21 Oct. 1779, describing the capture of Porto Omoa. It was made known in England on 18 Dec. 1779.

Preparatory to the exhibition of the new scenes, Mr. Bannister and Mr. Vernon have each a new song, neither of them very striking, but Mr. Vernon's having for its burthen 'Britons, strike home', was received with applause.

The performers did their duty; but the scene men blundered egregiously all through the entertainment. During the siege of the fort so much gunpowder was fired off, that the stage was so filled with smoke, that the officers, men, etc., were scarcely discernible from the boxes.[1]

It is difficult to know who was responsible for the topical part of this entertainment, but only an outline of the incidents and a few songs were required. The double aim was to please the spectators with splendid scenery and patriotic ardour. Since Sheridan had had a share in *The Camp*, he may have had some part in this. It seems almost certain that he wrote the words of the song 'The Midnight Watch',[2] but provincial advertisements suggesting that he did more than that must be received with the usual caution. For example, Birmingham Theatre advertised '*An Interlude* written by R. B. Sheridan, Esq. Taken from the pantomime of *Fortunatus* representing the Storming and Taking of Fort Omoa. In which will be introduced songs by Mr. Linley.'[3] It is possible that this is accurate, but I have not seen any evidence that can be considered conclusive.

The newspaper reference to a song with the chorus, 'Britons, strike home', was to the following:[4]

> Chearly, my hearts, of courage true,
> The hour's at hand to try your worth,
> A glorious peril waits for you,
> And valour pants to lead you forth;
> Mark where the enemy's colours fly, boys;
> There some shall conquer, some must die, boys;
> > But that appals not you nor me,
> > For our watch word it shall be,
> 'Britons, strike home!'

CHORUS

'Britons, strike home! revenge your country's wrong!'[5]

[1] *The London Chronicle*, 1–4 Jan. 1780.

[2] For the words, see p. 764 above. Rhodes, iii. 238–9, quotes a version from *The Beauties of Sheridan* (1834?), p. 49.

[3] Quoted by Rhodes, iii. 239, from *Aris's Birmingham Gazette*.

[4] From the *Town and Country Magazine*, xii (1780), 14. Cf. also Rhodes, iii. 239–40, quoting from *The Beauties of Sheridan*, pp. 49–50; and a sheet in the British Museum, catalogued as '1797?', and entitled: 'Chearly My Hearts of Courage, True, | Sung at the Theatres Royal | Written by | R. B. Sheridan, Esqr. | Composed by the late Mr. Linley | Price 1s. | London Printed and Sold by Preston, at his Wholesale Warehouses, 97, Strand.'

[5] Rhodes and Preston read 'and some' (l. 6 of the song) and 'or' (l. 7). Preston alone reads 'shall' (l. 6) and 'wrongs' (l. 11).

When rolling mists their march shall hide,
At dead of night a chosen band,
List'ning to the dashing tide,
With silent tread shall print the sand:
Then where the Spanish[1] colours fly, boys;
We'll scale the walls, or[2] bravely die, boys;
    For we are Britons bold and free,
    And our watch-word it shall be,
'Britons, strike home!' *etc.*

The cruel Spaniard,[3] then too late,
Dismay'd, shall mourn th'avenging[4] blow,
Yet, vanquish'd, meet the[5] milder fate
Which mercy grants[6] a fallen foe.
Thus[7] shall the British banners, fly, boys,
On yon proud turrets rais'd on high, boys;
    And while the gallant flag we see,
    We'll[8] swear our watch-word still shall be,
'Britons, strike home!' *etc.*

It is generally attributed to Sheridan.

The Generous Impostor (22 November 1780)

Application to perform this five-act comedy by Thomas Lewis O'Beirne[9] was sent to the Lord Chamberlain on 6 November 1780, and the play was produced at Drury Lane on 22 November. Larpent MS. 536 'contains a few passages not printed',[10] but no changes in Sheridan's hand.

Sheridan's part in this can be better appreciated from item 187 in Sotheby's Catalogue of 22 March 1855: 'T. L. OBeirne, *The Generous Impostor*, five act comedy in the autograph of the author. Played with much success at Drury Lane in 1780, having been previously prepared for the stage by R. B. Sheridan, by whom it contains numerous notes in his autograph.' It was sold to G. Smith for six shillings, but its present location is not known.

Robinson Crusoe (30 January 1781)

The first act was made up of nine scenes that followed Defoe's story closely, though introducing Harlequin Friday, Pantaloon, and Pierrot.[11]

---

[1] The Preston version reads 'Gallic'.   [2] 'We'll conquer or we'll . . .'
[3] 'The haughty Tyrants . . .'   [4] 'th'avengeful'.   [5] 'a milder'.
[6] 'Which Britons grant . . .'   [7] 'Then'.   [8] 'We'.
[9] 1748?–1823. Naval chaplain and political pamphleteer, who became Bishop of Ossory.   [10] MacMillan, p. 90.
[11] *London Chronicle*, 30 Jan. 1781.

The second act was set in Spain, and had little connection with Defoe. A newspaper report[1] gives us an idea of its content:

To Colombine, her Lover, and Mother, the Clown enters in haste, and informs them of Pantaloon's arrival; on which they all hasten to meet him. Scene changes to a port in Spain, where mutual congratulations are interchanged. Colombine falls in love with Friday, and begs him of Robinson Crusoe, who reluctantly agrees to part with him, and directly sets sail for England, after which nothing more is ever heard of him.—The succeeding business is composed of the customary distresses of Harlequin and Colombine relieved by the powers of magic. In the two last acts the principal circumstances are the two friars from the *Duenna*, one transformed into a cask for refusing his dress to Harlequin, with which a variety of pleasant tricks are played, such as, a fat Friar shrinking very small, and passing through a cask, leaving his clothes behind him, which Harlequin dresses himself in, and so gains admission.—The Clown taps the cask and draws wine; the Friar cries out of the cask, they tumble it down, it rises of itself, and produces a laughable effect. It is played with too long. At one time Harlequin is discovered in it; they seize him, and he lengthens at least four yards, and instantly draws up again. The scenery is perfectly adequate to the fanciful situations of Robinson Crusoe's cave, his bower, his boats, etc. Mr. Loutherbourgh's abilities appear to have been exerted to the utmost advantage in aid of the suffering mariner.

The changes of scenery most striking were from the outside of a convent to a windmill, when the Clown is tied to one of the wings and whirled round with great velocity. From a chandler's shop to a dyer's shop. An *auto da fé*, in which Harlequin is led to the stake, and no sooner tied up than it changes to a garden and temple. The music is composed mostly from the opera dances, and well selected.

Four songs appear to have been sung: 'The bottle's the sun of our table' (from *The Duenna*), 'There was a maid and she went to a mill', 'A lovely lass to a friar came', and 'Come, come, my jolly lads'.[2] It has been suggested that the last of these was by Sheridan to music by Shield.[3] The words[4] were printed in the *London Chronicle*, 27 Feb.–1 March 1781, 'from a correct copy':

> Come, come, my jolly lads,
>   The wind's abaft,
> Brisk gales our sails shall croud;
> Come bustle, bustle, bustle, boys,
>   Haul the boat,
> The Boatswain pipes aloud:

---

[1] Ibid.

[2] See Rhodes, iii. 339, quoting *The Lady's Magazine*, Jan. 1781.

[3] Rhodes, iii. 340. *The Overture, Comic-Tunes, & Song in the Pantomime of Robinson Crusoe* (S. A. & P. Thompson) says it was set by Linley, sung by Gaudry.

[4] See also a brochure called *A Short Account of the Situations and Incidents Exhibited in the Pantomime of Robinson Crusoe at the Theatre Royal, Drury Lane. . . . Printed for T. Becket, No. 186, Pall-Mall, 1797. (Price Sixpence.)*.

The ship's unmoor'd,
All hands on board;
The rising gail,
Fills ev'ry sail,
The ship's well mann'd and stor'd.

CHORUS.

Then sling the flowing bowl,
Fond hopes arise,
The girls we prize,
Shall bless each jovial soul;
The cann, boys, bring,
We'll drink and sing,
While foaming billows roll.

II

Though to the Spanish coast
We're bound to steer,
We'll still our rights maintain;
Then bear a hand, be steady, boys,
Soon you'll see
Old England once again:
From shore to shore
While cannons roar,
Our Tars shall shew,
The haughty foe,
Britannia rules the main.

CHORUS.

Then sling, *etc.*

When the pantomime was revived at Christmas-time 1796, *Bell's Weekly Messenger* reported that it had been a favourite exhibition some years ago: 'The second act, however, was always reckoned indifferent, and Mr. Sheridan has given it a considerable lift with his pen.'[1] It gave no details, and we have to turn to the *Morning Post*[2] for them: 'After a variety of changes and escapes Harlequin at last gets into the prison of the Inquisition, which is a very capital Scene, and from thence he is relieved by a Black Magician and transported back to the Island, to which he conveys Columbine: and the Piece concludes with a Grand Dance of Savages.' The brochure of 1797 gives an account of the twelve scenes of the first act in detail, but dismisses the second act with the words: 'Friday being invested with the powers of Harlequin, after many fanciful distresses, and the usual pantomimical revolutions, receives his final reward in the hand of Columbine.'[3]

[1] 25 Dec. 1796. [2] 27 Dec. 1796. [3] p. 21.

Thomas Moore,[1] Michael Kelly,[2] and the *Thespian Dictionary* (1802) agree in stating that Sheridan was responsible for this pantomime. *The European Magazine* clearly thought it was his, saying that it was inferior to the worst created by Messink, pantomimist at Covent Garden: 'and a proof that even the greatest genius will sink beneath contempt, when he contends with a mechanic in his own profession.'[3] However inferior it may have been as a story, it was undoubtedly popular, and was a useful vehicle for impressive scenery, fine dancing, and mime.

Besides, it is by no means certain that it was devised by Sheridan. When it was revived once again in 1809,[4] it was declared to be the production of 'the late Mrs. Sheridan and co.'[5] Quite independently, her brother supported this idea: ' "Robinson Crusoe", too, I have every reason to believe was Mrs. Sheridan's pantomime, as was one of very great originality in point of story, called "Harlequin Junior, or, the Magic Cestus" '.[6] Since the pantomime of this period included little dialogue, the question of authorship concerns the invention of situations and songs. It remains an open one. It is possible that Sheridan put them together in an idle moment to show that he could do so,[7] and equally possible that his share was a very small one. He may merely have revised, or 'given a lift to', something produced by his wife and her circle, for the common good.

Cobb, *The Haunted Tower* (1794–7)

This comic opera by James Cobb was produced at Drury Lane Theatre on 24 November 1789. At some later date, Sheridan wrote to Greenwood,[8] scene-painter at the theatre, saying:

Suspend other Operations a little—and look to the Scenery of 'the *Haunted Tower*' which I am wit[t]ling down into an after-Piece and have good hopes of it —it will be brought out on Saturday sev'night and tell Johnson from me to look after his Part of it. I think we might use some of our first of June Sea-Scenery in the opening of the first act—or if anything could be done so as to say new Scenery without expence it would be well—[9]

[1] Moore, ii. 251; *Journal*, iv. 222.   [2] Kelly, ii. 322.
[3] Quoted by Rhodes, iii. 339, from the *European Magazine*, Feb. 1782.
[4] See *The British Press*, 6 Jan. 1809, for some new characters that had been introduced into the cast, in the planter and planter's man.
[5] Meaning, I suppose, her sister, Mary, and Mary's husband, Richard Tickell. The phrase comes from 'Notes for a Life of Sheridan' by 'F.L.', in the Victoria and Albert Museum Library 48. E. 42.
[6] See A. R. Bayley, 'A Note on Sheridan', *Notes and Queries*, 11th ser., x (1914), 62.
[7] Provincial managements were glad to attribute it to him. Exeter Theatre, in 1781, declared: 'This admired Entertainment is (with strict adherence to the original history) compiled and adapted to stage representation by R. B. Sheridan, Esq. (Author of the Drama, *The School for Scandal*).' See Eric R. Delderfield, *Cavalcade by Candlelight* (Exmouth, 1950), p. 26.
[8] Thomas Greenwood, senior, died in 1797.   [9] *Letters*, iii. 322.

The Glorious First of June was given its initial performance on 2 July 1794.[1]

No other details of this revision have come to hand.

Kotzebue, *The Stranger* (24 March 1798)

In the autumn of 1796, one A. Schink approached Drury Lane Theatre with a translation of Kotzebue's *Menschenhass und Reue* (1788). The managers kept it eight or ten days, according to him,[2] then returned it stating they did not think it would succeed.

Schink said he was satisfied with the answer until he heard (in March 1798) that a translation of Kotzebue's play was to be produced after all. When he saw it acted, he found 'scarcely any alteration' from his own work, except in the names of the characters and 'the addition of a Song[3] and some Dancing, entirely unconnected with the subject'. His version seemed superior because 'most of the nonsense, which was hissed off the stage, is omitted', and the tedious last scene was considerably shortened. He insinuated that Sheridan had stolen his work and made it worse.

Schink's grievances are of importance because they suggest a date when an interest in Kotzebue began to be felt in the English theatre, as well as bring the real translator to the public eye to explain what had happened. Four days after the first performance, Benjamin Thompson pointed out that the charges were preposterous and that the suggestion (made by other critics) that he enjoyed personal influence at Drury Lane was untrue. He added later:

at the time I transmitted the Stranger to Drury-lane Theatre, I was totally unknown to any of the proprietors, and had no introduction to them, but through the play itself. Mr. Grubb, to whom I sent with a few lines, put it into the hands of Mr. Sheridan, who was so kind as to improve its effect by several alterations and additions. To both these gentlemen I acknowledge my grateful obligations. . . .[4]

Drury Lane Theatre paid Thompson fifty pounds for his work on 15 May 1798,[5] and that was the end of the transaction as far as he was concerned.

What we have now to discover is the extent of Sheridan's share in the version put on in the theatre. Since he knew no German, his business was merely to give the translation dramatic life. A few days before the first performance, he wrote: 'we are resolved to have the Stranger out on Saturday, and yet if I desert it it will not be. I have to finish my song,

---

[1] See pp. 753–5 above.
[2] 'Address to the Publick', signed 'S****k.' in *The Stranger: A Comedy Freely Translated from Kotzebue's German Comedy of Misanthropy and Repentance* (1798).
[3] 'I have a silent sorrow here' to music by the Duchess of Devonshire.
[4] *The German Theatre Translated by Benjamin Thompson, Esq.* (4th edn., 1811), i. 5.
[5] Add. MS. 29710, f. 115.

to alter an Epilogue we have got at last from Lewis to be spoken by Suett as a Gypsey and to touch up many things in the Play. . . .'[1] When the first performance was noticed in *The Times*, the translation was praised but a need for further revision was also suggested:

The translator has so successfully executed his task, that the Play is marked, unless in some few passages, with all the characteristics of English composition. For the ultimate polish and mechanism of the Piece, the public are indebted to the taste and discrimination of Mr. Sheridan, and to Mr. Kemble's skill in producing Stage effect. . . .[2]

Two complaints were voiced: one against the vulgarity of language in the lighter scenes, and the other saying that the play was 'full an hour too long'. After the second performance, *Bell's Weekly Messenger*[3] stated that it was 'divested of most of its objectionable qualities. . . . Many judicious alterations and curtailments have taken place'; but *The Times* still found it too long: '[it] might be easily abridged by retrenching the superfluous vulgarities of Solomon; and omitting the least interesting passages in the last scene between Mr. Kemble and Mrs. Siddons.'[4] The introduction of a new character, and a dénouement 'more consistent with English notions of virtue and honour', were reported in *The Times*, 19 April. For Mrs. Siddons's benefit night, *The Stranger* 'with alterations and an additional scene' was advertised. On the day of performance, the theatre had to admit that the extra scene was not ready and that the play would be given as usual.[5]

At some date during this period—either before or after the first performance—Sheridan mentioned to John Grubb that he was 'doing this d——d alteration of the Stranger'.[6] The tone of exasperation suggests that a considerable amount of work was involved. Was it as much as Moore recorded? 'S[heridan] said to him [Samuel Rogers] *twice* that every sentence in the "Stranger", as it is acted, was written by him. Can this be true?'[7] Moore's question remains unanswered. An argument has been advanced that Sheridan merely cut Thompson's translation and added some songs and dances to the entertainment,[8] but P. G. Patmore[9] discovered that there was in existence 'a single act of Thompson's version . . . part of the prompter's copy of that version, with numerous erasures, alterations, and interlineations, evidently in Sheridan's hand'. Sotheby's Catalogue, 12–17 May 1851, seems to identify it when noting that part of lot 1077 was 'the facsimile of "The Sheridan Autograph," being the 5th Act of the Stranger, with numerous alterations and additions by him'.

[1] *Letters*, ii. 85.   [2] *The Times*, 26 Mar. 1798.
[3] 1 Apr. 1798.   [4] 27 Mar. 1798.   [5] *The Times*, 18, 23 Apr. 1798.
[6] *Letters*, ii. 86.   [7] Moore, *Journal*, iv. 222.
[8] D. MacMillan, 'Sheridan's Share in *The Stranger*', *M.L.N.* xlv (1930), 85–6.
[9] *My Friends and Acquaintance*, iii (1854), 271–2.

There would therefore appear to be a case for saying that Sheridan revised at least one act thoroughly. It is impossible to go beyond that, at the moment, but it is worth recalling that the 'Programme' included 'The Stranger' among his authentic works.[1] When the text of the play 'as it is acted' becomes available,[2] we shall be able to decide whether this is wholly justified or not.

Ward and Colman, *The Forty Thieves* (8 April 1806)

The first edition was published in New York in 1808, and bore the legal declaration:[3]

... David Longworth, of the said District [of New York], hath deposited in this office the Title of a Book, the right whereof he claims as Proprietor, in the words following, to wit—

THE FORTY THIEVES;
A Grand Romantic Drama, in Two Acts.

BY

R. B. SHERIDAN and COLMAN the younger.[4]

The available evidence indicates, however, that Sheridan's part in this work was small, and that it may more properly be attributed to Colman and C. W. Ward.[5]

The earliest references to the subject belong to late October and early November 1804, when Charles Ward accompanied Sheridan to Lymington[6] and wrote home apologizing for his protracted absence: 'he [Sheridan] cannot possibly extend his stay beyond a day and I shall have the advantage of a tete a tete to finish our Ali Baba'.[7] *The Times*, 24 November 1804, stated that Sheridan was 'busily employed on a most difficult task, the dramatising of *Forty Thieves*', but he was soon diverted from it by the quarrel between the King and the Prince of Wales. Ward recognized the superior importance of this matter, and wrote, 'How can he devote hours to consider Scene shifting and artificial mules?'[8]

[1] See p. 19 above, and pp. 843–4 below.
[2] The Lord Chamberlain's MS. has not been located.
[3] The title-page reads: 'THE | FORTY THIEVES: | A | *GRAND ROMAN-TIC DRAMA* | IN | TWO ACTS. | BY | R. B. SHERIDAN AND COLMAN *the younger*. | [Short rule] | (WITH ALL THE ORIGINAL SONGS AND CHORUSSES.) | [Double rule] | NEW-YORK: | PUBLISHED BY DAVID LONGWORTH, | At the Dramatic Repository, | *Shakspeare-Gallery* | [Short rule] | 1808.' The declaration is on the verso.
[4] George Colman the younger (1762–1836).
[5] Charles William Ward, husband of Sheridan's sister-in-law, Jane Linley.
[6] *Letters*, ii. 223–5; Clementina Black, *The Linleys of Bath* (rev. edn., 1926), p. 267.
[7] C. Black, op. cit., p. 268.
[8] C. Black, op. cit., p. 270. Cf. *Letters*, ii. 231–2.

At this point, Michael Kelly seems to have come into the enterprise, and Ward reported:

Kelly and I are going on well together, he has proposed to get the music according to the sentiment and for me to write the words. I have consented and he goes on upon velvet, for he steals without let or hindrance. I gave him the idea of the Chorus beginning
                    Join the festive dance and song,
he forgot the words, but retaining some idea of them wrote down
                    Let the festive *foot* prepare
                    Songs of mirth and songs of Glee
is not that excellent?[1]

By 13 December, *Ali Baba* (as it was also called for the time being) was ready for rehearsal, but little more is heard of it until 3 October 1805, when *The Times* stated: 'The expected drama of *The Forty Thieves* was not, as reported, written by Mr. Sheridan, but by the Gentleman who married a sister of the late Mrs. Sheridan. Mr. Sheridan, however, is said to have given the piece some animated touches.' The touches (if given) were not animated enough, and Kelly persuaded Colman to revise the work.[2] When it was eventually produced on 8 April 1806, it was a spectacular success, in every sense of the word.

Years later, Thomas Moore sought to discover the truth about Sheridan's part in it, and was told by Ward: 'the skeleton of the "Forty Thieves" was Sheridan's; then he (Ward) filled it up, and afterwards George Colman got £100 for an infusion of jokes, etc. into it.'[3] We may prefer to think that the skeleton came from *The Thousand and One Nights*, and that Sheridan really wrote another 'outline of incidents'. This is what Moore found among Sheridan's papers, and he also provides us with a sketch of one of the scenes as drafted by Sheridan:

Bannister called out of the cavern boldly by his son—comes out and falls on the ground a long time, not knowing him—says he would only have taken a little gold to keep off misery and save his son, etc.

Afterwards, when he loads his asses, his son reminds him to be moderate— but it was a promise made to thieves—'it gets nearer the owner, if taken from the stealer'—the son disputes this morality—'they stole it, *ergo*, they have no right to it; and we steal it from the stealer, *ergo*, our title is twice as bad as theirs.'[4]

The remainder of the outline has not been available since Moore saw it, but the specimen he gives is sufficient to define the nature of Sheridan's contribution. He may, too, have revised Ward's dialogue a little, but by the time Kelly and Colman had been at work on the script, Sheridan's

[1] C. Black, op. cit., pp. 270-1. Cf. Kelly, ii. 213.
[2] John Adolphus, *Memoirs of John Bannister, Comedian* (1839), ii. 14.
[3] Moore, *Journal*, ii. 355.   [4] Moore, ii. 251-2.

part in it must have been quite small. Consequently, I do not print this piece in the canon.[1]

The Siege of St. Quintin, or, Spanish Heroism
(10 November 1808)

Application to present this three-act drama was made by Drury Lane Theatre to the Lord Chamberlain on 4 November 1808.[2] The play itself was an adaptation by Theodore Hook[3] of Pixérécourt's *Les Mines de Pologne*.

The Sheridans seem to have taken some trouble over this production. Tom Sheridan made a number of comments and corrections on a manuscript of the second act,[4] and his father contributed six characteristic notes:

> [f. 150ᵛ] Shorten and mend the writing
> old and stale
> [f. 154ᵛ] something of ironical humour might be introduced in the description of this apartment
> [f. 155ᵛ] How much this ought to be shorten'd I can't attempt to say as I have not had the enterprize to attempt to read it
> [f. 158ᵛ] all all too long
> [f. 163ᵛ] shorten

Manuscript versions of the third act were also extant at one time, and were described in Sotheby's Catalogue, 12–17 May 1851, item 1077, as

> R. B. Sheridan—the Third Acts of a Play, entitled, *St. Quintin*. Two copies of it, each containing marginal notes, additions and alterations in the autograph of Sheridan and his Son, 'Tom Sheridan'.
> Sheridan, in giving directions as to the acting of the play, writes:—'Tom knows better now how to manage it than I do.'

After the play was produced on 10 November, the *Monthly Mirror*[5] referred to Sheridan as 'the dramatist defunct': 'The scene between the *two English*, *Sir Leinster* and Captain MacEntire . . . is written by the author of the *School for Scandal*, and is the worst in the piece. As some other little touches have been given to it by Mr. Sheridan we are tempted to ascribe to him a share in the opening of the third act . . .' See p. 839 below.

---

[1] Rhodes, ii. 308–63, prints it from the edition of 1814 'by J. Charles of Dublin under the title of *Ali Baba; or, The Forty Thieves*'. The Lord Chamberlain's MS. is now Larpent MS. 1480 in the Huntington Library, but bears no sign of Sheridan's hand. An unacted piece, 'The Forty Thieves. A Musical Drama', by E. Green, and on paper bearing the watermark '1794', was among the Drury Lane MSS. found by P. G. Patmore, and is now Add. MS. 25919.

[2] MacMillan, p. 259. Larpent MS. 1559.   [3] 1788–1841.
[4] Add. MS. 42721, ff. 149–70.   [5] New ser., iv (1808), 316.

PLAYS NEVER PERFORMED

Ixion

NATHANIEL HALHED[1] was at Harrow with Sheridan, and when he went on to Oxford University secured his friend's interest in a burlesque that he had written. A copy of it is in the British Museum,[2] and from it we can learn that Jupiter wooed Major Amphitryon's wife and that Sir Richard Ixion pursued Juno. The quality of the entertainment and the verse may be seen in Juno's lines after Ixion leaves her:

> ... the Coxcomb by his breath is rotten.
> Puppy!—Jove's sister to assault, and wife t'him
> I'll play old Gooseb'ry with Him all his Life time.
> Sure for his Master I am Meat—a Brute
> To think I'd listen to his scurvy suit.
> He push a face here?—He make Jove a cuckold?—
> I'll put the Doctor on him, if my Luck hold.[3]

He sent it to Sheridan for revision, and with complete confidence in his ability. In a later letter, he remarked: 'every correction of yours would be an *emendation* and every addition a new perfection'.[4] Sheridan seems to have cut it drastically,[5] using its lines for a play-rehearsal scene and anticipating some of the effects of *The Critic*.

Very little of the revised play is available,[6] and we have to depend entirely on Moore's extract[7] for our knowledge of it:

SIMILE. Sir, you are very ignorant on the subject,—it is the method most in vogue.
O'CUL. What! to make the music first, and then make the sense to it afterwards!
SIM. Just so.
MONOP. What Mr. Simile says is very true, gentlemen; and there is nothing surprising in it, if we consider now the general method of writing *plays* to *scenes*.
O'CUL. Writing *plays* to *scenes*!—Oh, you are joking.

---

[1] Orientalist (1751–1830).   [2] Add. MS. 25935.   [3] Add. MS. 25935, f. 6ʳ.
[4] *Halhed's Letters to Sheridan, 1770–71* (Privately printed by R. B. Sheridan of Frampton, 1872), p. 13.
[5] Cf. Jupiter's song in Add. MS. 25935, f. 11, with Moore, i. 21.
[6] Rae, *Sheridan*, i. 108, n., remarks: 'Moore had before him the manuscript of *Jupiter* as prepared for the stage by Sheridan, but he may not have seen Halhed's *Ixion*, upon which it was based. Unfortunately, the manuscript of *Jupiter* is one out of several papers which were not returned to the Sheridan family after Moore had finished the 'Memoirs' of Sheridan; consequently, I am unable to verify the accuracy of what he has already given to the world.' It is still missing.   [7] Moore, i. 18–22.

MONOP. Not I, upon my word. Mr. Simile knows that I have frequently a complete set of scenes from Italy, and then I have nothing to do but to get some ingenious hand to write a play to them.

SIM. I am your witness, Sir. Gentlemen, you perceive you know nothing about these matters.

O'CUL. Why, Mr. Simile, I don't pretend to know much relating to these affairs, but what I think is this, that in this method, according to your principles, you must often commit blunders.

SIM. Blunders! to be sure I must, but I always could get myself out of them again. Why, I'll tell you an instance of it.—You must know I was once a journeyman sonnet-writer to Signor Squallini. Now, his method, when seized with the *furor harmonicus* was constantly to make me sit by his side, while he was thrumming on his harpsichord, in order to make extempore verses to whatever air he should beat out to his liking. I remember, one morning, as he was in this situation, *thrum, thrum, thrum,* [*moving his fingers as if beating on the harpsichord,*] striking out something prodigiously great, as he thought,—'Hah!' said he,—'hah! Mr. Simile, *thrum, thrum, thrum,* by gar here is vary fine,—*thrum, thrum, thrum,* write me some words directly.'—I durst not interrupt him to ask on what subject, so instantly began to describe a fine morning.

> Calm was the land and calm the seas,
> And calm the heaven's dome serene,
> Hush'd was the gale and hush'd the breeze,
> And not a vapour to be seen.

I sang to his notes.—'Hah! upon my vord vary pritt,—*thrum, thrum, thrum,*—stay, stay,—*thrum, thrum,*—Hoa! upon my vord, here it must be an adagio,—*thrum, thrum,*—oh! let it be an *Ode to Melancholy*.'

MONOP. The Devil!—there you were puzzled sure.

SIM. Not in the least,—I brought in a *cloud* in the next stanza, and matters, you see, came about at once.

MONOP. An excellent transition.

O'CUL. Vastly ingenious indeed.

SIM. Was it not? hey! it required a little command,—a little presence of mind,—but I believe we had better proceed.

MONOP. The sooner the better,—come, gentlemen, resume your seats.

SIM. Now for it. Draw up the curtain, and [*looking at his book*] enter Sir Richard Ixion,—but stay,—zounds, Sir Richard ought to over-hear Jupiter and his wife quarrelling,—but, never mind,—these accidents have spoiled the division of my piece.—So enter, Sir Richard, and look as cunning as if you had overheard them. Now for it, gentlemen,—you can't be too attentive.

Enter SIR RICHARD IXION, *completely dressed, with bag, sword, etc.*

IX.   'Fore George, at logger-heads,—a lucky minute,
           'Pon honour, I may make my market in it.
           Dem it, my air, address, and mien must touch her,
           Now out of sorts with him,—less God than butcher.
           O rat the fellow,—where can all his sense lie,
           To gallify the lady so immensely?

Ah! *le grand bête qu'il est!*—how rude the bear is!
The world to two-pence he was ne'er at *Paris*.
Perdition stap my vitals,—now or never
I'll niggle snugly into Juno's favour.
Let's see,—[*looking in a glass*] my face,—toll loll—
    'twill work upon her,
My person—oh, immense, upon my honour.
My eyes,—oh fie,—the naughty glass it flatters,—
Courage,—Ixion flogs the world to tatters.[1]   [*Exit* IXION.

SIM. There is a fine gentleman for you,—in the very pink of the mode, with not a single article about him his own,—his words pilfered from magazines, his address from French valets, and his clothes not paid for.

MACD. But pray, Mr. Simile, how did Ixion get into heaven?

SIM. Why, Sir, what's that to any body?—perhaps by Salmoneus's Brazen Bridge, or the Giant's Mountain, or the Tower of Babel, or on Theobald's bull-dogs, or—who the devil cares how?—he is there, and that's enough.

.   .   .   .

SIM. Now for a Phoenix of a song.

Song by JUPITER

You dogs, I'm Jupiter Imperial,
    King, Emperor, and Pope aetherial,
        Master of th'Ordnance of the sky.—

SIM. Z——ds, where's the ordnance? Have you forgot the pistol? [*to the* ORCHESTRA.]

ORCHESTRA. [*to some one behind the scenes.*] Tom, are not you prepared?

TOM. [*from behind the scenes.*] Yes, Sir, but I flash'd in the pan a little out of time, and had I staid to prime, I should have shot a bar too late.

SIM. Oh then, Jupiter, begin the song again.—We must not lose our ordnance.

[JUP.]   You dogs, I'm Jupiter Imperial,
            King, Emperor, and Pope aetherial,
                Master of th'Ordnance of the sky; etc. etc.[2]
        [*Here a pistol or cracker is fired from behind the scenes.*]

SIM. This hint I took from Handel.[3]—Well, how do you think we go on?

O'CUL. With vast spirit,—the plot begins to thicken.

SIM. Thicken! aye,—'twill be as thick as the calf of your leg presently. Well, now for the real, original, patentee Amphitryon. What, ho, Amphitryon! Amphitryon!—'tis Simile calls.—Why, where the devil is he?

Enter SERVANT.

MONOP. Tom, where is Amphitryon?

---

[1] Ixion's speech is entirely from Halhed's version, where two further lines are added:
        To Her, Ixion—To Her—wherefore funk ye?
        Faint Heart ne'er won a Lady fair, you monkey—
                                    (Add. MS. 25935, f. 4)

[2] This song is from Halhed's version, and runs to twelve lines. See Add. MS. 25935, f. 11.

[3] Kettledrums are used to suggest guns in *Judas Maccabaeus*. See Otto Erich Deutsch, *Handel* (1955), p. 640.

SIM. Zounds, he's not arrested too, is he?

SERV. No, Sir, but there was but *one black eye* in the house, and he is waiting to get it from Jupiter.

SIM. To get a black eye from Jupiter,—oh, this will never do. Why, when they meet, they ought to match like two beef-eaters.

This then was part of a play, in three acts, and called 'Jupiter', and Sheridan was given the task of finding a producer. Through a London friend named Lewis Ker, approaches were made to Foote, but they came to nothing, possibly through Sheridan's dilatoriness.[1] Halhed urged that Colman should be asked to consider the play, and in another letter referred to an attempt by Sheridan to interest 'G——' [Garrick?] 'in the affair of the Rehearsal', presumably meaning *Jupiter*. Nothing came of these negotiations, and when Halhed prepared to go off to service in India, he asked Sheridan to 'manage as you will about Ixion, and agree with Foote if possible'.[2] Their use of different titles makes for some confusion.

The last reference to the play that I have found occurs in a letter by their common friend, C. Horne,[3] to Sheridan, on 22 December 1771:

I have submitted Ixion to the perusal of my Brothers in a Family way, but to go no farther—they are much pleas'd with it and have laugh'd much over it for these two days past—I suppose now poor Halhed's gone the entire property devolves on you. You will therefore give me your instructions what to do with it whether to return it to you, or to any body in Town.

'The Caravan'

Grétry's three-act opera, *La Caravan du Caire*, was produced at Fontaine-bleau in 1783, and was a great success. As early as 1784, Sheridan 'announced that his opera of The Caravan should speedily appear, and rival the Duenna'.[4] By 1790, Le Texier, the elocutionist,[5] had translated the work, and Thomas Linley 'had adapted the original French music to English poetry',[6] but Sheridan's version was still not ready for production. Twelve months later, a statement that it was to appear had an ironical inflection,[7] and in January 1793 *The Thespian Magazine* reported[8] that 'the Caravan so long talked of, is first expected'.

Sheridan never completed his revision, but the early stages of the task may be seen in the Yale University Library MS., an anonymous, forty-page free translation of the French with a few pages of corrections and new dialogue by Sheridan. Some of the text is deleted in Sheridan's

[1] See Rae, *Sheridan*, i. 125–30. The original letters are in Yale University Library.
[2] *Halhed's Letters to Sheridan*, pp. 11, 23, 28, 34–8.
[3] In the possession of the Marchioness of Dufferin.
[4] Boaden, *Kemble*, i. 274.   [5] His monologues were popular.
[6] Kelly, i. 347.   [7] Folger MS. T. a. 124.   [8] iii (1793), 38.

characteristic manner,[1] using heavy downward strokes, and there are a few crosses in the margins, too; but three pages only bear the weight of his hand. The most interesting example is the following passage, altering Huscah's lines that read: 'Yes, I believe I do; but do you know, at the last Fair, I was fool enough to buy two Friars and a French Marquis—mere drugs—all bad Bargains—they lie upon my Hands, like good Advice, nobody will take them.' In their place Sheridan inserts this piece of dialogue about slave-trading:

HUSCAH. Yes, I believe I do;—but at this last Fair, I have been fool enough to buy more than I believe I shall find chapmen for—There are some Lots I fancy I shall dispose of in a Hurry—see those two Friars—what do you think I shall get by them?

NEBI. Not much I fear—no—they'll lie a dead weight upon your hands—

HUSCAH. If it were a dead weight the matter wouldn't be so bad—but the Rogues will have as burly Stomachs as if they were prime Goods and bid for every day. Ah friend Nebi it is a scandalous thing when a Slave can't fetch his Price that he should keep his appetite.

NEBI. It is unconscionable indeed.

HUSCAH. Yes but the selfish Rogues have no consideration. They never reflect what trouble or risk we are at to get them nor care what Price we give for them—and at last you shall sell them for double their worth and the ungrateful Knaves shall never thank you.

NEBI. Aye—or let them go for common dru[d]gery at half Price and they shall have no Feeling for your loss—Oh! they're an unfeeling crew that's the Truth on't

HUSCAH. I can say nothing for 'em—

Clearly Sheridan derived some ironical amusement from the woes of the slave-trader, but found little else in *The Caravan*[2] that stimulated his imagination.

'*A Fairy Opera*' (Add. MS. 25937)

This was found by P. G. Patmore, and described by him in some detail.[3] He was certain that it was by Sheridan, and added that the songs were based on music by Cimarosa, Portogallo,[4] Paisiello,[5] and Gugliemi.[6] He quoted one of them, and also noted: 'the blank verse of the Fairy portion of the piece is greatly superior to what might have been expected, even from the high reputation which Sheridan enjoyed in his own day as a

---

[1] pp. 11–12, 26–31, 35.

[2] A literal translation of the French libretto is among the Drury Lane plays that P. G. Patmore found. It is now Add. MS. 25958.

[3] *My Friends and Acquaintance* (1854), iii. 300–12.

[4] Marcos Portogallo (1762–1830), Portuguese conductor and composer.

[5] Giovanni Paisiello (1740–1816), Italian composer.

[6] Pietro Alessandro Gugliemi (1728–1804), Italian composer.

writer of elegant and graceful verses.[1] His high opinion of the opera was supported by Sichel, who, referring to it as 'King Arthur, a Fairy Opera', thought it was 'probably prompted by Dryden's extravaganza'.[2]

He is wrong in his conjecture, for the theme of *A Fairy Opera* unquestionably comes from Parnell's poem 'A Fairy Tale'.

Once we make this correction, we are naturally cautious about accepting Sichel's other point: 'There is no reason to doubt Sheridan's authorship; many of his corrections and most of the songs are in his handwriting, while he has rewritten part of the text.'[2] A close examination of the manuscript reveals that Sheridan rewrote part of the text and corrected some of the lines. I find that these changes are made in twenty places[3] in one hundred and nineteen leaves. Usually he appears to be revising with imminent production in mind. He supplies words where the copyist fails, suggests words for songs, and furnishes stage directions. He has practical details and stage business very much in his thoughts:

f. 1: Fairies dress'd in white and silver with Pink scarfs and crowns of roses

Oberon and Mab white and Gold blue scrap [? scarf] Robin Goodfellow purple

f. 22: New Scene—as passing thro' the court to the meadow—necessary to set the 3d Scene—

f. 57: Robin drives the two knights into the ruins

f. 58: [Fairies' dance] Music original by Ferari[4]

f. 109: the marches should be play'd by bands on the stage and advancing by degrees from a distance

It may be that he had a hand in the composition of this piece,[5] but the available evidence only permits the conclusion that he revised it thoroughly for production. The fact that it was not produced may incline us to the view that he did not write it.

By the list of characters, he has written suggestions for casting, and Elizabeth Farren's name was one of them. This must mean that the notes were written before her retirement in 1797. Since some of the paper bears the watermark '1795', it follows that Sheridan worked on the manuscript between those two years.

Patmore plays

Add. MS. 25933: F. Reynolds, *The School for Daughters.*

There are corrections and comments by Sheridan on ff. 2, 3ᵛ, 4ᵛ, 12ᵛ.

---

[1] P. G. Patmore, op. cit., iii. 306, quoting from f. 43.   [2] Sichel, i. 481.

[3] On ff. 1, 2, 3, 4, 7, 22, 29, 33, 34, 42, 57, 58, 82, 101, 109.

[4] Giacomo Gotifredo Ferrari (1763–1842), Italian composer.

[5] It is obviously pasticcio. For example, f. 55 contains a note that Robin's song was to be 'the Fairy Song in Relicts of Ancient Poetry'. This is the second stanza ('More swift than lightening can I flye') in Percy's *Reliques* (2nd edn., 1767), iii. 203.

Add. MS. 25938: *The Cobbler of Preston.*
Patmore thought the whole manuscript was by Sheridan, but I find only one entry by him: 'Accepted. . . . Rejected. . . .'

Add. MS. 25940: Thomas Sheridan, *The Strolling Company* (Watermark: 1802).
Sheridan has written in three words 'good' and 'very' (f. 9); and 'Ladies' (f. 18).

Add. MS. 25939: [John Dent] *The Statesman.*
Sheridan makes corrections on ff. 3, 4, 11, 16, 20, 26. See p. 841 below.

Add. MS. 25941: [Thomas Sheridan?] *The Untutored Savage* (Watermark: 1797), ff. 1–37. This is followed by *The Savage in Europe*, ff. 38–79.
Sheridan's hand is seen on ff. 1, 14^v, 16^v, 35, 37^v, 47^v, 48^v, 49, 53, 60, 62–5, 67–70, 73–9.
On f. 58, Sheridan wrote: 'Act II | Mr. Fenwick— | To the transcriber. The Scene of the Singing Girls is to be struck out of the 1st Act.'

Add. MS. 25949: *Adrastus.*
Three words are added by Sheridan on ff. 18, 43.

Add MS. 25954: *The Buccanneers or Merchant of Bruges.*
Sheridan has written on this:
Dialogue—1 Hour
Airs 1½—
_____
2½ Change of Scenes and time between the Acts included

Add. MS. 25956: *The Castles of Athlyn and Dunbayne.*
Sheridan has written on ff. 25, 35, 45, 46, 54, 57. On f. 55^v he adds: 'Peasant must be introduced or spoken of—otherwise he will be totally forgot before his entrance.' Some notes (on ff. 3^v, 6^v, 7^v, 9^v, 11^v, 12^v, 17^v, 18^v, 19^v) that Patmore thought were by Tom Sheridan, I think are by his father. They make the wording simpler, and introduce names in place of vague descriptions. For the theme, cf. Ann Radcliffe's novel *The Castles of Athlin and Dunbayne* (1789).

Add. MS. 25969: *The French Strollers.*
Sheridan's minor corrections are on ff. 1, 4, 16.

Add. MS. 25989: *Ormandine or the Captive Knights.*
Sheridan's hand is to be seen on ff. 9^v, 10, 11^v, 27. On f. 9^v, he adds, 'Jump the Trick of dividing the Horse.'

Add. MS. 25993: *Picturesque Incidents, a farce.*
This contains many corrections by Sheridan, with the aim of cutting and tightening the action.

Add. MS. 26000: *Scotch Œconomy, A Comic Opera of Two Acts.*
The 'Dramatis Personae' on f. 2, is in Sheridan's hand.

Add. MS. 26017: *Opera without Title.*
There are corrections by Sheridan on ff. 44ᵛ, 52ᵛ, 59ᵛ. A stage direction (f. 47), 'Enter Baroness from the Cave' is criticised by Sheridan (f. 46ᵛ) as follows: 'no reason why the Baroness whom we left escorting out of the Cave is still there.'

Add. MS. 26018: *Comedy without Title.*
There are minor corrections by Sheridan on ff. 4–6, 8–9, 11, 14, 32, 34, 43, 48, 71, 87, 119. The play would appear to be of early date from the fact that Sheridan alters (f. 43), 'He'll deny later like a pickpocket, before Justice Fielding' to 'before Sir John'. Fielding died on 4 Sept. 1780.

Add. MS. 26019: *A Farce without Title.*
Corrections by Sheridan on ff. 19, 20, 23, 25, 34, 39, 50, 54. One of them is curious: the change from 'my own servant' to 'one of my Gentlemen of the Stud'.

Add. MS. 26034: *Portion of a Comedy.*
Sheridan has written on f. 16ᵛ: 'Bannister should also speak as the Soothsayer opposing his [Longbow's] being let out—it being dark.'

OTHER MATERIAL

'The Vicar of Wakefield'

VERY early in his career, Sheridan tried his hand at dramatizing freely part of Goldsmith's *The Vicar of Wakefield* (1766). The manuscript, in his own hand, is now in Yale University Library, and reads:

Dramatis Personæ

Men	Women
Mr. Primrose	Mrs. Primrose
Burchell	Olivia
Thornhill	Sophia
Arnold	two ladies of the town
Farmer Flamborough	
Farmer Williams	
Moses	
Steven	

Scene I

THORNHILL and ARNOLD.

THORN. Nay pr'ythe' Jac no more of that if you love me. what shall I stop[1] short with the game in full view, faith I believe the fellow's turned puritan, what think you of turning methodist Jack, you have a tolerable good canting countenance and if escaped being taken up for a jesuit you might make a fortune in moorfields.

ARN. I was serious Tom.

THORN. Splenetic you mean. come fill your glass and a truce to your preaching; here is a pretty fellow has let his conscience sleep for these five years and as[2] new has pluck'd morality from the leaves of his Grandmother's bible, and begins to declaim against what he has practised half his lifetime. why I tell you once more my schemes are all come to perfection. I am now convinced Olivia loves me; at our last conversation she said she would rely whol[l]y on my honour.

ARN. And therefore you would dece[ive her]

THORN. why no—deceive her—why indeed—as to that. but for god sake let me hear no more on this subject in faith you make me sad. Jack if you continue your admonitions I shall begin to think you have yourself an eye on the girl. you have promised me your assistance and when you came down to the country were[3] as hot on the scheme as myself. but since you have been two or three times with me at Primrose's have fall'n off strangely. no encroachments Jack on my little rose-bud, if you have a mind to beat up game in this quarter there's her sister—but no poaching.

---

¹ MS. 'spop'.　　　　² MS. 'has'.　　　　³ MS. 'where'.

ARN. I am not insensible to her sister's merit, but have no such views as you have. well however you have promised me if you find that real vertue—which you so firmly deny to exist in the sex in this lady that you will give up your pursuit and foregoing the dirty consideration of fortune, make atonement by marriage.

THORN. Such is my serious resolution.

ARN. I wish you'd forego the experiment but you have been so much in raptures with your success that I have had as yet no clear account how you came acquainted in the family.

THORN. Oh I'll tell you immediately you know Lady Patchet.

ARN. What is she here?[1]

THORN. 'twas by her I was first introduced. It seems last year at some of the wat[e]ring places her ladyship['s] reputation began [to] suffer a little so that she thought it prudent to retire a little, till people learn'd better manners, or got worse memories she soon got acquainted with this little family and as the wife is a prodigious admirer of quality, became in a short time very intimate an[d] as she imagined she might one day make her market of the girls, has much ingratiated herself. she introduced me. I drank and abused the degenerate with the father promis[ed] wonders to the mother for all [her] brats, praise[d] her gooseberry wine ogled the daughters and in three days made the progress I related[2] to you.

ARN. You have been expeditious indeed I fear where that devil Lady Patchet's concerned there can be no good, but is there not a son.

THORN. Oh the most ridiculous creature in nature. he has been bred in the country a bumkin all his life 'till within this six [months] when he was sent to the university at which the misfortunes that have reduced his father fell out, and he returned the most ridiculous animal you ever saw a concei[te]d disputing blockhe[a]d—so there's no great matter to fear from his penetration. But come let us begone and see this m[o]ral family we shall meet them coming from the field, and you will see a man who was once in affluence, maintain[in]g by hard labour a numerous family

[ARN.] O Thornhill can you wish to add infamy to their poverty—

Scene II

PRIM. Come my children, we have had a good day's work, our harvest goes on apace and the time demands refreshment [Here] is Moses returned from the fair. Well Moses what news?

MOSES. I've sold pieball father for forty pound, but I could get but forty shilling for the colt.

PRIM. W[h]y so.

MOSES. Why you would have laugh'd to have heard how they abused em both but the chief objection against the colt was that he was near eighteen years old, one said he was blind etc etc so that at least I was so ashamed I was glad to get rid of him and so threw him into the bargain with pyeball.

PRIM. Ah Moses you'r[e] a simple bargainer

MRS. P. Oh he is an untoward youth he'll never come to anything allways poring over his books with his round squares etc. and he'll never come to good I fear we must make a Parson of him all

[1] MS. 'hear'.   [2] MS. 'relaided'.

MOSES. Why no Mother you are always gibing me because I was six months at the university, it would be better if you would take a little care of my sister and not let her be filling her head [with] novels.[1] I never knew any good come of such stuf[f], they get their heads so plaguy full of pu[r]ling streams and dying swain that w[h]ere they can't find an Oroondates they'll pack of[f] with Thomas.—

SOPHIA. pray Good Mr. Wiseacre to what purpose is your reading or how much better do men employ their time etc.

MOSES. Why as for that Sister, you have a specimen in six months I read six books of Euclid I learned that fire would not burn nor water drown—that all was spirit and all matter and that there neither was spirit [n]or matter. why now I suppose you beleive because the sun rose yesterday that he will rise again mis[s?] I tell you it is no such thing but your mind's not capable of such things no there I learn'd to beleive in nothing and doubt everything. unless you think[?] and then tis ten to one but you'r[e] alive.

PRIM. Come a truce to your dispute. Son Moses you have employ'd [your time] most excellently.—But why is my Olivia silent. you were wont to be my prattler you are grown so grave of late—that I shall begin to suspect you find some truth in your brother's remark come tell me Olivia what's the matter?

OLIV. Indeed father I am not melancholy, or if I am it proceeds only from my anxiety for your affairs and my fears least the partial hand of adversity should still more oppress you.

PRIM. O fie my daughter! do not name such a cause. can I while I am blest with health while the sun rises to show me such a family do you know[2] so little of you[r] father as to think that hard care can reach him thro' such blessings. but who has seen our poor friend Burchell. there's a man for you Olivia, he has felt the chilling adversity, but stoops beneath the load.

MRS. P. Ah I wish he was here husband he is so merry a companion he would raise my Olivia's spirits

MOSES father I believe yonder he's coming I know him by his belt and skirt coat

Enter BURCHELL[3]

Insipid bon-ton—speak with the utmost impartiality
Nephew abuse Uncle.
Nephew disclaim the affair.
Nephew providing for younger children
Uncle—fudge
Moses—Duel.
Scene—Olivia and Burchell
look on me if your eye dare
O these old eyes should not be full of tears.

---

[1] MS. 'noveles'.   [2] MS. 'no'.
[3] The dialogue ends here. Sheridan has then added some notes for later development, never carried out.

[*'A Scotchman'*]

An early piece of dialogue in Sheridan's own hand is to be seen in Yale University Library. It runs:

M[ANAGER]. Sir I have read your Comedy and I think it has[1] infinite merit. but pray don't you think it rather Grave.

S[COTCHMAN]. Sir you say true it is a Grave Comedy. I follow the Opinion of Longinus, who says Comedy ough[t] always to be sentimental. Sir I value a sentiment of six lines in my piece no more than [a] nabob does a rupee. I hate those dirty paltry equivocations who go by the name of puns and pieces of wit. no Sir it ever was my opinion that the stage should be a place of Rational entertainment, instead of which I am very sorry to say most people go there[2] for their diversion, accordingly I have formed my commedy so that It is no laughing gig[g]ling piece of work, He must be a very light man that shall discompose his muscles from the beginning to the end.

M. but don't you think it may be too grave.

S. O never fear, and as for hissing mon they might as well hiss the common prayer book, for there is the viciousness of vice and the virtuousness [of virtue] in every third line.

M. I confess there is a great deal of moral in it but Sir I should imagine if you tried your hand at tragedy——

S. no mon there you're out I'll relate to you what put me first on writing a comedy. you must know I had composed a very fine tragedy abut the valiant Bruce. I showed it to my Laird of Mackintosh. and he was a ver candid mon and he said my genious did lye in tragedy. and I took the hint and as soon as I got [home] I began my comedy.[3]

'A Drama of Devils'

This is a manuscript[4] of sixty-seven pages of writing in Sheridan's hand, and it has long been recognized[5] that some of the characters and scenes were suggested by Sir John Suckling's play, *The Goblins*.[6] As might be expected of an early piece of work, the theme in general is derivative, and Moore saw some resemblance at one point to Fielding's *A Journey from this World to the Next*.[7]

---

[1] MS. 'is'.   [2] MS. 'their'.

[3] Moore, i. 25, commented: 'we have here some of the very thoughts and words, that afterwards contributed to the fortune of Puff; and it is amusing to observe how long this subject was played with by the current of Sheridan's fancy. . . .'

[4] In Yale University Library.

[5] See the *Gentleman's Magazine*, N.S., xiii (1840), 127; J. W. C[alcraft], 'The Dramatic Writers of Ireland: Sheridan', *Dublin University Magazine*, xlvi (1855), 53.

[6] An edition of Suckling's *Works* in two volumes was published by Thomas Davies in 1770. *The Goblins* is in vol. ii, pp. 281–356.

[7] Moore, i. 316.

He printed a number of extracts, and improved on the hastily written text when he found it defective. The following passage from the opening of the scene in the Devils' cave contains a number of differences from the one transmitted[1] by him:

1ST DEV. Come, Urial, here's to our Resur[r]ection

2ND DEV. It is a t[oa]st I'll scarcely pledge in compliment—by life I think we're happier here.

3RD DEV. So think I—by Hell I would despise the Man who would but wish to rise again to earth unless we were to lord there. What sneaking pitiful in Bondage [among] vile money-scraping foes[?] deceit treacherous Friends or fawning Flatterers—or worse the treachery of Mistresses. Shall [those] who reign Lords have land again to swell the trains of Tyranny and usurpation. By my Old Father's memory, I'd rather be the blindest Mole that ever sculk'd in darkness and lord of one poor hole where He might say 'I'm master here'.

2ND DEV. You are too Hot—where shall concord be found, if e'en the Devils disagree.—Come [fill] the Glass and add thy Harmony— for my Part I think we're lords of the World.—And while we've Wine to enlighte[n] us, the Sun be hang'd.—I never thought it gave so fine a Light for my Part—Then be there vile inconvenience[s] I think. There are high Winds and Storms Rains dreadful Rains and Floods. Not to Speak of Frost and Snow, with dewes and Damps not a little—O Curse it living on the Outside of the Earth is like sleeping on Deck when one might have a good Birth in the Cabin.

It is in these scenes of rather crude but wry humour that something of the real Sheridan emerges. He is much less at home in pastoral scenes that imitate—at a very great distance—*The Tempest* and *A Winter's Tale*, as Moore's extracts show;[2] but in rustic humour even his carelessly composed first scene reveals the way in which he was to develop, not of course at his best, but in the opening lines of *The Rivals* and *The Camp*.

Many years later, William Linley recalled hearing his mother say that this piece was originally by his sister Elizabeth,[3] Sheridan's first wife, that it was called 'The Haunted Village', and that Thomas Linley and his son Tom had begun to write music for it.[4]

'The Foresters'

All that we really know about this piece is to be found in Thomas Moore's account (i. 319–23):

In a more crude and unfinished state [than 'A Drama of Devils'] are the fragments that remain of his projected opera, 'The Foresters'. To this piece, (which appears to have been undertaken at a later period than the preceding one,) Mr. Sheridan often alluded in conversation—particularly when any regret was expressed at his having ceased to assist Old Drury with his pen,—'wait (he

[1] Ibid., 314–15.   [2] Ibid., 308–14.
[3] For some allusions to her in it, see Sichel, i. 274–5, 478–80.
[4] A. R. Brayley, 'A Note on Sheridan', *Notes and Queries*, 11th ser., x (1914), 62.

would say smiling) till I bring out my Foresters.' The plot, as far as can be judged from the few meagre scenes that exist, was intended to be an improvement upon that of the Drama just described—the Devils being transformed into Foresters, and the action commencing, not with the loss of a son but the recovery of a daughter, who had fallen by accident into the hands of these freebooters. At the opening of the piece the young lady has just been restored to her father by the heroic Captain of the Foresters, with no other loss than that of her heart, which she is suspected of having left with her preserver. The list of the Dramatis Personæ (to which however he did not afterwards adhere) is as follows:

> Old Oscar.
> Young Oscar.
> Colona.
> Morven.
> Harold.
> Nico.
> Miza.
> Malvina.
> Allanda.
> Dorcas.
> Emma.

To this strange medley of nomenclature is appended a memorandum—'*Vide* Petrarch for names.'

The first scene represents the numerous lovers of Malvina rejoicing at her return, and celebrating it by a chorus; after which, Oscar, her father, holds the following dialogue with one of them:—

osc. I thought, son, you would have been among the first and most eager to see Malvina upon her return.

COLIN. Oh father, I would give half my flock to think that my presence would be welcome to her.

osc. I am sure you have never seen her prefer any one else.

COL. There's the torment of it—were I but once sure that she loved another better, I think I should be content—at least she should not know but that I was so. My love is not of that jealous sort that I should pine to see her happy with another—nay, I could even regard the man that would make her so.

osc. Haven't you spoke with her since her return?

COL. Yes, and I think she is colder to me than ever. My professions of love used formerly to make her laugh, but now they make her weep—formerly she seemed wholly insensible; now, alas, she seems to feel—but as if addressed by the wrong person, &c. &c.

In a following scene are introduced two brothers, both equally enamoured of the fair Malvina, yet preserving their affection unaltered towards each other. With the recollection of Sheridan's own story fresh in our minds, we might suppose that he meant some reference to it in this incident, were it not for the exceeding *niaiserie* that he has thrown into the dialogue. For instance:—

osc. But we are interrupted—here are two more of her lovers—brothers, and rivals, but friends.

Enter NICO *and* LUBIN.

So, Nico—how comes it you are so late in your enquiries after your mistress?

NIC. I should have been sooner; but Lubin would stay to make himself fine—though he knows he has no chance of appearing so to Malvina.

LUBIN. No, in truth—Nico says right—I have no more chance than himself.

OSC. However, I am glad to see you reconciled, and that you live together, as brothers should do.

NICO. Yes, ever since we found your daughter cared for neither of us, we grew to care for one another. There is a fellowship in adversity that is consoling; and it is something to think that Lubin is as unfortunate as myself.

LUBIN. Yes, we are well matched—I think Malvina dislikes him, if possible more than me, and that's a great comfort.

NICO. We often sit together, and play such woeful tunes on our pipes, that the very sheep are moved at it.

OSC. But why don't you rouse yourselves, and since you can meet with no requital of your passion, return the proud maid scorn for scorn.

NICO. Oh mercy, no—we find a great comfort in our sorrow—don't we, Lubin?

LUBIN. Yes, if I meet no crosses, I shall be undone in another twelvemonth—I let all go to wreck and ruin.

OSC. But suppose Malvina should be brought to give you encouragement.

NICO. Heaven forbid! that would spoil all.

LUBIN. Truly I was almost assured within this fortnight that she was going to relax.

NIC. Ay, I shall never forget how alarmed we were at the appearance of a smile one day, &c. &c.

Of the poetical part of this opera, the only specimens he has left are a skeleton of a chorus, beginning 'Bold Foresters we are,' and the following song, which, for grace and tenderness, is not unworthy of the hand that produced the Duenna:—

> We two, each other's only pride,
> Each other's bliss, each other's guide,
> Far from the world's unhallow'd noise,
> Its coarse delights and tainted joys,
> Through wilds will roam and deserts rude—
> For, Love, thy home is solitude.
>
> There shall no vain pretender be,
> To court thy smile and torture me,
> No proud superior there be seen,
> But nature's voice shall hail thee, queen.
>
> With fond respect and tender awe,
> I will receive thy gentle law,
> Obey thy looks, and serve thee still,
> Prevent thy wish, foresee thy will,
> And, added to a lover's care,
> Be all that friends and parents are.

There are a number of references to 'The Foresters' over a period of twenty-two years. The *Morning Post*, 19 October 1780, said it was to appear at Drury Lane Theatre in the following season,[1] but another allusion, two years later, suggested that it had been so long on the stocks that its timber had perished.[2] In 1785 Mary Tickell wrote to her sister to say, 'Sheridan would be almost tempted to give us the poor Forresters if he saw what a pretty Boy Mrs. Jordan makes.'[3] *The Times*, 26 January 1799, reported that 'Mr. Sheridan promises to finish his Opera of the *Foresters* in time to be brought out this season', and much the same statement was printed in *The English Chronicle*, three years later: 'Mr. Sheridan's long promised opera of *The Foresters* is said to be that to which he is now putting a finishing hand. The music is to be a compilation, like that of the *Duenna*.'[4] Sheridan was very good at puffing, but it hardly seems likely that reports of this kind going on for so many years were based on so small a fragment as that quoted by Moore. Consequently we are ready to accept a description of something more finished, even when it appears in as unreliable an account as 'An Octogenarian's' *Sheridan and his Times* (1859). The writer declares:[5]

We have seen and read the two first acts entire, abounding in interest, sparkling with wit and liveliness of satire. Some idea may be formed of his design and the construction of his plot from the imperfect sketches which Mr. Moore has given to the public, and we think unfairly, in evidence of the labour employed in pruning and preparing his first thoughts in fitting language. The contrary was the fact, for Sheridan could not endure the fatigue of correction and revision. The design was novel, the development of the scene natural, threading out the plot with many startling effects, highly wrought and of great artistic skill. In its construction, adapting itself to public taste, while it combined the keenest wit with admirable satire and the exciting glow of the great masters of the Elizabethan age, rich in imagery and redolent in beauties, it displayed powers peculiar to the pen that wrought it. It was Sheridan in every line, yet in its construction was unlike anything he had ever written. Is it possible that the manuscript can have been lost or destroyed, and that all that is left to us are the mere fragments of its skeleton, with the loose scraps on which first thoughts were dotted down, and no other evidence is left of its existence?

The question remains unanswered.

'*Affectation*'

Sheridan long meditated a comedy on this subject, but never seems to have gone beyond the stage of jotting down ideas. Some of them may be seen in manuscript in the Yale University Library, and are in his early neat hand as well as later scrawl.

---

[1] See pp. 12, 19 above.   [2] Winston papers, 1782–4.   [3] Folger MS. Y. d. 35, f. 171.
[4] 21–23 Oct. 1802.   [5] ii. 283–4.

A number of references to it appear in the period between 1779 and 1784. In the anonymous satire, *Coalition. A Farce* (1779),[1] 'Brainsley Junior' (Sheridan) says, in dismissing his wife, 'I wou'd have you finish the *touchings* of the first act of Affectation as soon as possible.' The *Morning Chronicle*, 16 October 1780, reported that 'Mr. Sheridan has promised his friends that he will this season not only produce his *Forresters*, but also his new comedy called *Affectation*.' The *Morning Post*, 6 November 1781, noted, 'Mr. Sheridan has made considerable progress in his new comedy of "Affectation", which will succeed the opera of Mr. Tickell, the parts of which are already distributed.' Tickell's *Carnival of Venice* was presented on 13 December 1781, but *Affectation* was never staged and was probably not completed. One note declares that it was not even on paper and was therefore unlikely to be finished soon.[2] Michael Kelly refers rather vaguely to 'an act or two of a comedy, which he never finished'.

The small notebook that Yale acquired in 1954, had been found by William Linley after Sheridan's death.[3] It was made available to Thomas Moore for his work on Sheridan, and he summarized it in a pencil-note on the fly-leaf, as 'Curious and elaborate memorandums of jokes kept by Sheridan so dull and far-fetched most of them that how they came to find favour for an instant in the head of a man of real wit seems almost inconceivable.' He was more cautious in his phrasing in the biography, remarking that Sheridan 'was desirous of making the vintage of his wit as rich as possible, by distilling into it every drop that the collected fruits of his thought and fancy could supply. Some of the jests are far-fetched, and others, perhaps, abortive—but it is pleasant to track him in his pursuit of a point, even when he misses. The very failures of a man of real wit are often more delightful than the best successes of others.'[4] He printed extracts from the notebook,[5] and some jottings that do not now appear in it, but since some pages have been torn out and the stubs show writing, the notebook may have been more complete when Thomas Moore copied out the passages he needed.

To date the notebook with exactness is not possible. Many of the entries are in an early hand, but a couple of references to the *Morning Post* show that these jottings must have been written in or after 1772, when the newspaper was founded. Rhodes thought that a number of phrases were reminiscent of *The Camp* (1778),[6] but one of his examples, 'a rondeau of circumvallation', has a parallel in 'a circumvallation of hoop' in *St. Patrick's Day* (1775). The allusion to Vestris, the dancer, may

[1] p. 9.
[2] Winston papers in the British Museum (press-mark C 120 h, 1782-4).
[3] See p. 9 above, and Add. MS. 29764, f. 26.
[4] Moore, i. 325.
[5] Moore, i. 324-34.
[6] Rhodes, iii. 296.

belong to 1781, when he gave his first performances in this country, rather than to 1791, the year of his return. One page contains figures dated 18 October 1804, concerning bank notes lent to one Atwood, and shows that the notebook was in use as late as that year.

A few words appear both in *Affectation* and a draft of part of *The School for Scandal*. They are 'Babble Bore', 'Dodsley's Grey's Elegy',[1] and 'The Critick—when he gets out of his Carriage should always recollect that his Footman from behind is gone up to judge as well as himself.' If they were copied into the notebook after the draft had been used, this would support Rhodes's contention that Sheridan began to work upon *Affectation* as soon as *The School for Scandal* had been performed; but my own guess, based on the handwriting, is that *Affectation* was begun as early as 1772–3, and that the notebook was little used after 1781.

I transcribe the notebook as it now appears,[2] omitting the money items and Moore's comment:

An Affectation of Business.
            of Accomplishments.
            of Love of Letters and Wit.
                  Music.
            of Intrigue.
            of Sensibility.
            of Vivacity.
            of Silence and Importance.
            of Modesty.
            of Profligacy.
            of Moroseness.

S[i]r Babble Bore
S[i]r Peregrine Paradox
Feignwit
—The Templar he the Colonels Brother—
                or Dodd
L[or]d A—x.—
An affected delicate robust woman—nervous.
A universal Lover—left to talk with the Aunt. makes love to her
Ah, by the bye an't I in love with you?
Dodsley's Grey's Elegy
City—Gates—shut
Aunt coming in the Neice's Place—lock'd up in the closet—
Lover there confesses—his attachment

The Letter I forgot to lose
A Pharoah-Bank

[1] See pp. 288–9, above.
[2] Moore has altered or completed some of the jottings in his transcription.

In the Cadence—eight loses—nine wins
—an Italian to sing.—
ombres chinoises
I shall order my valet to shoot me the very first thing he does in the morning
shall you be at Lady —— I'm told the Bramin is to be there and the new French
Philosopher—no it will be pleasanter at Lady —— Conversatione there—
A man intriguing with so many, that he forgets the particular situation of things
in which He left off with particular woman—
makes love to the mother—
to the maid as she passes—
A man intriguing only for the Reputation of it. To his Confidant Servant.—
'who am I in love with now—'—'The Newspapers give you to so and so.—you
are laying close seige to Lady L. in the morning Post and have succeeded with
L[ad]y G in the Herald
S[i]r T is very jealous of you in the Gazetteer—
—remember tomorrow the first thing you do to put me in Love with Mrs C.—
make love as I visit—
where was my carriage waiting last night—
—I forgot to forget the Billet doux at Brooks—
L[a]d[y] dy has promised to meet me in her carriage tomorrow—where is the
most public Place?
A Fellow one could scarcely intrigue with much less keep company with
I hear she is the Fashion

Character:—MR. BUSTLE

A Man who Delights in Hurry—and interruption—will take any one's Business
for them leaves word where all his Plagues may follow him—governor of all
Hospitals—and share in Ranelagh. speaker from the vestry to the House of
Commons.
—'I am not at home—gad now He has heard me and I must be at home—'
'Here am I so plagued—and there is nothing I love so much as Retirement
and Quiet'—'you never sent after me'—'nothing but the window Tax'—
(or let the servants call in with such message as that. He coming in a Room that
communicates.) young man tells—his important Business in the middle of
fifty trivial interruptions—and the calling in of Idlers—as Fidlers—wild beast-
men—Foreigners with recommendatory Letters—etc. answers Notes on his
knee—'and so your Unckle died—for your obliging enquiries—and left you
an Orphan—and to cards in the Evening
contrast with the man of Indolence—Brother—
So Brother just up—and I have been etc etc.
you mustn't meddle—with those Papers—'twill be Shorter
to pay the Bill than look for the Receipt
And Files Letters answer'd—unanswer'd—
Here are more unopen'd—than answer'd.
Z——ds! Here's the Letter unopen'd—
one will give his mon[e]y from Indolent Generosity—the other his time
from restlessness.
can I do anything for anybody at any Place?

I can't bear to be doing nothing—
The most active Idler—and laborious Trifler.
I have been to the secretary—written to the Treasury—no if you had
    but written one Line
what is the sum? I'll give it.
I promised to meet the commissioners and to write Mrs Prues[?] little
    Stage exercise[?][1]
Ha! ha! Did my Lord say what that I was always busy being—what
    plagued to Death!
He does not in reality love Business only the appearance of it—
—Keeps all his Letters—and copies—mem.—to meet the Hackney-
    Coach commissioners to arbitrate between etc.
One who always changes sides in all arguments the moment any one
    agrees with him—wants to have three sides to a Question—
One who agreeing with every one—will speak their sentiments for them—
    so fond of Talking that He does not contradict only because He can't
    wait to let any one go thro' what they are going to say—

These two Brothers Guardians to the son of a Third—

He regulates every Action by a Love for Fashion—will grant annuities tho'
He don't want money appear to intrigue tho' constant to drink tho' sober—
(He has some fashionable vices—affects to be distress'd in his circumstances—
and when his new vis a vis[2] comes out procures a judgment to be enter'd against
him. want to lose—but by ill luck wins five thousand Pounds.

A Plan of a public Flirtation—not to get beyond a Profile must I be Jealous? no
    old aunt softly
How could you be so wicked—you base

If alone with a pretty woman to be sure you can't taking
Virtue—for civility is due to the sex
    she thinks you are in Love with her—only because—how vain some women are
    you were rude to her
O no upon my soul—I made love to her directly

What are the Affectations you chiefly dislike—
There are many in this company so I'll mention others
To see two[3] People affecting intrigue—having their assignations in Public
    Places only. He pretending a warm assault—and the Lady acting the Hesita-
    tion of retreating virtue
'Pray ma'am don't you think'—while neither Party have
words between 'em to conduct the Preliminaries of Gallantry[4]
nor Passion to pursue the object of it.—
Then I hate to see one to whom Heav'n has given real Beauty setting her
    Features—at the Glass of Fashion—while she speaks—not thinking so
    much of what she says—as how she looks while she is speaking—and more
    careful of the action of her Lips than what shall come from 'em—I hate
    to see a prettying woman studying—Looks and endeavouring to recollect

---

[1] Moore reads 'Mr. Price's little boy's exercise.'
[2] See p. 592.   [3] MS. 'too'.   [4] MS. 'Gallown'.

an ogle, like Lady——who . . .[1] and oblig[e]s her ogle in all degrees—having le[a]rned to play eyelids like a venetian Blind.

Then I hate to see an old woman putting herself Back to a girl—

There is nothing ridiculous in being Fat once, but when I see you are yourself affected and don't know it—you would pass for morose.

He has no pleasure in the company there at the opera—yet sits with an implicit smile[2]—anticipating the Laugh not halting after the sense.   two wits are hobnobbing jokes—
    or a man studying to be conisscentie or labouring to be an amateur.

An old man who affects intrigue and writes his own lies reproaches in the morning Post—trying . . .[1] edge himself into the reputation of being young as if he could obscure his age by blotting his Character, tho' never so little need'd as when he's abusing himself.
    who pays for the valuable Decay of a Picture—

Learning is a pretty Ballast[3] for a woman but not the Freight.—

Affection of Prudery in an ugly woman, a hard task . . .[1] if she smiles.

A profess'd Wit—who has the exclusive Privilege of being[4] plag[u]ed with attention which he is afraid to disappoint and the . . .[1] laughs which he will add—calculates his expence for the company—and generally thre[e] or four . . .[1] Laughs into the Bargain—

A true train'd wit lays his Plan like a General—foresees the circumstances of the Converzation surveys the ground and contingencies—detaches a Question to draw you tho etc. where an a[m]buscade joke—detaching a Question to draw you into the palpable Ambuscade after ready made Joke—

Laughing—hear—what was it[5] I laugh'd at—

There is a natural civility in your nature that prevents your ever being a well-bred man.

S[i]r Peregrine Paradox
Fiction

I see them dance together—both taught by Vestriss—her twisting near sinking into herself—as you shut up an opera Glass.—

When she wore at the corner she pad[d]led like a Turtle turning to look up in his Face—a Dutch Madon[n]a

—discharging at the same time a most apoplectic Ogle—which being shot Parallel killed him about the middle of his waist.

A fat woman trundling into a Room on Castors—her sitting was a leaning—rises like a Bowl on the wrong Bias—rings on her Fingers—and her fat arms strangled with Bracelet—which belted them like corded Brawn—rolling and heaving when she laugh'd with the rattles in her Throat and a most apoplectic ogle—you wish to draw her out like opera-glass—married to . . . yet affecting

A long lean Man—with all his Limbs rambling—no way to reduce him to compass unless you could double him like a Pocket rule—with his Arms spread

---

[1] Illegible.   [2] MS. 'simile'.
[3] MS. 'Pallast'.   [4] MS. 'peing'.   [5] MS. 'at'.

He'd lie on the Bed of Ware like a Cross on a Shrove Tuesday good Friday Bun. standing still he is a Pilaster without a Base—he appears roll'd out or run up against a wall—so thin that his front Face is but the moiety of a Profile—if he stands cross-leg'd he looks like a caduceus and put him in a fencing attitude and you'd take him for a piece of chiveaux-de-Frieze. to make any use of him it must be as a Spontoon or a Fishing-rod—when his wife's bye he follows like a note of admiration—see them together one's a mast and the other all Hulk—she's a Dome and He's built like a Glass-House. when they Part you wonder to see the Steeple separate from the Chancel—and were we to see them embrace he must hang round her Neck like a skain of thread or a Lace makers Bolster. to sing her Praise you should chuse a Rondeau, and to celebrate him in verse you must write all alexandrine.

Her prudish Frowns and resentful looks are as ridiculous as 'twould be to see a Board with notice of Spring-Guns set in a high-way or steel-Traps in a common. such must be meant as insinuation that there is something worth plundering where no one would suspect it.

The expression of her Face is at once a Denial of all Love-suit and a confession that she never was ask'd—the sourness of it arises not so much from her aversion to the Passion, as from her never having had an opportunity to shew it—her Features so unfortunately formed that she could never dissemble or put on sweetness enough to induce anyone to give her occasion to shew her bitterness. I never saw a Woman to whom you would more readily give credit for perfect chastity.

A Prude in her Teens a wanton in grey hairs She kept her virtue as long as she could claim any merit in Denying—it was then a crime and effect of Passion to endeavour to seduce her which she punish'd by rejecting, but when her age made it *charity* to make Love to her she properly rewards it by compliance—and parted with [it] only when she gave others an opportunity of shewin[g] their Charity in—

it would have been an unhandsome thing in Providence to have made such difference in Womens Face—if it had not exactly fitted her humility to her countenance—they are never covetous or avaricious in this Point but each content—there would be no such Passion possible as envy if we could conceal our perceiving a Difference—all Glasses reflect but one Face—which is just what it should be—and if Providence [had not willed?] it would never have suffer'd the invention of mirrors.

A Poetical Beauty

I made regular approaches by Sonnets and Rebusses—a rondeau of circumvallation her Pride sapp'd by an elegy and her Reserve surprised by an impromptu proceeding to storm with odes, she at last saved the farther effusion of Rhime by a capitulation—
　　to a Lady who affects Poetry.

I wouldn't give a Pin to make fine men in love with me—every coquet may do that—and the Pain you can give these creatures is very trifling—I love out of the way conquests—and as I think my attractions are singular I would draw singular objects—

The Loadstone of true Beauty draws the hardest substances—not like the warm Dowager—who prate[s] herself into heat to get the notice of a few Papier maché Fops as you rub dutch sealing wax to draw Paper

If I were inclined to flatter

No I think you are so unlike other women that you ought not to be won as other women are every woman is to be gain'd by time wherefore you ought to be by a sudden impulse. sighs, Devotions, attention weigh with other women— but they are so much your due with all that that no one should ever claim merit from them, and it is even presumption to pay them—and to claim merit from good temper is insolent supposing you have not the Power to reform the worst— time is doubling your discernment attention making you mercenary I [n?] love

so that I would [have] everything the effect of your Beauty and not by my super- fluous Deserts make it a Debt and so lessen the obligation and my Gratitude— in short every woman follows her inclination but you above all things should take me if you don't like me

and you will have the fashionable satisfaction of knowing that we are certainly the worst match in the Kingdom—a match that must be your own work— in which fate could have no hand, and no Foresight could have [corrected?]

A happy Casuist—who veers by others breath gets on to information by tacking between the two sides like a Hoy, not made to go straight before the wind

The more he talks the farther he is off the argument—like a Bowl on a wrong Biass—

You should not be sway'd by common motives—how heroic to marry one for which no human being can guess the Inducement what a glorious unaccount- ableness. all the world will wonder what the Devil you could see in me—and if you doubt the singularity of it I pledge myself to you that I never yet was enslaved by a woman.

no man thought more generall[y] disagreeable.

An irresolute arguer—to whom it is a great misfortune that there are not three sides to a Question—a libertine in Argument conviction like enjoyment palls him and his rakish understanding is soon satiated with Truth—as matrimony more capable of being faithful to a Paradox.—I love Truth as I do my Wife— but Sop[h]istry and Paradoxes are my mistresses—I have a strong Domestic Respect for her, but to the other [give] the Passion due to a mistress—

his Regard for Truth is not lessen'd by his love of Paradox. to be sure not as a man always makes a better Husband for keeping a mistress.—

no if there is no medium but a man most absolutely wedded to truth, I had rather lie and be a Paradox.—why hang it no my moral is not the less to be taken because I now and then embroider a little deal in Figures—if I were wedded to truth I shouldn't love her so well

a harmless Lyar

Love of truth not natural all men [take] a Pleasure in Lying

He merely wanted to be singular and happen'd to find the character of morose- ness unoccupied in the society he lived with.

One who knows that no credit is ever given to his assertions has more right to contradict his words in the suburbs of an old manuscript.—the Suburbs of her head.

She might have escaped in her own cloaths but I suppose she thought it more Romantic to put on her Brother's Regimentals.—

Go and if thou darest outlive this wrong

make me the object of his Deliberate extacys, and methodical Raptures—

I'll go and pity him—directly—

Moore, i. 333, prints part of a passage that is not in the notebook, but is among the Frampton Court MSS. in Yale University Library:

Plate-Glass-manufactory

Mr. Bustle—Lady Clio—

Track him thro' the Day—laborious Idler

What News—do you hear—Cambridge—?

L[ady] C[lio]. What am I reading? I have put you into—is it verse or Prose Have I drawn nothing down lately? is the workbag finished?—I had forgot How accomplish'd I am! put me into the second volume. does it look as if I had been playing on it? has the man been to untune the Harpsichord.—Shall I be ill to Day—? shall I be nervous—your Ladyship was nervous yesterday.— was I? then I'll have a cold—I haven't had a cold this Fortnight—a cold is becoming—ahem—no I'll not have a cough—that's fatiguing—no—no this Bow[1] is very clumsy—psha!—it isn't becoming—here take it [a]way—I'll be quite well—you become sickness—your La'ship always looks vastly well— when you're ill.—leave the book half read—and the Prose half finish'd—you know I love to be caught in the Fact.

breed my own Footmen—only 90 of your select Friends and a whist Party of 100

I have not been able to find four extracts that Moore (i. 330–3) printed from *Affectation*. Possibly they were on pages that have now been ripped out of the book. They read:

He goes the western circuit, to pick up small fees and impudence.

A new wooden leg for Sir Charles Easy.

An ornament which proud peers wear all the year round—chimney-sweepers only on the first of May.

In marriage if you possess any thing very good, it makes you eager to get every thing else good of the same sort.

He certainly has a great deal of fancy and a very good memory; but with a perverse ingenuity he employs these qualities as no other person does—for he employs his fancy in his narratives, and keeps his recollections for his wit—when he makes his jokes you applaud the accuracy of his memory, and 'tis only when he states his facts, that you admire the flights of his imagination.

---

[1] MS. 'Beau'.

'The Wonders of Derbyshire' (8 January 1779)

The *Morning Post*, 28 December 1778, noted: 'The new pantomime entertainment, which has been so long preparing at Drury Lane Theatre, is, we hear, to be called *The Wonders of Derbyshire; or, Harlequin in the Peak*, and is expected in point of scenery, to be the greatest exhibition that was ever produced at a Theatre.' De Loutherbourg was paid to visit the Peak District and make suitable designs for scenery,[1] and when they were exhibited on 8 January 1779, they were thought 'infinitely superior to every thing that has been seen since those of Servandoni', and their 'sublime style' seemed to awe the genius of buffoonery.[2]

The Lord Chamberlain's MS.[3] contains only a few songs and choruses, amounting to fifty-six lines of poor verse, sung by 'Little Fairy', 'Salmandor',[4] Columbine, and the Genii. The entertainment's real attractiveness lay in the music and spectacle.[5]

The only suggestion that Sheridan was responsible for its lines comes from a recent writer,[6] who has observed that no payment for its libretto is recorded in the Drury Lane Theatre accounts. He assumes from that fact that Sheridan was the author. This is possible, but it is also worth saying that the lines were so few and so indifferent as not to deserve payment. The title is not in the 'Programme'.

'Renaud d'Ast'

Sichel thought that the British Museum manuscript bearing this title[7] was an original work by Sheridan,[8] but it can now be proved to be Mrs. Sheridan's adaptation of a popular French opera of the day.

The French libretto (based on Lafontaine) was by Dalayrac to music by J. B. Radet and P. Y. Barré, and the work was very successfully given at the Comédie-Italienne in Paris from 19 July 1787 onwards.[9]

On 6 October [1788?], Mrs. Sheridan wrote to her friend Mrs. Canning to say:

. . . Texier has brought a Translation of a French piece to us, in the style of Richard [Coeur de Lion]—Sheridan thinks it will succeed with a little of our

---

[1] Folger MS. W. b. 282: 15 Nov. 1779, 'Mr. De Loutherbourg for Expences to Derbyshire and Coxheath, £160'. [2] *General Evening Post*, 7–9 Jan. 1779.
[3] Larpent MS. 465. [4] 'The Genius of the Peak'.
[5] See the report in the *London Chronicle*, 9–12 Jan. 1779. A list of scenes is given by S. Rosenfeld and E. Croft-Murray, 'A Checklist of Scene Painters . . .', *Theatre Notebook*, xix (1965), 108–9. Ralph G. Allen gives a full appreciation in '*The Wonders of Derbyshire: a Spectacular Eighteenth Century Travelogue*', *Theatre Survey* (New York, 1961), pp. 54–66.
[6] G. W. Williams, 'A New Source of Evidence for Sheridan's Authorship of *The Camp* and *The Wonders of Derbyshire*', *Studies in Philology* (Chapel Hill), xlvii (1950), 624–7. [7] Add. MS. 25936. [8] Sichel, i. 7 n. 3, 610–11.
[9] A. Loewenberg, *Annals of Opera, 1597–1940* (2nd edn., Geneva, 1955), i. 445.

Assistance, and I have been employ'd in translating the French into English Verse, and adapting the Music to them, wh[ich] I assure you is no easy task, but nobody c[oul]d do it but myself or my Father, and I could not bear that he sh[oul]d be puzzleing his poor Head at this time.[1]

Thomas Linley had suffered a 'paralitick attack in his head', and it was independently reported that Elizabeth Sheridan was 'now working hard at some music they are preparing for Drury Lane to save him the labour as much as possible'.[2] If the French piece were 'Renaud d'Ast', as seems likely, it would be easy to understand why Sheridan did not take it up. Early in the following November, his energies were engrossed by 'the Regency crisis', and when this was over, the opera was no longer so attractive.

There can be no doubt, however, that the British Museum manuscript is in Elizabeth Sheridan's hand. If anyone queries this, he should look at a note in the text, obviously directed to her husband:

(then follows a love scene between Allan and Martha which you must fill up and make entertaining for the performers I cannot—the words of the Duet are the worst of all, but you must alter them, the tune is the beautiful one, that was sung last year at the opera by the   [3] this though so pretty is so odd I assure you it is very difficult to make any words that will go to it)[4]

This is the most interesting passage in the manuscript, since it reveals so clearly the working relationship of Sheridan and his wife.

'Richard Coeur de Lion' (24 October 1786)

Although this appears in the list of plays by Sheridan,[5] I have not been able to find any manuscript or other evidence to confirm the attribution. The French libretto was written by Sédaine[6] but there is some divergence of opinion about the English translator. Kelly says that Burgoyne 'had translated it, and Mrs. Sheridan adapted it to the English stage'.[7] Georgiana, Duchess of Devonshire, declared in an unpublished letter: 'Richard Coeur de Lyon . . . was translated by Mrs. Sheridan and her sisters but this is a secret.'[8]

Sheridan may possibly have had some hand in the main change that was introduced: 'the discovery of Richard's confinement being now given to Matilda in place of Blondell; as well as to increase the interest of the

---

[1] W.T.
[2] *Betsy Sheridan's Journal*, ed. W. LeFanu (1960), pp. 121–3.
[3] Several words have been heavily crossed out.   [4] Add. MS. 25936, f. 6.
[5] See p. 18 above.
[6] To music by Grétry. Thomas Linley adapted it for the English performance.
[7] Kelly, i. 289.   [8] Chatsworth MS. No. 765.

situation, as to avoid the less affecting interposition of the heroine in the latter part of the drama.'[1] There is nothing, however, to prove that he had any hand in it at all.[2]

'A Dramatic Proverb'

This is included in the list of plays by Sheridan, and its description suggests that it had some connection with the Pic-Nic theatre of 1802.[3] Possibly it was of a farcical nature, for *The Times*, 18 March 1802, reported: 'it is said Mr. Sheridan is writing a farce upon the new theatrical entertainments.' I have not been able to find any completed work or even fragment on the subject.

Unidentified Plays

Several pieces revised by Sheridan are mentioned in the following Sotheby's Catalogues:

12–17 May 1851, lot 1079:
    The third and fifth acts of two plays with numerous corrections and alterations in the autograph of R. B. Sheridan.[4]

5 August 1851, lot 60:
    The Third Act of a play, occupying many 4to sheets, *entirely autograph*.

'Prelude on Opening Covent Garden next Season'[5]

This appears to have been presented on 20 September 1775, and is described in the *London Chronicle*, 19–21 September 1775:

In the Prelude, the curtain rising, discovered the different performers of the theatre, comparing notes together on their various successes, cast of parts, droll accidents, etc. etc. which they experienced during their different summer excursions:—*Mattocks* gives an account of the Sailors levelling their great guns on the Liverpool theatre; when *Dunstall humorously* replied 'they would point them much truer at a Frenchman or a Spaniard.'—*Lee Lewis* diverts them with

---

[1] Oulton, i. 154.

[2] It is odd to find in Add. MS. 25915, a claim by James Cobb on Drury Lane Theatre 'For Richard Coeur de Lion sent for from Paris at my expence, and translated at the express desire of the Manager, but which Translation was never produced'.

[3] See *Letters*, ii. 170–4, for Sheridan's opposition to these aristocratic entertainments. 'Dramatic Proverbs' were frequently given at them. Oulton, p. 72, describes these proverbs as being an imitation of the French, 'who are very fond at times of giving some little incident in the support of an old favourite saying'.

[4] Sichel, i. 610, mentions that 'among the Sheridan manuscripts are some scenes of an Italian tragedy quite beyond the scope of the satirist's powers.' It has not come to light.   [5] See p. 18 above.

the manner of their performing Hamlet in a company that he belonged to, when the hero who was to play the principal character had absconded with an innkeeper's daughter; and that when he came forward to give out the play, he added, 'the part of Hamlet to be left out, for that night;'—after a variety of these curious stories, Miss *Barsanti* informs them, that the Managers have totally mistaken her talents, as she is calculated for deep tragedy, and immediately gives a fair specimen of mimicry, both in voice and action, in which the tragical conceits of Miss Y[ounge] are admirably hit off.

One of them now asks his brother if he has seen what they are doing at Drury-lane, telling him 'they have not left a bit of the old covering on, and that even the Old Rose Tavern had put on a masquerade upon the occasion.' The other, in answer, laments the loss of their late dapper manager, 'who,' he said, 'would have forestalled all their fine similies upon this *painting* occasion, etc. and not left his rival a single word to say on his own alterations.'—After this the stage being left to Mr. Hull and Lewes, the latter asks the former about the health of poor Ned Shuter; and Hull shakes his head, and tells him he fears he is in great danger, but hopes that the candor of the town will receive their old favourite, and make allowances for so deserving an actor.

I have not been able to find a manuscript copy of the piece.

Other Prologues and Epilogues

John Britton remarked, Sheridan's 'prologues and epilogues certainly eclipse any similar compositions of contemporary genius. They are sportive, satirical, elegant, and pathetic.'[1] The epilogue to *The Rivals* was particularly admired and, from time to time, Sheridan was asked to write prologues or epilogues to other people's plays. He composed several but, on at least one occasion, quite failed to carry out his promise.[2]

The 'Programme' mentions 'two or three prologues and epilogues' given in 1775. In that year, Sheridan was responsible for the prologues and epilogue to *The Rivals* and the prologue to *St. Patrick's Day*, but if these are not counted, only one piece is known to be his: the epilogue to *Edward and Eleonora*. For 1776–7, the 'Programme' notes 'two or three' again, referring to the epilogue to *Semiramis*, the prologue to *Sir Thomas Overbury*, and to some lines in memory of Henry Woodward. This source is even vaguer for the period 1778–98, and merely records 'several prologues and epilogues'. Only three are known, and one of those is an uncertain attribution: the prologue to *The Miniature Picture*, and epilogues to *The Fatal Falsehood* and to *The Fair Circassian*. *The Sun*, 14 March 1797, reported the possibility of another one: 'Reynolds's new Comedy is to be brought forward at Drury-lane Theatre, in about three weeks. Sheridan has promised an Epilogue, and, no doubt, he will as rigidly keep his word in this respect, as in all others.' The newspaper was politically opposed to Sheridan and was only too willing to score

---

[1] *Sheridan and Kotzebue* (1799), p. 59.   [2] *Letters*, i. 99.

off him, but this time its irony was justified. Reynolds's comedy, *The Will*, was presented at Drury Lane on 19 April 1797, and its epilogue was not by Sheridan. The printed text declared it to be the work of M. P. Andrews; Reynolds himself stated that the basic idea and some of the lines were written by Samuel Rogers.[1]

The 'Programme' does not mention any prologue or epilogue by Sheridan belonging to the period after 1798, and that may be enough to dismiss from serious consideration the claim that the epilogue to *The Land We Live In* was Sheridan's. It depends on a statement in *The Times*, 13 December 1804: 'The Epilogue to Mr. Holt's new Comedy comes from the Pen of Mr. Sheridan.' At the first performance on 29 December, the play was so badly received that Mrs. Jordan did not speak the epilogue. *The Times* defended her in its issue of 31 December: 'Whatever her duty to the public might have been, it was not to be expected that she should hazard her reputation and torture her feelings, for the possible chance of rescuing incapacity or presumption from merited reprehension.' Further evidence will be needed before we can prove that Sheridan wrote the epilogue to this play.[2]

For bibliographical notes on the plays from which the prologues and epilogues have been quoted, see Williams, pp. 214–18, 224, and his article in *The London Mercury*.

Epilogue to Edward and Eleonora:

Mrs. Barry 'hinted a wish' that James Thomson's tragedy, *Edward and Eleonora*, should be altered for performance, so Thomas Hull (the Covent Garden prompter) cut out the 'exceptionable' passages and added some additional dialogue. The play was acted on 18 March 1775 at Covent Garden Theatre, with an epilogue by Sheridan. The copy-text is to be found in the first edition (published by C. Bell, 1775), and it has been collated with the earliest version printed in the newspapers—that in the *Morning Post*, 28 March 1775. It reads:

> Ye wedded Criticks [*To the Pit*], who have mark'd our Tale,
> How say you? does our Plot in *Nature* fail?
> May we not boast that many a *Modern* Wife,
> Would lose her own to save a *Husband's* Life?
> 5 Would gladly die—O monstrous and ill-bred,
> There's not a Husband here but shakes his Head!

[1] *The Life and Times of Frederick Reynolds. Written by Himself* (2nd edn., 1827), ii. 249.

[2] Moore, i. 334–6, quotes fragments from what he believes was an epilogue to be spoken in the character of a woman of fashion and another dealing with female gamesters. The reference to Palmer's mail coaches leads Rhodes, iii. 287, to conjecture that the first verses were written 'within a reasonable time of 1784'. It seems to me possible that these lines were part of the poem on women that Sheridan mentioned in 1778, but may have added to from time to time, without ever publishing.

But you, my Gall'ry Friends [*To the First Gallery*]—Come,
what say you?
    Your Wives are with you—shake their Noddles too!

10   Above there—hey Lads [*To the Second Gallery*]—You'll not
treat us so—
    You side with us?—They grin and grumble *No*!

Yet hold—tho' these plain Folkes traduce their Doxies,
Sure we have *Eleonora's* in the Boxes?

15 Inhuman Beaux!—why that ill-natur'd Sneer?
What then you think there's no such Ideot here?

There are, no Doubt, tho' rare to find I know;
Who could lose Husbands, yet survive the Blow;
Two years a Wife—view *Lesbia*, sobbing, crying,
20 Her Chair is waiting—but my Lord is dying;
Preparing for the worst! she tells her Maid,
To countermand her Points and new Brocade;[1]
'For O! if I should lose the best of *Men*
Heav'n knows when I shall see the *Club* again.
25 So, *Lappet*,[2] should he die while I am out,
You'll send for me at Lady *Basto's*[3] Rout;
The Doctor said he might hold out 'till Three,
But I ha'n't Spirits for the *Coterie*!'

Now change the Scene—place Madam in the Fever,
30 My Lord for Comfort at the Scavoir Vivre;[4]
His Valet enters—Shakes his meagre Head,
'Chapeau—what News?'—'Ah! Sir, me Lady dead.'
'The deuce!—'tis sudden, faith—but four Days sick.—
Well, Seven's the Main—(poor *Kate*)—Eleven's a Nick.'[5]

35   But hence Reflections on a senseless Train,
Who, lost to real Joy, should feel no Pain;
'Mongst *Britain's* Daughters still can *Hymen's* Light
Reveal the Love which charm'd your Hearts to Night,

22 Points] *1st ed.*; point *Morn. Post*   29 Fever] *Morn. Post*; Fevre *1st ed.*

---

[1] Cf. Pope, *The Rape of the Lock*, ii. 107:
       Or stain her honour, or her new brocade.
[2] Cf. p. 334 above.   [3] Basto: the ace of clubs.
[4] A gaming club. Hannah More reports that 'A most magnificent hotel in St. James's
Street was opened last night for the first time, by the name of the "Savoir Vivre"; none
but people of the very first rank were there, so you may conclude the diversion was
cards; and in one night, the very first time the rooms were ever used, the enormous sum
of sixty thousand pounds was lost! Heaven reform us.'
[5] Cf. p. 336, n. 3.

Shew beauteous Martyrs—who would each prefer,
40 To die for *him*, who long has liv'd for *her*;
Domestic Heroines—who with fondest Care
Outsmile a Husband's Griefs—or claim a Share;
Search where the rankling Evils most abound,
And heal with Cherub-Lip the poison'd Wound.

45 Nay such bright Virtues in a royal Mind
Were not alone to *Edward*'s Days confin'd,
Still, still they beam around *Britannia's* Throne
And grace an *Eleonora* of our own.

Epilogue to Semiramis:

George Edward Ayscough's adaptation of Voltaire's *Semiramis* (1748) was given its first performance at Drury Lane Theatre on 14 December 1776, with Mrs. Yates in the title role. Ayscough himself wrote the prologue, and Sheridan, the epilogue. The *Whitehall Evening-Post* commented:

'The Epilogue was remarkable for its beauty. It began with the same idea which John Hume has with great simplicity and force held out in the epilogue to *Douglas*, but pursued it with a strain of chaste imagery and fine poetry which we do not remember to have heard equalled but in an Epilogue by the same writer. We mean Sheridan's Epilogue to the Comedy of *The Rivals*.'[1]

My copy-text is to be found in the printed edition (1776) of Ayscough's tragedy, and it has been collated with an eighteenth-century manuscript version in the Huntington Library (MO 4974). The latter reverses the order of lines 16–17.

Dishevell'd still, like *Asia*'s bleeding Queen,
Shall I with jests deride the tragic scene?
No, beauteous mourners!—from whose downcast eyes—
The Muse has drawn her noblest sacrifice!
5 Whose gentle bosoms, *Pity*'s altars—bear
The chrystal incense of each falling tear!
—There lives the Poet's praise!—no critic art
Can match the comment of a feeling heart!

When gen'ral plaudits speak the Fable o'er—
10 Which mute attention had approv'd before,
Tho' ruder spirits love th'accustom'd jest
Which chases sorrow from the vulgar breast,
Still hearts refin'd their sadden'd tint retain—
—The sigh is pleasure! and the jest is pain!—

42 Outsmile] *1st ed.*; Outsmiles *Morn. Post*

---

[1] Quoted in Rhodes, iii. 272.

—Scarce have they smiles to honour Grace or Wit,
—Tho' *Roscius* spoke the verse himself had writ!
Thus thro' the time when vernal fruits receive
The grateful show'rs that hang on *April*'s eve:
Tho' ev'ry coarser stem of forest birth
20 Throws with the morning-beam its dews to earth,
—Ne'er does the gentle *Rose* revive so soon—
But bath'd in Nature's tears, it droops till noon.

O could the Muse one simple moral teach,
From scenes like these, which all who heard might reach!
25 —Thou child of Sympathy—whoe'er thou art,
Who with *Assyria*'s Queen hast wept thy part—
Go search, where keener woes demand relief,
Go—while thy heart yet beats with fancy'd grief;
Thy lip still conscious of the recent sigh,
30 The graceful tear still ling'ring in thy eye—
Go—and on real misery bestow
The blest effusion of fictitious woe!—

So shall our Muse, supreme of all the Nine,
Deserve, indeed, the title of—*Divine!*—
35 Virtue shall own her favour'd from above,
And *Pity*—greet her—with a sister's love.

Prologue to Sir Thomas Overbury:

Richard Savage's tragedy, *Sir Thomas Overbury*, was altered by William Woodfall for performance at Covent Garden Theatre on 1 February 1777. The prologue was by Sheridan.

My copy-text has been found in the first edition of Woodfall's alteration, which was published on 13 February. It has also been collated with the version published in the *St. James's Chronicle* of the same day.

Too long the Muse—attached to regal show,
Denies the scene to tales of humbler woe;
Such as were wont—while yet they charm'd the ear,
To steal the plaudit of a silent tear,
When Otway gave domestic grief its part,
And Rowe's familiar sorrows touch'd the heart.

A scepter'd traitor, lash'd by vengeful fate,
A bleeding hero, or a falling state,
Are themes, (tho' nobly worth the classic song)
Which feebly claim your sighs, nor claim them long;
Too great for pity, they inspire respect,
Their deeds astonish, rather than affect;
Proving how rare the heart, that woe can move,
Which reason tells us, we can never prove.

Other the scene, where sadly stands confest,
The private pang that rends the Sufferer's breast;
Where Sorrow sits upon a Parent's brow,
When Fortune mocks the youthful Lover's vow—
All feel the tale—for who so mean but knows
What Fathers' sorrows are!—what Lovers' woes!

On kindred ground, our Bard his fabric built,
And plac'd a mirrour there for private guilt;
Where—fatal union!—will appear combin'd
An Angel's form—and an abandon'd mind?
Honour attempting Passion to reprove,
And Friendship struggling with unhallow'd Love!

Yet view not, Critics, with severe regard
The orphan-offspring of an orphan bard,
Doom'd, while he wrote, unpitied to sustain
More real mis'ries than his pen could feign!
—Ill-fated Savage! at whose birth was giv'n
No parent but the Muse, no friend but heav'n!
Whose youth no brother knew, with social care
To soothe his suff'rings, or demand to share;
No wedded partner of his mortal woe,
To win his smile at all that fate could do;
While at his death, nor friend's nor mother's tear,
Fell on the track of his deserted bier?

So pleads the tale,[1] that gives to future times
The Son's misfortunes, and the Parent's crimes;
There shall his fame (if own'd to-night) survive
Fix'd by the hand, that bids our language live!

[*Prologue to the Memory of Henry Woodward*]

Woodward, a fine Harlequin and the first Jack Absolute, died on 17 April 1777. Six days later, *Caractacus* and *The Royal Chace; or, Harlequin Skeleton* were given at Covent Garden Theatre for the benefit of Charles Lee Lewes, who, before the harlequinade, spoke a prologue in his memory. Part of it was quoted in the *Morning Chronicle*, 22 May 1777:

But hence with tragic strains, unless to mourn,
That LUN[2] and MARPLOT[3] here shall ne'er return;
The Comic Muse, who still with anxious pride
The claim of motley Pantomime denied,
Now humbly hangs o'er Woodward's recent bier,
See the fantastic mimic mourner there,
Yet deigns to join in grief, and sheds a kindred tear.

[1] The printer's own note reads: 'Life of Richard Savage by Dr. Samuel Johnson.'
[2] John Rich, the greatest harlequin of the eighteenth century.
[3] The title role, played by Woodward, in Mrs. Centlivre's *The Busy Body*.

The newspaper described them merely as 'Additional lines by Mr. Sheridan, spoken by Mr. Lee Lewes, on his Benefit Night, in the Character of Harlequin.' Boaden, in his *Life of Mrs. Siddons* (1827), i. 107, is responsible for the term 'Prologue'.

Epilogue to The Fatal Falsehood:

Hannah More's tragedy, *The Fatal Falsehood*, was acted at Covent Garden Theatre on 6 May 1779. The *Morning Chronicle*, 7 May, declared that the epilogue 'was written by Mr. Sheridan, and had great merit, though it was rather a comic poem than an Epilogue. It was spoken in the character of a trading author, and it was evident that the actor dressed as the Editor of one of the Reviews. . . . Lee Lewes spoke the Epilogue with great humour and propriety.'

My copy-text is taken from the first edition of the play, that was advertised for publication on 1 December 1779. It, too, recorded that the epilogue was written by Sheridan. Other printings are to be found in the *Morning Chronicle*, 5 January 1780, and *Felix Farley's Bristol Journal*, 8 January 1780, but they are obviously lifted from the first edition.

> Unhand me, gentlemen, by Heaven, I say,
> I'll make a ghost of him who bars my way [*Behind the scenes.*]
> Forth let me come—A Poetaster true,
> As lean as Envy, and as baneful too;
> On the dull audience let me vent my rage,
> Or drive these *female* scribblers from the stage:
> For scene or history, we've none but these,
> The law of Liberty and Wit they seize
> In Tragic—Comic—Pastoral—they dare to please.[1]
> Each puny Bard must surely burst with spite,
> To find that women with such fame can write:
> But, oh, your partial favour is the cause,
> Who feed their follies with such full applause;
> Yet still our tribe shall seek to blast their fame,
> And ridicule each fair pretender's aim;
> Where the dull duties of domestic life,
> Wage with the Muse's toils eternal strife.
>
>   What motley cares *Corilla*'s mind perplex,
> While maids and metaphors conspire to vex!

---

[1] The reference to *Hamlet* in the first two lines and in this one, led Rhodes, iii. 275, to see a play on Polonius's 'for the law of writ, and the liberty, these are the only men.

In studious deshabille behold her sit,
A letter'd gossip, and a housewife wit;
At once invoking, though for different views,
Her gods, her cook, her millener and muse,
Round her strew'd room, a frippery chaos lies,
A chequer'd wreck of *notable* and *wise*;
Bills, Books, Caps, Couplets, Combs, a vary'd mass,
Oppress the toilet, and obscure the glass;
Unfinish'd here an Epigram is laid,
And there, a mantua-maker's Bill unpaid;
Her new-born Plays fore taste the town's applause,
There, dormant Patterns pine for future gauze:
A moral Essay now is all her care,
A Satire next, and then a Bill of Fare:
A Scene she now projects, and now a Dish,
Here's Act the First—and here—remove with Fish.
Now while this Eye in a fine phrenzy rolls,
That, soberly casts up a Bill for Coals;
Black Pins and Daggers in one leaf she sticks,
And Tears and Thread, and Bells and Thimbles mix.

Sappho, 'tis true, long vers'd in epic song,
For years esteem'd all household studies wrong:
When dire mishap, though neither shame nor sin,
Sappho herself, and not her Muse, lies in.
The virgin Nine in terror fly the bower,
And matron Juno claims despotic power;
Soon Gothic hags the classic pile o'erturn,
A caudle-cup supplants the sacred urn;
Nor books, nor implements escape their rage
They spike the ink-stand, and they rend the page;
Poems and Plays one barbarous fate partake,   ⎫
Ovid and Plautus suffer at the stake,   ⎬
And Aristotle's only sav'd—to wrap plumb cake.   ⎭

Yet, shall a *woman* tempt the Tragic Scene!
And dare—but hold—I must repress my spleen;
I see your hearts are pledg'd to her applause,
While Shakespear's spirit seems to aid her cause;
Well pleas'd to aid—since o'er his sacred bier   ⎫
A female hand did ample trophies rear,   ⎬
And gave the greenest laurel that is worshipp'd there. ⎭

Epilogue to The Fair Circassian:

Samuel Jackson Pratt's tragedy, *The Fair Circassian*, was performed at Drury Lane Theatre on 27 November 1781, and was published on the following 12 December. The epilogue was anonymous, but M. J. Young (in *Memoirs of Mrs. Crouch*, 1806, i. 125) stated that it was 'written by the Hon. Mr. Fitzpatrick'.

In 1924 Iolo A. Williams[1] argued that Sheridan was the probable author. The weight of his case rested on a sentence in an undated letter from Pratt to Sheridan, reading, 'The press stands still for the Epilogue of which I have got a copy and wait only to know whether I may join the name of the most excellent author, or only say in my printed Tragedy by a friend.' William also noted that though Pratt did not particularize Sheridan's assistance in his preface to the play, he certainly acknowledged it in general terms.

Now it is possible that Sheridan merely acted as an intermediary for Pratt with Fitzpatrick, but it seems more likely that the prologue was his. Sheridan had just been elected to parliament, and the opening lines recapture something of the novelty of the experience. Their pointed wit is in his manner.

The copy-text is taken from the first edition of the tragedy, and has been collated with a manuscript of the prologue in the hand of an amanuensis, now Huntington Library MS. LA 576. I refer to them in the notes on variants as, respectively, '1781' and 'LA'.

> Of late at Westminster,[2] in order due,
> A gracious speech first made, debates ensue.
> Ere then, in this *full house*, our author's fate
> Becomes the subject of your warm debate—
> 5   Ere yet you opposition-criticks rise
> To move for censure, and refuse supplies;
> Or partial friends pour down corrupt applause,
> By *orders* pension'd in the author's cause,
> From either party—none will sure impeach
> 10   My sovereign title to pronounce the speech.
>
>   Thro' me the muse her *loyal subjects* greets—
> Tho' I speak standing, and you keep your seats—
> Pleas'd that so full a house attends the summons—
> Pit—Box—and Gallery—Peers and faithful Commons—
> 15   With deep concern she bids me here relate
> What dangers threaten the dramatic state—
> What hosts of foes her tottering realms invade,
> By fashion muster'd, and by folly paid:
> While *Taste*, her old ally, unmov'd we see,
> 20   And *Spleen* preserves an *arm'd neutrality*.
> See first come on—all arm'd in whale-bone hoops—

1 Of late] *1781*; This day *LA*   3 and 5 Ere] *1781*; E'er *LA*   13 the] *1781*; her *LA*

---

[1] 'Bibliographical Notes and News', *The London Mercury*, x (1924), 412–16.
[2] The first edition contains the note, 'The first night's representation happend on the opening of parliament.'

The tuneful leaders of Italian troops.
Long have they wag'd—too oft with conquest crown'd—
The doubtful conflict between sense and sound.
Allied with these—in hostile bands advance   25
The light-heel'd legions of invading France.

    To point her thunders on our British coast,
Year after year, has been vain Gallia's boast.
Their troops embark—the bold attempt is plann'd—
Their *heroes threaten*—and their *dancers* land.—   30
These only put their threats in execution,
And lay all London under contribution
Immortal chiefs! who on one leg can do
What yet no warrior has atchiev'd on two.
Like Rome's proud victor, in their fierce attack,   35
They come, they see, they conquer, and—go back,
And, modern Jasons, as of old in Greece,
Sail home triumphant with the golden fleece.

    Before such dangers shall we prostrate fall?
Or, like true Britons, boldly brave them all?   40
If fairly led, we'll bid their host defiance,
Dissolv'd a late *unnatural alliance*;
Our leader too shall now assistance lend,
Not promise succours, and delay to send:
But chiefly *hers*—our hopes and courage lie   45
In *you*, our truest friend and best ally—
Support our Bard to-night, and on his part
Receive the *tribute* of a grateful heart—
Thro' me receive, and here again I'll meet ye,
Act as ambassadress, and sign the treaty.   50

23 they] *1781*; the *LA*   30 dancers] *1781*; Dances *LA*   34 What] *1781*;
Who *LA*   39-50 omitted in *LA*.

POSTSCRIPT

SOME material of interest has come to hand while the present work was in the press. Since it amplifies or corrects earlier statements, I give it in the following pages in some detail.

AFFECTATION

Mrs. Christina Colvin's *Maria Edgeworth: Letters from England, 1813–1844* (Oxford, 1971), p. 92, contains an allusion to this play.

Lewis O'Beirne had mentioned *Affectation* to Maria Edgeworth, and she took an opportunity, in 1818, of asking Thomas Grenville what he knew about it. He replied: 'Yes—he [Sheridan] did half write it. I met him one day when he was in great pecuniary embarrassments. He shook my hand joyfully. "It is all settled and I have made a provision for Tom—£200 a year." "Indeed! How?" "An annuity from the money I am to get from the new comedy I am finishing!"' Maria Edgeworth adds, 'It never went further.'

BETTER LATE THAN NEVER

Early in his career, Frederick Reynolds collaborated with M. P. Andrews in writing a five-act comedy called *Better Late than Never*. 'Our agreement was, that I should receive one half of the profits, and Andrews have all the fame.'[1] Edward Topham, too, seems to have made some contributions.

When the comedy was acted at Drury Lane Theatre on 17 November 1790, a dull scene in the middle of it was made even more tiresome by Dodd's performance, but Mrs. Jordan's spirited playing in the last scene brought it some success. Reynolds describes,[2] perhaps too vividly, what happened immediately afterwards, and reveals the casual nature of its authorship:

. . . Andrews was much mortified; indeed, so was I, and we were still in the box, staring at each other, not in the best of all possible humours, when the Duke of Leeds (who wrote our prologue,) Sheridan and Topham entered together, all speaking at once, and all proposing alterations. Topham, however, took the lead, and in a friendly but decided tone exclaimed—

'Omit, in the first place, that deadly, dull, stupid comet scene.'

'Which scene, my dear Sir?' cried Andrews with particular irritation.

'Why,' continued Topham, 'the scene where Dodd fatigues the audience with his nonsense about telescopes, and the Zodiac and. . . .'

---

[1] *The Life and Times of Frederick Reynolds. Written by Himself* (1827), ii. 79.
[2] Ibid., 81–2.

'Stop, my dear Sir, stop,' interrupted Andrews, bursting with spleen, 'you are tiresome, Sir. You wrote that whole scene yourself, Sir, at Dartford. Did he not, my dear Reynolds?'

I replied in the affirmative.

'Well!'—exclaimed Topham, for an instant somewhat posed; but he immediately added, 'Probably in the multiplicity of my affairs, and engagements, I may forget many things; but if, as you say, I did write that scene, Reynolds, or you, afterwards marred it, no doubt—In fact—I have always thought Dodd a wretched first night actor; but,' he added, twirling his whiskers, 'he will be better tomorrow; so, try the scene again!'

The Duke of Leeds, and Sheridan, then took their turns, and gave their advice; and the result was, that the comedy having undergone many of the proposed alterations and curtailments, was received on its second appearance, with considerable approbation.

Sheridan's part in this appears to be small, but once again he is to be seen as a play-doctor, eager to cut and correct to secure a theatrical success.

THE CAMP

The Clare Sheridan MSS., sold at Sotheby's on 29 November 1971, included as lot 209 part of a prompt-copy of *The Camp*, consisting of twenty-one pages. It ends in the middle of the second scene of the first act, and also omits the text of two songs that should appear in the opening portion of the entertainment: 'Now coaxing, caressing', and 'Great Caesar'. Apart from seven words (two of them corrections in Sheridan's hand), the text is the same as that printed above on pages 725 to 734 (line 21). The manuscript also contains part of the cast list for the play in Sheridan's hand (one of the spellings being 'Bleuard'), and a reminder by Sheridan to himself of 'Bloodspill' in connection with the King of Prussia's eye. This note indicates that the manuscript is the one mentioned by Sichel,[1] though he does not say that it was incomplete when he examined it. I believe it to be a fair copy in the hand of Richard Tickell, but find nothing in it to help us to make a firm decision about the original author. Richard Brinsley Sheridan of Frampton inserted an opinion on the manuscript to the effect that the entertainment was 'the production of Mr. Tickell', but his source is clearly stated to be Moore's biography.

CAPE ST. VINCENT

To celebrate the naval victory of Sir John Jervis off Cape St. Vincent on 14 February 1797, Drury Lane Theatre gave a musical entertainment on 6 March. The performance was described in identical terms by *The Sun* and *The True Briton* of 7 March: 'A Musical Piece in one act, called *Cape St. Vincent*, altered from the Glorious First of June, and adapted

[1] See p. 709 above.

to the late signal Victory over the Spaniards, closed the entertainments of the evening. The loyal sentiments and sea-songs were well received, as was also a representation of the Action between the British and Spanish Fleets. The House was very crouded.'

The piece was not published, nor was a copy submitted to the Lord Chamberlain for licensing. It seems certain that it was made up of some material taken from *The Glorious First of June*, with topical additions. It is difficult to discover what share Sheridan had in the adaptation, but he was fond of making a figure in naval matters and may have made some contribution.

The songs were available in a brochure entitled, 'Songs, Duetts, Chorusses, &c., in an OCCASIONAL ENTERTAINMENT, call'd CAPE ST. VINCENT; or British Valour Triumphant, Altered from the Dramatical performance performed in 1794. And Acted by Their Majesties Servants at the Theatre Royal, Drury Lane. C. Lowndes, 1797.'[1]

A CHRISTMAS TALE

Willoughby Lacy, one of the proprietors of Drury Lane Theatre, thought of selling his moiety in the autumn of 1776 to Langford and Thompson, but Garrick's solicitor, Albany Wallis, warned him that first refusal should be given to his fellow-proprietors, Sheridan, Linley and Ford.[2] Disagreement grew warm and William Hopkins, the prompter, noted in his diary for 10 October: 'This Morning at Rehearsal Lacy came and told Sheridan that he could not be off from his Agreement with Mr. Langford and Captain Thomson. Sheridan told him, if he did not agree, that he would withdraw himself from the Management of the Theatre—accordingly at eight this Evening he sent me with a Letter to Lacy confirming what he told him, and ordered me to receive my orders from Mr L—— and that he withdrew the Christmas Tale, as he had altered, for a Farce, it was his Property. . . .'[3]

The disagreement was patched up, and Sheridan's adaptation of the entertainment by Garrick was presented in three acts at Drury Lane on 18 October 1776. Hopkins's diary again provides a useful source of comment: it 'was received with very great Applause—it is too long, and must be shortened.'[4]

A comparison of Garrick's version of 1774[5] with Sheridan's adaptation

---

[1] Pickering and Chatto's *The Book-Lover's Leaflet*, no. 202, item 11276.

[2] See *Letters*, i. 104–8.

[3] Quoted from the Folger MS. in *The London Stage, 1660–1800, Part 5 : 1776–1800* (ed. C. B. Hogan, Carbondale, Ill., 1968), p. 25. [4] Ibid., p. 28.

[5] A NEW / DRAMATIC ENTERTAINMENT, / CALLED / A Christmas Tale. / IN FIVE PARTS. / AS IT IS PERFORMED AT THE / THEATRE-ROYAL / IN DRURY-LANE. / Embellished with an Etching, by Mr. *Loutherbourg*. / [Printer's ornament] / LONDON: / Printed for T. BECKET, in the Strand. / MDCCLXXIV. / [Price One Shilling and Six-pence.]

in 1776,[1] seems to me to indicate Sheridan's intentions. Many lines in the 1774 edition are omitted in the 1776 version, because Sheridan wanted to cut it down into an afterpiece.[2] Occasionally he provides linking passages between the cuts, or amplifies a sentiment. Sometimes omissions are made to achieve a greater propriety of tone. Sheridan leaves out the line, 'If I had not so much tenderness in my composition, I would play the devil among those petticoats,' and the flippant remark, 'I thought to make away with myself, and quite forgot it.'[3] He also deletes eight songs or choruses, and makes some of the jocose dialogue more muscular.

THE CRITIC ♦

Another presentation copy is mentioned in Maggs's *Mercurius Britannicus*, no. 37 (1937), item 255. A first edition of *The Critic* (without half-title) is described there as 'A very interesting Association copy, having been presented by Sheridan to Anna Seward, the "Swan of Litchfield." On the fly-leaf Sheridan has written "From the Author," and the recipient had added "To Anna Seward." '

'A GERMAN PLAY'

The *Morning Post*, 3 January 1800, reported that 'Mr. Sheridan is at present amusing himself adapting a play from the German to the English stage.'

I have not been able to discover which play this was. In view of the astonishing success of his adaptation of Kotzebue's work in *Pizarro*, I am inclined to believe that Sheridan was busy with another play by the same author. Hoare's adaptation of the comedy, *Armuth und Edelsinn*, had been performed at the Haymarket on 30 August 1799 as *Sighs; or, The Daughter*. Possibly Sheridan thought of challenging it by improving M. Geisweiler's[4] translation, called *Poverty and Nobleness of Mind*. In the same year both Anne Plumptre and Benjamin Thompson published translations of Kotzebue's *La Peyrouse*, and it is not impossible that Sheridan was interested in one of them. At the moment, however, there are not any facts available to connect him with them. Nor is there anything to prove that he had a hand in Thomas Dibdin's *Of Age To-morrow*, adapted from Kotzebue's *Der Wildfang* and presented at Drury Lane Theatre on 1 February 1800, with music by Kelly.

---

[1] A / DRAMATIC ENTERTAINMENT, / CALLED / A Christmas Tale. / IN THREE ACTS. / AS PERFORMED AT THE / THEATRE-ROYAL / IN DRURY-LANE / [Double rule] / LONDON: / Printed for T. BECKET, the Corner of the Adelphi, / in the Strand. / MDCCLXXVI.

[2] The following pages in the 1774 edition are heavily cut: 16–17, 19, 22, 23, 30, 31, 34, 36, 38, 39, 41, 42, 44, 46, 50–2, 60, 62, 66, 69–71, 73–6.

[3] pp. 2–4.

[4] Cf. p. 645 above.

THE GLORIOUS FIRST OF JUNE

The Clare Sheridan MSS., sold at Sotheby's on 29 November 1971, included in lot 199 an item docketed by Thomas Moore, 'A Sketch for a Piece which seems to have been intended as a Sequel to No Song no Supper, and probably meant as an occasional allusion to the War.'

It is an amplification in four and a half folios of the slightly earlier outline quoted above.[1] Most of it provides a scenario (without dialogue) for the first scene, and the remainder of the entertainment is summarised even more briefly than in the first outline. The whole of it is in Sheridan's hand.

LOVE FOR LOVE

The *Morning Chronicle*, 11 May 1775, printed a letter from 'No Flatterer', which described *Love for Love* as 'a play, one act of which contains more real wit, than can be found in all the acts of all the comedies which have been produced for ten seasons past. What a pity it is that Mr. Colman, or some other able writer, does not take the trouble to clear Congreve's ore from his dross'. I am unable to tell whether Sheridan wrote this letter or not, or even read it, but he certainly set himself the task of revising the play very early in his management at Drury Lane Theatre. He presented it there on 29 November 1776, and J. P. Kemble afterwards noted on a playbill of the performance, 'Love for Love was revived with Alterations by R. B. Sheridan Esqre.'[2]

The nature of the changes[3] that Sheridan made may be seen in a notice of a provincial performance given some years later. The *Morning Chronicle*, 15 November 1782, printed an extract of a letter from Bath, dated 11 November and reading: 'Our Company of performers, who are now come here for the season, are certainly taken altogether the best we ever had, nor is there any performance that does them more reputation than that of Congreve's Love for Love, which by Mr. Sheridan's judicious alteration, still retains its sterling wit and humour, without the alloy of its indecency.'

Possibly Sheridan did not cut the text very much for he complained, many years later, that *Love for Love* 'had been so much altered and modified for the more delicate ears of modern audiences that it was quite spoiled'.[4]

---

[1] pp. 753–4.

[2] See the uncatalogued volume of bills, lettered 'Drury Lane, 1776–77', f. 46ᵛ, in the Huntington Library.

[3] Probably they were on the same lines as J. P. Kemble's alterations of the edition of 1710: 'whoremaster' is deleted; 'pox' becomes 'plague'; double entendre is toned down, and some rather wordy lines are cut out. Kemble's copy is now Covent Garden prompt book, vol. 3, at the Newberry Library.

[4] Kelly, ii. 310, and see p. 556 above.

THE OLD BATCHELOR

The *Morning Post*, 24 August 1776, noted that 'the new managers of Drury Lane Theatre have got several old English comedies altered, that they intend to get up, the ensuing season, which are so cast, as to afford entertaining characters to all the capital performers'.

Sheridan's knowledge of *The Old Batchelor* is evident in some allusions to be found in *The Rivals*,[1] so it is not at all unexpected to find Congreve's comedy presented by him at Drury Lane Theatre after an absence of many years. It was given on 19 November 1776, and William Hopkins noted in his diary, 'This Play is revived with Alterations (by R. B. Sheridan Esq). . . .'[2]

Possibly the corrected text is the one found in the edition printed by W. Lowndes and others in 1788, as 'Marked with the Variations in the Manager's Book at the Theatre Royal in Drury Lane.' When this version is collated with the one printed by Peter Buck in 1693, a few changes for the sake of delicacy may be observed. 'Pox!' (p. 7, l. 39) becomes 'Pshaw!', and 'O Pox!' (44, 8), 'O ay'. Several phrases are completely omitted: 'For she only stalks under him to take aim at her husband' (2, 30); 'my Members' (9, 7); 'as a Clap is to the Pox' (22, 41); 'Ah! I wish he has lain upon no-bodies stomach but his own' (41, 27). The texts, in general, are not very different, but the 1788 version also gives in inverted commas passages that were deleted—probably for other reasons—in the stage performance.

RICHARD COEUR DE LION

Sichel thought Sheridan contributed both ideas and songs to this production.[3] Some of the ideas are to be seen in a description of the differences between this version and the French original: 'Richard is not allowed to sing more than a couplet; and the Queen, who is here called Matilda, instead of Margaret, performs the part allotted to Blondel, appearing in the disguise of a blind minstrel, and using the same stratagem to entrap the Governor. It must be confessed, that these variations are the most judicious improvements that could be imagined in this opera; the character of a warbler being rather a disgrace to the royal dignity, and the sentiments of love sympathizing more with our feelings, than those of friendship. The part of Blondel is preserved; but he comes at the end of the first act, in the habit of a pilgrim just arrived from Palestine.'[4]

[1] See pp. 79, 84, 116, 142, above.
[2] Quoted in *The London Stage, 1660–1800: Part 5: 1776–1800* (ed. C. B. Hogan), p. 37, from the Folger MS. J. P. Kemble's note, repeating this, is to be found in 'Drury Lane Playbills, 1776–7', f. 37ᵛ, in the Huntington Library.
[3] I. 34.
[4] The *London Chronicle*, 24–26 Oct. 1786.

For Sheridan's other contribution to the piece, we have to turn to some letters written by Mary Tickell to him and, more especially, to her sister Elizabeth. The Sheridans were on a visit to Chatsworth, and Mary sent them full news of what went on at Drury Lane. She remarked on 18 October 1786, 'by the bye having seen some of the *poetical* altera- tion in the prompt Copy w[hi]ch T[ickell] has had written out I must own with all humility I think some of them infinitely for the *worse*, Oh Law Sir! I beg ee pardon but in good truth I do.—'[1] I assume that Sheridan was the author of the '*poetical* alteration', though what was altered is not clear. The most popular songs in the Drury Lane version were 'O Richard! O my love!' and 'The God of Love a bandeau wears', and the latter was, as Rhodes says, the neater.[2] Both were simple adapta- tions of the French lyrics, 'O Richard! ô mon Roi' and 'Un bandeau couvre les yeux': there is no particular reason why they should be attributed to Sheridan.

A little earlier, Mary Tickell had mentioned that she and her husband were 'jumbling our Brains together all the Morning to make out two Verses for Decamp—as when we arriv'd yesterday to dinner—there was my Father [Thomas Linley] in a mighty fuss for Words to a little french song w[hi]ch it seems they have all chose in preference to the Dance and he said it would be in vain to wait for S[heridan]s Words—however make him send them at all Events, as nothing will be easier than put[t]ing one song for another when he is ready.'[3] Miss Decamp, as Julie, sang 'Let me treat you to comply,'[4] but whether this was by Sheridan or the Tickells remains a problem.

From Mary Tickell's other letters of the period, it is obvious that Sheridan had earlier superintended the production, chosen the scenery and directed the players' movements.[5] His opinions were still required, as may be noted in a letter by Mary of 23 October 1786: 'I think there might be some parings in the Dialogue too, here and there, for example, the Joke of the Rabbit in Bannister's mouth I'm afraid won't have much effect and it w[oul]d shorten the Scene to cut it out but T[ickell] is afraid of interfering, unless he c[oul]d have S[heridan]s Opinion.'[6] When the play was eventually presented, she wrote to say 'you may rest assured that Richard will be, and is, the most popular Afterpiece we have had since the Camp.'[7] The manager, then, seems to have had a considerable hand in the production, if not in the actual writing.

[1] Folger MS. Y. d. 35, f. 274.
[2] III. 325; and cf. p. 818 above.
[3] Folger MS. Y. d. 35, f. 266.
[4] *The Songs, Duets, Trios and Chorusses of the Historical Romance of Richard Coeur de Lion as performed at the Theatre Royal in Drury Lane* . . . (Thompson, n.d.), pp. 44–5.
[5] Folger MS. Y. d. 35, ff. 250, 268, 274, 276, 278.
[6] Folger MS. Y. d. 35, f. 278.
[7] Folger MS. Y. d. 35, f. 288.

It may be worth adding that no alterations or additions that can be seen to be Sheridan's are found in the copy submitted to the Lord Chamberlain for licensing, now Huntington Library MS. LA 746.

THE SCHOOL FOR SCANDAL

Clare Sheridan MSS.

Lot 204 in the Sotheby sale of 29 November 1971 was described as 'a collection of contemporary prompt copies of different acts of *The School for Scandal*, the manuscript of Act I containing Autograph corrections and annotations to the text by Sheridan including the alteration of two names in the Dramatis Personae (e.g. Shargl to the final form of Trip) with further autograph corrections (less extensive) by Sheridan to Acts II, III and IV *c.* 260 *pages, sewn or unbound, some pages frayed and soiled 4to.*' There appear to be three different and incomplete sets of manuscripts in this collection. One of them was described by Rae[1] long ago, as having been found 'among a mass of tattered and begrimed papers,' and he printed some of the variants.[2] I shall call it the 'Spunge MS.' since Trip appears by that name in the list of characters. In another manuscript Trip is called 'Shargl' and Snake, 'Tricke'. I propose to describe both texts in greater detail on p. 850 below. The third manuscript is dated '1778' and consists of sixty-four leaves. It is a fair copy in the hand of a scribe, and such corrections as it contains bring it into conformity with other texts.

Flack-Fawcett MS.

I have mentioned above[3] that a manuscript of *The School for Scandal*, bound by Flack and annotated by Fawcett, was once in existence. I have now located it in the Huntington Library.[4] Since the paper of the last lines of the play is watermarked '1811' and M. Flack's bill to Fawcett is dated 4 July 1815, we may comfortably assume that the manuscript was written out at some date between 1811 and 1815. The title-page records that it was 'Copied from the Prompter's Book of the Theatre Royal Drury Lane', and the verso contains the lines, 'The Prompter's Book was *preserved* from the late fire in Drury Lane,—by being out of the House.' A cast list of a Drury Lane production is also written in and proves to be that of a performance on 26 February 1787.[5] This may

[1] *Sheridan*, i. 332–5.
[2] See p. 341 above, and pp. 360, 361, 364, 368, for variants.
[3] p. 349.   [4] HM 2546.
[5] See *The London Stage, 1660–1800 : Part 5 : 1776–1800* (ed. Hogan), p. 955. The manuscript gives details of two minor roles not noted by Dr. Hogan: 'Servant to Joseph', Benson, and 'Servant to Lady Sneerwell', Chaplin. No one is named for the part of Sir Toby.

suggest that the copy was made from a manuscript transcribed in 1787, ten years after the original production.

As we might expect, the text of the Flack-Fawcett MS. is similar to that in the Scott MS., originally owned by Fawcett.[1] They agree in a large number of unfamiliar readings and in more elaborate stage directions. Among the latter are the following: I. ii opens at 'Lady Sneerwell's House' with 'Pembroke Table, and Tea-things'; and a little later an instruction reads, 'Card Table—Six striped Chairs before the Scene'. At the beginning of III. ii, we find 'At Charles's House—Drop Chamber'. The 'Picture Room' at Charles's house (IV. i) is furnished partly by the note: 'Settee on. Pedigree hung up.' The setting of the Screen scene (IV. iii) is briefly described: 'Screen at upper Wing. Pembroke Table—Books on it. Two Chairs before the Screen—and one behind it.'

The Flack-Fawcett MS. also bears some resemblance to the Buckinghamshire MS. Its mixed origin is suggested too in the fact that, like the Scott and Georgetown Crewe MSS., it reads 'Novel';[2] and like the Scott MS. and the pirated first edition, indicates that Moses is a Jew when 'than that' is rendered, 'as dat'.[3]

The manuscript runs to 185 pages, but does not include the prologue or epilogue. It contains nothing in Sheridan's hand.

The Lilly MS.

This is a quarto manuscript, now in the Lilly Library of the University of Indiana, and it contains the armorial bookplate of George Chetwynd. The title page bears the impressed stamp of a crest and 'Grendon Hall 1850'. I have already mentioned[4] that this house belonged to Sir George Chetwynd and that he owned the manuscript of *The School for Scandal* that was sent to an ancestor of his for licensing. How he obtained the second copy is not clear, but he may well have bought it out of sheer interest in the subject. Unfortunately the Lilly MS. is of much less importance than the one sent to the Lord Chamberlain's office.[5]

It contains a note reading, 'The Corrections etc. are made evidently by Sheridan himself,' but this is inaccurate, for no trace of the dramatist's hand is to be seen and the text itself is very corrupt. Cousin Ogle's face 'resembles a Table ordinary at the German Spa'. Sir Oliver hates to see 'Prudence clinging to the Green Sickness of Youth'. Moses greets Sir Oliver and Rowley with 'Sarvant Gentlemens'. The real extent of the changes is best revealed, however, in Charles's last speech:

---

[1] See p. 344 above.

[2] See p. 374, l. 25, above.

[3] The pirated first edition was printed in Dublin in 1780, and is difficult to find. A facsimile reprint of the Bodleian copy was published at Menston in 1969, and the passage alluded to appears on p. 28.   [4] See p. 337 above.

[5] Professor David Randall kindly confirmed my impression of the manuscript.

As for reforming, Sir Peter; Bless'd as I am in your forgiveness and happy in the Possession of my adored Maria, I hope for the future to distinguish between liberality and Extravagance and without deviating into the wilds of dissipation or sinking into the narrows of meanness still remember that Benevolence when guided by prudence is the first great duty of Man. I want words to express my Love to Maria—and my sense of obligation to you—(To Sir Peter and Lady Teazle) To you (to Sir Oliver) And you (To the audience)

> You can each Doubt, each anxious Fear remove
> For even Scandal dies, if you approve.

The manuscript contains 139 numbered pages of text together with a further page bearing the title and the list of dramatis personae.

THE SIEGE OF ST. QUINTIN

I have already described Sheridan's corrections of the second act of Hook's play,[1] and have now come upon the text of the first act bearing a number of notes in his hand. It is to be found in the Special Collections (100 Box 124) of the Powell Library, University of California at Los Angeles.

The manuscript has a watermark dated 1805, and consists of thirty-three folios. The opening page contains a note, 'Dear Sir The whole— next week T. Hook', written from Taunton and above the title, 'a Play in Three Acts Act 1.' The signature 'Theo Hook' appears below.

Sheridan's first comment is written by the side of 'Philip I—King of Spain' in the 'Dramatis Personae' (f. 2^r): 'out with him if you can.' Hook's text is on the rectos that follow, and Sheridan's corrections are written between the lines or (with his remarks) on the blank facing pages. His main aim seems to have been to cut down the speeches and, at the same time, to give them greater liveliness. There are many examples of this, but perhaps the point may be supported by comparing one of Egmont's replies to Alvarez (f. 5^r) in its two states:

Hook	*Corrected by Sheridan*
Imprudent?—is it imprudent Sir to hazard every thing to guard the rights of Nations and protect the Kings we Love: we are oppressed a Foreign power would make us slaves—subvert our constitution Lay new duties and prescribe new Laws—the contest is a great one I allow—but what are	Prudence is always a virtue and often a Duty—but there are moments and occasions, when a valorous rashness nobly and justly supersedes her mandates—A foreign Power violating every principle of justice gratitude and humanity resolves to crush our constitution—to tear the Sceptre from

---

[1] See p. 792 above.

an hundred or a Thousand Slaves matched to the power of a Single Sword that strikes for Liberty—The Foe *once* fallen and their Force subdued again shall smiling peace maintain her lenient sway o'er all our states, our Vines shall flourish and our fields look green—again the willing Son of Labor shall delight in toil and sweet contentment gild his happy hours—shall we then heed remonstrance to create resistance—with such a prospect is there an obstacle too great to be surmounted a force too strong to be opposed—No my Countrymen—When we contend for Conquest and for gain we are but men and Soldiers but when the Struggle is for Freedom we are Lions in the fight

our monarch's grasp—in one word, to make US SLAVES a condition of existence to which the great creator never meant his creature man, should forf[e]it nature's charter by a base submission. This is a crisis when a cold Prudence must not be allow'd to check the daring of that desperate spirit which looks to the flag of Liberty as his banner or his shroud.

The need for improvement is apparent, and it is not surprising to find in later pages that Sheridan urged that lines should be cut drastically: 'make this [speech of fourteen lines] into a speech of four lines' (f. 6); 'shorten two thirds' (ff. 7–8); 'shorten' (f. 11^r); 'Shorten Shorten The tediousness while nothing is doing is ridiculous' (f. 11^v); 'ridiculous Length —and little worth having' (f. 14^v); 'all this scene to be reduced to one third of its present length' (f. 16^v); 'all this of course must be altered' (f. 20^v). Some pages have had all their lines crossed out, and in others twenty-one out of twenty-seven are deleted, yet Sheridan thought it was necessary to hammer home his criticism and wrote (on f. 32^v), 'assuming every curtailment I have suggested to be adopted this act would still be twice the length it ought to be, reduce it now as much as you can and then let a fresh copy be made and go to work again.—' The direction may have been meant for Hook, but I think it more likely that it was intended for Tom Sheridan.

Three of his comments are of greater general interest. One of them lays down a basic law in writing for the theatre: 'The Power of Coligny and many previous Circumstances which are here assumed to be known by the audience must in the course of this act be better explained. The Story does not tell itself—and it is always unsafe to presume that Historical facts are known. Shakespeare's historical Plays shew how well *He* managed this.' (f. 32^v)

When Kildare is made to say (f. 10^r), 'I am by birth a Briton—I have the honor to serve in the English Army under the Earl of Pembroke am by rank a Knight and General', Sheridan clearly thought that the author had lost an opportunity of bringing in some suitably Irish allusions.

He writes: 'I have no objection especially with reference to *present F[ac]ts*[1] to the introduction of an Irish Character—but this must be much mended—every Irishman's allusion t[o] his *Milesian* Origins is so obvious and so sure of producing effect that it is strange the Author should have miss'd it   consult J Johnston.'[2]

Another comment proves that he had become much more tolerant of Roman Catholicism during the course of his life. When *The Duenna* was presented in 1775 some critics deplored that Sheridan had shown the friars as pious frauds.[3] It is worth noting, therefore, that when Hook followed his example, Sheridan reproved him, saying, 'among many faults in the writing and some in the construction of this act nothing is so ill conceived as lugging in the stale ridicule of attacking a hypocritical Friar—and at this moment it is particularly ill-placed.—The Public sentiment is generally making head against the no Popery cry, and half the Patriotic enthusiasm in Spain is created and led by their Priests.' He added, 'out with this totally—it is easy enough to substitute something better'.

When we compare this manuscript with the text submitted to the Lord Chamberlain for licensing,[4] we find that Sheridan's suggestions and corrections have largely been followed. For example, Sir Leinster's speech is altered to read: 'As for myself I have the honour to be in the English army under the Earl of Pembroke—the good fortune to be by rank a Colonel—the satisfaction to be by name Sir Leinster Kildare, and the glory to be born an Irishman and your Countryman.'[5]

Accompanying this manuscript is one of nine folios of Act III. The sheets bear the watermark '1812', but contain no corrections in Sheridan's hand.[6]

THE STATESMAN

Lot 206 at the Sotheby sale of 29 November 1971 was listed in the catalogue as a 'contemporary manuscript of Act I of a play entitled "The Statesman" with EXTENSIVE AUTOGRAPH REWORKINGS, ANNOTATIONS AND ADDITIONS BY SHERIDAN, 22 PAGES, 4TO, SEWN, SOILED AND DAMPSTAINED'. It is clearly the one that Sichel noted among the Frampton Court papers,

---

[1] Early in 1808 Sheridan had declared that he would bring in a motion on Ireland in the Commons as soon as it met: see *Letters*, iii. 25 n., and Add. MS. 41857, f. 75. Sichel, i. 118, suggests that 'it was expressly to benefit the poor that he championed Catholic emancipation'.

[2] John ('Irish') Johnstone: the *Monthly Mirror* (1808, p. 317) said Sheridan wrote the 'wretchedly drawn' Irish part for him.   [3] See pp. 211–12 above.

[4] Huntington Library MS. LA 1559.   [5] Ibid., f. 9.

[6] The ill success of this play seems to have made a strong impression on Tom Sheridan, and we find him writing to Charles Ward about another play in February 1809 and urging him to '*remember St. Quintin* and make a damnable noise and Bustle what ever you do' (Egerton MS. 1976, f. 25).

and described as containing dialogue that was in the main mediocre though written, he believed, by Sheridan.[1]

Now that this manuscript has come to light again, Sheridan's contribution to the first scene cannot be disputed. The original author (believed to be John Dent) wrote out his dialogue quite neatly, and Sheridan set about improving it with judicious deletions or new lines.

The opening situation resembles the one with Young Fashion and Lory at the beginning of *A Trip to Scarborough*. Sprightly is a penurious young army officer, who wants to win over the father (Sir Peter Parade) of his beloved Emily, but knows he hates all army men. Sprightly decides to pretend to be Sir Harry Sash, while his man Fertile will act the part of the London alderman who is the favoured suitor. The piece of dialogue that now ensues is entirely Sheridan's work as is clear from the Frampton MS., though it is in fact quoted below from the fair copy, Add. MS. 25939, ff. 6–10:

SPRIGHTLY. But how can you hope to personate old Shrub, when Sir Peter was formerly acquainted with him?

FERTILE. O Sir Peter has not seen him for a great number of years, and it is notorious that the Alderman is much alter'd tho' he does not know it himself— and thinks that he is as young as ever—this with a certain Talent of Mimicry I have will do the Business, I'll answer for't.

SPRIGHTLY. But are you sure Sir Peter may not remember you?

FERTILE. O, Lud, no, Sir—when Sir Peter Parade lived in London—I was it is true in Alderman Shrub's service—but his Visits were not very frequent— and the cares of the world since—crosses in Love—hard living—and the honor of your service, Colonel have no doubt made some alteration in your humble Servant.

SPRIGHTLY. Poor Fertile—But Sir Peter Parade my Father-in-Law that is to be—I don't thoroughly understand his character—tho' I hear he is an oddity.

FERTILE. I'll give it you in a Minute—His Father carried a Greyhound at his Button as one of the King's messengers and his Mother kept a Coffee-House by the Court of Requests—So he was born a Politician on both sides— He served half an Apprenticeship to an Attorney's Desk and then Rose to be a Train-Bearer's Deputy—to one of the Judges. By the Interest of an old Friend of his Mother's he soon after got into a Clerkship in one of the public Offices—from whence by marrying a Woman whose Brother had married a Girl whose Uncle had a Relation whose first Cousin had Interest in a Borough he rose till he became a Commissioner of Hackney-Coaches—Here he received a disappointment from Government—and having a good Fortune with his Wife he procured himself to be Knighted—and retired in disgust.

SPRIGHTLY. Ha! ha! ha! But is he so ridiculous in his manner of living as I have heard?

FERTILE. Nothing can exceed it—my Landlord here, who knew me when I lived with old Shrub and from whose Distillery he has all his best Wine— tells me that Sir Peter is the Ridicule of the whole Country—His House

[1] i. 537–8.

stands just out of the Town—and he is a justice of the Peace, and in the Militia—both which however he thinks beneath his abilities and ambition— He manages his Estate and his Family as if he were a Minister in Office conducting the Affairs of a great Kingdom. He has his Councils, Cabinets, efficient Cabinets, Boards and Subordinate Boards—Cruet his Butler is his Principal Secretary—His other Servants he calls all either Clerks, Contractors, Controllers or Commissioners. Nay his very Coach Horses have Constitutional Names—in short his Life is a continual round of the Mimic Consequence of a Mock Minister.

SPRIGHTLY. Well, I shall know how to humour him, and Lady Parade you know is in my interest—but if we fail.

FERTILE. Zounds, Sir, we can't fail if you will only do as I bid you—which I think is no great matter for a servant to ask of his master in our Circumstances.

SPRIGHTLY. Well be you the leader then and yet Fertile I am afraid I shall want a little of your assurance to carry thro' my own part.

FERTILE. Dear Sir, you are pleased to Compliment—but you shall never want my Countenance depend on't—So now I'll step and write a Letter to Sir Peter in his own Style as from Alderman Shrub to announce my arrival and then prepare to visit him— [*going.*

SPRIGHTLY. Dispatch then or I shall be there before you—

FERTILE. And if only we succeed remember what I am doing for you, Sir— I am going even to tell a lie—lord forgive me!—for your service—Aye, Sir, to practice deceit—which I never did before in my life since my name was Fertile.

SPRIGHTLY. Go, you Rogue!

FERTILE. Nor wou'd do it, Sir, for my own Brother if I thought I shouldn't get something by it myself. [*Exeunt severally.*

The second scene discovers Sir Peter and Lady Parade at breakfast, with a large map and several newspapers spread over the table. The dialogue contains a few corrections and amplifications by Sheridan, and he has added a few speeches in subsequent pages. This much can be noted from the Frampton Court MS. but once it peters out, the reader can recognize comparatively few alterations by Sheridan in the remainder of the play given in the fair copy, Add. MS. 25939.

Rhodes noted[1] that it was never acted, in spite of the announcement in *The Gazetteer*, 21 December 1781, that 'a new farce of two acts called *The Statesman* is in rehearsal and will be performed in the course of a few days'. Politics now engrossed Sheridan, and it is possible that his initial interest in the play had waned, and that he could not find time to give it life.

THE STRANGER

I have mentioned above[2] the difficulty of discovering how large a share Sheridan had in this play when it was presented at Drury Lane Theatre in March and April 1798. The facsimile I then described has now come

---

[1] R. C. Rhodes, *Harlequin Sheridan* (Oxford, 1933), p. ix. [2] pp. 788–9.

to hand in the Huntington Library in some pages of an unidentified nineteenth-century magazine that must have been published before the Sotheby catalogue of 12–14 May 1851.

The facsimile consists of lithographs of a manuscript of the first two scenes of the fifth act, with many corrections in Sheridan's hand. I believe that the scenes may belong to the second stage of revision, for it seems likely that Sheridan had earlier hacked down Thompson's original submission. If that were the case, the theatre copyist would have been instructed to write out the corrected version, the one I think may have been the basis of the text in the lithographs. Then would have come further changes by Sheridan, and, after the play was performed, more again.[1] The last point is really[2] confirmed by *The Times*, 19 April 1798, when it mentions that 'a new character [is] introduced,[3] and the dénouement, more consistent with English notions of virtue and honour. It is a novelty in theatricals thus to change the features of a piece that has such firm possession of the Town; but we guess from whence the alterations come, or we should be doubtful of their success, and reprobate the attempt.'

A collation of the two scenes in the lithographed text with those published by Thompson in *The German Theatre* (4th edn., 1811) reveals some changes of a minor nature. The most important of them is the omission in *The German Theatre* of the first twenty-five lines of the lithographs. There are also some seventeen slight differences in phrasing. It is possible that Sheridan was responsible for them but proof is lacking. Nor can we be certain that the version in *The German Theatre* was an accurate transcription of the Drury Lane prompt-copy as it appeared for performance on 19 April 1798. What Sheridan claimed was that he had written every sentence in *The Stranger* 'as it is acted', and if that still seems a little extravagant, the evidence suggests that he had a greater share in the play than has usually been acknowledged.

For an amplification of this argument and a transcription of the lithographed scenes, see my article, 'Sheridan at Work on *The Stranger*', *Neuphilologische Mitteilungen*, lxxiii (Helsinki, 1972), 315–25.

'TWO POSTHUMOUS WORKS'

In *The Stage: Both before and behind the Curtain* (1840), Alfred Bunn mentioned[4] that

an offer, previously made, was renewed, of two posthumous works by Sheridan,

[1] See p. 789 above.

[2] Since it conflicts with the note in the previous day's issue (given on p. 789 above), we may reasonably assume that Sheridan made the revisions hastily and at the last moment.

[3] L. F. Thompson, *Kotzebue* (Paris, 1928), p. 121, notes that one character from Kotzebue's original had already been excluded, and says, 'This disagreeable and jealous lady's maid affords good comic relief, and furthermore is an original creation.'

[4] III. 153–5.

for which, it may be reasonably supposed, a considerable, but not too large, a sum of money was required. The former stipulation of not giving up the MSS. until the money was paid (on the prudent plan laid down by Sir E. L. Bulwer) was subsequently abandoned; and I had therefore an opportunity of consulting a gentleman on the subject, quite capable of decyphering one of the charms which it was stated the said MSS. contained, viz. Sheridan's handwriting. Mr. Dunn[1] knew as much of Sheridan as any man in existence—living at one time under the same roof with him, and being always in his fullest confidence. Pretty pickings from the said confidence, if one could only extract them! Billy drops an instalment now and then, and there are plenty of people ready to pick it up. It was Mr. Dunn's opinion that a part of one of the pieces was in Sheridan's handwriting, but that the rest decidedly was not. He moreover had never heard either work named, or even remotely hinted at; and wound up his observations by one of his usually shrewd remarks, which settled my enthusiasm in a minute. He stated that, to the best of his belief, not only had Sheridan raised every farthing he possibly could on every line he had ever written, but that there were wags to be found capable of asserting that he had raised a great deal upon what he had never written. This may be all erroneous, and God forbid that I should underrate any composition, particularly one supposed to emanate from such an inspired source; and as the dramatic productions in question are still, I presume, in existence, and if so, still of course to be purchased, I should be sorry to undervalue them.

The plays may have been written by others and partly corrected by Sheridan, or may have been original work of his own, but it is impossible now to identify them with any certainty. Since Sheridan ran the Drury Lane Theatre for over thirty years and had a fondness for amassing papers,[2] the problem will only be solved when a handlist of the materials he possessed is available, and that will have to include the books and manuscripts he put in pawn.

Even then we should need to have full details about the items.[3] This is apparent when we consider Sichel's description of a manuscript that he found among the Frampton Court papers: 'some scenes of an Italian tragedy quite beyond the satirist's powers.'[4] They have not come to hand recently, but a very brief outline that may just possibly refer to them, was in lot 199 at Sotheby's sale of 29 November 1971. I am not

---

[1] William Dunn was assistant in the Treasury at Drury Lane Theatre, and later became treasurer and secretary of the Drury Lane company. As such, he was called to give evidence in 1832, before the Select Committee on Dramatic Literature.

[2] See *Letters*, i. xxi.

[3] There are occasions, however, when references to Sheridan's signature in connection with a manuscript play may only mean that he has signed a letter of application to the Lord Chamberlain to put on a performance. I conjecture that this is the case in lot 238 of Puttick and Simpson's catalogue of 30 November 1908: 'Mr. Hough, Second Thought is Best, a Musical Entertainment, the Original MS., with autograph signature of R. B. Sheridan.' It was performed at Drury Lane Theatre on 30 March 1778.

[4] I. 610.

sure that it alludes to the same play because Sichel's note is so uninfor-
mative.[1]

What is clear from the many drafts and revisions of his plays and other
people's, is that Sheridan could scribble out dialogue at any time. This
trait is confirmed in a letter to his second wife that appeared in lot 190
at the same sale: 'When I have fix'd my Characters and the construction
of my Plot I can go on with the Dialogue travelling, visiting, walking,
anyhow or anywhere.'

VERSES TO THE MEMORY OF GARRICK

The four-page brochure that I have mentioned on p. 453 is to be found
in the Newberry Library and the British Museum. It gives an outline
of the text, and was presumably issued for free distribution at Drury
Lane Theatre before performances. The title-page reads:

The AIRS and CHORUSSES, / IN / The MONODY, / On the
DEATH of / Mr. GARRICK. / Set to MUSIC by Mr. LINLEY.

The text is as follows:

INTRODUCTORY SYMPHONY.

RECITED

If dying Excellence deserves a Tear, etc.

CHORUS

His Fame requires we act a tenderer Part;
His Mem'ry claims the Tear you gave his Art!

AIR

Great SHAKESPEAR's Image from its hallow'd Base,
Seem'd to prescribe the Grave, and point the Place.[2]

RECITED

Amid the Arts which seek ingenuous Fame, etc.

AIR

Each gaudy Bloom and dazzling Light subdu'd,
The pictur'd Form with equal Awe is view'd,
E'en Beauty's Portrait wears a softer Prime,
Touch'd by the tender Hand of mellowing Time.

---

[1] Sheridan's allusions to his own work can be even vaguer. Look at his letter to
Peake of 12 October 1802, in which he promises to 'bring home good Grist for the Mill
with me,—which I should not have finish'd either in London or Polesden' (*Letters*,
ii. 190).

[2] The Chorus then repeats the couplet, 'His Fame . . . Art!'

AIR

Grac'd by Defect, and worship'd in decay;
The sculptur'd ruin rises into Day.

TRIO

How dearer still that best applause
    The Poet's Lays impart;
Diffusive Fame his toils reward
    Superior as his Art,
A sacred Glory breath'd around
    Shall mark his hallow'd tomb
And ev'ry Laurel planted there,
    With Flowers eternal bloom.

RECITED

Such is THEIR meed—THEIR Honor's thus secure, etc.

DUETT

With thoughts that mourn—nor yet desire relief,
With meek Regret, and fond enduring grief;
Oh! lovliest Mourner, gentle MUSE! be thine
The sad delight to guard his hallow'd shrine.

AIR

By the hush'd wonder which his Accents drew!
By the applauding Tear bestow'd by you!
By the lone sigh the poor Man's sorrows gave,
By the last look when parting from his Grave;

CHORUS

Oh! lovliest Mourner, gentle MUSE; be thine
With sad delight to guard his hallow'd shrine.

CHORUS

So shall thou raise the Glory of his Tomb,
And vest its Laurels with eternal Bloom.

Airs and Chorusses contains some variants not to be found in *Verses to the Memory of Garrick*, and indicates something that we have found to be true of other work by Sheridan: that the text for a performance differs in a number of ways from the 'literary' version to be offered to readers. This is at its most obvious in the repetition of the chorus lines. What is even more interesting is the introduction of the 'Trio'. The notice of the first performance of 11 March 1779, in next day's *Morning Chronicle* (see p. 447 above), criticises the monody because it was 'written entirely in unvaried measure'. Since the 'Trio' introduces some variety, we are bound to wonder why the reviewer ignored its contribution to the general effect. Possibly he did not have the brochure in hand when he made his comment.

PROLOGUE TO THE MINIATURE PICTURE

Lady Craven's *The Miniature Picture* was first performed privately at her country house, Benham, and was afterwards given at the Town Hall, Newbury, for the benefit of the poor.[1] It was acted at Drury Lane Theatre on 24 May 1780, and the text (including the prologue by Sheridan) was printed by Riley in 1781. In the 'Advertisement' Lady Craven remarked: 'The Author of it publishes it at the Request of several of her Friends, who saw it *mis*-represented on the Stage, at *Drury-Lane*; as she chuses to submit Faults which are really her own, to the Judgment of the World, rather than be accused of those which she never committed.'

A manuscript version of the prologue in Sheridan's hand is extant, and is Huntington Library MS. LA 525. It contains a number of alternative readings, thus bearing out Moore's statement that Sheridan corrected and altered this piece of verse over and over again.

I have accepted the text in the first edition as copy-text, in the hope that it contains Sheridan's final thoughts, but have also collated it with the Huntington holograph. I omit the first thirty lines of the poem because they already appear in the present edition on p. 654. In printing the variants I have abbreviated the titles of the sources so that the first edition is described as '1781', and the holograph, as 'S'.

> But if this plea's denied, in our excuse
> Another still remains, you can't refuse;
> It is a Lady writes—and hark!—a Noble Muse!
> But see a critic starting from his bench—
> 'A noble Author?'—Yes, Sir, but the Play's not *French*:   35
> Yet if it were, no blame on us could fall,
> For we, you know, must follow Fashion's call:
> And true it is, things lately were *en train*
> To woo the Gallick Muse at Drury-lane;
> Not to import a troop of Foreign elves,   40
> But treat you with French actors—in ourselves:
> A Friend we had, who vow'd he'd make us speak
> *Pure flippant French*—by contract—in a week,

34–5 But . . . *French*] *1781*; *om. S.*   36 could] *1781*; should *S*   38 *train*] *S*; *traine* 1781   39 at] *1781*; in *S*   40 Not] *1781*; No *S*   42 he'd] *1781*; to *S*   43 *Pure flippant*] *1781*; authentic *S*

---

[1] A. M. Broadley and Lewis Melville, *The Beautiful Lady Craven* (1916), i. xxx.

Told us 'twas time to study what was good,
Polish, and leave off being understood; 45
That crouded audiences we thus might bring
To Monsieur Parsons and Chevalier King:
Or should the Vulgars grumble now and then,
The Prompter might translate—for Country Gentlemen.
Straight all subscribed—King's, Gods, Mutes, Singer, Actor,— 50
A Flanders Figure-dancer our Contractor.
But here, I grieve to own, tho't be to you,
He acted—e'en as most Contractors do;
Sold what he never dealt in, and th'amount
Being first discharg'd, submitted his account: 55
And what th' event? their industry was such,
Dodd spoke good Flemish, *Bannister* bad Dutch;
Then the rogue told us, with insulting ease,
So it was foreign it was sure to please:
Beaux wou'd applaud, as Fashion should command, 60
And Misses laugh—to seem to understand—
So from each clime our soil may something gain:
Manhood from Rome, and sprightliness from Spain:
Some *Russian Roscius* next delight the age,
And a Dutch *Heinel*[1] skate along the stage. 65
Exotic fopperies, hail! whose flatt'ring smile
Supplants the Sterner Virtues of our Isle!
Thus while with Chinese firs, and Indian pines,
Our nurs'ries swarm, the British oak declines:
Yet vain our Muse's fear—no Foreign laws 70
We dread, while native beauty pleads our cause:
While you too judge, whose smiles are honours higher,
Than verse should gain, but where those eyes inspire.
But if the men presume your pow'r to awe,
Retort their churlish Senatorial law: 75
This is your House—and move—the gentlemen withdraw:
Then they may vote, with envy never ceasing,
Your influence has encreas'd and is encreasing;
But there, I trust, the resolution's finish'd;
Sure none will say—*It ought to be diminish'd*.[2] 80

---

50 Mutes] *1781*; Mute *S*   59 it] *1781*; He *S*   to] *1781*; 'twould *S*
60 wou'd] *S*; Wits *1781*   70 Muse's] *1781*; Muses *S*   71 We dread]
1781; She dreads *S*   74 But] *1781*; And *S*   80 none will] *1781*;
they'll not *S*

---

[1] An allusion to the very popular ballet-dancer, Anne-Frédérique Heinel (1753–1808),
who made her début in Paris in 1768, and in London in 1771.

[2] John Dunning (1731–83) moved in the Commons, on 6 Apr. 1780, a resolution to
the effect that 'the influence of the Crown has increased, is increasing, and ought to be
diminished'.

FURTHER VARIANTS IN THE SCHOOL FOR SCANDAL

The Clare Sheridan MSS. of this play (described on p. 837 above) have fortunately come into the possession of the British Theatre Museum, and I am obliged to the Museum authorities and to Mr. Jack Reading for an opportunity of examining the manuscripts more carefully. Two of them (the 'Shargl MS.' and the 'Spunge MS.') deserve to be described in greater detail because they contain a number of variants in Sheridan's hand.

The Shargl MS.

This comprises one notebook with a separate sheet loosely inserted. The leaves are numbered one to eighteen and take us to the end of the first act: some of them bear writing on both sides. The version appears to be a very early one, coming between the Frampton Court and the Larpent MSS. Sheridan set about improving the dialogue but found himself in two minds about some of his changes. His indecision can be seen at the opening, in the lines that follow Lady Sneerwell's question, 'Did you circulate the Report of Lady Brittle's Intrigue with Captain Boastall?':

VERJUICE. Madam by this time Lady Brittle is the talk of half the town—and I doubt not but in a Week the Men will toast her as a Demirep.

Sheridan altered 'I doubt not but in a Week the Men will toast her' to 'I shall have her toasted', then wrote 'Stet', and afterwards deleted the three lines from the text. They are not to be found in the Larpent MS.

There is also evidence to suggest that some of the changes which now appear in the Shargl MS. had not been made in it by Sheridan when the Larpent MS. was copied. Consequently its transcribers had to make the necessary corrections after their copy was completed.

Some variants make their first appearance in the Shargl MS.: 'favored' becomes 'beloved' (p. 360, l. 27 above); 'a postchaise', 'the York Diligence' (365, 21); 'traduced', 'attack'd' (366, 11); 'on his arrival', 'whenever he returns' (369, 9); 'Bounty', 'Liberality' (372, 14). One variant is to be found otherwise only in the 'Spunge MS.': 'all Principle' (369, 15).

The Spunge MS.

This is also an early prompt copy, and it has an interesting stage direction at the opening: 'New Scene and B[ackcloth?] 2d gr[oove] Toilette 2 Chairs.' The text is not complete but comprises Acts I and II, Scene I (pp. 359-380, l. 26, above); Act III, omitting eight-and-a-half lines in the second scene (396, 4–12), and breaking off early (399, 20) in the third scene. It begins again in Act IV, Scene II (409, 26), then goes on to the end of Act V.

I have collated this version with the text printed above (pp. 359–441), and can add the following variants to Rae's short list:

Text above   Spunge MS.

p. 359, l. 11: Report] reports
p. 360, l. 11: Yes] [*They rise*] Yes
    26: Ladyship] Ladyship's
    28: you, the] YOU—a
p. 361, l. 1: widow . . . jointure] a widow, your own mistress, and indepen-
            dent in your Fortune
    2: passion] addresses
    3: more] still more
    24: Knave] knave, while with Sir Peter, and indeed with all who are
      of his acquaintance he passes for a Youthful miracle of
      prudence, good sense, and benevolence
    25: Yet] Yes, I know
p. 362, l. 3: Maria] Maria—while poor Charles has no friend in the house,
      tho' I fear he has a powerful interest in Maria's heart
      against which we must direct our schemes
    16: discernment] discernment and general—
p. 363, l. 3: true—I'll] true so I was indeed—I'll
    10: devoted—Lady] devoted—and most faithful—Lady
    16: he] Snake
    24: slipt . . . run] made my escape and have run
    28: severe] ill-natured
p. 364, l. 12: To be sure] Undoubtedly
p. 366, l. 5: Lord!] Heav'ns!
    17: Mr. Nickit] Mr. Pharo
    18: Acquaintances] friends and acquaintances
p. 367, l. 15: Ma'am] Miss
    20: Kind] species
p. 368, ll. 23, 30, 32, and p. 369, l. 1: Shepherd] Piper
p. 368, l. 25: O] *om.*
p. 369, l. 4: Strange] Ha! ha! Strange
    15: Principle] all principle
    17: egad] faith
p. 370, l. 3: O] *om.*
    18: going] *returns*
    21: going] *returns*
    24: certain] certain (*going*)
    25: going] *returns*
    30: Abuse . . . more] Abuse in the present case was not more
    36: Sentiments] Sentiment
p. 371, ll. 6–7: that . . . wedlock] *om.*
    21: Oh] *om.*

p. 372, l. 12: Rowley—on] Rowley you are wrong—on
16: Life] life, that much I may say.—
30: 'Egad] Fore Gad!
31: together] together—hours of rough mirth, and jolly scrapes which I dare swear He has not forgot
p. 373, l. 1: ah] so
2: at me] —yes Oliver will laugh
p. 374, l. 25: Novel] Sermon
25: or to be] or be
p. 377, l. 24: La'ship] Ladyship
26: Cards] Picquet
p. 378, l. 15: of a] of at
p. 388, l. 15: But why] But pray why
19: Interest] own Interest
p. 395, l. 31: couldn't] could
p. 397, l. 30: Sir Toby Bumper] Sir Harry[1]
30: Beauty] Beautys
p. 398, ll. 11–22: Sheridan reverses the order of the stanzas.
p. 416, l. 19: it—what] it—For my Lady Teazle—Lady Teazle I say—what
p. 417, l. 6: *goes to the screen*] *om.*
22: very] *om.*
p. 418, ll. 20–1: or . . . Husband] *om.*
p. 419, l. 35: *half aside*] *om.*
p. 420, ll. 3–4: *Enter . . . Strangers*] SIR PETER. And in future perhaps we may not be such Strangers.
SERVANT. (*to* SURFACE) Sir, Lady Sneerwell is below and says she will come up.
p. 423, l. 22: ROWLEY] Rowley as Stanley
p. 424, l. 1: Sentiments] Sentiment
p. 426, l. 13: *reads*] *reading*
p. 437, l. 18: Pshaw] Nay if you desert your Roguery in its Distress—and try to be justified—you have even less principle than I thought you had
p. 439, l. 10: I wish . . . Negotiation] *om.*
p. 440, ll. 16–17: SIR OLIVER. Well . . . fear] *om.*
18–19: yet . . . Critic] *om.*
p. 441, l. 14: *to the Audience*] *om.*
16: approve] approve. (*to the Audience*)

Clearly the Spunge text has much in common with *Cb* and *B*.

[1] The manuscript originally read 'Careless', but Sheridan altered it in his own hand to 'Sir Toby Bumper'. This was afterwards crossed off and 'Sir Harry' was written in by another hand. The same changes were made in line 32, but Sheridan began by altering 'Careless' to '1st Gent', then to 'Sir Toby'.

INDEX OF FIRST LINES OF SONGS AND VERSES BY A VARIETY OF AUTHORS

INDEX